The Half Has Never Been Told

# THE
# HALF HAS NEVER
# BEEN TOLD

---

## SLAVERY AND THE MAKING
## OF AMERICAN CAPITALISM

---

EDWARD E. BAPTIST

BASIC BOOKS

A Member of the Perseus Books Group

*New York*

Designed by Timm Bryson

Baptist, Edward E.
    The half has never been told : slavery and the making of American capitalism /
Edward E. Baptist.
      pages cm
    Includes bibliographical references and index.
    ISBN 978-0-465-00296-2 (hardcover : alk. paper) — ISBN 978-0-465-04470-2
(e-book)
    1. Slavery—United States—History. 2. Slavery—Economic aspects—United
States—History. 3. African Americans—Social conditions—History. I. Title.
    E441.B337 2014
    306.3'620973--dc23
                                        2014012546

10 9 8 7 6 5 4 3 2 1

*For Ezra and Lillian*

# CONTENTS

# 6. BREATH
## *1824–1835*
### 171

# 7. SEED
## *1829–1837*
### 215

# 8. BLOOD
## *1836–1844*
### 261

# 9. BACKS
## *1839–1850*
### 309

# 10. ARMS
## *1850–1861*
### 343

# 11. AFTERWORD: THE CORPSE
## *1861–1937*
### 397

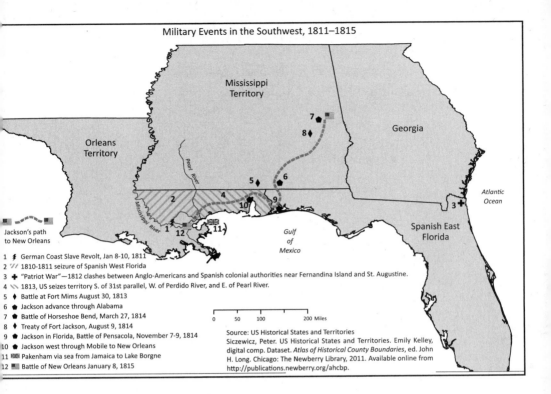

## Military Events in the Southwest, 1811–1815

Mississippi Territory

Orleans Territory

Georgia

7 ◆

8 ◆

*Pearl River*

5 ◆

6 ◆

4

9

10

*Mississippi River*

1

12

11

Atlantic Ocean

3 ✚

Spanish East Florida

Gulf of Mexico

⌁⌁⌁ Jackson's path to New Orleans

1 ⚡ German Coast Slave Revolt, Jan 8-10, 1811
2 ⬜ 1810-1811 seizure of Spanish West Florida
3 ✚ "Patriot War"—1812 clashes between Anglo-Americans and Spanish colonial authorities near Fernandina Island and St. Augustine.
4 ⬜ 1813, US seizes territory S. of 31st parallel, W. of Perdido River, and E. of Pearl River.
5 ◆ Battle at Fort Mims August 30, 1813
6 ◆ Jackson advance through Alabama
7 ◆ Battle of Horseshoe Bend, March 27, 1814
8 ◆ Treaty of Fort Jackson, August 9, 1814
9 ◆ Jackson in Florida, Battle of Pensacola, November 7-9, 1814
10 ◆ Jackson west through Mobile to New Orleans
11 ⬜ Pakenham via sea from Jamaica to Lake Borgne
12 ⬛ Battle of New Orleans January 8, 1815

0    50    100         200 Miles

Source: US Historical States and Territories
Siczewicz, Peter. US Historical States and Territories. Emily Kelley, digital comp. Dataset. *Atlas of Historical County Boundaries*, ed. John H. Long. Chicago: The Newberry Library, 2011. Available online from http://publications.newberry.org/ahcbp.

## Major US Acquisitions of Cotton Land from Native American Nations, 1814–1840

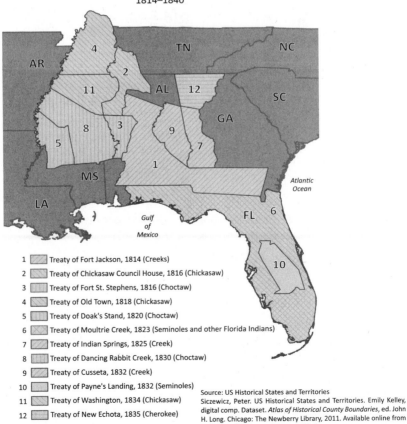

AR

4

TN

NC

2

11

AL

12

SC

8

3

9

GA

5

7

MS

1

LA

FL

6

Gulf of Mexico

Atlantic Ocean

10

1 ⬜ Treaty of Fort Jackson, 1814 (Creeks)
2 ⬜ Treaty of Chickasaw Council House, 1816 (Chickasaw)
3 ⬜ Treaty of Fort St. Stephens, 1816 (Choctaw)
4 ⬜ Treaty of Old Town, 1818 (Chickasaw)
5 ⬜ Treaty of Doak's Stand, 1820 (Choctaw)
6 ⬜ Treaty of Moultrie Creek, 1823 (Seminoles and other Florida Indians)
7 ⬜ Treaty of Indian Springs, 1825 (Creek)
8 ⬜ Treaty of Dancing Rabbit Creek, 1830 (Choctaw)
9 ⬜ Treaty of Cusseta, 1832 (Creek)
10 ⬜ Treaty of Payne's Landing, 1832 (Seminoles)
11 ⬜ Treaty of Washington, 1834 (Chickasaw)
12 ⬜ Treaty of New Echota, 1835 (Cherokee)

Source: US Historical States and Territories
Siczewicz, Peter. US Historical States and Territories. Emily Kelley, digital comp. Dataset. *Atlas of Historical County Boundaries*, ed. John H. Long. Chicago: The Newberry Library, 2011. Available online from http://publications.newberry.org/ahcbp.

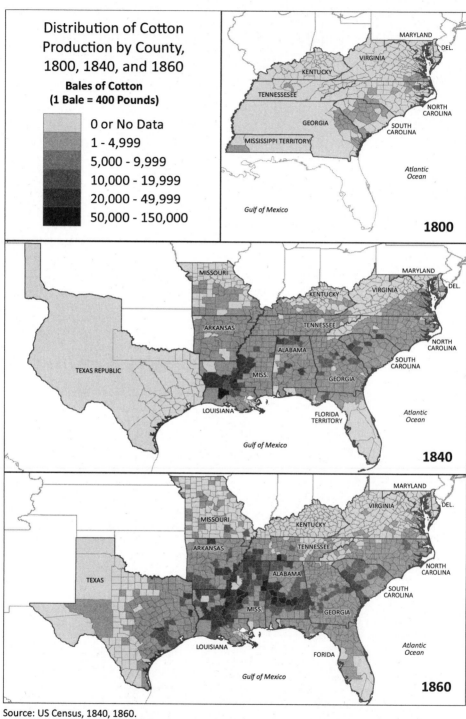

Distribution of Cotton Production by County, 1800, 1840, and 1860

**Bales of Cotton (1 Bale = 400 Pounds)**

- 0 or No Data
- 1 - 4,999
- 5,000 - 9,999
- 10,000 - 19,999
- 20,000 - 49,999
- 50,000 - 150,000

1800

1840

1860

Source: US Census, 1840, 1860.
Gray, L. C., and Esther Catherine Thompson, *History of Agriculture in the Southern United States to 1860.*
Washington, DC: The Carnegie Institution of Washington, 1933.

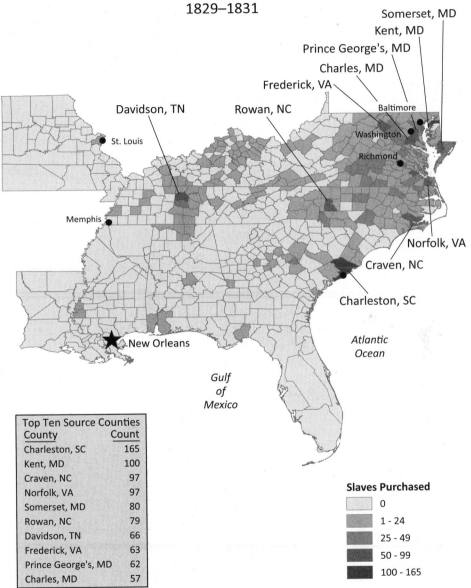

# Domestic Slave Trade:
## Slave Purchases, by County, for Resale in New Orleans, LA, 1829–1831

Somerset, MD

Kent, MD

Prince George's, MD

Charles, MD

Frederick, VA

Rowan, NC

Baltimore

Davidson, TN

Washington

St. Louis

Richmond

Memphis

Norfolk, VA

Craven, NC

Charleston, SC

New Orleans

Atlantic
Ocean

Gulf
of
Mexico

| Top Ten Source Counties | |
| --- | --- |
| County | Count |
| Charleston, SC | 165 |
| Kent, MD | 100 |
| Craven, NC | 97 |
| Norfolk, VA | 97 |
| Somerset, MD | 80 |
| Rowan, NC | 79 |
| Davidson, TN | 66 |
| Frederick, VA | 63 |
| Prince George's, MD | 62 |
| Charles, MD | 57 |

**Slaves Purchased**

| | |
| --- | --- |
| | 0 |
| | 1 - 24 |
| | 25 - 49 |
| | 50 - 99 |
| | 100 - 165 |

Source: US Historical Counties
Siczewicz, Peter. US Historical Counties. Dataset. Emily Kelley, digital comp.
*Atlas of Historical County Boundaries*, ed. John H. Long.
Chicago: The Newberry Library, 2011. Available online from http://publications.newberry.org/ahcbp.

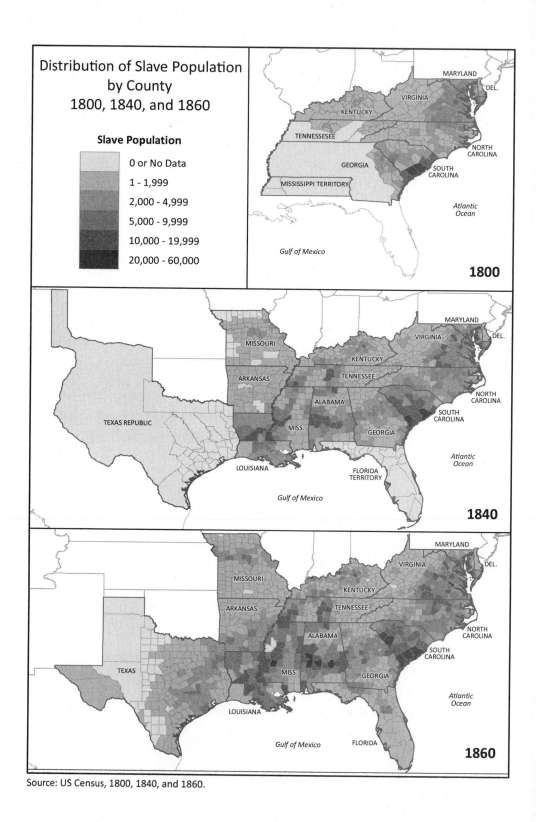

Distribution of Slave Population by County 1800, 1840, and 1860

Slave Population

- 0 or No Data
- 1 - 1,999
- 2,000 - 4,999
- 5,000 - 9,999
- 10,000 - 19,999
- 20,000 - 60,000

Source: US Census, 1800, 1840, and 1860.

# INTRODUCTION: THE HEART

## *1937*

A BEAUTIFUL LATE APRIL DAY, seventy-two years after slavery ended in the United States. Claude Anderson parks his car on the side of Holbrook Street in Danville. On the porch of number 513, he rearranges the notepads under his arm. Releasing his breath in a rush of decision, he steps up to the door of the handmade house and knocks.

Danville is on the western edge of the Virginia Piedmont. Back in 1865, it had been the last capital of the Confederacy. Or so Jefferson Davis had proclaimed on April 3, after he fled Richmond. Davis stayed a week, but then he had to keep running. The blue-coated soldiers of the Army of the Potomac were hot on his trail. When they got to Danville, they didn't find the fugitive rebel. But they did discover hundreds of Union prisoners of war locked in the tobacco warehouses downtown. The bluecoats, rescuers and rescued, formed up and paraded through town. Pouring into the streets around them, dancing and singing, came thousands of African Americans. They had been prisoners for far longer.

In the decades after the jubilee year of 1865, Danville, like many other southern villages, had become a cotton factory town. Anderson, an African-American master's student from Hampton University, would not have been able to work at the segregated mill. But the Works Progress Administration (WPA), a bureau of the federal government created by President Franklin D. Roosevelt's New Deal, would hire him. To put people back to work after they had lost their jobs in the Great Depression, the WPA organized thousands of projects, hiring construction workers to build schools and artists to paint murals. And many writers and students were hired to interview older Americans—like Lorenzo Ivy, the man painfully shuffling across the pine board floor to answer Anderson's knock.

Anderson had found Ivy's name in the Hampton University archives, two hundred miles east of Danville. Back in 1850, when Lorenzo had been born in Danville, there was neither a university nor a city called Hampton—just an American fort named after a slaveholder president. Fortress Monroe stood on Old Point Comfort, a narrow triangle of land that divided the Chesapeake Bay from the James River. Long before the fort was built, in April 1607, the *Susan Constant* had sailed past the point with a boatload of English settlers. Anchoring a few miles upriver, they had founded Jamestown, the first permanent English-speaking settlement in North America. Twelve years later, the crews of two storm-damaged English privateers also passed, seeking shelter and a place to sell the twenty-odd enslaved Africans (captured from a Portuguese slaver) lying shackled in their holds.

After that first 1619 shipload, some 100,000 more enslaved Africans would sail upriver past Old Point Comfort. Lying in chains in the holds of slave ships, they could not see the land until they were brought up on deck to be sold. After the legal Atlantic slave trade to the United States ended in 1807, hundreds of thousands more enslaved people passed the point. Now they were going the other way, boarding ships at Richmond, the biggest eastern center of the internal slave trade, to go by sea to the Mississippi Valley.

By the time a dark night came in late May 1861, the moon had waxed and waned three thousand times over slavery in the South. To protect slavery, Virginia had just seceded from the United States, choosing a side at last after six months of indecision in the wake of South Carolina's rude exit from the Union. Fortress Monroe, built to protect the James River from ocean-borne invaders, became the Union's last toehold in eastern Virginia. Rebel troops entrenched themselves athwart the fort's landward approaches. Local planters, including one Charles Mallory, detailed enslaved men to build berms to shelter the besiegers' cannon. But late this night, Union sentries on the fort's seaward side saw a small skiff emerging slowly from the darkness. Frank Baker and Townshend rowed with muffled oars. Sheppard Mallory held the tiller. They were setting themselves free.

A few days later, Charles Mallory showed up at the gates of the Union fort. He demanded that the commanding federal officer, Benjamin Butler, return his property. Butler, a politician from Massachusetts, was an incompetent battlefield commander, but a clever lawyer. He replied that if the men were Mallory's property, and he was using them to wage war against the US government, then logically the men were therefore contraband of war.

Those first three "contrabands" struck a crack in slavery's centuries-old wall. Over the next four years, hundreds of thousands more enslaved people widened the crack into a gaping breach by escaping to Union lines. Their movement weakened the Confederate war effort and made it easier for the United States and its president to avow mass emancipation as a tool of war. Eventually the Union Army began to welcome formerly enslaved men into its ranks, turning refugee camps into recruiting stations—and those African-American soldiers would make the difference between victory and defeat for the North, which by late 1863 was exhausted and uncertain.

After the war, Union officer Samuel Armstrong organized literacy programs that had sprung up in the refugee camp at Old Point Comfort to form Hampton Institute. In 1875, Lorenzo Ivy traveled down to study there, on the ground zero of African-American history. At Hampton, he acquired an education that enabled him to return to Danville as a trained schoolteacher. He educated generations of African-American children. He built the house on Holbrook Street with his own Hampton-trained hands, and there he sheltered his father, his brother, his sister-in-law, and his nieces and nephews. In April 1937, Ivy opened the door he'd made with hands and saw and plane, and it swung clear for Claude Anderson without rubbing the frame.[1]

Anderson's notepads, however, were accumulating evidence of two very different stories of the American past—halves that did not fit together neatly. And he was about to hear more. Somewhere in the midst of the notepads was a typed list of questions supplied by the WPA. Questions often reveal the desired answer. By the 1930s, most white Americans had been demanding for decades that they hear only a sanitized version of the past into which Lorenzo Ivy had been born. This might seem strange. In the middle of the nineteenth century, white Americans had gone to war with each other over the future of slavery in their country, and slavery had lost. Indeed, for a few years after 1865, many white northerners celebrated emancipation as one of their collective triumphs. Yet whites' belief in the emancipation made permanent by the Thirteenth Amendment, much less in the race-neutral citizenship that the Fourteenth and Fifteenth Amendments had written into the Constitution, was never that deep. Many northerners had only supported Benjamin Butler and Abraham Lincoln's moves against slavery because they hated the arrogance of slaveholders like Charles Mallory. And after 1876, northern allies abandoned southern black voters.

Within half a century after Butler sent Charles Mallory away from Fortress Monroe empty-handed, the children of white Union and Confederate soldiers united against African-American political and civil equality. This compact of white supremacy enabled southern whites to impose Jim Crow segregation on public space, disfranchise African-American citizens by barring them from the polls, and use the lynch-mob noose to enforce black compliance. White Americans imposed increased white supremacy outside the South, too. In non-Confederate states, many restaurants wouldn't serve black customers. Stores and factories refused to hire African Americans. Hundreds of midwestern communities forcibly evicted African-American residents and became "sundown towns" ("Don't let the sun set on you in this town"). Most whites, meanwhile, believed that science proved that there were biologically distinct human races, and that Europeans were members of the superior one. Anglo-Americans even believed that they were distinct from and superior to the Jews from Russia, Italians, Greeks, Slavs, and others who flooded Ellis Island and changed the culture of northern urban centers.

By the early twentieth century, America's first generation of professional historians were justifying the exclusions of Jim Crow and disfranchisement by telling a story about the nation's past of slavery and civil war that seemed to confirm, for many white Americans, that white supremacy was just and necessary. Above all, the historians of a reunified white nation insisted that slavery was a premodern institution that was not committed to profit-seeking. In so doing, historians were to some extent only repeating pre–Civil War debates: abolitionists had depicted slavery not only as a psychopathic realm of whipping, rape, and family separation, but also as a flawed economic system that was inherently less efficient than the free-labor capitalism developing in the North. Proslavery writers disagreed about the psychopathy, but by the 1850s they agreed that enslavers were first and foremost not profit-seekers. For them, planters were caring masters who considered their slaves to be inferior family members. So although anti- and proslavery conclusions about slavery's morality were different, their premises about slavery-as-a-business-model matched. Both agreed that slavery was inherently unprofitable. It was an old, static system that belonged to an earlier time. Slave labor was inefficient to begin with, slave productivity did not increase to keep pace with industrialization, and enslavers did not act like modern profit-seeking businessmen. As a system, slavery had never adapted or changed to thrive in the new industrial economy—let alone to play a premier role as a driver of economic expansion—and had been little more than a drag on the explosive growth that had built the modern United States. In fact, during the Civil War, northerners were so convinced of these points that they believed that shifting from slave labor to free labor would dramatically increase cotton productivity.

It didn't. But even though the data of declining productivity over the ensuing three score and ten years suggested that slavery might have been the most efficient way to produce the world's most important crop, no one let empirical tests change their minds. Instead, historians of Woodrow Wilson's generation imprinted the stamp of academic research on the idea that slavery was separate from the great economic and social transformations of the Western world during the nineteenth century. After all, it did not rely upon ever-more efficient machine labor. Its unprofitable economic structures supposedly produced antique social arrangements, and the industrializing, urbanizing world looked back toward them with contempt—or, increasingly, nostalgia. Many whites, now proclaiming that science proved that people of African descent were intellectually inferior and congenitally prone to criminal behavior, looked wistfully to a past when African Americans had been governed with whips and chains. Granted, slavery as an economic system was not modern, they said, and had neither changed to adapt to the modern economy nor contributed to economic expansion. But to an openly racist historical profession—and a white history-reading, history-thinking public obsessed with all kinds of race control—the white South's desire to whitewash slavery in the past, and maintain segregation now and forever, served the purpose of validating control over supposedly premodern, semi-savage black people.

Such stories about slavery shaped the questions Claude Anderson was to ask in the 1930s, because you could find openly racist versions of it baked into the recipe of every American textbook. You could find it in popular novels, politicians' speeches, plantation-nostalgia advertising, and even the first blockbuster American film: *Birth of a Nation*. As president, Woodrow Wilson—a southern-born history professor—called this paean to white supremacy "history written with lightning," and screened it at the White House. Such ideas became soaked into the way America publicly depicted slavery. Even many of those who believed that they rejected overt racism depicted the era before emancipation as a plantation idyll of happy slaves and paternalist masters. Abolitionists were snakes in the garden, responsible for a Civil War in which hundreds of thousands of white people died. Maybe the end of slavery had to come for the South to achieve economic modernity, but it didn't have to come that way, they said.

The way that Americans remember slavery has changed dramatically since then. In tandem with widespread desegregation of public spaces and the assertion of black cultural power in the years between World War II and the 1990s came a new understanding of the experience of slavery. No longer did academic historians describe slavery as a school in which patient masters and mistresses trained irresponsible savages for futures of perpetual servitude.

Slavery's denial of rights now prefigured Jim Crow, while enslaved people's resistance predicted the collective self-assertion that developed into first the civil rights movement and later, Black Power.

But perhaps the changes were not so great as they seemed on the surface. The focus on showing African Americans as assertive rebels, for instance, implied an uncomfortable corollary. If one should be impressed by those who rebelled, because they resisted, one should not be proud of those who did not. And there were very few rebellions in the history of slavery in the United States. Some scholars tried to backfill against this quandary by arguing that all African Americans together created a culture of resistance, especially in slave quarters and other spaces outside of white observation. Yet the insistence that assertive resistance undermined enslavers' power, and a focus on the development of an independent black culture, led some to believe that enslaved people actually managed to prevent whites from successfully exploiting their labor. This idea, in turn, created a quasi-symmetry with post–Civil War plantation memoirs that portrayed gentle masters, who maintained slavery as a nonprofit endeavor aimed at civilizing Africans.

Thus, even after historians of the civil rights, Black Power, and multicultural eras rewrote segregationists' stories about gentlemen and belles and grateful darkies, historians were still telling the half that has ever been told. For some fundamental assumptions about the history of slavery and the history of the United States remain strangely unchanged. The first major assumption is that, as an economic system—a way of producing and trading commodities—American slavery was fundamentally different from the rest of the modern economy and separate from it. Stories about industrialization emphasize white immigrants and clever inventors, but they leave out cotton fields and slave labor. This perspective implies not only that slavery didn't change, but that slavery and enslaved African Americans had little long-term influence on the rise of the United States during the nineteenth century, a period in which the nation went from being a minor European trading partner to becoming the world's largest economy—one of the central stories of American history.

The second major assumption is that slavery in the United States was fundamentally in contradiction with the political and economic systems of the liberal republic, and that inevitably that contradiction would be resolved in favor of the free-labor North. Sooner or later, slavery would have ended by the operation of historical forces; thus, slavery is a story without suspense. And a story with a predetermined outcome isn't a story at all.

Third, the worst thing about slavery as an experience, one is told, was that it denied enslaved African Americans the liberal rights and liberal subjectivity of modern citizens. It did those things as a matter of course, and as injustice, that denial ranks with the greatest in modern history. But slavery also killed people, in large numbers. From those who survived, it stole everything. Yet the massive and cruel engineering required to rip a million people from their homes, brutally drive them to new, disease-ridden places, and make them live in terror and hunger as they continually built and rebuilt a commodity-generating empire—this vanished in the story of a slavery that was supposedly focused primarily not on producing profit but on maintaining its status as a quasi-feudal elite, or producing modern ideas about race in order to maintain white unity and elite power. And once the violence of slavery was minimized, another voice could whisper, saying that African Americans, both before and after emancipation, were denied the rights of citizens because they would not fight for them.

All these assumptions lead to still more implications, ones that shape attitudes, identities, and debates about policy. If slavery was outside of US history, for instance—if indeed it was a drag and not a rocket booster to American economic growth—then slavery was not implicated in US growth, success, power, and wealth. Therefore none of the massive quantities of wealth and treasure piled by that economic growth is owed to African Americans. Ideas about slavery's history determine the ways in which Americans hope to resolve the long contradiction between the claims of the United States to be a nation of freedom and opportunity, on the one hand, and, on the other, the unfreedom, the unequal treatment, and the opportunity denied that for most of American history have been the reality faced by people of African descent. Surely, if the worst thing about slavery was that it denied African Americans the liberal rights of the citizen, one must merely offer them the title of citizen—even elect one of them president—to make amends. Then the issue will be put to rest forever.

Slavery's story gets told in ways that reinforce all these assumptions. Textbooks segregate twenty-five decades of enslavement into one chapter, painting a static picture. Millions of people each year visit plantation homes where guides blather on about furniture and silverware. As sites, such homes hide the real purpose of these places, which was to make African Americans toil under the hot sun for the profit of the rest of the world. All this is the "symbolic annihilation" of enslaved people, as two scholars of those weird places put it.[2] Meanwhile, at other points we tell slavery's story by heaping praise on those who escaped it through flight or death in rebellion, leaving the listener to wonder if those who didn't flee or die somehow "accepted" slavery. And everyone who teaches about slavery knows a little dirty secret that reveals historians' collective failure: many African-American students struggle with a sense of shame that most of their ancestors could not escape the suffering they experienced.

The truth can set us free, if we can find the right questions. But back in the little house in Danville, Anderson was reading from a list of leading ones, designed by white officials—some well-meaning, some not so well-meaning. He surely felt how the gravity of the questions pulled him toward the planet of plantation nostalgia. "Did slaves mind being called 'nigger'?" "What did slaves call master or mistress?" "Have you been happier in slavery or free?" "Was the mansion house pretty?" Escaping from chains is very difficult, however, so Anderson dutifully asked the prescribed questions and poised his pencil to take notes.

Ivy listened politely. He sat still. Then he began to speak: "My mother's master was named William Tunstall. He was a mean man. There was only one good thing he did, and I don't reckon he intended to do that. He sold our family to my father's master George H. Gilman."

Perhaps the wind blowing through the window changed as a cloud moved across the spring sun: "Old Tunstall caught the 'cotton fever.' There was a fever going round, leastways it was like a fever. Everyone was dying to get down south and grow cotton to sell. So old Tunstall separated families right and left. He took two of my aunts and left their husbands up here, and he separated altogether seven husbands and wives. One woman had twelve children. Yessir. Took 'em all down south with him to Georgia and Alabama."

Pervasive separations. Tears carving lines on faces. Lorenzo remembered his relief at dodging the worst, but he also remembered knowing that it was just a lucky break. Next time it could've been his mother. No white person was reliable, because money drove their decisions. No, this wasn't the story the books told.

So Anderson moved to the next question. Did Ivy know if any slaves had been sold here? Now, perhaps, the room grew darker.

For more than a century, white people in the United States had been singling out slave traders as an exception: unscrupulous lower-class outsiders who pried apart paternalist bonds. Scapegoaters had a noble precedent. In his first draft of the Declaration of Independence, Thomas Jefferson tried to blame King George III for using the Atlantic slave trade to impose slavery on the colonies. In historians' tellings, the 1808 abolition of the Atlantic trade brought stability to slavery, ringing in the "Old South," as it has been called since before the Civil War. Of course, one might wonder how something that was brand new, created *after* a *revolution*, and growing more rapidly than any other commodity-producing economy in history before then could be considered "old." But never mind. Historians depicted slave trading after 1808 as irrelevant to what slavery was in the "Old South," and to how America as a whole was shaped. America's modernization was about entrepreneurs, creativity, invention, markets, movement, and change. Slavery was not about any of these things—not about slave trading, or moving people away from everyone they knew in order to make them make cotton. Therefore, modern America and slavery had nothing to do with each other.

But Ivy spilled out a rush of very different words. "They sold slaves here and everywhere. I've seen droves of Negroes brought in here on foot going South to be sold. Each one of them had an old tow sack on his back with everything he's got in it. Over the hills they came in lines reaching as far as the eye can see. They walked in double lines chained together by twos. They walk 'em here to the railroad and shipped 'em south like cattle."

Then Lorenzo Ivy said this: "Truly, son, the half has never been told."

To this, day, it still has not. For the other half is the story of how slavery changed and moved and grew over time: Lorenzo Ivy's time, and that of his parents and grandparents. In the span of a single lifetime after the 1780s, the South grew from a narrow coastal strip of worn-out plantations to a subcontinental empire. Entrepreneurial enslavers moved more than 1 million enslaved people, by force, from the communities that survivors of the slave trade from Africa had built in the South and in the West to vast territories that were seized—also by force—from their Native American inhabitants. From 1783 at the end of the American Revolution to 1861, the number of slaves in the United States increased five times over, and all this expansion produced a powerful nation. For white enslavers were able to force enslaved African-American migrants to pick cotton faster and more efficiently than free people. Their practices rapidly transformed the southern states into the dominant force in the global cotton market, and cotton was the world's most widely traded commodity at the time, as it was the key raw material during the first century of the industrial revolution. The returns from cotton monopoly powered the modernization of the rest of the American economy, and by the time of the Civil War, the United States had become the second nation to undergo large-scale industrialization. In fact, slavery's expansion shaped every crucial aspect of the economy and politics of the new nation—not only increasing its power and size, but also, eventually, dividing US politics, differentiating regional identities and interests, and helping to make civil war possible.

The idea that the commodification and suffering and forced labor of African Americans is what made the United States powerful and rich is not an idea that people necessarily are happy to hear. Yet it is the truth. And that truth was the half of the story that survived mostly in the custodianship of those who survived slavery's expansion—whether they had been taken over the hill, or left behind. Forced migration had shaped their lives, and also had shaped what they thought about their lives and the wider history in which they were enmeshed. Even as they struggled to stay alive in the midst of disruption, they created ways to talk about this half untold. But what survivors experienced, analyzed, and named was a slavery that didn't fit the comfortable boxes into which other Americans have been trying to fit it ever since it ended.

I read Lorenzo Ivy's words, and they left me uneasy. I sensed that the true narrative had been left out of history—not only American history in general, but even the history of slavery. I began to look actively for the other half of the story, the one about how slavery constantly grew, changed, and reshaped the modern world. Of how it was both modernizing and modern, and what that meant for the people who lived through its incredible expansion. Once I began to look, I discovered that the traces of the other half were everywhere. The debris of cotton fevers that infected white entrepreneurs and separated man and woman, parent and child, right and left, dusted every set of pre–Civil War letters, newspapers, and court documents. Most of all, the half not told ran like a layer of iridium left by a dinosaur-killing asteroid through every piece of testimony that ex-slaves, such as Lorenzo Ivy, left on the historical record: thousands of stanzas of an epic of forced separations, violence, and new kinds of labor.

For a long time I wasn't sure how to tell the story of this muscular, dynamic process in a single book. The most difficult challenge was simply the fact that the expansion of slavery in many ways shaped the story of *everything* in the pre–Civil War United States. Enslavers' surviving papers showed calculations of returns from slave sales and purchases as well as the costs of establishing new slave labor camps in the cotton states. Newspapers dripped with speculations in land and people and the commodities they produced; dramatic changes in how people made money and how much they made; and the dramatic violence that accompanied these practices. The accounts of northern merchants and bankers and factory owners showed that they invested in slavery, bought from and sold to slaveholders, and took slices of profit out of slavery's expansion. Scholars and students talked about politics as a battle about states' rights or republican principles, but viewed in a different light the fights can be seen as a struggle between regions about how the rewards of slavery's expansion would be allocated and whether that expansion could continue.

The story seemed too big to fit into one framework. Even Ivy had no idea how to count the chained lines he saw going southwest toward the mountains on the horizon and the vast open spaces beyond. From the 1790s to the 1860s, enslavers moved 1 million people from the old slave states to the new. They went from making no cotton to speak of in 1790 to making almost 2 billion pounds of it in 1860. Stretching out beyond the slave South, the story encompassed not only Washington politicians and voters across the United States but also Connecticut factories, London banks, opium addicts in China, and consumers in East Africa. And could one book do Lorenzo Ivy's insight justice? It would have to avoid the old platitudes, such as the easy temptation to tell the story as a collection of topics—here a chapter on slave resistance, there one on women and slavery, and so on. That kind of abstraction cuts the beating heart out of the story. For the half untold was a narrative, a process of movement and change and suspense. Things happened because of what had been done before them—and what people chose to do in response.

No, this had to be a *story*, and one couldn't tell it solely from the perspective of powerful actors. True, politicians and planters and bankers shaped policies, the movement of people, and the growing and selling of cotton, and even remade the land itself. But when one takes Lorenzo Ivy's words as a starting point, the whole history of the United States comes walking over the hill behind a line of people in chains. Changes that reshaped the entire world began on the auction block where enslaved migrants stood or in the frontier cotton fields where they toiled. Their individual drama was a struggle to survive. Their reward was to endure a brutal transition to new ways of labor that made them reinvent themselves every day. Enslaved people's creativity enabled their survival, but, stolen from them in the form of ever-growing cotton productivity, their creativity also expanded the slaveholding South at an unprecedented rate. Enslaved African Americans built the modern United States, and indeed the entire modern world, in ways both obvious and hidden.

One day I found a metaphor that helped. It came from the great African-American author Ralph Ellison. You might know his novel *Invisible Man*. But in the 1950s, Ellison also produced incredible essays. In one of them he wrote, "On the moral level I propose we view the whole of American life as a drama enacted on the body of a Negro giant who, lying trussed up like Gulliver, forms the stage and the scene upon which and within which the action unfolds."[3]

The image fit the story that Ivy's words raised above the watery surface of buried years. The only problem was that Ellison's image implied a stationary giant. In the old myth, the stationary, quintessentially unchanging plantation was the site and the story of African-American life from the seventeenth century to the twentieth. But Lorenzo Ivy had described a world in motion. After the American Revolution—which seemed at the time to portend slavery's imminent demise—a metastatic transformation and growth of slavery's giant body had begun instead. From the exploitation, commodification, and torture of enslaved people's bodies, enslavers and other free people gained new kinds of modern power. The sweat and blood of the growing system, a network of individuals and families and labor camps that grew bigger with each passing year, fueled massive economic change. Enslaved people, meanwhile, transported and tortured, had to find ways to survive, resist, or endure. And over time the question of their freedom or bondage came to occupy the center of US politics.

This trussed-up giant, stretched out on the rack of America's torture zone, actually grew, like a person passing through ordeals to new maturity. I have divided the chapters of this book with Ellison's imagined giant in mind, a structure that has allowed the story to take as its center point the experience of enslaved African Americans themselves. Before we pass through the door that Lorenzo Ivy opened, here are the chapters' names. The first is "Feet," for the story begins with unfree movement on paths to enslaved frontiers that were laid down between the end of the American Revolution in 1783 and the early 1800s. "Heads" is the title of the second chapter, which covers America's acquisition of the key points of the Mississippi Valley by violence, a gain that also consolidated the enslavers' hold on the frontier. Then come the "Right Hand" and the "Left Hand" (Chapters 3 and 4). They reveal the inner secrets of enslavers' power, secrets which made the entire world of white people wealthy.

"Tongues" (Chapter 5) and "Breath" (Chapter 6) follow. They describe how, by the mid-1820s, enslavers had not only found ways to silence the tongues of their critics, but had built a system of slave trading that served as expansion's lungs. Most forms of resistance were impossible to carry out successfully. So a question hung in the air. Would the spirit in the tied-down body die, leaving enslaved people to live on like undead zombies serving their captors? Or would the body live, and rise? Every transported soul, finding his or her old life killed off, faced this question on the individual level as well: whether to work with fellow captives or scrabble against them in a quest for individualistic subsistence. Enslaved African Americans chose many things. But perhaps most importantly, they chose survival, and true survival in such circumstances required solidarity. Solidarity allowed them to see their common experience, to light their own way by building a critique of enslavers' power that was an alternative story about what things were and what they meant.

This story draws on thousands of personal narratives like the one that Lorenzo Ivy told Claude Anderson. Slavery has existed in many societies, but no other population of formerly enslaved people has been able to record the testimonies of its members like those who survived slavery in the United States. The narratives began with those who escaped slavery's expansion in the nineteenth century as fugitives. Over one hundred of those survivors published their autobiographies during the nineteenth century. As time went on, such memoirs found a market, in no small part because escapees from southern captivity were changing the minds of some of the northern whites about what the expansion of slavery meant for them. Then, during the 1930s, people like Claude Anderson conducted about 2,300 interviews with the ex-slaves who had lived into that decade. Because the interviews often allowed old people to tell about the things they had seen for themselves and the things they heard from their elders in the years before the Civil War, they take us back into the world of explanation and storytelling that grew up around fires and on porches and between cotton rows. No one autobiography or interview is pure and objective as an account of all that the history books left untold. But read them all, and each one adds to a more detailed, clearer picture of the whole. One story fills in gaps left by another, allowing one to read between the lines.[4]

Understanding something of what it felt like to suffer, and what it cost to endure that suffering, is crucial to understanding the course of US history. For what enslaved people made together—new ties to each other, new ways of understanding their world—had the potential to help them survive in mind and body. And ultimately, their spirit and their speaking would enable them to call new allies into being in the form of an abolitionist movement that helped to destabilize the mighty enslavers who held millions captive. But the road on which enslaved people were being driven was long. It led through the hell described by "Seed" (Chapter 7), which tells of the horrific near-decade from 1829 to 1837. In these years entrepreneurs ran wild on slavery's frontier. Their acts created the political and economic dynamics that carried enslavers to their greatest height of power. Facing challenges from other white men who wanted to assert their masculine equality through political democracy, clever entrepreneurs found ways to leverage not just that desire, but other desires as well. With the creation of innovative financial tools, more and more of the Western world was able to invest directly in slavery's expansion. Such creativity multiplied the incredible productivity and profitability of enslaved people's labor and allowed enslavers to turn bodies into commodities with which they changed the financial history of the Western world.

Enslavers, along with common white voters, investors, and the enslaved, made the 1830s the hinge of US history. On one side lay the world of the industrial revolution and the initial innovations that launched the modern world. On the other lay modern America. For in 1837, enslavers' exuberant success led to a massive economic crash. This self-inflicted devastation, covered in Chapter 8, "Blood," posed new challenges to slaveholders' power, led to human destruction for the enslaved, and created confusion and discord in white families. When southern political actors tried to use war with Mexico to restart their expansion, they encountered new opposition on the part of increasingly assertive northerners. As Chapter 9, "Backs," explains, by the 1840s the North had built a complex, industrialized economy on the backs of enslaved people and their highly profitable cotton labor. Yet, although all northern whites had benefited from the deepened exploitation of enslaved people, many northern whites were now willing to use politics to oppose further expansions of slavery. The words that the survivors of slavery's expansion had carried out from the belly of the nation's hungriest beast had, in fact, become important tools for galvanizing that opposition.

Of course, in return for the benefits they received from slavery's expansion, plenty of northerners were still willing to enable enslavers' disproportionate power. With the help of such allies, as "Arms" (Chapter 10) details, slavery continued to expand in the decade after the Compromise of 1850. For now, however, it had to do so within potentially closed borders. That is why southern whites now launched an aggressive campaign of advocacy, insisting on policies and constitutional interpretations that would commit the entire United States to the further geographic expansion of slavery. The entire country would become slavery's next frontier. And as they pressed, they generated greater resistance, pushed too hard, and tried to make their allies submit—like slaves, the allies complained. And that is how, at last, whites came to take up arms against each other.

Yet even as southern whites seceded, claiming that they would set up an independent nation, shelling Fort Sumter, and provoking the Union's president, Abraham Lincoln, to call out 100,000 militia, many white Americans wanted to keep the stakes of this dispute as limited as possible. A majority of northern Unionists opposed emancipation. Perhaps white Americans' battles with each other were, on one level, not driven by a contest over ideals, but over the best way to keep the stream of cotton and financial revenues flowing: keep slavery within its current borders, or allow it to consume still more geographic frontiers. But the growing roar of cannon promised others a chance to force a more dramatic decision: slavery forever, or nevermore. So it was that as Frank Baker, Townshend, and Sheppard Mallory crept across the dark James River waters that had washed so many hulls bearing human bodies, the future stood poised, uncertain between alternative paths. Yet those three men carried something powerful: the same half of the story that Lorenzo Ivy could tell. All they had learned from it would help to push the future onto a path that led to freedom. Their story can do so for us as well. To hear it, we must stand as Lorenzo Ivy had stood as a boy in Danville—watching the chained lines going over the hills, or as Frank Baker and others had stood, watching the ships going down the James from the Richmond docks, bound for the Mississippi. Then turn and go with the marching feet, and listen for the breath of the half that has never been told.

# 1
## FEET

*1783–1810*

NOT LONG AFTER THEY heard the first clink of iron, the boys and girls in the cornfield would have been able to smell the grownups' bodies, perhaps even before they saw the double line coming around the bend. Hurrying in locked step, the thirty-odd men came down the dirt road like a giant machine. Each hauled twenty pounds of iron, chains that draped from neck to neck and wrist to wrist, binding them all together. Ragged strips flapped stiffly from their clothes like dead-air pennants. On the men's heads, hair stood out in growing dreads or lay in dust-caked mats. As they moved, some looked down like catatonics. Others stared at something a thousand yards ahead. And now, behind the clanking men, followed a marching crowd of women loosely roped, the same vacancy painted in their expressions, endurance standing out in the rigid strings of muscle that had replaced their calves in the weeks since they left Maryland. Behind them all swayed a white man on a gray walking horse.

The boys and girls stood, holding their hoe handles, forgetful of their task. In 1805, slave coffles were not new along the south road through Rowan County, here in the North Carolina Piedmont, but they didn't pass by every day. Perhaps one of the girls close to the road, a twelve-year-old willow, stared at the lone man who, glistening with sweat and fixed of jaw, set the pace at the head of the double file. Perhaps he reminded her of her father, in her memory tall. A few years back, he'd stopped coming to spend his Saturday nights with them. The girl's mother said he'd been sold to Georgia. Now in the breath of a moment, this man caught her staring eyes with his own scan as he hurried past. And perhaps, though he never broke stride, something like recognition flashed over a face iron as his locked collar. This man, Charles Ball, a twenty-five-year-old father of two, could not help but see his own daughter ten years hence, years he knew she'd pass without him. Then he was gone down the road, pulling the rest of the human millipede past the girl. As the women's bare soles receded—the white man on the horse following last, looking down, appraising her—the overseer on the far side of the field called out "Hey!" to her stock-still self, and she would surely have realized that the coffle carried her own future with them.[1]

There are 1,760 yards in a mile—more than 2,000 steps. Forty thousand is a long day's journey. Two hundred thousand is a hard week. For eighty years, from the 1780s until 1865, enslaved migrants walked for miles, days, and weeks. Driven south and west over flatlands and mountains, step after step they went farther from home. Stumbling with fatigue, staggering with whiskey, even sometimes stepping high on bright spring mornings when they refused to think of what weighed them down, many covered over 700 miles before stepping off the road their footsteps made. Seven hundred miles is a million and a half steps. After weeks of wading rivers, crossing state lines, and climbing mountain roads, and even boarding boats and ships and then disembarking, they had moved their bodies across the frontier between the old slavery and the new.

Over the course of eighty years, almost 1 million people were herded down the road into the new slavery (see Table 1.1). This chapter is about how these forced marchers began, as they walked those roads, to change things about the eastern and western United States, like shifting grains moved from one side of a balance to another. It shows how the first forced migrations began to tramp down paths along which another 1 million walkers' 1.5 trillion steps would shape seven decades of slavery's expansion in the new United States. And it shows how the paths they made on the land, in politics, and in the economy—the footprints that driven slaves and those who drove them left on the fundamental documents and bargains of the nation—kept the nation united and growing.

For at the end of the American Revolution, the victorious leaders of the newly independent nation were not sure that they could hold their precarious coalition of states together. The United States claimed vast territories west of the Appalachian Mountains, but those lands were a source of vulnerability. Other nations claimed them. Native Americans refused to vacate them. Western settlers contemplated breaking loose to form their own coalitions. East of the Appalachians, internal divisions threatened to tear apart the new country. The American Revolution had been financed by printing paper money and bonds. But that had produced inflation, indebtedness, and low commodity prices, which now, in the 1780s, were generating a massive economic crisis.

TABLE I.I. NET INTERNAL FORCED MIGRATION BY DECADE

| IMPORTING STATE | 1790–1799 | 1800–1809 | 1810–1819 | 1820–1829 | 1830–1839 | 1840–1849 | 1850–1859 | TOTALS |
|---|---|---|---|---|---|---|---|---|
| Alabama | -- | -- | 35,500 | 54,156 | 96,520 | 16,532 | 10,752 | 213,460 |
| Arkansas | -- | -- | 1,000 | 2,123 | 12,752 | 18,984 | 47,443 | 82,302 |
| Florida | -- | -- | 1,000 | 2,627 | 5,833 | 5,657 | 11,850 | 26,967 |
| Georgia | 6,095 | 11,231 | 10,713 | 18,324 | 10,403 | 19,873 | -7,876 | 68,763 |
| Kentucky | 21,636 | 25,837 | 18,742 | -916 | -19,907 | -19,266 | -31,215 | -4,173 |
| Louisiana | -- | 1,159 | 20,679 | 16,415 | 29,296 | 29,924 | 26,528 | 124,001 |
| Mississippi | -- | 2,152 | 9,123 | 19,556 | 101,810 | 53,028 | 48,560 | 234,229 |
| Missouri | -- | -- | 5,460 | 10,104 | 24,287 | 11,406 | 6,314 | 57,571 |
| South Carolina | 4,435 | 6,474 | 1,925 | -20,517 | -56,683 | -28,947 | -65,053 | -158,366 |
| Tennessee | 6,645 | 21,788 | 19,079 | 31,577 | 6,930 | 4,837 | -17,702 | 73,154 |
| Texas | -- | -- | -- | -- | -- | 28,622 | 99,190 | 127,812 |
| *Decade Total* | *38,811* | *68,641* | *123,221* | *134,365* | *211,241* | *140,650* | *128,791* | *845,720* |

*Source:* Michael Tadman, *Speculators and Slaves: Masters, Traders, and Slaves in the Old South* (Madison, 1989), 12. Some states not included.

There was no stable currency. The federal government—such as it was—had no ability to tax, and so it also could not act as a national state.

Between the arrival of the first Africans in 1619 and the outbreak of Revolution in 1775, slavery had been one of the engines of colonial economic growth. The number of Africans brought to Maryland and Virginia before the late 1660s was a trickle—a few dozen per year. But along with white indentured servants, these enslaved Africans built a massive tobacco production complex along the Chesapeake Bay and its tributaries. Over those formative fifty years, settlers imported concepts of racialized slavery from other colonies (such as those in the Caribbean, where enslaved Africans already outnumbered other inhabitants by the mid-seventeenth century). By 1670, custom and law insisted that children were slaves if their mothers were slaves, that enslaved Africans were to be treated as rights-less, perpetual outsiders (even if they converted to Christianity), that they could be whipped to labor, and that they could be sold and moved. They were chattel property. And everyone of visible African descent was assumed to be a slave.[2]

After 1670 or so, the number of enslaved Africans brought to North America surged. By 1775, slave ships had carried 160,000 Africans to the Chesapeake colonies, 140,000 to new slave colonies that opened up in the Carolinas and Georgia, and 30,000 to the northern colonies. These numbers were small compared to the myriads being carried to sugar colonies, however. Slave ships landed more than 1.5 million African captives on British Caribbean islands (primarily Jamaica and Barbados) by the late 1700s and had brought more than 2 million to Brazil. In North America, however, the numbers of the enslaved grew, except in the most malarial lowlands of the Carolina rice country. By 1775, 500,000 of the thirteen colonies' 2.5 million inhabitants were slaves, about the same as the number of slaves then alive in the British Caribbean colonies. Slave labor was crucial to the North American colonies. Tobacco shipments from the Chesapeake funded everyone's trade circuits. Low-country Carolina planters were the richest elites in the revolutionary republic. The commercial sectors of the northern colonies depended heavily on carrying plantation products to Europe, while New England slave traders were responsible for 130,000 of the human beings shipped in the Middle Passage before 1800.[3]

Now, however, the consequences of war and independence were threatening the economic future of the enslavers. Marching armies had destroyed low-country rice-plantation infrastructure. Up to 25,000 enslaved Carolinians had left with the British. Britain blocked North American trade from its home and imperial markets. Though tobacco markets in continental Europe were still open, the price of that product went into free fall in the 1780s.[4]

Slavery was also caught up in the most divisive political issues raised by the Revolution. The weak federal government was buried in debts owed to creditors all over the nation and Europe, but southern and northern representatives to the Continental Congress disagreed over whether the apportionment of tax revenue by population should count southern slaves. More broadly, the Revolution raised the question of whether slavery should even exist, since rebellion had been justified with the claim that human beings had a God-given right to freedom. Petitions flooded northern state legislatures in the 1770s and 1780s, charging that slavery violated natural rights. And Thomas Jefferson, who admitted that "the Almighty has no attribute which can take a side with us" against the demands of the enslaved, was not the only prominent southerner who acknowledged the contradictions.[5]

Yet during the 1780s and 1790s, the possibilities that enslaved people represented, the wealth they embodied, and the way they could be forced to move themselves would actually forge links that overrode internal divisions. Marching feet increased the power of enslavers, and the beginning of forced movement south and west created new financial links and new kinds of leverage. And even among a million pairs of feet one can find the first steps: the moves and decisions that opened up new territories to slavery after the American Revolution. Kentucky and Mississippi could have been closed to slavery. Instead, during the 1780s, the early days of the American republic, decisionmakers in Philadelphia, New York, at Monticello, and elsewhere took crucial first steps that would allow slavery to spread.

BACK-AND-FORTH RAIDING DURING THE Revolution had stopped white settlement short of the mountains in South Carolina and Georgia. Few settlers had crossed the Appalachians into the Virginia and North Carolina districts that would become Kentucky and Tennessee. But potential migrants knew something about what lay beyond the bloody fringe of settlement. Since the early eighteenth century, white traders had walked deep into the woods of present-day South Carolina, Georgia, and Alabama, their mules laden with beads, guns, and liquor. Sometimes these merchants walked with enslaved African or African-American assistants. Those who returned alive told of rich soil and broad rivers. Further north, a trickle of settlers began to follow hunter Daniel Boone's reports of rich lands across the mountains that rose west of the Shenandoah Valley.[6]

Only after the American victory did waves of migration begin to surge west across the mountains. By the early 1780s, settlers were sending word back east of Kentucky acres that yielded a hundred bushels of corn apiece, an "Elysium . . . the garden where there was no forbidden fruit." But Native Americans called the region the "dark and bloody ground," a land of rich hunting over which they had long fought. In 1782, Indians began to raid the settlements, taking slaves with them as they retreated. Potential settlers became wary of the land, and of the journey there. The "Wilderness Road" through the mountain passes was slow, difficult, and dangerous. Shawnee and Cherokee killed dozens of travelers on the Wilderness Road every year. In winter, there were fewer Indian war parties about. But on their winter 1780 trip, John May and an enslaved man passed thousands of thawing horse and cattle carcasses in the "rugged and dismal" mountains, casualties of failed cold crossings.[7]

That year North Carolina enslaver Thomas Hart wondered whether he should send slaves to clear the land that he claimed in Kentucky: "to send a parcel of poor Slaves where I dare not go myself" seemed a kind of extreme taxation without representation, not in keeping with the ideals of the ongoing Revolution. But Hart changed his mind. He brought enslaved pioneers across the mountain road, even though the toil he planned for them to do in the woods, cutting down the forest and planting clearings with corn and tobacco, left them exposed to danger. "Lexington, Kentucky, August 22," read a 1789 newspaper story based on a letter from the western frontier. "Two

negro children killed and two grown negros wounded at Col. Johnson's."
Sometimes the Shawnees scalped prisoners, and sometimes they took them
back alive. Three Indians captured an enslaved man from a forge on the Slate
River in Kentucky during 1794. They bound his arms, made him walk, and
told him they were taking him to Detroit (where the British still maintained
a fort, in defiance of the Treaty of Paris) to sell him for "taffy"—tafia, cheap
rum. When they stopped to rest near the Ohio, they untied him and sent him
to gather firewood, which was when he escaped.[8]

Over the 1780s, the invaders from the coastlands fought hundreds of
battles. One such fight took place in 1786. Virginia-born migrant Abraham
Lincoln (the sixteenth president's grandfather) was clearing a field on his
land west of Louisville. The regular *thunk* of the axe was suddenly broken by
the crack of a musket. Lincoln fell. The Indian emerged cautiously from the
forest. Abraham's son Thomas, who had been playing in the field, crouched
behind a log. The sniper searched. Where was the little white boy with the
dark hair? Suddenly, another *crack*. The Indian, too, dropped dead. Lincoln's
teenage son Mordecai had shot him from the window of a log cabin on the
clearing's edge. And as the settlers won more and more little battles like this
one, eventually fewer and fewer Shawnee came south across the Ohio.[9]

Back on the east side of the mountains, meanwhile, slavery in the old Virginia and Maryland tobacco districts was increasingly unprofitable, and even
some enslavers were conceding that enslavement contradicted all of the new
nation's rhetoric about rights and liberty. In his 1782 *Notes on the State of
Virginia*, Virginia governor Thomas Jefferson complained that slavery transformed whites "into despots." Jefferson's first draft of the 1776 Declaration
of Independence had already railed against British support for the Atlantic
slave trade. Despite his ownership of scores of enslaved African Americans,
Jefferson recognized that the selling of human beings could turn his soaring
natural-rights rhetoric into a lie as sour as the hypocrisies of old Europe's
corrupt tyrants. Eventually, Jefferson embraced the hypocrisy, even failing
to free the enslaved woman who bore his children. "Sally—an old woman
worth $50," read the inventory of his property taken after his death. Yet in
1781, his Declaration's claim that all were endowed with the natural right to
liberty provided a basis to push the Massachusetts Supreme Court into conceding—in the case of a runaway slave named Quock Walker—that slavery
was incompatible with the state's core principles.[10]

Virginia politicians shot down Governor Jefferson's feeble suggestions of
gradual emancipation, but as he moved into the new nation's legislature, he
still hoped to ensure that the western United States would be settled and

governed by free, self-sufficient farmers—not an oligarchy of slave-driving planters. In 1784, a committee of the Continental Congress, headed by Jefferson, proposed an "ordinance" for governing the territories across the Appalachians. Many in Congress feared that the western settlements might secede or, worse yet, fall into the arms of European empires. As Britain's Indian allies raided south from their base at Detroit, Spain claimed the English-speaking settlements around Natchez. In 1784, Spain also closed the mouth of the Mississippi at New Orleans, the main trading route for western US territories. Eastern states also disagreed vehemently over how to sort out their overlapping claims to blocks of western land, which legislators hoped to sell in order to pay bonds issued during the Revolution. In the area that became Kentucky, still technically part of Virginia, the confusion generated by the uncertain government made it hard for small farmers like the Lincolns to make hard-won homesteads good. There was no logical system of surveying, so claims overlapped "like shingles." Old Dominion attorneys steeped in Virginia's complex and arcane land laws swarmed across the mountains to sort out conflicts—in favor of the highest bidder.[11]

The western issues that the Continental Congress faced in 1784 thus had implications for everything from the grand strategy of international relations to everyday economic and legal power. Jefferson's Ordinance of 1784 aimed to define them in favor of young Thomas Lincoln and everyone like him. It proposed that the territory between the Appalachians and the Mississippi River would become as many as sixteen new states, each equal to the original thirteen. And a second act that Jefferson drafted—the Ordinance of 1785—created a unified system of surveying, identifying, and recording tracts of land. This design eliminated the possibility of shingling over post-Kentucky territories with contradictory claims.[12]

The small farmer whom Jefferson imagined as the chief beneficiary of western expansion was as white as Abraham Lincoln, but the 1784 proposal also stated "that after the Year 1800 of the Christian Era, there shall be neither slavery nor involuntary servitude in any of the said states." That would have put Kentucky and what eventually became Tennessee on the road to eventual emancipation, perhaps along the lines of the statewide emancipations already under way in New England. The cluster of farms and plantations near Natchez on the Mississippi relied even more heavily on slavery. By 1790, there were more than 3,000 enslaved Africans in the disputed Natchez District. If Jefferson's proposal passed, presumably emancipation would have been mandated there as well. Yet under the Articles of Confederation, the wartime compromise that shaped the pre-Constitution federal government, a majority of state delegations in Congress had to consent for any proposal to become law. A majority of delegations, including his own Virginia one, rejected Jefferson's antislavery clause even as they accepted his other principles—that Congress should make rules for the territories, that the territories could become states, and that rational systems of land surveying and distribution should prevail. Frustrated, Jefferson sailed off to France to take up the position of American minister.[13]

Jefferson returned from France in September 1789. He had watched the Bastille torn down stone by stone, and he had seen ominous hints that the French Revolution would turn murderous. He had also started a relationship with a young enslaved woman. But the political changes he found upon his return gave him perverse incentives to think differently about the question of planting slavery in the western United States. Support for slavery's expansion had already become one of the best ways to unite southern and northern politicians—and Jefferson wanted to build a national political alliance that would defeat the older networks of power dominated by Federalist planting and mercantile gentries.

Congress had in the meantime taken one action to prevent slavery's expansion. In 1787 it reconsidered Jefferson's 1784 ordinance and passed it for the territories north of the Ohio, with the antislavery clause included. Perhaps this was no great moral or political feat. Few, if any, slaves had been brought to Ohio. Moreover, a handful of people would remain enslaved in the Northwest for decades to come, and the ordinance contained internal contradictions that left open the option of extending slavery into the states carved from the territory. Still, the ordinance became an important precedent for the power of Congress to ban slavery on federal territory.[14]

Yet in the four years between the end of the American Revolution in 1783 and the establishment of the Northwest Territory by Congress in 1787, the Congress had been able to accomplish precious little else to stabilize matters on either the western or the eastern side of the mountains. Chaos ruled: thirteen different states had thirteen different trade policies, currencies, and court systems. The Articles of Confederation, created as a stopgap solution for managing a war effort by thirteen different colonies against the mother country, had never allowed the federal government to have real power: the power to coerce the states, the power to control the currency, the power to tax. The result was not only economic chaos but also, wealthy men with much to lose feared, the impending collapse of all political and social authority. In rural Massachusetts, former Continental soldiers shut down courts after judges foreclosed on farmers who couldn't pay debts or taxes because of economic chaos. In other states, angry majorities elected legislatures that were ready to bring debt relief to small farmers and other ordinary folk even if it meant economic disaster for creditors.

So after Congress adjourned in early 1787, delegates from twelve states converged on Philadelphia. Their mission was to create a stronger federal government. The participants included future presidents George Washington and James Madison; Alexander Hamilton, who did more to shape the US government than most presidents; and Benjamin Franklin, the most famous American in the world. As May ended, they went into Independence Hall, closed the shutters, and locked the doors. By the time they emerged in late summer they had created the US Constitution, a plan for welding thirteen states into one federal nation. Once it was approved by the states, its centralizing framework would finally give Congress the authority it needed to carry out the functions of a national government: collecting revenue, protecting borders, extinguishing states' overlapping claims to western territory, creating stable trade policy, and regulating the economy. A deal struck between the big states and the small ones allowed representation by population in the House of Representatives while giving each state the same number of delegates in the Senate.[15]

But the Constitution was also built from the timber of another bargain. In this one, major southern and northern power-brokers forced their more reluctant colleagues to consent to both the survival and the expansion of slavery. The first point of debate and compromise had been the issue of whether enslaved people should be counted in determining representation in the House. Representing Pennsylvania, Gouverneur Morris warned that this would encourage the slave trade from Africa, since the importing states would be rewarded with more clout in the national government. In the end, however, every northern state but one agreed that a slave could count as three-fifths of a person in allocating representation. The Three-Fifths Compromise affected not only the House, but also the presidency, since each state's number of electoral votes was to be determined by adding two (for its senators) to its number of representatives in the House. One result was the South's dominance of the presidency over the next seventy years. Four of the first five presidents would be Virginia slaveholders. Eight of the first dozen owned people.

Over the long run, those presidents helped to shape the nation's policy of geographic and economic growth around the expansion of slavery. But those policies were not just enabled by the consequences of compromise over representation. Their roots grew out of the Constitution itself. As Gouverneur

Morris had suggested, the convention had to consider the issue of the Atlantic slave trade, the cause of a continual influx of people destined for slavery in the New World society. By the 1780s, many white Americans and a growing cadre of British reformers believed that modern civilized nations could no longer engage in the brutalities of the Middle Passage. In the Constitutional Convention itself, Virginia slaveholder George Mason bragged that Virginia and Maryland had already banned the "infernal traffic" in human beings. But, he worried, if South Carolina and Georgia were allowed to import slaves, the greed of those states would "bring the judgment of Heaven" on the new nation. Mason charged that "every master of slaves is born a petty tyrant," and yet the curse might spread. "The Western people"—by which he meant the people of Kentucky and other newly settled areas—"are already crying out for slaves for their new lands," he said, "and will fill that country with slaves if they can be got thro' S. Carolina and Georgia."[16]

Mason's critique infuriated politicians from the coastal areas of the deepest South, who leapt to their rights. Mason claimed to be a freedom-loving opponent of slavery, but he was speaking from self-interest, charged South Carolina's Charles C. Pinckney: "Virginia will gain by stopping the importations. Her slaves will rise in value, and she has more than she wants." Pinckney hinted at something new in the history of New World slavery: the possibility of filling a new plantation zone with slave labor from American reservoirs. This was possible because the Chesapeake's enslaved population had become self-reproducing. Pinckney then defended slavery in the abstract. "If slavery be wrong," he said, "it is justified by the example of all the world. . . . In all ages one half of mankind have been slaves." The Carolinas and Georgia threatened to abandon the Constitutional Convention.

Just as the already hot, shuttered hall neared the boiling point, Oliver Ellsworth of Connecticut—a future chief justice of the Supreme Court—rose to dump ice water on the Chesapeake delegates. Having "never owned a slave," Ellsworth said, he "could not judge of the effects of slavery on character." Rather than simply attacking the international slave trade's morality, or bewailing the effects of slaveholding in the moral abstract, let the economic interest of white Americans dictate whether the Atlantic slave trade should be closed. And, "as slaves also multiply so fast in Virginia and Maryland that it is cheaper to raise than import them . . . let us not intermeddle" with internal forced migrations, either. Concurring with Ellsworth, South Carolina's John Rutledge—another future chief justice—insisted that "religion and humanity [have] nothing to do with this question." "Interest alone is the governing principle with nations," he said. "The true question at present is whether the

Southern States shall or shall not be parties to the Union. If the Northern States consult their interest, they will not oppose the increase of Slaves which will increase the commodities of which they will become the carriers." New plantations within US borders could fill the role of the British sugar islands, to which northeastern merchants had lost access in the American Revolution. So the convention made a deal: Congress would ban the slave trade from Africa, but not for at least another twenty years.[17]

Years later, Illinois politician Abraham Lincoln, named for his grandfather who had been killed in the Kentucky field, would argue that a possible slave trade ban—however delayed—was a concession made by men ashamed of slavery. The Constitution, he pointed out, did not even include the words "slavery" or "slaves." Instead, it used circumlocutions, such as "Person held to service or labor." Perhaps, however, it was Ellsworth and Rutledge who were right: interest was the governing principle shaping the Constitution. In the interest of both profit and unity, they and most other white Americans proved willing to permit the forced movement of enslaved people. In straight or in twisted words, the outcome was plain: the upper and lower South would get to expand slavery through both the Atlantic trade and the internal trade. Meanwhile, the Northeast would earn profits by transporting the commodities generated by slavery's growth.

There were many Americans, even many white ones, whose interests were not served by those decisions, at least not directly. Yet the consequence of not accepting the deal would be disunity, which would be devastating to their interests in other ways. Allowing slavery to continue and even expand meant political unity. So black feet went tramping west and south in chains, and the constitutional compromise helped to imprint an economy founded on the export of slave-made commodities onto a steadily widening swath of the continent. Slavery's expansion soon yielded a more unified government and a stronger economy based on new nationwide capital markets. In fact, instead of finding slavery's expansion to be something that they just had to accept, to avoid ushering in a kind of conflict that could break the infant bonds of nationhood, white Americans soon found in it the basis for a more perfect union. Southern entrepreneurship and northern interest were going to be yoked together for a very long time.

IN EARLY 1792, VIRGINIA enslaver John Breckinridge was worried. He owned considerable land across the mountains, in Kentucky. He knew that over there was sitting a convention tasked with writing a constitution that would enable Kentucky to emerge from its territorial chrysalis and become a separate state of the Union. And he had heard that some in the convention might have the same doubts that Thomas Jefferson and George Mason had.

Breckinridge had no such doubts. He once advised a female relative: "Your land & Negroes let no person on this earth persuade you to give up." She wouldn't, however, be forced to do that by federal decisions. After the 1789 ratification of the US Constitution, the first Congress gathered in New York and immediately began to try to stabilize the chaotic territories. Congress confirmed the Northwest Ordinance's ban on slavery in what would eventually become Ohio, Indiana, Illinois, Michigan, Wisconsin, and Minnesota. No one thought those areas would make the commodities that John Rutledge had promised back at the Philadelphia Convention. South of the Ohio, the new Congress left open a massive new region for enslavers, organizing the Tennessee Territory in 1790 by passing a Southwest Ordinance that was an exact copy of the Northwest one—except that it left out the clause banning slavery.[18]

In the Natchez District along the Mississippi, slaves were already growing massive quantities of indigo. And in Kentucky, the first national census in 1790 had counted 61,000 whites and more than 12,000 enslaved Africans. Kentucky was not becoming Jefferson's dream republic of land-owning white yeomen—especially since the territory's constitutional convention decided that all land disputes would be referred to a statewide court of appeals staffed by three elite judges. The twenty-one speculators who owned a full quarter of all Kentucky land surely approved. Meanwhile, convention delegate David Rice—both a slaveholder and a Presbyterian minister—told the convention that slavery inevitably produced theft, kidnapping, and rape. Although a given owner might be a good man, debts could force him to break up families. Rice also insisted that slavery weakened the new republic by incorporating a group of people against whom citizens had effectively declared war. But the other delegates rejected his emancipation proposal, concluding that slavery actually strengthened Kentucky because it attracted wealthy settlers who would buy land from speculators.[19]

Once he heard the good news, John Breckinridge prepared to move his slaves west across the mountains. He wasn't sure if he would avoid "the perplexity of a Plantation" by hiring out his slaves. He'd heard that in the labor-hungry West, "the hire of your Negroes & rent of your land will far exceed any annual income you ever enjoyed." Reluctant to do the job himself, he convinced his neighbor John Thompson to lead the Breckinridge slaves across the mountains to his Kentucky properties. By the morning of April 3,

Thompson was at Fluvanna County on the James River, ready to leave, with Breckinridge's eighteen enslaved people in tow.[20]

Francis Fedric remembered such a morning—a morning on which he, too, had begun a forced march to Kentucky. As those who were about to be led away formed up before dawn, he saw men and women fall on the damp ground behind the old I-style house "on their knees[,] begging to be purchased to go with their wives or husbands." Some were "abroad husbands," men owned by other enslavers, but who had been allowed Saturday night visits with their wives—and who were now watching the dawn end their marriages. Some were abroad wives who had risen at 3 a.m. to walk to the plantation, bringing the last change of clothes they would ever wash for their husbands. Holding the hands of parents who were staying were sobbing sons and daughters. Begging was "of no avail," remembered Fedric. The man guiding the slaves out to Kentucky—well, this was not his first time. When he was ready, off they went, walking down the road toward the Blue Ridge looming in the distance.[21]

They walked, indeed. For as long as John Breckinridge owned people on both sides of the mountain, he also owned the connections between them. He held the carrots, and he held the sticks. For instance, Breckinridge had inherited a man named Bill from his father-in-law, Joseph Cabell. Breckinridge decided that Bill would have to go to the Kentucky farms. So would Bill's sister Sarah. This was when Bill and Sarah's mother, Violet, went to her owner Mary Cabell, Breckinridge's mother-in-law. Don't let Sarah "go to Cantucky," Violet begged, not unless "Stephen her husband," owned by another enslaver, could go with them. Violet had Mary Cabell's ear. However, Stephen cost more money than Breckinridge wanted to spend. Keeping Sarah in Virginia was the way for Breckinridge to save himself grief in his own family. So Sarah stayed. But Bill marched up the Wilderness Road, knowing that if he ran away along the trail, all bets were off. Sarah, and any children she might have, would be gone from Violet's life. The best he could do was to make the utilitarian calculations of the unfree, so he traded himself for his sister's marriage and his mother's last years.[22]

Thompson led Breckinridge's slaves across the Blue Ridge by the same pass where I-64 now soars over the mountain to connect Charlottesville in the Piedmont to Staunton in the Shenandoah Valley. Then they marched up the valley until, as Fedric remembered from his own journey, they saw the Alleghenies looming "in the distance something like blue sky." Looking for the shortest line through the folded hills to the Monongahela River in Pennsylvania, the flatlanders climbed up "through what appeared to be a long winding valley": "On every side, huge, blue-looking rocks seemed impending," thought Fedric—who feared that, "if let loose, they would fall upon us and crush us." It was April, but a late winter spell lowered upon Breckinridge's forced migrants. Snow or cold rain came almost every day, and by night, tired bodies shivered around roadside fires. Wolves howled at an uncertain distance. In the mornings, anger about forced separations bubbled up. "Never till then," wrote Thompson, "did I know the worth of whiskey." Indeed, it was valuable all day long: "When the Negroes were wet and almost ready to give out, then I came forward with my good friend whiskey and Once every hour, unless they were asleep I was obliged to give them whiskey."[23]

Sleep, however, was broken. Fedric remembered that "two or three times during the night . . . one of the overseers would call our names over, every one being obliged to wake up and answer." The men were not chained together, and the enslavers still worried that some wouldn't refuse the opportunity to escape—even with all the cards enslavers held over the migrants' families back east of the Blue Ridge. A slave named Mary, for instance, ran away from Jonathan Stout of Kentucky after Stout got her to the Ohio River. She had fled with a mulatto man, and they crossed the river together and struck out into the Northwest Territory. The causes of her run for freedom were written on her skin, as her enslaver's advertisement (in a newspaper called the *Herald of Liberty*) revealed: "She is stout made, with a scar over one of her eyes, and much scarified on her back."[24]

Some forced migrants marched through the mountains to Wheeling (in Virginia then, but now in West Virginia) on the Ohio River, while others floated down the Monongahela in Pennsylvania. Although Pennsylvania's glacial emancipation plan allowed slavery to exist for decades more, by the 1790s some white Pennsylvanians along the route to Kentucky had allegedly organized a "negro club" that sought to free enslaved people. In 1791, three Virginia slave owners, named Stevens, Foushee, and Lafon, on a flatboat with a group of enslaved men and women, heard someone on the shore calling them to come "take a dram." A chance to knock back a shot of whiskey and trade news in the wilderness sounded like a damn good idea. Soon the boat was scraping onto the gravel of the riverbank. That's when the white men on the bank pulled one of the slave men out of the boat and ran with him into the woods. The slave owners shoved hard on their steering poles, propelling the boat into the downstream current, while catcalls rang from the trees. In another case, when winter weather trapped a party of slaves and their owner at an inn in Redstone, Pennsylvania, three enslaved people slipped away. The

Virginia enslaver accused local whites of "seducing" the African Americans to escape. He returned to Redstone with allies, and local authorities arrested him for trying to recapture the people who had been "kidnapped" from him. The Redstone incident developed into a federal-level confrontation between Virginia and Pennsylvania. In 1793, southerners in Congress solved the crisis by passing the first comprehensive fugitive slave act.[25]

Once enslavers got their captives through the mountains and onto the Ohio River, these escape attempts declined. The flatboats didn't stop until they reached the growing frontier port of Louisville. From there, travelers made their way to Lexington and the Bluegrass region. This area was beginning to look like a more prosperous Piedmont Virginia, complete with economic winners and losers. In the counties around Lexington, 60 percent of all whites owned no land. There were two slaves for every white man over the age of twenty. Enslaved people toiled in fields that were lusher than Virginia's, growing tobacco, corn, and wheat. They also raised hemp, which enslaved workers made into cordage and rigging at the "rope-walks" around Lexington and Louisville. The US government, newly empowered by the federal constitution, rewarded Kentucky enslavers for their willingness to stay in the union by working to open the mouth of the Mississippi River to trade. The Treaty of San Lorenzo, signed with Spain in 1795, enabled planters to export shipments of tobacco, rope, and other products by taking them down the Mississippi to the world market via New Orleans.

The 1792 state constitution had made it illegal to bring slaves into Kentucky just to sell them, but this ban proved as porous as dozens of similar ones that would follow it. In 1795, William Hayden—a nine-year-old boy who would spend the next thirty years in the slave trade, first as commodity and then as a slave trader's employee—was sold at Ashton's Gap in Virginia. The man who purchased him brought him along the Wilderness Road and then sold him to Francis Burdett of Lincoln County, Kentucky. At his new owner's place, Hayden comforted himself by watching the reflection of the rising sun every morning in a pond, as he had done with his mother back in Virginia. He told himself that somewhere, she was watching, too. Meanwhile, slave buyers spread across the Southeast as far as Charleston, where Kentucky-based purchasers bought Africans from the Atlantic trade and marched them west to toil in the lead mines north of Lexington.[26]

The fact that slavery was now thriving in Kentucky enabled the new state to attract more people like John Breckinridge, folks whom George Nicholas, one of the key forces behind the 1792 state constitution, called "valuable emigrants from the five S. states." Such emigrants tuned the state's institutions

to help them maintain an ever tighter grip on human property. "Associations"—regional groups of Baptist and other churches—began to punish
ministers who preached against slavery. Ordinary white farmers, discour-
aged by the wealthy settlers' control over the processes of land law, moved
away. Thomas Lincoln, whose father had been murdered in the field as the
boy played, was now grown, and he hoped to have a farm of his own. But he
repeatedly lost claims on land he had cleared and planted in lawsuits launched
by speculators who lived as far away as Philadelphia. In 1816, he moved
his young family, including seven-year-old son Abraham, across the Ohio.
Thomas's retreat was part of a wider defeat for a vision of Kentucky as land
for yeoman farmers rather than as a region for high-capital speculation in
land and human bodies. And as young people like Francis Fedric and William Hayden marched west, another set of forced migrations started coming
out of Maryland and Virginia.[27]

ON A BRIGHT SPRING Maryland morning in 1805, Charles Ball rode com-
fortably on the board seat of a wagon, the lead rope of his owner's yoke of
oxen in his hands. He was driving the team to a little town on the bank of the
Patuxent River. Ball's latest owner—he'd had five in his twenty-five years—
was a hard man: Mr. Ballard would make a slave work in the woods on the
snowiest of days, with no boots. But Ball had hopes. All through the neighborhood, he was known as a strong, intelligent worker with a steady temper,
unlike his irascible African grandfather or his runaway father. Charles Ball
had been hired out to the Washington Navy Yard—and had come back, instead of running away like so many others had done when they had worked
"abroad." Ball could figure out faster, smarter ways to do any job. He had
incentives: a wife and children, owned by another white man. Ball's extra
hours supplied his family with food and clothing. Although he would later
laugh at his younger self, the twenty-five-year-old Charles Ball hoped for his
own and his family's freedom. And he was not alone. In Maryland's decaying
tobacco economy, enslavers were allowing many African Americans to buy
their freedom. The free constituted 5 percent of the state's 111,000 people of
African descent in 1790, and 22 percent of 145,000 by 1810. Maryland was
becoming a "middle ground" between a slave society and a free one.[28]

When Ball reached the little town, he followed his master's instructions,
tying the team of oxen up by the store that Ballard owned there. His owner
eventually appeared on horseback, went inside, and sat down to breakfast
with the storekeeper. Soon Ballard emerged and told Ball to come in and

finish the leftovers. As Ball sat down, he saw, through the wavy glass of the kitchen window, his owner talking emphatically with another white man.

Uneasily swallowing a last mouthful, Ball stood up and walked slowly out. He began hitching up the oxen, fumbling with the leather and rope. Suddenly he felt the presence of several people looming around him. He turned. As out of nowhere, a dozen white men had surrounded him. Before his eyes had time to flicker from one hard face to the next, his head jerked back as someone seized him by the collar from behind. "You are my property now!" a voice shouted in Ball's ear, and as Ball whipped his head around, he saw the man with whom Ballard had been whispering. "You must go with me to Georgia!" the stranger snarled.[29]

Ball stood in shock. White men grabbed and bent his arms. Quickly someone knotted his hands together behind his back. Mr. You Are My Property Now abruptly shoved Ball forward, and he stumbled. The crowd giggled. The enslaved man was suddenly helpless, barely able to stay on his feet. Playing desperately for time, Ball asked to see his wife and children. "You can get another wife in Georgia," countered his captor. Ball "felt incapable of weeping," and so, he later said, "in my despair I laughed loudly."

Proslavery writers later sneered at reformers who depicted slave transactions as sentimental tragedies, as if to say: "They laugh when they are sold—how bad can it be?" In their daily lives, enslavers understood that a laugh could be the only way to keep alive the ability to express something, anything. But behind the laugh, the word "Georgia" was racing through Ball's mind. Every African American in Maryland knew that word. By 1805, almost every slave had a personal Georgia story. Ball's was the only thing he remembered about his mother. In 1784, when Charles was four, his mother's owner went broke as tobacco prices collapsed. Doing the only thing he could do to escape his debts, the man died. And when the day came for the sale of the dead man's property, Charles, his mother, and his older brothers and sisters stood in the yard in front of the old Calvert County, Maryland, house.

Ball's father, who was owned by another man, was not allowed to leave work to see them before they were sold off. This was for safety's sake. A man who had to see his son stand naked before buyers might do anything. But among those who showed up were several men who had traveled a long way to Maryland. They came from South Carolina and Georgia. These men wanted to buy workers to work in the rice swamps and indigo fields and to fell the interior forests as the Catawba Indians retreated. Although by 1784 they hadn't yet figured out what they would plant on that raw new upcountry soil, they could pay a higher price than any Maryland buyer—what local sellers called a "foreign price." Several Carolina men divided up Ball and his brothers and sisters. A Georgia man bought his mother. Charles was too young to be worth carrying five hundred miles. A Maryland man bought the little boy and wrapped him in his own child's spare gown. Putting Charles up in front of him, the buyer turned his horse's head toward home. Before he could leave, Charles's mother came running up, weeping. She took Charles down into her arms, hugged him, and pleaded through tears for the man to buy them all. She only got a moment to make her case. Down came the Georgia man, running in his heavy boots, wading into her with his whip, beating her shoulders until she handed Charles over. The Georgia buyer dragged her screaming toward the yard. The crying boy clung to the Maryland man, his new owner.[30]

Only about 5,000 enslaved people were made to walk down the old Indian-trading trails to South Carolina and Georgia during the 1780s. But their significance was greater than their numbers suggest. They were the trickle that predicted the flood. As tobacco prices plummeted in the 1780s, the prices of long-staple, or "Sea-Island," cotton rose. Then, in the early 1790s, Carolina and Georgia enslavers started to use a new machine called the "cotton gin." That enabled the speedy processing of short-staple cotton, a hardier and more flexible crop that would grow in the backcountry where the long-staple variant would not. Suddenly enslavers knew what to plant in the Georgia-Carolina interior. Down south, enslaved people in Maryland and Virginia began to whisper to each other, you had to eat cotton seed. To be sold there "was the worst form of punishment," wrote a man who ran away after hearing that a "Georgia man" had bought him.[31]

These were rumors on the grapevine, not witness testimonies. Black people did not come back from Georgia. "Georgia-men" like John Springs did, and he brought so much gold for buying slaves that his bouncing saddlebags bruised his horse's sides. Georgia-men also brought information about opportunities that lay even farther southwest. Georgia, for instance, claimed the territory that eventually became the states of Alabama and Mississippi. Beginning in the late 1780s, state officials and northern investors launched multiple schemes to sell millions of southwestern acres to a variety of parties. Southwestern and northeastern entrepreneurs were using the allure of investment in future commodity frontiers developed by enslaved labor, and in the process they created a national financial market for land speculation. The North American Land Company, owned by American financier Robert Morris, a signer of the Constitution, purchased 2 million acres of what was

Image 1.1. "The First Cotton Gin," *Harper's Weekly*, December 18, 1869, p. 813. This image of the creation of one of the founding technologies of slavery's post-Revolution expansion was drawn after the Civil War by an artist who—judging by the grinning workers and watching child—couldn't decide whether slavery was businesslike or idyllic. Library of Congress.

at best infertile pine-barrens, and at worst simply fictitious. However, even bigger schemes were to follow, and some speculated on land that was both rich and real—although the multiple claims of states, empires, and Native Americans contradicted each other. The land at stake was the 65 million acres that became Alabama and Mississippi. In the breezy shorthand of land speculators and con men, the region was called "the Yazoo," after a river in present-day Mississippi.[32]

There were two chief Yazoo schemes. The first was launched in 1789, when it began to seem likely that Georgia would surrender the land south of Tennessee to the federal government. Indeed, the ratification of the US Constitution, and North Carolina's relinquishment of Tennessee to the federal government, made this step seem imminent. To establish a claim to as much of this land as possible, financiers put together three investment companies: the South Carolina Yazoo Company, the Tennessee Yazoo Company, and the Virginia Yazoo Company. The last was headed (on paper) by revolutionary firebrand Patrick Henry. Each was, boosters claimed, a company of most "respectable" gentlemen, whose endeavors would open up a vast and "opulent" territory for the "honor" of the United States. The companies struck a deal with the legislature of Georgia, acquiring 16 million acres for $200,000: twelve and a half cents an acre. And what a land it was rumored to be. Boosters claimed that it could produce all the plantation crops a North American reader could wish for in 1789. Indigo, rice, and sugarcane grew luxuriantly in the Yazoo of the mind: two crops a year! The most fertile soil in the world! A climate like that of classical Greece! Land buyers would flock there! And, "supposing each person only to purchase one negro," wrote one "Charleston," as he called himself in a Philadelphia newspaper, this would eventually create "an immense opening for the African trade." Charleston suggested that each planter of tobacco and indigo could trade slave-made crops for more slaves: "After buying one negro, the next year he can buy two, and so be increasing on."[33]

In 1789, investors' expectations already marked off the Yazoo for slavery, and investors attracted by Yazoo expectations counted on slavery's wealth-generating capacity to yoke together the interests of many parties across regional boundaries. People from the free states who might dislike the political ramifications of the Three-Fifths Compromise had few qualms about pumping investment into a slave country; they expected to make money back with interest from land speculation, from financing and transporting slaves, and from the sale of commodities. Investors nationwide bought the bonds of these land companies and put their securities into circulation like paper money.[34]

The 1789 Yazoo sale eventually collapsed, but within six years, the Georgia legislators found a second set of pigeons. Or perhaps it was the Georgia power-brokers who were the ones conned. Or, yet again, maybe the citizens of Georgia were being fleeced. In 1795, the Spanish government signed the Treaty of San Lorenzo, surrendering its claim to the Yazoo lands. A newly formed company—the Georgia-Mississippi Land Company—moved quickly to make a new deal. The roster of the company's leaders included a justice of the US Supreme Court, a territorial governor, two congressmen, two senators (Robert Morris of Pennsylvania and James Gunn of Georgia), and Wade Hampton of South Carolina, who was on his way to becoming the richest man in the country. Since the federal government would surely soon extinguish Georgia's western claims, speculators then would be dealing with a legislature that would be more expensive to bribe than a state. So the company sent Senator Gunn swooping down on Augusta, the Georgia state capital, with satchels of cash.[35]

Within days, Gunn persuaded the legislature to sell 35 million acres of land between the Chattahoochee and the Mississippi Rivers for $500,000 in gold and silver. The Georgia-Mississippi Land Company immediately sold the titles to other speculative entities, especially the Boston-based New England–Mississippi Land Company. That company, well provided with venture capital, broke up land into smaller parcels, which it then sold in the form of paper shares to investors. These Yazoo securities created a massive scramble in Boston, driving up the price of stock in the New England–Mississippi Land Company and creating paper fortunes. But in Georgia, people were furious. James Jackson, Gunn's fellow senator and political rival, pronounced the entire operation a fraud. Although he was a notorious land speculator in his own right, Jackson organized resentment of the Yazoo sale into a tidal wave at the next state legislative elections. In 1796, new representatives passed a statute overturning the previous legislature's land grant. They literally expunged by fire the record of sale from the 1795 session book of the legislature.[36]

The legal consequences of the sale itself remained unsettled. What was clear, however, was that people around the United States were willing to pour money onto slavery's frontier. They anticipated that slave-made commodities would find a profitable market. So did migrant enslavers, and so they demanded more slaves. In 1786, John Losson wrote to a Virginia planter whose Georgia land he managed. Crops were fine, he reported, impending war with the Indians promised more land acquisitions, and "likely negroes is the best trade for land that can be."[37]

Indeed, access to large supplies of "surplus" slaves from the Chesapeake was the best form of currency for buying land that one could possess. To get land in Wilkes County, Georgia, Virginian Edward Butler traded the promise of "three likely young negroes" who were still in Virginia. The buyer wished, Butler reminded himself in his diary, "one of the S[ai]d three negroes to be a girl or young wench." Back in Virginia, Butler hired Thomas Wootton to transport thirteen more enslaved people down to Georgia. Wootton delivered three "likely young negroes" to their purchaser and settled the rest on Butler's thus-purchased land. In this kind of process, less wealthy white men, such as Wootton, perceived a growing opportunity for those who were willing to buy slaves in the Chesapeake and march them south for sale. Such white men began to strike out on their own in greater numbers with each year in the 1780s and 1790s. So the "Georgia-man," an all-too-real boogeyman, became a specific type of danger in the oral book of knowledge of enslaved African Americans.[38]

Thus, as he sat mute and bound in the bow of a rowboat that had been hired to take him across the Patuxent River from Ballard's Landing, Charles Ball already knew his fate. The way enslaved African Americans talked about "Georgia" and "Georgia-men" was their way of describing the new economic, social, and political realities that were destroying the world they had built in the Chesapeake. Yet twenty years of fearing the Georgia-men did not make the instantaneous demolition of his family and future any easier. And while he had always feared the slave trade, Ball was beginning to realize that the Georgia-man who faced him across the body of the sweating oarsman was building a machine even more cunning than he had imagined.

Now, as they neared the other side, Ball saw a group of African Americans huddled on the bank. They were his fifty-one fellow captives. Nineteen women were linked together by a rope tied to the cord halters that encircled their necks. Thirty-two men were in a different situation, and Ball was about to be joined to them. A blacksmith waited with iron for him: iron collar, manacles, chains. The buyer cut loose the tight cords around Ball's wrists. Ball stood "indifferent" to his "fate," as he later remembered, while the two white men fitted the collar on his neck and slid the hasp of an open brass padlock through a latch in the front. Then they passed a heavy chain inside of the curve of metal and pushed the hasp and the body of the padlock together. Click.

The same heavy iron stringer now joined Ball to the other thirty-two men, sliding like fish strung through the gills. Then, for the last step in the process, the blacksmith took two bands of iron, put them around Ball's wrists, and pounded down bolts to fasten the manacles. He attached the manacle on Ball's right wrist by a short chain to the left manacle of the next man on the neck chain. The two of them would have to walk in step and next to each other. Ball was now becoming one moving part of something called a "coffle," an African term derived from the Arabic word *cafila*: a chained slave caravan. The hammer pounded hard, and the bolt pinched the wrist of Ball's chainmate, who began to cry. Ball sat stoically, but on the inside, his emotions ran just as wild. His mind raced uncontrolled, from "the suffering that awaited" him in a place that he believed had long since killed his mother to even more despairing internal sentences: *I wish I had never been born. I want to die. I cannot even kill myself, because of these chains.*[39]

They waited on the bank. The blacksmith yawned. By the time a flat-bottomed boat approached the bank, Ball's heart had stopped racing. "I concluded," he said as an old man, telescoping a recovery in reality more painfully won, "that as things could not become worse—and as the life of man is but a continued round of changes, they must, of necessity, take a turn in my favor at some future day. I found relief in this vague and indefinite hope."

In the boat was the returning Georgia-man, who ordered them all on board. The women—Ball now noticed that a couple of them were obviously pregnant—and the sixteen pairs of men, plus one, clambered in with a chorus of clinking. The scow set off toward the south bank of the Patuxent. The slave rowers pulled. Probably they didn't sing this song that one white traveler heard Chesapeake watermen chanting: "Going away to Georgia, ho, heave, O! / Massa sell poor negro, ho, heave, O! / Leave poor wife and children, ho, heave, O!"[40]

A man or woman who discovered that he was being taken south might be desperate enough to do anything. Some ran. Some fought like tigers. William Grimes tried to break his own leg with an axe. No wonder sellers and buyers schemed to take men like Charles Ball unawares. And once buyers bought, no wonder they bolted fetters on men and ran links of iron through padlocks. Men could march together carrying their chains. But there was no way that they could all run together. There was no way they could leap off a boat and swim to shore, no way thirty-three men hauling one thousand pounds of iron could hide silent in the woods. The coffle-chains enabled Georgia-men to turn feet against hearts, to make enslaved people work directly against their own love of self, children, spouses; of the world, of freedom and hope.[41]

When the scow scraped bottom in the shallows on the other side of the river, and the people awkwardly staggered out, the Georgia-man led them up the bank and onto a road that they walked until evening fell, heading southwest. They stopped at a rough tavern. The proprietor put them in one large room. Fifty-two pairs of mostly manacled hands managed to share a large pot of cornmeal mush before it was too dark to see.

That night, Ball, nestled between the two men chained closest to him, lay awake for many hours. When at last he slept, his son came to him. In Ball's dream the little boy tried to break the chain between his father's manacles to set his father's hands free, so that he could fix the boy's broken world. But the iron held. Charles's son faded. Then Charles's grandfather appeared. Born in Africa in the 1720s, he'd been kidnapped as a teenager, and sold to men who brought him across the salt water to Maryland. There they renamed him, and by the time Charles had known him, "Old Ben" was gray with half a century in slavery. Ben never surrendered his own version of Islam, or his contempt for either the enslavers or the enslaved people who behaved submissively. Charles's father, in contrast, had tried to play a less defiant part. But after the

1785 sale of his wife and children, the father changed. He spent his free time at Old Ben's hut, talking about Africa and the wrongs of slavery. The owner grew worried that the younger man would run away. He arranged a posse to help seize Charles's father for a Georgia trader. But Old Ben overheard two white men talking about the plan. He crossed three miles of woods in the dark to Charles's father's cabin. Handing his son a bag of dried corn and a jug of cider, Ben sent him off toward Pennsylvania. No one in Calvert County ever heard from Charles's father again.

Ben would have come for his grandson, too. But the old man was dead ten years gone, and these locks and chains would have defeated even his survivor's cunning. When the sun came up, it found Ball stumbling forward, trying to keep time with the rest of the coffle.

In the days to come, Ball and the other men gigged on the Georgia-man's line marched steadily southwest, covering ten to twenty miles a day. The pregnant women complained desperately. The Georgia-man rode on. After crossing the Potomac, he moved Ball, who was physically the strongest of the men, from the middle of the chain and attached his padlocked collar to the first iron link. With Ball setting a faster pace, the two sets of double lines of people hurried down the high road, a dirt line in the Virginia grain fields that today lies under the track of US Highway 301.

Ball's emotions continued to oscillate. Yet slowly he brought his interior more in line with the exterior face that men in coffles tried to wear. "Time did not reconcile me to my chains," Ball recalled, but "it made me familiar with them." Familiar indeed—at night, as everyone else slept, Ball crawled among his fellow prisoners, handling each link, looking for the weak one. He found nothing. But sometimes slave traders were careless—like the ones who were taking Jack Neal down the Ohio River in 1801. They had shackled him to the side of the boat, but one night Neal worked loose the staple that fastened iron chain to wood. He crept along the deck to his sleeping captor, slipped the white man's loaded pistol from his pocket, and blew the man's brains out. Neal then went to the far end of the boat, where another white man was steering, and announced, "Damn you, it was your time once but it is mine now."

Neal was recaptured on the Ohio shore and executed. Others had already tried the same thing, such as the enslaved men who in autumn 1799 killed a Georgia-man named Speers in North Carolina. He'd spent $9,000 buying people in northern Virginia—money embezzled from the Georgia state treasury by a legislator, as it turned out. If Speers had brought the men all the way to the end of the trail and sold them, perhaps the money could've been replaced, and no one would have been the wiser. But he forgot to close a lock one night, and as a newspaper reported, "the negroes rose and cut the throat of Mr. Speers, and of another man who accompanied him." Ten slaves were killed in the course of local authorities' attempts to recapture them.[42]

Every enslaved prisoner wanted to "rise" at one point or another. Properly closed locks disabled that option. Cuffs bound hands, preventing attack or defense. Chains on men also made it harder for women to resist. Isolated from male allies, individual women were vulnerable. One night at a tavern in Virginia's Greenbrier County, a traveler watched as a group of traders put a coffle of people in one room. Then, wrote the traveler, each white man "took a female from the drove to lodge with him, as is the common practice." Ten-year-old enslaved migrant John Brown saw slave trader Starling Finney and his assistants gang-rape a young woman in a wagon by a South Carolina road. The other women wept. The chained men sat silently.[43]

Chains enabled another kind of violence to be done as well. Chains saved whites from worrying about placating this one's mother, or buying that one's child. Once the enslaved men were in the coffle, they weren't getting away unless they found a broken link. For five hundred miles, no one had to call names at night to ensure they hadn't run away.

Men of the chain couldn't act as individuals; nor could they act as a collective, except by moving forward in one direction. Even this took some learning. Stumble, and one dragged someone else lurching down by the padlock dangling from his throat. Many bruised legs and bruised tempers later, they would become one long file moving at the same speed, the same rhythm, no longer swinging linked hands in the wrong direction.

Of course, though they became a unit, they were not completely united. Relationships between the enslaved could play out as conflict, or alliance, or both. People were angry, depressed, despairing, sick of each other's smell and the noises they made, how they walked too fast or slow, how no one could even piss or shit by themselves. At night, lying too close, raw wrists and sore feet aching, men in chains or women in ropes argued, pushed, tried to enforce their wills. John Parker, chained in the coffle as a preteen, remembered a weaker boy named Jeff who was bullied until John came to his aid, helping him stand up against a big teenager who was taking food from the younger children.[44]

None of that mattered to the Georgia-man as long as the chain kept moving, and Ball led the file down through Virginia into North Carolina at a steady pace. As the days wore on, the men, who were never out of the chains, grew dirtier and dirtier. Lice hopped from scalp to scalp at night. Black-and-red lines of scabs bordered the manacles. No matter: The Georgia-man

Image 1.2. Coffle scene, from Anonymous, *The Suppressed Book About Slavery* (New York, 1864), facing p. 49. The coffles marched south and west, with men linked together by a long chain, manacled hands, and women following them, under guard. Fiddles, songs, and whiskey were typical expedients to keep the chain moving forward.

would let the people clean themselves before they got to market. In the meantime, the men were the propellant for the coffle-chain, which was more than a tool, more than mere metal. It was a machine. Its iron links and bands forced the black people inside them to do exactly what entrepreneurial enslavers, and investors far distant from slavery's frontier, needed them to do in order to turn a $300 Maryland or Virginia purchase into a $600 Georgia sale.

At some point after they crossed the Potomac, Ball decided that as long as he was in the coffle, he could only do two things. The first was to carry the chain forward like a pair of obedient, disembodied feet. That, of course, benefited the Georgia-man, and a whole array of slave-sellers, slave-buyers, and financers-of-the-trade, while carrying him farther from home and family, and he had to do it whether he wanted to or not. The second thing, unlike the first, was something he could choose whether to do or not do. Charles decided to learn about his path, because understanding the path might eventually be for his own benefit. So he carefully watched the dirt roads of Virginia and North Carolina pass beneath his feet. He whispered the names of rivers as he lay in irons at night. He noted how far the cornfields had gone toward making ears as May crawled toward June. And he tried to draw out the grim man who sat on the horse clop-clopping beside the line. Day after day, Ball emitted a stream of exploratory chatter at the Georgia-man's ears, blathering on about Maryland customs, growing tobacco, and his time in the Navy Yard.

Enslaved people trained themselves all their lives in the art of discovering information from white people. But Ball couldn't pry loose even the name of the man who played this role of "Georgia-man." That role already did not have the best reputation among white folks in Virginia and Maryland. Some resented the way coffles, driven right through town, put the most unpleasant parts of slavery right in their faces. Others resented the embarrassment the traders could inflict. In the 1800 presidential election, Thomas Jefferson defeated the incumbent, John Adams, and the federal government shifted to the District of Columbia—and so the heart of the United States moved to the Chesapeake. Clanking chains in the capital of a republic founded on the inalienable right to liberty became an embarrassment, in particular, to Virginia's political leaders. Northern Federalist newspapers complained that Jefferson had been elected on the strength of electoral votes generated by the three-fifths clause of the Constitution—claiming, in other words, that, Virginia's power came not from championing liberty, but from enslaving human beings.[45]

Sometimes both Georgia-men and the enslaved intentionally irritated that particular sting. A few years after Ball was herded south, a slave trader marched a coffle past the US Capitol just as a gaggle of congressmen took a cigar break on the front steps. One of the captive men raised his manacles and mockingly sang "Hail Columbia," a popular patriotic song. Another such occasion relied for its emotional punch not on the sarcasm of captives but on the brashness of captors. Jesse Torrey, a Philadelphia physician, was visiting the Capitol when he saw a coffle pass by in chains. A passer-by explained that the white "drivers" of the caravan were "Georgy-men." The doctor walked up to one and inquired (in what must have been an accusatory tone), "Have you not enough such people in that country yet?" "Not quite yet," was the sneering reply.[46]

Another incident even became something of a media scandal. In the early nineteenth century, Americans were redefining the role of women, arguing that mothers needed to teach their sons the principles of self-sacrifice if the young men were to grow up to be virtuous citizens of the young republic. In December 1815, an enslaved woman named Anna dramatized the way in which slavery's expansion did not allow her to do that. Sold to a Georgia-man, separated from her husband and all but two of her children, she had been locked in a third-floor room at George Miller's tavern on F Street in

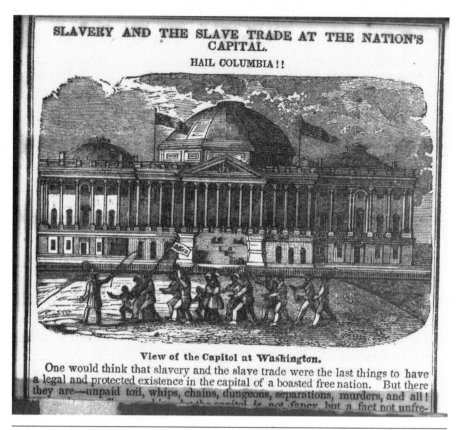

Image 1.3. "Hail Columbia!! View of the Capitol at Washington," illustration from Theodore Weld, *American Slavery As It Is* (New York, 1839). Though published in 1839, this image attempts to depict an incident that was first reported in the late 1810s. A coffle of enslaved people marching through Washington, DC, in plain view of congressmen taking a cigar break on the Capitol steps, saluted those representatives of a free people with an ironic rendition of the patriotic American song "Hail Columbia."

Washington, DC. Squeezing through a garret window, she was either trying to escape or jumping from despair. Whichever it was, gravity took over and Anna fell twenty-five feet, breaking her spine and both arms. Dragged into a bed, she said before dying, "I am sorry now that I did it, they have carried my children off with 'em to Carolina."[47]

Jefferson and his allies wanted to neutralize discussion of slavery. With the help of northerners, they were eventually able to do just that. Jefferson and his allies had fought their Federalist opponents over many things in the 1790s: the French Revolution; the Federalists' perceived desire to centralize power in the federal government; whether political opposition to the president was treason. But they almost never fought over slavery. During the 1800 election, a few northern Federalists charged Jefferson with keeping a "harem" of enslaved lovers at Monticello, but southern Federalists—and most northern ones—kept the slavery question sheathed. They did so because of interest. Slavery's expansion was one topic in which political leaders from all sides could find common interest. In Congress, prominent southern Federalists, led by Robert Goodloe Harper of South Carolina, blocked Georgia's 1796 attempt to repeal the Yazoo sale. Together with northern advocates for financial capital, such as Jefferson's nemesis Alexander Hamilton, Harper insisted that a contract was a contract, and a sale was final. Both investors and the cause of developing the southwestern United States should be protected from a legislature elected by popular demagoguery and out to overturn a legal transaction.[48]

The debate over the Yazoo claims might seem straightforward: big money versus small farmers meant Federalists versus Jeffersonians, nationalists versus states' righters. Yet things were not so simple. Many northern Republicans had invested in Yazoo bonds. Many Georgians recognized how they could benefit if the sale stood. And there was a potential quid pro quo on the table. In 1798, Congress was debating whether to organize the Mississippi Territory—the land sold off by the Georgia legislature in 1795. Several northern Federalists attempted to add the Northwest Ordinance's Article VI to the bill, proposing to outlaw slavery in a land where it already existed—especially around Natchez. Although the territory would obviously become at least one Jefferson-leaning state, Federalist Robert Goodloe Harper gathered an interregional coalition of both Federalists and Republicans to defeat the amendment. These were not only southerners, but also northerners who knew that trying to ban slavery could jeopardize Georgia's surrender of land claims to the federal government. That would delay the survey and sale of land, and thus the time when Yazoo investors could recoup their investments. And the investors knew that these millions of acres would yield much more value if purchasers could count on setting slaves to labor on them.[49]

Many congressmen examined their direct financial interests and chose to ensure that Mississippi became a slave territory. To soothe their consciences, some of Jefferson's followers began to claim that expanding slavery would actually make it more likely that slavery could eventually be eliminated. "If the slaves of the southern states were permitted to go into this western country," argued Virginia congressman William Branch Giles, "by lessening the number in those [older] states, and spreading them over a large surface of country, there would be a greater probability of ameliorating their condition, which could never be done whilst they were crowded together as they now are in the southern states." If the slaves were "diffused," enslavers would be more likely to free them, for whites were afraid to live surrounded by large numbers of free black people. Thus, moving enslaved people into new regions where their enslavement was more profitable would lead to freedom for said enslaved people. Make slavery bigger in order to make it smaller. Spread it out to contain its effects. And those most eager to buy this bogus claim were the Virginians themselves. Jefferson became the most prominent advocate of diffusion. The notion provided a layer of deniability for liberal enslavers who were troubled by slavery's ability to undermine their self-congratulation. Diffusion answered the clanking figures who sang "Hail Columbia," and the knowing sneer of the Georgia-man who knew the price of every soul.[50]

In 1798, Georgia ceded its lands to the federal government, and Congress organized the land between the Chattahoochee and the Mississippi Rivers into the Mississippi Territory, with slavery included. Congress proved unable to decide whether the Yazoo claimants had a right to the land bought in 1795. In the House debate, Virginia Federalist John Marshall was one of the claimants' most vigorous promoters. Long an advocate for investors who speculated on southwestern lands, Marshall would soon be appointed chief justice of the Supreme Court by President Adams.[51]

Once Jefferson was elected, he tried to settle the troubled waters of the political nation by proclaiming, in his 1801 inaugural address, "We are all Federalists, we are all Republicans." He might as well have argued, "We are all diffusionists, we are all Yazoo speculators." And then he could have added, reassuringly, "We are none of us Georgia-men." Yet, in 1805, the man on the horse directed Charles Ball and his coffle around Richmond, Virginia's capital. Perhaps he did so to spare the eyes and the consciences of those who weren't fully persuaded by diffusionism's sloppy logic. But Georgia-men didn't have to explain themselves to the likes of Charles Ball. Or to anyone, so long as the enslavers were willing to supply a stream of men and women to the backcountry. And the existence of Georgia-men allowed those who reacted to the ugliness of diffusion-in-actual-practice to waste their heat on an enemy who didn't care what they said.

So Ball and the coffle crossed the river on a ferry west of the city. The two lines, men in chains and women in ropes, walked southwest from Richmond for weeks. One day in southern Virginia, they passed a road leading up to a low house surrounded by sandy tobacco fields. A hundred men, women, and children toiled out there under the gaze of a white man with a long whip. The

Georgia-man stopped another white man coming up the road. "Whose land is that?" he asked. "Mr. Randolph, a member of Congress."

The coffle kept on. They crossed the Roanoke River, entering North Carolina's Piedmont. Next came a week of hard marching through this land of small farms, passing cornfields and the boys and girls toiling in them. Then water was sloshing around Ball's feet on the deck of an overloaded flat as a Yadkin River ferryman pulled on the rope: one trip for the men, going back for the women. Three days' marching later, and the Georgia-man told them they had entered South Carolina—a placename that was part of the greater Georgia in Ball's geography. Night fell. Thoughts of death returned.

In the morning, just to make sure they all understood that they had marched into a different part of the world, the Georgia-man pried open his compressed lips and made a little speech. They were now too far from Virginia or Maryland to ever get back again, he told them. They must give up all hope of returning. And there was much truth to what the Georgia-man said. These fifty-two enslaved African Americans had now walked into a place that the coffle-chain had inked onto the map with streaks of iron oxide from sweat and dirty manacles. Beside the road, they began to see a strange crop growing in the early summer fields: "It looked not unlike buckwheat before it blossoms," Ball remembered. This was the cotton plant. In this place where chains marched past plants that looked like food but turned into fiber, they were trapped in a deeper slavery, one shifted into being by two decades of Georgia-men traveling to and from the Chesapeake. When the American Revolution had ended, 20,000 enslaved people had lived in the South Carolina backcountry. Now 75,000 were there. Meanwhile, the Georgia slave population was growing, too, increasing from 30,000 in 1790 to 107,000 in 1810.[52]

The next day, as they walked, a stranger rode up, matching the Georgia-man's pace. "*Niggers* for sale?" He wanted to buy two women. The two men negotiated, argued, and insulted each other a little. The new man stared at the women and told them what he thought he'd do with them. The coffle kept moving. The white men rode along, bargaining. Maybe the deal could be sweetened, allowed the Georgia-man, if the South Carolinian paid to have the chains knocked off the men. One thousand dollars for the two, plus blacksmith fees. They stopped at a forge, and they kept arguing. The new man stated for everyone's benefit that he had worked African men to death in iron collars. The blacksmith came out, and he asked what "the two gentlemen were making such a *frolick* about," Ball later said. Frolicking: Down there, Ball realized, the Carolinians' play, the time when they were most fully themselves, was evidently when they were arguing, negotiating, dealing, and intimidating the enslaved.

For $2.50, the blacksmith would take off the chains. As he knocked off the bolts and the Georgia-man unkeyed the locks, the South Carolina buyer took the two women away. One was a Calvert woman, the mother of four. Ball had known her most of his life. He hoped he wouldn't end up with a man as frightening as the one who had taken her.

Freed of the heavy iron, Ball was giddy, but not happy. Five weeks in the chains had changed him just as surely as it had changed his location on the map. The enslaved people toiling in the fields kept their heads down as the new feet from Maryland walked past. He could see that more power hung over them, and now him, too.

White people now treated Ball as a different kind of property. Under Virginia and Maryland law, the slave had been chattel since the seventeenth century. Slaves could be sold by their owners, moved by their owners, and separated from others by their owners. Georgia and Carolina cut-and-pasted many aspects of the Virginia slave code into their laws. But in practice, the laws were implemented differently. Almost all of the slaves down here were new to the whites who owned them, and they used them without constraint. The Chesapeake enslavers were bound by many different considerations when it came to buying or selling human beings: family ties between enslaved people that were important to other whites, fear of angry slaves, fear of one's evangelized conscience, fear of foreign criticism of the land of the free. Still, by 1805 the coffle-chain was breaking that pattern, even back in Virginia. Up and down the path that ran from east to west, north to south, the chain made a person's feet work against him or her. The person in irons became more truly owned by someone else, more easily separated from family, and more easily traded and commodified.

The coffle helped make Ball's enslavement deeper and more flexible; it linked his marching feet to the needs of the nation's most successful people. It provided defenses for those who did not want to deal with their own half-hearted moral failure, with the inclusion of slavery in new state constitutions. The existence of the "Georgia-man" and the "Yazoo" as options also made a chained Ball into a movable piece in the political economic puzzle of the young United States. For although coffles got no closer than Pennsylvania Avenue to the room in which John Marshall read out his 1810 decision in *Fletcher v. Peck*, their chained footprints walked all over the case file. The technical issue before the Court was whether the Georgia state legislature could overturn a contract of sale into which a previous session had entered.

Marshall and the Court ruled that the people of Georgia could not overturn the sale. The contract might have been accomplished by bribery. It may have contravened the will of the majority of white Georgians. But the sale to the investors' land companies was a sale of property all the same, and property rights, by the chief justice's interpretation of the contract clause of the Constitution, were absolute. The people who invested in the company—mostly New England money-market types and bankers—should be repaid from the sale of the land, which was now held by the federal government.

Federalists were happy. But so were many of Jefferson's party. In Massachusetts, in New York City, and in Philadelphia were large nests of Jeffersonians whose financial fortunes were as invested in the development of stock and bond markets as those of their local Federalist rivals. Congress now had to compensate the Yazoo bondholders. The payout to speculators who had bought up the bonds would in turn strengthen confidence in all American capital markets. The Court was providing security that would bring more money into the southwestern territories over time. Some southern Jeffersonians felt betrayed by the Court's Republican appointees. Georgia politicians were furious in public. Tellingly, though, neither Jefferson nor his protégé, President James Madison, had attempted to influence the outcome of the Yazoo situation in favor of Georgia's desire to overturn the earlier legislature's sale of half of Alabama and Mississippi.

The principle that a contract is inviolable and that property is absolute was now the accepted conclusion of the federal constitution. In the *Fletcher* decision, the chief justice never mentioned slavery. But the Court's decision made possible the survey and sale of more than 20 million acres for slavery's expanding footprint. Marshall's ruling also gave every future defender of slavery and its expansion an incredible tool. Consider this: If the people of Georgia couldn't overturn a contract born from obvious corruption, how could a legislature or any other government entity take slaves away from owners? Enslaved African Americans were property acquired by contract, according to the law of slave states. Nor, the decision implied, could legislatures constrain enslavers' right to treat said property as being as absolute, as mobile, and as alienable as they liked.

The interlinked expansion of both slavery and financial capitalism was now the driving force in an emerging national economic system that benefited elites and others up and down the Atlantic coast as well as throughout the backcountry. From Jefferson and Madison's perspective, the soon-to-be states of the Mississippi Territory would yield votes in the Electoral College and Congress, votes to use against the Federalists—and more than they would have gained by courting hard-core states' righters. One of the latter was Jefferson's onetime lieutenant, the increasingly erratic Yazoo-hater John Randolph—whose whip-wielding overseer had seemed to Charles Ball like an omen of the Georgia looming up at the end of his road. Instead, the Republicans now formed a pro-finance, pro-expansion coalition that ingested many onetime Federalists and dominated US politics until, by the 1820s, it became a victim of its own success. Randolph was one of the few southern enslavers consistent enough to insist that both the stigmatization of Georgia-men and the diffusion scam were hypocrisies. That kind of truth-telling drives an implicated man mad, and Randolph, once Speaker of the House, eventually spiraled into a level of insanity remarkable for even a Virginia politician.

More typically hypocritical was Bushrod Washington, George's nephew and a Supreme Court justice. This classic Virginia gentleman, who inherited Mount Vernon in 1799 when his uncle died, had concurred with Marshall in 1810. Perhaps he had done so because of the sweet reasonableness of the chief justice's arguments. More likely, the principle of property and contract offered men like Washington a series of un-trumpable "outs." Such justifications came in handy in 1821, for instance, when it became public knowledge that Washington had sold fifty-four people from Mount Vernon to a slave trader who had then taken them through the Yazoo territories. In response to a newspaper editor who complained that the Father of Our Country's nephew had sold human beings like "horned cattle," Bushrod Washington wrote "on my own behalf and on that of my southern fellow citizens to enter a solemn protest against the propriety of any person questioning our right; *legal or moral*, to dispose of property which is secured to us by sanctions equally valid with those by which we hold every other species of property."[53]

Men like Washington the younger could use the property story underlined by *Fletcher v. Peck* to slip away from confronting the contradictions of slavery's expansion, even if singing coffles and snickering Georgia-men waved the contradictions under Congress's collective nose. Having said of himself in 1788 that "nobody will be more willing to encounter every sacrifice" to bring about emancipation, in 1814 Jefferson ruefully shook his head and said that the old generation had moved too slowly. Now, instead of finding that "the generous temperament of youth" raised the new generation "above the suggestions of avarice," he realized that the young men of this new day dawning had digested the lessons of Georgia and were racing to create fortunes from slavery's expansion.

Bushrod Washington also got good mileage from Jefferson's diffusion story. His decision to sell off enslaved people was, he insisted, not a tale of greed but a demonstration of how forced migration protected white lives. As the African Americans living at Mount Vernon grew in number, he claimed, they had become insubordinate. A couple of Washington's slaves escaped to the North, using their feet to undermine his right to property. The rest came to believe that when he died they would be free. And the justice began to fear that they were speculating about where the sharpest knives were, and how they might hide poison in his food. No more Bushrod, no more slavery. Jefferson had blurted analogous fears, famously speaking of a possible "reversal of fortunes" and describing the situation of Chesapeake slaveholders as being like riding a "wolf [held] by the ears[;] . . . we can neither hold him, nor safely let him go." Even if whites had agreed to general emancipation, whites had "deeply rooted prejudices," and blacks "ten thousand recollections." "New provocations" would divide and whip them into an apocalyptic race-war crescendo. These "convulsions" would end only with "extermination of the one or the other race."⁵⁴

So Jefferson and Washington and other white Virginians stuck to a third choice, a financially profitable one: to "diffuse" enslaved African Americans south and west. And the existence of the Georgia-men allowed such respectable leaders to draw alleged emotional and moral distances between themselves and the unpleasant side of "diffusion." They wrung their hands as coffles and Georgia-men passed. Or they asserted that slaves lived better in the new states than in the old. But while Washington contended that forced migration was carried out for the benefit of enslaved people, one observer, who stood in Leesburg in August 1821 and watched as Bushrod Washington's coffle went by, saw "unhappy wretches," among whom were "husbands [who] had been torn from wives and children, and many relatives left behind." Those left at Mount Vernon whispered bitter words to tourists who visited the national father's home.⁵⁵

BETWEEN THE END OF the American Revolution and the *Fletcher v. Peck* decision in 1810, slavery's expansion linked the nation together. The needs of the nation encouraged the growth of a complex of institutions and patterns—and, just as significantly, excuses—that made national political and financial alliances possible. The needs of individual enslavers and others who hoped to profit from the expansion of all sorts of economic opportunities encouraged the growth of a more powerful set of national capabilities, more market-friendly laws, and more unified markets. The needs of national expansion, plus the ability of chained people to walk, trapped enslaved people as absolutely held property in the political compromises, political alliances, and financial schemes of the United States and in the very map of the young country. Slavery, and specifically, the right of enslavers to sell and to move their slaves into new territory, became a national practice: as a strict definition of property under constitutional law, as habit and expectation, and as a pattern of political compromise.

Turning this wheel of cause and effect were moving feet—those of Charles Ball, of the thirty-two other men to whom he was connected, of the nineteen women roped together behind them, and others still growing toward sellable height. From old Maryland and Virginia, which were crumbling beneath the glossy veneers offered to the world by their politicians, the coffle-chains and the people who toted them clanked across hundreds of miles into a new world where everything was flux and frolic. Forced migration and the expansion of slavery became a seemingly permanent and inevitable element of the mutually-agreed-to structure of lies that, defended by the agile legal realism of Marshall and the myth of diffusion, made the nation. To put the machine in motion, Washington could now rely on a set of chaining experts, Georgia-men who took the financial and physical and status risks of moving enslaved people. Charles Ball could now be moved more easily in every sense, with less political, ideological, legal, and personal friction.

Thus the coffle chained the early American republic together. In South Carolina, Charles Ball's neck and hands were finally freed of the coffle's chains, but only so his owner could finish the chain's work of converting Charles and the other remaining Maryland slaves into market goods. Because they had left sweat from pores and pus from blisters on the road, and had drawn down their meager stores of body fat, the Georgia-man rested them for twenty days at a property owned by a cotton farmer. Ball and his companions were given butter to eat so they would become sleek and "fat." The lice were driven from their bodies and clothes by repeated washing. And soon, white people began to come and examine them, ask them questions, speculate on their bodies. Here, the Georgia-man was among people who respected him, calling him "merchant" instead of "negro driver" or "Georgia trader." Here he was needed, and not as the scapegoat for other enslavers' sins. He even let his name drop from his tight lips: "My name is M'Giffin, sir," he said in response to a prospective buyer's inquiry.[56]

After two weeks, M'Giffin moved the drove of slaves south into Columbia. There, on the Fourth of July, the local jailor auctioned them off in front of a crowd of hundreds who had just finished eating a fine banquet and listening to a patriotic speech. The sale eventually narrowed down to the last three, the stoutest men, including Ball. The jailor now theatrically announced that if M'Giffin did not get $600 for each man, he would take them to Georgia and sell them there. An "elderly gentleman" announced that he would pay that amount for "the carpenter." Ball was not really a carpenter, but many lies were told on that day that celebrated freedom from tyranny: not one of the slaves for sale had ever run away, or stolen from their masters, or been whipped. Each was sold by a fine Maryland or Virginia gentleman who had sadly fallen into debt.

The other whites deferred to this "elderly man." Ball pegged him as a major slave-owner. He was actually one Wade Hampton, among other things a major Yazoo investor. Having inherited rice plantation wealth in the low country, Hampton was in the process of shifting his slaves into cotton—for now, on acres he owned near Columbia, South Carolina. Later, his quest for wider vistas would lead him into Georgia, Mississippi, and Louisiana endeavors. Today, however, Hampton was drinking, and celebrating the Fourth. He told Charles to find a corner of a stable and go to sleep. The next day, they would make the trip to Hampton's nearby property—one last step of the journey that Ball's feet had made from the old to the new.

## 2

# HEADS

## *1791–1815*

T HE LOGS BOBBED AROUND the pilings of the customhouse. The hut
stood on legs, a chicken up to its drumsticks in shallow water, besieged
by a continent's stew. Anything that could last a month in water ended up
down here at the "Balize," the flats at the Mississippi's mouth: bark; sticks;
whole trees, if they didn't get hung up along a thousand miles of snags. Deer
and drowned wild cattle didn't make it; catfish and turtles ate them long
before they could come this far. The heaviest load of all flowed under the
rippling corduroy of forest waste: a mighty subsurface plume of water, fresh
but not sweet, sagging with its load. Iron from the far north, silver from
Rocky Mountain lodes, and most of all, dirt. Humus rinsed from the banks
of ten thousand forest tributaries, tumbled past Jefferson's would-be sixteen
states, stirred with black soil from the delta. For an eon the river had piled
up silt, marching its outlet southward on its own. But for the past decade, the
runoff slurry had been thickening. Upriver, someone was plowing, planting,
harvesting.

It was the beginning of 1807. Looking over the side of the *Adventine*, as it
bobbed at anchor in the ship channel, was a short, dark man. He had been the
only slave on board since Charleston. The crew paid him no mind. He was
neither a threat nor the main cargo. He still didn't understand what they said,
and they did not understand him. But they no longer feared that he'd jump,
like the Africans they'd wrestled back over the rails on Atlantic crossings.
There were two startling things about him. One was that when he slept, he
always curled up in the same position. The other was that he wore an iron collar around his neck, inscribed with the words, "Property of Hugh Young."[1]

Behind his eyes, he remembered. Coming from Africa to South Carolina,
he had gone through what 10 million other forced migrants to the New World

had already survived: captured or kidnapped, or simply bought, marched to the coast, sold by strange men to even stranger men (some milky-colored, some angry red, some tan with dark curly hair). Out of the darkness of the dungeon in chains, hand and foot, one of a whole stick of African men bundled by the white sailors into the big coastal canoe. Feeling the salt spray as it flushed over the gunwales. They plunged through rough waves to a floating structure and were hauled on board the Rhode Island ship. Herded below with shoves, they took dainty, quick steps to stay balanced under a four-foot ceiling, too short for even these men, who barely averaged five feet. The air stank from men already curled on the floor in front of them. Their predicament showed the new arrivals how to lie: spoon-fashion, on the left. Easier on the heart that way, captains believed.

In 1787, the Constitutional Convention had allowed the trade to go on. In the twenty years since, citizens of the new nation had dragged 100,000 more people from the African coast. Always, some fought. They clung to the doorposts of the dungeons and barracoons. They threw themselves in chained groups over the gunwales of the boats to drown together in the surf. They grabbed at the clubs the sailors used to beat them down onto the slave deck. They rushed the barricade when the crew let them out for exercise. Ten percent of Atlantic slave-trade voyages experienced major rebellions. But resistance almost always failed. Sailors fired grapeshot cannon into surging masses of desperate men and women in the midships. The scuppers ran with blood. The sharks ate.[2]

Now the man remembered how he had lain in vomit and shit and piss. How he had eaten from the bucket they brought. He heard the women on the other deck crying for a dying baby or sister; heard them fight as the sailors took them into the crew's quarters one by one, to be raped. He saw them drag out men who had gone stiff and grinning. The angel's fingers clawed at him, too. He puked up everything down to the bile, barely survived the dysentery that emptied out a hundred, sweated from cargo fevers. He panted, waiting for the water pail's ladle. He could've died like millions of others. But he lived on.

Perhaps he was lucky. At last the ship dropped anchor in Charleston harbor. Then, they sold him to a New Orleans merchant's local agent, who locked him into the iron collar that bore the merchant's name. Another white man walked him up East Bay Street toward the *Adventine*'s dock. Signs creaked in the wind that brought the stench of his old ship from Gadsden's Wharf. The buzzards lighting and flapping on the other side of the Cooper River knew where the harbor current piled bodies against the sandbar. That year alone, seven hundred Africans died on the twenty-five different ships that spent time waiting there in quarantine.[3]

Now, after another voyage, the rowboat eased up to the *Adventine*'s hull. The white customs officer scrambled up the rope ladder. The man in the iron collar watched everything. He could tell that the slave who rested on the oars had gone through dark waters, too. Behind unblinking eyes, the oarsman gave back the collared man's gaze, and remembered the feel of the slave deck's sweating wood pressing against his ritually scarred cheek.

Yet this new arrival's experience would be different. Slavery itself was changing from the first story, the sugar-island model that had shaped everything in the New World to this point. This man would carry his collar not to an island or to an isolated belt of settlements clinging to the coast. He was headed into a vast continent. Behind the mists on the mud flats, enslavement would find no geographical limit, only political ones—and enslavers had structured politics to their advantage. Citizens, not colonials, would own him. Owners' property interests—owners who got to vote and run for office and govern—would drive decisions about him, not the plans of distant imperial bureaucrats. And because the man in the iron collar and all who followed him into the depths of the continent would make not a luxury product but the most basic commodity in a new kind of endlessly expanding economy, there would also be no limit to the market for the product of his labor. This meant that there was no numerical limit to the number of enslavers, or to the number of investors who would want to chase enslavement's rewards. Only conscience, or the inability of the world's investment markets to deploy enough savings, could impede the transfer of capital to slavery's new frontiers.

All of this was certain, but for the doubt raised by one big question: whether the United States and all the entrepreneurs who wanted to expand slavery into the great river valley in the middle of the continent could actually hold onto North America's interior. That outcome was still in doubt, even in 1807. In fact, it had been in doubt since the 1790s, and would continue to be so for almost a decade more. For this reason, slavery's expansion was not a foregone conclusion. And four great episodes of violence, three of them played out along the river system whose flow rocked the *Adventine* at anchor, would decide its fate.

As of 1807, four out of every five people who came from the Old World to the New had come from Africa, not Europe; chained in the belly of a ship, not free on its deck. Huddled masses in steerage class, yearning to breathe free of the famine and poverty of Ireland, Italy, or Russia's shtetls—they came later. Ten million Middle Passages of African captives had shaped the New World and its interactions with the Old. The only other shift on a similar scale was the death of millions of the hemisphere's original inhabitants. From the twin realities of demographic catastrophe and Middle Passage, empires emerged to dominate the first three centuries of American history: Spanish, Portuguese, French, and British. Once all the gold and silver had been thoroughly stolen, the empires found even greater sources of wealth by laying a belt of plantation colonies from Brazil north to Virginia. Many were small in size, but all were huge in economic and political significance. In 1763, in the first Treaty of Paris, France traded all of Canada for the island of Guadeloupe.[4]

What was made on such islands, and what made much of Europe's new wealth before 1807, was sugar. The Portuguese brought sugarcane to Brazil at the beginning of the sixteenth century. They'd already learned how to crush it, boil the sap, and crystallize it on Atlantic islands such as Madeira or Sao Tomé. There, Europeans had first combined the volatile ingredients of sugarcane, fertile land, chattel slavery, and enslaved Africans carried far from their homelands. In Brazil, this solution precipitated not only crystallized sucrose from vats of bubbling cane juice in the brutally demanding *safra*, or sugar harvest, but also immense revenue. Prestige consumers in the economies of late sixteenth-century Western Europe ate sugar and more sugar. Brazil was, for a time, early modern Europe's Silicon Valley, the incubator of techniques for making massive profits, a synonym for sudden wealth. Robinson Crusoe was going to become a Brazil planter when shipwreck cast him on his desert island.[5]

Within fifty years, Barbados shoved Brazil from the top of the sugar heap. The heyday of Barbados lasted only a few decades, for Jamaica rose next to command credit and fame. On island after island, Europeans and their pathogens killed the natives, slave ships appeared on the horizon, and cane sprouted in the fields. Streams of survivors crawled forth from slave ships to replenish the cane-field work gangs of men and women as they died. But enslavers grew fabulously rich. On each island, the richest crowded out others. Then a new island came online, offering entrepreneurs the chance to get in on the ground floor with fresher soil, offering investors novelty that attracted new credit. The sugar-island process of destruction and implantation shaped the geopolitics, economics, and culture of the first three centuries of the New World. Virginia and South Carolina were different from the islands, yet they were channels of the same current. The northern colonies were irrelevant until they evolved trades that the islands needed—shipbuilding, grain-growing, and livestock-raising—and started distilling sugarcane molasses into rum, carrying slaves, and trading in slave-made products.[6]

In European shops and kitchens, sugar started as a luxury for the rich. By 1700, it was becoming the sweetener for the new middle class's coffee and tea, also imperial tastes. By 1800 the English poor could sometimes indulge in sugar as a luxury, as a stimulant that got one through a hard day of labor, or a treat to quiet the crying child. Sugar and slavery quickened European trade, broadened the financial capital available to entrepreneurs, whetted the appetite for profit, and increased the revenue and power of centralizing states. But sugar and slavery had not definitively lifted the economies of Western Europe above those of the rest of the planet. China, which also consumed sugar, remained the massive gravitational center of world trade during much of the eighteenth century. Like the rest of the world, most Europeans were only one bad season from starvation. They all grew food by local traditions of agriculture that in technological complexity, efficiency, and productivity were closer to the year 0 than to 1900. The great masses of the poor and the peasantry were as short as the man in the collar, for living standards for most people had not risen since the dawn of the agricultural era.[7]

On the quarterdeck, the white customs officer huddled with the captain. They walked over and stared at the man in the iron collar together, talked gibberish. The captain signed a paper, and the customs officer clambered back down. The man was still unnamed in white folks' documents, but ink had captured his presence again. The rowboat slipped back toward the house. The *Adventine*'s sailors pulled and hoisted. Anchors clanked and sails flapped. The wheel spun. The brig slid out into the ship channel.

The man in the iron collar watched from the rail. The mist peeled back and a low, flat landscape came into view. For the next few days, the *Adventine* tacked with the river's winding turns through the new land made by the Mississippi. Slowly the banks rose. Low levees protected the flat land that lay behind. Mud gave way to green cane. First he saw occasional huts, and then large houses surrounded by huts. Three days later, the river turned right and straightened, and a small forest grove of masts came into view. They were at New Orleans.

In 1800, French traveler Pierre-Louis Duvallon had seen a smaller forest of masts. But he saw enough to prophesy that New Orleans was "destined by nature to become one of the principal cities of North America, and perhaps the most important place of commerce in the new world." Projectors, visionaries, and investors who came to this city founded by the French in 1718 and ceded to the Spanish in 1763 could sense the same tremendous possible future. Sitting at the mouth of a river system greater in economic potential, according to Duvallon, than the Nile, the Rhine, the Danube, or the Ganges,

New Orleans would be "the great receptacle" of the "produce" of half a continent. Even "fancy in her happiest mood cannot combine all the felicities of nature and society in a more absolute degree than will actually be combined" in New Orleans, Duvallon said.[8]

Yet powerful empires had been determined to keep the city from the United States ever since the thirteen colonies achieved their independence. Between 1783 and 1804, Spain repeatedly revoked the right of American settlers further upriver to export their products through New Orleans. Each time they did so, western settlers began to think about shifting their allegiances. Worried US officials repeatedly tried to negotiate the sale and cession of the city near the Mississippi's mouth, but Spain, trying to protect its own empire by containing the new nation's growth, just as repeatedly rebuffed them.[9]

Spain's stubborn possession of the Mississippi's mouth kept alive the possibility that the United States would rip itself apart. Yet something unexpected changed the course of history. In 1791, Africans enslaved in the French Caribbean colony of Saint-Domingue exploded in a revolt unprecedented in human history. Saint-Domingue, the eastern third of the island of Hispaniola, was at that time the ultimate sugar island, the imperial engine of French economic growth. But on a single August night, the mill of the first slavery's growth stopped turning. All across Saint-Domingue's sugar country, the most profitable stretch of real estate on the planet, enslaved people burst into the country mansions. They slaughtered enslavers, set torches to sugar houses and cane fields, and then marched by the thousand on Cap-Français, the seat of colonial rule. Thrown back, they regrouped. Revolt spread across the colony.[10]

By the end of the year thousands of whites and blacks were dead. As the cane fields burned, the smoke blew into the Atlantic trade winds. Refugees fled to Charleston, already burdened by its own fear of slave revolt; to Cuba; and to all the corners of the Atlantic world. They brought wild-eyed tales of a world turned upside down. Europeans, in the throes of epistemological disarray because of the French Revolution's overthrow of a throne more than a millennium old, reacted to these events with a different but still profound confusion. Minor slave rebellions were one thing. Total African victory was another thing entirely—it was so incomprehensible, in fact, that European thinkers, who couldn't stop talking about the revolution in France, clammed up about Saint-Domingue. The German philosopher Georg Hegel, for instance, who was in the process of constructing an entire system of thought around the idealized, classical image of a slave rebelling against a master, never spoke of the slave rebellion going on in the real world. Even as reports of fire and blood splattered every weekly newspaper he read, he insisted that African people were irrelevant to a future that would be shaped by the newly free citizens of European nation-states.[11]

Yet the revolution in Saint-Domingue was making a modern world. Today, Saint-Domingue is called Haiti, and it is the poorest nation in the Western Hemisphere. But Haiti's revolutionary birth was the most revolutionary revolution in an age of them. By the time it was over, these people, once seemingly crushed between the rollers of European empire, ruled the country in which they had been enslaved. Their citizenship would be (at least in theory) the most radically equal yet. And the events they pushed forward in the Caribbean drove French revolutionaries in the National Assembly to take steadily more radical positions—such as emancipating all French slaves in 1794, in an attempt to keep Saint-Domingue's economic powerhouse on the side of the new leaders in Paris. Already, however, the slave revolution itself had killed slavery on the island. An ex-slave named Toussaint Louverture had welded bands of rampaging rebels into an army that could defend their revolution from European powers who wanted to make it disappear. Between 1794 and 1799, his army defeated an invasion of tens of thousands of antirevolutionary British Redcoats.[12]

By 1800, Saint-Domingue, though nominally still part of the French Republic, was essentially an independent country. In his letters to Paris, Toussaint Louverture styled himself the "First of the Blacks." He was communicating with a man rated the First in France—Napoleon Bonaparte, first consul of the Republic, another charismatic man who had risen from obscure origins. Napoleon, an entrepreneur in the world of politics and war, rather than business, used his military victories to destroy old ways of doing things. Then he tried to create new ones: a new international order, a new economy, a new set of laws, a new Europe—and a new empire. But after he concluded the Peace of Amiens with Britain in 1800, the ostensible republican became monarchical. He set his sights on a new goal: restoring the imperial crown's finest jewel, the lost Saint-Domingue. In 1801, he sent the largest invasion fleet that ever crossed the Atlantic, some 50,000 men, to the island under the leadership of his brother-in-law Charles LeClerc. Their mission was to decapitate the ex-slave leadership of Saint-Domingue. "No more gilded Africans," Napoleon commanded. Subdue any resistance by deception and force. Return to slavery all the Africans who survived.[13]

Napoleon had also assembled a second army, and he had given it a second assignment. In 1800, he had concluded a secret treaty that "retroceded"

Louisiana to French control after thirty-seven years in Spanish hands. This second army was to go to Louisiana and plant the French flag. And at 20,000 men strong, it was larger than the entire US Army. Napoleon had already conquered one revolutionary republic from within. He was sending a mighty army to take another by brute force. As for the third republic, when his second army landed in Louisiana, its presence at the head of the Mississippi would destabilize the United States along the fracture line that divided west and east.[14]

In Washington, Jefferson heard rumors of the secret treaty. To keep alive his utopian plans for a westward-expanding republic of independent white men, he was already compromising with slavery's expansion. Now he saw another looming choice between hypocritical compromise and destruction. No memory rankled Jefferson more than a humiliation he had endured back in 1786, when he and John Adams had been presented to the British royal court as the rebel republic's ambassadors. When a periwigged herald had brayed out the American envoys' names, George III, still furious, ostentatiously turned and waddled away as courtiers snickered. And yet, as Jefferson now instructed his envoy to Paris, Robert Livingston, "there is on the globe one single spot, the possessor of which is our natural and habitual enemy. It is New Orleans." Jefferson had to open the Mississippi one way or another. Should a French army occupy New Orleans, wrote Jefferson, "we must marry ourselves to the British fleet and nation."[15]

Napoleon had his own visions. He ignored Jefferson's initial offer for the city at the mouth of the Mississippi. So the president sent future president James Monroe with a higher bid: $10 million for the city and its immediate surroundings. Yet, in the end, Paris would not decide this deal. When Le-Clerc's massive army had disembarked in Saint-Domingue, the French found Cap-Français a smoldering ruin, burned as part of scorched-earth strategy. LeClerc successfully captured Toussaint by deception and packed him off to France to be imprisoned in a fortress in the Jura Mountains. Resistance, however, did not cease. The army Louverture had built began to win battles over the one Napoleon had sent. French generals turned to genocide, murdering thousands of suspected rebels and their families. The terror provoked fiercer resistance, which—along with yellow fever and malaria—killed thousands of French soldiers, including LeClerc.

By the middle of 1802, the first wave of French forces had withered away. Napoleon reluctantly diverted the Louisiana army to Saint-Domingue. Then this second expedition to the Caribbean was also destroyed. So even as Toussaint Louverture shivered in his cell across the ocean, the army he left behind became the first to deal a decisive defeat to Napoleon's ambitions. "Damn sugar, damn coffee, damn colonies," the first of the whites was heard to grumble into his cup at a state dinner. On April 7, 1803, Louverture's jailer entered the old warrior's cell and found the first of the blacks seated upright, dead in his chair. The same day, Monroe's ship hove into sight of the French coast. And on April 11, before Monroe's stagecoach could reach Paris, a French minister invited Livingston to his office.[16]

Napoleon's minion shocked Livingston almost out of his knee breeches with an astonishing offer: not just New Orleans, but all of French Louisiana—the whole west bank of the Mississippi and its tributaries. Now the United States was offered—for a mere $15 million—828,000 square miles, 530 million acres, at three cents per acre. This vast expanse doubled the nation's size. Eventually the land from the Louisiana Purchase would become all or part of fifteen states. It still accounts for almost a quarter of the surface area of the United States. By the late twentieth century, Jefferson's windfall would be feeding much of the world. One imagines that Livingston found it hard to hold his poker face steady. He immediately agreed to the deal.[17]

So it was that as 1804 began, two momentous ceremonies took place. Each formalized the consequences of the successful overthrow, by enslaved people themselves, of the most profitable, most fully developed example of European imperial sugar slavery. One of the ceremonies took place in Port-au-Prince and was held by a gathering of leaders who had survived the Middle Passage, slavery, revolution, and war. On January 1, they proclaimed the independence of a new country, which they called Haiti—the name they believed the original Taino inhabitants had used before the Spaniards killed them all. Although the country's history would be marked by massacre, civil war, dictatorship, and disaster, and although white nations have always found ways to exclude Haiti from international community, independent Haiti's first constitution created a radical new concept of citizenship: only black people could be citizens of Haiti. And who was black? All who would say they rejected both France and slavery and would accept the fact that black folks ruled Haiti. Thus, even a "white" person could become a "black" citizen of Haiti, as long as he or she rejected the assumption that whites should rule and Africans serve.[18]

Not only did Haitian independence finish off Napoleon's schemes for the Western Hemisphere, but it also sounded the knell for the first form of New World slavery. On the sugar islands, productivity had depended on the continual resupply of captive workers ripped from the womb of Africa. Many Europeans who had not been convinced of the African slave trade's immorality were now convinced that it had brought destruction upon Saint-Domingue, by filling it full of angry men and women who had tasted freedom at one point in their lives. British anti-slave-trade activism, frightened into a pause in 1791 by heads severed by the Saint-Domingue rebels and Paris guillotines, became conventional London wisdom. In 1807, the British Parliament passed a law ending the international slave trade to its empire. In the near future, Britain's government and ruling class, confident that their own abolition of the trade had provided them with what historian Christopher Brown has aptly called "moral capital," would use the weight of their growing economic influence to push Spain, France, and Portugal toward abolishing their own Atlantic slave trades.[19]

Meanwhile, the US Congress had already been pushing forward its own bill to ban the international slave trade to the United States—starting in 1808, the first year that the Constitution permitted it. But this slave-trade ban, urged by Thomas Jefferson in his 1806 annual message to Congress, was a political possibility in part because the Middle Passage was no longer seen as an economic necessity. Feet marching west, south, and southwest enabled slaveholders in the new western districts of South Carolina, Georgia, and elsewhere to buy from an endless coffle of people like Charles Ball. Thus, the bill's passage did not mean that the southern representatives who voted for it believed that slavery was wrong. As one of them insisted proudly, "A large majority of people in the Southern states do not consider slavery as a crime."[20]

In any case, the Haitian Revolution had already made it possible for the United States to open up the Mississippi Valley to the young nation's internal slave trade. About ten days before the declaration of independence in Port-au-Prince, on December 22, 1803, Louisiana's new territorial governor had accepted the official transfer of authority in New Orleans. American acquisition depended on the sacrifices of hundreds of thousands of African men, women, and children who in Saint-Domingue rose up against the one social institution whose protection appeared to be written into the US Constitution—the enslavement of African people. This reliance on the success of the Haitian Revolution was a profound irony. Jefferson, whose argument for "diffusion" relied in part on exploiting white fears of slave revolt, did not acknowledge that Toussaint's posthumous victory made the nation's—and slavery's—expansion possible. The only voice pointing out that the republican president was an emperor without clothes came from Jefferson's old rival Alexander Hamilton, who wrote that "to the deadly climate of St. Domingo, and to the courage and obstinate resistance made by its black inhabitants are we indebted. . . . [The] truth is, Bonaparte found himself absolutely compelled"—and not by Jefferson—"to relinquish his daring plan of colonizing the banks of the Mississippi."[21]

Even today, most US history textbooks tell the story of the Louisiana Purchase without admitting that slave revolution in Saint-Domingue made it possible. And here is another irony. Haitians had opened 1804 by announcing their grand experiment of a society whose basis for citizenship was literally the renunciation of white privilege, but their revolution's success had at the same time delivered the Mississippi Valley to a new empire of slavery. The great continent would incubate a second slavery exponentially greater in economic power than the first.

SO THE MAN IN the iron collar was a sign not of the passing of an old forced migration, but of the conception of a new one. Yet acquisition of territory doesn't automatically translate to control. Potential wealth doesn't translate automatically into floods of money. To convert possibility into reality in the Mississippi Valley, enslavers would have to work together across linguistic and cultural difference; find new sources of slaves, especially after 1807; and defeat challenges to their power. And had we been able to interview William C. Claiborne, governor of the Orleans Territory, on May 15, 1809, he might have had a pessimistic assessment of their chances. On that day, he was frantically scrawling a letter from his desk in the Cabildo, a white stone structure that stood on the Place d'Armes in New Orleans. Built by the Spanish, the Cabildo now houses the Louisiana State Museum, but in the years after the 1804 "change of flags" it was the nerve center of government on the frontier of empire.

Claiborne was a man in a hurry. The breakneck pace of his political career had rushed forward frenetically with the expansion of the new United States. Born in Virginia in 1775, he had moved to Tennessee and was in 1795 elected the youngest US representative in history. Powerful Virginia allies had secured him the appointment as federal governor of the newly acquired Orleans Territory, as present-day Louisiana was then termed. But here everything he wanted to accomplish seemed to run aground. Some of it was his fault. He refused to learn French, for instance. He was brusque and tactless, in an existential hurry like his nation. Even now he leapt up from his seat to look out the window toward the river, then strode hastily back to the desk to scribble, twitching, again.[22]

For the governor had just received the troublesome news that ships full of slaves had arrived from Cuba and were trying to dock at the port of New

Orleans, in contravention of the ban on importing slaves into the United States. The question of importing slaves threatened to amplify rivalries inherent to the nature of this territory. French-speaking residents, conscious of cultural difference, fought in the New Orleans streets with English-speaking Protestants about which dances should be performed at a ball—the ones fashionable in England or the ones popular in France. "American" women (and a few men) complained that here, wealthy white men sometimes lived with mulatto women until it came time to marry a respectable white one. Such things happened in Virginia—Claiborne knew Thomas Jefferson quite well—but they were usually kept under wraps. Meanwhile, new American arrivals used capital from outside the territory to dominate business that came from New Orleans's now-unimpeded access to the products and profits of the interior. French Louisianans could only fall back on their control of the territory's fixed capital, and some tried to shut out American emigrants by refusing to sell them land.[23]

Cultural conflict kept alive uncertainty about the loyalties of the newly incorporated peoples of Louisiana. The Spanish Empire still loomed on both the western and eastern frontiers, refusing to give up West Florida. Rumors of plots to detach the Mississippi Valley from Washington's control implicated Spain, French Louisianans who were disloyal to the United States, and overambitious English-speakers. The most notorious was the 1806 scheme supposedly organized by former vice president Aaron Burr and General James Wilkinson—a plan to establish a breakaway republic in Louisiana. Although Wilkinson was a paid agent in the service of Spain, he was not arrested. Burr was, but his subsequent trial for treason devolved into a disaster for Jefferson. The president came out looking like a man eager to twist evidence in order to inflict revenge on a rival (the junior partner on Jefferson's 1800 ticket, Burr had allegedly tried to steal the presidency by cooperating with Federalists to drive the election into the House of Representatives).[24]

Most uncertain of all in the wake of the revolution in Saint-Domingue was the future of slavery in Louisiana. The legal records of the Orleans Territory from 1804 through 1810 show a count of 15,927 enslaved people, and scholars have found enough information to make an ethnic identification in 5,527 of the cases. Of those, 61 percent seem to have been born in Africa, 27 percent in Louisiana, 6 percent in the Caribbean, and 6 percent in Anglo North America (see Table 2.1). Ears in New Orleans marketplaces heard dozens of African tongues. Eyes there noted strange "country marks," tribal scarifications carved in the faces of men and women coming in from the cane fields. "Strange negroes" from Africa seemed particularly prone to resistance. "Our Quondam friend *Mandingo Charles* alias *Goliah* has again absconded from the

TABLE 2.1. ORIGINS OF ENSLAVED PEOPLE
FOUND IN NEW ORLEANS RECORDS, 1804–1810

| ORIGIN* | NUMBER | PERCENTAGE OF THOSE IDENTIFIED |
|---|---|---|
| African | 3,387 | 61.3 |
| Louisiana Creole | 1,482 | 26.8 |
| Anglo | 338 | 6.1 |
| Caribbean | 304 | 6.1 |
| Other | 16 | -- |
| Unidentified | 10,400 | -- |
| *Totals* | *15,927 [5,527]* | *100.0* |

*Source:* Hall Database, www.ibiblio.org/laslave/.
* Search on variable "Origin," except for number of African groups, in which variable "Birthplace" was used.

plantation[;] also an Ebo man named *Cracker*," wrote John Palfrey in 1810 from his property Cannes Brûlées (Burnt Cane) in St. Charles Parish, fifty miles upriver from New Orleans. Palfrey, a merchant from Massachusetts, had moved to Louisiana in the 1790s to take over his brother-in-law's sugar operation. At the end of 1810, unable to pull the enterprise out of debt, he sold out to New Orleans entrepreneurs William Kenner and Stephen Henderson and launched a cotton-growing operation in the Attakapas region of Louisiana. Cracker stayed in the St. Charles woods.[25]

Saint-Domingue was present, in spirit, in the Louisiana that Claiborne was trying to govern. Most of the white constables in the streets of New Orleans had been born on the French island. Sugar and sugar specialists had come to Louisiana from the burned colony, too. In 1794, refugee sugar artisan Antoine Morin helped Etienne Boré become the first Louisiana planter to granulate sugar from cane. A little Saint-Domingue sprang up along the great river's "German Coast," which stretched from St. James Parish down to the city itself. Fields of cane replaced fields of corn. Seventy-five sugar mills were in operation by 1804. Along these one hundred miles of development, army officer Amos Stoddard saw "scenes of misery and distress." He added, echoing Jefferson, "Wounds and lacerations occasioned by demoralized masters and overseers, most of whom exhibit a strange compound of ignorance and depravity, torture the feelings of the stranger, and wring blood from his heart. . . . Good God! Why sleeps thy vengeance!"[26]

Seemingly unable to think beyond a playbook that had already ended in vengeance, Saint-Domingue refugees and their French- and Spanish-speaking compatriots demanded more slaves. From their perspective, the

Louisiana colony had been long starved of enslaved Africans, having imported fewer than 2,000 in the decade before American acquisition. When Claiborne arrived in 1804, bringing the news that Congress would probably block the international slave trade to the territory, he discovered "an almost universal sentiment in favor of this inhuman traffic." "The prohibition thereof," he reported, was "a great source of discontent" among French-speakers, but even English-speaking residents agreed that "*they must import more slaves or be ruined forever.*"²⁷

Ruined! And forever! "No subject seems as interesting to their minds," wrote one of Claiborne's deputies, "as that of the importations of brute Negroes from Africa." *Nègres bruts*, people recently stolen, or, as they also called them: *têtes*, heads. Claiborne reported that a reopened trade would "better reconcile" French residents "to the government of the United States than any other permission which could be extended"—though he worried that enslaved Africans would turn Louisiana into "another Santo Domingo." In July 1804, however, Louisiana whites learned that Congress was also planning to ban the internal slave trade from other parts of the United States to Louisiana. New Orleans erupted. Public meetings rang with threats of secession. Community leaders besieged Claiborne: "The most respectable characters cou'd not, *even in my presence* suppress the Agitation of their tempers, when a check to that Trade was suggested."²⁸

Enterprising types rushed in before the October implementation of the slave-trade bans, not bringing the "thousands of African Negroes" that Claiborne had predicted, but 463 in six ships from Africa and 270 in three from Jamaica and Havana. But the next year, Congress passed a law raising Orleans to the same territorial status as Mississippi. The territory's attorney general, James Brown, a Virginian who owned a German Coast sugar plantation, pounced on the loophole this law opened. Mississippi could import enslaved people from other states. Mississippi could even import African slaves transshipped from other ports. Therefore, he insisted, so could the enslavers of the Orleans Territory. Jefferson allowed the ruling on the ground to stand. Slave imports resumed.²⁹

By ones, like the man in the iron collar, by twos, and by whole shiploads sent from Africa via Charleston, traders brought hundreds, or perhaps even thousands, of *nègres bruts* to New Orleans before the legal Atlantic slave trade closed at the end of 1807. In addition, enslavers—including a Tennessee judge named Andrew Jackson—were sending English-speaking enslaved people down the Mississippi River. The new flows of enslaved people into New Orleans began to meet the demands of new arrivals, refugee planters,

TABLE 2.2. SLAVES SOLD IN NEW ORLEANS, 1800–1819, BY HALF-DECADE INCREMENTS

| | MALE | | FEMALE | | TOTAL | |
|---|---|---|---|---|---|---|
| | *Row %* | *Count* | *Row %* | *Count* | *Row %* | *Count* |
| 1800–1804 | 54.0% | 1,036 | 46.0% | 882 | 100.0% | 1,946 |
| 1805–1809 | 56.4% | 3,103 | 43.6% | 2,399 | 100.0% | 5,632 |
| 1810–1814 | 56.3% | 4,119 | 43.7% | 3,196 | 100.0% | 7,458 |
| 1815–1819 | 51.9% | 6,497 | 48.1% | 6,022 | 100.0% | 12,771 |
| *Total* | *54.1%* | *14,755* | *45.9%* | *12,499* | *100.0%* | *27,807* |

*Source:* Hall Database, www.ibiblio.org/laslave/.

and old Creole entrepreneurs alike. In a single year, 1804 to 1805, the number of people sold in New Orleans increased almost five times over, and average prices dropped as supplies rose (see Tables 2.2 and 2.3). Not all sellers—or buyers—were white. John Palfrey's overseer reported that he'd bought a "negro winch" from "a Quadroon named John Chassier." Chassier was, Palfrey noted, very persistent in collecting his debt.[30]

Thanks to decisions made in London and Washington, the boom didn't last. Great Britain insisted on searching and seizing American merchant ships bound for her enemy France, often kidnapping some of the vessels' sailors into the British navy. In 1807, Jefferson banned all foreign trade. His theory was that Britain and France would suffer so much that they would agree to respect neutral shipping and allow American vessels to carry American cargoes of tobacco, sugar, and other crops wherever they could find the best market.

For eighteen months, the government struggled to enforce Jefferson's policy. Rampant smuggling punched holes in the embargo and undermined the presidency's claim to authority at home and abroad. But smuggling couldn't preserve the export-dependent economy of New Orleans, and the embargo chilled slave sales throughout 1808. Finally, three days before Jefferson left office, on March 1, 1809, Congress replaced the embargo with the Non-Intercourse Act, which attempted to ban US trade with Britain and France only.

So now we are back to May 15, 1809, with Claiborne in his office on the verge of panic because, as the letter he was writing informed his superiors in Washington, a ship from Santiago, Cuba, "with a number of French passengers and thirty-six slaves," was near the city. Many Saint-Domingue refugees had moved to Spanish Cuba. Some of these French nationals had helped

TABLE 2.3. SLAVES SOLD IN ORLEANS PARISH, 1804–1811:
INDIVIDUAL SALES

|      | MALE SLAVES | MEAN PRICE IN DOLLARS | FEMALE SLAVES | MEAN PRICE IN DOLLARS | TOTAL NUMBER SOLD | MEAN PRICE IN DOLLARS |
| ---- | ----------- | --------------------- | ------------- | --------------------- | ----------------- | --------------------- |
| 1804 | 75          | 537                   | 53            | 486                   | 128               | 514                   |
| 1805 | 340         | 489                   | 296           | 469                   | 636               | 480                   |
| 1806 | 241         | 564                   | 199           | 520                   | 440               | 544                   |
| 1807 | 341         | 576                   | 288           | 536                   | 629               | 558                   |
| 1808 | 255         | 599                   | 222           | 503                   | 477               | 555                   |
| 1809 | 627         | 575                   | 414           | 494                   | 1,041             | 539                   |
| 1810 | 521         | 568                   | 446           | 507                   | 967               | 539                   |
| 1811 | 420         | 562                   | 396           | 525                   | 816               | 544                   |

Source: Hall Database, www.ibiblio.org/laslave/.

to incubate the new Cuban sugar industry. But at the beginning of 1809, when Napoleon invaded Spain, the Spanish Empire retaliated by expelling the refugees from its possessions. Now a shipload of these twice-refugees had crossed the bar at the Balize, seeking asylum. A fast messenger boat had run the news up and was waiting for instructions from the governor.

Claiborne did not know what to do. The city's many former refugees would be deeply sympathetic to this latest wave, many of whom had left coffee plantations and sugar mills behind them in Cuba. But some brought slaves, and to welcome them in would violate federal law. And before the governor could even finish his first letter to Washington—a letter that was irrelevant, since it wouldn't bring a response in time to solve the immediate crisis—the local French consul arrived with news that another 6,000 people were on their way. Claiborne hustled the consul back out as soon as possible, broke the seal on the first letter to Washington, and scrawled a despairing postscript: "So great and sudden an Emigration to this territory, will be a source of serious inconvenience and embarrassment to our own Citizens."[31]

Claiborne could easily tick off the difficulties the situation presented. There was the problem of finding food, shelter, and employment for 9,000 people in a city that normally supported 15,000. There was the legal problem of bringing slaves. And then again, there was the fact that a third of the refugees were free people of color, forbidden to immigrate to the United States and unwanted by whites in New Orleans—particularly by English-speakers who preferred the ostensible clarity of their own American pattern in which all black people were assumed to be enslaved. Yet over the next few days, the white people of New Orleans held meetings and wrote petitions insisting that they wanted Claiborne to admit the refugees.[32]

Sympathy drove them, but so did other forces of attraction. "I have no doubt," the mayor of New Orleans wrote to Claiborne, carefully pressing him to admit the refugees, and their slaves, "that the result would be the settling of many new plantations, which would give large crops of cotton and other produce before three years time." More trade, more connections with other markets, and—this was implied—more unity between white citizens, whatever their native language. Allowing slavery's expansion, the mayor and other wealthy Louisianans insisted, made white New Orleans and white America more prosperous and more united, binding states and factions together. So Claiborne capitulated. The refugees poured up the river. Congress would (when it heard) quibble, but it backed down and consented to this post facto exception to the 1807 international slave-trade ban. The governor himself enforced only a single law. Following territorial regulations to the letter, he expelled all free males of color over the age of fifteen who had entered on the refugee ships. Women and children could stay.[33]

"To the arrivals from Cuba," is how A. Bonamy, a Louisiana enslaver, directed his advertisement in the New Orleans newspaper *Moniteur de la Louisiane*. "I will hire thirty *nègres de la hache*"—"slaves of the axe" might be a rough translation—"and a number of laboring negresses for long leases." In 1809, the number of slaves sold in New Orleans surged sharply upward. Close to one-third of the slaves brought from Cuba were cashed in by enslavers who needed ready funds for a new start. As ever in histories of displacement, people who were ready and able to make profit out of distress did well. One was Christian Miltenberger, a physician of French extraction, who had been kicked out of Cuba in 1809. Right before he boarded the ship that would take him to Louisiana, he had bought a man named Pierre Louis from fellow refugee Marie François. Pierre Louis had been born a slave in Saint-Domingue and transported to Cuba when his owner fled there at some point between 1791 and 1804, during the revolution. Miltenberger sold some people once he reached New Orleans, which allowed him to restart his career as a planter, but he didn't sell Pierre Louis. Using the cash from other slave sales, Miltenberger established a small sugar plantation, where he put Pierre Louis to hard labor.[34]

The refugees' arrival injected new enslaved laborers and new buyers for land in lower Louisiana. Hard times and cultural dissonance between English and French, and distance from Washington, had slowed the newest West's incorporation into the United States. The incorporation of the refugees helped

TABLE 2.4. SLAVES IMPORTED TO LOUISIANA, 1809–1811

| ORIGIN | NUMBER LISTING AN ORIGIN POINT FOR JOURNEY* | PERCENTAGE |
|---|---|---|
| Louisiana | 176 | 19.9 |
| Eastern United States | 251 | 28.3 |
| Western United States (not including Louisiana) | 287 | 32.4 |
| Caribbean (not including Cuba and Saint-Domingue) | 28 | 3.2 |
| Saint-Domingue Refugees | 144 | 16.3 |
| *Totals* | *886* | *99.9* |

*Source:* Hall Database, www.ibiblio.org/laslave/.

* The variable used was "Via," which records the place from or by which the seller brought the slave to New Orleans; 9,157 other sales and/ or probate records contain no entry for this variable.

smooth over those sources of friction. The refugees' slaves accounted for a full quarter of the growth of the Orleans Territory's slave population, from 22,701 to over 34,000, between 1806 and 1810, and for 16 percent of the 3,000 people sold as slaves in New Orleans between 1809 and 1811 (see Table 2.4). The American empire expanded instead of devolving into a squabble between local slaveholders over scarce resources.[35]

NOT EVERYONE IN THE Mississippi Valley was willing to cooperate. Rival empire Spain still hoped to block the growth of the United States. So did Britain. And 50,000 Native Americans, who did not plan to surrender the rich soil under their feet, still lived on the millions of acres that Yazoo companies and other speculators had successfully turned into paper on the financial exchanges of America's northeastern cities. These conflicts were coming, and soon. Even sooner, in 1811, the enslaved people who had been brought in such diversity to the Mississippi Valley as "heads" and "slaves of the axe" would make their own attempt to change the course of things.

Along the river's east bank above New Orleans, on the German Coast, dozens of slave labor camps stretched back from the river in French-surveyed "long lots," narrow strips of land that ran a mile or two across cleared ground to a dense belt of forested swamps. Their pattern, still visible from the air today, gave the maximum number of large landowners access to the Mississippi. Each holding had a slice of the incredibly rich soil that lay between the levee and the swamps. The swamps themselves were almost impassable, full of alligators, snakes, panthers, and bears. Runaways sought refuge in the swamps, hiding from overseers and free black slave-catchers. Forty-year-old Phillip, also known as Coles, ran away from Kenner and Henderson's new place—John Palfrey's old Cannes Brûlées—in early November 1810 as the sugar harvest's intense labor began. He'd been brought down the river on a flatboat from Natchez and sold to Kenner and Henderson just that year. A few miles closer to the city was a huge labor camp that still survives as the show plantation "Ormond." Pennsylvanian Richard Butler and his business partner Samuel McCutcheon had recently bought dozens of new enslaved people for Ormond, one of whom was six-foot-tall John. He, too, had run to the woods in November, and he had not returned. And somewhere back there, as 1811 dawned, John Palfrey's runaway "Cracker" still lurked.[36]

The sugar harvest ended at the beginning of January. For weeks, overseers and owners had pushed the enslaved drivers, who in turn had pushed the cane cutters, the loaders, and the women who fed the mill with cane in double shifts all day and night. The sugar makers, the artisans (free or slave) who supervised the artful process of boiling, skimming, and crystallizing cane juice into sugar, had also driven their subordinates around the clock. Now some of the enslaved spent their days loading hogsheads of sugar and molasses onto flatboats and pirogues for transport to New Orleans. Most of the thousands brought in the previous ten years from Africa and the Caribbean, local-born Louisianans, and a few from Virginia and Maryland as well labored at dreary January tasks such as digging up minefields of sharp-cut sugarcane stubble so the next crop of cane could be planted.

Had you been out walking near midnight on Saturday, January 5, 1811, you would have heard, from the river side of the levee that protected Manuel Andry's land from spring floods, the murmuring of men's voices in mixed Creole French and broken English. These men were not just sitting around trading stinging pulls from a jug of tafia, the harsh raw rum made from cane juice. Nor were they simply alternating complaints about women with ragged growls about this overseer or that slave owner. The men were planning what would become the biggest slave rebellion in the United States before the Civil War.

They hailed from many places. Based on his name, for instance, we could guess that Amar was born in the Muslim-influenced Sahel region of West Africa. The mulatto Harry, owned by William Kenner and Stephen Henderson, was probably from the Chesapeake. Quamana, owned by territorial attorney James Brown, may have been from present-day Ghana, and had probably been pulled here by his owner's success in opening the international slave trade to Louisiana. As for Charles Deslondes, who would be credited and blamed as the leader and instigator of the revolt, we don't know precisely who he was. He might have been "Creole"—Louisiana-born, in other words. But many contemporary accounts said he was born in Saint-Domingue, and that he served as Andry's *commandeur*, or enslaved overseer. We do know that in 1809, before leaving Santiago as a refugee, Auguste Girard had bought a man named Charles. This Charles had been born in Saint-Domingue in 1787, and was thus old enough to remember a little bit of 1791. When Girard reached New Orleans from Cuba, he sold eleven slaves. One was Charles. Manuel Andry was the buyer. Perhaps this Charles, raised in the vortex of both slave and sugar-making revolution, was the same one to whom Andry had given the task of organizing his field slaves in the coordinated process of harvesting and refining sugarcane. Perhaps Girard's Charles was the Charles Deslondes who supposedly called the meeting on the levee on that night of the 5th.[37]

As is almost always the case with slave revolts and allegations of revolt conspiracies, we only know what we know from confessions made by some of the captured rebels. Perhaps "know" is not the right verb to use when the information comes from tortured people desperate to save their own skins. From what one can gather, however, it seems that after the gathering under the levee, the leaders—Amar, Quamana, Harry, and others in the fraternity of *commandeurs* and sugar refiners up and down the German Coast—went back to their respective plantations to spread the word among those whom they trusted. Except for Charles—he headed down the river toward the long lot owned by Etienne Trepagnier. A mile and a half later, Charles reached the Trepagnier place, where "his woman" lived. Charles, as a *commandeur*, would have been selected for charisma, for the strength of mind and body to impose his will on those who were supposed to follow him, for the intelligence and discretion to know when to push and when to back off from pushing. These qualities probably made him attractive to many women. These qualities also made him well suited to lead a revolt.[38]

By Sunday evening, Charles and a few others were traveling, under cover of darkness, back up the river toward the Andry place. Augustin, one of Trepagnier's slaves, later claimed that he only went with Charles because the *commandeur* held a gun on him. Perhaps Charles feared that Augustin was a traitor. Or perhaps Augustin concocted the gun story to save his own skin. Whatever the case, most of this core group hid in the woods near the Andry place, while Charles went back to work under the nose of Manuel Andry and his adult son Gilbert. As the fugitives waited, perhaps they discussed an event they all knew something about: the revolt in the Plaine du

Nord of Saint-Domingue. That revolt had also been planned by high-status slaves like *commandeurs*. There, too, the leaders had gathered in a nighttime ceremony. And there the rebels had also relied on amassing a powerful force from the sugar plantations in order to overwhelm the white opposition before it could coalesce.

The key of the plotters' 1811 strategy was a march straight on to New Orleans. They apparently believed that they outnumbered whites by enough on the German Coast to sweep all before them. Then they could take the city, the hinge of slaveholder power in the southwestern United States, and hold it as the heart of a slave coast in revolt. Some of the *commandeurs* and house servants would have understood that 1811 was a particularly propitious moment because of Louisiana's confrontation with Spain on the borders of "West Florida," the land from Mobile in Alabama to the north shore of Lake Ponchartrain. The United States claimed that this was actually its property. Governor Claiborne had ordered General Wade Hampton—the same Hampton who had bought Charles Ball in South Carolina, now seeking to gain both glory and access to new land as a recently mobilized officer of the US Army—to march his troops away from their usual post in New Orleans and plant the US flag in West Florida. On January 6, however, someone— whether premature rebels or a runaway—attacked a mail coach. Hearing this news, Claiborne ordered Hampton to delay his scheduled march toward West Florida. Late on Monday the 7th, he sent another note to Hampton describing what he knew "relative to the movements of the Insurgents" and ordering Hampton to keep his troops near the city.[39]

The sun rose and set on Tuesday, January 8. Upriver, behind the Andry barracks, Charles gathered the enslaved people who would follow him. At midnight they marched to Manuel Andry's front door. They hewed it down with an axe and burst in. They searched for Manuel, the man who called himself their master. His son blocked the way, so they cut the young man down. A glancing axe stroke pursued the father as he hurled himself out the window, but he hit the ground running and reached a boat by the levee. Andry cast out into the river for the west bank of the Mississippi, where he planned to raise the alarm.[40]

On the east, the rebels were already moving toward New Orleans by the river road. At each property they passed, recruits joined them. On Andry's place, Jupiter was among the first. Why? Later he would say he wanted "to go to the city to kill whites." Two parishes lay in between them and the city, a little more than fifty miles as the river bends. Next, the rebels stormed onto the land of parish judge Achille Trouard, who had heard them coming. He hid in the cane fields with his nieces as the band swept by. As the sun rose, the rebels pushed into St. Charles Parish and through plantation after plantation: Picou, Kenner and Henderson, Trepagnier, and Delhomme.[41]

At 6:30 on the morning of January 9, the *commandeur* Pierre woke up his enslaver Hermogène Labranche. Slaves from the Delhomme place just up the river had told Pierre that a rebel army was marching. Later, Pierre would say the messengers had fled the rebels, but they could have been scouts who wanted to know if Pierre would have the residents prepared to join when the "brigands" appeared at Labranche's slave quarters. Pierre chose instead to alert Labranche, who leapt out of bed and fled to the woods with his wife and a slave named François. Yet as the rebels poured through Labranche's sugar operation, ten joined.[42]

They marched on. Lindor (owned by Kenner and Henderson) strode in front playing the drum. Mathurin, claimed by the Broussards, held his sword like an officer. So did Dagobert, the *commandeur* from Joseph Delhomme's cane fields. Hyppolite found a horse and mounted it. Raimond, who joined at Labranche's, carried a musket. Others bound cane knives on long poles, like pikes. Some improvised banners. Born in Louisiana, Kentucky, Saint-Domingue, Jamaica, the Congo, Ibo villages east of the Niger delta, and Virginia, the five hundred rebels marched downriver out of a cloud of smoke rising from burning houses and cane sheds.

For the past decade, white men had been hustling "heads" through the streets of New Orleans in strings of *nègres bruts*. Now the roles had changed. By afternoon, most of the whites of the German Coast had either fled or were fleeing. When one stubborn enslaver—Jean-François Trepagnier, Etienne's relative—stayed put, one of his own house slaves, a young man named Cook, chopped off his head with an axe. The rebels threw the body over the levee and kept moving. By the time night closed in they had overrun the Destrehan property just west of the town that today bears the same name. They made camp at the Jacques Fortier place just over the Jefferson Parish line, less than twenty miles from the one spot on earth that both they and the United States needed to control.[43]

The first panicked rider had galloped into the streets of New Orleans at 10 a.m. on January 9. Throwing down his reins in the Place d'Armes, he ran up the stairs of the Cabildo, banged on Claiborne's door, and poured out his news. The governor immediately ordered a 6 p.m. curfew, closed the gates of the French Quarter, and shuttered the arsenal—today the site of the US Mint museum. (One Louisiana historian argues that Claiborne did so because city-based allies of the rebels had made an attempt to break in and seize its weapons.) Claiborne also dispatched several different groups of armed men up the River Road toward the rebel army.

January 10, early morning, before dawn. The rebels' camp was cold. Fires lit early in the evening had been extinguished earlier, when a few shots rang out in the middle of the night. For the rest of the night the rebels lay behind a picket fence that enclosed Fortier's sugar house and storage buildings. But now a louder rustling told Charles and his men to prepare: noise from the river road, but now also from the levee, and from the north. Men peered over the fence. In the gathering light they saw, advancing up the road, Wade Hampton's regulars and "volunteers" from New Orleans. From the levee on the right, seamen on foot, and from the swamp to the left, more volunteers. From behind, they suddenly heard horses snorting, hooves clopping. They were caught in a trap. Obeying a command or a previously made plan, the rebels rose from behind the fence. A few who had horses mounted up. The rest turned and ran, thundering full speed but without a shout back up the river road. Shots rang wildly, and the mounted cavalry from the west bank scattered as the rebels passed through them and disappeared into the mist.[44]

Embarrassed, the cavalry tried to regroup. Hampton's infantrymen were already marching in pursuit of the rebels. They had come more than fifteen miles, tramping all night, but he was determined to end this rebellion before it could spread. The bands of soldiers set off up the road, stomping past a body that lay in front of Fortier's house: it was Télémacque, a *vieux nègre* (old Negro), who had been enslaved by Destrehan until he had joined the rebellion the previous afternoon.[45]

Fifteen miles the rebels ran, stumbled, walked, and ran again over the next four hours. Some slipped off across ragged fields and headed for the swamps, but strays risked being run down by the horse-mounted rulers of the German Coast who bayed at their heels. Far behind the rebels and the harassing horsemen tramped Hampton and his men: armed (unlike many of the rebels, who had thrown aside their pikes), trained, and determined.

At last, the cavalry came riding back to Hampton with news. The rebels, too tired to run anymore, were making a stand in a grove of trees at Bernard Bernoudy's plantation. Only about one hundred were left. The rest were hiding, caught, or lying dead along the road. Hampton's troops quickened their pace. Soon they were at Bernoudy's. They formed up next to the cavalry and then charged the rebels' improvised line. The rebels scattered, dodging saber blows and bullets. Cracker, the longtime Ibo runaway; Dawson, who was Butler and McCutcheon's sugar refiner; and a dozen more fell. Others surrendered—some the whites killed on the spot, others they bound. They prodded Amar into line with the rest. He had survived the militia charge, but he had been slashed across the throat.[46]

The militia marched the captives back down the river road toward the Destrehan plantation, while a white resident of St. John the Baptist named Charles Perret marshaled a group of men on horseback who swept even farther back up the river, going from labor camp to labor camp. They ordered *commandeurs* who had not gone with the rebels to drive their slave forces out into the fields to work. Make them act as though nothing had happened, even as squads of militia combed the woods for fugitives, forcing those they caught to point out fellow rebels who were trying to melt back into the ranks of laborers.[47]

On the 12th, Perret and his men returned to the Andry house from one such expedition, carrying the heads of rebels Pierre Griffe and Hans Wimprenn. Andry showed Perret and his troops—who included several free men of color—his own trophies. In a circle of lamplight, surrounded by a dark yard full of white men with muskets and bayonets, Andry had three men tied up: Barthelemy, who had been Trepagnier's sugar artisan, a man called Jacques Beckneil (Jack Bucknall?), and, prize of prizes, Charles Deslondes. There were enough white landowners present for a "court," said Perret. A US Navy man who was present reported what came next. Deslondes "had his hands chopped off" with an axe—we can imagine Andry, who had lost his son to one of these so recently, delivering the blow through the wrists, onto the chopping block. "Then shot in one thigh, and then the other, until they were both broken—then shot in the Body." But what else to do? Quickly, before Charles bled to death, someone broke open a bale of straw. They threw the writhing man into the straw, scattered it on him, and thrust in the torches—and so Charles Deslondes died with the flames crackling his skin.[48]

The next day, the 13th, German Coast enslavers convened a more organized mechanism of judgment at the Destrehan plantation. Over the next forty-eight hours, they brought thirty-two captured rebels one by one to stand before them on the brick floor. Some tried to defend themselves as part of a large group—so large that it would surely be impossible to execute them all. Guiau, once owned by John Palfrey, now by Kenner and Henderson, was implicated by others, who said he stole a horse and led others off the plantation; he deflected blame by saying that "all the negroes . . . of Kenner and Henderson had followed the brigands." The message from those who sat in judgment was clear: sell out other rebels, name their names, and thus save your life. Some talked. Cupidon, owned by the Labranche brothers, and Louis, of Trepagnier, implicated dozens of men, some dead and some alive.

Once Cupidon and Louis had pointed at so many of those in custody, others had less to sell.

A final group played their last cards very differently. Quamana stood before the tribunal on the 14th. According to the tribunal's notes, he "avowed that he had figured in a remarkable manner in the insurrection." What it meant for him to "avow" is unclear. Did he confess voluntarily? Was he tortured? Did he say something else, and did the judges simply write what they wanted? Only one thing is definitive: "Il n'a denoncé personne." He named no one. Nor did Robin, nor Harry, Hyppolite, Cook, Ned, or Etienne. Then the judges had Amar brought out before them. They accused him of being a "chief of the brigands, denounced by many." He said nothing in response. Perhaps he couldn't speak, even had he tried. Perhaps nothing would come from him but the wind whistling through the hole in his throat as he struggled for breath.[49]

On the morning of the 15th, the judges pronounced the sentences. Twenty would die. Even Cupidon and Louis did not save themselves. They, too, were to be executed, just like the silent ones. Death was to come by firing squad. Each convicted rebel was to be taken to his respective home plantation, to be executed in front of all the gathered slaves. Over the next day or so, the militia carried out the sentences, shooting the condemned and decapitating their corpses while silent crowds watched. In New Orleans, meanwhile, eight were hanged for alleged complicity in the insurrection. Another seven, including Charles Deslondes, had already been executed by the "court" convened at Andry's. Enslavers claimed compensation for at least ten others executed, making at least forty-five condemned and killed by the state. Together with the people killed during and after the battles of January 10, at least sixty-six, and probably close to one hundred, enslaved people lost their lives. Gilbert Andry and Jean-François Trepagnier may have been the only whites killed by the rebels.[50]

Both the 1811 rebellion and the Haitian Revolution began as conspiracies organized by a few *commandeurs* in the most densely cultivated area of the sugar district. Both were launched at a time when the enslavers were divided and facing internal and external threats. Yet despite the high cost they paid in lives, the 1811 rebels had failed to capture New Orleans or seriously threaten US or slaveholder rule in the Lower Mississippi Valley. And they failed for reasons that prophesied much about the second great era of slavery in the history of the modern world, an era that not only would be very different from the first, but would shape a different, wider, more modern world.[51]

The swift and ruthless response to the 1811 rebellion tells us that enslavers in the southwestern United States were different from those in the Caribbean.

They were wiser in their power, for they had been taught by many lessons: those of the Haitian Revolution, seen from afar by most (though some of the enslavers in Louisiana had been there); those of the American Revolution, which still was not that long ago; and those of the seemingly endless wars against Native Americans. They were more numerous than their island counterparts, and they were better at war. They were more clever in their cruelty. They were more ruthless and decisive in a crisis. And whites in the most slavery-dominated districts could call on two key elements of force that Saint-Domingue whites had lacked. The first was a white majority in the regional and national theaters. Even though enslaved people outnumbered free whites in many plantation districts in the United States—such as in the German Coast, where they had a 70 percent majority—they never formed the 90 percent supermajorities common on the sugar islands. The second was a federal government dominated by enslavers that was committed to putting down slaves' collective resistance. Federal troops were the key to suppressing the 1811 revolt. The government protected the enslavers' enterprises, and they, in turn, extended the power of the American state by occupying and developing territory.[52]

By reputation, slaveholders were stubborn traditionalists who forgot nothing and learned nothing; in reality, they continued to learn and adapt to promote their own interests. But after the 1811 revolt, they increased their regulation and surveillance of the slave population, taking them to new heights. Local militia trained more intensely. Patrols swept slave quarters with new regularity. Claiborne, anxious as ever, now put the area on alert whenever he heard a rumor of revolt—like the one that came to his ears right before Christmas in 1811. Louisiana's state government rewarded informers with freedom. Free people of color in the United States were always a tiny minority who sided with the white majority during crises, in contrast to Saint-Domingue, where many had joined the rebellion.[53]

Supporters of Louisiana statehood in Congress used the insurrection as an argument for their cause, suggesting that a territory that was exposed to peculiar dangers but that produced great wealth for the nation should have a sovereign voice in the councils of the republic. As a few northern congressmen warned, this meant that the entire nation was now more compelled than ever to defend slavery in Louisiana. But Congress agreed to take on the responsibility, and Louisiana became a state in 1812. This step, like all the measures taken and lessons learned, would be of crucial importance in the next few years.

Violence in Saint-Domingue had won the Mississippi Valley for the United States and for the new, dynamic form of slavery whose expansion would in turn drive the nation's growth. Violence, marching down the road toward New Orleans, had been the climax of threats from within to the dreams of the new entrepreneurs of a transformed slavery. Violence from without was about to challenge enslavers and their allies once again.[54]

THE MILITIA STOOD AMAR up in the yard at the Widow Charbonnet's place. Herded into an audience, the men, women, and children who knew him had to watch. The white men took aim and made Amar's body dance with a volley of lead. In his head, as he slumped and fell, were 50 billion neurons. They held the secrets of turning sugarcane sap into white crystals, they held the memories that made him smile at just such a joke, they held the cunning with which he sought out his lover's desires, they held the names of all the people who stood circled in silence. His cheek pressed on earth that his own feet had helped to pack, his mouth slackly coursing out blood, as gunpowder smoke gathered in a cloud and blew east. A white officer's sideways boots strode toward him. The dancing electrons in Amar's brain caressed forty-five years of words, pictures, feelings, the village imam with his old book, his mother calling him from the door of a mud-brick house. The memory of a slave ship or maybe more than one, the rumor of Saint-Domingue—all this was there, was him—but his cells were cascading into sudden death. One last involuntary wheeze as a soldier raised an axe sharpened by recent practice and severed Amar's head from his body.

Six weeks later, a merchant drifting down the river on a flatboat spied strange fruit growing. "Along between Cantrell and the Red Church I saw a number of Negro Heads sticking on Poles on the Levee," he wrote. On the pike, Amar's face stared out over the water. The buzzards and the crows had already taken what they could. Slowly, as his jaw became unstrung, his mouth gaped. In terror of what would happen if they were caught taking him down, in fear of his unquiet spirit, his people left him up there. Perhaps some thought he had done wrong, that his choices, and those of dozens of others whose heads now stretched up and down the levee for fifty miles, had brought disaster upon themselves and their people. Perhaps others thought him a martyr, an avatar of revolution, of pride and resistance.

Amar had done no more than answer the call that came to him, to choose when he had a choice. And half a century would pass before anyone like him would face such an opportunity to choose again. By that time, his skull had long since crumbled in the sun. Yet before they turned to dust, Amar's empty sockets may have gazed on another school of flatboats, which came down the river in the last weeks of 1814. The vessels were packed to the gunwales not with the usual cargo of pork, tobacco, and corn, but with an army of white men from Tennessee, a force eight times as large as the one that had followed *commandeurs* to defeat.

Already, on December 1, Andrew Jackson, commander of US army forces in the southwestern region, had ridden into New Orleans on the old Chef Menteur Road that went out along the Gulf Coast toward Biloxi. He had come from Mobile in ten days of forced marches, with 1,000 soldiers and a long string of victories trailing him. As he entered a city that stood again as the contested prize of impending mass violence, young boys, black and white, ran shouting the news that General Jackson was here at last.

In the Place d'Armes, where Cesar, Daniel Garret, and Jerry had all been hanged for participating in the 1811 insurrection, white New Orleans residents gathered again—this time called more by fear than by spectacle. After Claiborne (who had been reconfirmed as governor by the voters after Louisiana achieved statehood) said a few words, Jackson stepped forward, attended by the wily politician Edward Livingston—who stood ready to translate the general's remarks into the French still preferred by most of the people in the city.[55]

The blue uniform with its golden epaulets seemed to fit the tall man in ways beyond measurements and cut, but not because he was handsome. He was not. Jackson's hatchet face—the Creek Indians called him "Sharp Knife"—was topped with a shock of once-red, now gray hair. He was tall for the time at 6'1", but extremely thin—140 pounds in the prime of his life, and less now. Jackson had spent the past eighteen months on the warpath, and along the way he had contracted a terrible case of dysentery. Days still passed when he felt too sick to eat. Street fights and duels had left pistol balls embedded in his flesh. Pieces of his bullet-shattered humerus had worked themselves out through the wiry fibers of his bicep a few months earlier.

Physically, Jackson was a wreck. But an incredible will to dominate, which Jackson channeled into a determination to defeat everyone whom he saw as an enemy, kept him standing straight as a spear. Not a shred of doubt floated in Jackson's eyes. In one anecdote from his time as a judge in Tennessee, a criminal had refused to come into the courtroom to face his charges, and then cowed a posse that Jackson sent out into the street after him. At last Jackson stepped down from the bench and came out himself. He stared down the man, a giant of a village bully, who then meekly entered the courtroom.

Why? the defendant was later asked. Because, he replied, "when I looked him in the eyes, I saw *shoot*."

Thomas Jefferson had known a younger Andrew Jackson during the latter's brief term as senator, and had noted that Jackson's passion controlled him: "He could never speak on account of the rashness of his feelings. I have seen him attempt it repeatedly, and as often choke with rage." Some of Jackson's ferocity came from mysterious sources within. Some came from the rage generated in 1781, when a British sweep of backcountry South Carolina guerrilla strongholds ended in the capture of fourteen-year-old Andrew and his older brother Robert. Andrew was beaten with the flat of a cavalry saber for refusing to clean a British officer's boots like a slave, and Robert died in prison. But Andrew had survived. And he grew. Now he wielded his anger as a disciplined weapon. Jackson's habit of command was also reinforced by his ownership of dozens of enslaved African Americans on his labor camp outside of Nashville. Their toil had made Jackson's fortune and raised him to the prominence that won him election as the head of Tennessee's militia. He now bore a regular army commission and was the US government's only hope for protecting the Gulf Coast against invasion in the third year of a war that had gone remarkably poorly.[56]

Jackson told the crowd gathered at the square that would one day bear his name that he would save the city. Rumors held that tens of thousands of British veterans were coming, and Lord Wellington, who had defeated Napoleon, was commanding them. The whites of New Orleans feared not only the massive British invasion army bearing down upon them from the sea, but also the disruptions and slave revolts that might come with becoming the seat of war. And they feared that the divisions between French, Spanish, and English speakers, sutured by business deals that brought in more slaves, and then by mutually suppressing slave rebels, might open like old wounds under the stress of invasion. But Jackson told them he would throw the enemy into the sea or die trying.[57]

A cheer went up. It was not only Jackson's unyielding assurance, nor his patriotic rhetoric, that calmed his anxious audience. Since the War of 1812 had begun, victories had been unexpectedly few and far between. In 1812, after trying various strategies to push Britain into allowing American trade more freedom on the high seas, President James Madison had caved to pressure exerted by Republican congressmen and asked for a declaration of war. The most vehement congressmen were the so-called War Hawks, mostly young representatives from western states. They believed that now, while Britain's fleets and armies were tied up in the struggle with Napoleon, was the time to finish dismembering the British Empire in North America by annexing Canada. (As it turned out, Canadians did not want that.) Southern congressmen also imagined that war with Britain would permit them to seize additional territories from Spain. They had just annexed "West Florida," the strip of land from Mobile to the "Florida Parishes" of Louisiana. Now the rest of Florida was in their sights.

By 1814, American nationalists had suffered many disappointments. The huge Royal Navy had bottled up the tiny American fleet in its ports. Canadians and British troops inflicted a series of stinging defeats on US forces on the northern border. An attempted coup (later shined up with the name "Patriots' War"), led by English-speaking planters living on Spanish-ruled Florida's Atlantic coast, failed. Irritation at westerners' dominance in the decision for war turned the northeastern states toward open undermining of war efforts. And in 1813, dozens of Creek villages in Georgia and Alabama rose against white settlers in a war called the "Red Stick," after the emblem of war that militants carried from town to town. On August 20, 1,000 warriors broke into a huge frontier stockade called Fort Mims, where 700 white settlers and enslaved African Americans sheltered. In less than an hour they slaughtered 250 men, women, and children. Only a few whites escaped, though the Creeks—the most powerful of whom owned African-descended slaves and cotton plantations—kept black prisoners alive.[58]

In Tennessee, Andrew Jackson reacted to the news of Fort Mims by gathering the state militia and marching them south into Alabama. The brutal campaign that followed displayed both Jackson's domineering personality and southwestern whites' determination to do anything necessary to secure fertile soil for slavery's expansion. Jackson maneuvered to keep his command out of the control of political rivals back in Tennessee, shot deserters, and eventually pinned 2,000 Creeks into a loop of the Tallapoosa River called Horseshoe Bend. On March 27, 1814, his troops breached the enemy's log walls and ran amok, killing 900 Creek warriors at a cost of only 70 of the attackers. Then, Jackson called all Creek leaders—including the ones who had opposed the Red Sticks—to a meeting at Fort Jackson. There he bullied them into signing a treaty that conceded 23 million acres (36,000 square miles), an area as large as Indiana. The friendly Creeks protested, but he had the army, the victory, and the power. They signed away over half of their lands in Alabama, much of it on the rich black soil of the central part of the territory. The land, already speculated upon several times as part of the vast Yazoo claim, could be surveyed and sold again—this time to actual white settlers.[59]

Jackson's victory at Horseshoe Bend was one of the two real American triumphs of the War of 1812, even though the fact that it was fought against Indians and deep in the southwestern interior means that many forget to think of it as part of that war. Measured by numbers killed—almost 1,000 between the two sides combined—it was the deadliest battle fought in the war. Horseshoe Bend's casualties do not compare, of course, to those generated by the massive armies that had for a quarter century fought in Europe, though it was among the 100 deadliest battles of the Napoleonic Wars. And considered by its outcome, it ranks among the most significant. The Treaty of Fort Jackson permanently handed far more land, and more valuable land, to the enslavers of the United States than all the blood and treasure poured out by France had won for her. The strong-arm robbery of the Creeks set the stage for millions of other profitable transactions that would ensue over the next half-century. White slave-owning settlers' military dominance over the southwestern Indians rendered inevitable the eventual loss of all their remaining land in Alabama, Georgia, and Mississippi.

What Jackson was in the process of doing now would be just as significant. Haiti's defeat of the invincible French army had opened the entire Mississippi Valley to an American expansion driven by the productive force of slavery. In the suppression of the 1811 revolt, slaveholders and the US government had shown themselves willing to defend that opportunity ruthlessly. In the new environment of the now-open southwestern regions, slavery was changing, becoming something different from what it had been in the old states or the old Caribbean. But from the perspective of Britain, the Treaty of San Ildefonso was illegitimate, and therefore so was the Louisiana Purchase. Napoleon had no right to sell a territory to which he had no title. Now—having raided the Chesapeake coast and burned Washington to the ground, British Admiral Sir Alexander Cochrane was on his way to the Gulf to seize New Orleans, return greater Louisiana to Spain, and leave the United States caged behind the Mississippi.

Already humiliated by his scampering retreat from the White House, President Madison desperately needed help if he was to prevent British forces from overturning his mentor's most significant achievement. Jackson was the man for the job. After imposing his treaty on the Creeks in August, he had pursued remaining Red Sticks into ostensibly neutral Spanish-held Florida. He seized Pensacola, sending British marines and a flotilla of warships reeling backward. He also fortified Mobile, another target of British invasion plans. The British, meanwhile, shifted troops to a staging base at Jamaica. They believed Louisiana was low-hanging fruit: divided by ethnic conflicts and filled with slave owners who would surrender before risking a fight that could disrupt their "property arrangements." When Jackson heard in late November that a massive invasion force was about to leave Jamaica, he sent word to units from Tennessee and Kentucky to descend down the Mississippi to New Orleans as quickly as possible. He had left Mobile on the 22nd. Now, he was here. Over the next weeks he would gather more troops, fortify the approaches to the city, and continue to stiffen the sometimes-flagging resolve of the wealthier residents. But the British were coming.

IF YOU DRIVE OUT from New Orleans's Vieux Carré, the French Quarter, Rampart Street turns into St. Claude Avenue as you enter "the Marigny"— the old Faubourg that was literally outside of the city in Jackson's day. Once St. Claude passes over the canal, the neighborhood changes from white to black. You cross Andry and Deslonde, streets that, a few blocks north of here, run through a landscape once blown bare of houses by the explosive force of water. Keep going, though. There was already enough encoded in the street names of the Lower Ninth Ward to make you weep without thinking, too, of bare concrete pads and naked sidewalks. Soon the road becomes St. Bernard Highway, and in a single minute you are at the battlefield. And yet you are only five miles from the Quarter.

Today the swamps are filled in, but in the first days of 1815, the Chalmette property on which the Battle of New Orleans was fought was a narrow neck of 1,000 yards of sugarcane stubble that covered the gap between the almost impassable wetlands and the Mississippi. The invaders' fleet had balked at the attempt to get their troops up the winding and fortified river. Instead the British army landed almost in the rear of New Orleans on Lake Borgne, and passed by canal and path through the woods over the course of December 22 and 23. Some 5,500 regulars under Edward Pakenham, a thirty-seven-year-old veteran of the Napoleonic wars, now stood almost within sight of New Orleans, five miles from the destruction of American empire west of the Appalachians.[60]

Although Jackson could deploy 4,000-odd men in the bottleneck of Pakenham's path to New Orleans, American militia had historically performed poorly in pitched battle against trained European regulars. Yet those units had not been commanded by Andrew Jackson. He shamed backbone into the city fathers of New Orleans, who (when the British army arrived at their gates) begged him to retreat upriver from the city and declare it open so they would not be burned and looted for resisting. The majority of his troops came from Tennessee and Kentucky. There were also two battalions of free men of color from lower Louisiana, one of which was composed of refugees from Saint-Domingue. Jackson warned them all that the enemy, who supposedly promised freedom to the hundreds of slaves who had escaped to their lines in the two weeks since they had arrived, "avows a war of vengeance and desolation, proclaimed and marked by cruelty, lust, and horrours [*sic*] unknown to civilized nations." Only victory, he suggested, would prevent the unleashing of the fires of Saint-Domingue in the slave societies of the Mississippi Valley.[61]

Jackson had chosen his ground well, anchoring his lines in as good a defensive position as one could find between the Appalachian and Rocky Mountains. As January 7 turned into January 8, he and his troops lay entrenched behind the ten-foot-wide Rodriguez Canal that separated the lands of Chalmette from those of Benjamin Macarty. At one in the morning, Jackson woke his aides. He could smell the attack. Four years to the day after the *commandeurs* had launched their attack on the most thickly planted center of enslavers' power, Pakenham's troops stirred and moved.

Dawn revealed 4,000 men drawn up in menacing formation across Chalmette's long lot. Then, drums beating, cannon firing, the red line began to advance on Jackson's lines in perfect step, ominous and beautiful. They embodied the discipline that had ruled European battlefields for the past century. But as they came into range, splitting into two prongs to avoid a huge mire in the middle of Chalmette's field, Jackson's troops began to empty a carefully aimed storm of lead into the British ranks. Cannon fire ripped holes in the red formation. Pakenham himself, riding forward to see why his lines had shuddered and stalled, was hit multiple times. He bled to death by the edge of the swamp.[62]

By 8 a.m. it was all over. Two thousand British soldiers lay as casualties on the Chalmette plain, of whom at least 300 were dead. The Americans lost a mere thirteen killed. Still, Jackson wisely refused his subordinates' pleas for him to pursue the retreating British army, which still held 2,000 trained men in reserve. Instead, he let the enemy pack their bags. On January 25, the invaders departed, taking with them almost 800 enslaved people who had, in effect, emancipated themselves.

Although mighty armies disrupted slaveholder power more effectively than the slaves' revolt had, enslavers had won this round, too. The loss of 800—for whom Britain would after many years consent to reimburse Louisiana enslavers—was not even a dent in the solidity of slavery at the mighty river's head. Within hours of the American triumph, meanwhile, a rider with news of this most significant of American victories between the Revolution

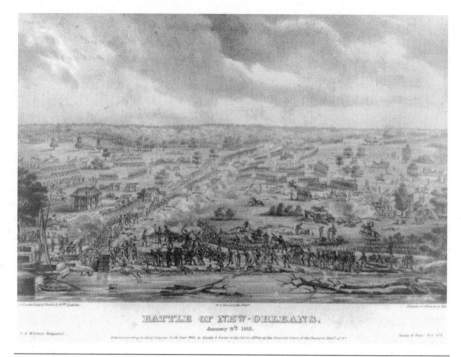

BATTLE OF NEW-ORLEANS.
January 8ᵗʰ 1815.

Image 2.1. Jackson's victory at New Orleans in January 1815 was the capstone to twenty-five years of violence that ensured United States enslavers would control the Mississippi Valley. This illustration shows the way the swamps to the north and the river to the south constricted British options and forced them to attack Jackson's cotton-bale-protected defenders across the muddy ground of a winter sugarcane field. "Battle of New Orleans," Hyacinthe Laclotte, 1820. Library of Congress.

and the Civil War whipped his horse into a gallop past Fort St. Charles, turned left just past where one last head had sat on a pike for so long, and headed up the Chef Menteur Road. Another went up the river road, past all the still-standing posts. It took weeks—until February 4, in fact—for news on horseback to reach the national capital. But when it did, a mighty flood of joy poured out.

The elation was undiminished by the simultaneous arrival of the news, from Europe, that American negotiators had signed a peace treaty with Britain at the neutral city of Ghent on December 22, 1814, even as British troops disembarked from their ships at Lake Borgne. The terms of the treaty essentially returned everything to the starting position of 1812, giving captured territory back to its owner. Some have claimed that the treaty rendered Jackson's victory at New Orleans irrelevant, except for enshrining Jackson as a nationalist icon. But with the prize of the Louisiana Territory in their hands, the British would have been entitled, according to their own interpretations, to hold onto it or give it back to Spain. In fact, Article IX of the Treaty of Ghent obligated the United States to return land taken from Britain's Indian allies—who included the Red Stick Creeks. Thanks to Jackson's victory, however, the United States was in no position to feel compelled to reverse the Treaty of Fort Jackson and remand 36,000 square miles to Creek custody. So the Battle of New Orleans protected the windfall the United States had caught when the sacrifices of the Haitian Revolution shook the tree of empire, and it confirmed Jackson's great land grab from the Creeks as well. Slavery's expansion could now proceed unchecked.

The man in the iron collar had come to slavery's new frontier, a place created by violence. Revolution in Saint-Domingue overthrew the old pattern of early modern slavery, which had driven one kind of economic development in the Atlantic world. Haiti's revolutionaries had offered the world a radically new concept of human rights, the right of all to become equal citizens. But this vision did not become reality, either in independent Haiti or elsewhere. Indeed, the death of the old slavery cleared room for something quite different: a new, second slavery. Constructed first in the southwestern United States, this modern and modernizing process brought benefits and rights to ever wider groups of people while stripping them, with great violence, ever more radically from others. At the Mississippi's mouth, brutal force defended this infant process from the efforts of the enslaved to block it, marking the ramparts of its cradle with the severed heads of rebels. Next, Jackson completed American possession of the southwestern frontier with victories that opened thousands of square miles. Now a continental empire was possible, one that had vast resources within its reach. But to create vast and sweeping dominions out of the chaos that their own violence amplified, the victors would still need many things: credit, land, markets, crops, authority, and hands—above all, hands, hands to write, to buy, to reach, to grasp, to plant, and to harvest.

## 3

# RIGHT HAND

## *1815–1819*

FROM THE DECK OF the brig *Temperance* to the grass-clotted soil of the New Orleans levee stretched a long narrow plank. It bent under the weight of the four men as they filed across it, bent under Rachel's, too, as she followed.

Throughout the morning of January 28, 1819, one white man after another had boarded, talked with Captain Beard, and walked back down the gangplank. One had taken a couple of the brig's twenty-four enslaved passengers. Rachel, standing by the deck rail in her new clothes, had watched them disappear between the huge piles of cotton bales on the levee.

The opposite deck rail had showed her the river. Hundreds of masts were in sight, seagoing brigs and barques and sloops and schooners moored along the levee like the *Temperance*. River flatboats by the hundred were here to unload their Ohio corn and hogs, Mississippi cotton, and Kentucky tobacco. She could see the stacks of a dozen steamboats. And working its way across the muscular brown chop of the Mississippi had come one little rowboat. A slight, black-suited white man sat upright in the stern. And a black man worked the oars.[1]

Now, at the end of the plank, Rachel put her feet on Louisiana. On unsteady legs she climbed the levee to the southwest. She'd been six weeks on the water since the *Temperance* had left Baltimore. That was where merchant David Anderson had purchased her for consignment to his New Orleans partner Hector McLean. Anderson had also bought William (tall, dark, age twenty-four), George, Ellis, and Ned Williams. Rachel now followed them up the slope. Her head rose over the top of the levee. As she reached out to balance herself, her hand found a bare post driven into the dirt, one in a long series stretching upriver, each one separated from the next by a mile or so.

Nailed to it was, perhaps, a placard. Its words were everywhere in New Orleans: tacked to walls and posts, printed in directories and newspapers. "AT MASPERO'S COFFEE HOUSE. . . . PETER MASPERO AUCTIONEER, *Informs his friends and the public that he continues to sell all kinds of* MERCHANDISE, REAL ESTATE, AND SLAVES . . . *in Chartres Street."* And at the bottom: *"Looking-glass and Gilding Manufactory. P. Maspero."*[2]

From the levee, Rachel could see a city in the midst of full-tilt growth. Populated by 7,000 people at the time of American acquisition in 1803, New Orleans now claimed 40,000. Already this was the fourth-largest city in the United States, behind New York, Philadelphia, and Baltimore. In commercial dynamism, Jefferson's "one spot on Earth" was equaled only by New York. From every quarter hammers pounded on the ear, nailing timbers of broken-up flatboats together into storefronts. To the east, downriver of the *Temperance*'s mooring-point at the French Quarter, stretched the Marigny district, a mostly French-speaking "Faubourg," or suburb. To the west spread the rapidly growing "American Quarter," or Faubourg St. Mary. As Rachel followed the others down the levee's other slope, they passed a chain gang—"galley slaves," New Orleans residents called them, slaves who for the crime of running away were locked in the dungeons behind the Cabildo at night and brought out to build up the levee by day. The city government could punish resistance while simultaneously using rebellious slaves' labor to protect the city from the giant river that crested each spring.[3]

At the bottom of the levee, parallel to it, ran a dirt avenue—Levee Street—and as they stepped onto it the five entered a city whose vortex had been sucking at their feet ever since Maryland. Here, women of every shade called out in French, English, Spanish, and Choctaw, selling food and trinkets, but beneath the patter was another hum, that of bigger business—and it was booming. On corners, under the awnings of new brick buildings, white men gathered, talking. Heads turned, appraising. Before the War of 1812, enslaved people from other US states had been relatively scarce in New Orleans. But from 1815 to 1819, of those sold, about one-third were new arrivals from the southeast—Virginia, Maryland, North Carolina (see Table 3.1). Another 20 percent came down the river from Kentucky. A few hundred came from northern states such as New Jersey and Pennsylvania, slipped out in contravention of gradual emancipation laws that contained provisions designed to keep masters from liquidating in a going-out-of-business sale.[4]

One turn left, and they headed up a muddy street. In the middle: a ziggurat of cotton bales, taller than the men who muscled them up, too wide for carts to pass. It being January, the crop was coming down at full tide on

TABLE 3.1. SLAVES IMPORTED TO AND SOLD IN NEW
ORLEANS, 1815–1819

| ORIGIN | NUMBER LISTING AN ORIGIN POINT FOR JOURNEY* | PERCENT OF TOTAL |
| --- | --- | --- |
| Chesapeake and older South | 705 | 32.9 |
| KY, TN, and MO | 423 | 19.7 |
| Southwest (AR, MS, AL) | 314 | 14.7 |
| Northeast and Northwest | 22 | 1.0 |
| Caribbean | 89 | 4.2 |
| Other Louisiana | 591 | 27.6 |
| *Totals* | *2,144* | *100.0* |

*Source:* Hall Database, www.ibiblio.org/laslave/.

* The variable used was "Via," which records the place from or by which the seller brought the slave to New Orleans; 6,698 other sales either contain no entry for this variable or record Orleans Parish.

flatboats and steamers. Even as the employees of cotton dealers piled bales high, teamsters hired by cotton buyers chipped them back down: pulling bales out, checking letters branded on cotton wrapping, hauling the 400-pound cubes of compressed fiber toward the river.

If Rachel could've followed the bale, she'd have seen it loaded from the levee onto oceangoing vessels. These would carry the bales across the Atlantic to Liverpool on England's northwestern coast, where dockworkers moved the bales to warehouses. After sale on the Liverpool cotton market, they went by canal barge to Manchester's new mills. Textile workers—often former operators of hand-powered looms, or displaced farmworkers—opened the bales. Using new machines, they spun the cleaned cotton fibers into thread. Using other machines, they wove the thread into long pieces of cloth. Liverpool shipped the bolts of finished cloth, and they found their way into almost every city or town in the known world, including this one.

Cotton cloth was why New Orleans was booming, why the world was changing. White entrepreneurs here—like the customers in the shops Rachel was passing, the men on the corners, the sellers and buyers on the ships along the levee—were participating in, even driving, this worldwide historical change. Building on the government-sponsored processes of migration and market-making taking place in Georgia, and the battles fought by the slaveholders' military to open up the Mississippi Valley, after 1815 a new set of entrepreneurs had begun to use Rachel and all the others brought here against their wills to create an unprecedented boom. It linked technological

Image 3.1. On the New Orleans levee, bales came off river-going steamboats and were loaded onto oceangoing vessels. Thus cotton grown in southwestern fields connected to world commodity and credit markets here, but New Orleans also became the nexus of other network-driven processes glimpsed on the levee, such as the forced migration of enslaved people to slavery's frontier, or the development of new African-American cultures of performance. "View of the famous levee of New Orleans," from *Frank Leslie's Illustrated Newspaper*, v. 9, no. 228, April 14, 1860, p. 315. Library of Congress.

revolutions in distant textile factories to technological revolutions in cotton fields, and it did so by combining the new opportunities with the financial tools needed to make economic growth happen more quickly than ever before. This boom was changing the world's future, and these entrepreneurs who used Rachel were establishing themselves and their kind as one of the most powerful groups in the modernizing Western world that cotton was making.

BEFORE THE LATE EIGHTEENTH century, all societies' economies were preindustrial. Almost all of their inhabitants were farmers or farm laborers. Whether European, Asian, American, or African, such economies rarely grew by as much as 1 percent per year. So it had been since women and men had invented agriculture ten millennia earlier. Most of what people made fell into a few categories: food, fuel, and fiber. The pace of innovation was glacial. And when preindustrial societies did begin to grow—whether through technological advances, increases in access to resources through conquest or trade, or changes in weather conditions, such as the warming that took place in Europe between 800 and 1300 AD—the increasing prosperity led people to have more babies. Babies grew into more farmers, who could grow more food, and more purchasers, who would buy their products. But the increasing number of mouths to feed began to exceed the maximum output possible under preindustrial methods of agricultural production. The easily accessible firewood was being burned up; and the acres needed for raising the flax or wool to clothe the increasing population was being turned over to marginal subsistence agriculture. Costs rose. Living standards dropped. Famine, epidemic disease, war, political instability, and full-scale social collapse were next.

English clergyman Thomas Malthus wrote about this cycle in a famous 1798 pamphlet. Food production, he argued, could increase arithmetically at best, while population could expand geometrically. Thus, no increase in the standard of living was sustainable. It would always run up against resource limits. Western societies acquired massive new resources between 1500 and 1800. Conquistadors stripped the Incas and Aztecs of their gold and silver. The creation of the first slavery complex, with its "drug foods"—sugar, tobacco, tea, coffee, and chocolate—stimulated Western Europe's desire to seek out and consume still more resources. The massive Atlantic slave trade required ships, trade commodities, and new structures of credit, and growth spilled over into sectors less directly linked to sugar. Many in Western Europe began to work longer hours in order to get new commodities, in what is sometimes called an eighteenth-century "Industrious Revolution."[5]

Yet neither the first slavery, extended hours of labor, or the theft of resources could permanently relieve Malthusian pressures. Even Thomas Jefferson, who hoped that the Louisiana Purchase would delay the collapse of his yeoman paradise for a hundred generations, knew that such solutions eventually ran out of arithmetic. Malthus and Jefferson's pessimistic reading of human history from 10,000 BC until 1800 was the realistic one.[6]

But even as Rachel climbed the levee, the ground was shifting. The global economy was launching an unexpected and unprecedented process of growth that has continued to the present day. The world's per capita income over the past 3,000 years shows that a handful of societies, beginning with Great Britain, were shifting onto a path of sustained economic expansion that would produce higher standards of living and vastly increased wealth for some—and poverty for others (see Figure 3.1). The new trajectory created winners and losers among the different societies of the world. Until the late twentieth century, we could simply state these with a catchy phrase: the West and the Rest.

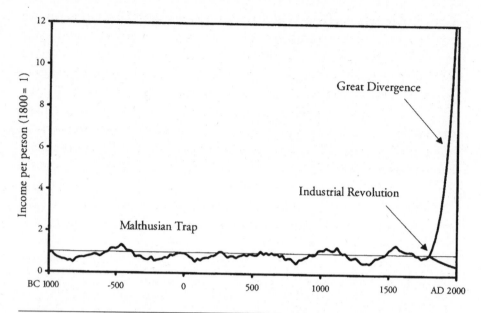

*Source:* Gregory Clark, *A Farewell to Alms: A Brief Economic History of the World* (Princeton, NJ, 2008).

People have called this incredible shift in human history by a variety of names: modernization, the industrial revolution, the Great Divergence. In those societies that it benefited the most, this transformation built fundamentally upon one key shift: increasing the amount of goods, such as food or clothing, produced from a given quantity of labor and land. This is what allowed the standard of living not only to keep up with a growing population, but for many, also to improve. By 1819, it was dramatically evident that mechanical innovations and a new division of labor could result in increased production of goods at lower cost in labor and resources than ever before. And exhibit number one was northwestern England's cotton textile industry.

Until late in the eighteenth century, cotton fabric had been a luxury good woven on handlooms in Indian villages. But by 1790, British inventors had begun to create new machines that spun cotton into thread at a rate that human hands could not approach. The machines were less expensive to acquire and operate than the human hands, too. Within seven decades, Manchester factory workers running the new machines could make cloth five or ten times faster than laborers alone working by hand. A new class of factory-owning entrepreneurs emerged. They extracted massive profits from textile manufacturing, but textile revenues also boosted and transformed the entire

British economy. Wealthy landowners borrowed cotton-generated invest-ment capital and commercialized agriculture. Surplus rural laborers, pushed into factory towns, became wage-earning factory workers.[7]

The evidence of transformation surrounded the white customers Rachel saw in the stores. Imagine one of them, his fingers checking out one bolt of cloth after another, sensing its weight, its texture, the elaborate variety pumped out by Manchester mills and promoted in newspaper ads: "Superfine broad cloths," "white flannels," "Cambrick and jaconet muslins." Lower in quality were ready-made and standard-sized "Negro shirts" pieced together from cotton "Negro cloth." Piled on bales of slaves' blankets were iron pots and casks of "trace chains" for hitching mules to plows; stacked up on count-ers were saws, log chains, balance beams called "steelyards" for weighing cotton; piled in corners were "West India" and "Carolina" hoes for sugar-cane and cotton, respectively. These non-textile goods were mostly made in British workshops. Designed for the new markets of plantations and growing cities, they were what economists call "knock-on effects" pushed by the pis-tons of the cotton textile engine. On the shelves were breakables meant for consumption and not production: hundreds of "packages" of "earthenware (chiefly blue printed)," perhaps made by Wedgewood, the first large-scale British maker of "china"; "first rate gold watches"; dozens of cases of guns; "2 cases looking glasses" (putting Maspero out of one business); "elegant pianos"; decanters of "Cristal [*sic*] and cut glass."[8]

In enclaves like this store, this city, this network of enclaves that stretched to New York and Liverpool and London and so on, men like this man were changing their worldviews. Increasingly, they anticipated that progress would carry them and their society ever upward and onward to positions of unprecedented power. And for the next eighty years, they would use in-dustrial power and technology to subdue the rest of the world. By the end of the nineteenth century, only half a dozen independent non-Western nations would survive on the globe as colonialism expanded. Even nature surren-dered, as William N. Mercer, a physician who traveled to New Orleans in 1816, predicted. "Steam Boat navigation" would conquer "the western coun-try," taming the immense distances and "deep and impetuous" currents of the Ohio and Mississippi Rivers. Steady improvement in machine technol-ogy became a popular metaphor; it depicted change as unending progress, change in which machines extracted power from nature and yielded it to human beings.[9]

But the move from arithmetical to geometric economic growth wasn't only caused by the greater efficiency of British machines. All the new efficiencies, all the accelerating curves of growth, would have been short-circuited if embryo industries had run out of cotton fiber. And that nearly happened. Before 1800, most of the fiber came from small-scale production in India, from the Caribbean, and from Brazil. The price of raw cotton was high, and it was likely to rise higher still, because the land and labor forces available for producing cotton were limited, and their productivity was low. High raw material costs constrained the expansion of the British textile industry.

The North American interior, on the other hand, had thousands of acres of possible cotton fields, thousands for each one in the Caribbean. And the invention of the cotton gin in the early 1790s helped to uncork one of the bottlenecks to production by allowing the easy separation of cotton fiber from seeds. But even with the dramatic increase in the amount of cotton produced in South Carolina and Georgia that followed, and even with the growing labor force supplied by coffle-chains and marching feet, southeastern enslavers still were not close to meeting the world market's growing demand for raw cotton. In hindsight, we see that the greater Mississippi Valley was the obvious answer. Yet the Mississippian who wrote that New Orleans would be the "port of exit for the redundant produce of the upper country—its sugar, tobacco, cotton, hemp"—was typical before 1815 in thinking that cotton came in third. He imagined that Louisiana's main function would be to replace Saint-Domingue in the world circuit of sucrose. Before 1815, New Orleans lagged well behind Charleston as North America's main cotton port.[10]

On May 19, 1815, four months after Jackson's victory, New Orleans cotton entrepreneur William Kenner reported that "upwards of Thirty vessels were in the River" on the way to the city, because "Europe must, and will[,] have cotton for her manufacturers." His Liverpool cotton brokers predicted that cotton prices "will not decline." Before 1815 was half over, 65,000 cotton bales, made on slave labor camps in the woods along the Mississippi and its tributaries, arrived in New Orleans by flatboat. This was 25 percent of the total produced by the entire United States, and the land and dominion that southwestern slaveholders won in battles against the enslaved, against Native Americans, and against the British prepared them to launch even greater expansions in raw cotton production.[11]

In fact, the cotton supply was about to increase even more rapidly. By the time four more years had passed, and Rachel arrived in New Orleans, 60,000 more enslaved people had been shifted into Louisiana, Mississippi, and Alabama from the older South. By 1819, the rapid expansion of Mississippi Valley slave labor camps had enabled the United States to seize control of the world export market for cotton, the most crucial of early industrial commodities.

And cotton became the dominant driver of US economic growth. In 1802, cotton already accounted for 14 percent of the value of all US exports, but by 1820 it accounted for 42 percent—in an economy reliant on exports to acquire the goods and credit it needed for growth. New Orleans had become the pivot of economic expansion, "the point of union," as one visitor wrote, between Europe and America, industry and frontier. Its proliferating newspaper columns were filled with long lists of ship landings and departures, ads for goods imported, brokers' pleas for more cotton, offerings of commercial credit, and notices of bank directors' meetings. Economic acceleration loomed over Rachel in mountain ranges of cotton bales.[12]

THESE WERE THE CHANGES that flowed through the man's hands like the warp and weft of fine cotton, and these were the changes that swept Rachel and the others, five droplets in a human flood, past him and around the corner onto Chartres. The cathedral loomed above the roofs of the stores to the right. Two blocks more, and they reached the intersection with St. Louis Street. On their right stood a two-story stucco building. A wooden box, the height of a bench, waited by its exterior wall. The white man leading them opened the door and stepped inside under a swinging sign that said, simply, "Maspero's." Last of all, Rachel caught the door with her left hand and stepped over the threshold.

In 1819, it was hard to come to the city without being taken to Maspero's "Coffee-House." If New Orleans was the pivot of southwestern and even national expansion, much of the city's commerce rotated around this specific point—a "coffee-house" that was nothing like Starbucks. One visitor complained that "as this is a coffee-house, you can here find all cordials but coffee." Whiskey fumes cut through tobacco haze, revealing to Rachel the waist-high bar running the length of the back wall; behind it—hovering—a middle-aged man of Mediterranean origin. His eyeglass manufactory straggled on next door, but Maspero spent most of his time chasing cash over here. He'd sell you a glass of wine or liquor. He'd even sell you, if the right chance presented. Only a year or two after Rachel came to Maspero's, when an immigrant German "redemptioner," or indentured servant, died in rural Louisiana, the man's little white daughter would allegedly be sold as a slave here—like hundreds of other daughters.[13]

For the past few years Maspero's main trade had been providing a place for others to meet and speculate, and today, several dozen white men were seated at the tables scattered around the sand-covered floor that eliminated the need for spittoons. Some of the men turned toward the newcomers when the door opened. Rachel took inventory. Some were in their twenties, some older. Some wore hats, some did not. Most dressed in the styles of the time: long trousers, dark jackets over white shirts with cravats. One man of narrow frame wore all black. Rachel might have recognized him from earlier. He was the man in the rowboat.

Rachel would also have seen how they *looked*—how they gazed at *her*, and yet through and beyond her, too, appraising her and fitting her into calculations that stretched on to the future's horizon. Here's how William Hayden felt on the receiving end of that gaze. Sold to Kentucky as a boy in the 1790s, he was dealt again in 1812 to a man named Phillips. This new owner, a Mississippi Valley version of a Georgia-man, carried people down the river to sell them from his flatboat to planters in Natchez, at New Orleans, and in small Louisiana towns. One day a merchant named Castleman came to talk to Phillips. Castleman "was anxious to secure me," Hayden remembered, and his smile revealed "the joy that the wolf feels when pouncing upon a lamb."[14]

Wolves. Rachel felt their eyes. The key to all the commodities sold at Maspero's, even cotton, was flesh. When she had boarded the *Temperance*, she had already known that she was going to be sold in New Orleans. African Americans in Maryland were learning about "New Orleans" just as they had learned about "Georgia." Rachel could now see the line of men, women, and children standing against the far wall, and she saw that Maspero's was the place where the sale would happen. But even had she been blind, the palpable anticipation in the air would have revealed the place's nature. That desire was not for her alone as a slave, or as a woman—though both of those desires were part of the combustible mixture. The anticipation was part of the identity of the specific white men who waited in the room. They weren't slave traders in the same sense that the term describes either a Georgia-man like M'Giffin or a Phillips, or their successors who would work in New Orleans in later years. Those were people who specialized in buying enslaved people in one place, taking them to another, and selling them there. As of 1819, professional slave traders were rare in New Orleans. No specialist kept a private jail, like the two dozen that would cluster by the 1850s along Gravier and Baronne Streets, just southeast of where the New Orleans Superdome now stands. Nor would one find at the levee in 1819 dedicated slave ships like those that eventually plied the waters between the Chesapeake and the Mississippi.[15]

On an 1817 journey down the Mississippi, an Englishman noticed that in the taverns where businessmen met along the way to New Orleans, "there are many men of real, but more of fictitious capital. In their occupations they are not confined to any one particular pursuit, the same person often being farmer, store and hotel-keeper, land-jobber, brewer, steam-boat owner, and slave dealer." Most important: "All are speculators; and each man anticipates making a fortune, not by patient industry and upright conduct, but by 'a lucky hit.'" Such were the men who collected here at Maspero's. Take the one in black, sipping cold water, for John McDonogh was an abstemious Presbyterian. McDonogh had come from Rachel's own Baltimore, two decades earlier—not as goods for sale, but with a cargo owned by merchant employers. He sold it, remitted the proceeds, and struck out on his own. Rivals claimed that McDonogh and his business partner, Richard Shepherd, intentionally planted land-sale rumors in Maspero's, gossip that raised the price of McDonogh's own property holdings, which covered much of Louisiana. Yet McDonogh was neither a landlord, nor—though he bought and sold slaves—a slave trader. McDonogh was an entrepreneur. He modestly clothed his desires in solemn black broadcloth. But he was a disruptive, destructive force that broke and remade the world, just like a more flamboyant man whose gaze Rachel also crossed.[16]

No single man was more influential in shaping the New Orleans cotton trade into the world's biggest one than Vincent Nolte. He first came at the behest of the Anglo-Dutch firm Hope and Company before 1812, bringing half a million pounds in paper backed by the Bank of England. With this stake he built a circuit of cotton and capital between the Old World and the New. After the War of 1812 ended, he linked up with Baring Brothers, the massive London commercial bank that had financed the US purchase of Louisiana, and whose pressure had convinced American and British negotiators to swallow pride and sign the Treaty of Ghent at the end of 1814. Barings' money allowed Nolte to accumulate huge piles of cotton on the levee after 1815, and by 1819 he was buying 20,000 to 40,000 bales per year—4 to 8 percent of US exports, and up to a quarter of what passed through New Orleans.[17]

One could argue that as much as any great inventor, factory owner, or banker, it was Vincent Nolte who made modernization possible. He shaped the patterns and institutions of the most important commodity trade of the nineteenth century, the one that fed Britain's mills with the most important raw material of the industrial revolution. The huge quantities of money he channeled from Britain into this room at Maspero's stimulated greater and greater cotton production along the river valleys that fed New Orleans. Nolte's modernization of the trade incidentally made it both more efficient and more open to new players. He gathered and disseminated information about the state of Mississippi Valley markets by creating a printed circular that quoted the going price for all sorts of goods in New Orleans—what his contemporaries called a "Price-current."[18]

Usually we think of the architects of modern capitalism as rational. They might be greedy and they might be profit-seekers, but they reject gambling and achieve accumulation through self-denial and efficiency. Accounts of economics usually teach that people are driven by calculations about "utility" and price, and that market behavior is predictable and rational. Nolte, however, was unquestionably a gambler. He didn't care about efficiency; he wanted piles of money, and he wanted to win. Make no mistake: He didn't think he was trusting to luck. He believed that he understood the game of speculation well enough to know its secrets. But he rolled the dice. Over the decades, Nolte gained and lost vast sums of money. He even put his life at stake for his prospect of gain, fighting four duels with business rivals in 1814 and 1815.[19]

If Nolte wanted to make an incomparable fortune, it wasn't because he thought success equaled salvation, or because profit was an end in itself, exactly. Nolte's actions spurred economic modernization—ever-more-efficient exploitation of ever-greater amounts of resources—by stimulating the production of enormous quantities of cotton. In the real history of the real modern world, change has been jolted forward again and again by people like Nolte, who in their dice-rolling bids to make massive profits disturb existing equilibriums by introducing new elements. The new elements they introduce as levers of dominance might be technological innovations, but entrepreneurs rarely create these innovations themselves. Instead, they figure out how to reap their benefits in order to rip market share and profits away from other capitalists who are invested in status-quo technologies and staler business models. They are architects of the dynamic of "creative destruction" that iconoclastic economist Joseph Schumpeter identified as the core engine of capitalism's growth. Creative destruction produces wrenching shocks, devastating depressions following dramatic expansions, wars and conquests and enslavements. Here, in New Orleans, cotton—and slaves—enabled creative destruction to produce the modern economy.[20]

Nolte said he did what he did because of something he wanted to feel— what he called "the charm," the spell he wove upon himself by knitting a "vast web of extended commerce" with himself at the center. And Maspero's was a room full of Noltes, for whom creative destruction was motivation as much as process. Along with McDonogh and Shepherd and Nolte, their ranks at the tables included such men as Beverley Chew and Richard Relf, William Kenner, Stephen Henderson, and French-speakers like merchant

Louis Lecesne and broker P. F. DuBourg, who cut deals with Creole planters. They, too, loved the sense of power they got from exerting what Nolte
called the "enterprising mercantile spirit": cutting out rivals, knowing that
people far away were bending to their wills. They bought cotton from the
interior and shipped it to Liverpool. They bought cargoes from England and
Germany and sold their contents to stores strung like beads on the rivers all
the way up to Louisville.[21]

Using geographical position, special knowledge, and special access to essential commodities, these nonspecialized, flexible entrepreneurs organized
from scratch a massive increase in the global economy's most important raw
material. Over the course of the five years that began in 1815, southern cotton became the world's most widely traded commodity, and New Orleans
became the gravitational center of the system of buying and distributing it.
The city doubled the amount of cotton it shipped, soon surpassing the southeastern ports of Charleston and Savannah.

Maspero's was the first center of the New Orleans cotton trade. It was also
the site around which another new market was coalescing. As the *Gazette de
la Louisiane* reported, at Maspero's you could buy a cargo of Irish and English cloth; a pilot-boat; a piece of land on Chartres Street; a brick house; a
plantation (that of Madame Andry, Manuel's widow, in fact), and *les esclaves*.
One could buy people here, on any day save Sunday, by bidding at auctions
or negotiating with these entrepreneurs. In addition to their other activities,
all these men sold and bought substantial numbers of slaves there. Kenner
and Henderson sold at least 150 slaves at Maspero's between 1815 and 1820.
McDonogh's trading partner Shepherd sold 97. Scottish cotton merchant
Thomas Urquhart sold 76 people. And so on. And as with cotton, at Maspero's these creative destroyers established access to supply, stimulated demand,
and created a place where a purchaser could always count on finding what
he wanted. In other words, they made a market, one that—though centered
in the Lower Mississippi Valley—stretched far beyond this specific place to
creep tendrils of incentive reaching into Maryland farms, Alabama cotton
docks, New York banks, and London parlors. This slave market would continue to develop over the next four decades in dynamic relationship with the
development of the cotton economy.[22]

As we trace Rachel's path, we can see how that market-making happened.
Her transport depended on the actions of federal and state governments. The
compromises of the Constitution permitted the transport of slaves across
state lines. Congress also protected transport with its 1793 law that blocked
non-slaveholding states from sheltering runaways. Meanwhile, like most

other enslaved people transported from the southeast to New Orleans in the pre-1820s period, Rachel came by a route that resembled the paths of other commodities to the levee. Southwestern entrepreneurs asked their southeastern contacts to buy them slaves. Sometimes these were specific requests—a blacksmith from Maryland for Stephen Minor of Natchez, for instance—but usually they were general, as in, "Procure [me] hands from Virginia." For now, the people procured were sent on regular merchant ships, such as the *Clio*, on which Benjamin Latrobe sailed from Norfolk in 1818. The *Clio* also carried regular merchandise and one Doctor Day, who was moving to the Red River to become a cotton planter. While Day transported twelve of his own slaves, the ship also bore Tom, who had been consigned, like Rachel, by Baltimore merchant David Anderson. Tom cost Anderson $800, plus a fare of $30, but he died off the coast of Florida. Watching the *Clio*'s sailors throw his body into the water, white passengers speculated that he would have brought close to $1,200 in New Orleans. Anderson's New Orleans consignee had lost quite an investment.[23]

After reaching New Orleans, slaves like Rachel and tall William were often kept on board their vessels until they could be sold. In other cases, entrepreneurs locked captives in stables, in the city jail, or with other commodities in counting-houses and warehouses. William Kenner kept people at his own slave labor camp until he considered them "seasoned" enough to sell. Slave-sellers also locked people in Maspero's—in the ballroom adjacent to the bar, or upstairs in the meeting room, the same one where Andrew Jackson had berated the gathered city fathers for quailing in the face of Pakenham's redcoats. But Maspero's made a poor jail. In October 1819, the Roman brothers, local enslavers who branded any person they bought, purchased a woman named Maria for the high price of $1,500. They left her in Maspero's keeping while they finished their town business. Reluctant to endure the hot iron the Romans were paying so much to inflict on her, Maria escaped. Seven weeks later, she was still running.[24]

Yet despite its inadequacies as a cage, Maspero's was the pole around which the market in enslaved people orbited between 1815 and 1819. Even if the man or woman wasn't physically present, the buyer could read the enslaved person's name in the *Louisiana Courier* as he sat here. He mentally compared the description to the others who were paraded here. The seller came here to meet him and arrange the sale. The papers changed hands here in the barroom. The forces generated in this long, low, smoky room changed the lives of thousands of Rachels and Williams. The acts of New Orleans entrepreneurs also changed their own lives, and not simply by enriching their account balances. For men like the entrepreneurs in Maspero's, the birth of the modern world opened access to powers that few who were not absolute monarchs had ever felt before.

These sensations were generally only available to those with the luck of being born white, male, in the right place, and to the right family. Still, old mercantile alliances and families were being bypassed as new men created new money-making empires. Imagine the luck of a boy like Henry Palfrey, son of a failed father, who became a clerk for Beverley Chew and Richard Relf of New Orleans at age twelve. As Palfrey grew to manhood in the environment of Maspero's, internalizing its desires, he would write commands and requests. He sent them as letters, and in consequence things happened that his father, a frustrated merchant of an earlier generation, could not make happen. Huge quantities of cotton bales moved. People were sold away from their families, piles of cloth and iron loaded, money transferred.[25]

The way entrepreneurs assimilated that environment's values and came to see those values as normal reveals much about why they devoted their lives to creating an "extended commerce" in the southwestern United States. They spoke as if their own bodies were doing the things that their deals—sales of cotton, purchases of land or slaves, payments of money on the other side of the ocean—made happen. Yet not their whole bodies. There was one specific part of the body they talked as if they were using. They wrote notes and letters that informed their correspondents that they held slaves "on hand" and money "in hand." Important letters "came to hand." They got cotton "off [their] hands" and into the market. In 1815, waiting for prices to rise, John Richards offered the Bank of the State of Mississippi a note to ensure that he would not yet have to sell "the cotton that I now have in hand." Individual promises-to-pay that drew upon credit with other merchants were "notes of hand."[26]

Few parts of the body have a more intimate and direct connection to the mind than the hands, and when entrepreneurs used words to grasp the control ropes of the new economy, they described the sensation as if the new world's powers were held in their own like puppet strings. They produced concrete results at distance, using words that their hands wrote on pieces of paper. The fingers at the end of the writer's arm might not actually hold the material thing—the bales of cotton, the stacks of coin, the ship whose captain and crew were directed to carry them—that the figurative language of trade said it grasped. But in a very real sense, the writer controlled these things, these people.

These writers' hands could grasp much more than the hands of merchants and traders in the past because the new dynamic growth of Western capitalism was producing massive quantities of what the great twentieth-century theologian Robert Farrar Capon called "right-handed power": the strength to force an outcome. Capon identified right-handed power as being like the idea of God held by many believers of many religions: a deity working in straight-line ways, exerting crushing force, throwing the wicked into the flames, drowning the sinful earth. Right-handed power is the power of domination, kings, weapons, and the letter of the law. In the early nineteenth century, those societies and individuals who were winning in the sorting-out of power and status accumulated unprecedented right-handed strength. They got more guns and bullets, more soldiers, the ability to knock down other peoples' defenses and force them to trade on the terms most favorable to the West. They dominated other peoples to a degree unprecedented in human history, and within victorious new modernized nations, right-handed power was increasingly distributed in a lop-sided fashion. Members of the new leading classes—people like the men at Maspero's, but also the cotton-mill owners of Manchester, the merchants of New York, the bankers of London—got most of that power in their hands.[27]

So if one had to pick the hand to which letter-writers referred as they sat there at Maspero's, one might say "right." Even though the effects of entrepreneurs' decisions sometimes played out a long way from the places where the decisions were taken, they were still straight-line effects. The letter is written and sent, the Maryland trading partner reads it, deposits the bill of exchange, goes to the probate auction, buys a woman advertised as a house servant, and takes her to the next Louisiana-bound ship. So the exchanges of the cotton economy, wrote one white man (to whom Louisiana success, he said, had given a new "sense of independence"), "put it in *your* power"—into your hands, he told his relative—"to enrich yourself." A man presses a button (with his *right* index finger) on the machine of the trading world, with its new markets and opportunities, and things happen to benefit him—things involving sterling bills, a huge pile of cotton, or a long roster of slaves. The emerging modern world strengthened the right hands of these men, offering them the opportunity to make everything new and different, to shape it along the lines of their desires.[28]

Much of the muscular power in right hands was nerved by credit, itself a phenomenon almost as magical-seeming as the idea that one could direct far-off events with one's hands. Credit is *belief* (the word comes from the Latin *credere*) that brings value today in exchange for a promise to pay in the future. Credit allowed entrepreneurs and others to spend tomorrow's money today, accomplishing trades and investments that would (the borrower believed) make more wealth tomorrow. When granted on easy terms, credit was what allowed trade to spread, to move smoothly, and to enrich people around the Atlantic basin.

New Orleans entrepreneur William Kenner, for instance, could use bills of exchange, promises to pay that originated with a British merchant firm, to buy cotton bales from his planter trading partner John Minor. Kenner could then ship the bales to Liverpool and sell them there to a merchant house, which would in turn credit Kenner's account and "redeem" the bills of exchange from the original firm. The merchant house could allow Kenner to "draw" on his account by writing checks, or "drafts." It could also, if its partners believed in Kenner's financial future, allow him to write his own notes of hand and "negotiate" them in the United States, using them as his source of credit. Kenner could sell such a note for cash here at Maspero's, or trade it for goods—or people—if the seller believed that the Liverpool firm would "honor" Kenner's hand. How much the person accepting the note of hand believed in it—how much he or she *credited* its magic—determined not only whether he or she would accept it as money, but also how much money one believed it to be. Bills traded at a "discount" on the face value of the note, a floating value that also served as an interest rate. (One might give $96 for a bill that one could then, in six months, exchange for $100. One has just lent and been repaid at about 8 percent annual interest, in other words.) The buying and selling of promises to pay was itself a business. Vincent Nolte's newspaper advertisements proclaimed his willingness to buy "exchange" on Paris, New York, or London—notes that were payable in those cities, which Nolte could send to pay his own bills there.[29]

But belief in credit must be created. People must come to trust in its institutions and in the reliability of their trading partners in order for credit to spring into life as money and serve as fuel for explosive growth. And like every other faith, credit has a history, and Rachel came to Maspero's at an important moment in that story.

Jeffersonian Republicans had killed off the first Bank of the United States in 1811, but during the War of 1812, financial chaos made it very difficult for James Madison's government to raise the money it needed to fight the war. Following the country's close call, in 1816 the Republicans chartered (for twenty years) the Second Bank of the United States. The "B.U.S." was intended, in fact, to anchor the broad economic program advanced by the "National Republican" faction—a group of young leaders who were elbowing out the old Jeffersonians. They included Henry Clay of Kentucky and John Calhoun of South Carolina's cotton frontier, and their plan to use federal power to create a modern economy in the United States pivoted on the bank's ability to lure foreign investment in its bonds, stabilize the financial system, and feed credit into entrepreneurs' hands. Their "American system," as Clay termed it, also included a planned network of "internal improvements": canals, roads, and river-clearance projects to lower the cost of transportation and encourage production for distant markets. A tariff that protected domestic textile production would allow the American economy to follow the British model of industrialization.[30]

The new B.U.S., headquartered in Philadelphia, also established branches in major trading centers such as New Orleans. But most of the branches ignored their mandate to regulate financial flows. Instead, as local banks sprang up like fungus—the Kentucky state legislature chartered forty banks in 1818 alone—the B.U.S. allowed credit to slosh into every cranny of the expanding nation. In the short term, a runaway burst of prosperity silenced traditionalists, who warned that paper money and banks were scams. In April 1814, there were 38 flatboats from upriver tied up alongside the New Orleans levee; four years later, there were 340. Financial giants Baring Brothers, Hope and Company, and other European cotton buyers injected millions of pounds of credit to pay Nolte and his peers. Textile and other merchants looking to unload their wartime backlog of goods advanced millions more in merchandise to American distributors. The B.U.S. directly lent huge amounts of credit to land speculators, and the bank's directors and employees borrowed from the cashbox for their own endeavors.[31]

For enslaved people like Rachel, the sudden growth in financial confidence did not mean liberation, but the opposite. The bank helped both white Americans and overseas investors to have faith in a future in which the debts of slave buyers would be paid off by ever-growing revenues from the cash-earning commodities that industrializing Britain wanted. One could see the visible signs of this quickening right-handed power all across the southwestern United States, not just in Maspero's but also, for instance, in Huntsville, Alabama, a frontier village into which a dust-caked Virginian named Francis E. Rives rode on the same January 1819 day on which Rachel and William arrived on the levee. Soon Rives would sit in the state legislature in Richmond, but today he was leading a train of twenty-odd enslaved people whom he and his employees had marched from Southampton County, Virginia. Rives and the employees who helped guard the coffle were explorers of a new country of credit and trade. Searching out ways to extract new yield from human energy stored in the slave cabins of Virginia's Southside, their expedition extended Georgia trades west by hundreds of miles. Following

Cherokee trails from the left corner of North Carolina across the spine of the Smoky Mountains, they had now descended into the valley of the Tennessee River, which flowed by Huntsville.[32]

The Tennessee could carry cotton-laden flatboats into the Mississippi, so Huntsville was tied to the invisible cord of trade and credit attached to New Orleans. And thanks to the investments channeled through the Bank of the United States and the possibilities of trade, the valley that lay before Rives's coffle was suddenly blooming with both schemes and cotton. Anne Royall, an acerbic Pennsylvania travel writer who went to Alabama in 1818 to get material for a new book, found that her usually dismissive authorial voice cracked when she crested the same ridges that Rives's forced migrants now descended into Huntsville. "The cotton fields now began to appear. These are astonishingly large; from four to five hundred acres in a field!—It is without a parallel! Fancy is inadequate to conceive a prospect more grand!"

"There has not been a single . . . person settling in this country who has anything of a capital who has not become wealthy in a few years," claimed Virginia-born migrant John Campbell. He clearly suffered from the "Alabama Fever," as people called it—the fervent belief that every white person who could get frontier land and put enslaved people to work making cotton would inevitably become rich. And it was credit that raised their temperature. Most of the settlers in Alabama were squatting on land that had once been included in the Yazoo purchase, had later been surrendered by the Creeks at Fort Jackson, and was now being sold by the federal land office in Huntsville to purchasers who typically relied on credit. By the end of 1818, the land office had dealt away almost 1 million acres, which officially brought in $7 million. But speculative purchasers, including Andrew Jackson, James Madison, and the chief employees of the local land office, paid only $1.5 million up front. Of that amount, $1 million was in the form of scrip that the federal government had given to investors who had received compensation after the 1810 *Fletcher v. Peck* decision. Thus government-supplied credit had financed 93 percent of the cost of the land in the valley before Rives—money that would have to be repaid from sales of cotton not yet planted by slaves not yet bought. No wonder Rives marched these enslaved people to Huntsville. Here was a prime hunting ground for slave sales.[33]

Credit appeared to be turning enslavers' Alabama dreams into reality. Alabama was already third in the United States in total cotton produced and first in per capita production. And not just Alabama enslavers: between 1815 and 1819, settlers transported nearly 100,000 unfree migrants to southern Louisiana, central Tennessee, and the area around Natchez, Mississippi.

These slaves cleared fields bought on spec, grew cotton to make interest payments and keep new loans flowing, and served as collateral besides. The dramatic increase in the ability of would-be entrepreneurs to borrow money had extended their right-handed reach across time and space, over mountains, and across seas.[34]

BACK IN NEW ORLEANS, where plenty of credit was available for the right hands of those who bought and sold, the bells of the St. Louis Cathedral on the Place d'Armes—just around the corner from Maspero's—rang out at noon, resounding through the conspiratorial coffee-house buzz. Then one of the wizards of the credit process arose. This was Toussaint Mossy, one of the city's most popular auctioneers. Until now he had been sitting at a table, observing the people who leaned in a rough line against the wall, puffing on his pipe and glancing occasionally at a sheet of paper. On it were written names, ages, and phrases, some of which might be true. Standing, he turned to face the room. In French-accented English, he explained to the expectant audience that twenty-three slaves would now be sold by auction. The newspaper had simply said "terms will be made known at the time of sale." Enslaved people sold as part of an estate often were sold on longer-term credit of a year or more granted from local seller to local buyer, usually with a mortgage to protect the lender. Sellers like McLean, who had probably bought his slaves in the Chesapeake with short-term credit that soon would be due, wanted bank notes or easily traded credit in the form of bills of exchange. Mossy then explained that the auction would take place outside. He turned and walked out the door.[35]

Rachel and William blinked in the sunlight that beat down on the St. Louis Street wall. The first person to be pulled out might have been John—at about fifty, the oldest in the group. Mossy pointed him to the low bench. Tall and light-skinned, John stepped up on the box as white folks filed out of Maspero's and surrounded him in a semicircle. Passers-by paused: women with market baskets, men striding up from other stores, children white and black, flatboat men from up the river. Enslaved people stood at the back of the crowd, faces blank. A hush settled, broken by creaking wagon wheels and muffled shouts from stevedores on the levee. The moment was here, the one that made trees fall, cotton bales strain against their ropes, filled the stores with goods, sailed paper across oceans and back again, made the world believe.[36]

Mossy began to speak. But not in everyday talk. Auctioneers persist long past Mossy's day. One knows what they sound like, but their skills seem antique in a time when most auctions are held impersonally online. But there are two important things to remember about Mossy's job. First, an auction is the purest moment of supply meeting demand and thus sorting out prices in the capitalist market economy. John, facing the crowd, was a test of the demand for a fifty-year-old male human being in New Orleans on a Thursday in January when cotton sales had been strong and credit elastic. Buyers and sellers who heard its outcome would hang a whole array of prices on the amount paid for him. This lesson would shape private sales, affect bidding in later auctions, weigh the numbers inked by slaves' names on estate inventories. Mossy's cajoling, whispered collusions between potential buyers in the crowd, nods and raised hands that signified bids, prices of credit and cotton—all were shaped by and in turn blew back and forth the cloud of information and belief that was the market for slaves.

Second, auctioneers then as now were expected to weave a spell of excitement about the act of purchasing. Mossy wanted to get the highest possible price, but he also created a community of buyers and sellers there at Maspero's. This kind of market-making trained buyers to think about the enslaved in certain ways. As Mossy announced key numbers for John and each of the other subjects of sale who would follow him onto the bench—height, age, and price—he also taught buyers how to see the features this community considered most valuable in an enslaved person. Height was the easiest to learn. You could see it. Enslavers usually paid more for tall men than for short ones. Height was less important for shaping women's prices, but age mattered for both men and women. Enslavers generally paid their highest prices for young men between eighteen and twenty-five, or for women between fifteen and twenty-two. At going rates in January 1819, McLean might realize between $900 and $1,100 for Ned or William, while women of the same age usually sold for at least $100 or $200 less. Mossy would have to work to get $400 for fifty-year-old John.[37]

Although enslaved people born in the southwestern United States were considered less likely to die from disease than were new migrants to the region, African Americans from Virginia and Maryland were already important to this market, too. There were simply not enough local prime-age men and women available to meet the demand. And unlike seasoned but savvy locals, a youngster from Virginia might seem like a malleable piece of one's right-handed dreams: Alexander McNeill, for example, told the man selling teenager Henry Watson that he "wanted to bring up a boy to suit himself." Moreover, in Maryland at about this time, enslaved men in their early twenties sold for about $500. In New Orleans, Ned or William might bring twice the Chesapeake price. Transport costs averaged less than $100 per slave, so

Image 3.2. At auctions, enslavers and the credit that they wielded formed a community of entrepreneurs, who here stand—both men and women—around the main event. But the auction also shaped a market that measured people as commodities—like the men, women, and children who slump on the bench in the foreground, waiting their turns. George Bourne, *Picture of Slavery in the United States of America* (Middletown, CT, 1834), 144–145.

entrepreneurs who secured enslaved people from older states could undersell locals while still pocketing a huge profit.[38]

The transactions of the auction, and indeed of any sale, were more complicated than a simple sale of good $x$ by seller (1) to buyer (2) for price $y$ or $z$. Going by fifties, tens, or smaller numbers still, bidders competed with each other in ways that were sometimes more about proving oneself than about buying a slave. Methodist minister Wilson Whitaker reported what happened at a North Carolina auction when John Cotten battled with a man the preacher knew only as "Dancy." The two first clashed over who would win a cornfield. Then they ran the price of a male slave up to $1,400—New Orleans prices, in North Carolina. Dancy could go no higher. But then he called Cotten "a dam'd scoundrel," and went for the winner with a whip. So Cotten pulled out his pistol and shot him. The victor fled, leaving a friend to take possession of the enslaved man.[39]

At the same time, the auction was a place for finding out how malleable an enslaved person would be in the buyer's right hand, how well they suited the buyer's schemes. Young Louis Hughes remembered how the buyers pressed him and dozens of other slaves who stood in a formation at a Richmond slave

Image 3.3. Inspection was part of the process of establishing a human being as a "hand" available and ready for sale. This was serious business, but here the enslaved person was required to play a role—standing still, not resisting, answering questions with the most market-friendly responses and behaviors. *Illustrated London News,* February 16, 1861, p. 138.

pen. Shoppers "passed up and down between the lines looking the poor creatures over, and questioning [the women,] . . . 'What can you do?' 'Are you a good cook? seamstress? dairymaid?' . . . [and to the men,] 'Can you plow? Are you a blacksmith?'"⁴⁰

Private sales, made not in public auctions but in one-on-one negotiations, sometimes gave a person the chance to size up his or her would-be consumer. On the one hand, if the scuttlebutt in the warehouse told you a prospective buyer lived near the place where you had heard your wife or child or parent had been sold—well, then make yourself the brightest-eyed and most compliant in the bunch. On the other hand, you might not want to be noticed in some cases. To the frightened teenager Henry Watson, Alexander McNeill appeared "the very man . . . from whom I should shrink, and be afraid . . . sharp, grey eyes, a peaked nose, and compressed lips." "He was a very bad-looking man," Watson said years later, and Watson "never wish[ed] to look upon his face again." But be careful: If the seller caught you not "selling yourself," you would get whipped.[41]

At auctions, the number of white eyes concentrated on one slave's body emboldened questioners and intimidated the questioned. Interrogations replaced coy flirtations: "What sort of work can you do? Have you ever run away?" The seller might have primed the slave with answers, but a room full of aggressive entrepreneurs pressed, trying to get slaves to stumble and spill the truth: "Who taught you how to lay brick?" John might have been struck off in five minutes so that Mossy could get to the more delectable parts of the bill of fare, but others had to endure half an hour or even longer before they could step down. This was too long to game the questions and answers. To add to the pressure, when whites sensed fatigue, they'd press a man on the block to share a fake-companionable swig of brandy, forcing the enslaved to lower his or her defenses and submissively swallow the spit of the people who sold them.[42]

No, on the block, only the most desperate plays had a chance. At fifteen, Delicia Patterson gave this speech, literally from the stump: "Old Judge Miller," she said, "don't you bid for me, cause if you do, I would not live on your plantation, I will take a knife and cut my own throat from ear to ear before I would be owned by you." Others wailed from the lines where they waited—keep me near my children; buy me, man who is not as harsh as that other one, I will be a good worker. Some tried a bravado approach, laughing and joking—see, you cannot break me. But while Judge Miller dropped his bid for Delicia, when the young woman's father begged his current owner to buy his daughter, the man cited her public defiance and refused. Stubbornness could also lead to physical assault. Martha Dickson, sold at an auction in St. Louis, refused to speak when she was ordered to describe herself. The auctioneer had her whipped until she talked.[43]

So auctions not only set prices, but also destroyed the façade of negotiation with the enslaved and established a community of right-handed power. The most useful advice was what Charlotte Willis's grandfather discovered on a Mississippi block: "Better keep [your] feelings hid." Some channeled pain and fear into silent fury: as he "ascended the auction-block," remembered one man, "there was hate mingled with my humiliation." The grim satisfaction of focusing on a tightly controlled kernel of hate—this was all most enslaved survivors of the auction could take away as profit from the sale of their own bodies and futures. But uncertainty, humiliation, and threats stunned most minds on the block. Eventually their bodies revealed the terror. Mothers wailed. Some, physically overwhelmed, couldn't quite follow what was happening. Incoherent, they could barely stand before eyes that measured them, planned for them. "I's seen slaves" on Napoleon Street in New Orleans, remembered Elizabeth Hile, fellow slaves "who just come off the auction block." Staggering away from Maspero's behind their new owners, they "would be sweating and looking sick."[44]

This day, when seventeen-year-old Mary climbed onto the bench after John stepped down, a buzz probably rippled through the crowd. From Mary the crowd sought a particular kind of compliance and entertainment. She was wrapped in a different set of codes than the ones that a man signaled. Dredging up the memory of the auction of his half-white half-sister, which he had to witness in 1830, Tabb Gross recalled that "her appearance excited the whole crowd of spectators." "Fine young wench!" a woman remembered hearing, on another occasion: "Who will buy? Who will buy?"[45]

Rachel watched. She had been leered at, too—when she came through the door, all the way back to the point of her sale in Baltimore. It had been going on ever since she reached puberty, but sale time was when the forced sexualization of enslaved women's bodies was most explicit. Before the 1830s, and sometimes after, whites usually forced women to strip. Robert Williams saw women required to pull down their dresses: each one "would just have a piece around her waist . . . her breast and things would be bare." In the middle of Smithfield, North Carolina, said Cornelia Andrews, slave sellers "stripped them niggers stark naked and gallop 'em over the square." In Charleston, enslaved women stood, wrapped only in blankets, on an auction-table in the street. The "vendue-master" described their bodies, and a white bidder who took a woman back into the auctioneer's shop could take off the blanket.[46]

Auctioneers and bidders would turn a woman around, raise her skirt, slap "and plump her to show how fat she was." William Johnson remembered that "bidders would come up and feel the women's legs—lift up their [g]arments and examine their hips, feel their breast, and examine them to see if they could bear children." For white people, seeing Mary up on the bench was one of the rewards of membership in the fraternity of entrepreneurs. Men asked questions of a woman that they did not put to John or William, questions that attempted to force her to acknowledge everything that was being bought and sold. Women who refused to play along could expect white anger, as one observer noted: "When answers were demanded to the questions usually put by the bidders to slaves on the block, the tears rolled down her cheeks, and her refusal to answer those most disgusting questions met with blood-curling oaths." Of course, not all white bidders minded resistance. Some relished overcoming it. It was all part of the game.[47]

SHE KNEW HER TURN was coming. But as Rachel waited, she heard, punching through the auctioneer's patter, through the probing questions of the men in the crowd, one word that recurred in the murmurs of the prospective buyers lining up credit with the lenders who would back them. This strange but ordinary word floated and hummed around her, bubbling up her ear canal and knocking on the door of the mind. Likewise, it crawled out of pen nibs and spoke on the papers on which some of the men who were still sitting inside Maspero's were writing. It rested quietly in the darkness of folded letters, sailing out in leather letter-satchels in the holds of ships, sealed behind wax but ready to burst off the page and into the world. It spoke of a deeper order, a value structuring the seething water of price-setting and price-changing. But it also carried its own chaos: dreams of creation, destruction, greatness, order, progress; machine, metal, fear-sweat and field-sweat, desire amid the hot cotton bales stacked in the shed.

Hand. By the time the auctioneer finished off Mary and announced that William was next, Rachel had heard that word more times that day than she could count. It is a very ordinary word. It was being used in a sense different from the way that entrepreneurs used it when they wrote about their notes of hand and so on—different, but as interlaced with that meaning as a fist. Enslavers' use of the word "hand" as a metaphor for the right-handed power that they experienced through participation in modernization seems "normal." Pull the thread of "hand" in Mossy's auction-talk, and we will find that it was so deeply embedded in the language and practices of the emerging slave market that we have incorporated it into our history of slavery ever since as if it were a natural term. We miss its non-neutrality in our first pass across a sentence, for we are embarrassingly literate in hand-talk. After two centuries, we still translate without thinking John Brandt's 1818 offering of "Five likely Negro fellows, prime field hands."

You see five men like William, standing in line beside the bench, don't you? But try to read William Robertson's 1816 advertisement literally. He's planning an auction, at a New Orleans church, of "20 or 30 Negroes, just arrived from Tennessee, consisting principally of working hands." Or take just as literally the precise language of the *Louisiana Gazette*'s booster-ish description of the riches that those willing to take the plunge and become planters in its reading area had already gained. Nicholas Lorsselle had "7 hands only," and yet "he" made forty bales of cotton, and $593 to the hand. A man with *only* seven hands. Imagine carpals, metacarpals, nails assembled together and coated with seven sets of muscle and skin. See disembodied hands working, but never holding themselves out for payment.[48]

When Mossy said the word "hand," white people saw not an appendage with five fingers, but four simple letters that pulled a freight of metaphor and real-world effects. Two thousand years earlier, the Greek philosopher Aristotle called the slave the "instrument" of the owner, "a living tool." Aristotle gave formal recognition to the idea that the slave was the master's right-handed will embodied: his hand grasping in the world (*his*, though *shes* were enslavers, too). The slave reached when the owner said "reach," took when the master's brain sent an impulse down the nerves of social power, all without thinking or reflecting.[49]

In important ways, Aristotle's story had always been a lie. Through centuries of slave revolts and endless days of resistance, slaves insisted that they had their own wills. Those wills, in the shape of enslaved Africans, were so strange to Europeans in the first couple of centuries of New World slavery that they did not use the idea of the hand to describe the people whom they held captive. That does not mean they did not try to create as reality the relationships of absolute right-handed power that "hand" implied. But they also developed an ideology claiming that Africans were radically different from Europeans in order to explain away the gap between seemingly unbridgeable cultural difference and resistance, on the one hand, and the dream of the slave as a pure tool, on the other. You can see this in the names they gave to the people whom they drove off of Middle Passage ships and into sugar and tobacco fields, titles that emphasized the otherness of the African—*bossales*, saltwater slaves, *têtes*, "heads."

In the 1810s, however, as right-handed power expanded explosively in the southwestern United States, the word "hand" began to replace "head." A clerk working for William Kenner quoted prices to customers: "Negroes have sold here lately," he wrote in 1816, perhaps from a table at Maspero's, "at 600 [and] 500 dollars per head, for common field hands." The word began to carry a set of newly possible promises about the people whom it labeled. Hand was the ideal form of the commodity "slave," just as white crystals are the ideal commodity form of "sugarcane." Each person for sale was a commodity: alienable, easily sold, and, in important ways, rendered effectively identical for white entrepreneurs' direct manipulation.[50]

Bidders could fit a William, for instance, into the box of the concept "hand," an idea that experienced entrepreneurs told newbie Natchez planter

John Knight was the archetype he should look for in the slave market. "The qualities and requirements to make <u>first-rate</u> plantation hands," they told him, began with this: "They should be <u>young</u>, say from 16 to 25 years old, stout and active, large deep chest, wide shoulders & hips &c." To make sure his reader did not miss the point, he underlined and bold-inked his summary: "I wish first-rate hands, young and stout." Enslavers in the Lower Mississippi Valley wanted to buy those who looked strong enough to bear intense physical labor. Here was William, looking young and stout. And they'd force him to be "active," because white men made plans for returns and revenue by the hand, anticipating the amount of value they could extract from a human being straitjacketed into the role of commodity. One calculated power and possibility by the number of hands needed to fell an acre of trees, one denominated the rate of return from ground cleared or cottonseed planted by the hand. E. B. Hicks used hands as a unit of accounting and "put as many hands on the river plantation" as his business partner.[51]

The word delivered because it was continually recalculated from a thousand different economic relations. As he was buying enslaved people, the white man, in his mind's eye, saw himself working them, reselling them, mortgaging them, making them into money, putting them "in his pocket"— to use the words of slave owners' threats to many a "hand." And here at Maspero's, sellers, auctioneers, buyers, and bidders did specific things to make whole people look and in certain ways to *be* like the obedient right hands of enslavers' future endeavors. They worked to assure buyers that the person on the bench, brought so many miles from home by coffle-chain, could call on no sources of external power countervailing against that of the purchaser. "It is better to buy <u>none in families</u>, but to select <u>only choice, first rate, young hands from 16 to 25 years of age</u> (buying no children or aged negroes)," those same old Natchez planters quoted above told John Knight. Before American acquisition, Louisiana enslavers had bought children, adults, and older adults in percentages proportionate to their presence in the population. But after the purchase and the establishment of new trade routes and robust systems of credit, entrepreneurs bidding at Maspero's began to demand that eastern sellers send them young adults ready to start work right away, and able to produce profits for years to come. By the five-year period starting in 1815, almost 45 percent of the enslaved people bought from other states were between the ages of fourteen and twenty-five: more than twice as many as the number between twenty-six and forty-four, and significantly more than the children aged thirteen and under (see Tables 3.2 and 3.3).[52]

Enslavers wanted to buy people who had no claim to a special status— who were as unformed as Henry Watson had been in the eyes of Natchez

TABLE 3.2. AGE GROUP DISTRIBUTION OF ENSLAVED PEOPLE SOLD IN NEW ORLEANS, 1800–1804

| AGE GROUPS: | 0–13 | 14–25 | 26–44 | 45 AND UP | TOTAL |
|---|---|---|---|---|---|
| Known to be imported | 72 | 59 | 37 | 4 | 172 |
| | 41.9% | 34.3% | 21.5% | 2.3% | |
| Not known to be imported | 573 | 514 | 565 | 120 | 1,722 |
| | 32.3% | 29.0% | 31.9% | 6.8% | |
| Total in column | 645 | 573 | 602 | 124 | 1,944 |
| | 33.2% | 29.5% | 31.0% | 6.4% | |

TABLE 3.3. AGE GROUP DISTRIBUTION OF ENSLAVED PEOPLE SOLD IN NEW ORLEANS, 1815–1820

| AGE GROUPS: | 0–13 | 14–25 | 26–44 | 45 AND UP | TOTAL |
|---|---|---|---|---|---|
| Known to be imported | 769 | 1,125 | 555 | 73 | 2,522 |
| | 30.5% | 44.6% | 22.0% | 2.9% | |
| Not known to be imported | 2,756 | 4,003 | 2,837 | 612 | 10,208 |
| | 27.0% | 39.2% | 27.8% | 6.0% | |
| Total in column | 3,525 | 5,128 | 3,392 | 685 | 12,730 |
| | 27.7% | 40.3% | 26.6% | 5.4% | |

*Source:* Hall Database, www.ibiblio.org/laslave/. "Known to be imported" includes those with a non-Louisiana origin, as noted by the database. "Not known to be imported" clearly includes a large number of those imported. Some of these we can identify from newspaper advertisements. If they have a similar age profile to those in the "Known to be imported" group, and were moved to that group, then the difference between the two rows might be even starker.

buyer Alexander McNeill. This characteristic made it much easier to talk about them as disembodied hands. But many of those sold at Maspero's had in fact acquired various kinds of specialized expertise in the East. In the Chesapeake and Carolinas, enslaved men rose in status by learning trades. They might be blacksmiths or coopers, teamsters or house servants. Women could become servants, cooks, or weavers. Such skills could gain one respite from incessant field labor, or even give hired-out slaves the possibility of keeping some of the earnings. Artisans were even important in Louisiana. Sugar making, for instance, required a class of trained enslaved experts who supervised the boiling process. They sold for high prices. Whites identified 5 percent of local slaves sold in New Orleans from 1800 to 1820 with a specific skill.[53]

Skills meant that one could claim some authority over a task and tools, a kind of capital accumulated during a unique past. African Americans sent to New Orleans came to Maspero's with individual job-related identities. But they came out with those skills erased, at least from the perspective of a claim that they could make on the enslaver. Many a newspaper advertisement for a man from the Chesapeake stated these skills. For example: "ANTHONY, 23," who was to be sold January 5, 1819, at Maspero's, was identified as a "sawyer, plough man, driver and good axeman" who had been "working in a brickyard." "NORA, 22," was advertised as an "excellent house servant, good seamstress, washer and ironer, good disposition and careful mother." All fifteen women advertised for that particular sale were described as possessing house-servant skills—washing, cooking, cleaning, ironing, caring for children. Yet none appeared as a house servant on the bill of sale. Of the thirty-four men offered, the newspaper advertisement claimed that twenty-seven possessed skills: carpenter, cooper, blacksmith, teamster, and so on. Not a single one had a skill listed upon his sale document, even though enslavers listed skills on similar bills for enslaved people of local origin. Only 1.5 percent of the bills of sale for enslaved people shipped from Norfolk and sold in New Orleans in 1815 to 1820 list a skill. The other 98.5 percent might not have come from the fields, but field hands they now were.

The "handness" of Virginia and Maryland slaves—the English (not French) names of the men, their greater stature, the plain kerchief of the women (not an artfully tied chignon like the ones Anglo visitors to New Orleans always noted), the claim that every one of them was raised waiting the table of a Virginia gentleman who had fallen on hard times—such narratives suggested that here was a standard story who could be forced to become a standard hand: "Very smart and willing. . . . [You] can turn his hand to anything. . . . [A] most valuable subject." You could take away their pasts and make them seem both the ready instrument and the object of the entrepreneur's right-handed power. Enslavers counted on the massive geographic shift over land and water to the southwest, the separations, the silencing, the distance, and the shock of the process of sale to produce isolation and helplessness. That made human beings look—to buyers—like hands. Resistance to handification certainly happened. Many forced migrants from Chesapeake and Kentucky ran away from purchasers in the Lower Mississippi Valley in the late 1810s, as numerous newspaper ads testify. But they also seem to have been far more likely than locals to be caught quickly, to return, or to die in the process. They had fewer—or no—places to hide, and surely fewer people to help them hide.[54]

"The sugar and cotton plantations[,] . . . we knew all about them," said Lewis Hayden, remembering a childhood in Kentucky in the 1810s. "When a friend was carried off, why, it was the same as death." One way or another, the sale at Maspero's marked one as a hand and meant that an old life was over. Right here, on this January day, for instance, William was about to be torn from the last few people who had known him in Maryland. As the bidding on him crept upward—six hundred, seven hundred—something piqued the interest of a white man in the crowd. Though several bidders already contested the prize, when Louisiana enslaver James Stille made his entry, he did so with determination. The numbers rose higher as Mossy chanted. When Stille's bid hit nine hundred, a typical price at this time for a man of William's age, a hush settled on the crowd. Would someone go higher? At last Mossy's hammer came down to break the silence. (Where did it hit—the wall of the building? Perhaps he tapped it on William's head. Some auctioneers did this, infuriating the people they sold.) A white helper stepped forward to lead William down off the bench and walk the new hand back into the shop as Stille continued shopping. After the sunlight, the darkness disoriented William. The white man sat him down against a wall. Beyond a new clamor outside, William could surely hear the earlier-sold people who now sat next to him: perhaps a woman sobbing, a man panting. Or was he making those noises himself?[55]

Meanwhile, Rachel stepped up, onto the bench.

IF SHE COULD GET her eyes to focus, Rachel tried to read the faces. In the East, the constant exchange of information among the enslaved made it possible for the people being sold to know the reported characters of many possible masters. But Rachel was trapped in full view in a new place where the face of every enslaver was unknown to her. She did not know, for instance, as the auctioneer's voice rose, that one of the men bidding for her was William Fitz, a merchant trading here and in Baton Rouge.

Whether Rachel experienced the minutes through which she stood on the bench as hate, shame, terror, or exposure, she had to face the crowd. And she faced it alone. If Rachel had a husband, he does not appear to have come in the *Temperance* with her. Neither did any children. Yet, given her age—about twenty-five—and the average age of first childbirth for an enslaved woman in the Chesapeake—just over twenty—the odds are good that she had children. She was not alone in being alone. Of the twenty-eight slaves sold by McLean at Maspero's on January 28, only two—twenty-three-year-old Sophie and her young child—had any discernable family relationship to each other.[56]

Throughout the history of slavery in the Southeast, infants and mothers had typically been sold, given, moved, granted, and deeded together. The infant followed the mother in condition, since the womb was "slave" and the child of a slave mother was thus also the enslaved property of her owner. Often the infant literally followed the mother from place to place. Here, however, the ideal hand did not come with a family. Slave sellers and buyers conspired to break attachments between parents and children—usually before their removal to New Orleans, but sometimes at Maspero's itself. Out of 2,567 women twenty-one years old and up sold by enslavers in New Orleans between 1815 and 1820, we can prove that at least 553 came from outside the city. Of these, enslavers bought 525 without children. Whether women like Rachel did or did not leave children behind in Maryland, they stood on the block alone. Meanwhile, only in 6 of 553 cases did New Orleans sellers deal the women's husbands with them. Even if one includes those whose origins we cannot demonstrate from the records of sale, between 1815 and 1820 only 8 women of 2,567 were sold with their husbands, and only 3 with both husband and child. Clearly, more than 1 percent of all the enslaved women over twenty, whether in Louisiana or throughout the South, were married with children.[57]

During boom times like these, southwestern buyers were more interested in extracting value now than in the long-term accumulation strategy that healthy childbirth and well-fed childhoods represented. A woman who was alone would waste none of her labor on children. And men were universally sold without family members. So were many children. On January 5, just three weeks before Rachel was sold, sixty-one slaves from the Chesapeake had been auctioned at Maspero's. Among the "smart promising boys" of whom may "be anything made of," as the ad put it, were young brothers Ruffin, eight, and Harry, six. Ruffin went to Jean Armand, up in St. James Parish. Nicholas Hanry bought Harry. Ruffin and Harry probably saw each other for the last time at the back wall where William now leaned his weight against the interior bricks. From 1815 to 1820, in fact, New Orleans saw 2,646 sales of children under the age of thirteen, of whom 1,001 were sold separately from any family member. Their average age was nine. Many were younger—some much younger.[58]

Brothers broken apart, mothers taken from daughters and vice versa—all were easier to move, to "be anything made of," individual units ready to come to hand in entrepreneurial dreams. To make the parents into mere individuals, children were left back in the Chesapeake to be reared by grandparents and aunts and uncles. So African-American households back East paid the cost of increasing right-handed power in the southwestern United States,

Image 3.4. The New Orleans market pre-ferred young people with no attachments. Both in the selling states and in the buying states, the forces of this demand led to sep-arations of parent from child and brother from sister—like Isaac and Rosa, ex-slave children from New Orleans, photographed in 1863 after the Union capture of New Or-leans ensured that they would not be sold apart from each other. Library of Congress.

just as those did who now stood on the block. Purchasers who made complete the conversion of mother into hand did not have to pay, at least not now. They only needed the belief of those who granted them credit, and that could be bought with the promised future value imputed by a person made hand.

As they created the patterns and expectations of a slave trade that made a uniform commodity—hands—perpetually available, men like William Ken-ner and Hector McLean were doing more than making profits for themselves. Such entrepreneurs—none of whom were slave-trading specialists—were creating a market for future slave trading, though other entrepreneurs would wrest it from their hands even as it emerged. The appearance of Francis E. Rives in Alabama—he also made two trips to Natchez in 1818 and 1819— foretold the future. Without planning to do so, the merchants of New Orleans had paved the way for a later, more organized "domestic" trade that linked the techniques of the Georgia-men to the much greater distances and emerg-ing markets of the Mississippi Valley. They were laying the connecting rails of a national domestic slave market. Before enslaved people were marched to the ship or the flatboat that took them to New Orleans, and long after their first sale at Maspero's, the patterns of exchange and newly habitual assump-tions there made them the perpetual objects of enslavers' plans.

An increasingly efficient market for hands was the core of the process that enabled the new men of New Orleans, from Vincent Nolte to Toussaint Mossy to James Stille and William Fitz, to knot together a nexus of cotton, slaves, and credit. The effects of their endeavors reached far beyond both Maspero's and the expanding southwestern United States itself. Cotton bales were the cheap oil of the nineteenth century. Here their outflow met the influx of credit to yield a new thing: ever-increasing production and thus ever-increasing economic growth. And to keep schemes and trades bubbling along from Manchester to Liverpool to New Orleans to the newly-staked-out faraway tracts of plantation-land-to-be way up the Tennessee River in Alabama required a mighty belief. The flow of hands into the market made would-be lords of commerce and new planters believe. As hands, Rachel and William were also credit: promissory notes on their sellers' and buyers' future possession and use of right-handed power.

There was one more crossroads here at the corner of Chartres and St. Louis. But to map this one, we cannot look in the documents that slave-buyers had to file after they won the auction. Instead, we must use a slave-sale memory handed down to us, one that originated with a woman who stood up above this crowd to be the object of inspection and bidding. Forty years after the year when Rachel stood on the bench, a dying grandmother (we do not know her name) reached up from the corn-shuck mattress where she lay under the roof of a Louisiana slave cabin. She grabbed her frightened granddaughter Melinda by the wrist, and she said the last words Melinda would ever hear her speak: "First thing I can remember is that I was standing on a slave block in New Orleans alongside my ma." The place must have been Maspero's. The time was the moment of sale that had separated her from her mother and everything that had come before. Maspero's shaped the rest of her life, and she had to pass that moment on to her own granddaughter in order for Melinda to know her and herself. Here was the crossroads of time and space where Melinda's family history had to begin again. So would it be for thousands of other family histories.[59]

TOUSSAINT MOSSY BROUGHT DOWN the hammer. The last heartbeat of Rachel's old life trickled out of its chamber. Her past and her future had just been killed for the profit of others. William Fitz won her at about $800.

Fitz had bought one other person—a man named Frank Boyd—and Fitz was ready to walk his two new slaves back toward the levee and the boat that would carry them up to Baton Rouge. People sold could sometimes hold on to small things that helped them to remember: a pair of gloves worn by a dead mother; a small blanket, split with a sister. Perhaps Rachel had an opportunity to say goodbye to William and the others from the *Temperance*. But from this point forward, she disappears from known documents.[60]

Not so for William, at least not quite yet. He had to wait for James Stille to arrange payment for Perry, a young man from the *Emile*'s cargo. At the same auction, McLean also sold Stille a young woman named Maria and her infant daughter, America, consigned by Virginian William Coles. And over the next few days, Stille also bought Jacob, Murray, Jefferson, and the nine-year-old boy Braxton, plus eleven slaves from New Orleans merchants Jackson and Reynolds, and six from Virginia residents John Stiles and Thomas Wily. So in less than a week, Stille spent over $20,000—mostly on credit—on new "hands."[61]

A day or two later, Stille collected the twenty-five people whom he had purchased from the city jail and the warehouses where they had been stowed while he shopped. He marched all twenty-five back to the levee. The chained city slaves leaned on their shovels, watching a different sort of coffle pass. Past the posts, the leaflets flapping in the wind, William walked across a different gangplank onto a steamboat that could churn steadily upriver against the current. Hands loaded barrels purchased by upstream customers. The bell rang, steam rose, the boat began to back away from the levee. The last passengers sprinted to leap the widening gap, papers fluttering in their hands. The steamer gathered headway upstream past moored flatboats and sailing ships.[62]

From its deck the bound passengers watched the landscape unroll. Behind the levee, each mile studded with a bare pole, they saw rectangular fields of stubbled cane stretching back. Right before the Red Church, they passed Destrehan's manor, the double galleries that belted the house shining with new paint. More big houses were visible now than before 1811. Near each were cabins and long, low barracks in sprawling clusters.

After the first day the cotton fields began to appear. Gangs of laborers moved slowly among the winter-brown and bare stalks, hoeing them under. The boat passed Iberville Parish, and there were few sugar plantations. By the time it reached Baton Rouge, there were only cotton fields and woods. But by then, Stille had already disembarked his hands. William and all the rest had vanished into the slave country, a land populated almost entirely by walking, working hands.

# 4

# LEFT HAND

## *1805–1861*

ON JULY 5, 1805, almost fifteen years before William disappeared into the cotton country with James Stille, Charles Ball jogged down a South Carolina road. Ball had carried iron chains on his wrists and neck for five hundred miles down to South Carolina. Then the slave trader, M'Giffin, had sold him to Wade Hampton at a Columbia inn as part of the local Fourth of July celebration. Now it was late the next morning. Hampton sat low between the two wheels of a stylish horse-drawn chaise, periodically flicking a long, thin whip. He had told Ball to keep up, so Ball and the horse ran. Years later, Ball bragged that in his youth he could cover fifty miles a day. Still, he surely began to flag after two or three hours. What Ball eventually remembered most about that long day's run, however, was not his ragged breath, but the groves of huge trees through which the road periodically wound. He anticipated each one, grateful that he'd be jogging in the shade for a few minutes. The smell of the trees reached him before he even saw them. Once he was under them, the magnolias' sweet, musky odor overwhelmed him.[1]

Ever since the Civil War, magnolias have signaled plantations, and in popular understandings of what slavery was like—movies, novels, tourism, the pages of *Southern Living*, and even many historians' scholarly accounts—plantations were places where things didn't change. But as he ran out of the magnolias' shadow, Ball passed one newly cleared field after another. On the left was one full of stumps and piles of logs and brush, on the right a black wreck of charred logs and ashes. He jogged past still another, this one covered with rows of nearly waist-high green plants, slaves among them, bending and rising in lines between the rows.[2]

The night before, he had sat outside the inn and talked with an enslaved man who had once lived just across the Potomac River from where Ball had grown up, a part of Maryland where slaves whispered rumors to each other, saying that down south where the Georgia-man took you, you'd have to eat cottonseed instead of food. The man told Ball that no, he'd have meat and meal. But the man assured him that his work in the cotton fields would be far more difficult and draining than the long hours of labor he had served in Maryland.[3]

The kind of slavery that Ball was encountering and that was emerging on the frontiers of the early nineteenth-century South was inherently new. For centuries, slavery in the New World had expanded by a process of extension: adding new slaves, clearing new fields from the next sugar island. The southwestern frontier was expanding—in part—via a similar strategy, though on an unprecedented geographic scale: it was not an island, but a subcontinent's rich interior stripped from its inhabitants. And not mere battalions, but whole armies of slaves were being moved to new soil. By 1820, whites had already transported more than 200,000 enslaved people to the South's new frontiers in the years since 1790 (see Table 1.1).

What made this forced migration truly different was that it led to continuous increases in productivity *per person*—what economists call "efficiency." The two ways out of the Malthusian trap were either to incorporate more "ghost acres"—land outside of industrializing core regions like Britain or, soon, the northeastern United States—or to create systematic increases in efficiency of production. The first slavery had not yielded continuous improvements in labor productivity. On the nineteenth-century cotton frontier, however, enslavers extracted more production from each enslaved person every year.

The source of this ever-rising productivity wasn't a machine like the ones that were crucial to the textile mills. In fact, you could say that the business end of the new cotton technology was a whip. And the fact that slave labor was unpaid, and compelled by brute force, was not new. That reality was as old as the human institution of slavery itself.

Just as old was the fact that those who were compelled to knuckle under to right-handed power used the art of secret resistance—such as slowing the pace of work when overseers were out of sight—to undermine the sway of the dominant. It had been the same in traditional societies for all those millennia when serfs, peasants, and slaves made up most of the labor force of most societies. Their craft was much like what Protestant reformer Martin Luther in the sixteenth century called "left-handed" power: the strength of the poor and the weak, the secret way of seemingly passive resistance to evil. Peasants and servants broke employers' tools, lied, played dumb, escaped from masters. At the same time, they kept their secrets about all their crafts. In older slave regions like the Chesapeake, where Charles Ball had learned to cut and cradle wheat, a secret way of doing or making was a treasure that gave an enslaved man or woman a kind of leverage in his or her dealings with enslavers.[4]

Yet in the fields past the magnolia grove, the dynamic of right-handed domination and left-handed resistance, a struggle as old as the Pyramids, was changing. Something profoundly new was happening. Enslavers were finding ways to turn the left hand against the enslaved. Entrepreneurs redirected left-handed power by measuring work, implementing continuous surveillance of labor, and calibrating time and torture. All of this repeatedly accomplished enslavers' ongoing goal of forcing enslaved people to invent, over and over, ways to make their own labor more efficient and profitable for their owners.

New techniques that extracted ever-greater cotton efficiency radically changed the experience of enslaved people like Charles Ball and the 1 million who followed him into the cotton fields. But they also transformed the world beyond the fields. The amount of cotton the South grew increased almost every single year from 1800, when enslaved African Americans made 1.4 million pounds of cotton, to 1860, when they harvested almost 2 billion pounds. Eighty percent of all the cotton grown in the United States was exported across the Atlantic, almost all of it to Britain. Cotton was the most important raw material of the industrial revolution that created our modern world economy. By 1820, the ability of enslaved people in southwestern frontier fields to produce more cotton of a higher quality for less drove most other producing regions out of the world market. Enslaved African Americans were the world's most efficient producers of cotton. And they got more efficient every year, which is why the real price of the most important raw material of the industrial revolution declined by 1860 to 15 percent of its 1790 cost, even as demand for it increased by 500 percent (see Table 4.1). Cotton also drove US expansion, enabling the young country to grow from a narrow coastal belt into a vast, powerful nation with the fastest-growing economy in the world. Between the 1790s and 1820, the United States acquired a near-monopoly on the world's most widely traded commodity, and after 1820, cotton accounted for a majority of all US exports. And all of the transformations that spun from these facts depended on changes inflicted on the left hand.

A little while before sunset, the chaise finally stopped in the drive before Hampton's house near the Congaree River. Ball bent over, panting and retching. When he finally raised his head, Hampton's teenaged son was staring at

TABLE 4.1. COTTON PRODUCTION IN THE UNITED STATES

| YEAR | COTTON MADE IN US (MILLIONS OF BALES) | COTTON MADE IN WORLD (MILLIONS OF BALES) | US SHARE OF WORLD PRODUCTION OF COTTON | US SHARE OF ALL COTTON IMPORTED TO BRITAIN | COTTON AS SHARE OF ALL US EXPORTS | REAL PRICE OF COTTON (INDEX, 1820 = 100) |
|---|---|---|---|---|---|---|
| 1791 | 2 | 469 | > 0.01 | 0.01 | -- | 191 |
| 1801 | 48 | 531 | 0.09 | 0.34 | 0.14 | 116 |
| 1811 | 80 | 556 | 0.14 | 0.42 | 0.22 | 78 |
| 1821 | 180 | 630 | 0.29 | 0.63 | 0.49 | 73 |
| 1831 | 354 | 820 | 0.43 | 0.73 | 0.42 | 53 |
| 1841 | 644 | 1,044 | 0.62 | 0.69 | 0.52 | 48 |
| 1851 | 757 | 1,482 | 0.67 | 0.99 | 0.63 | 46 |
| 1860 | 1,390 | 2,500 | 0.66 | 0.88 | 0.61 | 48 |

*Source:* Stuart Bruchey, *Cotton and the Growth of the American Economy, 1790–1860: Sources and Readings* (New York, 1967).

him. The boy sneered with contemptuous menace and asked Ball if he knew how to pick cotton. Just then the elder Hampton walked past. He ordered Ball to put the horse away and help the gardener. In the garden, Ball pulled weeds as his body cooled from the run. As the sun set, a boy came with a message: come to the overseer's house to find out where to stay that evening. As they walked away from the big house where Hampton lived, they heard the oncoming tramp of feet. From the lowering dusk strode the slave labor camp's white overseer. After him straggled 170 black men, women, and children. Behind them, night fell on the fields.[5]

BEFORE SUNRISE, A LOUD, braying noise shattered Ball's sleep. When the overseer's horn blew for the second time, his bare feet hit the dirt floor. He stumbled out of the hut to which he had been assigned, rubbed his eyes, and looked around to see something new. Around him, shaping up like day laborers, was the army he'd seen the previous evening. In Maryland and Virginia, labor crews usually numbered only a dozen or so. These people also looked different. Even after a month-long march south, "it could be seen that my shirt and trowsers had once been distinct and separate garments. Not one of the others had on even the remains of two articles of clothing." Many of the men wore only long, tattered shirts. Many women only had skirts. Some teenage boys and girls were completely naked. And the state of the bodies thus exposed worried Ball even more. Their skin was reddish and ashy, their hair matted and stringy. Bones stood out. Skin hung slack where muscle had atrophied.[6]

As Ball took in his new peers, the overseer stepped into their midst. Here was a tightly contained white man, of a type much like M'Giffin the Georgia-man. He turned, beckoned silently, and the crowd followed. "A wretched-looking troop we were," Ball said years later, picturing the moment, still watching them (and himself) marching toward the fields of green, waist-high plants that soon loomed up in the gloaming. They trudged past uncounted rows, through a mile of clods drying from the hoe. Beyond a grove of trees, the rising sun showed that a vast field opened beyond. On its edge the overseer stopped them. He announced eleven men as "captains" for the day, and from his slate named fifteen laborers to follow each. Ball was to go with Simon. Marching his troop to a section of planted furrows, Simon posted his soldiers: one adult or two children to the head of each row.

Every forced migrant whose story has survived tells us that when they crossed the threshold of the fields of a new slave labor camp, they entered a world that was fundamentally different from the one in which they had toiled before. As Ball lined up by the first waist-high cotton plant of his row, he was about to learn a new way of working, one meant to occupy most of the waking moments remaining to him on earth. He saw Simon take a row, lift his hoe, and begin to work rapidly down the side of his furrow. Everyone else began to do the same, in a great hurry. Ball could see that each of them had to chop all the weeds in their row without damaging the cotton plants. But then the man in the next row warned him that no one was allowed to fall behind the captain. Ball realized that thus "the overseer had nothing to do but to keep Simon hard at work, and he was certain that all the others must work equally hard." And the overseer was already stalking across the rows, whip in hand. Ball put his head down and kept his hoe moving, trying to keep up with Simon's furious pace.[7]

By the time he reached the end of the first row, Charles Ball had been exposed to crucial differences between the forms of enslaved labor demanded in Maryland and the new ones on the cotton frontier. Survivors identified these differences not as idiosyncrasies, but as a new system of enslaved labor. Most forced migrants had been brought up working according to the rules of one of two southeastern regimes. In some regions, a "task" system had prevailed, as in the South Carolina and Georgia "low country." In those rice swamps, each day enslavers assigned each worker a specific job. Custom fixed the volume of each daily piece of labor, so that a man knew that on a day when he had to chop weeds, his "task" was to cultivate an acre of rice and no more. As historians have pointed out, a long history of "negotiations" between masters' power and the cunning of the enslaved had created the task system. It contained benefits for both left hand and right. Those who finished early could tend their own gardens, help others to work, or simply relax for an hour or two. Without direct supervision, forced labor was usually inefficient, but tasking relieved enslavers of this dilemma by offering diligent slaves an incentive: free time. No wonder owners who tried to increase customary tasking levels and limit free time faced direct or covert resistance.[8]

Yet most enslaved migrants marched to places like Congaree did not come from the low country. They came from the greater Chesapeake of Virginia, Maryland, and their North Carolina and Kentucky offshoots. A watercolor sketch made in 1798 by Benjamin Latrobe, designer of the US Capitol, shows the prevalent form of labor on Chesapeake tobacco farms. A white overseer stands on a stump, a pipe in his mouth and his whip under his arm, supervising a "gang" of enslaved women as they cultivate tobacco plants. This gang system relied on direct surveillance of labor, but by whom? Tobacco planters often grew their crop on many small and widely scattered plots of land. They had to coordinate complex operations carried out by small groups. Most had no choice but to delegate surveillance to black drivers who led labor crews outside of direct white observation. And while enslavers in the Chesapeake pushed slaves to carry out their field work quickly, drivers had their own incentives. Workers moved across Chesapeake fields in ragged disorder set by divergent individual paces, not ranks formed up in lockstep like the ones that marched that July morning at Congaree.[9]

The best-known innovation in the history of cotton production, as every high-school history student knows, is the cotton gin. It allowed enslavers to clean as much cotton for market as they could grow and harvest. As far as most historians have been concerned, the gin is where the study of innovation in the production of cotton ends—at least until the invention of the mechanical cotton picker in the 1930s, which ended the sharecropping regime. But here is the question historians should have asked: Once enslavers had the cotton gin, how then did enslavers produce (or *have* produced, by other hands) as much as the gin could clean? For once the gin shattered the processing bottleneck, other limits on production and expansion were cast into new relief. For instance, one constraint was the amount of cheap, fertile land. Another was the lack of labor on the frontier. So enslaver-generals took land from Indians, enslaver-politicians convinced Congress to let slavery expand, and enslaver-entrepreneurs created new ways to finance and transport and commodify "hands." And, given a finite number of captives in their own control, entrepreneurs created a complex of labor control practices that enslaved people called "the pushing system." This system increased the number of acres each captive was supposed to cultivate. As of 1805, enslavers like Hampton figured that each "hand" could tend and keep free of weeds five acres of cotton per year. Half a century later, that rule of thumb had increased to ten acres "to the hand." In the first minute of labor Charles Ball had encountered one of the pushing system's tactics, in which overseers usually chose captains like Simon to "carry the fore row" and set the pace.[10]

We do not know who invented the pushing system. But it was already present when Charles Ball got to Congaree in 1805. And slavery's entrepreneurs carried it west and south, sharing it as they went, like Johnny Cottonseed. "You find the Virginian upon Red River, you find the North Carolina man, the South Carolina man, the man from Georgia, alongside of him," wrote one enslaver about the new neighborhoods in which greenhorns from tobacco or rice regions learned from their peers how to extract the maximum number of acres from each hand. On early-summer visits to town, migrant entrepreneurs began their street-corner conversations by asking "Well, how does your cotton look?" Thus, wrote another migrant planter, "any increased quantity of product, by any new course of cultivation, spreads like the fire of the American prairie"—all the way up to ten acres to the hand.[11]

Enslavers shared innovations because the world cotton market was an example of what economists call perfect competition. In fact, it was *the* example—it was used later in the nineteenth century as the archetype in which the great British economist Alfred Marshall discovered the famous concepts of supply-and-demand curves. The market was so big that no individual producer could control even 1 percent of the total. This meant that individual producers had no reason to hoard innovations in the extraction of labor from neighbors, for a neighbor's increase in production did not change the price the innovator received by a visible amount. Enslavers also had a vested interest in the ability of their neighbors to suppress their own slaves' resistance. So planter-entrepreneurs readily shared their labor-control innovations: "The intercourse of experience," wrote one enslaver, is the "solder" of slaveholders' communities, in which "every individual is bound not only by his duties to others, but by his own interests, to extend and nourish this useful interchange of systems."[12]

Innovation in violence, in fact, was the foundation of the widely shared pushing system. Enslaved migrants in the field quickly learned what happened if they lagged or resisted. In Mississippi, Allen Sidney saw a man who had fallen behind the fore row fight back against a black driver who tried to "whip him up" to pace. The white overseer, on horseback, dropped his umbrella, spurred up, and shouted, "Take him down." The overseer pulled out a pistol and shot the prone man dead. "None of the other slaves," Sidney remembered, "said a word or turned their heads. They kept on hoeing as if nothing had happened." They had learned that they had to adapt to "pushing" or face unpredictable but potentially extreme violence. Enslavers organized space so that violent supervision could extract the maximum amount of labor. "A good part of our rows are five hundred and fifty yards long," wrote one Tennessee cotton planter in the 1820s. He had created a space in which he could easily identify stragglers. He also simultaneously ensured that when he inflicted exemplary punishment, he did so in clear view of a large audience.[13]

THOUGH THE ROWS WERE long and Simon's pace was hard, Ball was getting his wind back at seven a.m., when they all paused to eat a breakfast of cold cornbread. Charles Ball and Simon exchanged a few grunted words as they returned to their side-by-side rows. Already, the captain recognized that Ball was one of the few in the field physically capable of keeping up without panicked effort. Both returned to their toil, hoes swinging like metronomes, sweat rolling down arms and backs. The overseer kept the time. Once an hour he allowed the men, women, and children to walk over to a wagon loaded with water barrels and drink a ladleful of water.[14]

At noon the hands at Congaree ate another hurried meal: more cornbread, a little salt, one radish each. Ball was catching on to other ways in which the pushing system maximized the amount of labor extracted from him—for instance, the tricks that filled every minute of daylight with money-making labor. At the end of a row, Simon whispered to Ball to conserve what strength he could, for they would have to work until it was too dark to tell cotton from weed. There would be no leaving the field in time to make the evening meal. In fact, the overseer had assigned an old woman to stay back in the quarter and bake everyone's suppertime cornmeal ration. Likewise, when, thirty years later, Henry Bibb was transported up Louisiana's Red River to a slave labor camp, his new enslaver ordered slaves to gorge themselves with a heavy breakfast two hours before sunlight. They were then allowed but one break before nightfall.[15]

If Ball got ahead of Simon for a moment, stood up straight to wipe off the sweat of this long afternoon, and looked around at the bodies behind him, he'd see two more pushing-system elements that enabled entrepreneurs like Wade Hampton to plant and cultivate more and more acres of cotton over time. First, almost everybody who lived in Wade Hampton's huts—men and women, children and adults—was in the field. Second, they were all doing the same job. In 1827 a Virginia-born enslaver wrote to his business partner asking him to procure "a number of slaves sufficient to make 40 working hands—which you know in a cotton country will be much less than in a grain country." Chesapeake slave quarters had large numbers of nonworking children and old people as well as those who did some kinds of labor and not others. But cotton entrepreneurs worked men, women, and older children together for most of the year at jobs that were identical.[16]

In labor camps like Congaree, a few men became "captains" or even "drivers." But torn between the interests of enslavers, their own interests, and those of their peers, drivers were subject to frequent demotions. Women, meanwhile, usually did not even have these options. The flattening of the job hierarchy made men, women, and even children roughly equal in the sense that they did the same kind of labor. Many women and children could accomplish some elements of cotton labor just as well as many men. The elimination of most distinctions among the enslaved, and the curtailment of possibilities for independence, put into practice the theory incipient in the way entrepreneurs sold people at Maspero's. Everyone had a uniform status—that of cotton "hand."[17]

The product of their labor was also uniform. When the row was finished, the long line of red dirt Ball had turned over disappeared into the sameness of hundreds of identical rows of identical green plants. And the rows stretched on ahead. Simon's crew finished one set and started another, still moving at his pace as he carried the lead row. Slowly, slowly, the shadows extended out from the trees on the field's western borders. The vast gang of "hands" toiled on, all straining to hear the same sound.

At last, as dark settled, the overseer called a halt. The laborers shouldered their hoes and turned for home. Along the way, Ball fell into step with a slow-walking woman. She told him her name was Lydia. Worn and haggard, she carried a baby on her back in a sling of cloth. The baby had been fathered a year ago, soon after she had arrived from Ball's own Maryland. They talked as the others outpaced them. But as Ball began to ask her how she had adapted to life in the cotton fields, the overseer's horn blew. "We are too late, let us run," Lydia blurted.

Ball arrived back at the slave cabins just as the overseer finished his roll call. Lydia came toiling up a minute later, with the baby bouncing on her back. "Where have you been?" the overseer demanded. "I only stopped a while to talk to this man," she said, "but I shall never do it again." She began to sob. The overseer ordered her to lie down on her stomach. Handing her baby to another woman, she complied. The white man pulled up her torn shift, exposing her buttocks and back. Then he drew from his belt the lash he had been carrying folded there all day.

The whip, ten feet of plaited cowhide dangling from a weighted handle, was, Ball realized, "different from all other whips that I have ever seen." The impression it made would never leave him. Many other migrants reported the same feeling of shocked discovery. In Virginia and Maryland, white people used cat-o'-nine-tails, short leather whips with multiple thongs. These were dangerous weapons, and Chesapeake enslavers were creative in developing a repertoire of torment to force people to do what they wanted. But this southwestern whip was far worse. In expert hands it ripped open the air with a sonic boom, tearing gashes through skin and flesh. As the overseer beat Lydia, she screamed and writhed. Her flesh shook. Blood rolled off her back and percolated into the packed, dark soil of the yard.[18]

Those who had seen and experienced torture in both the southeastern and southwestern regions universally insisted that it was worse on the southwestern plantations. Ex-slave William Hall remembered that after he was taken to Mississippi, he "saw there a great deal of cotton-growing and persecution of slaves by men who had used them well" back in the Southeast. Once "the masters got where they could make money[,] they drove the hands severely." White people also recorded the way that southwestern captivity distilled and intensified slavery. On a sheet of lined notepaper saved by small-time cotton planter William Bailey survives a strange set of lyrics in the voice of an enslaved migrant, a man moved to the cotton frontier: "Oh white folks, I hab crossed de mountains / How many miles I didn't count em." Perhaps Bailey wrote down verses he heard. Perhaps he wrote them as a "darky song" parody. Either way, they tell us what people at both ends of the whip understood as its purpose. "Oh, I'se left de folks at de old plantation / And come down here for my education," he wrote. What did the "singer" define as his "education"? "De first dat I eber got a licken / Was down at de forks ob de cotton picken / Oh it made me dance, it made me tremble / I golly it made my eyeballs jingle."[19]

Survivors of southwestern torture said their experiences were so horrific that they made any previous "licken" seem like nothing. Okah Tubbee, a part-Choctaw, part-African teenager enslaved in Natchez, remembered his first time under "what they call in the South, the overseer's whip." Tubbee stood up for the first few blood-cutting strokes, but then he fell down and passed out. He woke up vomiting. They were still beating him. He slipped into darkness again.[20]

Under the whip, people could not speak in sentences or think coherently. They "danced," trembled, babbled, lost control of their bodies. Talking to the rest of the white world, enslavers downplayed the damage inflicted by the overseer's whip. Sure, it might etch deep gashes in the skin of its victim, make them "tremble" or "dance," as enslavers said, but it did not disable them. Whites were open with those whom they beat about the whip's purpose. Its point was the way it asserted dominance so "educationally" that the enslaved would abandon hope of successful resistance to the pushing system's demands.

"Their plan of getting quantities of cotton," recalled Henry Bibb of the people who drove him to labor on the Red River, "is to extort it by the lash." In the context of the pushing system, the whip was as important to making cotton grow as sunshine and rain. That's exactly what Willie Vester, a Mississippi overseer, told his friends back in North Carolina. He hoped to ride back home for a visit on a nice new horse, sporting a suit of fine clothes. To do so, he needed to "make a little more [money]." The way to do that was to "walk over the cotton patch and bring my long platted whip down and say 'who prowd[,] boys[?]' and see a fiew more bales made." Likewise, in 1849 a migrating North Carolina planter hired a "Mississippi overseer" to ensure that his "hands" would be "followed up from day break until dark as is the custom here." The overseer would drive each "fore row" in a vast and easily surveyed field, and he would "whip up" those who fell behind. All that pushing, the owner calculated, would force "my negroes [to do] twice as much here as negroes generally do in N.C."[21]

Finished with beating Lydia, Hampton's overseer turned to Charles Ball, who stood frozen on the edge of the lamplight. "When I get a new negro under my command," he said, "I never whip at first; I always give him a few days to learn his duty. . . . You ought not to have stayed behind to talk to Lydia, but as this is your first offence, I shall overlook it." Ball nodded mutely and "thanked master overseer for his kindness." As he chewed his cornbread, he reflected on his new reality: "I had now lived through one of the days—a succession of which make up the life of a slave—on a cotton plantation," he later wrote.[22]

IN THE COURSE OF surviving his first day, Ball had discovered the new pushing system: a system that extracted more work by using oppressively direct supervision combined with torture ratcheted up to far higher levels than he had experienced before. Between 1790 and 1860, these crucial innovations made possible a vast increase in the amount of cotton grown in the United

TABLE 4.2. INFANT DEATH RATES ON SELECTED SOUTHWESTERN
SLAVE LABOR CAMPS

| LABOR CAMP | STATE | YEARS OF RECORD | NUMBER OF BIRTHS | TOTAL NUMBER OF CHILD DEATHS | INFANT DEATH RATE PER 1,000 |
|---|---|---|---|---|---|
| Magnolia | MS | 1838–1855 | 54 | 29 | 430 |
| Watson | AL | 1843–1865 | 157 | 81 | 280 |
| McCutcheon* | LA | 1832–1863 | 221 | N/A | 213 |
| Minor | LA | 1849–1863 | 217 | N/A | 184 |

*Sources:* R. C. Ballard Papers, Southern Historical Collection, University of North Carolina, Chapel Hill; Henry Watson Papers, David M. Rubenstein Rare Books and Manuscripts Library, Duke University, Durham, North Carolina; Richard H. Steckel, *The Economics of U.S. Slave and Southern White Fertility* (New York, 1985).

\* In the McCutcheon documents, only 14.6 percent of all recorded infant deaths occur in the first twenty-eight days after birth, whereas other statistics suggest that a rate of 50 percent is much more typical. This fact, in turn, suggests a substantial under-enumeration of both births and deaths. The real infant death rate was probably about 350.

States. They did so at an immense human cost, which could be calculated in many ways. We could count those who caught malaria in the fields of a more intense disease environment, or those who died young, their bodies malnourished by insufficient food and intense labor. The rate of infant mortality in the new slave labor camps was extraordinary: one of every four children born died before reaching his or her first birthday. This is five times the rate of present-day Haiti, the same as the rate that would have been found in the most malaria-infested parts of nineteenth-century West Africa or the Caribbean (see Tables 4.2 and 4.3). And every burst of forced migration produced a decrease in the average life expectancy of African Americans, not just for infants, but for the whole population.[23]

But other costs cannot be measured. Although Ball had been able to keep up with Simon, he foresaw that the pace of work on coming days would be difficult and unvarying. He could tell that his clothes would wear down to rags. He also clearly ran the constant risk of suffering violent, humiliating assault. Ball had not been beaten since he was fifteen. Back in Maryland, he had been what owners called "a well-disposed negro" who tried to build a life within the system. Anyway, the pathological bullies that white supremacy bred in such high numbers preferred easier targets than someone as large and strong as Ball. But he could see that on the Congaree, if white folks thought that doing so would result in more cotton, they would find a way to bend even the toughest black man to the new bullwhip.[24]

TABLE 4.3. COMPARATIVE INFANT DEATH RATES

| GROUP | APPROXIMATE DEATH RATE PER 1,000 INFANTS BORN |
|---|---|
| All African Americans, 1820–1860 | 256 (girls) / 296 (boys) * |
| Enslaved infants on two South Carolina cotton plantations, 1800s | 181 ** |
| Jamaican slaves, 1820s | 255 (girls) / 296 (boys) *** |
| Nineteenth-century whites (US) | 162 † |
| United States, 2006 | 6.43 †† |
| Haiti, 2006 | 71.65 †† |

*Sources:* * Jack Ericson Eblen, "Growth of the Black Population in Ante Bellum America, 1820–1860," *Population Studies* 26 (1972): 273–289.

** Richard H. Steckel, *The Economics of U.S. Slave and Southern White Fertility* (New York, 1985), 88–89.

*** B. W. Higman, *Slave Populations of the British Caribbean, 1807–1834* (Kingston, Jamaica, 1995), 319.

† Actuarial estimate for 1830–1860 made in 1895. See Michael R. Haines and Roger C. Avery, "The American Life Table of 1830–1860: An Evaluation," *Journal of Interdisciplinary History* 11 (1980): 11–35, esp. 88.

†† Central Intelligence Agency, *World Fact Book*, https://www.cia.gov/library/publications/the-world-factbook/index.html.

Intimidated, Ball strove hard in the days that followed to labor at the torrid tempo of the southwestern pushing system. By the time July rolled toward its close, he had begun to outpace Simon. The "hands" had chopped weeds from every cotton row three times over, and now the plants were "laid by"—tall enough to shade the rows and keep down the growth of weeds. Now Ball began to look around. One Sunday, exploring, he found a body dangling in the woods—a runaway, despairing of escape, unwilling to return. Through his own long march he had stuck to his resolution to stay alive for something better to offer itself. So now, as he hilled sweet potatoes, he calculated how many he could carry in his shirt if he slipped off for Maryland. As he pulled leaves from the corn stalks, fodder for the livestock, he looked at swelling ears and mentally mapped the months when they would be ripe on the stalk on the banks of all the rivers he'd counted and named on his route south.

July turned to August. Carbohydrates sweetened in the corn kernels. But something was happening in the cotton fields, too. The plants strained up to man height and added leaves. The branches grew "squares," or buds. And white people began to dole out pennies to slaves in exchange for baskets woven by firelight. They inspected cotton-gin machinery. They checked the weighting of whips. They went to town and bought sacks, new slates, chalk, ledgers, pens, and ink. And they mailed off expectant, calculating letters that yammered on, as the wife of a Louisiana planter complained in 1829, about nothing but how the profits of the cotton now in the fields would let them continue "buying plantations & negrows."[25]

"Cotton! Cotton! Cotton! . . . is the theme of nearly all the conversations now a days," wrote one migrant to Florida. "Even the Ladies talk learnedly upon the subject. . . . If you see a knot of Planters engaged in earnest conversation, without even approaching, you may [know] the topic of their discourse. Get within earshot of them, and, I will guranty, that the first word that you will hear will be *cotton*." As planters talked, the squares grew and swelled behind cream-and-yellow blossoms. Growing heavier every day, they tilted this way and that until stalks arched and groaned. One day the first boll exploded open, and then the next one, and then the next, millions. A white blizzard settled on the green fields. One more night, and another first day in the life of a hand was here.[26]

ON AN EARLY MORNING at the beginning of September, the overseer ordered the enslaved people at Congaree back into the cotton fields. He gave each man, woman, and child a long sack and ordered them to take a row and start picking. As Ball bent over the plants in the gloam of near-dawn, wetting his shirt with cotton-leaf dew, he found that picking required sharp eyes, speedy hands, and good coordination. Slip up and the hand clutched a leaf, or fingers pricked on the hard points of the drying "square" at the base of the boll. Grab too much, and a mess of fiber and stem sprung loose in one's hand. Grab too little and the fingers twisted only a few strands. Finally reaching the end of his first row, Ball emptied his sack into his own large basket. Suddenly he realized that women and even children were already far down the neighboring rows. As the pickers bent in ever-more hurried motion, their hands were blurs. Not just their right hands, in the fastest cases, but their left as well. But when Ball tried to set both hands to work, his arms flailed like disconnected parts. His fingers lumbered. For the first time since he was a boy, he felt out of control of his body. Muscular strength could not solve this task.[27]

The sun crawled in a slow parabola across the sky. All day long the sound of click, click, click rose from almost-silent fields, as nails tapped on hard pods and fingertips pulled bolls. The overseer rode his horse slowly across the rows, whip in hand. By late afternoon, Ball was exhausted and anxious.

Image 4.1. This 1853 illustration shows men and women picking furiously. The men wear palmetto hats made in New England. "Picking cotton in Louisiana," *Harper's New Monthly Magazine*, March 1854, p. 456.

Looking left and right at the baskets of others, he felt shrunken, "not equal to a boy of twelve or fifteen years of age." Cotton-picking had little to do with physical strength. It broke down distinctions of size and sex. Women were sometimes the fastest pickers in a cotton slave labor camp. Young migrants could learn picking more quickly than their elders. In fact, Ball heard that "a man who has arrived at the age of twenty-five before he sees a cotton field will never, in the language of the overseers, become a *crack picker.*"[28]

In their heads, in conversations, and on paper, planters obsessively calculated equations of hands and cotton, always coming up with the same solution: wealth. A visitor reported that according to Florida calculations, "a hand generally makes from 5 to 6 bales weighing 400 lbs—at 15 [cents per pound] five bales to the hand will give $300—and at 15 six bales will give you $360, at 10 five bales will give you $200 and 6 bales at 10 cents will give $240." Looking at the soil of Mississippi's Yazoo River district, Clement Jameson concluded, "I shall make close to $250.00 to the hand." In Alabama, wrote a woman from North Carolina, "a thousand witnesses will attest that you may average on each hand about four to six hundred dollars clear of expense." Making more money allowed one to buy more slaves, thus harvesting more cotton, which meant yet more money. Mississippi farmer L. R. Starks asked a slave-dealer to send a young man he wanted to buy at "the first opportunity. . . . I have purchased five very likely negroes this season. We have raised great crops the last season. I am planting 130 acres in Cotton. I shall not be able to pay for the boy forthwith perhaps, but can make the money sure upon time."[29]

Yet as the acres of plants grew and the squares ripened into bolls, the key unknown variable was the speed at which hands would pick. As early as 1800, enslavers deploying the pushing system could make their captives raise more acres of cotton than they could harvest between the time the bolls opened and the time one had to begin planting again. Picking was now the bottleneck: the part of the cotton production process that took the most labor, and the part that determined how much money enslavers would make. And as Ball was discovering, picking was difficult, and picking fast was very difficult.

In 1820, Mississippi enslaver John Ker reminded himself that because his brother-in-law's "hands" were "unaccustomed to the cultivation and picking of cotton [it] would render it prudent that I not make large calculations on the profit of their labor." Yet enslavers made optimistic calculations nonetheless, because, despite the real difficulty of learning, the amount of cotton that enslaved people picked increased dramatically over time. From 1805, when Charles Ball first dragged his cotton sack down a Congaree row, to 1860 in Mississippi, the amount of cotton the typical "hand" harvested during a typical day increased three, four, six, or even more times over. In 1801, 28 pounds per day, per picker, was the average from several South Carolina labor camps. By 1818, enslaved people on James Magruder's Mississippi labor camp picked between 50 and 80 pounds per day. A decade later, in Alabama, the totals on one plantation ranged up to 132 pounds, and by the 1840s, on a Mississippi labor camp, the hands averaged 341 pounds each on a good day—"the largest that I have ever heard of," the overseer wrote. In the next decade, averages climbed even higher. A study of planter account books that record daily picking totals for individual enslaved people on labor camps across the South found a growth in daily picking totals of 2.1 percent per year. The increase was even higher if one looks at the growth in the newer southwestern areas in 1860, where the efficiency of picking grew by 2.6 percent per year from 1811 to 1860, for a total productivity increase of 361 percent (see Figure 4.1).[30]

Almost as remarkable as this dramatic rise in productivity is the fact that the history of the modern world, of industrialization and great divergences,

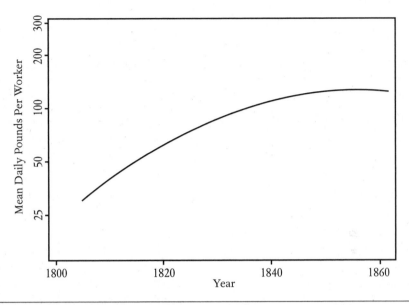

Figure 4.1. Increase in Picking Productivity Over Time
*Source:* Alan L. Olmstead and Paul W. Rhode, "Biological Innovation and Productivity Growth," NBER Working Paper No. 14142, National Bureau of Economic Research, June 2008.

of escape from the Malthusian trap, has almost never noticed it. Or perhaps that should be no surprise. This increase confounds our expectation that dramatic, systematic gains in labor efficiency depend on new machine technologies, such as the continuous series of innovations in spinning and weaving machines that were increasing the productivity of Manchester's textile workers. Some of the climb in cotton-picking efficiency may be attributable to a kind of "bioengineering"—new breeds of cotton, especially the "Petit Gulf" seed introduced from Mexico in the 1820s. Yet if heavy-yield and bigger cotton bolls of these breeds made picking individual bolls easier, the richer yield also meant more reaching and bending and moving and grabbing and lifting and carrying. And more expectations.[31]

Anyway, picking totals rose continuously. They rose before Petit Gulf. They rose after it. Moreover, while some planters obsessively chased the latest fad for cotton-seed varieties (they were marketed with names like "Mastodon," "100 Seed," "Sugar Loaf," and "Prolific"), others argued that new breeds added nothing to the "picking qualities" of Petit Gulf. So something that cannot be explained by the seeds happened to produce a continuous increase in productivity. That increase had huge consequences for global history. Cotton, like oil later on, was the world's most widely traded commodity, but that analogy doesn't even begin to explain how crucial the ever-growing efficiency of cotton-picking was to the modernizing world economy. Neither Britain nor any other country that followed it down the path of textile-based industrialization could have accomplished an economic transformation without the millions of acres of cotton fields of the expanding American South. To replace the fiber it imported from American slave labor camps with an equivalent amount of wool, Britain in 1830 would have had to devote 23 million acres to sheep pasture—more than the sum total of the island's agricultural land.[32]

The expanding cotton plantations of America's southwestern region allowed the textile industries to escape Malthusian constraints, and not just by adding additional acres and laborers. Consider this: The total gain in productivity per picker from 1800 to 1860 was almost 400 percent. And from 1819 to 1860, the increase in the efficiency of workers who tended spinning machines in Manchester cotton mills was about 400 percent. Meanwhile, the efficiency of workers in weaving mills improved by 600 to 1,000 percent (see Table 4.4). Therefore, even as textile factories harnessed increasingly complex machinery to more powerful non-human energy sources, even moving from water to steam power, cotton pickers produced gains in productivity similar to those of cotton factories. And those gains created a huge pie, from which many other people around the world took a slice. Lower real cotton prices passed on gains in the form of capital reinvested in more efficient factory equipment, higher wages for the new industrial working class, and revenue for factory owners, enslavers, and governments. Cheaper cotton meant cheaper cloth and clothing. Thus productivity gains in cotton fields also translated into benefits for consumers of cloth. Most of the world eventually acquired clothes made in the industrial West from cotton picked in the US South.[33]

There would be no mechanical cotton picker until the late 1930s. In fact, between 1790 and 1860, there was no mechanical innovation of any kind to speed up the harvesting of cotton. There was nothing like the change from scythe to mechanical reaper, for instance, that by the 1850s began to reshape the Chesapeake wheat fields Ball had left behind. Even slave-operated Louisiana sugar mills were more factory-like than the cotton labor camps were. And the nature of human bodies, the only "machine" that worked in the cotton fields, did not change between 1805 and 1860. Still, the possibility that enslaved people might have picked more cotton because they picked faster, harder, and with more efficient technique does not come readily to our minds. In fact, during the late antebellum years, northern travelers insisted that slave

TABLE 4.4. COTTON-PICKING PRODUCTIVITY AND BRITISH COTTON
TEXTILE—MAKING PRODUCTIVITY OVER TIME

| YEAR | COTTON-PICKING INDEX (1820 = 100) | SPINNING PRODUCTIVITY INDEX (1820 = 100) | WEAVING PRODUCTIVITY INDEX (1820 = 100) | COTTON IMPORTED BY THE UK (MILLION £) | INDEX OF REAL PRICE OF RAW COTTON (1820 = 100) | VALUE OF BRITISH COTTON TEXTILE EXPORTS (MILLION £) |
|---|---|---|---|---|---|---|
| 1790 | 54 | — | — | 2.57 | 191 | 2.1 |
| 1800 | 66 | — | — | 4.20 | 172 | 9.65 |
| 1810 | 81 | — | — | 4.77 | 100 | 17.4 |
| 1820 | 100 | 100 | 100 | 7.27 | 100 | 17.9 |
| 1830 | 123 | 159 | 161 | 7.08 | 60 | 19.7 |
| 1845 | 168 | 284 | 514 | 11.79 | 47 | 25.8 |
| 1850 | 187 | 318 | 756 | 19.63 | 58 | 30.4 |
| 1860 | 230 | 379 | 994 | 34.60 | 48 | 49.0 |

*Sources:* Cotton-picking index derived from Alan L. Olmstead and Paul W. Rhode, "Biological Innovation and Productivity Growth," NBER Working Paper No. 14142, National Bureau of Economic Research, June 2008, www.nber.org/papers/w14142, accessed January 8, 2014, using mean annual increase of 2.1 percent. Spinning and weaving indexes derived from D. A. Farnie, *The English Cotton Industry and the World Market, 1815–1896* (Oxford, 1979), 199. Figures for 1790 through 1810 are unknown. Value of exports is derived as midpoint of decade values from Ralph Davis, *The Industrial Revolution and British Overseas Trade* (Leicester, UK, 1979), 15. Davis's figures are averages for three-year sets, such as 1784–1786, 1794–1796, etc. While not precisely accurate for this specific year, this does map trends with accuracy.

labor was less efficient than free labor, a point of dogma that most historians and economists have accepted.[34]

The same northern observers who proclaimed that slave labor was inefficient had great faith in the idea that free people who were motivated by a cash wage would work harder and smarter than coerced workers. Occasionally, under special circumstances, some enslavers did pay people a wage. In 1828, Edward Barnes paid eight of the twenty-seven people enslaved on his Mississippi cotton labor camp a total of $28.32 for picking on Sundays, the day of the week when it was technically illegal for enslavers to force field labor. These positive incentives, however, accounted for only 3 to 5 percent of the raw cotton that Barnes's hands harvested in 1828, a year in which he sold eighty-one bales. In fact, enslavers typically only paid for Sunday picking, if they ever used wages. Most enslavers never used positive incentives at all. And perhaps most conclusively, after the Civil War, when many cotton planters would pay pickers by the pound at the end of a day's work, free labor

Image 4.2. Late in the year, the pickings grew slimmer. "Picking Cotton Near Montgomery, Alabama," J. H. Lakin, 1860s. Library of Congress.

motivated by a wage did not produce the same amount of cotton per hour of picking as slave labor had.[35]

What enslavers used was a system of measurement and negative incentives. Actually, one should avoid such euphemisms. Enslavers used measurement to calibrate torture in order to force cotton pickers to figure out how to increase their own productivity and thus push through the picking bottleneck. The continuous process of innovation thus generated was the ultimate cause of the massive increase in the production of high-quality, cheap cotton: an absolutely necessary increase if the Western world was to burst out of the 10,000-year Malthusian cycle of agriculture. This system confounds our expectations, because, like abolitionists, we want to believe that the free labor system is not only more moral than systems of coercion, but more efficient. Faith in that a priori is very useful. It means we never have to resolve existential contradictions between productivity and freedom. And slave labor surely was wasteful and unproductive. Its captives knew it wasted the days and years and centuries extorted from them. They would never get those days back. Yet those who actually endured those days knew the secret that, over time, drove cotton-picking to continually higher levels of efficiency.

BY THE EVENING OF his first long day of picking cotton in the Congaree field, Charles Ball hadn't discovered the secret. Not yet. His hands had struggled and shuffled against each other as he observed his fellow slaves moving as frantically as if some demon pursued them. As afternoon moved toward evening, the sun finally neared the western trees. The toiling bodies hunched across the fields, heads bowed, arms moving back and forth between branch and bag, legs shuffling forward down the row. The only sound was the occasional hoarse cry of "Water, water!" Children ran back and forth, buckets resting on their heads where within a few weeks a circle of hair would wear off in a ring, visible until February.[36]

Dusk now settled, achingly slow, over the field's white glow. At last, tired eyes could not tell boll from leaf. The overseer grunted. Men, women, and children straightened their stiff backs. They trudged to the ends of their rows, emptied their last sackfuls into their cotton baskets, and hefted the wicker containers onto their heads—Ball, too. He arched his tired spine to bear the weight and began swaying slowly back toward the open shed that held the cotton. A long half-mile later, the final drops of sweat squeezed out of pores, lining tracks in the dust that caked the pickers' bodies. The outbuildings of the camp loomed up from the now-full dark.

Another day was almost done. Ball had almost survived it. But now, in the yard in front of the cotton-shed, he would learn the secret that made hands pick cotton like machines.

In a semicircle outside the "stand," the open shed that sheltered the gin, Ball and the others put their baskets down. They waited while drivers hung each basket by its handles on a "steelyard," a balance-beam scale that measured their day's picking. The overseer called out the weight and then chalked the numbers by the picker's name on his slate. Ball had thirty-eight pounds—at least ten less than most of the other men, even though they were not as strong with the axe or as swift with the hoe. Yet some, and some women and teenagers who had also picked more than Ball, were being taken to the patch of ground where Lydia had been beaten.[37]

Twenty years after Ball's first day of picking, Israel Campbell went through his own first season at a Mississippi slave labor camp. Try as he might, Campbell could pick no more than ninety pounds between first light and full dark. But the planter, "Belfer," had told the young man that his daily minimum was one hundred pounds—and that on this day he would "have

Image 4.3. Carrying the cotton from the fields to the gin stand for the weigh-in, at the end of the day. *Harper's New Monthly Magazine*, March 1854, p. 457.

as many lashes as there were pounds short" in the "draft of cotton" recorded beside the name "Israel" on the Irish-born overseer's slate. (A "draft" was a check that paid off a debt, in the commercial lingo of the time.) On the hard-packed earth of Belfer's cotton yard, between the rough-hewn timbers of the gin stand and the packing screw that squashed cleaned cotton into bales, a kind of accounting took place. It used slate and chalk, balance beam, and one more tool as well. And as Campbell brought his cotton up in the growing darkness, he knew that his weight left him with a negative balance. Desperate to avoid a reckoning, he set his basket down and silently slipped behind the other slaves lining up outside the circle of torchlight where the Irishman was weighing baskets. He went to hide in the hut where the slaves did their cooking. But just a few moments later, the door opened, and looming back-lit on the threshold stood Belfer—lantern in one hand, four stakes and the bullwhip in the other: "Well, Israel, is that you?" The Irishman had weighed Campbell's basket. The account was negative. "I will settle with you now," Belfer said.[38]

We can find this system of accounting, experienced by Campbell and Ball, reported again and again by people who were moved to the southwestern cotton fields. Southern whites themselves sometimes admitted that enslavers used the vocabulary of credit and debit accounting to frame weighing and whipping—like this Natchez doctor, who in 1835 described the end of a picking day: "The overseer meets all hands at the scales, with the lamp, scales, and whip. Each basket is carefully weighed, and the nett weight of cotton set down upon the slate, opposite the name of the picker. . . . [O]ccasionally the countenance of an idler may be seen to fall": "So many pounds short, cries the overseer, and takes up his whip, exclaiming, 'Step this way, you damn lazy scoundrel,' or 'Short pounds, you bitch.'"[39]

Charles Ball's first-day total on his slate became the new minimum on his personal account. He understood that if he failed on the next day to pick at least his minimum, thirty-eight pounds, "it would go hard with me. . . . I knew that the lash of the overseer would become familiar with my back." In contrast to the task system of the South Carolina rice swamps, on the cotton frontier, each person was given a unique, individual quota, rather than a limit of work fixed by general custom. The overseer, wrote one owner in the rules he created for his Louisiana labor camp in 1820, "shall see that the people of the plantation that are fit to pick cotton shall do it and to Pick clean as much as possible and a quantity conforming [to] their age[,] Strength & Capacitys."

Sarah Wells remembered that near Warren County, Mississippi, where she grew up, some slaves picked 100 pounds a day, some 300, and some 500. But if your quota was 250 pounds, and one day you didn't reach it, "they'd punish you, put you in the stocks," and beat you. If a new hand couldn't meet the set quota, that hand would have to improve his or her "capacity for picking," or the whip would balance the account. "You are mistaken when you say your negroes are ignorant of the proper way of working," wrote Robert Beverley about a new crew transported from Virginia to Alabama. "They only require to be made to do it . . . by flogging and that quite often." A few years later, having received another batch of people, he wrote, "They are very difficult negroes to make pick cotton. I have flogged this day, you would think if you had seen it[,] without mercy."[40]

Learning how to meet one's quota was difficult, and those who met it before sunset still had to keep picking. As William Anderson moved toward his quota in a Mississippi field, his new enslaver repeatedly knocked him down with a heavy stick, claiming William was lagging. In Alabama in the 1820s, "Old Major Billy Watkins" would "stand at his house, and watch the slaves picking cotton; and if any of them straitened their backs for a moment, his savage yell would ring, 'bend your backs.'" In 1829, also in Alabama, Henry

Gowens saw an overseer force slow women to kneel in front of their cotton baskets. Shoving their heads into the cotton, he would pull up their dresses and beat them until blood ran down their legs.

Women were disproportionately targeted. Enslavers who were obsessed with getting crops to market were not interested in hearing about recovery from childbirth or gynecological problems. "To make money men are required[,] or boys large enough," wrote one frustrated enslaver, and another, "[Because] we have not a pregnant woman on the plantation[,] the females are the better pickers and have saved much the larger portion of the crop." Women nursing babies in the shade where they had been laid, or toddlers among the cotton plants—all could become flashpoints for white fury. "Gross has killed Sook's youngest child," wrote a white woman to her slave-trader cousin. "He took the child out to work (it was between one year and eighteen months old) & because it would not do its work to please him he first whipt it & then held its head in the [creek] branch to make it hush crying."[41]

So, afraid of what lurked behind their bent backs, afraid of the scale and slate that lay before them, enslaved people kept picking till the end of the day. When the weighing and account-balancing by whipping was done for the evening, they tried to salve their wounds. Yet as they slept, the enslaver sat in his house. By the light of a candle, he transferred chalk totals into the more lasting ink and paper of a ledger. Then he erased the slate. And then, he wrote down new and higher minimums. After Israel Campbell figured out how to meet his quota, Belfer raised Campbell's requirement to 175 pounds per day. John Brown remembered that "as I picked so well at first, more was exacted of me, and if I flagged a minute the whip was applied liberally to keep me up to my mark. By being driven in this way, I at last got to pick a hundred and sixty pounds a day," after starting at a minimum requirement of 100.[42]

Cotton-picking increased because quotas rose. In 1805, Wade Hampton and his henchmen gradually increased their demands on Ball until he was picking 50-odd pounds a day. By the late 1820s, enslavers in Mississippi and Tennessee demanded 100 pounds. Five years later, that total had gone up another 30 pounds. Hands now moved "like a bresh heap afire"—"as if," a Mississippi planter wrote, "some new motive power was applied in the process." As if, in other words, mechanical engines hummed inside the enslaved, as if the disembodied hands of whites' language moved by themselves over the cotton plants in the field. By the 1850s, ex-slaves reported, enslavers demanded 200 pounds or more of most slaves on some places, and even 250 on others.[43]

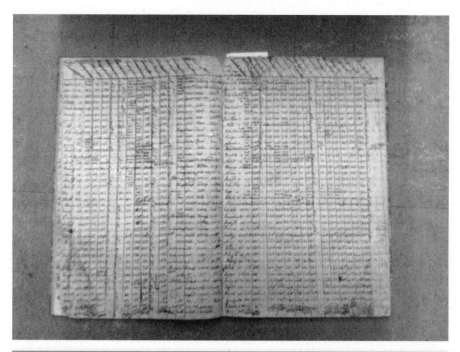

Image 4.4. Enslavers used cotton-picking records to measure and record each enslaved person's output. Such ledgers served, along with the scale and the whip, as key parts of the "whipping-machine" system that raised cotton output steadily over time. Here we have two pages of the picking record used in 1852 on the Laurel slave labor camp in Warren County, Mississippi, owned by R. C. Ballard. R. C. Ballard Papers, Folder 447, University of North Carolina.

Thus enslavers extracted a massive rise in cotton productivity from the 1790s to 1860. While planter-entrepreneurs did not publish their method for making cotton-picking as efficient as possible in a textbook or an agricultural journal, they created practices, attitudes, and material goods—whips, slates, pens, paper, and the cotton plant itself—that made up the method's interlocking cogs. White overseers also played an important role, and not just as the ones who often put this system of violent labor rationalization into hour-by-hour practice. They probably invented many of the practices of accounting and torture as they carried their slates and bullwhips ever west and south. Eager to impress their employers, associating with each other, they, too, shared ideas and pushed their peers to conform to an ideal of absolute control over their captives through a commitment to violence. But whoever created the pushing system and the dynamically increasing picking quotas, they were crucial to what one overseer called this "great revolution in the commerce and manufactures of nations," the continuous increase in cotton productivity that shaped the nineteenth-century transformation of the world.[44]

In 1861, the basic mechanics of arms, backs, and fingers remained as they had been in 1805, when Charles Ball came to Congaree. They were unchanged from the time when human beings invented agriculture. Nor could enslaved people imagine, when they were confronted by ridiculously high quotas, how they would pay their debt from their hands and not their skin. Often, their first solution was to try to fool the weight and cheat the whip. They hid rocks, dirt, and pumpkins in their baskets in order to make them heavier. Sometimes it worked. Israel Campbell hid watermelons in his baskets to cover the ten pounds he could never quite make. He got away with it for a year. Another method took teamwork: distracting the overseer as he manned the scale, taking advantage of the darkness outside the circle of his lamp to swap a heavy basket for a light one. "Such tricks as these will be continually practiced upon an overseer who is careless or 'soft,'" wrote one planter.[45]

Overseers, however, were selected for their "hardness." If they caught enslaved people trying to short the scales on their daily cotton debt, the punishment was severe. Surveillance and physical intimidation in the fields also made it difficult for pickers to cheat the scale by loading in field rocks, or to run away before weighing time. Sometimes, fast workers tried to help slower ones by putting cotton in their baskets, or taking their rows for a while. But enslavers usually made rules against cooperation, and enforced them. Instead, as minimums increased for all over time, entrepreneurs and exploiters forced individual enslaved people to marshal the forces of their own creativity against their own long-term health and independence, and even against each other. So, fearing punishment or even death, minds scrambled to come up with ways to speed hands. And the dramatic increase over time in the quantity picked reveals that somehow they succeeded.[46]

But how? Look at enslavers' language. It assumed that some human beings could be reduced to appendages of others. Yet it also mirrored the words that formerly enslaved people used to describe the experience of picking cotton. For they remembered that to pick quickly enough to turn cotton entrepreneurs' calculations about profit into reality, one had to disembody oneself. Picking all day long until late at night, even by candlelight, they had to dissociate their minds from pain that racked stooping backs; from blood running down pricked fingertips; from hands that gnarled into claws over a few short years; from thirst, hunger, blurred vision, and anxiety about the whip behind and before them. One had to separate mind from hand—to become, for a time, little more than a hand. Or two hands, like novice picker Solomon Northup's neighbor Patsey. While Northup lurched down his row, "the long cumbersome sack" making "havoc with [cotton] branches," and groping single cotton bolls with both hands, Patsey worked both sides of her row in perpetual motion, right and left. She reached with one hand and dropped cotton in the bag hanging from her neck with the other, "lightning-quick motion was in her fingers as no other fingers possessed," Northup later wrote. She moved like a dancer in an unconscious rhythm, though of displacement rather than of pleasure.[47]

Patsey's hands—both of them, right and left—each did their own thinking, like those of a pianist. For most of the laborers, however, the left hand was a problem. Symmetry can be beautiful to witness. In tests, people seem consistently attracted to more symmetrical faces and bodies. But in fact human beings are in crucial ways asymmetrical. Nine out of ten of us prefer to use the right hand for most tasks. Virtually all of us prefer one hand over another. And we know now that the left side of the brain controls the right hand, and vice versa. The left side of the brain is more heavily involved in analytical, detailed, specific processes and thoughts. These include language, and they also include skilled work with the hands. The right is more responsible for "global" processes, such as general perceptions of the world. Many believe it to be more artistic, more emotional. Of course, the reality is slightly more complex than a simple right/left spatial separation inside the brain. Nor is the nature of asymmetry always the same: in some left-handers, language faculties are primarily based in the right side of the brain, rather than the left. But either way, different sections of the brain play specific and distinct roles, and specific parts of the brain are linked in different ways to our dominant and nondominant hands. Right and left hand, right and left brain are neither equal nor interchangeable. Our hands are crucial elements of how we are wired to the world and the brain and the mind and the self.[48]

Our strong hand, whether we are right- or left-handed, is the dexterous partner of our conscious, planning mind. We write, we touch, we gesture, we take more with one hand than the other. And we also work with one hand more than the other, and that hand links our work to the mind and the self, making them all one whole identity. In the skilled tasks that Charles Ball did back in Maryland, the right hand always led his body. Like a woodcarver or a blacksmith, a man like Charles Ball often identified himself with the day's work he could do with an axe (led by one hand) or the scythe (ditto.) So would a cook, or a housemaid. She, or he, was more than that work. But in skilled labor in which one hand was the leader, the mind at work could sometimes express the self with mastery and joy—even if the work was forced and the product stolen.

On the cotton frontier, however, quotas kept rising. Now, there are switch-hitters in baseball, piano and guitar players with equally (though differently) skilled left and right hands. There are those who as a trick or because of an injury have learned to write with each hand. But these are specific skills, learned for the purpose of distinguishing and expressing the self. In reality, almost no one is truly ambidextrous. Enslaved people were only able to pick the required amount of cotton by learning how to unhook their nondominant hand from the tethers of bodily asymmetry and brain architecture that they had developed over the course of a lifetime. For eventually, only by using two hands that operated independently and simultaneously could they meet the rising quotas.

"Some hands can't get the sleight of it," said one white man, who had tried to whip a young woman to "make her a hand at cotton-picking." Enslavers and their victims sometimes described the skill of working with two hands that operated independently, with neither one dominant, as the "sleight" of picking cotton. The word means craft, cunning, the special knack or trick of something done too quickly for the eye to see. There is something left-handed about the word, something that is distinct from right-handed force. We think of sleight of hand as something employed by pickpockets, magicians, three-card monte dealers. But this sleight was different: extracted by power, it exposed and commodified hidden, individual skills. In the case of those who, like Patsey, developed the sleight of picking, what they achieved was not a mobilization of left-handed tricks to undermine right-handed power and entertain audiences, but a kind of detachment from their own consciousness. Patsey was beautiful as she moved, a sense that drips out of Northup's description of her performance between the rows. Yet her achievement was also a thing of horror; she was a person forced to toil in a hot field, but she was also one of the "hands" sketched in words written on paper by men sitting in cool, dark offices.[49]

Picking one cotton plant clean was much lighter work in terms of weight lifted or aerobic energy expended than cutting down a tree. Yet picking cotton was at the same time much harder labor than anything else enslaved people had to do. Here, for instance, is the rest of the story of the woman who didn't "get the sleight of it": "I whipped her, and if I did it once I did it five hundred times, but I found she *could* not; so I put her to carrying rails with the men. After a few days I found her shoulders were so *raw* that every rail was *bloody* as she laid it down. I asked her if she would not rather pick cotton than carry rails. 'No,' said she, 'I don't get whipped now.'" Repetitiveness, and above all the demand that one become a different person—or not even a whole person, but a hand, and the wrong hand at that—these things made cotton-picking horrible. People remembered it as "irksome" and "fatiguing." "I was never thoroughly reconciled to it," they said, for it never felt like their own work or their own body.[50]

To alienate one's hands and rewire them for someone else was torment. Enslaved people, however, discovered how to do it. They had no choice. So they watched and talked to others, learning from their speed. They created, on their own, new efficiencies that shortened the path from plant to sack and back in space and time. And above all, they shut down pathways in the brain so that the body could dance like a Patsey, could become for a time the disembodied "hand" of enslavers' fantastic language. The whole effort left permanent scars. Years after she learned to pick cotton in Alabama in the 1850s, an elderly woman named Adeline still couldn't stand to watch clerks weighing the meat she bought at the grocery store: "Cause I remembers so well that each day that the slaves was given a certain number of pounds to pick. When weighing up time come and you didn't have the number of pounds set aside, you may be sure that you was going to be whipped."[51]

The threat of torture drove enslaved people to inflict this creation and destruction on themselves. Torture walked right behind them. But neither their contemporaries then nor historians since have used "torture" to describe the violence applied by enslavers. Some historians have called lashings "discipline," the term offered by slavery's lawgivers and the laws they wrote, which pretended that masters who whipped were calmly administering "punishment" to "correct" lazy subordinates' reluctance to work. Even white abolitionist critics of slavery and their heirs among the ranks of historians were reluctant to say that it was torture to beat a bound victim with a weapon until the victim bled profusely, did what was wanted, or both. Perhaps one unspoken reason why many have been so reluctant to apply the term "torture" to slavery is that even though they denied slavery's economic dynamism, they knew that slavery on the cotton frontier made a lot of product. No one was willing, in other words, to admit that they lived in an economy whose bottom gear was torture.[52]

Yet we should call torture by its name. Historians of torture have defined the term as extreme torment that is part of a judicial or inquisitorial process. The key feature that distinguishes it from mere sadistic behavior is supposedly that torture aims to extract "truth." But the scale and slate and lash did, in fact, continually extract a truth: the maximum poundage that a man, woman, or child could pick. Once the victim surrendered that fact—opened up his or her left hand and revealed it, as it were—the torturer then challenged the enslaved person's reason once again, to force the creation of an even greater capacity to pick.[53]

Enslavers used torture to exert continuous pressure on all hands to find ways to split the self and become disembodied as a left hand at work. This was why many planters and overseers whipped even—or perhaps especially—their fastest pickers. In 1840–1841, Bennett Barrow, owner of a slave labor camp in West Feliciana Parish, Louisiana, kept a journal that he called his "Record of Punishment." In this ledger, which records both whipping and picking, Barrow revealed how he calibrated torture. Three-quarters of the 1840–1841 instances of torture were directed at those who did not meet their weight. Sometimes he focused on those who failed to meet a relatively low quota, as he did on the October day when he directed a "whipping frollick." He "whiped 8 or 10 for weight to day—those that pick least weights." But he actually beat the most productive cotton pickers more frequently than he did the least productive ones. He tortured his fastest male picker twice, and his three fastest women nine times between them, just as Edwin Epps beat Solomon Northup's friend Patsey until "her back bore the scars of a thousand stripes." This was how clever entrepreneurs extorted new efficiencies that they themselves could not imagine. They pressed their most skillful hands and contriving minds ever harder.[54]

Using torture, slavery's entrepreneurs extracted an amount of innovation virtually equal in numerical measure to all the mechanical ingenuity in all the textile mills in the Western world. The enslavers' choice was a rational one, if that which increases profitability and productivity is by definition rational. On the cotton frontier, Charles Ball said, torture was "practised with . . . order, regularity, and system" designed to convert "insufficient" production into sufficient production—sufficient, that is, until the next day, when it would be repeated. Henry Bibb's owner said "that he was no better pleased than when he could hear . . . the sound of the driver's lash among the toiling slaves," for then he knew that his system was working.[55]

Of course, not all of the benefits of torture for profit appeared in black and red ink. Some enslavers beat captives who lied, and then again, as one formerly enslaved person said, "when you tell them the truth, they whip you to make [you] lie." They beat captives who resisted. They beat those who did not. Enslavers beat the enslaved to assuage jealousy—yes, jealousy of a field hand who had to pick three hundred pounds a day. Edwin Epps envied the narrow transcendence of his power that Patsey's unconscious grace in the field revealed. Beyond the body he raped, the womb whose children he could sell, the back he flayed, there was part of her that danced, and he hated it. Meanwhile, "Captain Davis," the father of James Fisher's Alabama owner, carried a whip he named "The Negro Ruler." Making it a point to "conquer or kill every one he undertook to flog," he beat one man until brain damage prevented the victim from walking. He was eager to beat Fisher, too, but James managed to run away before the white woman consented to let her father do so.[56]

For many southwestern whites, whipping was a gateway form of violence that led to bizarrely creative levels of sadism. In the sources that document the expansion of cotton production, you can find at one point or another almost every product sold in New Orleans stores converted into an instrument of torture: carpenters' tools, chains, cotton presses, hackles, handsaws, hoe handles, irons for branding livestock, nails, pokers, smoothing irons, singletrees, steelyards, tongs. Every modern method of torture was used at one time or another: sexual humiliation, mutilation, electric shocks, solitary confinement in "stress positions," burning, even waterboarding. And descriptions of runaways posted by enslavers were festooned with descriptions of scars, burns, mutilations, brands, and wounds. Yet even slave owners' more "irrational" forms of torture could have "rational" outcomes. As ex-slave Henry Gowens pointed out, wild assaults "cramp[ed] down [the] minds" of their targets (if they survived) and other witnesses, who now acted as much like hands as they could.[57]

We don't usually see torture as a factor of production. Economics teachers don't put it on the chalkboard as a variable in a graph ("T" stands for torture, one component of "S," or supply). But here is something that may help reveal how crucial systematized torture was to the industrial revolution, and thus to the birth of the modern world. It's a metaphor offered by a man named Henry Clay, after the architect of the "American system." Born into slavery in the Carolinas, moved west as a boy, Clay recalled after slavery ended that his Louisiana owner had once possessed a machine which by his account made cotton cultivation and harvesting mechanical, rapid, and efficient. This contraption was "a big wooden wheel with a treadle to it, and when you tromp the treadle the big wheel go round. On that wheel was four or five leather straps with holes cut in them to make blisters, and you lay the negro down on his face on a bench and tie him to it." When the operator pumped the treadle to turn the wheel, the straps thrashed the back of the man or woman tied to the bench into blistered, bloody jelly. According to Clay, the mere threat of this whipping-machine was enough to speed his own hands.[58]

The contraption may have actually existed. More likely, however, the whipping-machine was not a material thing of wood and leather but a telling tale. Clay was using a metaphorical argument to say that every cotton labor camp carved out of the southwestern woods used torture as its central technology. Every single day, calibrated pain, regular as a turning gear, challenged enslaved people to exceed the previous day's gains in production. Planters and entrepreneurs rarely talked about how other human beings actually picked cotton, but they didn't need to. They had only to deploy and tune the technology of the whip, steelyard, and slate in order to force people to focus their minds on inventing new ways to perform repetitive and mind-numbing labor at nearly impossible speed. Fingertips hardened, but also became more subtle and swift. Enslaved people developed different tricks, ways to get down the row with as little wasted movement as possible. Some of the new discoveries they could teach to each other, but ultimately one also had to split one's own consciousness in half in order to generate unseen creativities of movement, new graces of speed.

Thus torture compelled and then exposed left-handed capacities, subordinated them to the power of the enslaver, turned them against people themselves. And thus untold amounts of mental labor, unknown breakthroughs of human creativity, were the keys to an astonishing increase in cotton production that required no machinery—save the whipping-machine, of course. With it, enslavers looted the riches of black folk's minds, stole days and months and years and lifetimes, turned sweat, blood, and flesh into gold. They forced people to behave in the fields as if they themselves were disembodied, mechanical hands that moved ever more swiftly over the cotton plant at the wave of the enslaver's hand. Enslavers forced the sleight of the left hand to yield to the service of their own right-handed power.

It was true that when entrepreneurs made plans, their desires sometimes ran away with them, and they counted on grandiose futures that might never come to pass. They looked at people with heads and arms and legs and could not "see anything but cotton bales," ex-slaves said. Mississippi enslaver Daniel Jordan, for example, made the wild prediction in 1833 that he would get "ten bales to the hand," speaking as if the people who picked his cotton were bizarrely disembodied "hands." Yet some of these plans did come to pass. The whipping-machine that enslavers built in the southwestern slave labor camps enabled them to reshape the world along the lines of their own fanciful calculations of people into hands, hands into bales, bales into money, money into hands again. Hard forced labor multiplied US cotton production to 130 times its 1800 level by 1860. Slave labor camps were more efficient producers of revenue than free farms in the North. Planter-entrepreneurs conquered a subcontinent in a lifetime, created from nothing the most significant staple-commodity stream in the world economy. They became the richest class of white people in the United States, and perhaps the world.[59]

ON THAT FIRST 1805 evening, Charles Ball still stood uncertainly outside the lantern-light's circle. The overseer had called out his thirty-eight pounds of cotton and warned him about the second day's number. The drivers took several others off to the side. Ball "stood by, with feelings of despondence and terror, whilst the other people were getting their cotton weighed." But when the overseer walked over to where Ball stood, he simply examined Ball's hands and then said, "You have a pair of good hands—you will make a good picker." This was both reassurance and threat. Your hands, he was telling Ball, will allow you to become a hand. We will make you make yourself into a good picker.

In the days that followed, Ball pushed himself frantically, willing his hands to move faster. After a couple of weeks he had reached an average level. The next day he increased his total by a few pounds, and then the white men who drove and measured him established a new, higher minimum. But Ball never excelled. He complained that he "was hardly regarded as a *prime hand*." In Maryland, though he was not free, Ball had taken pride in the good things his brain and body could do together. They made him a man, in his view, and an individual as well. They brought him a family. In South Carolina, he was never comfortable with the way cotton-picking required him to subordinate his inventive mind, and his muscles that were the product of ten thousand hours of hard labor, to the endless repetition of his hands. And it brought him nothing but an unwhipped back for one more day.[60]

The left-handed innovations that Ball had to surrender, imposing self-torture to avoid that done by others, was in 1805 a future through which millions of people would be compelled to pass. The woods that shadowed Ball at the end of the day stretched a thousand miles away west, finally running out in central Texas. Everything in between, and even beyond, was potentially cotton land. For the next half-century new fields ran west and south like wildfire from the Congaree, changing the world—one tree cut down, one field plowed, one bag picked at a time. Slave labor camps spread more quickly than any agricultural frontier had expanded in human history. Felled logs smoldered in countless new grounds. Fields widened. The processes of hand-making churned in a vast and ever-widening and thickening circle.

By the time William from Baltimore came to James Stille's place, which just happened to be right across the Mississippi River from Wade Hampton's new Louisiana slave labor camp, everything Charles Ball had to produce in

South Carolina had raised the ante for what William would have to do. A few months after his sale, William woke up and found that he, too, would have to make his hands learn to pick cotton. Of course, learning how to meet the daily demands of the overseers was measurably harder in 1819 than it had been in 1805.

Yet "hands" were not only white entrepreneurs' disembodied appendages. James Stille had bought men who had been transformed into commodities. He drove them hard, and by the beginning of August 1819, they had their first taste of cotton-picking and, no doubt, the brutality of the southwestern "negro whip." A few days into the picking season, however, four of Stille's "hands" crossed the river and went south fifty miles into the German Coast's sugar country. At William McCutcheon's slave labor camp—the same camp that in 1811 had been the source of many rebels—they tried to break into the storeroom. McCutcheon heard a noise, came out, and surprised the escaped captives. Two pointed guns at him. From five yards away, they snapped their triggers. But the powder was wet. The guns misfired, and McCutcheon sounded the alarm. Enslavers soon captured two of the runaways and killed a third. The fourth escaped into the tall August sugarcane.[61]

The whip drove men and women to turn all of their bodies and much of their minds to the task of picking faster and faster. But gang labor could never occupy every corner of every person's brain. There was always nighttime. So Charles Ball walked back to the small village of huts where the exhausted and bruised people among whom he had found himself were trying to survive. And a man—for all we know, Rachel's shipmate William—crouched in McCutcheon's cane field, trying to still his wildly thumping heart lest his pursuers hear.

# 5

# TONGUES

*1819–1824*

S HE HAD COME FROM far away. Her journey down from Kentucky,
all the tears she had cried when Robert Dickey bought her and left her
mother at New Orleans—they had drained her. Now she was dead. But her
body could not settle into death on a cooling board, couldn't take the slow
bumpy ride on the mule cart. Instead, morning after Louisiana morning, her
body shuffled into a sea of cotton. Her hoe rose and fell, rose and fell with the
others. The sun that beat on her was gray, not gold, though the sky burned
white-hot at three in the afternoon. Dust coated her legs and arms until they
looked as gray as the underworld that her vacant stare took in. Water from
the dipper scratched her tongue like sand. Her corpse grew thinner. Men
tried to speak to her. Their voices sounded far away, as if she lay at the bottom of the sea. Their faces shimmered over a surface she could not breach.
Some looked kind; some greedy for a new woman; some waiting to see if
she would gasp for help. But her dry tongue clove to the roof of her mouth.[1]

Wordless haunts like her wandered the landscape of slavery's southwestern frontier. They hid in abandoned corncribs, waited at crossroads, chased
children from places where blood had spilled. They were girls who killed
themselves after being beaten for leaving the onions out of the stew. They
were men who disappeared after the master caught them praying that slavery
would end. Slaves born in Africa told others that if you died outside God's
presence, perhaps because you were the victim of violence so horrifying that
even a deity couldn't bear to watch, half of your spirit might remain behind—wandering the crime site, thirsty for peace.[2]

Soon she would be another wisp on the night breeze. But as long as her
working body inched up one furrow after another, she was also another story
of the undead. Before the Haitian Revolution, Africans toiling in the sugar

fields of Saint-Domingue spread the story of the *zombi*. This was a living-dead person who had been captured by white wizards. Intellect and personality fled home, but the ghost-spirit and body remained in the land of the dead, working at the will of the sorcerer-planters. Any slave could be a *zombi*. She already was one, in fact. And after the spirit departed, the individual body that remained behind might not last much longer. It might shake to death with the country fever, or be beaten and killed by a furious overseer. She might waste away in the gray country until one morning the threat of whip couldn't rouse her, one more uncounted ghost whose spirit and body had wilted and died in the new ground of the southwestern frontier. But if individual bodies died, more kept coming. In the broader sense, the body of slavery, the system of slave trades and whipping-machines, of right- and left-handed power that enslavers were assembling—this kept growing.

Years later, she remembered her zombie days. And she never forgot the living men who called to her. They fished for her spirit, down in dark oceans of their own. Daughter sister wife lover they named her, for faces they remembered. Nights at the fire, they talked about her. They knew the cold terrain of the submerged city where she wandered. When they lay down, they wondered about her to themselves. Then they dreamed of their own lost people.

No name turned the key of their prison. They stopped talking and started singing. Out under the sun, corn-shucking songs that laughed to a fiddle's sawing beat just wouldn't do. Out here hands were turning their own muscles into someone else's cash. So every song was a question. (*Am I born to die, and lay this body down?*) Some say that songs talked in cipher about running away. (*On Jordan's Stormy Banks I stand, and cast a wishful eye / To Canaan's fair and happy land, where my possessions lie.*) Some say those songs just promised pie in the sky. But, either way, these songs acknowledged that tears watered any Eden their singers could imagine. For only once songs sounded the depths of the river could singers and listeners wade through the sorrow to walk on the other bank.[3]

So in the dead land the men sang to her. The sound faded across the rows of plants. The dusty mechanism of her arms rose and fell.

At last they tried a new tune whose wave carried across the gray field. The melody rose to joy and plunged to sadness and back again. Simple words named the brutality of their shared fates, and simple words promised that the world might have color once again, if the song could but sweep her up to the surface. *Hair as black as coal in the mine, little Liza Jane / Eyes so large and big and fine, little Liza Jane.* You are beautiful. We need you. You cannot go where you are trying to go. Come back up, and join us.

*You plant a patch of cotton, I'll plant a patch of cane / I'm gonna make molasses, to sweeten Liza Jane.* The singers kept one eye on the overseer. The other watched her. For they knew that no matter how they strove with their song, she would never see her mother again. As the men sang the verse again, they saw her bend down, holding onto the handle of her hoe for support. Here she was, all alone. Her chest lifted and fell in convulsions. She could not bring herself to go on living by herself. But they were asking her not to let herself die.

Sobs began to heave out of her mouth. The men came around to the chorus. They felt the pain in their own dead flesh, cracking as the part that wanted to live tried to break through. *Oh Liza, poor gal, Oh Liza Jane / Oh Liza poor gal, she died on the trail.* Liza, they sang. Lucy raised her head. Tears flowed down her face and she opened her mouth: "I got happy," Lucy Thurston remembered eighty years after her resurrection, "and sang with the rest."[4]

IN THE THIRTY-ODD YEARS since the 1780s, when slavery's survival as an institution had looked so imperiled, a complete reversal had taken place. The new zombie body of slavery, stretched by new kinds of power, new technologies of exploitation, new markets, and new forms of credit, was now growing at a metastatic rate. Individuals like Lucy, their lives ripped asunder so that their market value could be extracted, were watching as their links to hope and to each other dissolved. And what could bring an end to their ongoing torture? Enslaved people's opportunity for collective resistance along the lines of Saint-Domingue had been foreclosed by enslavers and governments. Nor could enslaved people call upon powerful allies who might help bring about a peaceful end to slavery's expansion. For virtually all white Americans were now interested, almost all profiting in some way—financially, psychologically, or both—from slavery's growing empire.

The bond between white people was about to be tested by the political controversy called the Missouri Crisis, in which northern and southern congressmen divided over the question of whether slavery should grow even more. The crisis lasted from 1819 to 1821, causing political insiders to panic—such as retired president Thomas Jefferson, who famously referred to it as a "firebell in the night." In the end, however, the crisis—itself a product of white people's successful conquest of half a continent—would by its outcome raise the question of how enslaved people could ever draw upon any resources beyond their own and those of the others in the same coffles and fields and slave quarters.

At the same time, if people like Lucy could not survive in body and mind, it was obvious that no reversal of history's course since the 1780s would be possible. And if survival by means of outside help was unlikely, survival through the efforts of the enslaved acting together may have seemed even more unlikely. To understand why, plumb the depths of loss that Liza and Lucy's chorus knew so well. Many of the people who came out of the chains and off the blocks, who couldn't make their weight in those first weeks in the cotton fields, had lost everything: their words, their selves, even their names. It was no foregone conclusion that Lucy Thurston would even remember her name, much less speak again. Forced migration to the frontiers of slavery took children from parents who named them and taught them to talk, brothers from sisters who carried them as babies, wives from husbands who had whispered to them in the night, men from friends who had taken whippings rather than betray them. Survival by means of joint effort would require strong bonds, and all existing strong bonds had been broken.

One woman on Joseph Shepherd's Mississippi plantation changed her name to "Silence." Another sold-off woman said she was no longer Sophia, but Sophia Nobody. Many found that when they reached back for essential memories, nothing was there. Margaret Nickens's mother and father, brought to Missouri from Kentucky and Virginia as children, forgot their own parents' names. Whenever they saw an adult slave who resembled their fuzzy memories, they asked: Are you my mother? Are you my father? A Tennessee girl lay in childbirth, when to her appeared a woman. Who are you, she groaned, not recognizing. "Don't forget the old folks," the ghost replied, and vanished. Only then did the daughter recognize her own dead mother. The midwife put an axe under the bed to cut the young woman's pain as the contractions grew harder. Soon she'd name her own newborn, a sword to pierce her own heart, another child sentenced to be sold from her mother.[5]

From the Atlantic ships ancestors had crawled, more dead than alive. Against all odds, strangers from one hundred different ethnic groups had learned to talk to each other, and become kin. Now another massive disruption was taking place, and it, too, was destroying families and social networks, sweeping away all of the relationships and statuses that made up the structure of social life. Like the earlier Middle Passage, the journey along the road southwest had given many reason to feel distrust of their peers—if not of relatives, then of the wider circle of the people who shared their badges of slavery. They'd been talked into coming in from hideouts in the Carolina woods, only to find they had been "sold running" to a trader. Slave traders' enslaved assistants doctored people up, blacked their hair, rubbed their skins slick with oil to grease prices higher. In the jails where coffles slept, bullies intimidated the small, stole food, and raped. Traitors betrayed plans for revolt. On new slave labor camps, the pushing system pitted migrants against each other. When picking season came, one person's skill could push up another's quota.

After weighing-up some might become friends. Others already planned to be enemies. One man might see in another a competitor for a woman, and in a woman a conquest; a woman, in turn, might see another woman as a rival. Small rewards of money or favor convinced captives to abandon incipient solidarity. William Anderson complained that "slaves are sometimes great enemies to each other, telling tales, lying, catching fugitives, and the like. All this is perpetuated by ignorance, oppression and degradation." When another captive saw Anderson, who had recently been transported from Virginia to Mississippi, eating a stolen fowl, he ran and told the overseer that William was "eating up all of the chickens on the place." Anderson got one hundred lashes.[6]

In the older states, many enslaved African Americans had believed that techniques from African spiritual traditions could enable one to exert some control over events. William Grimes, who had been sold to Georgia from his Virginia home in around 1800, consulted fortune-tellers; they reassured him, telling him he would one day be free. Henry Bruce remembered that some of the other people enslaved in Virginia with him had hired a slave "conjuror" to bury a little ball of what looked like dirt—a "jack," or "hand," a symbolic object—under the doorstep of an enslaver who was planning to move them to Alabama. When the white man changed his mind, at least temporarily, all of the African Americans congratulated themselves on their success.

Enslaved migrants brought these traditions to the frontier. Archaeologists have dug up little brass "hands" under doorsteps in the slave quarters of Andrew Jackson's "Hermitage" slave labor camp outside of Nashville. Yet Bruce, who was transported to Missouri, Mississippi, and Texas over the years—despite anything conjurors could do—noted that many enslaved people on the frontier had changed their minds about the efficacy of "voodooism," as he called it. With him, some now scoffed at their peers' claims that their once-magical hands could control white people's growing right- and left-handed power. And in their desperate, isolated circumstances, those enslaved people who could exert some control, magical or otherwise, often used it as what ex-slave Henry Bibb called "instrumentality"—a tool for getting what one wanted, no matter how it hurt other enslaved people. When Grimes got to Georgia, for instance, his enslaver told him he had to sleep in the same bed as an older woman who manipulated the slave owner. The teenaged Grimes complained to his owner that "Aunt Frankee" was a witch who was trying to ride him. The enslaver told Grimes to get back into bed and give the woman what she wanted.[7]

Even among those with goodwill, different origins could be a cause of conflict. Some people clung to the shreds of old identities, sometimes using them as walls to hold away or even abuse those among whom they were now enslaved. "Grandpa loved Virginia long as he had breath in him," said a woman born in a Mississippi labor camp. At Congaree, the enslaver forced Charles Ball's Maryland-born friend Lydia to marry a man from Africa. This man spoke only rough English. Enslavers made him "work with the other hands in the field, but as soon as he had come into his cabin, he took his seat." He refused to help Lydia with cooking, cleaning, child care, or the family garden patch. And he beat her.[8]

Many enslaved people spoke literally different languages. As of 1820, enslaved people in many Louisiana labor camps—like Île Breville on the Red River, for instance—spoke only French or creolized African-French hybrid tongues. Captives from the Chesapeake, including Charlotte Rogers of Virginia, couldn't communicate with them. Isolated, she imagined her mother was there singing beside her as she labored. She walked miles to meet a new arrival to Louisiana, one whom she had heard was from her own Virginia. Even in English-speaking districts, eastern seaboard accents sounded strange on slavery's frontier. Migrants from South Carolina's low country spoke the Gullah dialect or an African language. At Congaree in the Carolina interior, Charles Ball met an African-born Muslim man who prayed in Arabic. Elisha Garey remembered that his grandmother Rachel, whom "the Traders fotched [to Georgia] from Virginny" in the early nineteenth century, "never did learn to talk plain."[9]

Yet over the first half of the nineteenth century, enslaved people across the southwestern cotton frontier developed the "talking" that seemed "plain" to Elisha Garey. Nobody knows how long it took to create a common accent, vocabulary, and grammar. But enslaved migrants to the plantation frontier created this dialect, and it was what linguistic scholars call modern "Vernacular African-American English." The crucibles where they forged the new way to "talk plain" were places like the cabin to which the overseer assigned Charles Ball—a dwelling that already contained a man named Nero, his wife, and their five children. Nero surely could not have been overjoyed by this development—a young man moving in with him and his family—but he led Ball to his home with welcome anyway. They ducked through the cabin's low doorway, and then the man's naked four-year-old girl collided around her father's knees with an excited hug. She'd been baby-sitting her infant brother all day, and her father's return meant relief and food: "Now we shall get good supper!"[10]

Nero looked down at her for a moment and then turned back to Ball: "Did you leave any children at home?" Ball couldn't choke out a word. Nero fell silent, too. When his wife, Dinah, came in, followed by the couple's three older children, and heard the news that a new body would further crowd their tiny cabin, she simply went out to gather wild greens. These she boiled, and added them to the family's weekly cornbread ration. Ball sat down with them, and for a few minutes the world no longer seemed to swim around his eyes. After eating, he climbed into the loft of the cabin and rolled up in an extra blanket they had given him.

Soon Ball was drawing his own weekly ration of corn. But he piled it in Dinah and Nero's basket, and they shared it equally. A few days later, Dinah offered him some of the molasses that she and Nero had bought with money earned by weaving baskets for sale in the evenings. "I therefore proposed," Ball recalled three decades later, that as "a member of the family, I would contribute as much towards its support as Nero himself." The pennies he made from selling wooden bowls that he carved would go into the family pool. They shared the produce of their garden patch with him. The family traded ears of corn from Nero's patch for beans that Lydia had grown.

Families and communities do not run on the fuel of pure altruism. Everyone got something from these exchanges. People from different origins, collected together in a system designed to pit them against each other even when they were working in the same field, could have chosen not to help each other. Some at Congaree were selfish and grasping. But more saw that survival required them to make a new and different kind of family. Even those who stayed outside drew benefit. Ball helped Lydia's troublesome husband to dig a grave for their baby boy, because he knew of no other way to help Lydia. He watched the African man lay his son in the ground. Beside the tiny body, the father laid items for the boy's brave journey across the water to a place where the father's ancestors waited: "a small bow and several arrows; a little bag of parched meal; a miniature canoe, about a foot long, and a little paddle . . . a piece of white muslin, with several curious and strange figures painted on it in blue and red." By this, he told Ball, "his relations and countrymen would know the infant to be his son," and would welcome the boy back into his ancestors' kingdom. He put a lock of his own hair on his son's chest, scooped dirt into the grave with his hands, and told Ball and the others present that "the God of his country was looking at him, and was pleased with what he had done."[11]

Lydia's husband could not bring himself to reach out to the living people in his new world. Only the dead received his trust. But many others chose to treat unknown fellow migrants like brothers or sisters. After teenager John Brown was sold from Virginia to Georgia in the late 1820s, he endured vicious beatings at the hands of his new owner. "[I] used to wish to die, and only for John Glasgow I think it must have come to that very soon," he later reflected. Glasgow, an older man, led one of the work gangs. He taught Brown how to keep the pace in the cotton field, and he told the boy "not to cry after my father, and mother, and relatives, for I should never see them any more. He encouraged me to try and forget them, for my own sake." Death was here, but so was life, and Glasgow guided Brown toward the second. When the enslaver shattered Brown's nose and eye socket with a booted kick, Glasgow cleaned the teenager's wounds. With a careful hand and a warm ball of tallow, he massaged Brown's displaced eyeball back into place.[12]

Like the other things that enslaved people shared—food they cooked, bean plants in a garden patch, enough space for one more man to lie down in a cramped cabin, a piece of hard-won advice—caring hands helped migrants to come out of the first few days and weeks alive. After that, captives of the new slave labor camps began to work together. So as winter approached, Ball and Nero each bought three blankets with their small extra earnings. Cut up and sewn carefully, they made eight warm coats for Ball and the family. The small village on the edge of the cotton frontier built patterns that linked small groups together. Every Monday night, after weekly rations were distributed, one member of each household had to wait for a turn to grind corn at the hand mill in the yard. The last one did not finish until one in the morning. They assigned the sequence by lot. Each person ground his or her own corn and woke the next one.[13]

Not everything was collective. Enslaved people shared possessions, but they also used them to mark out boundaries, forming relationships and structures out of both contention and cooperation. I am more than a hand, said the little money-making tobacco patch that Jimmy planted in the Tennessee woods owned by his enslaver. I am more than what the law says, more than a body to be sold, beaten, raped, and divided from my children at the will of whites, said Myra, who wanted a calico coat so she could "show out" on Sundays. I am not cheap, worn-out, identical to a thousand others, I am unique, said the umbrella old Toby carried under his arm when he walked to town on a hot Mississippi Sunday, hoping to meet his next wife.[14]

Though scarcer on the southwestern frontier than back East, possessions shouted all the louder, because they now had to assert an identity for people who had not known one since birth. The things people made and claimed as their own even marked ties beyond the grave. While chopping firewood one day in the Alabama woods, Anthony Abercrombie became aware of a spectral presence hovering in a nearby tree. He dropped his axe and ran, but later realized that the ghost dropping nuts from the tree must have been Joe. Joe had promised Anthony twenty-five cents for helping him to shuck his corn. But before Joe could sell the corn, get the money, and pay Anthony, "Marse Jim" had shot Joe dead. Now Joe was back to fulfill his obligation, giving him something to gather and sell.[15]

WHILE ENSLAVED PEOPLE WITH almost nothing to divide were finding ways to make their mite into a basis for sharing, the first waves of slavery's expansion were creating tremendous gains for white Americans. The surge after 1815 was particularly lucrative. Many of the new dollars suddenly circulating through the US economy had been generated by the toil of people who had been commodified as hands and then put into the whipping-machine. Economic power meant political power. Since Jefferson's victory in 1800, an alliance between northern and southern pro-expansion white politicians who simply referred to themselves as "Republicans" had dominated American politics. John Quincy Adams, son of the only non-Virginia president to serve before the 1820s, had switched from the Federalists to the Republicans while representing Massachusetts in the Senate during Jefferson's second term. And the results of the Battle of New Orleans made the Federalists irrelevant.[16]

Heirs of Thomas Jefferson, critic and beneficiary of slavery, the Republicans had already presided over a massive extension of human bondage. Despite the claims of Virginians that the diffusion of slavery across the southwestern frontier would make the institution somehow dissipate, northerners who had traveled on business to New Orleans or Alabama understood that the opposite was happening. By the 1810s, thanks to the Constitution's bargains, seventeen southern congressmen represented three-fifths of the slave population—though, of course not the interests of the enslaved, but of the enslaver. This increment allowed southern politicians to dominate the Republican faction, and thus—with the loyalty of northern Republicans—the entire government. After all, cotton entrepreneurship passed on benefits to the North, expanding credit markets, supporting trade, and making markets for the new textile mills being established by John Quincy Adams's constituents. Adams was a good Republican soldier. He was now secretary of state for President James Monroe, another Virginia slaveholder. But he complained that the "slave representation . . . will be forever thrown into the Southern scale." In other words, the pounds of cotton that mounted up on the steelyards of new southwestern labor camps did more than tell the truth about an individual's daily picking. When the pounds were counted and multiplied by the number of the enslaved, they also created more money, more slavery, more southern congressmen and senators, and more legislation favorable to the South—and then, in turn, even more money, even more slavery . . . on and on in a continuous growing cycle. The ever-growing weight of slave owners' political power, worried the New Englander in Adams, "must forever make ours kick the beam."[17]

During the first two decades of the nineteenth century, tens of thousands of settlers from Virginia and Kentucky moved west of the Mississippi and north of what is now the state of Louisiana. The part of the country where the Missouri, the Mississippi, and the Ohio mingle the waters of half a continent and head south toward New Orleans rests on a major geological fault line, which in 1811 shifted, and destroyed the important Mississippi River port of New Madrid. But the Missouri Territory, as the region was now called, also rested atop another confluence of opposing forces. To the northeast lay the new state of Illinois, ostensibly free by virtue of its inclusion in the 1780s-era Northwest Territory, but in reality settled in part by southerners, who used a loophole in the state's law to hold African Americans in slavery. In 1821, in fact, those settlers would attempt to rewrite the Illinois state constitution to permit large-scale human bondage. To the north and west and south of Missouri, meanwhile, lay the vast Louisiana Purchase. Only one section of this area—Louisiana—had yet become a state. The status of the remaining 800,000 square miles was undecided.[18]

By December 1818, when a petition from the Missouri Territory's whites reached Congress for statehood, those settlers had established a thriving agricultural economy in the valleys west of St. Louis, one based on tobacco, hemp for cordage and sailcloth, and corn. And, of course, slaves. More than 10,000 enslaved African Americans lived in Missouri. Now Missourians were asking Congress to admit their territory as a state, so Congress took up the issue. Beginning with Kentucky in 1795, Congress had now admitted five slave states west of the mountains and south of the Ohio. Perhaps, given the growing anxiety among good northern Republican soldiers like John Quincy Adams, no one should have been surprised by what Representative James Tallmadge of New York said when he stood up in Congress on February 13, 1819. But they were surprised.[19]

For Tallmadge proposed two amendments to the Missouri statehood bill. The first banned the importation of more slaves into Missouri. The second proposed to free all enslaved people born in the new state once they reached twenty-five. And here is what might have surprised even savvy observers: as the clerk of the House counted the votes, it became clear that heavy northern support had passed Tallmadge's amendments over universal southern opposition. Some in the free states clearly feared that they were becoming mere junior partners in the government of the United States. They were choosing to draw a line, though not against slavery itself, or against the kind of slavery from which they profited most. Missouri was too far north for cotton to grow. Still, for the first time since the Congress had affirmed the Northwest Ordinance in 1789, a house of the national legislature had blocked slavery's expansion.[20]

In the Senate, matters were different. Over the previous decade, Congress had been admitting states in pairs, retaining a rough balance between North and South in the Senate. Southern senators turned back the House's bill and struck the antislavery clauses. In response, the House rejected the Senate's version of the Missouri statehood bill. And as speeches grew more heated, John Quincy Adams realized that they "disclosed a secret," a subterranean fault line—the fact that almost all northern representatives would, if pushed to the test, vote against more slavery expansion. Meanwhile, southern representatives were deciding that the right to expand slavery was inseparable from any other right that they possessed. John Scott, the nonvoting delegate from Missouri, insisted that restriction would deny Missouri whites their constitutional right to property. The right to expand was even the right of self-preservation. If slavery restriction blocked further expansion, southern representatives wailed, slave numbers would balloon until a black rebellion erupted, making a giant Haiti of the southern states. Thomas Cobb of Georgia warned that the friction of slavery restriction was "kindling a fire which all the waters of the ocean could not extinguish. It could only be extinguished in blood!"[21]

In the face of Cobb's implied threat of civil war, New York's Tallmadge replied that "if blood is necessary to extinguish any fire which I have assisted to kindle . . . I shall not forbear to contribute my mite." Back and forth the debate went, but when the spring session of Congress ended, nothing had been resolved. Congressmen from New York and New Jersey returned home to find that a flurry of public meetings were in progress supporting their anti-slavery-expansion stance. In such meetings, some constituents raised questions that went beyond mere sectional advantage. Wasn't slavery

a contradiction, asked the organizers of a New York meeting, to the principles of *"life, liberty, and the pursuit of happiness?"* But opposition to slavery
itself was not what brought most white attendees to those meetings, and the
idea of black equality would have been anathema to almost all of them. In
contrast to the abolitionist groups that would emerge years later, socially
conservative Federalists led these meetings. These old and prominent ministers, these long-established philanthropists, brooked little or no input from
African Americans. Instead, most of the complaints voiced by such meetings
were about sectional power balances. By the time William Plumer of New
Hampshire was on his way back to Congress for the next session, he believed
it had become "political suicide" for a free-state politician "to tolerate slavery beyond its present limits." Further concessions would make America "a
mighty empire of slaves" dominated by arrogant planter-politicians.[22]

The group that joined Plumer in the capital during the early winter of
1819 was a new Congress, elected in 1818. In the thirteen months between
the time of their election and the time of their seating—lame ducks lasted
much longer in those days—a major financial crisis had erupted. The Panic
of 1819 embroiled the administrators of the Second Bank of the United States
in scandals that demanded legislative attention. But the debate over Missouri
continued, too. Even though Kentucky representative and Speaker of the
House Henry Clay was working behind the scenes with a middle group of
congressmen from both free and slave states, trying to organize a compromise, tempers on the floor of the House grew more and more heated. Rumors
whispered that congressmen were carrying pistols into debate.[23]

John Quincy Adams—a New Englander in a southern administration,
trying to focus on his negotiations to acquire Florida from Spain—had assured an audience in the summer of 1819 that he believed the restriction of
Missouri slavery was unconstitutional. But while negotiations dragged on
into February 1820, and as Monroe used the power of the executive to lean on
northern Republicans to break from the slavery-restriction ranks, Adams had
a startling late-afternoon conversation with Secretary of War John C. Calhoun, a South Carolinian. Calhoun predicted that the Missouri crisis "would
not produce a dissolution" of the Union. "But if it should," Calhoun continued, "the South would of necessity be compelled to form an alliance . . . with
Great Britain." "I said that would be returning to the colonial state," replied
the shocked Adams, who remembered two wars with the old empire. "He
said, yes, pretty much, but it would be forced upon them."

Adams fell silent. But in his diary, his pen wrote thoughts that his voice
was afraid to breathe: "If the dissolution of the Union should result from the

slave question, it is as obvious as anything . . . that it must be shortly afterward followed by the universal emancipation of the slaves." For "slavery is the great and foul stain upon the North American Union." The opportunity of war would mean that "the union might then be reorganized on the fundamental principle of emancipation. This object is vast in its compass, awful in its prospects, sublime and beautiful in its issue. A life devoted to it would be nobly spent or sacrificed."[24]

Yet, just like Calhoun and all the other cabinet men, Adams was thinking not of self-sacrifice, but of the election of 1824, Monroe's retirement, and his own possible candidacy for president. In public his tongue stayed silent on this issue—for now. And by early 1820 Clay could offer the House an already-passed Senate bill that admitted Missouri as a slave state, and added Maine (sectioned from the northern coastlands claimed by Massachusetts) as a free state, to keep the Senate balanced. The bill also barred any more slave states from being carved out of the Louisiana Purchase above 36°30' north latitude, essentially Missouri's southern border. Southern senators thought this deal gave up little of practical importance. One could not grow cotton and sugar in the Dakotas. When free-state representatives in the House shot down the combined compromise bill, Clay divided it into separate Missouri statehood and restriction-line bills. Then southerners, plus a few northerners, voted for Missouri statehood (with slavery), while northerners passed the 36°30' restriction line. At last the crisis was over.[25]

With the Missouri statehood issue, the expansion of slavery had been presented as a stark choice, one uncomplicated, for instance, by the desire to bring Louisiana into the Union so that European empires could no longer block national expansion. Northern politicians had united almost instantaneously against it. The shock of this opposition helps explain, perhaps, why southern politicians reacted with their own startling level of emotion and threats of secession. Southern forces in Washington had relied on the Senate's balance between free-state and slave-state delegates to accomplish further expansion—and those who took a calculating view understood that northern money, especially that represented by New Englanders (who had lagged behind the anti-expansion zealots), was unlikely to slap away the hand that fed it. Merchant elites who depended on the shipping trade still dominated New England politics. While some southerners might complain that a wall of Spanish territory to the west of Louisiana now blocked further expansion, the compromise dealmaker, Clay, thought he could add Spanish Texas to the Adams-Onis Treaty—which already ensured that enslavers would get Florida. He wasn't able to do so, but southern leaders like

President James Monroe still believed that Texas would inevitably fall to the United States. And many, both North and South, now thought that the Missouri Compromise—as it came to be known—had established a precedent of dividing the West between free and slave territory. They would come to refer to the Compromise as a "sacred compact."[26]

The Missouri controversy caused many southern enslavers to become overly sensitive to future criticism; northern opposition to the expansion of slavery, however, dissipated when the crisis was over. Before 1819, there had been no such thing as an organized opposition to slavery or its expansion among northern whites. After 1821, northern whites returned to ignoring the rights of African Americans or the consequences of slavery and its expansion for the enslaved. The few northern whites who recognized that slavery raised important moral issues—issues that went beyond the question of whether it was a stain on the national honor—did not act, but rather cast off upon Georgia-men or other bad actors the moral weight of slavery's expansion. Moral discomfort and political interest did not coalesce into a lasting opposition to expansion. Indeed, by 1821, some southern leaders were realizing that they would have little trouble creating winning interregional coalitions that allowed for further exploitation of enslaved African Americans so long as they could make a claim that their policies supported increased democracy among whites. Northerners were doing their best to give that impression, at any rate. For instance, even as the ink dried on the Missouri bills, New York was holding a state constitutional convention. In the new document they created, delegates who wanted to undermine the power of the state's traditional elites eliminated property requirements for white men who wanted to vote, but increased the barriers for black men.

BY THE EARLY 1820S, it was simply the case in the United States that enslaved people could look to no one but themselves for help. And yet they were outnumbered and outgunned, so rebellion and direct resistance would lead only to certain defeat. They would have to change their world in different ways, but even building from within presented problems. Forced migration, which atomized groups and erased identities, required enslaved migrants to create new ties to each other in the constantly changing places where they found themselves. That would not be easy. But people, and indeed the world, can change from things as invisible and acts as ephemeral as words on the wind.

One Thursday evening in October, sometime around 1820, a Kentucky enslaver named Taylor waited on his porch. Between his barn and his house waited a huge pile of corn in the husk, which needed to be prepared for storage in his barn. Soon he heard muffled sounds: groups of enslaved men and women converging through the woods from their owners' property, singing as they came to shuck his corn.

In one of those columns was Francis Fedric, who in 1863 recorded what happened on that night four decades before. And at the head of his line strutted the night's star, a tall, quick-witted young man named Reuben. Reuben's cap bristled with sticks and feathers, decorations for the chosen champion of friends and cabin-mates who planned to test their skill and heart in a competition to see which gang could shuck Taylor's corn most swiftly. Soon, scores of men poured into the fire-lit circle where the corn lay heaped, while women moved around the edges to form an audience. The men who knew each other traded jokes and gave sizing-up glances to new ones. Reuben and another captain huddled to decide the ground rules. Then the selected pair chose up sides, who divided the corn pile in two. Taylor handed each captain the all-important jug of liquor.[27]

With a rush the men dived in, grabbing ears and pulling off the shucks, while each captain leapt to the top of the pile, and, turning to his team, took center stage. His job was to lead and encourage his team by making up humorous, catchy verses that the team would then repeat or answer even as they in ceaseless motion pulled off shucks, tossed the naked ears into the "clean" pile, and passed the jug. In corn-shucking competitions, captains sung out rhymes that ridiculed other enslaved people, present or absent, by name or by implication: "Dark cloud arising like [it] going to rain / Nothing but a black gal coming down the lane." Which dark-skinned woman steamed up with anger or sneered with contempt at these sour grapes? Other lyrics took different risks, slyly chanting half-praise of an owner. Still others talked politics in ways palatable to some owners but rankling to partisans of the other side: "Polk and Clay went to war / Polk came back with a broken jaw." Some even criticized, for those who had ears to hear—"The speculator bought my wife and child"—this was a slow dragged-out verse—"And carried her clear away." Or they demanded more of the liquor that fueled the long-night labor of shucking—"Boss man, boss man, please gimme my time; Boss man, boss man, for I'm most broke down."[28]

They worked on past midnight. Whiskey flickered in their bellies and laughter roared, keeping them warm despite the chilly fall air. The smell of the ox roasting a few dozen yards away urged on the rings of grabbing, tearing men. The piles shrank. The captains' hoarse voices sped the rhythm. At two in the morning, Reuben's band frenetically, triumphantly shucked their last ears and rushed to surround the others' sweating circle, waving their hats and singing to the defeated, "Oh, oh! fie! for shame!" But the shame did not sting for long, for now, behind Reuben, they all marched down to Taylor's house. He waited there on the porch with his wife and daughter. The enslaved men crowded around it and sang one last time to Reuben's lead: "I've just come to let you know / [Men] Oh, oh, oh! / [Captain] The upper end has beat / [Men] Oh, oh, oh! / . . . [Captain] I'll bid you, fare you well / [Men] Oh, oh, oh! / [Captain] For I'm going back again / [Men] Oh, oh, oh!" Then they all went back together to shuck the last ears in the losing team's pile, after which all the corn-shuckers sat down at long tables to feast.[29]

The fun and local fame that enslaved people won at such occasions were as fleeting as the meal. Two weeks later, thirty of the men who shucked corn at Taylor's on that night were sold to buyers who were now, in the late 1810s, beginning to comb Kentucky every December. Reuben was among the first "dragged from his family," recalled Fedric: "My heart is full when I think of his sad lot." Yet even as raw memories of his own sale from Virginia flooded his thoughts, Fedric could not forget Reuben's night of triumph, the way he had led more than one hundred men with virtuosity of wit and artistry of tongue. For that night those three hundred men had all ridden on his gift despite everything that hung over them. And Reuben had soared highest of all.[30]

Here is something that is no accident: the most popular and creative genres of music in the history of the modern world emerged from the corners of the United States where enslavers' power battered enslaved African Americans over and over again. In the place Reuben was being dragged to, and in all the places where forced migration's effects were most dramatic and persistent, music could not prevent a whipping or feed a single hungry mouth. But it did serve the enslaved as another tongue, one that spoke what the first one often could not. Music permitted a different self to breathe, even as rhythm and melody made lines on which the common occasions of a social life could tether like beads. Times like corn-shuckings, when people sang and played and danced, became opportunities for people to meet. There they mourned, redeemed, and resurrected sides of the personality that had been devastated by forced migration.

On such occasions—and perhaps even more so on Saturday nights when whites weren't watching—people animated by music and by each other thought and acted and rediscovered themselves as truly alive, as people who mattered for their unique abilities and contributions, as people in a common situation who could celebrate their own individuality together. Back

Image 5.1. Corn-husking: an opportunity for community-building, mutual recognition, and improvisational freestyle battling that showcased individual virtuosity. *Harper's Weekly*, April 13, 1861, p. 232.

in Maryland, Josiah Henson's father had played a banjo made from a gourd, wood, and string. This African instrument, Henson remembered, was "the life of the farm, and all night long at a merry-making would he play on it while the other negroes danced." But around 1800, Josiah's father ran afoul of his owner, who had the man's ear severed in punishment. Deformed and angry, the maimed man let his banjo fall silent. Soon the owner sold him south, far away from Josiah. "What was his after fate neither my mother nor I ever learned," Henson wrote decades later. But any southwestward course was likely to drain a man down into the great trap of New Orleans.

In 1819, as white people began to shout and threaten each other over Missouri, a visitor wandered on a Sunday to the open space on the northern border of the French Quarter. Today the maps call this place Louis Armstrong Park. The visitor had already heard it referred to as Congo Square. He saw men drumming in a circle while a wizened elder played a banjo. Two women danced in the middle while "squall[ing] out a burthen to the playing, at intervals." In the 1830s, William Wells Brown, then an enslaved employee of a slave trader, found Congo Square still thundering with African drumming. In each corner, a different African nation—the Minas, the Fulas, the Congos—played their own music and danced their own dances while others watched, nodded heads, and jumped in. Drums sped and slowed, talking in rhythms brought thirty years before from beyond the salt water. Dancers wove patterns that talked, too. If Henson's father had come there, he might have realized that he and they sang in the same family language.[31]

So perhaps he would have picked up his banjo again. Long-lost relatives had much to teach him and others from the Chesapeake and Carolinas, where the drum had long been outlawed. And southeastern migrants had much to teach immigrants from Africa or the Caribbean. The surging patterns of sawing fiddle and plunging banjo, and the stripped-down, charging syncopation of their music, were innovations produced over the course of two hundred hard years in the New World. Southeastern migrants' own personal experiences of exile and movement within the country spread and then transformed their performance styles again. One 1800s writer claimed that "the Virginian negro character therefore has come to prevail throughout the slave states," and that "every where you may hear much the same songs and tunes, and see much the same dances." Virginia's exiles now sang about what made them no longer Virginians. Their songs evoked the traumas of separation in a modernizing society in musical ways more complex than words alone could achieve.[32]

"Traveling through the South," wrote an early white commentator on nineteenth-century African-American music, "you may, in passing from Virginia to Louisiana, hear the same tune a hundred times, but seldom the same words. This necessarily results . . . from the habit of extemporizing, in which the performers indulge on festive occasions." Only one thing about these performances was fixed: that they were not to be fixed. Instead they mixed together even well-known components of rhythm, melody, lyrics, and motion in fresh ways. So, for instance, from 8 p.m. until 2 a.m., Reuben had kept his footing on the pile of corn because he had trained for it; he had gained, under the tutelage of peers and elders, the ability to sing a song that he continually made up, and revised, and created all over again.[33]

In the nineteenth century, white European and American authors began to claim that they had become uniquely individualistic, modern, not bound to repeat the old. And the modern Western world did seem to be celebrating the individual. Think of Walt Whitman, singing a song not about the greatness of the tradition he'd been handed, but of himself. By the time Reuben sat chained to the deck of the slave-trader's flatboat on his way from Kentucky to Louisiana, every state he floated past had opened up voting to almost every individual white man. Hence Whitman's song to himself, and the celebration of the self and of American individualism, which would be emphasized over the coming century in white art forms. When white people wrote about black culture in the nineteenth century, however—and often when they have written since—they placed African-American art forms with the traditional cultures of the premodern world, which supposedly did not have a concept of the autonomous self. White people's accounts depicted black dancers and singers as acting on tradition, or even instinct, rather than attributing individual genius to them—and these accounts served as just-so stories that had the added benefit of implicitly justifying slavery. Whites explained their own attraction to enslaved people's music by crediting African Americans with unusual "powers of imitation," the primitive ability to forget the self in bacchanalian revels. By the late nineteenth century, whites believed, as many still do, such quasi-biological myths—that African-descended peoples had a "natural," biologically innate, unchanging, common response to rhythm.[34]

But it was enslaved African Americans who were the true modernists, the real geniuses. The innovation that flooded through the quarters of frontier labor camps in the first forty or fifty years of the nineteenth century was driven by constant individual creativity in the quarters' tongues. In the real world in which people like Reuben were trying to survive, individual creativity improved an enslaved African American's chance of survival, and not just by enabling him or her to find a faster way to pick a pound of protection from the whip. Skillful words made one valuable to self and peers; they helped the enslaved to see themselves not as hands but as voices. And being a voice recognized by one's peers gave one a reason to live. So no wonder music and dancing on slavery's frontier emphasized individual improvisation, not imitation, and not unison. No wonder that at corn-shuckings, at log-rollings, and at every Saturday night party, people swept from every mooring by slavery's westward-rolling tsunami sought moments like the ones that seared the memory of Reuben into the folds of Francis Fedric's brain. They strove to loose their tongues from fear and anxiety, so that they could do something that marked them as unique, their words and steps as novel, themselves as worthy of their peers' respect. There always came a space in the gathering and a moment in the song where, like Reuben, the individual performer did his or her unique thing. And then the performer's peers reveled in his or her triumph, while "all the peoples," said Hattie Ann Nettles, "cut the high step," young and old, man and woman.

For not everyone was a virtuoso, but in contrast to the vast majority of whites, no one was a specialist non-performer. Everyone could sing and dance in the circle. Anyone willing to try could jump in the middle of a ring. Women and men both took the center. As was the case wherever African Americans gathered together in the young United States, not even the men expected the women to be modest and retiring. "You jumped and I jumped / Swear by God you outjumped me!" sang out the man at the corn-shucking. The workers, laughing with a man laughing at himself, sang back "Huh! Huh! Round the corn Sally!" Sally was a name from a song, but maybe Sally's stand-in danced while the men recognized that her boldness might outjump that of her husband or lover. Other women earned the reputation of the "fastest gal on the bayou" by "dancing down" one man after another in the center of the floor. Liza Jane was alive on every dance floor.[35]

Of course, if one could not hold the stage, someone else would break in, riffing on the songs as they sang them, even in the chorus—even familiar songs with known names like "Virginny Nigger Very Good." Listeners and singers at the corn-shuckings disdained song leaders who stuttered or ran out of rhymes. The tongues of the enslaved learned to keen or growl or laugh their songs a different way each time through. This was very different from white music and white people's songs, which stuck to the same lyrics for decades. White musical ensembles played one rhythm at a time, their dancers following steps that might as well have been painted on the floor. White musical culture was a formation that approved those who marched in time. Black culture was a ring, with space in the middle for anyone willing to try his or her step. And by nourishing, practicing, and training themselves in improvisation, enslaved masters of innovation learned to think creatively as new demands and new dangers emerged. To the extent that they could institutionalize anything while living in the midst of white-created chaos, enslaved African Americans made the encouragement of creative individual performance the center of gatherings. At Saturday night dances, "when a brash nigger boy cut a cute bunch of steps, the men folk would give him a dime or so," even though dimes were scarce.[36]

Dimes earned in that way, and the love implied by them, had taught Reuben as a boy—had taught him to teach himself. Their equivalent kept teaching him as a man. At the corn-shucking, it was his peers, the ring, who sang the base to guide and bear him up. Even his rivals were the steel on which

THE CHRISTMAS WEEK.

Image 5.2. Dances during the off-times and Saturday nights provided one type of social setting that allowed people divided and measured and sold, forced through what were in effect divorces—though against the will of each party—to perform the gender roles and individual personalities that they believed made them special. "The Christmas Week," from "Album varieties no. 3; The slave in 1863," Philadelphia, 1863. Library of Congress.

he sharpened himself. And it was no foregone conclusion that enslaved migrants would support each other in this process, that they would form a ring and clap, or sing the base from which others could improvise. Their traumas could have made them too selfish, too arrogant, too amoral, too self-isolating. They were desperately poor. Enslavers teased them with stolen abundance. On Sunday mornings, remembered George Strickland of his boyhood in Alabama, "they"—white folks—"would give us biscuits for breakfast, which was so rare that we'd try to beat the others out of theirs." Children fought for the taste of white flour, to the laughter of enslavers, and some enslaved people old enough to know better acted much the same when the music started.[37]

Yet in musical and social rituals that played out as rings surrounding a changing cast of innovators, enslaved people chose to act in ways that reinforced a sense of individual independence through the reality of mutual interdependence. And those choices mattered. Music can do things to our emotions, our thoughts, and our bodies in ways that analysis of the words of a song like "Liza Jane" cannot encompass. Those were the things about music that could, and did, save lives. Cold metal shackles now bound Reuben's hands, and he sat silent on the flatboat as the shoreline scrolled by him. But in his tongue, his memory, his spirit, and his spine were well-honed tools. In Louisiana, Reuben would wield once again his power to adapt old songs to new situations: to call out emotions, to urge his coparticipants to merge with and play off each other's voices and rhythms in greater collective effort that also allowed space for individuals to shine. What they did for themselves would do for him as well. For people made into commodities had a desperate need to resist the ways in which the rapidly changing world treated them like faceless units. Many had the creative capacity to do it, just as many had the creativity to survive the ever-increasing demands made on hands in the field.[38]

Eventually, white Bohemian communities of artists in Paris and New York and San Francisco would build on Whitman's ideals of individualism by trying to make life into art and vice versa. But they trailed behind Reuben in many ways, and his depths were deeper. His powers of observation and creation were more powerful, for he knew the weight of iron on his wrists. He drew on the old and the new more effectively, for change had cost him a price the white Bohemians might never comprehend. Nor could the man or woman who was about to buy him understand, and southwestern enslavers who compelled performance—such as the enslavers who forced marching coffles of captives to sing as they marched southwest in the slave trade—even found themselves the objects of ironic imitation. The circle became an opportunity for in-jokes, for sheltering together from the white stare, for facing outward together in defense.[39]

The circle, of course, became all the more fascinating to whites as it grew more impenetrable. Whites' belief that there was a distinct "Negro music" helped shape another commodity: this one something that some whites wanted to possess and inhabit as a put-on self. It began with a few black performers who had made their way to the North as sailors on cotton vessels. They became a sensation in New York's working-class theaters, playing their banjos, singing, dancing, and clapping rhythms with their hands and feet. In the increasingly fast-paced and novelty-seeking culture of commercializing cities, the impact of black performance was shocking yet entrancing. White men—including many working-class ones who had worked in the South as functionaries of the expanding cotton empire—began to imitate and demonstrate what they had learned on the Ohio River or in New Orleans. Former cotton-gin mechanics, flatboat pilots, and apprentice clerks sang, bucked, and jived while frailing their banjos in the most authentic way, often while (weirdly) blacked-up, "playing Negro."[40]

It was very strange for such white men to sing "Oh, Susanna, don't you cry for me"—the story of an enslaved man trying to find his true love, who'd been taken to New Orleans—when the losses of a million Susannas made jobs for such white men. But as these white imitators created the minstrel show genre, and "Oh, Susanna," the most popular song of 1847–1848, made Stephen Foster the nation's first professional songwriter, blackface became the quintessential American popular entertainment of the nineteenth century. Blackface also became the archetypal model for how non-black performers would sell a long series of innovations created by enslaved migrants and their descendants—ragtime, jazz, blues, country, rhythm and blues, rock and roll, soul, and hip-hop—to a white market. From that time forward, many whites saw African-American song and dance as mere instinct, and have not understood that it is really deep art in control of complex passion. That art took shape in the creation of new ways to talk and to sing and to dance, it took shape on the cotton frontier, and it took shape in the loss and transcendence that lies seven hundred miles deep in the words of "Old Virginia, Never Tire"—a song first sung by men and women whose personal histories pivoted around the endlessly repeated march from Virginia to the new ground. But over time, iterations and recombinations of what enslaved migrants created on the cotton and sugar frontiers gave birth to American and then global popular music. Musical elements from African cultural traditions surely explain some of this appeal, but what African Americans did to always make those roots new on slavery's frontiers made this musical tradition uniquely attractive.[41]

CHARLES BALL HAD EXPERIENCED the full array of devastations practiced upon his body and his life by the new kind of slavery growing on the South's frontiers. He contemplated the choice that almost swallowed up Lucy Thurston, whose first few weeks in the Louisiana field had been the death-in-life of the zombie. Like Lucy, Ball chose otherwise. Perhaps his survival, and perhaps Thurston's as well, were miracles. Then again, there were times when to those who struggled on, death seemed more merciful than these resurrections. But just as Lucy ended up singing with the men in the fields on Friday, on a Saturday night in 1805 Charles Ball danced until dawn in the yard between the slave cabins. Several men took turns playing the banjo. Everyone sang. The older people soon grew too tired to dance but they still beat rhythms with their hands. When the music slowed to a pause, they told stories of Africa. "A man cannot well be miserable, when he sees every one about him immersed in pleasure," Ball remembered. "I forgot for the time, all the subjects of grief that were stored in my memory, all the acts of wrong that had been perpetrated against me."

Singing in the circle was teaching the people on a thousand Congarees to speak in one tongue, despite their divergent origins. Beneath all their particular interests lay the fact that they were all slaves, all faced by a group that exploited them together. On fundamental questions that divided black and white, the circle gave its participants practice in acting and thinking together. This did not mean they would always get along harmoniously, that they would have no conflicts, that the circle was never broken by competition, or that no one would ever seek his or her own advantage by siding with the masters in a way that other enslaved people thought betrayed their own values. But Saturday night promoted survival, and not just the survival of one individual. What tongues sang, how they called out with joy, longing, or competition as bodies shifted in dance, all these sounds and movements drew together the bonds that would help the group to help its members. It taught most enslaved migrants that despite all their differences and conflicts, they needed each other if they were to survive. And already they were doing more than surviving together—they were shaping new ideas, new analyses of the world and how it worked, which would in turn shape future actions.

Ball himself acted—sooner rather than later. As soon as he settled in a bit at Congaree, in fact, he was given by Wade Hampton to the planter's recently married daughter. She and her husband deployed Ball on a new slave labor camp deep in the woods of frontier Georgia. Within a year, he became a driver, charged with forcing others to keep the pace. Ball did so well at this that by the summer of 1808 his owner's brothers-in-law began to feel he was getting too much confidence. They beat him severely. Ball resolved that the time had come to leave.[42]

Enslaved migrants ran away all the time, hiding in the woods to escape violence. The number, not surprisingly, peaked during cotton-picking season. But most of them eventually came back to the slave labor camp. Slave patrols caught them. Random whites caught them. Other slaves betrayed them. Most of them didn't know the way back to wherever they had come from. And in between stood thousands of armed white people who would not be their friends. As for the free states, they were even farther away. The number of enslaved migrants who made it from the depths of the cotton and sugar frontiers all the way to the free states probably numbered under a thousand during all the years of slavery. That amounts to one-tenth of 1 percent of all forced migrants. Most of those who did make it got away by hiding on steamboats, oceangoing ships, and later, on railways.[43]

In Georgia, Ball was six hundred miles by foot from Maryland's Calvert County. He decided to try anyway. In early August he packed a small bag with food, flint, and tinder. He tied his faithful dog, who he feared might give away a hiding place, to a tree near the cabins of the labor camp. He fed his pet one last time and set off north through the woods.

Night after night Ball walked, sometimes wandering in circles until he could find a road or get his bearings from Polaris through the ragged clouds. By day he hid in the woods. He stole ripe corn from the fields. When October came he was still only at Columbia, South Carolina. And his memory told him that it had taken him more than a month on the high roads coming south there from Maryland. There were many miles still to go.

Ball crept across North Carolina in the dark. Each morning the cold sunrise found him looking for groves of evergreen holly where he could shiver in safety through the day. A nighttime attempt to ford the frigid Roanoke River turned into a disaster. It was deeper and swifter than he remembered, and he had to swim for it. He made it to the other shore, but almost went into hypothermic shock before he could get a fire going. But now Ball was in Virginia. One day north of Richmond, a white man spotted him hiding near the high road. Within a few hours, Ball was locked in the Caroline County jail. The normal procedure was to try to ascertain where the runaway had come from and then "advertise" him or her in newspapers likely to be read there. Ball refused to say who he was, and no one there recognized him. He had already come farther than any of the jailers would have believed.

After thirty-nine days in jail, in early February 1809, Ball broke out of the flimsy building and headed northeast. At the Potomac, he found a small boat tied up on the shore. Rowing himself across, Ball hiked to the Patuxent and did the same thing. At one in the morning he reached the door of his wife's cabin. Ball stood there in shock. Perhaps he'd been replaced. Finally he summoned the courage to knock, and heard his wife respond "Who's there?" He said "Charles." And she said, "Who is this that speaks like my husband?" Like, but not the same. For his tongue sounded different now.

## 6

# BREATH

### *1824–1835*

THE COLD STARS OF the southern night glittered high above the quarters in the Tennessee cotton belt. Three hundred miles away, a man followed a northbound path by their light. Down here, the adults and youths were sitting on three log benches, pulled into a triangle around a fire that burned low. The younger children slept in the cabins. But there weren't many of them. Most of the young people were big enough to work all day. They'd been sold here away from their parents. So who would send them to bed? And things were being said that they needed to hear—and there were also things they needed to tell.

Iron spoons clanked on tin cups of cornmeal mush and rationed salt pork. It was almost contradictory that low laughs, punctuating rumbling speech, meant that what the speaker said wasn't funny. That night there were many grim chuckles. Now a girl's voice, tired from the field, began to tell a story that a child named Hettie Mitchell—not born, not even thought of yet— would eventually hear. This was the night when Hettie's one-day-to-be mother first told her own tale—how "she had been *stole*" from her parents in South Carolina. How the last sight anyone on the home place saw of her was a glimpse of a child getting bundled into a covered wagon. One hundred years later, Hettie herself would be telling the tale that got her mother to Tennessee. This night, the words her future mother spoke began to weave their way into the story of everyone else on the benches, of everybody scattered under the southern stars across ten thousand clearings like this one.[1]

If one could sit there with them, one would learn that as soon as forced migrants could understand each other's tongues, they tried to make sense of the destruction and chaos inflicted upon them. One would also hear them remembering the lost, hoping, too, that the lost would also not forget them.

For they were all lost. And one would notice another thing: the same phrases, again and again. "I saw them travel in groups. . . . They looked like cattle." "They was taking them, driving them, just like a pack of mules." "I seen people handcuffed together and drove along the Williamsburg Road like cattle. They was bought to be took south." The stories of those who endured coffle, block, and whipping-machine were as like to each other as two links forged as part of the same iron chain. But enslaved people also forged their own links. They borrowed catchphrases that resonated with their own or their relatives' experiences: "My mother and daddy done told me all about it. . . . Sold just like cows, honey, right off the block." Every teller owned a piece of this story, for the experiences and forces that the words tried to describe had shaped every teller's life. They did far better than professional historians have done at identifying the common ways that forced migration shaped their lives and that of the United States. Indeed, the storytellers concluded that forced migration was slavery's truest measure.[2]

Year after year, night after night, survivors talked and listened, creating a vast oral history that was also an argument about the nature of slavery. One million tongues were providing anyone willing to listen with an explanation for why these things had happened to them, and who was to blame. Their talking assembled them, at least for the time of the storytelling, into one body that breathed the vast and devastating common experience of slavery's expansion. For the way that enslaved migrants explained their common situation helped them to unite, cementing a baseline of solidarity that was fundamental to African-American survival. The stories that enslaved migrants whispered on the night air would also, when carried north on the tongues of intrepid messengers like Charles Ball, be powerful enough to breathe fire into the disparate elements of anti-slave-expansion sentiment in the free states. One day, enslaved people's own acts might thus bring allies to their beleaguered cause.

YET WHETHER THE POTENTIAL emergence of allies for tough but disarmed survivors could derail the most kinetically forceful economic phenomenon in the nineteenth-century world—the growth of cotton production and its transformation into textiles—was an open question that seemed to be closing in the wrong direction. For even as the disparate elements of enslaved African-American populations on slavery's frontier knitted together the words of a new common cultural tongue into a story, the powers of their world were growing even more menacing. There was no new day on the horizon on November 5, 1829, when Granville Sharp Pierce stood in the

New Orleans office of public notary William Boswell. Pierce was dealing in much more tangible transactions and effects than were the people who sat around fires talking. He was at the office to file two specific documents. Together those two pieces of paper left a trail that maps all we know about Ellen, the short seventeen-year-old woman whose name was on the documents Pierce handed to Boswell. The first document was a deed. It recorded his sale of Ellen to Barthelemy Bonny. In other states, slave sellers and buyers retained deeds of sale themselves, and most of those papers did not survive the passing years. Louisiana's Napoleonic legal code, however, required notaries to keep a record of every local slave trade. Almost all the New Orleans ledger books have survived, and they are now stored in the city's Notarial Archives on the fifth floor of the Amoco building on Poydras Street.

Pierce's transactions help to show how, even as Hettie's mother told her story, her story itself, and Ellen's too, was changing from the one Charles Ball or Rachel would have told. For the ways in which the enslaved were stolen and driven were changing. Through the 1820s, building on the ad hoc speculations of Georgia-men and Louisiana entrepreneurs, an emergent crop of professional slave traders knotted together an innovative trading system that would supply even more enslaved people to slavery's frontier and help keep slaveholding profitable everywhere. The new professionals had created a true national slave market, lungs to bring in huge gulps the oxygen of slave labor into the southwestern region, where enslavers were willing to spend the most for hands. Those lungs would keep inhaling until the end of the Civil War.

The documents accumulated by Louisiana notaries help give a clear picture of how the trade worked, in New Orleans and elsewhere, by the time Ellen got there in 1829. From 1804 to 1862, the 135,000 recorded New Orleans notarial sales map a fascinating overall profile of the changing price patterns of the slave trade at its pivot point, its biggest market. For instance, in 1820, the average price of a male "hand" between twenty-one and thirty-eight years of age had been $875 (see Figure 6.1). In 1824 that average had fallen to $498. By 1829, prices had risen again, to an average of $596. In fact, if we compare slave prices to cotton prices multiplied by the output of cotton per enslaved person—an output that was, as we know, rising under the influence of the whipping-machine—we can see that by the 1820s the price of slaves had begun to track closely with the revenue generated by the average cotton hand (see Figure 6.2). Demand from cotton-state slave buyers increased when the product of two factors multiplied together—the number of pounds picked times the price per pound—was high.[3]

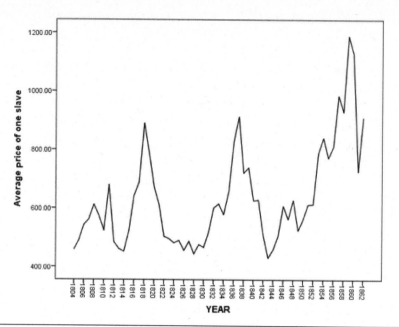

Figure 6.1. Average Price of Slaves, New Orleans, 1804–1862. *Source: New Orleans Slave Sale Sample, 1804–1862*, compiled by Robert W. Fogel and Stanley L. Engerman, University of Rochester, ICPSR07423-v2 (Ann Arbor, MI: Inter-University Consortium for Political and Social Research [producer and distributor]), 2008-08-04, doi:10.3886/ICPSR07423.v2. Price is an average of prices for all enslaved men between twenty-one and thirty-eight years of age.

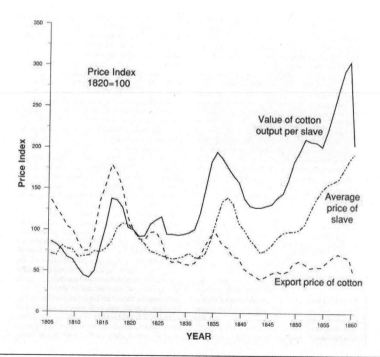

Figure 6.2. Price of Cotton, Price of a Slave, and Value of Cotton Output per Slave, 1805–1860. *Source:* Adapted from Roger Ransom, *Conflict and Compromise* (Cambridge, UK, 1989), 56.

But the legal documents of New Orleans allow us to take an even more accurate measurement of the new traders' creation—and they show that something else was happening in the 1820s. Whereas most 1815–1819 sales there had been made by entrepreneurs who traded in other goods as well, now specialized slave traders began to dominate the notarial records. These professional traders dramatically increased the scale of the forced migration of people. And when we combine the information from the first document that Boswell recorded—the deed or act of sale, which showed that Pierce was selling Ellen to Barthelemy Bonny of Orleans Parish for $420—with a second one, we can see that in the 1820s enslavers had also come as close to fully monetizing human bodies and lives as any set of capitalists have ever done. Starting in the fall of 1829, buyers and sellers also had to comply with a new Louisiana law that required everyone who imported an out-of-state slave for sale to create and file a "certificate of good character," which had to be witnessed by two property owners from the slave's home county. Louisiana state legislators were worried that the rapidly expanding trade between slavery's oldest states to slavery's newest ones was bringing in rebellious troublemakers. This certificate had to list the names of the original seller and purchaser, the sale site, and a general description of the person sold: name, age, sex, color, height. So we can see from the certificate Pierce filed with Boswell that Pierce bought Ellen in Davidson County, Tennessee—Nashville—on the 22nd of September, from Garrison Lanier. Lanier was a Davidson County resident who owned six slaves before selling Ellen.[4]

The law was in force until late 1831, and the trade concentrated mainly in the post-malaria months of late November to April, so the certificates give us two "selling seasons." In those two seasons, more than 4,200 certificates of good character entered the books of thirteen different New Orleans notaries. Add them all up, sort them, test them with statistical software, and they yield a census that is unique in the records of the internal slave trade in the United States. Such a database allows us to see, for these two years, precisely whom the slave trade pulled to the Mississippi's mouth, where they came from, and who had sold them back in the old states. This knowledge can shed new light on how professional slave traders replaced the multitasking entrepreneurs of the 1810s. The data from the notarial records can also contextualize the experiences of the people who were inside the slave trade, helping us to see what shaped the stories Ellen told when she got to Barthelemy Bonny's slave labor camp. (See Tables 6.1 and 6.2.)[5]

To begin with, the enslaved people sold in New Orleans in 1829–1831 by slave traders like Pierce were overwhelmingly from the older states that

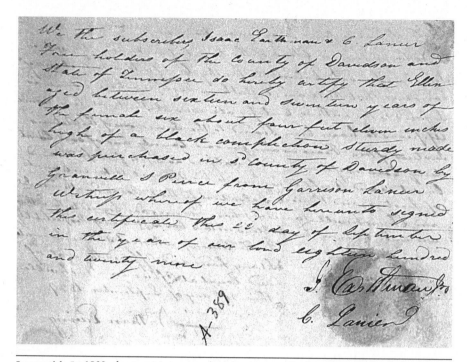

Image 6.1. In 1829, the Louisiana state legislature passed a law that required all enslaved
people brought into the state to be sold to be accompanied by a "certificate of good character." These contained personal information about the enslaved person in question, making
possible an unprecedented analysis of where they came from, when they had been sold to
the slave trader in question, and other key characteristics of their personal forced migrations. *Source:* New Orleans Parish, Acts of William Baswell, Vol. 7, p. 299, Certificate of
Good Character for Ellen, Notarial Archive, New Orleans.

constituted the heart of slavery and the African-descended population in the
United States. In 1815–1819, 33 percent of the enslaved sold in New Orleans
had come from the Chesapeake and the Carolinas. Now more than one-third
of all the certificates were issued in one state—Virginia—which one of its
natives, Louis Hughes, called the "mother of slavery." "When I was placed
upon the block," Hughes remembered, "a Mr. McGee came up and felt of
me and asked me what I could do. 'You look like a right smart nigger,' said
he, 'Virginia always produces good darkies.'" In fact, more than two-thirds
of the people transported to New Orleans between July 1829 and the end of
1831 came from the three states of North Carolina, Virginia, and Maryland.
The combined share for North Carolina and the Chesapeake—the oldest
districts of slavery in the United States—amounts to 3,009, or 77 percent of
the total (Table 6.2).[6]

TABLE 6.1. CERTIFICATE ORIGINS BY STATE, 1829–1831,
NEW ORLEANS, AND 1826–1834, NATCHEZ

| STATE OF ORIGIN | NEW ORLEANS | NATCHEZ | TOTAL |
|---|---|---|---|
| Unknown | 312 | 6 | 318 |
| | 7.4% | 0.5% | 5.8% |
| AL | 57 | 3 | 60 |
| | 1.3% | 0.2% | 1.1% |
| DC | 90 | 40 | 130 |
| | 2.1% | 3.2% | 2.4% |
| FL | 13 | 0 | 13 |
| | 0.3% | 0% | 0.2% |
| GA | 78 | 0 | 78 |
| | 1.8% | 0% | 1.4% |
| KY | 188 | 464 | 652 |
| | 4.4% | 37.2% | 11.9% |
| LA | 147 | 0 | 147 |
| | 3.5% | 0% | 2.7% |
| MD | 519 | 105 | 624 |
| | 12.3% | 8.4% | 11.4% |
| MI | 0 | 2 | 2 |
| | 0% | 0.2% | 0% |
| MO | 5 | 0 | 5 |
| | 0.1% | 0% | 0.1% |
| MS | 8 | 25 | 33 |
| | 0.2% | 2% | 0.6% |
| NC | 794 | 40 | 834 |
| | 18.7% | 3.2% | 15.2% |
| SC | 193 | 0 | 193 |
| | 4.6% | 0% | 3.5% |
| TN | 216 | 98 | 314 |
| | 5.1% | 7.9% | 5.7% |
| VA | 1,615 | 465 | 2080 |
| | 38.1% | 37.3% | 37.9% |
| *Total* | *4,235* | *1,248* | *5,483* |

*Source:* Baptist Database, collected from Notarial Archives of New Orleans and Port Register, Adams County, Mississippi (in private hands).
  * Number of persons
  ** Percent of column total

TABLE 6.2. CERTIFICATE ORIGINS BY GROUPS OF STATES, 1829–
1831, NEW ORLEANS, AND 1826–1834, NATCHEZ

| Groups of States | NEW ORLEANS | | |
| | Female | Male | Total |
| --- | --- | --- | --- |
| VA, MD, DC, NC | 1,036 (34.4%) | 1,973 (65.6%) | 3,009 (77.0%) |
| SC | 49 (25.7%) | 142 (74.3%) | 191 (4.9%) |
| KY, TN, MO | 150 (36.9%) | 257 (63.1%) | 407 (10.4%) |
| AL, GA, MS, LA | 79 (26.1%) | 224 (73.9%) | 303 (7.7%) |
| *Total* | *1,315 (33.6%)* | *2,596 (66.4%)* | *3,911* |
| | NATCHEZ | | |
| | Female | Male | Total |
| VA, MD, DC, NC | 275 (44.1%) | 349 (55.9%) | 624 (51.5%) |
| SC | 0 | 0 | 0 |
| KY, TN, MO | 279 (49.8%) | 281 (50.2%) | 560 (46.2%) |
| AL, GA, MS, LA | 18 (66.7%) | 9 (33.3%) | 27 (2.2%) |
| *Total* | *572 (47.2%)* | *639 (52.8%)* | *1,211* |
| | COMBINED | | |
| | Female | Male | Total |
| VA, MD, DC, NC | 1,311 (36.1%) | 2,322 (63.9%) | 3,633 (70.9%) |
| SC | 49 (25.7%) | 142 (74.3%) | 191 (3.7%) |
| KY, TN, MO | 429 (44.4%) | 538 (55.6%) | 967 (18.9%) |
| AL, GA, MS, LA | 97 (29.4%) | 233 (70.6%) | 330 (6.4%) |
| *Total* | *1,886 (36.8%)* | *3,235 (63.2%)* | *5,121* |

*Source:* Baptist Database, collected from Notarial Archives of New Orleans and Port Register, Adams County, Mississippi (in private hands).

In counties along the James, the Roanoke, and the Potomac, African grandparents, great-grandparents, and even further-back parents had, over the decades and centuries since they had survived the Atlantic slave trade, created the traditions and networks that enabled enslaved families to survive. They had even thrived, living longer and raising more of their own babies to healthy adulthood. But by the 1820s, enslavers had been pulling up stakes and heading southwest across the mountains to places where money could be made for three decades. As of 1850, 388,000 whites born in Virginia would live in other states. Human property, generated by enslaved people's own commitment to raising and protecting children, often represented for the enslavers who remained in the Southeast their only real wealth. Only markets in Georgia or Louisiana could render those slaves as liquid value. And by 1829, a new set of entrepreneurs was building on the earlier development of market institutions in New Orleans to create a powerful and efficient trade that unlocked the monetary value stored in the family bonds that enslaved people had built so richly in the Chesapeake and Carolinas.[7]

As early as the mid-1820s, people who visited the Mississippi Valley had been noticing this new breed of entrepreneurs. They were young men who were getting rich fast by specializing in one commodity—humans. Buying masses of enslaved people for low prices in Virginia and Maryland, these young men "thrust them into the prison-house for safe-keeping," drove their enslaved purchases "handcuffed through the country like cattle," and boated them down the rivers and around the cape of Florida to New Orleans or elsewhere to the southwest. The new entrepreneurs were efficiently connecting stored wealth to markets by handling the entire middle portion of the forced migration process. And African Americans gave them a new name. Robert Falls heard it from his mother, who told him that her enslaver sold her "to the slave speculators," who drove her and the rest of a coffle "like a pack of mules, to the market." They went through North Carolina, where, Falls later said, "she began to have fits. You see they had sold her away from her baby."[8]

One of the most famous speculators, Austin Woolfolk of Baltimore, created a number of innovations that produced increasingly efficient market connections between the old states and the slave frontier. He set up branches of his firm in both selling and buying areas, allowing his trading activities to run more or less continuously. In districts ripe with buyable slaves, such as Maryland's Eastern Shore, Austin Woolfolk and his brother John used advertisements to generate a groundswell of brand recognition. Soon competitors did the same, such as Samuel Reynolds, who came to Maryland's Eastern Shore in 1831 and placed an ad in the *Easton Republican Star*. It proclaimed that he wouldn't leave the Easton Hotel until he bought "100 NEGROES," "from the age of twelve to twenty-five years, for which he will give higher prices than any real purchaser that is now in the market." Young Frederick Douglass, who was sent back from Baltimore (where he had secretly learned to read) to rural Talbot County—Easton was the county seat—remembered that for those who didn't read the newspapers, Woolfolk's employees tacked up "flaming '*hand-bills*'"—printed in loud typefaces—"headed CASH FOR NEGROES." The Woolfolks, who bought Jacob Green's mother, paid cash. But they refused to haggle, Green recalled—they typically offered a standard rate for individuals of a particular age and sex.[9]

Just to the north of Talbot County was Kent County, another decayed rural area whose enslavers profited more from selling people than they did from selling tobacco. Thousands of whites left Kent County for greener pastures. So did African Americans, such as nine-year-old Henry Highland

Garnet, who escaped to Pennsylvania with his parents in 1824. Garnet grew up to become an advocate of African-American self-determination, famous for speeches like his 1842 "Address to the Slaves," which called for violent revolt. But most of the African Americans who left Kent County went south with speculators, not north to freedom. In 1829 through 1831, the certificates from New Orleans show, slave traders bought 100 slaves in Kent County and took them to Louisiana. Kent County at the time had about 10,000 people, 3,000 of whom were enslaved, so 100 sales equaled more than 3 percent of the enslaved.[10]

Look even closer: 97 of the Kent County slaves sold in New Orleans were between the ages of ten and thirty, and 79 were between fourteen and twenty-three, the age group that held most of those who were sold as "hands." Look with the eyes of Methodist minister and Kent County native John Dixon Long. He saw the result of these sales at the water's edge where those to be transported were to be loaded onto a ferry. A crowd of mothers, fathers, and friends waited to say goodbye to one out of every ten young men and women in the community. Armed white men kept the two crowds apart, for although a coffle-chain already bound the men and boys, everyone was a potential escape threat. Not even the women were allowed into the bushes. "I have seen [the men], at the Ferry," Long remembered, "under the necessity of violating the decencies of nature before the women, not being permitted to retire." They did the best they could, the opposite sex turning away in kindness. Then the barge grounded on the sand and the time came to say goodbye: "'Farewell, mother'; 'farewell, child'; 'farewell, John'; 'farewell, Bill.'"[11]

This scene was replayed at countless southeastern riversides and canal edges, crossroads, and eventually railroad depots every year up until the Civil War. In the 1820s, migrating enslavers and new traders moved approximately 35,000 enslaved people from Maryland and the District of Columbia; 76,000 from Virginia; and 20,000 from North Carolina—and that was only the beginning (see Table 1.1). Speculators repeatedly tapped areas that had large enslaved populations and anemic cash-crop possibilities, skimming off the cream of uncounted parents' lives: young men and women, boys and girls. Of the enslaved children aged ten and under in Virginia in 1820, only three of every four who lived would still be in Virginia ten years later. The figures for Maryland, Delaware, and North Carolina were all similar.[12]

Charles Ball had feared the Georgia-men, but beginning in the 1820s, the possibility of being sold to the southwestern interests increased dramatically. In a single year, a given person's risk might be lower than the 10 percent chance faced by young people in Kent County. But the cumulative risk of

UNITED STATES SLAVE TRADE.
1830.

Image 6.2. In the 1820s and early 1830s, the domestic slave trade from the Chesapeake and Carolinas expanded rapidly. Formerly enslaved people and white observers alike noted the upsurge in activity. This was one of the first graphical representations of both the domestic slave trade and the pervasive family separations it caused. Print c. 1830. Library of Congress.

being sold at some point in the course of the three decades of one's "salable" years was close to 50 percent for each individual. These odds also meant that many enslaved people experienced something like what Moses Grandy endured. Enslaved in eastern North Carolina during the 1820s, he watched as his wife, sister, and six children were all sold to the interstate trade. All in all, the nonstop siphoning-off stopped the demographic growth of Virginia's slave population in its tracks between 1820 and 1860.[13]

The new slave trade enabled eastern slaveholders to cash in potential wealth on distant markets. Some used the new trade to measure out their slave forces by the spoonful to the speculators, which allowed indebted planters to hold off creditors and stay in the Southeast. Other enslavers sold a few slaves to finance their own resettlement, or to set up one or more family members in the southwestern cotton-growing areas with young slaves so as to make a fortune that would save the old family establishment. "I have been disappointed in getting the negroes I expected of Mrs. Banister," wrote S. C. Archer, who was trying to get in on the slave-trade business. "She intends sending her son Robert out [to Mississippi] as soon as he is old enough to manage all of her negroes for her."[14]

Individual entrepreneurs penetrated different states in different ways and to different degrees. In South Carolina, collectively they produced a highly centralized output to interstate trade, in which most slaves destined for the New Orleans market were sold in Charleston. Judging from their height—65.3 inches, on average, for adult males, 3 inches shorter than southern white men—most of the South Carolina slaves who were sold came from the under-fed and malarial rice plantations of the low country (see Table 6.3). But that didn't stop Leon Chabert of New Orleans, the trader responsible for a large percentage of South Carolina purchases, from basing his business on them.

North Carolina, in contrast, was a terrain of vast rural stretches and little infrastructure. Its slave trade focused on a few towns, such as Salisbury in Rowan County in the western Piedmont. And here a series of men dominated the buying and transporting of slaves from the surrounding catchment area. In 1829–1830, it was James Huie. Within a few years Huie was displaced by local sheriff Tyre Glen and his confederates R. J. Puryear and Isaac Jarratt. Craven County, on the coastal sound, was the nexus of another significant trade, a concentration point for slaves brought in by sellers from outlying dis-tricts. A third major point was Chowan County in the northeastern swamps, where the county seat was the port town of Edenton.[15]

In Virginia the slave market was even more widespread. In 1829–1831, forty-one of the state's counties sent at least fifteen people to Louisiana for sale. The whole state was, in the words of a former slave, "a regular slave market." Professional slave-buyers traveled up and down every road and canal, peering into every courthouse town. Slave-selling financed the re-making of the Old Dominion's political economy: Francis Rives reinvested profits from his Alabama slave-trading journeys in a coal-dealing firm that eventually supplied early railroads and factories with fuel. Thus the market for human flesh funded a new economy that was to be less dependent on plantation-style production, although newly dug canals kept bringing boats from the foothills of the mountains to the slave market in Richmond.[16]

Well-supplied with tempting cash by profit-savvy southeastern banks, slave-buyers in the 1820s and onward disciplined sellers to bring in exactly the kind of people the southwestern market sought. For instance, when Jacob Bell sold twenty-year-old Lewis to slave trader John Maydwell on September 1, 1830, in Kent County, Maryland, Maydwell was getting Bell's most valu-able property. Perhaps Bell would've preferred to keep Lewis, his only adult male slave, to work for him in Kent County. But Lewis would yield Maydwell $500 in profit when he was resold in New Orleans two months later. And Lewis was typical of those whom the traders extracted from the old states' enslavers. First, he was young: 84 percent of those bought in the Southeast for New Orleans between 1829 and 1831 were between the ages of eleven and

TABLE 6.3. MEAN HEIGHTS OF ADULTS, BY STATE OF ORIGIN, FROM NEW ORLEANS SLAVE SALES, 1829–1831

| GROUPS OF STATES | | MEAN HEIGHT (INCHES) | NUMBER OF ADULTS | STANDARD DEVIATION |
|---|---|---|---|---|
| VA, DC, MD, NC | F | 62.86 | 397 | 2.512 |
| | M | 66.82 | 1,537 | 2.728 |
| | *Total* | *66.01* | *1,934* | *3.124* |
| SC | F | 63.40 | 31 | 2.082 |
| | M | 65.29 | 114 | 2.311 |
| | *Total* | *64.88* | *145* | *2.386* |
| KY, TN, MO | F | 64.38 | 114 | 2.860 |
| | M | 68.35 | 338 | 3.052 |
| | *Total* | *67.32* | *452* | *3.484* |
| AL, GA, MS, LA | F | 63.67 | 30 | 3.399 |
| | M | 67.18 | 77 | 2.817 |
| | *Total* | *66.20* | *107* | *3.370* |
| Total | F | 63.22 | 572 | 2.671 |
| | M | 67.00 | 2,066 | 2.850 |
| | *Total* | *66.18* | *2,638* | *3.215* |

*Source:* Baptist Database, collected from Notarial Archives of New Orleans.

twenty-four. Second, he was male, and third, he was sold alone. Two-thirds of those brought southwest to New Orleans were male, and most were sold solo, without family or spouses. Even among the women of childbearing age, 93 percent were sold without children. "One night I lay down on the straw mattress with my mammy, and the next morning I woke up and she was gone," recalled one former slave, Viney Baker.[17]

Austin Woolfolk's corporate organization included systematic channels of communication and exchange, widespread advertising, consistent pricing, cash payments, and fixed locations. He and his relatives concentrated people at fixed points in preparation for making large-scale shipments. Moses Grandy saw a set of Woolfolk's barges coming into Norfolk, Virginia, from the Eastern Shore. Or, rather, he heard the boats, "laden with cattle and coloured people," easing into the slack water by the docks. "Cattle were lowing for their calves, and the men and women were crying for their husbands, wives, or children." The Woolfolks also shipped slaves across the Chesapeake to Baltimore's Inner Harbor. Employees there offloaded enslaved passengers by night and marched them east up Pratt Street through the heart of today's downtown Baltimore. Their "dead, heavy footsteps" and "piteous cries" woke young Frederick Douglass, who was living there in his enslaver's townhouse. When the chained gang reached the end of the street, it was driven through an underground passageway that led up and out into the courtyard of a private "jail" designed for the trade. No more warehouses, barns, and taverns. From the jail, the Woolfolks sent slaves out to New Orleans by the sea route in regular dispatches, often renting entire vessels that carried one hundred or more people at a time. The vertical integration of this multistate enterprise enabled Austin Woolfolk, who had started as a mere Georgia-man, to pile up so much wealth that he could now play the grand gentleman. When University of North Carolina professor Ethan Allen Andrews visited Woolfolk at his Pratt Street pen in the 1830s, neighbors told him not only that Austin was "a most mild and indulgent master," but also that his cash payments and standard prices proved he was "an upright and scrupulously honest man."[18]

In the old Southeast, white people bought and sold black people on exceptional days. "It was customary," wrote ex-slave Allen Parker of the early nineteenth century, "for those having slaves to let, to take them to some prominent place, such as a point where two roads crossed, on the first day of the New Year." Quarterly court days also generated holiday crowds sufficient for community auctions, while Sundays, when gentlemen traded horses and people in the yard outside of the church, were also typical sale days. The certificates from New Orleans reveal, however, that from the 1820s onward traders like Woolfolk were buying slaves not on a traditional calendar of rural time, but in countless individual transactions throughout a new business year. Of the 4,000-plus certificates from southeastern states in the Notarial Archives, 89 percent were created on weekdays—Monday through Friday, which constitute only 71 percent of the week. One reason: individual sales on individual days in "business" places (such as the bar of the Easton Hotel, where Austin's brother, John, met sellers) eliminated a problem: the possibility of staged auction bids by locals who might collude with sellers to drive up the prices. Slave buying and selling was no longer extraordinary, but ordinary, something businessmen did on business days. For despite Austin Woolfolk's paternalistic act, his business was separating spouses and orphaning children. He and the new slave traders transformed the selling of human beings in the southeastern United States into a modern retrovirus, an economic organism that respected no ties or traditions and rewired everything around itself so that capitalism's enzymes of creation and destruction could flow unimpeded.[19]

At the same time, the new convenience of slave-selling also met sellers' desires and needs. Soon enough, authors building on free-floating cultural excuses would publish plantation novels that painted Chesapeake enslavers as reluctant slave-sellers who were driven by debt or other forms of catastrophe to send family property to the market in order to raise money. But the pattern of sales does not suggest that enslavers were paternalistic planters who had fallen on hard times, and who were thus being forced to sell off slaves to make ends meet. Instead, they were men and women who were extracting cash from small portions of their total reserves of human wealth whenever they wanted it. More than half of the slaves in the South were owned by whites who claimed twenty or more people as their property. Two-thirds of the sales in the 1829–1831 records were executed by slave owners who sold no more than four slaves during this time span. If they had been hit by catastrophe, surely they would have sold more slaves all at once. "I am in want of money," wrote B. S. King of Raleigh, North Carolina, in 1825, even as he mumbled about the moral repercussions of selling a man away from his wife. In the end, "I am in want of money" usually won. "You know every time they needed money they would sell a slave," said Robert Falls. Traders calibrated their innovations not only for southwestern entrepreneurs who wanted hands, but also to provide a highly useful service to southeastern white folks—the ability to turn a person into cash at the shortest possible notice.[20]

THE DOCUMENTS CREATED IN William Boswell's New Orleans notary office reveal another reason why the Missouri crisis was not even a blip on the long upward climb of slavery's expansion, which in the 1820s saw the transfer of 150,000 enslaved people from the southeastern states to the southwestern states and territories and an increase in US cotton production from 350,000 four-hundred-pound bales in 1819 to more than 800,000 in 1830. The name with which Ellen's seller acknowledged his receipt of Barthelemy Bonny's $450 was a strange one, especially for a man who fished the seas of Kent County and its surroundings. Granville Sharp Pierce's parents had chosen to name him after a different kind of disciple: the eighteenth-century Anglican priest Granville Sharp. That original Granville had been known for several things, including his research on the grammar of biblical Greek. But Sharp was most famous as an international abolitionist. In the early 1770s, James Somersett, an enslaved man born in Virginia, was brought by his enslaver to London. There he escaped and sought Granville Sharp's help: the runaway wanted to sue for freedom in a London court. Somersett won the case. The decision ruled that slaves became free the moment they set foot on Great Britain itself, although slavery remained legal in the rest of Britain's empire. Sharp next attempted to convince the British authorities to prosecute the captain of the slave ship *Zong* for ordering his crew to murder 122 Africans in the middle of the Atlantic when water supplies were running low. Sharp also helped to found the colony of Sierra Leone, where the Royal Navy (once the British government abolished British participation in the international slave trade in 1808) would land Africans recovered from captured slave ships.[21]

Granville Sharp was emblematic of an earlier generation of English-speaking antislavery activists. Their late eighteenth-century offensive targeted the first slavery, especially that of the sugar islands. That system depended, above all, on the Middle Passage, they charged, and they sought to limit slavery by ending the Atlantic trade. The American version of this long-gone antislavery movement had helped to emancipate slaves in marginal areas of the North. What these movements had in common was that they were composed of elite men who were trying to convince centralized power—Parliament, Congress, state legislatures elected by property-owning citizens—to mandate change through legislative or royal decree. Despite its elitism, Granville Sharp's generation did shift the center of polite society's opinion against the Middle Passage. By 1808, the governments of both the United States and Great Britain had outlawed their citizens' participation in the international slave trade. Sharp and his allies had concentrated on the international slave trade because they believed that without the continual importation of new slaves from Africa, the sugar plantations of the Caribbean would die out.[22]

Yet even as northern states were freeing most of their last slaves in the 1820s, the claim that slavery harmed the American political economy looked less persuasive every day in light of cotton's astonishing profits. The interstate slave trade mocked the hopes of the abolitionists that slavery would die on its own. And Granville Sharp's generation had not been replaced. No substantive opposition to the expansion of slavery existed among white Americans. After the Missouri Compromise, active white opposition to slavery dwindled toward the vanishing point. Most of those who conceded that slavery was morally wrong in the abstract refused to do anything concrete about it. It was easy to blame Georgia-men for "excesses," as all the while the speculator upgraded the Georgia-man. It was easy to propose the transportation of African Americans "back" to an Africa that they had never seen. It would never happen. John Quincy Adams, for instance, only needed to calculate on his fingers to see that hoping for an end to slavery through "colonization" was a "day-dream." And all the while, every new hand in every new cotton field meant markets for northern produce, more foreign exchange, cheaper raw materials for northern industry, and more opportunities for young Vermonters and Pennsylvanians who moved to Natchez. Slavery's defenders had won the arguments that mattered. Even a man whose parents had named him after Granville Sharp had become a speculator.[23]

In the 1820s, enslaved people on slavery's frontier faced the yoked-together powers of the world economy, a high demand for their most crucial commodity, and the creatively destructive ruling class of a muscular young republic. And they faced it all alone. For many years, enslaved people could only push back with hushed breaths around ten thousand fires on the southwestern cotton plantations—or in the Southeast, among those left behind. Although they had to keep them from white ears, the words that made up their critique of slavery mattered tremendously to them and to the future. Around the fires, or late at night with a mouth pressed to the ear of the person with whom one shared a bed, or coded in the testimony of the faithful at all-black religious meetings, enslaved people said the word "stole," and so described a history that undermined all of the implicit and explicit claims enslavers made to defend slavery. Among those with whom they now spoke a common tongue, they dared to disagree with the claim that slavery would expand, and that no one should do anything much to interfere. They rejected the claim that God, nature, or history had destined them for slavery. They exposed the assumption that white people's needs ought to trump their own, or the idea that money ought to trump conscience, pitting this word of their own against every word written on papers like the ones Granville Sharp Pierce carried with him to William Boswell's office.

"My mother and uncle Robert and Joe," said Margaret Nickerson of Florida, "[they] was stole from Virginia and fetched here." Lewis Brown explained his own genealogy in this way: "My mother was stole. The speculators stole her and they brought her to Kemper County, Mississippi, and sold her." Over and over, enslaved people said that when they were sold, or otherwise forced to move, they had been "stolen." In so telling their personal histories, they accomplished two things. First, they used a newly common tongue to make their own personal histories part of a larger story. And second, they made it clear that this common story was a crime story. Buying and selling people was a crime. Buyers and sellers were criminals.[24]

Critiques of slavery as theft had been made before. But the context was different now. The international slave trade was closed, and enslavers could pose as the architects of a "domesticated" system no longer sustained by wars of enslavement in Africa. Meanwhile, the New Orleans notarial records, like all the legal records of southern slavery, described the rupture that Granville Sharp Pierce imposed on Ellen's life as a legitimate transaction in legally held property. Most whites, whether in the North or the South, believed that slave owners had obtained their slaves by orderly business transactions, well recorded in law. And as the economy changed, they were suggesting that owners of property should be able to do whatever they wanted with what they legally owned. In such a context, when enslaved people said to each other, "We have been stolen," they were preparing a radical assault on enslavers' implicit and explicit claims to legitimacy, one that would lay an axe to the intellectual root of every white excuse—even ones that hadn't yet been dreamed up. For describing slavery and its expansion as stealing meant that slavery was not merely an awkward inconsistency in the American republican experiment, or even a source of discourse about sectional difference. Slavery was not, then, merely something that pained white people to see. Instead, "stealing" says, slavery is a crime.

One word, "stole," came to be a history—an interpretation of the past and how it shaped the present—from Maryland to South Carolina to Texas and everywhere in between. Enslaved people recognized that the slavery they were experiencing was shaped by the ability of whites to move African Americans' bodies wherever they wanted. Forced migration created markets that allowed whites to extract profit from human beings. It brought about a kind of isolation that permitted enslavers to use torture to extract new kinds of labor. It led to disease, hunger, and other kinds of deadly privations. So as these vernacular historians tried to make sense of their own battered lives, the word "stole" became the core of a story that explained. It revealed that what feet had to undergo, and the way the violence of separation ripped hearts open and turned hands against body and soul, these were all ultimately produced by the way enslavers were able to use property claims in order to deploy people as commodities at the entrepreneurial edge of the modern world economy.

In this critique, slaveholders were not innocent heirs of history, which is what Jefferson had made them out to be. Instead, slavery's expansion was consciously chosen, a crime with intent. Years after slavery ended, former slave Charles Grandy reflected on the motives of the enslavers who had shipped him from Virginia to New Orleans for sale. After a lifetime, he had made it back to Norfolk. Now he asked his interviewer, an African-American academic just like Claude Anderson of Hampton University, if the young man understood the significance of the statue of the Confederate soldier that loomed on a high pillar down by the harbor. Grandy himself had once passed the statue's eventual site in the hold of a slave ship. "Know what it mean?" Grandy asked. But the question mark was rhetorical, he already had an answer ready: it meant, he told the interviewer, "Carry the nigger down south if you want to rule him."[25]

The statue stood as a post-hoc justification for the same desires that had led whites to steal him from his Virginia life, or Hettie Mitchell's mother from her Carolina parents. For if you want to *rule* a person, *steal* the person. Steal him from his people and steal him from his own right hand, from everything he has grown up knowing. Take her to a place where you can steal everything else from her: her future, her creativity, her womb. That was the true cause working behind the history of the nineteenth century, Grandy insisted, from slavery's expansion to its political defense, and to the war that its proponents eventually started. Talk about "stealing" forces a focus on the slave trade, on the expansion of slavery, on the right hand in the market, on the left picking ever faster in the cotton fields. In this story there is no good master, no legitimate heir to the ownership of slave property, no kindly plantation owner, only the ability of the strong to take from others. Stealing can never be an orderly system undergirded by property rights, cushioned by family-like relationships. There is no balance between contradictory elements. There is only chaos and violence. So when enslaved people insisted that the slave trade was the crystalline form of slavery-as-theft, they ripped the veils off a modern and modernizing form of slavery, one that could not be stabilized or contained. Constant disruption, creation, and destruction once more: this was its nature.

"I heard this over again so many, many times before grandmother died," said Helen Odom of her grandmother's story about being taken to Arkansas and sold—"the greatest event in her life." Talking with each other night after night about how slavery's expansion had shaped their own lives, enslaved people, taken away or left behind, created a vernacular tradition of history that encouraged storytellers to bend every migration tale around the fulcrum of theft. And almost every tale fit. The standard methods used by slave traders were, indeed, much like kidnapping, just as the tales said. If you had been seized, tied to the saddle of a horse like a sack of meal, and ridden off without a chance to kiss your wife goodbye forever—this is what happened to William Grose of Virginia in the 1820s—you might compare your experience to that of being kidnapped.[26]

Some African Americans who toiled in the cotton and sugar fields had in fact been literally "stolen" even within the framework of whites' property claims. John Brown watched slave trader Starling Finney and his men abduct a girl from her owner in South Carolina. The thieves kept her in the wagon on the way down to Georgia, partly so that they could repeatedly gang-rape her, but also to hide her from potential pursuit by the girl's owner. Julia Blanks said that her grandmother was freeborn in Virginia or Maryland, but whites lured her into a coach in Washington, DC, drove her to the White House, and presented her as a gift to Andrew Jackson's niece. Still other slaves, who had been expecting freedom under the gradual emancipation laws of northern states, found themselves in Louisiana or Mississippi when unscrupulous owners sold them south before their freedom came. Between 1825 and 1827, Joseph Watson, the mayor of Philadelphia, pursued at least twenty-five cases in which free African Americans from his border-state area had been abducted and taken to Mississippi and Alabama. Most were children. Watson hired lawyers in Mississippi, wrote letters to slave-state government officials, and tried to organize prosecution of the alleged kidnappers, to little avail.[27]

Sometimes enslaved people conflated kidnapping and plain old-fashioned slave dealing because, like Carey Davenport's father, they were unsure of their actual legal status. Davenport's father was supposedly promised freedom by his "old, old master" in Richmond. But after the old man's death, his son "steal him into slavery again," said Davenport. People who claimed to be kidnapped free men or women might have been looking for some sort of individual "out" from the shame of slave origins. Not I, someone like James Green might suggest, I did not belong in slavery, because I, as an individual, was kidnapped. His father, he said, was a "full-blooded Indian." His mother's owner, "Master Williams," who "[called] me 'free boy,'" walked "free" James down the street to the Petersburg, Virginia, auction block one day and had him sold to Texas. Green spoke as if it had all been a mistake. *He* never should have been subjected to slavery's humiliations. But Green's daughter called him on his self-deception. She "took exception," remembered the interviewer who met them both, "to her father's claim that he was half Indian." She knew that her father's lighter skin and ambiguous status ("I never had to do much work [in Virginia] for nobody but my mother") revealed that "master Williams" had actually put his own son on the auction block.[28]

To the enslaved, only one other set of events in remembered history seemed as significant as the forced migration that was consuming their families and communities at an accelerating rate in the 1820s. Long after 1808, plenty of people in the South could still talk about how they had been stolen from Africa into the Middle Passage. In 1844, asked to give his age, an African-born Florida man replied, "Me no know, massa, Buckra man steal niggar year year ago." To understand and explain the expansion of slavery in which they found themselves, American-born listeners borrowed terms from African survivors who had told them of how the first slavery had been made. "They always done tell it am wrong to lie and steal," said Josephine Hubbard. "So why did the white folks steal my mammy and her mammy from Africa?" "They talks a heap 'bout the niggers stealing," said Shang Harris. "What was the first stealing done? It was in Afriky, when the white folks stole the niggers."[29]

In the 1820s and 1830s, as the new professional slave trade in hands became institutionalized and expanded exponentially, so did the stories and so did the number of tellers. The themes of theft, the indictment of whites, and the understanding that the personal disruptions drove a new form of slavery all deepened. Anyone, enslaved people came to understand, could be taken and transported southwest. All of those taken were in some way stolen, for the basic rituals of this emerging, modern market society were absurd disguises for thievery. So, for instance, implied the apocryphal tale of a woman named Venus, whose story circulated around southern fires for decades. Shoved onto the auction block by her enslaver, Venus scowled down at those who eagerly bid on her. Then she interrupted the auctioneer's patter with a sarcastic shout: "Weigh them cattle!" Such stories became classics, delivering again and again a powerful freight of indictment of whites, leading listeners from their own particular experiences into wider criticism of the absurdity of buying and selling human beings as property. "What was the law"—the one that should be, or even, in the case of children kidnapped from free states, the law that white people themselves had written—"what was the law, when bright shiny money was in sight?" asked Charley Barbour. "Money make the train go . . . and at that time I expect money make the ships go"—to New Orleans with slaves, to Britain with cotton. Instead of being individual misfortunes, enslaved people realized their own experiences were part of a giant historical robbery, a forced transfer of value that they saw every day in the form of widening clearings, cotton bales moving toward markets, and slave coffles heading further in.[30]

African Americans were not confused about what they thought of slavery's expansion. Yet in the 1820s enslaved people's vernacular history of being stolen was still hidden on the breath of captives. And these captives had been carried far away from any audience that had the political or economic power to do much about the situation of enslaved people, or about the endlessly multiplied theft that was still in progress. Forced migration taught enslaved people to call slavery stealing, and it provoked them to take extreme measures to escape. In 1826, an ad appeared in the *Natchez Gazette* offering $50 for anyone who could capture Jim, a slave who had escaped from owner

William Barrow. Purchased from Austin Woolfolk late the preceding fall at New Orleans, Jim had now run away, and Barrow suspected he'd try to "pass for free" on steamboats. Jim had a speech impediment, Barrow's ad pointed out. Geography also impeded escape. Most likely, Jim did not make it, although a few did. The same new technology that sped the passage of enslaved migrants up the rivers of the cotton country could also carry stowaways out.[31]

The enormity of what was happening in the cotton fields and traders' jails of the new South was still only beginning to leak out in the 1820s. Runaways would carry most of what was carried: it wasn't going to leak out with many whites. Most found ways to accommodate themselves to what they saw, to sweep the inconvenient fragments under the rug. "Mrs. Ann Anderson sat by her window and cried," remembered ex-slave Elisha Green, seeing in his mind again a white woman in the house where he'd worked back in Mayslick, Kentucky. Wagons filled with crying children came down the street as she watched, and then a clanking caterpillar of men in irons followed. The oldest, in the lead, "looked to be about seventy years old, and he sang: 'Hark from the tomb'"—a doleful hymn that in 1825 was already old-fashioned. So Mrs. Ann Anderson wept. And sat still.[32]

In the 1820s, a few scattered white dissidents were trying to raise the issue of slavery. But these white folks were in practical terms almost as powerless as white folks could be in this era of American history. For instance, there were the southern Quakers, or at least a few of them. Although Pennsylvania was the settlement of New World Quakers, members of the Society of Friends—as the Quakers officially denominated themselves—had lived in North Carolina since the early eighteenth century. During the late eighteenth and early nineteenth centuries, as other denominations of Protestants in the South accommodated themselves to slavery, many North Carolina Quakers chose slavery over their own religious identity. But a few reacted against slavery's deepening. There was Rachel Leonard, who became the first white woman to address a mixed male-female gathering on the subject when she read her "Address" to the North Carolina Manumission Society in the 1820s. Then there was Elihu Embree, an eastern Tennessee Quaker, who in the early 1810s saw enslaved people being driven in irons along the roads across the mountains. Embree couldn't sit by the window. He freed his own slaves and launched a newspaper called *The Emancipator*. His editorials rejected conventional excuses, such as Thomas Jefferson's claim that separation from loved ones mattered little to African Americans. No, insisted Embree, enslaved people had as much "sensibility and attachment" to their families as Jefferson did.[33]

These isolated dissidents were often unable to see beyond the assumptions that they took on board with their own self-identification as white. But at their best, they knew that slavery was changing and moving, and they knew that slavery's growth troubled them in ways that could not be dealt with in the sphere of normal political calculations and regional rivalries. At the same time, other white southerners began to see dissent as more problematic, especially after the Missouri crisis. By the time Embree died in 1820, some of his local associates, including fellow Quaker Charles Osborn, had already been forced out of Tennessee. Osborn moved to free-state Ohio and established *The Philanthropist*, the first newspaper to advocate the unconditional abolition of slavery. He also met a young New Jersey Quaker named Benjamin Lundy. At nineteen, Lundy had gone to the Ohio Valley to practice his trade of saddle-making. In Wheeling, Virginia, which linked the Virginia valleys to the Ohio River and ultimately New Orleans, he realized the extent of the slave-trade network. Wheeling, he wrote, was part of "a great thoroughfare for the traffickers in human flesh. Their *'coffles'* passed through the place frequently. My heart was deeply grieved. . . . I heard the wail of the captive; I felt his pang of distress; and the iron entered my soul." Lundy moved Embree's *Emancipator* to Baltimore and renamed it *The Genius of Universal Emancipation*.[34]

"Genius" meant "Spirit"—or "breath," and Lundy's paper was the first white-run abolitionist newspaper to keep breathing for more than a handful of issues. Initially, Lundy used it to support the program of the American Colonization Society (ACS), which in the 1820s was the only prominent white organization to make a claim to being against slavery. The ACS proposed to solve the problem of slavery by shipping emancipated slaves to Africa and elsewhere. Even this expedient was too antislavery for many whites. The escape of any African American, including the already-free, shrank the potential market in stolen humans. Perhaps that explains the murderous sentiment of the hired captain of an 1826 Quaker-sponsored voyage to resettle freed slaves in Haiti. He told his Quaker employer he'd prefer to tie the forty emancipated African Americans on the ship to the Quaker himself and drown them all in "the Gulph Stream."[35]

Most free African Americans despised the ACS, believing that the country of their birth was their country. A Quaker who interviewed free people of color in North Carolina learned that most were only considering transportation out of their home state because slave traders kept kidnapping their children. Once Lundy settled in Baltimore, African Americans convinced him to move from colonization to advocacy of the immediate and unconditional end of slavery. In the 1820s, Baltimore was the biggest center of the domestic slave trade on the East Coast. African Americans left behind there had much to say about the trade that had taken so many of their kinfolk. Their conversations with Lundy agitated him into confrontation with powerful pro-slave-expansion interests. Soon, Lundy was charging in the pages of *The Genius* that all slaveholders were "disgraceful whoremongers" who bred human beings for the market. He saved his greatest fury for the Woolfolks, describing the family as a set of lawless "pirates" whose "heart rending cruelty" caused "fatal corruption in the body politic."[36]

On January 9, 1827, Austin Woolfolk approached Lundy as the editor was locking up his print shop for the day. Woolfolk threw the Quaker to the ground and beat him severely, then walked away. Lundy pressed assault charges against Woolfolk. But when the case came to trial, the judge declared that the editor deserved "chastisement." He fined the slave trader one whole dollar and then gave a speech praising the slave trade's economic benefits to the state of Maryland. He added that Woolfolk also had removed a "great many rogues and vagabonds who were a nuisance in the state." (The government of Louisiana would have been unhappy to hear that the Maryland justice system encouraged the transportation of dangerous slaves to New Orleans.)[37]

Lundy had an apprentice, a young man from Newburyport, Massachusetts. His name was William Lloyd Garrison. Every day, as he set the type for the next issue of *The Genius*, Garrison listened thoughtfully to local African-American men—men such as William Watkins and Jacob Greener, who came to the printing shop to talk with Lundy and each other. What they said "revealed," as Garrison later put it, "the radical doctrine of *immediate, unconditional* emancipation." Lundy began to travel more, and his extended absences gave Garrison a chance to run the paper himself. It quickly became clear that the apprentice had a stronger taste for confrontation—and unlike the diminutive Lundy, Garrison was built like a linebacker. When Garrison labeled Francis Todd, a Massachusetts shipowner whose vessel had transported seventy-five slaves to Louisiana, a "highway robber and murderer" and an "enemy of the human species," Todd decided the courts were the better part of valor. He sued Garrison for libel and won. Garrison couldn't pay his fine, so he was sentenced to six months in jail. After his release, Garrison headed north—another slave-trade-driven migration. Settling in Boston, he launched a new paper, called *The Liberator*.[38]

Free African Americans were already using the boom in newspaper publication and readership to spread what they had seen and heard from those who had survived forced migration. In 1827, Samuel Cornish began to publish the New York *Freedom's Journal*. Cornish, an African American who had been born free in Delaware, had spent 1819 as a missionary to enslaved people on Maryland's Eastern Shore, just as the long-distance trade to New Orleans was beginning to drain hands from places like Kent County. The newspaper's first issue contained a harrowing account of something he'd seen there: the sale of a man to a trader Cornish identified as "Mr. W*."[39]

*Freedom's Journal* was the first African-American newspaper in the United States. It was not Cornish, however, but his Boston subscription agent who made the most influential case that slavery was getting worse and bigger, not better and smaller. Born free in North Carolina, David Walker had also lived in Charleston. There, in 1822, he saw panicked whites torture and execute over thirty enslaved men who had allegedly conspired with a free black man named Denmark Vesey to launch a slave revolt. Fearing for his safety, Walker moved to Boston, where he established a secondhand clothing shop in the city's African-American neighborhood. (Garrison, who relied heavily on black subscribers and donors in order to publish *The Liberator*, established his printing shop in the same neighborhood.) Walker's store was the end of the cotton chain, and as he sat in it, he breathed the dust of frayed fibers that had originally been pulled from the boll by southwestern hands.[40]

The fibers had a tale to tell, as did the free black sailors who shopped in Walker's store. When night fell, he wrote these stories down in his office at the back of the narrow shop. He shaped his thoughts into four devastating essays and put them between the covers of one book—and when *An Appeal to the Coloured Citizens of the World* appeared in September 1829, it was like nothing anyone had ever read before, though it had all been said around a thousand fires. In it, Walker ferociously assailed slavery, slaveholders, and their enablers. Most whites, he charged, either directly or tacitly supported slavery and were thus "our natural enemies"—though slave traders were particular "*devils*."

Walker insisted that the dynamism of nineteenth-century slavery made it worse than earlier forms: the ancient Spartans did not lock the Helots in coffles and drag them "from their wives and children, children from their parents, mothers from their suckling babes." In 1776, "there were but thirteen States in the Union," but after half a century, "now there are twenty-four, most of which are slave-holding States, and the whites are dragging us around in chains and in handcuffs, to their new States and Territories to work their mines and farms, to enrich them and their children." He'd read, in white Carolinians' newspapers, stories decrying the way the Turks denied the Greeks their independence, and "in the same paper was an advertisement, which said 'Eight well built Virginia and Maryland *Negro fellows* and four *wenches* will positively be sold this day *to the highest bidder!*'"

"Americans! I ask you candidly," wrote Walker, "was your sufferings under Great Britain one hundredth part as cruel and tyrannical as you have rendered ours under you?" Turning to black readers, he proclaimed that "freedom is your natural right." Walker was playing with fire. He knew how dangerous whites could become. Even white abolitionists feared that violent resistance would turn white audiences against emancipation. But whites had treated enslaved Africans as if it were no crime to bind them "with chains and hand-cuffs," and then "beat and murder them as they would *rattle-snakes*." Thus black people had the same right to defend themselves against crimes and oppressions claimed by America's revolutionaries. "It is no more harm for you to kill a man who is trying to kill you than it is for you to take a drink of water when thirsty." And so he praised "Hayti[,] the glory of the blacks and the terror of tyrants . . . men who would be cut off to a man, before they would yield to the combined forces of the whole world." So: "Act like men." Prepare, Walker commanded slavery-survivors in the tones of an Old Testament prophet, to inflict the consequences of sin if justice was not done, even if that meant facing one's own death in the effort. Once the battle was joined, once they saw that victory was possible, slaves would be willing to pay the cost: "Let twelve black men get well armed for battle, and they will kill and put to flight fifty whites. . . . Once you get them started, they glory in death." For enforced submission disguised mighty rage beneath: "As Mr. Jefferson wisely said, they have never *found us out*."[41]

Walker's statements required real courage in an era when Granville Sharp had morphed into Granville Sharp Pierce. "If any wish to plunge me into the wretched incapacity of a slave, or murder me for [telling] the truth, know ye, that I am in the hand of God," he wrote. "What is the use of living, when in fact I am dead." Hoping to get a rebellion started, Walker stuffed copies of the pamphlet into the pockets of pants and jackets that he sold to sailors. Some knowing, some not, they carried the spore of Walker's words into the harbors of the slave states, where almost all American merchant ships made annual pilgrimages to pick up cotton bales.[42]

In March 1830, authorities in Savannah, New Orleans, and Charleston began to find copies of Walker's *Appeal* in the possession of free blacks. They immediately went into panic mode. Seeking to quarantine the pamphlet like a contagious disease, southern state governments banned free black sailors from disembarking from their merchant vessels. They panicked at rumors of slave revolts from New Bern, North Carolina, to the other end of the pipeline of stolen people in Opelousas, Louisiana. Georgia and Mississippi passed laws imposing the death penalty on free black people who disseminated antislavery materials. State legislatures planned to ban the teaching of literacy to enslaved African Americans. Instruction in basic mathematics would remain legal, however, so that black drivers would be able to subtract the number of pounds of cotton picked from the quota, thus deriving the requisite number of lashes to deliver.[43]

Unlike other political questions, abolition talk carried with it the seed of revolutionary violence. Therefore, southern officials and newspaper writers claimed, it was not protected speech. Savannah's mayor sent a letter to his Boston counterpart, Harrison Otis, asking the conservative New England politician to arrest the old-clothes dealer for publishing "such a highly inflammatory work." Though sympathetic to the request, the Boston mayor had to refuse. Walker had broken no Massachusetts law. Rumors in Boston claimed that various southern state governments had put a bounty of $3,000 on Walker's head—double that if he was brought south still alive. In August 1830, at the age of thirty-three, he collapsed in the doorway of his shop and died in convulsions. Many African Americans in Boston believed that he had been poisoned, though no direct evidence for this survives. The official cause of death was consumption—probably what we would call tuberculosis. Or perhaps Walker had simply breathed too much cotton dust.[44]

Even with Walker dead, and black sailors locked on board their ships, the language of being "stolen" was already making its way by secret pathways out of lands that were being remade by the whipping-machine and the speculators who fed it with human flesh. Beginning in the mid-1830s, an abolitionist movement finally emerged. Much of its moral force and most trenchant analysis came from former slaves such as Frederick Douglass and other African Americans living in northern communities, including David Walker's Boston. Of them, many, like Douglass, were Southern refugees who had been pushed to escape from the slavery zone, usually as fugitives, by the new expansion of the slave trade. The new movement would also be led by white allies, most especially William Lloyd Garrison and the host of white women who signed petitions and wrote books. However, the white abolitionists would always be a small minority inside a white northern population that mostly wanted to ignore slavery.[45]

But in contrast to earlier, more half-hearted white critics, the new abolitionists now agreed that slavery needed to end, and it needed to end as soon as possible. Much of the new urgency now pulsing in their veins had been transmitted to them from formerly enslaved people who had survived the new slave trade—many of whom also became significant actors in the movement. Running beneath abolitionist activity and critique, like the spinal plates under a mountain range, were the words that forced migrants them-selves chose to use to understand their history. The language of being "stole" was everywhere in those words, so that in 1849, African-American abolition-ist William Wells Brown would assert that his "master" was in fact merely a "man who stole me as soon as I was born." Brown had first heard that phrasing not in the printed rhetoric of abolitionists, but in the philosophy of the illiterate forced migrants among whom he had once been numbered.[46]

YET THE ABOLITIONISTS' HOPE for a dramatic change was implicitly premised on the idea of converting a significant portion of the nation's white majority to their antislavery cause. In the meantime, could anything limit the damage being inflicted by the juggernaut of slavery expansion, in whose path still lay more than 2 million lives? To many enslaved African Americans, only one phenomenon seemed to offer much immediate help. And this phe-nomenon, this ally in the cause of ending slavery, came with several draw-backs: it was invisible, it was lacking in physical power, it was prone to giving commands unenforceable by law, and it was often silent.

Go back to the sale that Samuel Cornish witnessed on Maryland's Eastern Shore, but do not focus on Cornish, an educated free man confronted by the hypocrisies of the slave republic. Put aside the mental maps that draw lines of correspondence and credit to connect nodes like Baltimore to New Orleans. Brush aside, for a moment, price curves of hands sold by a professionalized slave trade. Instead, focus on the existential situation of the man that Mr. W* bought: William, a member of the Methodist church. "[Woolfolk] ordered William to stretch out his hands in order to be tied. [William] rather shrank from this, as every *honest* man would do[;] however[,] with much piety and resignation, he submitted." Watching this, his friends, fellow church mem-bers, "began to weep bitterly." William turned: "Don't cry for me! God is everywhere!" Then Woolfolk led him away.[47]

William believed that underneath the surface world, where all the powers of the world arrayed themselves against him, lay a world of the spirit where the real value would be measured. It was perhaps the same world through which an enslaved girl moved in a vision she had at a Tennessee prayer meet-ing, one which, as an old woman, eighty years later, she would recount to an interviewer. Clear as day, she remembered what she had seen: "I was travel-ing along a big road. Down on each side I saw the souls in torment. Many of them were people I had known in life. They were just roaming and stagger-ing along. They were saying 'Oh, how long?' I met on the road a great host, some walking, some on mules, some going down to hell."[48]

Image 6.3. White abolitionists and enslaved migrants both focused on the possibility—and for thousands of individuals, the reality—that free African Americans in the Chesapeake and border states were being kidnapped by criminals attracted by the new profits offered by the market in human beings. The man who has been kidnapped here wears respectable work clothes no different from those who have seized him and plan to sell him to the cotton frontier. George Bourne, *Picture of Slavery in the United States* (Middletown, CT, 1834), 120.

For those taken, for those left behind and bereaved, for all who knew that they, too, could be stolen, the acceleration of slavery's expansion was hell—separation from all that gave life in the world meaning. By the late 1820s, hell was more real than ever. William professed his faith that God was everywhere, but surely he must have wondered if God would come with him on the road through hell, into the holds of the ships tacking around Florida into the Gulf, if he would climb with William onto the block and stand beside him in the notary's office in New Orleans.

David Walker, writing in his old-clothes shop in Boston, saw the coffles in his mind's eye, and prophet-like, predicted that God would arrive on the frontier. And when he did, he would come in the form of an angel of slave rebellion to drown sinners in fire and blood, a right-handed avenging God bringing justice through the sword. Yet the failure of the 1811 revolt on Louisiana's German Coast illustrated what most individuals who had been stolen away to the frontier of slavery had breathed in as knowledge taught from the cradle. Redemption by revolt was impossible. So many enslaved migrants chose a different exit from hell on earth.

The vast expansion of slavery in the United States happened in tandem with the emergence of evangelical Protestantism. At the time of the American Revolution, most Americans had not participated actively in organized religion. Though most were nominally Protestant, few outside of New England attended church services on a weekly or even monthly basis. But by the 1850s, half or more of all white Americans had come to participate regularly in some sort of church. The vast majority were in evangelical denominations, among which the Methodists and Baptists were the most popular choices. This evangelical Christianity was not exactly like the twenty-first-century version. Unlike many of its descendants, it was usually not fundamentalist in theology. Yet like its twenty-first-century descendants, it did use an informal liturgy. And the evangelical preachers who spread across the continent (and eventually, across the oceans) insisted that those who would be redeemed needed to undergo an individual conversion experience. Instead of placing their faith in a special ceremony or in some sort of inscrutable predestination, evangelical theologies made the believer's individual choice to come to God for forgiveness the key moment of salvation.[49]

Along with millions of individual choices, the growth of slavery helped to make evangelical Protestantism the hegemonic pattern of American religion. Yet the relationship between the two expansions was complex. As of 1790, although Africans and their children had been slaves in North America for more than 160 years, few enslaved people had converted to the staid, planter-dominated Anglicanism of their enslavers. Sometime around 1770, however, the first evangelical Protestant preachers—many of them exiles from theological struggles within the churches of New England—began to travel through the South. Though the planter gentry of the Chesapeake persecuted these "New Light" ministers, other Virginians and Carolinians flocked to their revival meetings. Many enslaved people were at those gatherings. Their presence often galvanized the already emotional New Light revivals into something electric. Enslaved people born in Africa—still in the late 1700s a significant percentage of Chesapeake slaves—came from a part of the world where it was common for gods to throw people on the ground, to breathe in and through them, to ride worshippers' spirits and remake their lives. These new converts demonstrated the same intensity of conversion, and their fervor was catching. White converts modeled their conversions on enslaved people's behavior, learning that shouting and singing were appropriate responses to the breath of the divine. Some who expected to scoff with amusement at a slave preacher's sermon found themselves lying on the ground, soaked in sweat, not quite sure what had happened. Evangelical church communities adopted enslaved men and women as spiritual brothers and sisters, even as experts and guides.[50]

After the Revolution, Thomas Jefferson and James Madison framed the Virginia Statute on Religious Freedom, the law that did away with all established churches and served as the intellectual foundation for the First Amendment. "God Almighty hath created the mind of man free," began the two slave owners, and so man's government was not to impose any specific religious dogma on its citizens. But white evangelicals, prime beneficiaries of the disestablishment of the state churches that had characterized most of the prerevolutionary colonies, increasingly concluded that God Almighty was just fine with keeping the bodies of some men and women unfree. Many of the early white Baptists in Virginia had moved to Kentucky to escape religious persecution. But those same people, charged Kentucky Baptist minister David Barrow, saw no sin in separating "husband and wife"—indeed, they did so "without the least apparent signs of fellow feeling." William Thompson, enslaved in Virginia, remembered how the hypocrisy of "Christian" enslavers had spoiled his taste for evangelical religion: "I went to meeting on a Sunday after I had seen the gang chained, but the preaching did me no good." In Virginia, before the beginning of the forced migrations west, one-quarter of all Methodists had been black. In Kentucky, only 10 percent were. On Sundays at Congaree, where Charles Ball lived in South Carolina, an enslaved migrant from Virginia named Jacob led religious meetings—but most of Wade Hampton's captives preferred to spend the Sabbath raiding orchards for fruit to supplement their limited diets. And when Betsey Madison, a Virginia woman transported to Natchez in the 1790s, tried to spread her version of the faith, cotton planters tried to stop her from preaching. As Ball noted, enslavers feared that slaves "may imbibe with the morality . . . the notions of equality and liberty, contained in the gospel."[51]

Yet the power of African-influenced spiritual practices was too useful for white preachers to resist the temptation to borrow. African-American participation on the frontier would thus ultimately reshape the religious dynamic of the entire United States. In the summers of 1800 and 1801, Presbyterian, Methodist, and Baptist ministers in the Bluegrass region of Kentucky led a series of dramatic revivals. Thousands of free white and enslaved black settlers fell on church floors or wandered around shouting and jumping and praising God. They spilled out of the doors until the ministers decided to move their services outside. At the Cane Ridge meeting in August 1801, 10,000 attendees exploded into seven days of mass conversions, accompanied by fainting, ecstatic dance, visions, and unconsciousness.[52]

Soon, similar revivals broke out across slavery's frontier, dramatically increasing church membership in all denominations. Critics scoffed: "Some came to be at the camp meeting / And some perhaps to get good eating," rhymed a skeptical attendee; and as the preacher's tempo mounted, "the altar soon was filled with lasses / Some kicked so high they showed their a——." Enslaved migrants' influence also began to gall some observers. From "the *blacks'* quarter" of revival camps, complained Methodist John Watson, came Saturday-night music turned to religious purpose: extemporaneous verses "sung in the merry chorus-manner of the southern . . . husking-frolic method." Singers stomped rhythms, "the steps of actual negro dancing." We cannot "countenance or tolerate such gross perversions of true religion!"[53]

As mass revival and emotional individual conversion on the frontier reverberated back East, one could argue that enslaved migrants' influence was expanding, too. Especially after the Cane Creek revivals, a long-lasting nationwide boom of evangelical conversion transformed the American religious landscape. From zero in 1770, the number of Methodists in the United States climbed to a quarter million by 1820, and doubled in the next decade. From 1790 to 1820, the number of Baptist churches exploded, from 500 to 2,500. In some ways the process initiated by this evangelical take-off continued all the way into the twenty-first century. Continuously seeking new adherents—often by utilizing the most "modern" tools of marketing to spread their message—evangelicals have inhabited a process of constant transformation. True believers' competing claims have led to constant denominational splintering among evangelicals, with each group typically insisting that it possessed a truer fundamentalism than any other and that it was rebuilding the "primitive church" of Jesus's first followers. By the early twenty-first century, believers around the world had, in this process of creative destruction, created more than 30,000 Protestant denominations, most of which were born in the United States. Evangelical Protestantism claimed almost as many adherents worldwide as Catholicism or Islam. A young tradition, created in large part on slavery's frontier out of elements that included a healthy dose of West African religious practices, has become one of the most influential cultural exports in world history.[54]

Back to the early nineteenth century, however, and to an encounter between a white man and Pompey, a black Methodist preacher in Mississippi. Why, asked the white man, did the enslaved man sing hymns all day? "It makes my soul so happy," Pompey responded. "You simpleton," replied the white man. "A negro has no soul." New evangelical denominations have always drawn converts from the poor and the excluded—as in early twenty-first-century Brazil, for instance—because emotional conversion experiences and informal participatory services treat disempowered people as if they have souls equal in value to those of the powerful. Yet one of the fracture lines along which evangelical Protestant denominations have split has been the question of whether believers like Pompey should challenge structures of worldly power.

The "perfectionist" evangelicals who began to create and support moral reform movements in the North after 1830, including the new abolitionism, insisted that Jesus's instruction—"Feed my sheep"—required believers to improve their society and protect the weak from the sins of the strong. In the slave society, however, official theology's social prescription was slowly bent to a different frame. Over the first half of the nineteenth century, as conversion experiences and churchgoing became the expected thing for proper white citizens, most Christianized enslavers abandoned the claim that African Americans had no souls to be saved. Thus, they had to "consider the dreadful responsibility," as a Methodist minister told Natchez whites, that they "would incur if [they] prevented the Negroes from hearing the message sent by our gracious Creator to the whole family of the human race." From 1800 to the 1820s, mixed black-and-white frontier congregations emerged, and they welcomed new African-American members. When "Adam[,] a black brother," joined Louisville Baptist Church in Mississippi, all the members—white and black—greeted him with "the right hand of fellowship." As churches multiplied, more enslaved people could avoid worshipping with their masters on the Sabbath.[55]

"However sable their hue and degraded their condition in life," a group of Mississippi Baptist preachers reminded their fellow enslavers, enslaved African Americans "possess rational and immortal souls." Yet the pull of slavery distorted white evangelicals' theology, and by the 1820s whites in biracial churches were deleting rituals that recognized recently joined African Americans as "brother" and "sister." After the Missouri crisis, touchy enslavers claimed that a "Christian," paternalistic slavery would counter criticism of the South. Along with neutralizing the bad odor of the whipping-machine, ministers writing in new denominational magazines insisted that conversion to white-authenticated Christianity would not infect enslaved people with the idea that Jesus came to set the captives free. Instead, they generated a tame theology that was in many ways the Calvinist opposite of the early slave-frontier revivals, with their emphasis on a believer's decision to ask for forgiveness and faith. Even as famous northern evangelical Charles Finney told tens of thousands of converts in 1820s Erie Canal boomtowns that they could choose to turn to God for salvation, Mississippi Baptists were trying to ensure that the enslaved believed that nothing important in heaven or on earth was up to their choosing. God himself, the Baptists' state convention announced, had established their bondage: "However dark, mysterious, and unpleasant these dispensations may appear to you we have no doubt they are founded in wisdom and goodness." "The great God above has made you for the benefit of the Whiteman, who is your law maker and law giver," a Kentucky captor preached to his human property, whom he had gathered in his yard for his Sunday morning sermon.[56]

Enslaved people, however, believed otherwise. In 1821, one Georgia slave wrote a letter to a white preacher. "If I understand the white people," he wrote, "they are praying for more religion in the world." Well then, "If god sent you to preach to sinners did he direct you to keep your face to the white people constantly or is it because they give you money?" "We are carried to market and sold to the highest bidder," and whites "never once inquire whither you are sold, to a heathen or a Christian?" Yet enslaved people continued to flock to churches, even if ministers turned their backs on them, and to hold their own religious meetings as well. For in the story of Jesus, believers found kinship and a promise. Jesus was a god made mortal, a wrongly captured man who endured torture and violent death. Forced migrants already knew what it was like to journey into a grave. But the story told them that Jesus had risen from his tomb and returned to tell the captives of a new kingdom whose gate he had opened.[57]

So now one understands how that teenaged girl, the one interviewed as an old woman, had come to be in a Tennessee prayer meeting. She was agonizing over her future, specifically, over her inability to protect her first child, who had just been born, from violence, hunger, and separation. And one understands why, when the girl heard a voice no one else could hear and rose up from her knees in wonder, her own mother rushed to her side to guide her to the edge. "Pray on, daughter," she remembered the older woman telling her, "for if the Master has started to working with you, he will not stop until he has freed your soul." The mother had already traveled this road, and she pushed her fearful daughter against all the impending crucifixions she'd have to survive. "It wasn't long," the daughter remembered, before, collapsing to the ground, "I died."[58]

She fell into an abyss. But as the young woman plunged, a different voice, a new one, breathed in her ear. It told her that the thefts in her own life, and her own transcendence of them, mattered. Both, it told her, were part of the greatest drama in creation. And it told her not to hide from the pain and the fear, but to plunge into her own desolated emotions and powerless complicity, for the voice specifically said, "You must die and go to hell," or she could not live again. She twitched, and was fully in the dream.

She found herself walking down the slave trail. People who survived the southwestern daylight fields called the acres of cotton "Hell without fires" for the sad zombies and evil demons that stalked in them, but in the perpetual night on each side of this road, she could see the fires clearly. Flames raged unceasing in the cotton and logs and stumps. Beside her staggered stolen people, people lost in their chains. People who did not know their own names. She saw babies left on the ground by mothers. She heard mothers whose screams sounded like wounded animals.[59]

The coffle she was in came to the forks in the road. A little man stood there. He beckoned her to follow him up a narrow path. Because this was a dream, a vision, somehow she had come unlinked from the coffle, so follow him she did. She gasped for breath, lagging as she struggled up the path's dizzying switchbacks. So the man called down "a great multitude" of angels, and told them to sing to her as she climbed. "Mama, Mama, you must help carry the world," they chanted. What would become of her baby, what would become of her, she could not know. Somehow she had to care for, instruct, defend her child against forces too heavy to fight. She had a whole world to carry.

Then the angels began to sing her name. They sang her weary legs to the top of the stairs, where the last step emptied upon a high courtyard. There she stood, and somehow she knew she stood before God. A disembodied voice rang out. "How did she come?" Ranks of spirits flickered into sight, and they echoed the question in song. In her waking life, not even her mother knew how hard her path had been. But a second voice did know. It said what she couldn't: "She came through hard trials with the hell-hounds on her trail." She realized that voice had breathed in her ear all along. Mary and Martha, Jesus's helpers, came forward, clothed her with a new robe, and the first voice said: "You are born of God. My son delivered your soul from hell and you must go and help carry the world."

She awoke. She was alive. She believed that the most powerful forces in the universe could name the pains and fears that even she could not. These forces recognized her. From them, she was not stolen. All she had to do in return for this gift was to carry the whole world.[60]

The experience of spiritual death and rebirth reassured converted slaves that they had a value and a responsibility that went far beyond the number of dollars one could sell for, of pounds one could pick, or of babies one could bear for the market. They spoke of their own transformed spirits as being set free from the fear that their enslavers were, in the end, their final judges. "I heard a voice speak to me," said William Webb. "From that time I lost all fear of men on this earth."[61]

No matter how vigorously white preachers argued that conversion made slaves more docile, enslavers worried that freedom from fear might launch other quests for change. True, in the New Testament, as nineteenth-century Christians often heard it, the Spirit gave redemption from sin and commanded forgiveness. Many Christian slaves believed that God had commanded them to put violent vengeance aside, if only for their own souls' sake. But following the command to forgive one's enemies was a difficult task—"a lifetime job," said one ex-slave: "I don't care how long God lets me live, it will still be a hard job." And forgiveness did not mean that enslaved people believed that the thieving powers of this world would never bow, that the lowest would not one day be the highest, or that their kidnappers would never face judgment. "Him claiming to be a Christian! Well I reckon he's found out something about slave driving by now," mused ex-slave Robert Falls about his now-dead former owner, whom he believed was toiling on Satan's labor camp. "The good Lord has to get his work in some time."[62]

But there was another text available. In some books of the Old Testament, the Spirit kindled not forgiveness but the uncompromising fire of holy warriors like Sampson or Saul, commanding them to slay all the Lord's enemies down to the last man, woman, and child. And many enslaved migrants dreamed of that. "The idea of a revolution in the conditions of the whites and the blacks is the corner-stone of the religion of the latter," recalled Charles Ball of conversations among other captives of Wade Hampton. "Heaven will be no heaven" to the average slave, Ball said, "if he is not to be avenged of his enemies."[63]

Perhaps God demanded that his followers start to "get his work in," even if avengers lost their lives in the process. That impulse found fertile soil in Southampton County, Virginia, an old tobacco county where the accelerating growth of slavery carved deep scars in the 1820s. John Brown, born there around 1818—the year Francis Rives took his first coffle from Southampton to Alabama—belonged to an old white woman. She "used to call us children up to the big house every morning, and give us a dose of garlic and rue to keep us 'wholesome,' as she said, and make us 'grow likely for market.'" Then she "would make us run round a great sycamore tree in the yard, and if we did not run fast enough to please her, she used to make us nimbler by laying about us with a cow-hide."[64]

Throughout the 1820s, the new national slave market drained people like Brown from Southampton. Forty-eight of them, for instance, passed through the hands of New Orleans slave traders between late 1829 and early 1831. In Southampton, the enslaved despaired over the increasing destabilization of their temporal lives, and whites tried to extend their control over African Americans' spiritual lives. In 1826, an enslaved Southampton lay preacher named Nat Turner had told a white man named Ethelred Brantley of his religious visions. Brantley believed that Turner's touch cured him of a skin disorder. The two decided they wanted Turner to baptize Brantley at a local Methodist church, but the white church hierarchy would not let Turner perform the ritual. So Turner and Brantley went down to the river, where Turner baptized him. A crowd of whites gathered, and "reviled us." So the preacher later put it.[65]

By 1828, Nat Turner had stopped believing that he should leave vengeance in God's hands. Instead, he saw visions that he thought demanded violence: white people and black people fighting in the sky, blood condensing like dew on the corn, a voice like thunder telling him, "Such is your luck, such you are called to see, and let it come rough or smooth, you must surely bear it." Turner retreated into his wilderness. He later said, speaking to a local Southampton lawyer named Thomas R. Gray, who recorded Turner's words and published them as *The Confessions of Nat Turner*, "I heard a loud noise in the heavens, and the Spirit instantly appeared to me and said the Serpent was loosened, and Christ had laid down the yoke he had borne for the sins of men, and that I should take it on and fight against the Serpent, for the time was fast approaching when the first should be last and the last should be first." With his orders clear, Turner gathered a small group of angry, broken men into his confidence and waited for another sign. Then, in early 1831, a total eclipse blocked out the sun.[66]

THE FIRST HEADLINES DID not reach New Orleans until September 1831. But from there the news spread quickly up the river-veins of the slave frontier's network of steamboats and cotton landings. In Southampton County, on August 22, insurgent slaves had begun killing whites. Almost sixty had been slaughtered in a two-day rampage across Southampton. They included a baby in a crib and ten children in a log-cabin school. Then masses of white troops descended on Southampton and crushed the revolt. They executed, through shootings, beheadings, and torture, about fifty African Americans, many of whom had not participated in the rebellion. Turner himself was captured two months later, then tried, convicted, and hanged—but not before dictating his confessions to Gray.[67]

Southwestern whites suddenly realized that their system had inhaled tens of thousands of people who had been stolen from Southampton and similar counties that had been devastated by the professional slave trade over the past decade. Alabama's governor activated the state militia. Newspapers in New Orleans suppressed reporting of the rebellion until authorities could collect enough weapons to defeat copycat attacks, but word still got out. In Louisiana's West Feliciana Parish, a white widow heard a rumor that the slaves on a nearby labor camp "had armed themselves and claimed their liberty." "She instantly started screaming and crying as loud as she could," a calmer neighbor recorded in her diary. The widow demanded that a male neighbor go find out what was happening, but instead, he called out the members of the local militia, who assembled and marched to the alleged epicenter. There they "found the overseer and the Negroes very busy at gathering the crops," picking cotton "as peaceable as lambs."[68]

"The proper officers of the state should take measures to prevent the importation of slaves" from "the infected section of the country," wrote the *New Orleans Bee*. The editor had stopped trusting certificate laws to filter the old states' most rebellious enslaved people from the stream of the slave trade. Despite opposition from ambitious cotton and sugar entrepreneurs, an emergency session of the state legislature banned the slave trade. (Reading the writing on the wall, traders rushed in 774 more slaves before the special session ended.) The Alabama legislature also raced into session and prohibited the trade. The next spring, Mississippi held a constitutional convention. There were so many enslaved migrants around booming Natchez, said planter-banker Stephen Duncan, that "we will one day have our throats cut in this country." Elitist representatives from the Natchez area and delegates from the poor-white "piney woods" formed an unusual alliance and incorporated a slave-trade prohibition in the new constitution.[69]

Of course, buyers and sellers immediately began to poke loopholes in the slave-trade prohibitions. Buyers traveled to the Chesapeake. Traders filled out declarations swearing that the slaves they were transporting were for their own use only. Legislators from the newer cotton counties in Mississippi, who still wanted slaves, blocked implementation of that state's constitutional ban, so the biggest traders moved their headquarters from New Orleans to the "Forks in the Road" market just north of Natchez. But back East, Virginia—the site of the rebellion and still the home of the South's largest slave population—had called a state constitutional convention to consider emancipation. In the course of the deliberations, Thomas Jefferson's grandson Thomas Randolph proposed a statewide referendum of white voters on whether Virginia should initiate gradual emancipation.[70]

Randolph's plan would have made all slaves born after July 4, 1840, into state property upon adulthood. Virginia would then hire out these slaves, saving the wages to pay, ultimately, for the expenses involved in exiling them "beyond the limits of the United States." Under this plan, many Afro-Virginians would have still been enslaved in the early twentieth century, although Randolph assumed that before then, most enslavers would cash out by selling them south. Randolph was proposing to revive his grandfather's dream: the exile of Virginia's slave population and the creation of an all-white Old Dominion. Many, such as fellow delegate Thomas Marshall, son of John Marshall, the chief justice of the US Supreme Court from 1801 to 1835, supported Randolph's proposal, believing that slavery was "ruinous to whites." The "industrious population" of non-slaveholding whites was emigrating in order to flee a state whose biggest business was raising people for the southwestern market. And if they continued, Marshall predicted—invoking the fate of Saint-Domingue whites—"the whole country [of Virginia] will be inundated by one black wave . . . with a few white faces here and there floating on the surface."[71]

Yet other delegates warned that the state's entire economy depended on the price point of a single commodity: that of hands at New Orleans. If the Randolph plan passed, Virginia enslavers would rush to sell their human property south at one time and the price would plummet. Slave owners were vested in the slave market, and most of them wanted the government to defend and expand their right to nearly unfettered use of their property—not to limit it. The Virginia convention rejected Randolph and approved the status quo, though it added new limits on slave literacy and on free black life. Over the next three years, North Carolina, Tennessee, and Maryland imposed similar restrictions. Enslavers had already imposed the like in the southwestern states.[72]

Limits on literacy and on contact with free blacks aimed to restrict access to ideas about freedom. Proslavery politicians blamed the first appearance of Garrison's *Liberator* in January 1831 for Nat Turner's decision later that year to bathe Southampton County in white folks' blood. The Georgia legislature even offered a $5,000 reward for Garrison's apprehension. But enslavers also feared that African-American Christianity itself might generate danger from within. Governor John Floyd of Virginia wrote that "every black preacher . . . east of the Blue Ridge" had known about Turner's plot. Misguided white piety had permitted "large assemblages of negroes" at which black preachers had allegedly read out the "incendiary publications of Walker [and] Garrison." An Alabama newspaper warned of "shrewd, cunning" slave preachers. Should revolt break out in the southwestern region, "Some crispy-haired prophet, some pretender to inspiration, will be the ring-leader as well as the inspiration of that plot. By feigning communication from heaven, he will rouse the fanaticism of his brethren, and they will be prepared for any work, no matter how desolating and murderous."[73]

Southwestern enslaver-politicians decided to put an end to independent black Christianity. Mobile, Alabama, banned gatherings—including religious ones—of more than three slaves. The punishment for violation was "twenty stripes" on the back. The local newspaper wrote, "The managers of the Mobile Sunday School [have decided] that hereafter no colored person will be received for instruction who does not bring written permission to that effect from the owner." The Mississippi state legislature made it illegal for any "slave, free negro, or mulatto . . . to exercise the function of a Minister of the Gospel." All religious practice, aside from individual prayer, would now be kept under the eyes of enslavers and their henchmen—which is what evangelical ministers now volunteered to be. White ministers eagerly promised that they would henceforth work harder than ever to make Christianity into a tool that would help enslavers govern their society.[74]

With independent black preaching now illegal in most places, white Methodists, Baptists, and Presbyterians offered two legal religious options to the enslaved. The first one was to affiliate with white churches. There, African Americans could look forward to unequal status and discipline. In bigger churches, they'd sit in the upstairs galleries. In the log church that Annie Stanton attended in the Alabama woods, she actually had to sit outside the door with her fellow slaves on benches. After the white preacher's sermon was done, a black preacher would come out and talk to them, while whites supervised.[75]

The second strategy was the creation of "slave missions": white preachers, funded and regulated by white denominations, would be sent to preach to black congregations. The proslavery sermons that slave missions delivered were the South's interior version of the arguments that were to be, beginning in the 1830s, increasingly projected at the region's exterior critics. Ministers developed a theological argument that claimed that Christianity justified slavery. They leaned on the apostle Paul, with his admonitions to servants to obey their masters. Increasingly they also argued that a holistic view of the Bible showed that slavery was not sinful. In fact, they said, God had ordained that the Israelites, and white people in general, could enslave allegedly inferior "Hamitic" peoples (supposedly descended from Ham, one of Noah's sons), such as Africans, so long as they treated the latter with paternalistic goodness.

In this view, slavery's critics were willfully refusing to read the Bible closely enough to recognize that slavery was God-ordained; abolition doctrines were merely attempts to supplant the word of God with individual will. And this went for potential southern critics as well as northern ones. James Smylie, a prominent Presbyterian minister from Mississippi, and (by 1840) the captor of thirty men, women, and children, argued in 1836 that a slaveholder "whose conscience is guided, not by the word of God, but by the doctrines of men"—i.e., by the anxiety that antislavery Christians might have a point—"is often suffering the lashes of a guilty conscience." But he should not suffer. God had created some people unfit for freedom. Slavery was God's will. To worry about slavery was to doubt God. To oppose it was heresy.[76]

BY 1835, ISRAEL CAMPBELL, who had been transported from Kentucky to the cotton "system" of Mississippi, had become a "first-rate hand" and more. He drove a work gang on a slave labor camp near the little crossroads town of Mount Vernon. Campbell had been granted as much status as any white Mississippian was willing to give him. Yet one night, when someone pounding on his cabin door jolted him out of sleep, he woke up to discover how little protection he had. Stumbling out of bed, he unlatched the door and tumbled backward as two white men shoved their way in. One grabbed Campbell by the collar and pulled his throat toward the point of a bowie knife. "What do you know about Dr. Cotton's scrape?" the man growled.

"Nothing at all, sir," stammered Campbell. That was true. But he did know who Dr. Cotton was. And that had him shaking. Cotton was a white man who had come from up north to practice as a "steam-doctor"—a "Thompsonian" physician, who claimed he could treat many illnesses and complaints by having the patients inhale large quantities of steam and small quantities of medicine. Though Thompsonian homeopathy was less likely to kill the patient than the massive chemical doses prescribed in those days by traditional physicians, steam-doctors were thought of as itinerants from society's fringe. And somehow Cotton had given the impression that he was overly friendly with local African Americans. Emphasizing their questioning with a blade pressed against Campbell's throat, these men told him that "Dr.

Cotton and some mean white men and a great many of the negroes were laying plans to rise and kill off the white people and free the negroes." Then they said that they knew Campbell had recently attended a secret, illegal prayer session in the woods led by "Harris' old Dave, the negro preacher." Clearly, they suspected that Campbell was also involved in the alleged plot. How long had he stayed? Did he know if slaves had talked "about getting free and killing the white people?"

Campbell desperately denied hearing anything of the sort. Somehow he convinced the interrogators that he had nothing to do with a conspiracy. The knife moved away from his throat. The men offered him a convivial shot from their stoneware jug. Campbell's hand shook as he raised the brandy to his lips. It burned going down, like the drinks auctioneers gave men and women on the block, but the men watched with approval as he took their cup. Campbell wiped his mouth with the back of his hand. They warned him that anyone connected with the plot would be shot, and then they clattered off in the night. Campbell watched from the doorway as they rode away. He knew that the excitement and fear he'd seen mingled in their eyes was going to condemn some people to death before the sun rose.[77]

If there was a plot, all Campbell knew about it could probably be inferred from the tales he and his peers had told each other about their own stolen lives. The whites had their own feared storyline, which had been seared into their brains long before Southampton. To stop that one from coming to pass, all around the neighborhood that evening, groups of white men were dragging slaves out of cabins and questioning them. In terror, some charged others with crimes that never existed. When the night was over, when enough victims had been rounded up, the vigilantes—most of whom were local planters—began to hang the condemned in Mount Vernon. For two days, they dropped and strangled black preachers and worshippers from a pole between two high Y-shaped posts. They also strung up a few white men who, like Dr. Cotton, had crossed a racial barrier.[78]

Afterward, the vigilantes came back and got Campbell. This time, they only wanted him to wait tables at a banquet, where the planters of the area praised themselves for saving Mississippi from destruction. Walking home the morning after the party, Campbell saw the heads of hanged black preachers impaled on roadside stakes. And that was almost the last time Campbell saw Old Dave and his brothers. But not quite. He came face to face with them again once that fall. Not long before Campbell's owner moved his slaves yet again, this time to Tennessee, Campbell went into the little apothecary's shop that served as Mount Vernon's pharmacy, and there he saw the grinning skulls of Dave and his apostles displayed on its shelves.

Israel Campbell had been seeking God for a long time, "but in Mississippi there were so many drawbacks" that he could not "make my peace with God," he later said. Indeed, religious seeking had almost made him one of white Mississippi's bleached trophies. But Campbell was still drawn to chase the same God who didn't intervene when white people set the buzzards' table at Mount Vernon. In Tennessee, Campbell tried again. He and his wife attended every nearby religious meeting. Frenetically, he sneaked off twice a day to a "praying-ground" he had cleared at a secret place deep in the woods. On his knees he battled his fear that he was no more than chalk dust in someone else's hands. Then, late in the fall, a week of frantic cotton-picking earned the slaves of the devout a short break in the harvest: a few days timed to coincide with a nearby Methodist camp-meeting, where white preachers led and black "exhorters" were restricted to warming up the crowd and praying with individual seekers. Israel Campbell and his wife attended. For three days, they begged on their knees for the kind of ecstatic transformation they saw people having all around them. Finally, on the fourth night, Israel's wife stood up and began to shout with other new converts.

Campbell had seen others who shouted in ecstasy. He had heard others say they felt God's breath in their lungs. What was left of some of them gaped at customers in the apothecary's shop. It was hard to make peace with that. There were also the bleeding wounds that God had permitted wrong-doers to blast in his own life. Despite all his mother's prayers, something—whether God, or the universe, or fate—had torn Israel from her, strapped a young man who had once been an infant at her breast into the leather of the whipping-machine. Mississippi Baptists claimed that "dark, mysterious . . . dispensations" excused white Christians' complicity in slavery's outrages. But lives that were stolen—this was a crime, not a mystery to be accepted on faith. Perhaps even God was complicit.

Israel fell on his knees, almost alone. An older black preacher named Reeves stood behind his shoulder. Reeves had survived six weeks of marching in shackles. He had survived white folks' fear of him. He was thin, made of knots of starved, scarred muscle, draped in rags. He held his face—carved with lines dark from fifteen thousand days under the sunshine—utterly still. As Campbell prayed, Reeves looked straight ahead, impassive as a king. At last some moment only he could judge arrived. He bent down and breathed into Israel's ear: "Pray on, young brother."

# 7

# SEED

## *1829–1837*

S PRINGTIME. THE FIELD SPREADS open. Suddenly it feels as if the insects have always been buzzing here. As if gray January never was. Green crusts the tree branches. The rain falls. The ground drinks the rain. The world shines like a sun.

The entrepreneur looks out at the fields from the new porch on his cabin, talking. His employee listens, then walks over, picks up a clod of dirt. Smells it. Maybe tastes it. Puts it down.

The next day it rains hard in the morning, but when it stops the men bring the mules and the plows out. The spongy earth oozes into the hollows, sucking the metal plow points. "Fuck this mud," the men mutter.

*Fuck*. From an Old English word meaning: *to strike, to beat*. Before that, in an even older language: *to plow*. To tear open.

The seeds are waiting.

In the sack in the shed. Or maybe safe under the entrepreneur's high bed. The bed where he fucks his wife. Bed brought by wagon from the landing, bed bought with last year's crop. Maybe he didn't bring his wife. Maybe the sack is under the bed where he fucks the sixteen-year-old light-skinned girl from Maryland, also bought with last year's crop. Maybe she is the same girl who washes the bloodstains from the sheets in the morning. Who carries the chamber pot to the woods. Who turns it over, brings it back empty, sets it by his side of the bed. Bumps her toe on the bulging sack, full of tiny seeds.

Her toe feels their caress through cotton bagging sewn up with cotton thread. One hundred thousand DNA packets, each one encoding *Gossypium hirsutum*. One hundred thousand cotton seeds. Oily against each other, warm like Mexico's Tehuacan Valley, where five thousand years ago Indian women tamed these seeds' ancestors.[1]

Or, *to plant*. It is the next dry day. The employee brings out the bag. He cuts it open with his long knife. A double handful into her new apron. She lines up barefoot in the field with the rest. One hand pinches apron into pocket. One hand holds seed between thumb and forefinger. The next woman on drags a hoe up the row, trenching the broken dirt. Her turn now, she drops a seed, rakes damp black dirt over it with her naked left heel, presses the ball of her foot down to settle the seed in the dirt. She moves a few inches up the row.[2]

Underneath, all is dark. The layers of muck and humus have already quickened with their own yearly cycle. They hum the rhythms of their local history of biological alliances. The outsider seed sits quiet as a tick. In its hull, double helixes lie in suspended animation.

The next day, the rain falls. Water molecules leach through the seed coat. The helixes awaken. They twist, shudder, break apart, draw more molecules to their open spaces, building their own mirrors. From them march streams of chemical messengers; orders that compel whole cells to stretch and split into twins. The embryo plant bulges. It shatters the seed hull from within and forces the stem up toward unseen light.

Squatting in the creek, the girl washes herself frantically. She does not know that if the planter's seed is motile enough, it has already journeyed up into her hours ago, questing for her own. If this is her time, they will meet.

The green shoot breaches the surface. Tiny pores gasp carbon dioxide, and cell membranes gulp in the life-sustaining molecules. The first rounds of photosynthesis begin. Triumphantly the erecting stem spreads two cotyledons, baby leaves that all winter long have been tucked like arms on a fetus.

All across the field, thousands of other shoots are doing exactly the same thing. Now they can consume Mississippi's long arcs of sunlight, heavy rains, and the incredible chocolate soil that river and forest built. The local ecosystem struggles against this invader. But the cotton plant has plow and hoe as its allies. And it is rammed into this dirt by command of desires equipped with yet more powerful tools, hands that will keep these little plants clear of weeds for four months. For the four after they will dominate this field, shading out every other plant that challenges their possession, making this field a grid of revenue on which only one species lives. By mid-August they will explode into an unnatural whitescape that lasts until winter falls or picking finishes.

Yet whether the seed's seed will live on is an open question. Its DNA codes for a life cycle in which it grows into a tree that lives many years in a tropical climate. Here, though, this plant dies with the first winter frost. By that time most of its seed will have been picked with the cotton bolls, separated by the gin, and discarded. Already in the early 1830s many planters buy each year's seed from breeders who create new varieties and promise great yield. The white entrepreneur will risk many things, but not the chance that this hybrid kernel's own seed will fail to run true and leave his production anemic in a year of high prices.

This tree-turned-into-a-bush, in short, is fucked. So, too, is the soil. When the enslaved men broke it open for the entrepreneur, he fucked this dirt with them as his tool. He fucked this field. He might fuck their wives out in the woods, or in the corn when it is high. Or their daughter in the kitchen. Then the next new girl he buys at New Orleans.

But he fucks the men, too. He plants in all his hands the seeds of his dreams. In fact, he plants them all, men and women, in this place, just as he plants as those seeds. Plants, ecosystems, people strain to live their lives according to their own codes, but he twists their efforts into helixes of his own design. He takes their product, keeps it for himself. He breaks open the skin on their backs with his fucking lash, striking their lives with his power, marking them and their world with his desire.

So even as the cotton plant's internal programming raised two little leaves to flutter in the April breeze off the Mississippi River, entrepreneurs' desires dominated it. In a broader sense, much of this story about the expansion of slavery and how it shaped the lives of black folks and the wider world is driven by the white men who tried to impose their codes on everything around them. Those codes included, above all, their ideas about what made them men. White men's code of masculinity shaped all lives on slavery's frontier: shaped the costs of being black, the benefits of being white, the costs of being female. White men used the code as both weapon and motivator against each other in battles for political equality and access to the economic benefits of slavery. And the seed sowed by entrepreneurs sprouted in ways both cultivated and unforeseen: into the two-party political system emergent in the 1830s, the economic boom that shaped the years from 1829 to 1837, and ultimately the Civil War, which the boom's aftermath planted. By the time 1837 came, all would be different—national politics, slavery's economic status, the South's relationship to the rest of the United States, even how enslavers felt about slavery. Above all, this decade, perhaps the most pivotal in American history, unraveled and re-knit and scattered and chopped short and harvested and broke and consumed the lives of millions of enslaved people.

THE NEW CROP SPREAD far in space and in time, but to understand the DNA of the white men who planted it, one must look back to the old states where it was first synthesized. In an early 1832 letter to his business partner, North Carolina–based slave trader Tyre Glen coined a verb that cut straight to that essence. As an aside from an otherwise ordinary discussion of trafficking-in-humans, he noted that "because of a recent bill in the General Assembly, potterizing now carries the punishment of death."[3]

"Potterizing" was a neologism. It evoked the recent case of "Bob Potter," as Glen called him. Robert Potter had been born around 1800 into a poor family in Granville County, North Carolina. In the Granville of Potter's childhood, an old tobacco district with worn-out fields and an entrenched planter oligarchy, there was no economic mobility except by geographic migration. Indeed, while poor white men like his father were free, and white, they lacked key rights that distinguished the independent from the dependent. North Carolina's constitution, for instance, excluded most white men who did not own property from voting for the state legislature. Restricted voting perpetuated oligarchy. Planter legislators levied taxes on all to build infrastructure that carried little but planters' crops to market; established state banks that lent only to the wealthy; and created a state university that educated only planters' sons.[4]

Yet as a boy, Potter always stood out from Granville County's other second-class white citizens. A local gentleman took an interest in him, granting him unusual favors: a free classical education from his son's tutor, and later, appointment as a midshipman in the US Navy. The kinds of favors showered on Potter could easily co-opt a lower-class white man. Look at Henry Clay, another social climber. Born the son of a small Virginia slave-owner, Clay moved to Kentucky and became the best rich man's lawyer in the land-speculation game. Days after his first arrival in Congress, awed colleagues made Clay Speaker of the House. Later he became a senator, secretary of state, and presidential candidate. Above all, Clay was the architect of the "American System" of economic development. Development-minded elites loved his ideas for domestic markets, support for banks, and government funding of infrastructure projects.

But many less wealthy white men disliked the idea of the American System, fearing it shed benefits unequally. Even as they moved southwest, it seemed to them that the political system was widening the gulf between rich and poor. Although by the 1820s all white men in the new states could vote, except in Louisiana and Mississippi, rich men's concerns still set the political agenda. Mississippi's legislature, for instance, chartered the state's Planters' Bank in 1830, subsidizing it with $2 million of taxpayers' money.[5]

Potter spent his teenage years at sea, learning how to turn charisma into practical leadership. But when he returned to Granville in 1821, he found that things there were as they'd been when he'd left for the sea a decade before. In the zero-sum world of the decaying southeast, sustained by slave-trade remittances, Potter immediately ran into limits intended to remind him that he should defer to his betters. In 1824, Potter ran for the state legislature, but elite factions conspired to ensure victory for old-money planter Jesse Bynum. The furious Potter challenged Bynum to a duel. The victor declined, for Potter was no gentleman. Potter ambushed Bynum and cracked his skull with a stick.[6]

In Western Europe, from the fifteenth century to the start of the twentieth, the homicide rate plummeted from 41 per 100,000 to 1.4. In Western societies, the state claimed a monopoly on violence, and the law became the legally and culturally approved way to settle individual disputes. But the great outlier in this picture was the South. Even leaving aside the unmeasured violence committed against the enslaved, at the beginning of the nineteenth century the white-on-white homicide rate in Virginia was around 9 per 100,000—eight times that of New Hampshire.[7]

At the most basic level, white people fought and killed each other in the old slaveholding states to prove that they were not slaves. Enslaved men were not allowed to defend their pride, their manhood, or anything else. They had to endure the penetration of their skin, their lives, their families. Therefore, the best way to insult a white man was to treat him like a black man, as if he could not strike back, and the best way to disprove that was to strike back. In Robert Potter's North Carolina, courts often denied poor white men that right. There was much talk of charging Potter for assault and battery on Bynum. The court may have had the discretion to punish him with a slap on the wrist, giving him a sentence like Austin Woolfolk's one-dollar fine for beating up Quaker editor Benjamin Lundy—or may have done something much harsher and more humiliating.

Before any court case arose, it was time for the next legislative elections. Potter and Bynum met once more in electoral combat. This time, Potter won the majority of the county's votes. Granville's small farmers, desperately trying to hang on to their property, and with it their status as voting citizens, appreciated his combative unwillingness to accept the insults of privilege. They gave him the right to strike back, for he punched for them. As soon as he joined the legislature, Potter began to fire off impatient proposals that directly challenged wealthy slaveholders' grip on North Carolina. His first effort was an attempt to create a new state university: what he called a "Political College." This would train young men to be leaders, but would accept no student from a family whose property was valued at more than $1,000.

One hundred of these young men—one hundred Robert Potters—would graduate every year. His fellow legislators, educated at the state university in Chapel Hill, were shocked at the attempt to overturn their power and blocked his proposals.[8]

Potter then turned to the state-chartered banks, charging that they foreclosed on small farmers even as they rolled over debts for wealthy men. Potter's constituents—or most of them—liked his initiatives. In 1828 they elected him to Congress, and again in 1830. But during the summer of 1831, as he visited home between congressional sessions, things took a strange turn. Potter became convinced that his wife had committed adultery with both a Methodist minister and a seventeen-year-old neighbor from a wealthy family. On August 28, 1831, Potter kidnapped both of those men. He took them out into the woods. Then he castrated them. Then he released them.[9]

Within a day, Potter had been captured. He was then locked in a cell at Oxford, the county seat. But from behind bars, as he awaited trial, Potter penned a defense of his actions. His "Appeal" was, he said, an effort "as a man—as a member of society"—to explain himself "to the world," but especially "to you, *my constituents.*" He justified his castration of two white men, honored members of their society, as self-defense. They had tried to unman him first, "stab[bing] me most vitally—they had hurt me beyond all cure—they had polluted the very sanctuary of my soul." Their cuckolding left him "the most degraded man" in Granville, and he now "felt that I could no longer maintain my place among men." He had been subjected to the same humiliation that enslaved men had to endure. The only possible solution was to wipe off "the disgrace that had been put upon me, with the blood of those who had fixed it there." Like a proper gentleman who shot someone in a duel to erase an insult, Potter believed that only an act of greater violation than what had been committed against him would erase the unmanning mark.[10]

Rich men were almost never prosecuted for dueling. Poor men involved in less deadly fights could face long jail terms. But Potter's crime wasn't specifically listed on the law books, and the most serious charge that the local courts could find with which to charge him was "maiming," with a maximum penalty of two years' imprisonment. This was why the state legislature passed a new law punishing future castrations of white men with execution.

Two years was a long time to sit in a jail cell, however, and while he was in there, the legislature granted his wife a divorce. It also allowed her to change the last name of their two children. The law now said that Potter was not a father and his children were not his seed. In that way, too, he was like a slave. Still, the planters of northeastern North Carolina had not heard the name

Potter for the final time. After his 1834 release, Potter ran again for the state legislature. He won a contest marred with violence, which Granville County remembered as the Potter War. But the legislature soon contrived a bogus charge of cheating at gambling, and expelled him. This time Potter obliged his opponents and left. Like countless other troublemakers, Potter headed first for New Orleans. There, he would plant anew.[11]

Yet it was not certain that white men who came from Potter's origins would find escape on the frontier from the constricting economic, social, and political inequality of the old states. And if most of them had more ordinary gifts, many of them were still Bob Potters in their own way. This is one reason why, from the earliest days, violent conflicts over status, reputation, and pride of membership, access, and recognition were even more common on slavery's frontiers than in the older slave states. In the cotton counties of middle Georgia in 1800, for instance, the homicide level was approximately 45 per 100,000 whites, five times that of Virginia. Three decades later, the rate in Florida's cotton districts was 70 per 100,000, fifty times the northeastern rate.[12]

One North Carolina migrant wrote back home that in his new Alabama community, "no man [is] safe from violence, unless a weapon is conspicuously displayed on his person." In North Carolina, he continued, "it is considered disreputable to carry a dirk or a pistol. [But] in Alabama, it is considered singularity and imprudence to be without one: in fact, nine persons in ten . . . you will see with the dirk handle projecting from their bosoms." When pistols and dirks weren't handy, white men used anything and everything else to try to intimidate, humiliate, and kill each other: teeth, rocks, nails, cowhide whips, canes, pieces of lumber. Letters from the frontier are riddled with shootings, stabbings, cuttings, gougings, horse-whippings, and other brutal assaults on everyone who had the misfortune to meet them. So and so "had his thumb cut off . . . in consequence of a bite by Bob Hutchins at the races"; "he had the impudence to call my wife & mother whores, & I beat him"; "they will hardly hang a man here for willful murder, and they do not regard taking the life of a man anymore than I would a snake"; "he coughed up a buckshot"; there were "some angry words out in the yard, [then] Dudley shot Rowan in the right side"; "the woods were searched and the body of a man was found with two bullet holes in the forehead and the whole of the hind part of his skull stove in."[13]

"They're mighty free with pistols down there," an escaped slave told an audience in 1842. "If a man don't resent anything that's put upon him, they call him 'Poke-easy.'" The way white men saw it, being poke-easy was for men toiling in the field, and for the women out there, too—people either forced or willing to be the helpless target. Dirks, pistols, and physical assault asserted that one was un-poke-able. Little boys in the southwestern towns learned to fight for their honor as soon as they could walk. "Catch him down," said a Florida father watching his son fight another boy, "[then] bite him, chaw off his lip"—or else "you'll never be a man." A man must be ready to fight on almost any day, from cradle to grave. And old men dying of alcoholism scrabbled frantically under their beds for stashed revolvers, to shoot the phantoms that still rushed toward them.[14]

Wealthy men well-positioned to grab the right-handed rewards generated by ever-growing productivity in the cotton fields committed more than their share of frontier violence. But also characteristic was the type of Alabama employer-employee conflict that John Pelham described to his North Carolina uncle in 1833: "I had a falling out with Mr. Bynum (I was not quite as submissive as he would wish an overseer). He threatened to *cane me* (he has three sons grown). I told him the whole family could not *doe that* and *dared* them to try it." Bynum wanted deference, but Pelham refused to be submissive. He was an employee, but also, he asserted, an equal. You don't cane an equal. You cane someone to prove that they are not your equal. Pelham made Bynum back down, and now the rich man had to find another overseer. Meanwhile, Pelham found someone willing to give him credit—to believe his claim-to-status—"I had money and friends and determined to alter my business I went to Florence . . . and bought me a good assortment of grocerys and brought them to this place where I find I am doing a good business."[15]

In personal encounters, less wealthy white men who moved to the new states became increasingly confrontational toward those who dared to act like their betters. Tens of thousands of Pelhams, just like the original Potter, also wanted to force political recognition of their equality. When property-owning citizens in South Carolina and Kentucky decided in the 1790s to expand the franchise to all adult white men, regardless of their property-owning status, they probably assumed that educated, wealthy men from the upper class would still hold all offices and set the agenda of politics. This is essentially what happened at first. Many successful frontier politicians were like George Poindexter. He arrived in Mississippi from Virginia in the first decade of the nineteenth century and became the author of Mississippi's first legal code and the Natchez river–county elite's political champion. The "Natchez Nabobs" were few in number, but they controlled the state legislature, and so they made Poindexter their US senator.[16]

Yet, by the time Poindexter's star was reaching its zenith, the impact of poor white migrants from the old states on frontier elections began to change the political game. The 1832 Mississippi state constitution removed the last few restrictions on white male voting. The broadened electorate brought in a state legislature that told Poindexter to cast his Senate votes against banking policies that benefited his cronies. He responded with the claim that the common voter could not tell him what to do: "If . . . the people of Mississippi desire to be represented in the national legislature by a mere machine, to be wielded by the arm of [popular] power, they have made an unfortunate selection in me."[17]

Elite politicians also tried to distract attention from policy programs that served oligarchic factions by painting their opponents as poke-easies undeserving of voters' respect. Florida territorial governor Richard K. Call, leader of a clique of land speculators, described his campaign strategy as "riding" his opponent "with a stiffer bit and a ranker rowel" than he had been ridden before—verbally humiliating him and threatening violence until the opponent backed down, tail between legs.

Political honor-violence could be as meaningful to voters as policy programs and oratory. Yet new voters who built their log cabins on the poor land far from the rivers did not want their representative to tell them he wasn't going to listen to them. Sometimes voters could be as brutal with their rebukes as the Georgia constituent who assassinated a Yazoo-man state senator for giving away his birthright of land yet-to-be-stolen from the Creeks. Given the option, poor white men preferred politicians like Franklin Plummer. Plummer arrived in Mississippi with no more money than Poindexter, settling in the hardscrabble piney woods of the state's southeast, rather than Natchez. When he decided to run for Congress in 1829, the state's ruling factions "considered it a great piece of impertinence," as a fellow politico from those days later recalled. The Natchez machine sent notorious duelists to heckle him during speeches, seeking to humiliate him as an unmanly coward. Plummer "coolly took the stump and routed them" with clever mockery. His ability to connect with the common voter made him virtually invincible. During one election campaign, Plummer traveled the district in company with a competitor, and one night the two of them stayed at the same settler cabin. When Plummer's opponent walked outside early the next morning, he found the woman of the house milking, while Plummer—grinning at his rival—held the cow's hungry calf back by its tail. At another stop Plummer helped a farmer's family pick parasitic red bugs out of their toddler's hair. In a different campaign he printed up a mock advertisement that asked readers for help in locating opponent Powhatan Ellis's allegedly lost trunk, which supposedly contained such items as "6 lawn handkerchiefs; 6 cambric shirts; 2 [cambric] night [shirts]; 1 nightcap; 1 pr. Stays; 3 pr. Silk stockings." Ellis lost the election.[18]

THE KIND OF WHITE man who supported Franklin Plummer—or Bob Potter—wanted even more than mockery of the arrogant. That kind of white man wanted politics to change—to incorporate white male equality in both political practice and policy outcomes. Ironically, no Potterizing politician planted more fruitful seeds of that kind of change than a Tennessee cotton planter and slave trader, a man who on March 5, 1829, woke up aching in Washington, DC. The capital was in the middle of a long, deep cold snap. Local firewood stockpiles had gone up the capital's chimneys. Andrew Jackson's wiry old body felt the frost. He had never quite recovered from his campaigns, and under the knife scars that cicatrized his body was a void in his heart, where Rachel fit. Jackson believed that the scurrilous pamphlets published by John Quincy Adams's campaign had killed his wife. Mortified by charges that she had committed adultery when she took up with Andrew in the 1790s before finalizing her divorce from her abusive first husband, Rachel declined rapidly after Jackson's November victory.

Now, as Jackson rose to his feet, a slave waiting outside the door heard the old man and entered the room. A few minutes later, the president-elect emerged: washed, shaved, and buttoned into mourning-black pants, waistcoat, coat, and overcoat. On his head, where Jackson had once favored a white beaver hat, he settled a black one. At the bottom of the stairs he found a group of younger men whom he and Rachel, a childless couple, had essentially adopted. Many had served as his officers. As they breakfasted, people collected in the cold outside the hotel at Sixth Street and Pennsylvania Avenue. Right on time at 11 a.m., Jackson opened the front door. A deafening shout of joy erupted.

The president-elect and his soldiers pushed their way down the steps in a loose tactical formation. "A military chieftain," his critics had sneered, implying his appeal was that of the despot on horseback, whose forcefulness thrills the ignorant. But there was more to him. He and his allies and supporters were making a new kind of government. Not a dictatorship, not a republic, it built white men's equal access to manhood and citizenship on the disfranchisement of everyone else. Yet it was still the first mass democracy in world history. And as he proceeded onto Pennsylvania Avenue's frozen mud, Jackson didn't ride. He walked.[19]

Jackson and his supporters had fought through two bitter national elections to reach this day. In 1824, Jackson had won a plurality of the popular votes, but he had been outmaneuvered in Congress after no candidate won an electoral-college majority. By 1828, however, he had joined forces with New York's Martin Van Buren and his "Bucktail" faction. It was the Bucktails who had created the new state constitution in 1821, the one that disfranchised most property-owning African Americans and enfranchised all white men. New York votes were essential to Jackson's 1828 victory. Jackson had also let his northern allies in Congress lock in their states' votes in the spring of 1828 by passing a tariff bill laden with specific protections for Pennsylvania and New Jersey manufacturing districts. But his greatest strength came from slave-frontier states, including Kentucky, Alabama, and Tennessee. Here in the southwestern states, virtually universal support for the victor of New Orleans among non-planter white men made and sustained Jackson as a national force.

Previous inaugurations had attracted few spectators. But on this day, it seemed as if every single white rural laborer, tenant farmer, and urban workingman in the United States had come to Washington. The Jackson voters, sneered Massachusetts senator Daniel Webster, "really seem to think that the country is rescued from some dreadful danger." Uniformed officers flanked Jackson as he marched up Pennsylvania Avenue, but so did a self-nominated escort of firewood carts and farm wagons. When Jackson reached the Capitol and entered via a basement door, the ocean of citizens lapped around the base of the building. Then the east doors swung open. The inauguration party walked from the Senate chamber onto the portico. Twenty thousand people jostled forward a few steps.[20]

When the tall man emerged from the pack of dignitaries and stood before them, they began to shout: "Huzza! Huzza!" Suddenly every man in the multitude took off his hat at once; a sign of respect for the apotheosis of their equality, their sovereign citizenship, their manhood. Every breath was drawn in. Cannons erupted in a twenty-four-gun salute. The Marine band struck up a tune. And the hero of New Orleans stood erect above the mist of twenty thousand exhaled breaths, and looked at the upturned white sea of faces. Then he bowed low.[21]

Andrew Jackson had risen spectacularly. Yet he still lived as simply as possible for the owner of more than a hundred slaves. Rachel had even smoked a pipe. And instead of insinuating that his voters were beneath him, he used Potterizing violence to defeat attempts to dishonor either him or his white male constituents. They gloried in vicarious wish-fulfillment as they heard about his confrontational behavior, like the time when his steamboat narrowly escaped a collision, prompting the presidential candidate to run on deck to threaten the other vessel's reckless pilot with a loaded rifle. But Jackson also delivered more than the posture of white male equality. His victories at Horseshoe Bend and New Orleans had made Jefferson's paper empire for white liberty into fact. On the millions of Indian acres he seized, tens of thousands of white men now strove to escape crusty hierarchies by becoming landowners.

When Jackson became president, the symbolism of his actions would become even larger. In 1832–1833 he stared down South Carolina's elites (including his own vice president, John C. Calhoun) when they asserted that their state could simply "nullify" federal laws—in this case, the tariff of 1828. While claiming that he opposed tariffs in principle, Jackson took the nullifiers' action as a direct challenge to the power of a national majority. So did a Tennessee constituent, who said, delighting in Old Hickory's humiliation of the South Carolina planter elite, "The old chief could rally force enough . . . to stand on Saluda Mountain [in northwestern South Carolina] and piss enough to float the whole nullifying crew into the Atlantic Ocean." The way he saw it, Carolina's planters blustered about mobilizing the militia and blocking federal tariff enforcement until the collected penises of Jackson's supporters, like himself, cowed them, and they backed down.[22]

So Jackson stood tall before his supporters, symbolizing who they wanted to be—the unpretentious but assertive man who dominated his household and forced arrogant bullies into feminized submission. And as he took out his paper and began to read his first inaugural address, he was delivering to his faithful supporters a down payment of democracy, and not just in the pageantry of white male equality. His policies, he promised, would not cater to the powerful. He planned, he said, to correct "those abuses that have brought the patronage of the Federal Government into conflict with the freedom of elections." This reminded voters of the chicanery that had been carried out in the House of Representatives four years earlier, which overruled popular will and elected John Quincy Adams. More important than any specific measure, however, was the fact that while Jackson was in office, his politically innovative allies, such as Martin Van Buren, used Jackson's popularity to create new national political structures that put white male equality into gritty practice. They created the routines of a party system, welding ordinary citizens into mass electoral forces through precinct-level organization and emotional appeals for loyalty. The historical consequences of the Jacksonian reorganization of politics, which leveraged these Potterizing resentments on slavery's frontier, were momentous. They stretch from that cold March day to our own.

Yet while the people in their majesty removed their hats, and Jackson bowed, Jackson still had on his own hat. Under it Jackson couldn't help also carrying another set of programs. In fact, he often carried his ideas *in* his hat—seeds of thought jotted on scraps of paper and shoved into the interior band. And as his speech went on, Jackson signaled four policies that were destined to seed more slave labor camps on the southwestern frontier. These were not necessarily incompatible with the hopes and principles of common white men. But their outcomes would also deliver both financial benefits and unintended consequences to the entrepreneurs of the frontier.

First, Jackson announced that he planned to address the Indian issue according to the "feelings" of his countrymen. Almost 50,000 native people still lived on and held title to 100 million acres of land in Georgia, Alabama, Mississippi, and Florida. The "feeling" of Jackson's countrymen was that they wanted that land in order to launch expanded cotton-and-slavery-induced booms. And over the next eight years, Jackson's administrations forced all the surviving Indian tribes across the Mississippi to free up more land for white—and black—settlement.[23]

Jackson also said that "with foreign nations it will be my study to preserve peace and to cultivate friendship on fair and honorable terms," but he had already made it known that he believed that with the Louisiana Purchase, the United States had actually also bought most of what eventually became the state of Texas. The independent nation of Mexico claimed this territory, but Jackson wanted to redraw the boundary line that the United States and Spain had negotiated in 1819 to incorporate most of today's Texas as a new frontier for cotton seed.[24]

Jackson also mentioned his desire to adjust the tariff levied on foreign manufactured goods by the most recent Congress in 1828. This unwieldy compromise subsidized America's still-weak manufacturing sector by levying import duties, such as the 280 percent surcharge on cotton broadcloth. American factories could undersell some British goods, but the consumer paid the cost. Although the tariff protected some of Jackson's northern supporters, it hurt southern planter-entrepreneurs by taxing their consumption. South Carolina politicians were already pushing for a showdown over the issue. In his speech, Jackson suggested that the tariff was too high.[25]

Then there was "reform," Jackson's amorphous fourth goal. He was evasive in the short speech about what reforms he meant. Jackson would soon charge that the executive branch's Adams-era holdovers—a hundred or so clerks—embodied corruption. But we know that the president was more concerned about the Second Bank of the United States. Many branches of the B.U.S. had deployed financial resources in the service of the Adams campaign, and Jackson wasn't going to forget that. And although the B.U.S. had stabilized the nation's financial structure, allowing many to recover from the Panic of 1819, many other Americans were not getting wealthier. Most of those Americans had voted for Jackson. He left the harshest B.U.S. lines out of his inaugural address, but he would soon launch attacks on the bank, attacks pitched as a reform program that enhanced the egalitarianism of white manhood citizenship.[26]

So Jackson closed. Then he strode down the steps and through the crowd to the rowdiest inauguration party in history. That evening, thousands of his excited supporters crowded into the White House, overwhelming attempts at crowd control. They drank and ate everything, broke furniture, teacups, and noses, and almost smothered their hero against the back wall of the house. Jackson had to escape through a back window. He spent the night back at the hotel. The party raged on without him, for, as Washington hostess Margaret Bayard Smith sniffed, it was indeed "the People's Day."[27]

The inauguration set the stage for four years of raucous conflict. Among other things, Jackson faced down half the members of his Cabinet because they and their wives labeled the wife of another a whore. And though Congress moved toward lowering tariffs, it didn't move quickly enough for South Carolina politicians, who claimed that they could nullify the federal law. Some historians have claimed that the nullification movement anticipated the disunion threats of the South in the 1850s—threats that were issued in response to northern attempts to block the expansion of slavery—but this is false hindsight. In the late 1820s, South Carolina whites were scared. They had not mentally recovered from the alleged Denmark Vesey slave conspiracy of 1822, and they also sensed their decline relative to the southwestern region. In fact, few west of South Carolina supported threats of disunion, and in the winter of 1832–1833, Jackson demolished the logic of nullification in a brilliant defense of nationalism.[28]

Already in 1830, Jackson and his allies in Congress had proposed the Indian Removal Act, which forced southwestern Indians into present-day Oklahoma. Although some northerners criticized conquest and displacement as immoral, Congress passed the act, authorizing Jackson's government to evict the remaining eastern nations. By the end of his second term, the vast majority of the Native Americans who had lived in the southwestern cotton states in 1828 had been driven from their homes.[29]

Before a single Cherokee or Chickasaw was driven from his homeland, however, came the day in November 1829 when B.U.S. President Nicholas Biddle traveled from his Philadelphia headquarters to the White House. Biddle was a dapper, poetry-publishing aristocrat, as close to a Renaissance man as nineteenth-century America produced. He had rooted out the institutional dysfunction that had led to the Panic of 1819 and rebuilt the B.U.S. into a sophisticated financial machine that regulated credit-granting sectors. More than any other individual, Biddle ensured that the massive productivity increases in frontier cotton fields since 1790 would be converted into steady nationwide economic growth. In fact, since the 1820 trough of the post-panic depression, the national economy had already grown by 38 percent. But the polished Biddle was anxious to sound out the frontier general. For Jackson's source of power was his appeal to a newly enfranchised majority that was congenitally suspicious of the bank's octopus-like ability to reach into their lives.[30]

In the meeting, the president thanked Biddle for the bank's help in paying off the national debt. But Jackson also said something that struck Biddle as strange: "I do not dislike your Bank any more than all banks," said the president, "but ever since I read the history of the South Sea Bubble I have been afraid of all banks." Historians have used this exchange to depict Jackson as driven by a backward-looking broader cultural anxiety—the fear that the paper money printed by banks was not "real" in comparison to precious metals such as gold and silver. Yet Jackson also represented interest groups that had more practical reasons to resent Biddle's bank. All these sources of opposition would soon combine to fuel a confrontation between Jackson and the B.U.S. That struggle touched off a series of consequences that shaped both the process of slavery's expansion and the political drama that is the more conventional narrative of US history from Jackson to Lincoln.[31]

THE LINK BETWEEN THE cotton field and politics can be found in the strange alchemy of banks. Everyone knows that banks take in deposits and lend out money, but they don't always realize that when banks lend, they actually create money. We call that money *credit*. As we heard already, that means that money is based on "belief"—the root is the Latin *credere*, a verb meaning "to believe"—and people have to believe in the money for it to work, because banks lend out more money than they take in through deposits. This money has to be paper money, which in the nineteenth century the

state-chartered banks printed themselves, or it can be numbers added to borrowers' credit accounts on a paper ledger, loans against which the borrowers
could write checks. Paper is useful, of course, because it is light. With it you
can transfer large sums in an envelope, whereas even medium-sized amounts
of specie are cumbersome (recall Georgia-man John Springs's ride north to
Maryland's Eastern Shore in 1806, in which the gold in his saddlebags beat
up the sides of his horse).[32]

But more importantly, bank-created money has to be paper (or mere numbers on paper) because only then can money be created out of nothing. And
thus only paper money can lead to real economic growth. Imagine an economy that uses only gold and silver, also known as "specie." A bank in such
an economy could lend no more than it received in deposits, and that bank
would simply be a glorified mattress. It would actually reduce the amount of
money in circulation. If the money supply depended on the total amount of
gold and silver dug out of the ground, the money supply would not increase
as rapidly as the amount of goods and services being produced. The price of
goods would drop, and the price of loans would rise, disincentivizing investment in new production.

When banks create credit by lending out more money than they take in,
a small store of value—deposits—gets multiplied into more. Through this
miracle of leverage, wrote H. B. Trist in 1825, the newly established Bank
of Louisiana had "thrown a great deal of money into circulation" by issuing
$4 million in notes. The bank lent these notes to borrowers, who then made
new investments, buying land, supplies, and slaves. "The price of negroes
has risen considerably," Trist noted. Borrowers were making calculations
much like those of planter-entrepreneur Alonzo Walsh. In 1823, a Louisiana
merchant offered him a five-year loan of $48,000 at 10 percent annual inter-
est. For collateral, he'd mortgage what he called "from 90 to a 100 [sic] head
of first rate slaves," although some of those slaves would be bought with the
money he'd borrow.[33]

Walsh thought he was being offered a good deal. With the work of these
additional hands at Bayou Sara in Louisiana's West Feliciana Parish, he could
clear more fields, plant more cotton, and make the money to repay the loan
with interest. The merchant, who could borrow the money from the B.U.S. at
6 percent, would make 10 percent from Walsh, yielding a tidy net profit. For
the larger balance sheet of the United States, this was also a good deal—assuming that economic growth is always good. In this exchange, the creation
of credit would accelerate the pace of economic activity by convincing economic actors to take risks and employ new resources. However, left to their

own devices, banks sometimes made too many loans, disrupting prices and destroying confidence in the value of money. If people became convinced that a bank's policies were irresponsible, the result could be a "run" on the bank, in which depositors and creditors cleaned out the bank's reserves by demanding that it "redeem" its deflated paper with specie. Enough runs at one time would produce a panic in which all lenders demanded their money back from all banks and debtors, bringing the entire economy to a halt.[34]

Panic is what the B.U.S. had failed to prevent in 1819. Despite that, the Supreme Court's famous *McCullogh v. Maryland* decision defended the bank from angry state legislatures, meaning that, like the Federal Reserve of more recent US history, the bank had the capacity to control the supply of money in the economy. To do so, it first established its own paper notes as a reliable currency. The B.U.S. backed its $50 million (as of 1830) in circulating notes with a massive pile of gold and silver in its vaults—typically half the value of its paper money, so that everyone would know that they could take a B.U.S. bank note to one of the B.U.S.'s twenty-five branches and receive a gold dollar in exchange. Consequently, no one ever did. In fact, merchants like slave trader Isaac Franklin often charged a premium for those Mississippi customers who paid with non-B.U.S. paper money. Believable credit gave the B.U.S. great power to stimulate the economy by lending money. In an 1832 letter, for example, Franklin wrote, "The US Bank and the Planters Bank at this place has thrown a large amt of cash into circulation and the price of cotton has advanced a shade." Cotton buyers felt more comfortable bidding higher for the bales that planters brought to market, and prosperity reigned.[35]

At the same time, the B.U.S. made certain that growth was steady and safe by forcing state-chartered banks to keep a "fractional reserve" of gold or B.U.S. notes in their vaults. In the course of business, the B.U.S. regularly acquired huge stacks of bank notes issued by other banks. Then officers "presented" this paper to other institutions for "redemption." When Isaac Franklin deposited $5,025 of Planters' Bank of Mississippi notes at the Natchez branch of the B.U.S., the bank sent the notes to the Planters' Bank and demanded that it pay $5,025 in specie or B.U.S. This process forced smaller banks to restrain their printing and lending of money, which in turn made their bills more reliable. In 1829, for instance, bank bills from North Carolina were trading at a discount of 3.25 percent, even in far-off Baltimore. One could use a $1 bill issued by the Bank of Cape Fear, which funded Tyre Glen's slave-trading expeditions to Alabama, to buy 96 cents' worth of flour, cotton, or person in Baltimore—it was not a perfect "at par" currency, but far more reliable than paper money had been during the Panic of 1819. More broadly, the

confidence instilled by the B.U.S. meant that European lenders were willing
to inject their capital into American merchant firms, which in turn ensured
that each year's cotton harvest could move smoothly from southwestern fields
to the New Orleans levee to Liverpool-bound ships and finally to Manchester
mills.[36]

Yet despite all of Biddle's success in creating an environment conducive
to unprecedented steady growth, hostility to the bank was endemic. Many
Americans believed that the bank's power was fundamentally at odds with
democratic rule, and not just because it allegedly interfered in elections.
The B.U.S. was the banker for the federal government: holding its deposits,
handling every penny of Washington's $17.5 million budget. Yet the B.U.S.
was also a private corporation whose 4,000 stockholders reaped profits from
every financial exchange the bank carried out for Washington. And yet Biddle insisted that all of the bank's operations were exempt from the scrutiny of
the people's elected representatives, writing that "no officer of the Government, from the President downwards, has the least right, the least authority,"
to interfere "in the concerns of the Bank."[37]

Then there was the complaint that the B.U.S., which made 20 percent of
all the bank loans in the country in the 1820s, chose winners and losers in the
economy. For instance, on Tuesday, March 22, 1831, Natchez planter Francis
Surget borrowed $9,000 in short-term credit from the local branch of the
national bank, which he used to pay creditors, such as cotton broker Alvarez
Fisk. What distinguished Surget from aspiring planters out in the Mississippi hinterland was his established wealth and his connections. In 1830, he
owned ninety-five slaves, placing him in the top 1 percent of wealth in the
United States. Surget was also atypical because he was related by marriage to
Stephen Duncan, the power broker whose control over the Mississippi Planters' Bank and its pipeline of B.U.S. credit, via the national bank's Natchez
branch, made Duncan the center of that state's most powerful financial and
political circle. A state bank could be an ATM machine for those connected
to its directors, and by 1850, Surget had borrowed and bought enough to
increase his slaveholdings to over 2,200.

Yet the Duncan clique of insiders shut out other entrepreneurs. The Planters' Bank did not open branches outside the state's original settlement nu-
cleus near Natchez, leaving planters settling in newly opened areas without
access to bank capital. True, during Jackson's first term, Biddle amplified
the national bank's lending dramatically, especially via the New Orleans
and Natchez branches. By the time 1832 began, at least a third of all B.U.S.
capital had been allocated to merchants, planters, and local banks in the

southwestern states. If the bank wanted to increase its value to the major actors in the American economy, the new cotton empire where much of its dynamic activity was located was the place to concentrate B.U.S. efforts. But of all the 70,000 white people in Mississippi, only a few dozen received large B.U.S. loans. Therefore, despite the flood of credit poured into the cotton frontier, many of its aspiring entrepreneurs still disliked the B.U.S.—not because it made paper money, but because it did not make even more, and give it to them.[38]

The B.U.S. and its unelected cliques blocked the desires of less well-connected southwestern planters and merchants, leaving would-be speculators feeling as if they were treated as inferiors. And other simmering energies also led entrepreneurs to dislike the B.U.S. precisely because it prevented runaway speculation. The desire for risk, speculation, and boom drips from letters like this one to Tennessee Congressman James K. Polk: "A. C. Hays, H. M. Walker, Duncan & Dr. McGimsey have all returned from a visit to Miss. and *all* have *cotton making* fever the most imaginable. . . . Tis rumored that L. H. Duncan & Dr. McGimsey have made stipulations for *Cotton farms.* Our friend Hays is in perfect *ecstasy.*" Hays told another friend that "hands can make $500 each"—per year, which was ecstatic, fevered thinking indeed. Cotton would have to rise to 20 cents a pound and stay there, and the "hands" would have to make more of it than ever before. Enslavers wanted to experience again the surge that had reshaped the southwestern cotton market during the 1815–1819 expansion, but this time they wanted it *more so.* They desired risk more than ever. And to take the full measure of the volatility that characterized the slave frontier in the early 1830s, one must examine another layer of impulses and desires.[39]

JUMP FORWARD A FEW years. Pick through what sprouted from the fields cleared and seeds planted in the 1830s to find one obscure exchange that took place a few years after Andrew Jackson took on the Bank. Begin with a picture: Here's a man, a white man. He's sitting in his office in Louisville, Kentucky, close by the Ohio River. A folded letter has just been thrust into his hands. Looking up, William Cotton's eyes run over the white man who has just handed him the square of paper. Then they fall—and stick—on the woman next to the man. She is not hard on the eyes. Fine dress can't hide her figure, or the bonnet, the spill of tight brown curls over pillow-soft tan skin. Her child faces away as Cotton peers over the edge of the desk and down at the rich man's doings. A toddler, gender indeterminate from here. Cotton sees silky hair, black like that of the child's white father.

"It's for you," says Douglass. Cotton exhales as he breaks the seal, realizing now that he's been holding his breath. Unfolding, the merchant tilts the paper to catch August light spilling through the open window into the office. "This will be handed you by M. Douglass, who will deliver you Mr. Isaac Franklin's Girl Lucindy & child, to be left with you until you hear from him."

This letter told an old story. "Our friend"—meaning Isaac Franklin, until the mid-1830s one of the nation's greatest slave traders—had now, in 1839, "married a very pretty & highly accomplished young Girl." Some rich slave owner's white daughter. So, Mr. Cotton, please "assist in making all things easy. . . . [T]he tale must not get out on the Old Man." Douglass's eyebrows raise as Cotton's eyes glance up sharply at him, but Cotton silently returns to his instructions. Do what you want with her. But say nothing to Douglass, or to the boy as he grows. Keep him and Lucindy out of the way of Franklin's new bride and her wealthy Tennessee family. And don't send Douglass back with a bill for feeding the two. The young woman herself was "the means to pay with."[40]

Cotton had been chosen because he was "a smooth hand at Cuff," as Franklin's business partner, Rice Ballard, put it. "Cuffy" came from a common West African name that had become a generic and derisive term for black men in eighteenth-century America. Some slave traders used it to describe slaves as a commodity. In an 1834 letter to Ballard, for example, Isaac Franklin wrote: "The price of Cuffy comes on . . . they are very high through all the country." The "smooth hand" was the skill of wielding of power over the bodies, lives, and legal persons of enslaved people—a highly developed right-handedness that ruthlessly extracted maximum value. A smooth hand could always extort submission: fear, hope of reunion with someone stolen, hunger, promises of kindness or of a patient forced prostitution rather than a brutal rape—each body had its price.[41]

Slavery permitted unchecked dominance and promised unlimited fulfillment of unrestrained desire. That made the behavior of entrepreneurs particularly volatile, risky, profitable, and disastrous. Then, in the 1830s, as white people, especially men, tried to build southwestern empires out of credit and enslaved human beings, they sought out more and more risk. This behavior planted the seeds for a cycle of boom and bust that would shape the course of American history, and one cannot understand it without studying both careful calculation and passionate craving. Although modern economics often assures itself it is a science, assuming that people are perfectly rational actors who choose their actions based on a clear, even quantifiable understanding of their own economic self-interest, that assumption is false. People rarely have sufficient information to measure the consequences of one act or another. More to the point when planters talk about "fever" and "ecstasy": pure rationality does not always drive people's actions, even—and sometimes especially—their "economic" ones.

This is what the great British economist John Maynard Keynes was trying to explain to his readers when he wrote that "animal spirits"—emotions and desires—drive the ebbing and flowing financial tides. More recently, behavioral economists who run experiments on human test subjects have demonstrated seemingly hardwired connections between sexual desire and risk-taking decisions about buying and selling. When researchers expose men to images of attractive, presumably available women, their propensity to take financial risks increases dramatically. (When women see pictures of attractive men, they tend to use strategies to present themselves as selfless caretakers.) But whether it is evolutionary biology or something else that makes males more financially aggressive when their brains are "primed" by imagery of supposedly sexually available women, financial risk-taking and the sexualized commodification of enslaved women were, by the 1830s, in the minds and in the behavior of white entrepreneurs, tangled in a mutual-amplification relationship.[42]

Of course, Rachel could've predicted, from her perspective up on the auction block at Maspero's in 1819, that the legal right to rape one's human property would shape not only purchases of slaves but the broader behavior of entrepreneurs in the southwestern markets. For from the beginning of slavery in the Americas, if not before, white men had believed that when it came to enslaved women, purchase promised reward. Male enslavers justified themselves by saying that African-American women were more sexual, less moral, less beautiful, less delicate. Such claims allegedly excused rape, the rejection of children, the sale of lovers, and the practice of forcing black women to labor in jobs for which white women were ostensibly too delicate.

Thomas Jefferson admitted that unchecked power twisted white men's characters: "The man must be a prodigy who can retain his manners and morals undepraved by such circumstances." We don't know whether Jefferson thought his morals depraved when he fathered his first child with an enslaved teenager named Sally Hemings. And we can imagine reasons for his desire. Perhaps she looked something like his dead wife, who was, after all, Sally's half-sister. Jefferson left no words about his transactions with Hemings. But a document from another white man raised in the slave colonies of the eighteenth-century British Empire reveals more openly the intimate connections between white men's sexual and financial desires.[43]

In the 1790s, Bryan Edwards, a Jamaican planter who wrote a four-volume history of the West Indies, published something that seemingly didn't fit with his usual fare of trade laws and sugar statistics. This was a ribald poem about the "Sable Venus," an allegory depicting the slave trade as a nude black woman riding a shell pulled from Angola by harnessed fish. The woodcut on the facing page revealed that she wore as little clothing as Botticelli's goddess, but the Sable Venus was dark and voluptuous instead of pale and potbellied. And when she entered Kingston harbor, "wild rapture seized the ravish'd land" of Jamaica. Planters crowded the docks in a "scramble" as they did when they tried to grab the strongest sugarcane workers, but this was a stampede to worship at the throne of a goddess of love. The white men of Jamaica, "all, adoring thee . . . *one* deity[,] confess" that their fetish was this goddess who traveled the Middle Passage. Her skin was not the white of English poetry, but Edwards noted with a wink that there was "no difference—not at night." And he rhapsodized about pursuing the ideal Sable Venus through a sequence of names as stereotypically West African as "Cuffy": "Do thou in gentle Phibba smile / In artful Benneba beguile / In wanton Mimba pout / In sprightly Cooba's eyes look gay? / Or grave in sober Quasheba / I still shall find thee out."[44]

Edwards has pulled a sneaky move. He pretends that the Sable Venus is in charge of the planters, echoing the literary lover's plaint: I have lost control, I am exquisitely captive to the one I desire. Of course, his depiction of the Sable Venus as a goddess who lures white men into sexual bondage is nonsense. The poem is about buying slaves. Edwards was not ruled by Quasheba, Cooba, or Mimba. He could buy each of them. Or all. After purchase, taking, consuming, could replace longing.

Modern consumers who lust for Apple products or other fetishized commodities should be familiar with lies to the self. Likewise, researchers who analyze the psychologies of gambling addicts note the sense of omnipotence that a successful play generates: the universe seems to have abandoned the law of chance and submitted to the rule of the gambler. When Edwards or Jefferson chased the Sable Venus, they always played successfully. They took no risk. She couldn't reject them. Outside of poetry, women did sometimes fight back. But in eighteenth-century slavery, the dice were loaded, and most enslaved women ultimately found it vital to go along. Look at the long record of successful rapes, intimidations, and transactions left by a contemporary of Edwards, Thomas Thistlewood. The manager of a wealthy man's Jamaican plantation, Thistlewood recorded the names of 109 enslaved women with whom he coupled over thirteen years. He focused on teenage girls, not

Image 7.1. In this image, slaveholders imagine African women as sexualized goddesses who come west across the Atlantic to serve white men as slaves in the New World. All her divine panoply—the cherubs, the sea creatures pulling her half-shell chariot—is a wink that reminds the white male viewer how different her status is from that of white women symbolized by Venus, the goddess whose apotheosis this one mocks. "Voyage of the Sable Venus," from Bryan Edwards, *The History, Civil and Commercial, of the British Colonies in the West Indies* (London, 1801), vol. 2.

grown women, and on isolated, recently imported Africans, rather than the Jamaican-born. Sometimes he had sex publicly, in front of other enslaved people, demonstrating his dominance over all of them. Nor was he unusual. Sexual opportunity was one of the factors that drew white men to Jamaica.[45]

In the nineteenth-century US South, two factors stood in the way of white men who wanted to play out Edwards-style fantasies. One was the fact that American religious reformers had begun to identify nonmarital sexuality as a major social problem, in part as a reaction to the way the increased mobility of young adults brought new temptations into their lives. Commercial quickening turned New York and other cities into hunting grounds for prostitutes looking for traveling businessmen, and vice versa. The solution, said authors of literature on the topic, many of them female, was that girls and women needed to refuse sexual contact outside of the guarantee for the support that marriage provided. Young men, meanwhile, needed to learn the self-control such authors thought necessary to make the young republic a moral paragon by avoiding illicit sex and masturbation.[46]

The Victorian complex of ideas about sex soon became the consensus view of respectable society. And enslaved people themselves often resisted, setting limits on the ability of white men to fulfill their desires. Their resistance was strengthened by strategies developed over generations of experience in southeastern communities. African-American family networks and ties to white patrons gave some girls and women allies who could intervene to prevent horrific abuse. The best-known case is that of Harriet Jacobs, whose Edenton, North Carolina, enslaver pursued her from the time she began puberty in the mid-1820s. For a decade, Jacobs deflected his advances with the help of white and black allies. Ultimately, she sought refuge in the attic of her grandmother, a free woman of color.[47]

Of course, some women of African-American descent used their sexuality to create a little leverage for themselves. Nor was the shift toward a more "Victorian" way of thought the only reason why, for instance, white women felt anger and competition when their husbands had sex with enslaved women. And despite respectable condemnation of "concubinage," the coercion of enslaved women continued in the nineteenth century. In one case, South Carolina Governor James Henry Hammond bought a woman and her daughter. The mother became his sexual partner. When her daughter reached twelve, he made the girl his victim as well. (He also molested his four white nieces, creating a scandal that ruined their marital prospects. Its effects on him were temporary, however, and he was elected to the US Senate.)[48]

Still, men like Hammond became increasingly circumspect in the Southeast. But the southwestern region was different, in several key ways. Many migrant whites came with the idea already in their heads that slavery's frontier was a white man's sexual playground. "To be a gentleman here," wrote one visitor to New Orleans, "one must patronize a yellow miss. . . . [I]f a young buck has one or two discarded lemans, his credit rises in proportion to the number." Supposedly, in arrangements called *plaçage*, young white men contracted with mixed-race women for long-term sex work. More temporary associations were arranged at balls that were limited to white men and nightgown-clad women of color, who were, as one irate white woman fumed, "Heaven's last, worst gift to white men."[49]

The complaints about New Orleans reflected the fact that many southwestern whites wanted proper forms of sexual morality to govern the public culture of the region. But that plan collapsed. The explosive growth of the interstate slave trade relentlessly forced the commodification of enslaved women's sexuality into view. And no individuals were more directly responsible for that than the nation's biggest slave traders during Jackson's presidency: Tennessee-born Isaac Franklin and his partners—who included, in a way, both Nicholas Biddle and Andrew Jackson. During Jackson's first term in office, as impending Indian removal made it clear that new markets for slaves were about to open, Franklin's firm rode the rising demand to become the biggest slave-trading firm in the United States. By 1832, B.U.S. lending in the Lower Mississippi Valley was sixteen times the 1824 level, because that was where Biddle saw the opportunity to give "the great staple of the country"—cotton—"assistance in bringing [it] into the commercial market." The massive injection of capital directly and indirectly financed an equally massive expansion of the internal slave trade. The well-connected Franklin firm, for instance, drew up to $40,000 at a time from the B.U.S. to buy more slaves in the East. In fact, about 5 percent of all the commercial credit handled by the B.U.S. in 1831–1832 passed at some point through the smooth hands of this single slave-trading partnership.[50]

Yet somehow Franklin and his business partners John Armfield and Rice Ballard viewed themselves as lawless outsiders. When Ballard wrote Franklin asking for an infusion of cash to pay short-term debts, Franklin wrote back, "It would be hard if two such old robbers as yourself and John [Armfield] could not sustain yourselves." By "robber" Franklin meant a "smooth hand" at the entrepreneurial business of the frontier, including the various legal and quasi-legal ways to take money from other people. Ballard could expertly "financeer," "shave" notes (sell people's debt to third parties for a profit), lose $4,000 in one round of cards and take $5,000 on the next, and judge a hand in the market, then drive her hard once he bought her. Sure, they took risks, but "if they Loose everything" one day, said Franklin, on the next "they can Robb far more." Even their competitors, and the bill-brokers, land speculators, and bank schemers who populated their circles, were "robbers": "land pirates," they sometimes called each other.[51]

Perhaps land pirates viewed themselves as outsiders because some southeastern elites, reacting to the new abolitionist criticism of the early 1830s, were beginning to scapegoat slave traders again. Or maybe because Ballard was the sort of man who threatened to shoot a powerful Mississippi politician on sight if the man didn't start paying his debts. Politicians, meanwhile, passed laws restricting slave traders when it suited their needs, and Franklin and his friends habitually bent and broke those laws. And maybe the slave traders cultivated a sense of rule-breaking because of the way entrepreneurs at the cutting edge of economic expansion tend to sneer at old-fashioned risk-averse people. Less savvy slave-buyers were, to Ballard, "thick-headed gumps" who were not alert to the intricacies of skinning and shaving.[52]

The ultimate reason why the slave traders felt the kind of power experienced by an outlaw who gets away was half-hidden, but everybody knew about it. In 1834, Isaac Franklin wrote Rice Ballard from New Orleans, where Nat Turner panic had worn off and the trade in hands was once again going full tilt. Talking about himself in the third person—or not exactly as a person—Franklin wrote: "The way your Old One Eyed friend looked the pirate was a sin to Crockett," he said. "Sin to Crockett" was a slang term meaning "astounding"—Davy Crockett was a frontiersman-turned-stage-performer-turned-congressman and author of a spectacularly exaggerated autobiography. And "One Eyed friend"—well here, Franklin meant himself, but also, a penis.[53]

In the same vein, Franklin continued, "The fancy Girl from Charlottes-ville, will you send her out or shall I charge you $1100 for her? Say Quick, I wanted to see her. . . . I thought that an old Robber might be satisfyed with two or three maids." Starting in the early 1830s, the term "fancy girl" or "maid" began to appear in the interstate slave trade. It meant a young woman, usually light-skinned, sold at a high price explicitly linked to her sexual availability and attractiveness: "For Sale: A coloured girl, of very su-perior qualifications . . . what speculators call a fancy girl; a bright mulatto, fine figure, straight, black hair, and very black eyes; very neat and cleanly in her dress and person."[54]

Abolitionist Ethan Allen Andrews toured John Armfield's Alexandria, Virginia, slave pen in 1835 and reported that he was told that "though mulat-toes are not so much valued for field-hands, they are purchased for domestics, and the females to be sold as prostitutes." Ironically, it was a wave of new white abolitionists, inspired by William Lloyd Garrison and by the black voices he promoted in the pages of *The Liberator*, who did much to make sure everyone knew about the fancy. In a national campaign of pamphlets and antislavery books that blitzed the nation's postal networks in the 1830s, ab-olitionist critique focused on the way slavery disrupted family relationships and forced enslaved women into nonmarital sex. The concerns of white moral reformers about the sexualized sale of women, especially almost-white ones, probably revealed much about the critics' preoccupations and repressions. But they didn't make it up, and enslavers were also preoccupied. Even before Andrews's depiction of the trade as forced prostitution, the customers and the impresarios of the slave market were writing with a leer about the women they used. "I sold your fancy maid Alice for $800. There are great demand for fancy maid. I do believe that a likely Girl & a good seamstress could be sold for $1100," Isaac Franklin wrote to Ballard in 1833. He wanted Ballard to send more: "I was disappointed in not finding your Charlottesville maid that you promised me," he wrote in 1834, referring to Ballard's latest shipment from his jail at Richmond. Soon, though, Isaac would have his turn, and then James Franklin, who two months later wrote to Ballard: "The Old Man sent me your maid Martha. She is inclined to be compliant."[55]

Breaking the rules of evangelical public propriety delivered to these men the sense of illicit discovery that accompanies pornography. For many white southern men, and not just slave traders, the existence of "fancy girls" put a piratical middle finger in propriety's face, which mattered not only because it irritated meddling abolitionists but because it irritated white southern women. Calls for sexual morality implied that women were the arbiters of domestic moral authority. This struggle over who would rule was the real meaning of the "Petticoat War" in Jackson's Cabinet, and in it the president leveraged male resentment of female claims to power. Who were politicians' wives to say whether or not John Eaton was a moral man for marrying Peggy, a former waitress who had, rumors suggested, offered more than drinks? There was no better way to show pious white women that they governed nothing than by buying a woman for sex.

That was the meaning, for instance, of the gesture that slave trader Theophilus Freeman made when he received visitors to his New Orleans house while lying in bed with his purchased mistress Sarah Connor. Take that, conventional white society, he said. For you'll never stop buying slaves from me. The lip-licking letters of Franklin and Ballard's firm, meanwhile, reveal their gleeful disdain for white women's social authority: "I am getting dam[n]ed tired of company," wrote a Ballard employee, briefly trapped at the high-toned White Sulphur Springs resort in Virginia. "I tell you it would be a great relief to be at the forks of road among the darkies." After dining with a recently married couple, a Ballard associate, Bacon Tait, wrote that he "had not sit at table in a private house with [white] Ladies for more than twenty years." And Isaac suggested that two women he purchased "could soon pay for themselves by keeping a whore house . . . for the Exclusive benefit of the concern and its allied agents."[56]

Slave traders were not the only sexual pirates, they were just more likely than planters to testify about such things in their letters to one another. And dark-skinned women were no safer from this form of violence than "mulatto" ones, whether from slave traders or other white men. "Put a single man" on a plantation as an overseer, "and you will see trouble enough," wrote an Alabama planter, for "they become intimate with the negro girls, and then all order is at an end." The white men who initiated such encounters in the southwestern areas seemed to feel more entitled to them than those in the southeastern states, and less concerned about keeping such things secret. Louisiana planter Jacob Bieller carried on a lengthy relationship with "bright mulatto" Mary Clarkson, his slave. When Bieller's wife complained, he responded by threatening to beat her. In 1834, Mrs. Bieller finally ran away and sued for divorce. But to no small extent, the southwestern region was a free-fire zone where white men exerted power without rules.[57]

In the southeastern states, enslaved husbands and male lovers possessed limited power to defend women, but at least they were impediments that white men had to calculate. Southwestern male predators enhanced their power by stripping away husbands and other allies on whom women might call. At thirteen, Louisa Picquet was the property of a Mr. Cook, whose bankruptcy reduced him to living in a Mobile boardinghouse. He spent mornings sleeping off the previous night's drinking and gambling, and afternoons trying to get Louisa alone in his room. For a while, the white landlady protected Louisa. Instead of sending the slave girl, the woman took Cook the things he demanded: salt, a washbasin, his mended clothes. But eventually Cook's creditors caught up to him. They sold light-skinned Louisa at the Mobile slave market to a Mr. Williams of New Orleans. He paid $1,400, a "fancy" price. Then Williams told Louisa that "he and his wife had parted," and they boarded the next coastal steamer going to Louisiana. "Soon as we started for New Orleans, Mr. Williams told me what he bought me for," Louisa later said.[58]

The word "fancy" can mean something highly decorative, or one can "fancy" something—desire it, as something or someone to acquire. White men fancied a Louisa; white men used her to decorate their lives as commodities to be displayed. But being fancied carried over into the descriptions and pricing of all women, light or dark, house servant or field hand. Although descriptions of men emphasized size, and sometimes skills, evaluations of women discussed their attractiveness. "Girls and ordinary women" bring $350 to $400, wrote Isaac Franklin in 1832, "and a few of superior appearance at $500." "Two boys have a mother here," wrote a New Orleans dealer to a man who had already bought the sons. "[She is] about thirty six years old fine teeth without any grey hairs a mulatto—she is very anxious to go with them—shall I buy her? . . . She [is] very likely of her age and young looking." Another trader described a "13 year old Girl, bright color, nearly a fancy for $1135." She had potential. Another: "a girl[,] size of Gilmer's girl"—so far so good, evidently—"but rough faced," reducing her value. Even for field hands like John Knight's dark women, looks changed prices. Male buyers imagined times between days, hidden spaces between cotton rows.[59]

For the female half of the enslaved people traded and moved, sexual assault and exploitation shaped price and experiences. Traders manipulated buyers' fancies to make sales. "We anticipate tolerably tough times this spring *for one eyed men*," wrote James Franklin to Rice Ballard in 1832. "I have seen a handsome Girl since I left Va that would climb higher hills & go further to accomplish her designs than any girl to the North & she is not too apt to leave or loose *her gold* & the reason is because she carries her funds in her lovers purse or in Bank & to my certain knowledge has been used & that smartly by a one eyed young man about my size & age, *excuse my foolishness*." Franklin, a one-eyed man, would use her lover's purse until he could manipulate other men's single-focused desires and get them to transfer their funds to his bank account.[60]

To understand why a slave trader would call himself a one-eyed man, one must view him in the context of a slave-frontier world where white men saw their contests with other people as rendering the winner manly and the loser emasculated, enslaved, feminized. The slave trader, as a one-eyed man, wasn't just raping the women he bought and sold. He was also metaphorically raping his competitors. This was the same metaphorical world in which less wealthy white men opposed banks that used their deposits and taxes and pro-ductivity in order to create credit. Said banks then lent said credit to wealthy would-be aristocrats, men who wanted to replicate Granville County–style hierarchies on the frontier. This is why ordinary white men called on Andrew Jackson to save the country from inchoate but horrible threats to them as manly citizens. They wanted him to help Potterize the B.U.S., and all the other targets of resentment, before it raped ordinary male citizens. And just as consequentially for what happened in the 1830s, Franklin and Ballard slipped incessantly between talking about the financial risk-taking of credit and collections, on the one hand, and sex with enslaved women, on the other. The exploitation of enslaved women had existed since the beginnings of slav-ery in North America, but what was now emerging was different. The new trade branded and marketed the ability to coerce sexuality, priming white en-trepreneurs to believe that the purchase of enslaved-people-as-commodities offered white men freedoms not found in ordinary life. Fancy branded slave-trading as sexy for sellers and buyers.

From fancy maids to slave-trading in general, they went on to financial risk in general. In the 1830s, when the real-world test subjects on slavery's entrepreneurial frontier, primed by the sexual arousal built into the human-commodity market, met with opportunities to buy more slaves, take out loans to expand their operations, or sell cotton, they were more likely than ever to chase short-term gains with little thought for the future. North Carolina migrant Moses Alexander thought so, seeing the slave frontier as the epicen-ter of multiple types of profligacy. "To raise my children in Alabama, I may

Image 7.2. Auction of enslaved baby. African-American and white abolitionists identified family separations and the exposure of women to sexual abuse as two of the most devastating impacts of the domestic slave trade. Henry Bibb's autobiography described his own misery at being separated—like the parents and spouses crying and pleading here—from his wife and children. *Narrative of the Life and Adventures of Henry Bibb, an American Slave* (New York, 1849), 201.

possibly tell you my greatest objection—but I cannot write it," Alexander noted in a letter, but he saw southwestern sexual license as part and parcel of risky southwestern economic behavior. "Speculation is the order of the day and stalks abroad in the country," he warned. Events would reveal that his estimate of one-eyed enslavers was correct. Stimulated by the domestic slave trade to think of themselves as rule-breaking "one-eyed men" who could always have their fancy, southwestern entrepreneurs were planting the financial seeds of still more irrational choices. Enslavers would soon insist on taking on immense debt. But they underestimated the downside of that risk, and eventually not only because they had been trained to feel that the universe had loaded the dice in their favor. People almost always misjudge downside risk when the prices of assets (such as slaves) are rising. They know intellectually that asset prices that have climbed in the past—whether Dutch tulip bulbs, Yazoo Company stock, or subprime mortgage securities—have formed bubbles that eventually popped. But this time is always different.[61]

To most one-eyed men, the B.U.S. seemed like a maiden-aunt chaperone who frowned at any sign of a creeping hand. Enslavers benefited from bank-induced stability and steady credit expansion, but the B.U.S. limited credit expansion and favored only a few entrepreneurs. Of course, there were other important reasons—even "rational" ones—why enslavers wanted to borrow more money. The more slave purchases they could finance, the more cotton they'd make, and cotton was the world's most widely traded product. It had an unending market. So the more cotton they made, the more they'd sell, and thus the more money they'd make. Owning more slaves enabled planters to repay debts, take profits, and gain property that could be collateral for even more borrowing.[62]

At the same time, it made sense that people with money wanted to lend it to entrepreneurs on slavery's frontier. People who have money want to lend it if they can make still more money doing so, especially if they can feel certain of repayment. Lending to the South's cotton economy was an investment not just in the world's most widely traded commodity, but also in a set of producers who had shown a consistent ability to increase their productivity and revenue. In other words, enslavers had the cash flow to pay back their debts. And their debts were secure, since enslavers owned a lot of valuable collateral. In fact, they owned the biggest pool of collateral in the United States: 2 million slaves worth over $1 billion. Not only was that almost 20 percent of all the wealth owned by all US citizens, but it was the most liquid part of that wealth, thanks to the efficiency of markets manned by professional slave traders and supplied with credit by a B.U.S.-governed financial system (see Table 7.1).

Potential lenders—such as the banks of Western Europe and their investors, the old and new upper classes, whose savings Baring Brothers and the Bank of England pooled—wondered whether Biddle was perhaps not investing aggressively enough, or passing on sufficient profits to Europeans who bought B.U.S. bonds. Enslavers, meanwhile, wanted to transform their control over enslaved people's bodies into authority over their own credit. In 1827, a Louisiana enslaver had created a tool that might answer both tasks at once. J. B. Moussier was facing a lawsuit by Rogers and Harrison, Virginia-based slave-trading partners to whom he owed $21,000 for seventy men, women, and children he had bought on a short-term, high-interest loan. What if, Moussier wondered, planters used slaves as collateral to raise capital overseas, from people who needed American cotton and sugar, and then used the capital to build a lending institution that enslavers themselves could control? Moussier took his idea to New Orleans politician-entrepreneurs Edmund Forstall and Hugues Lavergne, who engineered it into the charter of the Consolidated Association of the Planters of Louisiana (C.A.P.L.), chartered by the state legislature in 1827.[63]

TABLE 7.1. ENSLAVED PEOPLE AND TOTAL US WEALTH

| YEAR | TOTAL US WEALTH (MILLIONS OF DOLLARS) | ENSLAVED POPULATION | WEALTH IN SLAVES (MILLIONS OF DOLLARS) | ENSLAVED PEOPLE AS SHARE OF ALL US WEALTH |
|------|------|------|------|------|
| 1790 | 1,150 | 800,000* | 200* | 0.174 |
| 1800 | 2,400 | 1,000,000* | 250* | 0.104 |
| 1810 | Unknown | 1,191,000 | 316 | — |
| 1820 | Unknown | 1,538,022 | 610 | — |
| 1830 | 3,825 | 2,009,043 | 577 | 0.151 |
| 1840 | 5,226 | 2,487,355 | 997 | 0.191 |
| 1850 | 7,135 | 3,204,313 | 1,286 | 0.180 |
| 1860 | 16,160 | 3,953,760 | 3,059 | 0.189 |
| 1870 | 26,460 | 0 | 0 | 0 |

*Author's estimate.

Source: *Historical Statistics of the United States: 1789–1945* (Washington, DC, 1949); Susan B. Carter, Scott Sigmund Gartner, Michael R. Haines, Alan L. Olmstead, Richard Sutch, and Gavin Wright, eds., *Cambridge Historical Statistics of the U.S.* (Cambridge, MA, 2006).

Here are the nuts and bolts of the C.A.P.L. First, potential borrowers would apply to buy stock in the "Association." Their application accepted, they could mortgage slaves and land to the C.A.P.L. in order to pay for the stock. The stock would entitle them to borrow C.A.P.L. bank notes of up to half the value of the mortgaged property. To ensure that people would take these bank notes at face value, the founders needed a large reserve of hard cash. They planned to raise it by selling bonds on the financial markets of the Western world. Each bond would be $500 in face value—about the average price, in the 1820s, of a young enslaved man. A bond would reach maturity in ten to fifteen years, and it would pay investors 5 percent in annual interest.[64]

Lenders always want security, though, so how would the C.A.P.L. assure potential investors that the bonds would be worth their face value plus interest? Thomas Baring of Baring Brothers helped Lavergne and Forstall to convince the state legislature to back the C.A.P.L.'s bonds with the "faith and credit" of Louisiana. If loan repayments from planters failed and the bank could not pay off the bonds, the taxpayers of Louisiana were now obligated to do so. The state's commitment convinced the European securities market. In 1828, the C.A.P.L. received from Baring Brothers, its European brokers, the first receipts from bond sales that would ultimately total $2.5 million in "sterling bills" redeemable for silver at the Bank of England. The bank started to

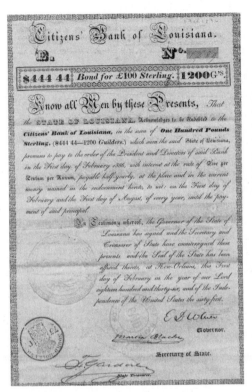

Image 7.3. In the late 1820s, southwestern states began to issue bonds that turned slave mortgages into securities that could be marketed to investors around the Western world. This helped pump credit onto slavery's frontier, where it was used to purchase large numbers of enslaved people from the southeast. Citizens' Bank faith bond, marketed in Europe. When first issued, the price was approximately that of a first-rate female slave in New Orleans. Louisiana Banking collection, Louisiana Research Collection, Tulane University.

lend out $3.5 million in new C.A.P.L. notes, printed by a London engraver, to planter-stockholders.[65]

For the next dozen years, entrepreneurs working with legislators in Louisiana, Mississippi, Alabama, Tennessee, and the territories of Arkansas and Florida replicated C.A.P.L. innovations in a series of new banks. Many were bigger, generated more capital, and sold even more bonds than the C.A.P.L. The tens of thousands of enslaved people named in their documents were still used as collateral mortgaged to a lender—which was now a local bank like the C.A.P.L.—but the banks' bonds securitized the slave mortgages. Securitization is the pooling of debt from many borrowers so that it can be sold off in uniform chunks, reducing the risks inherent in lending to one person at a time. Now, all bond-buyers would share in the profits of the C.A.P.L. while being shielded against the kind of catastrophic individual losses a single lender would suffer if, say, a borrower's slaves died en masse at a malaria-infested labor camp, or if floods destroyed a cotton crop.[66]

The financial product that such banks as Baring Brothers were selling to investors in London, Hamburg, Amsterdam, Paris, Philadelphia, Boston, and New York was remarkably similar to the securitized bonds, backed by mortgages on US homes, that attracted investors from around the globe to US financial markets from the 1980s until the economic collapse of 2008. Like the C.A.P.L. bonds, mortgage-backed securities shifted risk away from the immediate originators of loans onto financial markets while promising to spread out and thus minimize the consequences of individual debtors' failures. Investors who purchased latter-day mortgage-backed securities planned to share in streams of income generated by homebuyers' mortgage payments. Likewise, the faith bonds of the 1830s generated revenue for investors from enslavers' repayments of mortgages on enslaved people. This meant that investors around the world would share in revenues made by hands in the field. Thus, in effect, even as Britain was liberating the slaves of its empire, a British bank could now sell an investor a completely commodified slave: not a particular individual who could die or run away, but a bond that was the right to a one-slave-sized slice of a pie made from the income of thousands of slaves.

Typically, credit brings risk. For the borrower, there is the risk of not being able to pay, and for the lender, the risk that he will not be repaid. The C.A.P.L. model shifted risks away from both the immediate lender—a bank—and the borrower. In fact, the faith bonds shifted, or "socialized," risk onto two groups of people. The first was the enslaved. Their own hands would have to repay the loans. And if their owners did not pay their debts, the enslaved people themselves would be foreclosed upon.

Second, if neither bank revenue nor foreclosure sales of human collateral could pay back the bondholders, the citizens of the state would have to redeem the bonds with their own taxes. The fact that popularly elected legislatures repeatedly supported such bond schemes is therefore remarkable. After all, many elements of the intensely democratic frontier electorate saw banks as machines designed to channel financial benefits and economy-governing power to unelected elites. But advocates of the new banks often posed as competitors to much-resented factions favored by the hated B.U.S. When Mississippi's newly democratized legislature considered the possibility of chartering a new bank, its backers insisted that doing so would provide competition to Stephen Duncan's Bank of Mississippi. That bank's "aristocratic pack" of supporters "ridiculed the notion of anybody but Dr. Duncan and Gab. Tichenor knowing anything about Banking or even being able to put their feet in a Bank except as petitioners." Or so claimed a board member for the new institution.

Enhancing the effect of the rhetorical device of posing new banks as democratic blows against established cliques was the sudden increase in opportunities for putting credit to use. After the passage of Indian removal, the
US government imposed the Treaty of Dancing Rabbit Creek on the Choc-
taws, opening 11 million Mississippi acres to sale. Federal treaty-makers'
agreements with the Chickasaw, meanwhile, transferred another 7 million.
Potential bank-borrowers imagined what they would do with the land. "A
thousand avenues [are] wide open here for money making," as one Mississippi enslaver wrote, "such as planting shaving paper [buying and selling
other people's debt for profit] or speculating by buying & selling all kinds
of property." Robert Walker, a supporter of the new bank, wrote that "Kentucky's coming, Tennessee's coming, Alabama's coming, Georgia's coming,
Carolina's coming, Virginia's coming, and they're all coming to join the joy-
ous crowd of Mississippians."[67]

The new banks were bound to find themselves in conflict with the B.U.S.
monopoly on financial and monetary control, but the C.A.P.L. showed borrowers, bankers, slave traders, and other entrepreneurs an accessory pathway
around Nicholas Biddle. And they traveled in that direction hand in hand
with Andrew Jackson and his administration. Jackson supposedly hated all
banks, but his policies would lead to explosive growth in both new banks
and new lending. Even more ironically, Nicholas Biddle did at least as much
as Jackson to create a new financial environment in which C.A.P.L.-style
innovations could run as wild as one-eyed men demanded.

From 1828 onward, Biddle had tried to court both Jackson and other
southwestern entrepreneurs. Yet neither Biddle's visits to the Oval Office
nor a dramatic surge of B.U.S. credit into southwestern channels changed the
minds of the bank's opponents. These included not only resentful planters,
but also radicals like the members of the Philadelphia Workingmen's Party,
who attacked the disproportions of wealth that were emerging in eastern
urban centers. The bank's monopoly control over American credit, complained one "Workie'" spokesman, enabled "some men to live in splendor on
the labor of operatives." Then there were those who still resented the bank's
role in the troubles of 1819, such as Jackson's close adviser Amos Kendall.
Even Baring Brothers, long-term B.U.S. trading partners, were beginning
to perceive Biddle's regulatory power as an impediment to C.A.P.L.-style
endeavors.[68]

Biddle's administration contacts hinted to the bank that an extension of its
charter, which expired in 1836, was a real possibility. But Jackson kept his

cards close to the vest. By 1832, the uncertainty was driving Biddle crazy, and even though Jackson's more pro-bank counselors told the bank president to avoid pushing, Biddle made an unwise decision. The suave Kentuckian Henry Clay, Jackson's inevitable 1832 opponent for the presidency, persuaded the vulnerable Philadelphian to try to back Old Hickory into renewing the bank's charter before the election. Clay believed he could trap Jackson on a dilemma. If Jackson vetoed the recharter, Old Hickory would lose the electoral votes of pro-bank Pennsylvania. If Jackson signed the bill, he would blur the lines between himself and Clay, blunting the enthusiasm of his most fervent foot soldiers. In June, the Clay-manipulated Senate passed a bill reestablishing the B.U.S. for another twenty years. Southwestern senators split on the issue. Louisiana's delegation supported it. So did Mississippi's George Poindexter; B.U.S. loans financed his extravagant lifestyle. But Mississippi's other senator stood against it, with those of Tennessee and Georgia.[69]

On July 3, the House followed suit with its approval. The next day, Martin Van Buren, who was replacing Calhoun as the vice-presidential candidate on Jackson's ballot, found the president sick in bed. The old general squeezed Van Buren's hand and struggled to sit upright. "The bank, Mr. Van Buren, is trying to kill me, *but I will kill it*," he said. Back in 1815 at New Orleans, Edward Pakenham had also thought he had Jackson trapped. Pakenham died on a sugarcane field. Over the next week, alternating between his sickbed and meetings with a hard core of anti-bank advisers—Martin Van Buren, Maryland's Roger B. Taney, and Amos Kendall—Jackson worked up an essay that supported what he was about to do. On the 10th, he announced his veto of the bank recharter.[70]

This was an unprecedented act. No president, opponents would charge, had vetoed an act passed with overwhelming support by both houses, simply because he personally disagreed with the policy it enacted. Yet Jackson asserted an idea of power in a representative government that showed why less wealthy white men supported him with such ferocious loyalty. In the president's "Veto Message," he argued that all white male citizens were precisely equal in political rights and power. The government should not favor anyone, and in particular, it should not fulfill the self-interested wishes of the wealthy over the will of the majority. This was no mindless critique of government. He did not agree with, for instance, the "d—d tadpole eating crew," as one Tennessee Jacksonian called South Carolina's nullifiers. Instead, said Jackson, if government "would confine itself to equal protection, and, as Heaven does when it rains, shower its favors alike on the high and the low, the rich and the poor, it would be an unqualified blessing." But in Jackson's judgment, the bank did "not measure out equal justice." Instead, it used the government's favor to make "the rich richer and the potent more powerful." The federal charter, government deposits in the bank, and monopoly power over the workings of the economy enabled the B.U.S. to make its stockholders "a privileged order, clothed both with great political power and enjoying immense pecuniary advantages from their connection with the Government."[71]

Congress exploded. The reaction was so furious, in fact, that Biddle believed the electorate would punish Jackson at the polls. "One individual," wrote Biddle, has "opposed his will to the deliberate reflections of the representatives of the people." And indeed, the fall 1832 election was an epic moment that helped crystallize the coalitions of voting blocs and politicians into modern political parties. Henry Clay's supporters, outraged at the veto, included the "National Republicans" who had supported John Quincy Adams. They linked up with former Jackson supporters who thought the national bank was necessary and believed that the general's veto had broken all restraints on the executive branch. Also joining them were supporters of moral and economic improvement who believed that Jackson's followers ignorantly opposed progress. Young Abraham Lincoln, for instance, was the only reader in his family, the one who left his father Thomas's farm in the woods. He had walked all the way to the Illinois frontier town of Salem Creek to work in a store and read law. Abraham Lincoln was also the only one in his family who joined the brand new party of Jackson's opponents: the Whigs.[72]

Clay's opponents included most of Jackson's core constituencies from the 1828 election. In the veto summer their representatives united at the first-ever national convention of the Democratic Party. They included many southeastern and southwestern enslavers who lacked personal connections to merchants and bankers. The Democrats also included small farmers, tenants, and the rural landless of the southern and northwestern frontiers, urban workers, and Robert Potter sitting in the Granville County jail: everyone energized by Jackson's assertive refusal to accept anything less than white male equality.

The B.U.S. openly subsidized Clay's presidential campaign. In so doing, it did much to prove Jackson's points—which Biddle foolishly publicized by having tens of thousands of copies of the Veto Message distributed throughout the country. He thought that everyone who read it would agree that Jackson had produced a "a manifesto of anarchy," addressed to a "mob." But when all the votes were cast, Biddle's "mob"—or, in Jackson's terms, the "people"—had sustained the president's veto of the pro-bank Congress, reelecting Jackson by a clear majority in both popular and electoral votes.[73]

Anyone who understood at the subrational level why Robert Potter's support increased with each conflict he fought against the Granville County elite would also understand why Clay and Biddle and the B.U.S. went down to inglorious defeat in November 1832. The destruction of the B.U.S. definitively established popular but white-males-only democracy as a winning play in the US political competition. White men forced to the margins of the changing US economy usually chose the Democrats as their political home, and would do so for the next fourteen decades. Frontier enslavers, even if they were outside of the old bank cliques, didn't want the same kind of democracy that Jackson's hottest partisans among common white men wanted. But the two groups could cooperate, at least during good times.[74]

Yet even though Jackson believed he was acting to protect opportunity for all white men, his policies repeatedly gave the frontier's entrepreneurial elite exactly what most of them wanted: more Indian lands, more territories to the west for slavery, free trade for cotton, and, finally, destruction of all limits on their ability to leverage enslaved people's bodies as credit. The majoritarian philosophy of the new Democratic Party would be fatally alloyed by its commitment to both slavery's expansion and the unregulated, unstable economy that one-eyed entrepreneurs desired. But in the short term, the 1832 election convinced Jackson that the people now expected him to cut off the Monster Bank's power to divert the blessings of government to the well-connected. And Jackson's most fervently populist followers had long been anticipating a moment of confrontation with the nefarious powers who they thought were scheming to steal the independence and equality promised to white men by American citizenship. The B.U.S. charter allowed it to serve as the central bank until 1836, so Jackson pushed his advisers to find a legal or quasi-legal way to move against the bank. Finally, the president ordered Secretary of the Treasury Louis McLane to remove government deposits from the B.U.S. Instead, McLane issued a report showing that Biddle's staff had managed the deposits judiciously. So Jackson reshuffled his Cabinet. Roger Taney eventually became the secretary of the treasury, and in September 1833 he began to draw down the $10 million in federal money that was still sitting in the B.U.S. account.[75]

Needing somewhere to put federal money, the executive branch decided to distribute it among individual state-chartered banks. "Those which are in hands politically friendly will be preferred," wrote one of Jackson's most trusted political operatives. The opposition press called the recipients of federal money the "pet" banks. The Union Bank of Nashville was the chosen "pet" for Tennessee, for instance. It just happened to have been founded by the brother-in-law of James K. Polk, Jackson's main political lieutenant in the state. The ranks of the "pets" soon expanded to over thirty. While the eastern institutions that received federal deposits were conservative with the new influx of money, banks at the leading edge of southwestern expansion used government funds as an excuse to expand lending dramatically. The Mississippi pets' directors knew that after land sales in the Chickasaw and Choctaw cessions, government land offices would deposit hundreds of thousands of dollars. Anticipating these new reserves—which were also, they might have remembered, liabilities that could be withdrawn—the banks began to print and lend their own paper money. By late 1833, Mississippi banks had twenty times as much paper floating around the economy as they had gold in their vaults to back it up. From Columbus, Mississippi, a boom town in the state's northeastern corner, D. W. Jordan chortled, "Here I can make *money money*" to his North Carolina relatives. John Knight reported that Natchez cotton was 18 cents per pound. He wanted to buy a woman for his wife, and Isaac Franklin was now charging $1,000 for a well-schooled house servant. "We shall do well this season," Franklin wrote.[76]

Back in Philadelphia, however, the Monster Bank still had claws. After Jackson's withdrawal of the deposits, Biddle fought back. In November 1833, the B.U.S. began to call in all its loans. As he deliberately induced a massive recession, Biddle announced that "the other banks and the merchants may break, but the Bank of the United States shall not." Businesses closed down. Factories and workshops stood idle. Retail districts had no buyers. The slowdown threatened devastation to heavily leveraged planters and cotton merchants. Interest rates offered to the brokers who flocked to New Orleans every fall to buy the cotton harvest rose to 25 percent. Cotton purchases dropped, pushing the recession up the rivers into the Crescent City's vast watershed. In Mississippi, wrote one Natchez lawyer, "times are very hard, the mad course of the president has caused more ruin in the country than was ever known before." Now John Knight watched cotton prices plummet to 9 cents per pound. The price of slaves followed. "I tried every Bank in this City for a check on the North," wrote a panicked Isaac Franklin from New Orleans, "[but] none will." "The Bank [here] will not discount a dollar," confirmed his Natchez allies.[77]

Many blamed Jackson. Elite southwestern Jacksonians turned apostate. Robert Walker, previously one of Jackson's Mississippi political lieutenants, switched sides. Franklin Plummer was the only holdout, and he was reportedly wavering. Loyalist J. F. H. Claiborne expressed anti-bank views at a public meeting in Natchez, and was physically assaulted and beaten by the mostly wealthy crowd. A torrent of complaints poured into the offices of congressmen. Philadelphia businessman John Wurts wrote a letter imploring James K. Polk to use his "personal and political influence . . . to provide some remedy to check the impending evil." From Tennessee, John Welsh warned that "even the enemies of the Bank here freely admit that all this distress may be corrected by a return of the deposits to the U.S. Bank." Henry Clay, meanwhile, organized the Senate to censure Jackson for removing the deposits. But the president refused to quail. When a delegation of businessmen visited Jackson, he said: "What do you come to me for, then? Go to Nicholas Biddle. We have no money here, gentlemen. Biddle has all the money." The bank, Jackson believed, was confirming the warnings of his Veto Message. His loyal followers agreed: Jackson loyalist Terry Cahal told James K. Polk that Tennessee Bank allies were squealing that the "mob" was plotting a revolution in which "the rich [will be] plundered by the rabble." But this kind of talk reinforced the Jacksonian claim that B.U.S. supporters hated white men's democracy, while Jackson partisans cheered his attack on the bank: "*Crush it forever!!* It is a *Monopoly* which ought not to exist among us."[78]

The recession winter of 1833–1834 was difficult, but by spring the economy began to cooperate with Jackson. Good harvests in Europe and new supplies of precious metal for circulation in the Western economies raised consumer demand and lowered interest rates. But one of the most significant factors that turned the southwestern economic climate from bank war to boom was the replication of the C.A.P.L.'s slave bonds on a far vaster scale. The new banks began to appear right as the bank war began, starting with the Union Bank of Louisiana in 1832. Structured on the C.A.P.L. model but significantly larger, the bank sold $7 million in "faith bonds" through the agency of the Barings. The proceeds of the faith bonds were to fund the capital-intensive projects of shareholders—in other words, to help them buy slaves—and back a massive commercial credit operation that would help move the annual pile of cotton from steamboat landings to Liverpool docks. By 1834, the Union Bank was taking up a lot of the slack left in New Orleans by the retreat of the B.U.S. In November 1834, it became a pet bank, opening access to another pool of money.

Next, the state legislature established the Citizens' Bank of Louisiana with $12 million in faith bonds, and then authorized several other smaller institutions (for instance, the Atchafalaya Railroad and Banking Company, capital $2 million). Louisiana's orgy of bank-creation increased the number of the state's banks from four to sixteen and expanded the total amount of authorized capital from $9 million to $46 million. By 1836, New Orleans

Image 7.4. An elderly but still pugnacious Andrew Jackson as President, slaying the many-headed Hydra of the nefarious Second Bank of the United States. The head with the top hat is Nicholas Biddle. "General Jackson slaying the many headed monster," Henry B. Robinson, 1836. Library of Congress.

had the densest concentration of banking capital in the country, outpacing Philadelphia and New York and suggesting that Louisiana might become the nation's financial power center in the near future. The Florida territory, with fewer than 100,000 residents, launched multiple banks, including its own Union Bank, for which it issued faith bonds. Alabama also funded its banking system with bonds, selling most to the Rothschilds of Paris, Europe's most powerful bankers. In 1832, the total amount of the bank loans available to southwestern borrowers had been under $40 million, including $30 million lent by the B.U.S. By 1837, despite the retreat of the B.U.S, southwestern bank loans soared to more than $80 million—one-third of the national total and more than that of any other region. Southwestern legislatures had authorized significantly more banking capital in the 1830s than what the B.U.S. had earlier applied to the economy of the entire United States.[79]

Although some of the banks were ostensibly chartered to create investment in the state's infrastructure—including railroads, or, in the case of the New Orleans Gas Light and Banking Company, modern municipal utilities—the major purpose of the splurge was to rush seeds of growth into the fields of southwestern entrepreneurs' dreams. In the course of a mere four years, from 1833 through 1836, 150,000 enslaved people were moved from the old states to the new. They cleared and planted and harvested millions of new acres, and the US cotton crop doubled in size. Meanwhile, the bonds created by southwestern states—each one a guarantee of an income stream from the labor of mortgaged hands—found buyers in all of the major financial centers of the Western world—London, New York, Philadelphia, Amsterdam, Hamburg, Bremen, and Paris. Investors around the world voted their confidence in slavery's expansion. And rising London prices for southwestern securities, statistics demonstrate, pushed up slave prices in New Orleans.[80]

The irony is obvious, in hindsight. Andrew Jackson had mobilized common white male anger at arrogant, antidemocratic supporters of the B.U.S. and its allies. He and his followers, from the lowliest voter to loyal congressmen, metaphorically Potterized Biddle and George Poindexter and all the members of the old southwestern bank-vault factions that had monopolized frontier opportunity and tried to tell ordinary citizens to keep quiet. In fact, cartoons of the day even depicted Jackson chopping off the penile snakeheads of a hydra-headed Monster Bank.

Yet the destruction of the B.U.S. and the ensuing deployment of banking innovations didn't make the southern financial environment more democratic. For instance, when Franklin Plummer, the champion of the people of southeastern Mississippi, visited Natchez before the 1835 state elections, men who ran the new banks bought him a fancy carriage. Plummer then reversed his rhetoric against the use of state power to deliver bank goodies to insiders and campaigned for a slate of pro-bank candidates. When elected, these pro-bank state legislators sent Robert Walker to Washington as senator, deposing George Poindexter from office. Walker had depicted Poindexter as the servant of the Monster Bank, an arrogant opponent of white male equality. Now he and Plummer encouraged the Mississippi legislature as it chartered so many banks that by 1839 the state's total on-paper bank capitalization was $63 million—more than the national B.U.S. at its largest. And old insiders managed to remain insiders. Stephen Duncan, leader of the old Natchez-based Planters' Bank, launched a new bank, which the state legislature chartered. Henry Clay wrote his Mississippi allies in 1834, asking a Duncan ally to give his son a loan so that he could buy a Mississippi cotton plantation: "I have a number of surplus slaves here, principally young and well adapted to a cotton plantation." Banker and planter were often the same: ten of the top eleven borrowers from the Union Bank of Florida were members of its board of directors, or immediate relatives thereof. While some charters required new institutions to distribute loans in a more geographically equal fashion than had predecessor banks, the new banks did nothing different from the B.U.S. when it came to distributing credit to lower-class men. Thus, those who had derived political benefit from common white men's insistence on equal manhood replaced the B.U.S. with an insider-favoring banking system.[81]

"The people" thought they had slain the monster, but the stumps sprouted new heads that feasted on the huge sums of capital being imported via European sales of state bonds that securitized slave mortgages. All of these innovations planted a crop of dramatic consequences. Securitization's ability to export risk away from the immediate lender enabled unregulated borrowers to expand leverage without end. Here's how the equation worked. In 1835, a cousin told Anna Whitteker that "each of his hands made $500 last year, raising cotton" in Mississippi. If remotely true, that kind of revenue would mean a return of over 30 percent per year. Enslavers with access to bank credit could now borrow money on slaves at 8 percent. The margin between anticipated returns on borrowed capital and its cost to borrow was thus huge. And the direct risk appeared to be negligible. State-guaranteed slave-mortgage bonds dispersed much of the immediate risk of borrowing to others—to bondholders, to taxpayers, and, above all, to the enslaved. In addition, entrepreneurs themselves—including judges, politicians, and state officials—controlled debt collection in their states, making it less likely that elite borrowers would be foreclosed, even if they fell behind on payments. Banking elites had the recourse of socializing the losses—making the whole population pay off the debts of failed enterprises—just as the old Plummer (pre-carriage) and the old Walker (pre–bank war) had once warned. So as enslavers multiplied their leverage, they multiplied their revenue without increasing their individual risk. In response to these clear incentives, enslavers created still more ways to leverage slaves into still more leverage. They mortgaged the same collateral from multiple lenders. They used slaves bought with long-term mortgages to bluff lenders into granting unsecured commercial loans. Above all, they kept buying more slaves on credit. Even if they ran into problems, they figured they would still win, because they could sell their assets. For the slave prices were still rising.[82]

Yet the consequences of seemingly infinite and risk-free leverage were perverse, and not just because sexual predation helped stoke the risk-taking atmosphere. Securitization enabled both the immediate borrower and the immediate lender to escape the direct consequences of risk—economists call this "moral hazard"—even as they dramatically increased the total risk accumulated in the financial system. The multiplication of total leverage dramatically amplified the general consequences of a potential setback, such as a sudden decline in the cotton prices by which enslavers multiplied pounds picked per hand to calculate anticipated revenue. Yet by late 1834, few were thinking about such possibilities. The biggest boom yet seen in the history of slavery's expansion began to swell as money from the new southwestern banks seeded the region with enslaved hands ready to meet a sudden increase in European demand. In 1832, cotton brought 9 cents per pound. By 1834, a woman reported from the Huntsville slave market, "cotton [at] 13 cents . . . has turned their heads." In 1835 cotton hit an ecstasy-inducing 18 cents per pound. And demand for slaves kept soaring. "I have just returned from Charlottesville court, great many buyers[,] and negroes was scarce and high," reported Rice Ballard's employee from a buying trip along the Blue Ridge Mountains.[83]

"People here are run mad with speculation," wrote one visitor to the former Chickasaw land in northeastern Mississippi. "They do business in . . . a kind of phrenzy [sic]. [Gold] is scarce, but credit is plenty." In 1835, government land offices in Mississippi sold 2.9 million acres, more than had been sold in the entire nation in 1832. A few found frenzy worrisome. "We have not yet reached the neighborhood of a sufficiency of Banking Capital—but taking this as true I would prefer to approach the point gradually, and not with such rapid strides," wrote a Louisiana man in 1835, after the legislature chartered four banks in two days. Cheap land was vanishing, wrote a migrant to newly organized Noxubee County, Mississippi. "Speculators and cappitalist [sic] all have an idea to it. I have never in my life seen such a rush for land." Next, he predicted, came the forced migrants—"this country will be a perfect negro quarter"—who, underfed by gambler planters, "will kill your pigs hogs and cows, I feal the effects of it already."[84]

But the tunnel vision of one-eyed men seemed to be working. Banks were lending, and land bought by speculators at the government minimum of $1.25 sold at $20 per acre. The clanking of chains rose from the roadways leading into the courthouse towns; entrepreneurs looked at their ledgers, at bales stacked by the landing, and at the men and women trudging out to the springtime field; light-skinned women stood in front of tables where traders poured their drinks and negotiated a price. Prosperity trickled credit further down the chutes and slides of the southwestern economy into the pockets of slaveholders, overseers, and random white men with smooth tongues. Like Anne Royall cresting the hill and rounding the Alabama bend back in 1819, most white southwesterners thought they could see, spread out before them, a glorious future shining in a bubble. It looked like that first day when ten thousand little seedlings in the cotton field had obviously become a host of young plants. The green muscled its way upward, into the sight of the slave owner's focused eye. Who knew how miraculous the crop of his seed might become?

# 8

# BLOOD

## *1836–1844*

ERE WAS WILLIAM COLBERT'S awakening. In the middle of the night, a gruff white man's shouts splintered his child's deep sleep, and then, on a lower register still came his older brother January's voice in response. Some other antenna began to rattle. William was sensing that his parents were in distress. Whenever that happened, William always looked for big brother Jan, tall and unbroken. And now, William was out of bed and accelerating out the door of his parents' cabin toward the sound of January's voice.

He stopped like a braked wheel. The full moon shone on January tied to the pine tree that stood across the yard from the long row of shacks. The white man stood behind January with a bullwhip. A silent chorus of enslaved people watched from their porches. And the young man—caught on the way back from visiting a girl at the next labor camp—refused to cry.

January clenched his teeth, trying to endure any amount of pain rather than confirm submission with tears. On slavery's frontier, however, the blood that ran usually showed a white man's potency. And it was running down January's chest and back. Not for him was the right to say "enough"; to act on his own desires rather than his master's. Each stroke was meant to force him to crawl. But still he held out. "What's the matter with you, nigger?" growled the white man. "Don't it hurt?"

Maybe the slave owner's arm was getting tired. But after a decade in which millions of measured lashes had doubled cotton production, he knew that consummation was coming. William could remember his own agony at this moment, how with head on knees he had "sat on my mammy's and pappy's step a cryin'," sobbing with each choking grunt that came from his brother's clenched teeth. He could not articulate it, but William was coming to understand what the scene implied for him, and for the dreams he didn't even dream yet. The others had seen this script rehearsed a thousand times. "Some of 'em couldn't stand it; they had to go inside their cabins." Like the fathers and brothers in the cabins, January could not be for long the man that he had imagined himself becoming as he had returned, elated, from his rendezvous with that girl. "After a while January couldn't stand it no more hisself, and he say in a hoarse, long whisper: 'Massa! Massa! Have mercy on this poor nigger!'" Eighty years later, William cleared his throat, paused for a moment, and changed the subject.[1]

THE DRAMAS OF WHITE manhood inflicted havoc not only on black women's lives but on African-American men as well. Those dramas cut and stained enslaved men specifically *as men*, systematically denying them the opportunity to assert traditionally masculine roles. Lewis Clarke, an escapee from the whipping-machine, once told northern white audiences that his most visceral experience in slavery was learning that "A SLAVE CAN'T BE A MAN." Like free men, enslaved men also felt that manhood required them to defend self and family and other victims from violence. When Samuel Ford bullied the men on Jacob Bieller's cotton camp, deep in the Louisiana woods, they tried to puncture his domineering-overseer act. He told them he would whip them, and "they swore not a negro on the place should be touched for it. They have gone so far as to shake sticks over my head and threaten my life," wrote Ford to Bieller, his boss. All along slavery's frontier, African-American men pushed back against assault and humiliation, the two master teeth of the whipping-machine's gear: "Washington who was in the woods come up this morning," wrote a Louisiana overseer. "I undertook to whip him for his conduct, [and] he raised his hoe at me and swore I should not whip him."[2]

"Such conduct as that I cannot stand on a place that I have to manage," Ford had concluded in the letter to his employer. Enslavers might not have understood everything about enslaved men, but Ford and his peers knew that allowing assertive behavior to stand would only lead to further boldness both there and all along Bayou Boeuf. Leaving a threat unpunished also carved a wound in the enslaver's persona. Look at the letter written by enslaver Joseph Labrenty of Alabama: "Rather than take $700 for Alfred," a runaway who had escaped recapture, "I would rather go into the woods and mall [*sic*] rails for the next twelve months to pay the reward to have him shot. . . . I wish to god that I could get within 40 yards of him with a double barreled and if I did not stop him I am much mistaken."[3]

Image 8.1. William Colbert in the 1930s, about eighty years after the beating and humiliation of his brother. This photo was taken at the time of his interview by Works Progress Administration workers. Library of Congress.

Labrenty was "determined to spend double his value to conquer [Alfred]," showing that sometimes the needs of domination could not be comprehended by economic calculation. But all in all, enslaved men had to make different calculations. Sure, they, too, told stories about Potteresque "men of blood" who resisted attempts to humiliate them, like the ones Wiley Childress heard about "Fedd" from the older men. Fedd proved to his enslaver that he wouldn't crawl or beg, even under the heaviest whipping. When Fedd attempted to run away, some entrepreneurs captured him and figured out a new use for him: they made him their pet prizefighter. Now Fedd could use violence without punishment. He killed a slave from the local ironworks in a match. But looming larger were the stories like the ones told by skulls on display. Martha Bradley remembered how she learned that neither she nor the men she knew could respond to the things white men did and survive. An enslaved man in her neighborhood shot an overseer. Although he taunted his pursuers as he fled, the white folks caught him a few hours later. They tied him up and burned him alive. Martha—then a little girl—and all the other people from local labor camps were marched past his blackened bones.[4]

"You know if you was raised from birth like this you could stand it," said another formerly enslaved man, Peter Corn. Yet another, Robert Falls, remembered that in his Mississippi childhood, "We learned to say 'Yes Sir!' and scrape and bow, and to do exactly just what we was told to do, make no difference if we wanted to or not." Whites subjected boys to incessant behavioral modification techniques: making them watch whippings, scaling up physical pain for even the smallest evidence of resistant behavior. Then, when as a man someone tried to run away, the first things the trackers did once the dogs caught him was to re-inoculate him against the disease of self-assertion: "The hounds would bite you and worry you," remembered Henry Waldon, but the overseer, running up, called out, "If you hit one of them dogs, I'll blow your brains out!" "They would tell you to stand still and put your hands over your privates," Waldon said.[5]

"If I had my life to live over . . . I would die fighting rather than be a slave again," Robert Falls asserted, looking back across a whole century on Earth. The white world—and, perhaps, the voices inside Falls's head—insisted that men who submitted were not-men, men who deserved slavery. Then again, Ann Clark could look back, too, at the memory of her father, who always resisted whippings. When his Texas enslaver said it was time for him to take one, on the principle that no slave should remain unbeaten, Ann's father replied, "You can't whip me." Ann remembered the white man's reply, for she was never the same once she heard it: "But I can kill you." Ann, describing the incident, said: "He shot my poppa down. My momma took him in the cabin and put him on a pallet. He died." Thus, if one "fought like a hero," as did one Mississippi runaway man whom a slave-catcher cornered in a cave in 1848, they'd eventually bury another drained body in its chains. Or they could separate you from your blood another way. Robert Falls's own father, a famous fighter, had been on his way to the lead-bullet exit from slavery until his enslaver threatened him with sale away from his family unless he stopped fighting back.[6]

Falls's father changed. Robert grew up with a father. And so, to save their sons' blood, elders told young male slaves stories like the one about the man who ran away to escape torture. The dogs bayed after him for days. Eventually the slave catchers began to reel him in. Finally, jaws snapping at his heels, the young man burst out of the woods, into a clearing where men were making bricks, and ran straight into the blazing furnace. Run from hell and you might find yourself in even hotter pain. So, in the Mississippi night, after young Scott Bond heard such stories, he curled up in his single blanket and tried to sleep. He breathed slowly on his pallet. As the world quieted, he could hear, howling in the woods around him, "the blood hounds." And he thought about how he'd heard the white folks say that the *"music they made was the sweetest music in the world."*[7]

Never did the music ring out louder than it did by the time of the 1836 harvest. Never had white people loved it more. If one could draw a graph that mapped the intensity of the losses that all enslaved men had to suffer, its curve peaked in the 1830s, along with the curves of booming slave prices and cotton revenue per slave. More migration, more speculation, more financial leverage for one-eyed men: all meant more defeats for enslaved men. There were more first lickins at the forks of the cotton pickin, more old wives and new girlfriends taken away, more sons and daughters lost to the slave trade, more discoveries that being an axeman or coachman or wiseman or preacherman or simply any man who was a slave was only dust blown off the paper that named one as a hand. If white men planted their seed in the boom years, black men lost their blood—their link to the past, their connection to the future.

AS MARCH 3, 1837, turned into March 4—the day when Martin Van Buren would be inaugurated as the eighth president of the United States—Andrew Jackson sat quietly with a few friends in an upstairs room in the White House, celebrating eight years of gains. When the tall clock in the corner struck midnight, the president lit his corncob pipe and raised a glass of dark, thick, red Madeira wine. A recent flare-up of chronic digestive troubles, contracted in the 1814 campaign against the Creeks, had made him abstain for weeks. Tonight Jackson threw caution to the wind.

In two terms in office, Jackson had seen all his major goals fulfilled, and now a nation flooded by cotton and credit wallowed in economic high tide. On the crest of that boom, which enslavers and their political and financial allies themselves had engineered, rode triumphant the southwestern entrepreneurs in whose ranks Jackson was numbered. His administration's enforcement of the 1831 Indian Removal Act had driven 60,000 of the cotton frontier's original inhabitants across the Mississippi, opening 25 million acres (an area the size of Kentucky) for speculation and cotton production. His political allies had learned to steer the angry Potterizing resentments of overseers, small farmers, and public-land squatters into the channels of a new institutional party system. And that, in turn, helped southwestern entrepreneurs to convert rank-and-file Jacksonian voters' demands for an

assault on entrenched bank elites into a paradoxical flood of lending to enslavers and cotton speculators, this time pumped through innovative banks
that the entrepreneurs themselves controlled. The banks and their borrowers
socialized all the risks on distant investors, the general white southern public,
and, above all, enslaved people. The result was unprecedented growth. Even
factoring in 1833's Biddle-engineered recession, the economy expanded at an
unprecedented rate: 6.6 percent per year between 1830 and 1837.[8]

Jackson still believed that gold and silver were the only real money and
that banks were all scams. But if his precious-metal fetishism prevented him
from admitting the role of pet banks in fueling rapid expansion, he did not
object to taking credit for national prosperity. And just that morning, he had
told representatives from the Republic of Texas that the United States was
officially recognizing their independence. Observers believed this was the
first step in uniting the fledgling slave owners' nation to the much larger one
to its east. So even wider fields beckoned, ripe for planting with the seeds of
creative destruction. But actions have repercussions, and often not the ones
for which the actors hope. Over the decade or so that followed 1836, enslavers' overreach produced literal and figurative blood, pivoting the antebellum
history of the United States in unexpected directions.[9]

Seventeen years earlier, Connecticut-born Moses Austin had ridden from
Missouri to San Antonio, which was then one of the easternmost towns in
Mexico. Moses died not long afterward, but his son Stephen carried on the
Austin scheme of helping Americans emigrate to the vast spaces west of Louisiana. Stephen recruited many southerners, some of whom brought slaves
with them. Mexico had made emancipation its national policy, but Texas
was many miles from Mexico City. Enslavers also connived to import several boatloads of Africans bought in Havana harbor (Atlantic slave traders
brought more than 200,000 Africans to Cuba in the 1830s). By the end of
1835, almost 5,000 enslaved Africans and African Americans lived in Texas,
making up 13 percent of the non-Indian population. After a half-hearted 1829
attempt to enforce its emancipation laws in Texas, the central government
in Mexico City signaled in 1835 that this time it was serious about ending
slavery. Texas enslavers began to arm themselves, and in October, shooting
broke out between American settlers and Mexican soldiers.[10]

In March 1836, a convention gathered at the town of Washington and
declared Texas an independent republic. Although Texas rebels announced
they were fighting for "Liberty in opposition to slavery," it was southerners
who financed and staffed the quest for independence. Rebel commissioners
had already raised $300,000 from New Orleans entrepreneurs, and once

independence was declared, merchants advanced war supplies in exchange for freshly printed Texas bonds. Rebels also profited from the services of casualties from earlier waves of expansion. For instance, reeling from a divorce that ended his Tennessee political career, Sam Houston turned up in late 1835 and assumed command of the republic's fledgling army. Robert Potter also materialized at the Washington convention and proved to be one of the most aggressive proponents of Texas independence. ("He can only float in troubled waters," wrote one observer at the convention.) After troops under Mexican general Antonio López de Santa Anna slaughtered the entire garrison of a fort called the Alamo (save five enslaved men, and the women and children), every rumor about other alleged atrocities found an eager US audience. One rumor claimed that Mexican troops had captured the son of Ohio governor William Henry Harrison, castrated him, and then raped him to death with a spear. Each atrocity story brought angry new volunteers across the border to join the rebel army.[11]

In April 1836, Houston's forces routed Santa Anna's army at San Jacinto. Southern whites were overjoyed. "Everyone is speaking of emigration to the 'Far West,' either Mississippi or Texas," wrote John Lockhead from Southside Virginia's moribund tobacco lands. "I should prefer Texas as I feel that there is a greater field for enterprise than in any country at present. . . . All who go there certainly run the risk of stopping a bullet, but if they escape they are handsomely paid for that danger." Investors in the Texas cause now expected profit from the doors their ground-floor investment would open. "You must not be surprised to see me among you, in a few months," wrote one to a Texas contact. "I shall soon have a large Cotton farm, perhaps several of them under weigh in Texas."[12]

With the war's end, entrepreneurs of the domestic slave trade jockeyed to send "the tide of emigration . . . flowing rapidly to Texas," as a North Carolina enslaver put it. In the next five years, the number of slaves in Texas would grow from 5,000 to about 13,000. All Texas needed, enthused Virginia migrant James Cocke, was a bank to print up money and lend it to slave buyers. Credit would convert "floating speculators" into "well-settled planters," who could extract $1,000 in cotton per hand in a year. The bank could sell bonds on European financial markets, using the C.A.P.L. model of funding credit and a currency with slave-revenue securitization.[13]

The Texas Revolution also galvanized whites who had heard a different sort of news. Benjamin Lundy, William Lloyd Garrison, and others had awakened to the power of the ever-growing whipping-machine. They had awakened still others. Quietly, almost muted in the background by a national press devoted to the constant drumbeat of political debate over issues such as nullification, tariffs, the bank war, and the formation of new political parties, a small but dedicated group of black and white abolitionists had built up local associations across the North. Beginning in 1835, many of these abolition societies—composed, in many cases, primarily of churchly white women who saw slavery as an affront to morality—sent petitions to Congress, asking representatives to ban slavery in the federally administered District of Columbia.

Southern congressmen reacted with fury, insisting that the petitions could not be read into the public record. But that reaction itself helped the petitions gain a stubborn and canny legislative champion. John Quincy Adams, former president, was now the representative from his home district in Massachusetts, and he saw a chance to get revenge for critiques he'd suffered at the hands of southerners during his presidency. Adams argued that the right of citizens to petition their legislature went back to England's Magna Carta, and that the petitions should be read into the congressional record. Southerners, with many northern representatives concurring, responded by passing a "gag rule" that automatically tabled any petition referring to slavery. Yet Adams had a bag of parliamentary tricks that allowed him to keep forcing the petition issue into discussion in the House. And the petitions kept coming. By 1836, many echoed a claim that Benjamin Lundy was making in print: that "the slave holders of this country, (with land speculators and slave traders)," instigated the Texas Revolution "to open a vast and profitable SLAVE-MARKET therein, and ultimately to annex it to the United States."[14]

Adams told his constituents that whether they cared about slavery or not, the weight of this massive new slave territory would render New England forever politically irrelevant. And the southern congressmen were making it easy for him to claim that the slaveholders, with their zeal for hushing criticism of slavery, were sacrificing the basic political rights of other white Americans by stifling their rights of petition and free speech. The uproar over the petitions convinced Andrew Jackson to back away from immediate annexation. Still, by March 1837, the fear that Britain might make Texas its client state had enabled the president to manipulate Congress into recognizing the new republic as an independent country, separate from Mexico. So as Jackson sipped Madeira, almost eight years after his first raucous evening at the White House, he confidently expected that Texas would soon become one (or several) states.[15]

Perhaps the outgoing president was less sanguine about other recent developments. He was certainly eager to deny complicity in the flood of credit sloshing through the nation's economy. But one of the main reasons why the supply of money in circulation rose by 50 percent between 1834 and 1836 was that he had freed the banks from scrutiny by his veto of the Monster Bank. Now, wrote Burrell Fox from a new Mississippi town, "Everything is at its high water, there was five droves of negroes [sold] this fall . . . fellows at $1200 to $1400 and up . . . times appear to be brisk for everything that can come to market, even apples is selling at Vicksburg for $5 a barrel." A North Carolina migrant reported that his relatives along the Tombigbee in northeastern Mississippi were "all deranged on the subject of real estate." Even in the dormitories of the University of Alabama, reported a student, there was "more talk of speculation . . . than anything else. Every[body] is awake to the land speculation, money is plenty."[16]

Of course, if everyone was "awake," it was hard to see how one could continue to buy low and sell high. By 1836, the Alabama and Mississippi relatives of Pendleton County, South Carolina, enslaver Thomas Harrison had been pressing him to move his investments west for years. "Pendleton is a very happy and pleasant country," they wrote, but for all of its "pleasures and comforts," it was just the place to miss the chance: "Surely it must be very unprofitable to have money vested in land and negroes there." Hurry out, they told him, before the "speculators and capitalists" buy all the good cotton land. But Harrison feared that credit on slavery's frontier was now coming too easy, that "the immense floods of paper money with which the country is inundated if not checked will give a fictitious value to property beyond anything ever known." In fact, he noted, irrational increases in asset prices were already evident. He sent a group of his enslaved people out to Alabama so that a son located there could sell them off at the current high prices. On the way back from a visit, Thomas Harrison traveled through Kentucky, where people there assured him that the price of their land would "never fall again." Harrison wrote, "But this I do not believe. That the whole real property of a state so long settled should increase permanently in value 500 per cent in five years is impossible." Like a North Carolinian who warned his migrating son not to let "the wild extravagant speculating notions of these Southern people lead you astray," for "a reaction must take place," Harrison feared a calamity would soon "involve thousands in ruin."[17]

The term "bubble" gets used to describe a situation in which an important asset has become wildly overvalued compared to realistic predictions of future returns. From 1800 onward, the price of slaves—the most important asset in the southern economy—had always tracked that of cotton, or, more specifically, the rate of individual productivity times the price of a pound of cotton. In 1834, however, slave prices detached themselves from that of cotton and soared upward on a new trajectory (see Figure 6.2). By the time Louisiana's Jacob Bieller bought dozens of slaves on credit from Isaac Franklin and Rice Ballard in 1836, for instance, he paid over $1,500 each for the young men, more than twice the 1830 price, even though cotton prices had declined from a late-1834 peak to 1830 levels.[18]

For decades before the financial crisis of 2008, most economists dogmatically insisted that the behavior of the market and its actors was inevitably rational. Yet a few brave souls insisted that the history of bubbles, booms, and crashes showed a clear historical record of mass irrational economic behavior. Throughout history, in fact, when three conditions occur at the same time, an asset bubble—irrationally high prices for some category of asset— usually emerges. Thomas Harrison was observing all three. The first such condition is the elimination of market regulation. By 1836, Jackson's administration had destroyed the B.U.S., and replaced it with nothing. Nor did states try to control how much money banks printed and lent. Meanwhile, the national Whig Party, once the champion of the B.U.S., now tried to eliminate regulation altogether by passing the Deposit Act of 1836. This act shifted public land revenues from western banks to eastern ones, allowing the latter to increase their lending. The Whigs also doubled the number of pet banks.[19]

Lending by US banks had also increased dramatically since 1833 because of the second cause of bubbles: financial innovations that make it easier to expand the leverage of borrowers. C.A.P.L.-style bonds provided distant investors with opportunity to purchase shares in the income flows of thousands of slaves—to speculate, in effect, on future revenues generated by cotton and slaves. These securities drew cash into the southwestern region, inflating the value of all kinds of assets, especially enslaved "hands."

But one more factor makes a bubble run wild, and that is the euphoric belief that the rules of economics have changed, that somehow "this time is different" and asset prices will not return to their mean. "We can see nothing in the prospects of the Country to make it likely that [positive forecasts] will be disappointed," wrote merchants Byrne Hammond and Company in March 1836. "The whole Southern and Western country is in a most prosperous state and its products annually extending in a most extraordinary manner." Southwestern entrepreneurs, particularly prone to aggressive, risk-taking behavior, suffered an especially bad case of the strain of this-time-is-different thinking called "disaster myopia," meaning that they underestimated both the likelihood and the probable magnitude of financial corrections. Thus, a white migrant who wrote that the 1836 price of "fifteen hundred dollars

[for] ordinary field hands" was "extravagant" assumed in the next breath that prices would rise further, and he hoped to take advantage: "Cuff, for instance, would command sixteen hundred." Although "negroes are all out of character high," wrote Henry Draft in 1835, "I see no prospect of their falling. . . . I fully believe negroes will be higher." He believed it, for he needed to believe it. "I don't want them to fall at present, for I have Ten on hand," whom he hoped to resell for a profit.[20]

"Everybody is in debt neck over ears," wrote one young Alabama planter to his Connecticut father. The house of cards built by what Thomas Harrison called "the wild speculating notions of these Southern people" could collapse, and then "those who are making large contracts with all their show of wealth must come down." Yet in late summer 1836, the editor of the commerce-dedicated newspaper *New Orleans Price-Current* told his readers not to worry. True, there was a lot of debt hanging over Louisiana entrepreneurs and their banks: bank loans, dry goods "sold on credit to the upper country more than usual," major infrastructure projects in and around New Orleans (gas-lighting networks, railroads, levees, canals, steam-powered cotton presses), and "lands entered in the upper country and negroes purchased, to be paid out of the ensuing crop" of cotton, "for which the money has already been drawn from New Orleans." That all added up to $23 million, leveraged on the steelyard beam against the anticipated revenue to be generated from what hands were at that very moment picking in the fields. For "all of this deficit," insisted the *Price-Current*, "will soon be covered by the receipt of Cotton, Sugar, and the various products of the Western States, which we may assume with great safety will amount to at least sixty millions of dollars." Thus, even though a slave trader wrote from Alabama in December that "business seems dull," he added that "traders are not discouraged." Cotton was at 16 cents a pound, but "it will bear 25 cents before the crop is in."[21]

There was much more cotton in 1836 than there had been in 1828. Over eight years of seedtime, the US government, the states, banks, private citizens, and foreign entities had collectively invested about $400 million, or one-third of the value of all US economic activity in 1830, into expanding production on slavery's frontier. This includes the price of 250,000 slaves moved, 48 million new acres of public land sold, the costs of Indian removals and wars, and the massive expansion of the southwestern financial infrastructure. The number of hands on cotton plantations expanded dramatically, and the need to repay loans only accelerated the whipping-machine, collectively forcing the total picking that hands could accomplish just a little higher each day. In 1830, the United States made 732,000 bales. As the harvest kicked into high gear in the fall of 1836, men who made a living by gambling on cotton were predicting a deluge of 1.5 million bales, each one a 400-pound snowy semi-cube wrapped in canvas. This was 600 million pounds of clean cotton—or, expressed in a different way, more than six million person-days of picking under the hot sun.[22]

European and North American economies had been expanding and people were buying more, but consumers' demand for cotton goods simply could not keep up with this vast an increase in supply. In late summer 1834, the price of cotton at New Orleans was 18 cents per pound. After that, it began to decline, reaching 12 cents in early 1836. Unease with the slow downward trend in prices was beginning to shape decisions at the commanding heights of the transatlantic economy. By late 1836, Baring Brothers, the most influential commercial bank in the world, had been quietly restricting new investments for almost twelve months. And as that year's bumper crop began to reach market, one speculator privately ruminated: "Will prices in Liverpool continue to hold their own? We think not."[23]

The White House was also quietly alarmed, in its case by the dramatic expansion of speculation in public lands. Purchases had reached the figure of $5 million a month in the summer of 1836. In response, Jackson issued the "Specie Circular" in July, declaring that from August onward, only gold and silver would be accepted as payment for most government-owned lands. Jackson's advisers didn't want him to issue the Specie Circular. It was based on his old-fashioned misunderstanding of the nature of money and credit in a modernizing economy, and it clogged the economy's circulatory system. Heavy gold and silver had to be moved from the East Coast to Indiana and Mississippi and then back again. Land sales plummeted. Banks began to charge a premium for gold and silver, making everything else more expensive.

Still, by winter the flow of money, credit, and goods through the channels of the American economy had begun to adjust to Jackson's friction-creating policy. All other commodities—cotton, consumer goods, and slaves—continued to move on a paper money basis, helped by commercial banks like Brown Brothers of New York, which kept credit flowing to merchants and importers. And that was important, because the entire Atlantic economy now depended on the ability of the planters to cycle cotton revenues back through the system. Yet British textile mills already held high stocks of raw cotton, and layoffs at factories were increasing. Soon consumers would choose to wear their old clothes into rags rather than replace them. Demand for raw cotton was about to crater. The Bank of England, the source of credit for

British cotton-buying firms in Liverpool, began to get nervous. In late 1836, it began denying credit to those firms.[24]

It took a while for news of this decision to percolate back across the Atlantic. In February, as Martin Van Buren's inauguration approached, a few insiders were quietly coming to realize that this time was not, after all, different—unless by "different" one meant especially disastrous. "Against the judgment of others in whom I usually confide, I do not anticipate that the present prices of cotton will be fully maintained," a Washington correspondent warned John Stevens, a principal at the New York firm Prime, Ward, and King, which held millions in slave-backed securities issued by southwestern states.[25]

Even as Jackson lit his celebratory pipe, a dramatic chain reaction had already begun to ignite. In the wake of the Bank of England's credit-tightening, the annualized price of short-term business loans in Liverpool skyrocketed to 36 percent, making it impossible for cotton brokers to buy even as the full tide of the 1836 crop swept in. Cotton prices began a free fall that only ended in July 1837, when a dead-cat bounce took it to 6 cents a pound. In the meantime, collapsing British merchant firms had pulled each other down as they fell. Three of the top seven Liverpool cotton traders closed their doors by the end of February. And Le Havre, France's main cotton exchange, shut down completely.[26]

Into the hulls of westward-racing ships went bags of letters desperately calling in the mountains of debt owed by American trading partners. As soon as the news reached the Mississippi's mouth, arrays of interlinked debtors and creditors began to cascade down. One after another in the last week in March, the ten largest cotton buyers in New Orleans announced that they were insolvent. Some allegedly owed $500 for every $1 that they held in cash or collectible debts. The smaller firms were next. On April 20, the New Orleans *Picayune* wrote that there were "no new failures to announce," for by then "nearly all [firms] have gone." Shockwaves fanned out across the southwestern states and the frontier and backwashed over New York, where banks shut their doors to prevent runs on their own reserves of gold and silver. By the first week of May, no one in New York could borrow, collect debts, or carry out business at all.[27]

In the two most important trading centers of the United States a state prevailed that venerable former treasury secretary Albert Gallatin called "incalculable confusion." Yet no economic actors were hit harder by what soon became known as the "Panic of 1837" than the southwestern banks. They had lent far more paper money than their own reserves of cash justified.

Their currency now traded for well under its face value. They faced massive upcoming interest payments on bonds sold on worldwide financial markets. The cotton merchants who owed southwestern banks millions in short-term commercial loans had nothing but cotton, which was selling for less than the cost of transportation. On the other hand, the slave owners who owed the banks money did have tangible property. In one folder of the papers of the Citizens' Bank of Louisiana, which had hurriedly disbursed some $14 million in 1835–1836, are nineteen pages of inventories of mortgaged slaves, listing more than 500 people. And that was only a fraction of those who were mortgaged to southwestern banks, which had lent at least $40 million on mortgaged slaves. At the rate of 1 slave for every $500 of outstanding debt, this meant that 80,000 or more enslaved people were put at risk of another sale by the collapse of commodity prices and the southwestern banks. Thousands more, like the 29 people ("Phillip, Toney, Caesar . . . ") whom Champ Terry of Jefferson County, Mississippi, had put up as collateral for a loan made to him by entrepreneur Nathaniel Jeffries, were privately mortgaged. Working in the fields, sleeping at night, sitting in the quarters while they held a child, every person named on a debt document was under the auctioneer's hammer.[28]

If the worst came, wrote one Mississippi enslaver to his North Carolina relative, then an enslaved woman whom they both knew—"Old Dorcas"— would be "sold to the highest bidder," because "Duncan McBryde is in a peck of trouble." Human flesh had proved a liquid resource in times of trouble for many a white person like McBryde. Yet in the present crisis, the highest bid would be uselessly low. "I heard a gentleman say a few days ago," wrote William Southgate from Alabama, "that he saw a negro fellow sell in Missi. for $60.00 in specie—which negro cost something like $2,000." Those who tried to "dispose of some negroes to live on," as one bankrupt North Carolina migrant planned to do, found that "in many instances they are sold at ¼ the sum given or promised and the poor debtor left ¾ the sum to be raised from his other property if such there be."[29]

BY THE SUMMER OF 1837, the sudden shift to impotence left white men all across the South anxious and angry. Men accosted each other in the streets, demanding payment for debts. Accusers insisted that banks should open their books. Cashiers cut their own throats. Old men came out west to try to sort out the messes that their sons had made, but dropped dead of strokes when they saw how bad the messes were. When a zealous sheriff tried to press debt cases in Hinds County, Mississippi, local entrepreneurs chased him away and

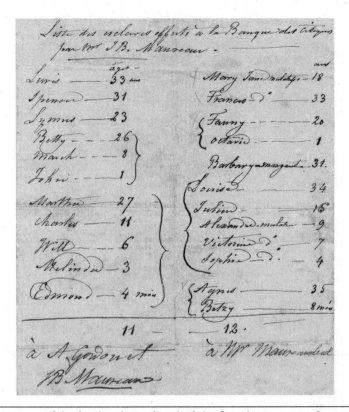

Image 8.2. Many of the family relationships built by forced migrants to the southwest—like the ones on this list of mortgaged human "property"—would be smashed by the same mortgages and financial operations that caused those relationships to be recorded on paper in the first place. Louisiana Banking collection, Louisiana Research Collection, Tulane University.

let everyone know they had "laid up a bowie knife for any man who attempts to execute the office." Instead of liquidating debts now, wrote one member of the Natchez banking circle to another in late 1837, everyone should play for time: "The debt to the banks in this state must amount to 33 million," but the crop of cotton now growing in Mississippi "will net probably *10 millions* of dollars." Four crop years like the one now under way would clear Mississippi planters of debt. This calculation convinced the Natchez man that creditors would rather take delayed payment than call on the collateral. Europe would surely soon want all the cotton Mississippi hands could make, and at a high price.[30]

The closing of both southwestern and New York banks had frozen the financial sector in a kind of induced coma. The temporary shutdown also kept southwestern banks on life support. The merchant firms of port cities such as Mobile and New Orleans, in contrast, were terminal. Most of these firms never reopened their doors. And there was another problem: when consumers and investors lack confidence that credit will be available, they save too much, turning their fear of deepening recession into a self-fulfilling prophecy. So during a deflationary crisis, sensible macroeconomic policymakers usually prescribe "priming the pump," in which the government's deficit spending encourages private investment. But the federal government had already signaled that it would not take such actions. Martin Van Buren called a special "Panic Session" of Congress in the late summer of 1837. He stood by Jackson's Specie Circular and argued for an "Independent Treasury" that would make it impossible for a private bank to use federal deposits to create leverage. His administration did issue new federal debt, in the form of "Treasury notes," to make up for the shortfall in federal revenue, which relied on tariff collections and land sales and thus had declined dramatically with the collapse of trade. But the president refused to underwrite the expansion of credit for the banking system.[31]

Yet, "In Missi.[,] there has been no absolute loss of capital," wrote Stephen Duncan. Enslavers still held the assets—the men, women, and children who produced the commodity around which the entire Atlantic financial economy revolved. But without enough credit to lubricate the circuits of American trade, bales made in 1837 might well sit on the levees and docks until the wind ripped their burlap wrappers into flags. So over the next twelve months, southern entrepreneurs asked investors to sink more long-term capital into their region, and to do so on the basis of slavery-backed securities. States and territories on slavery's frontier issued at least $25 million in new bank debt, most of it state-backed, between 1837 and 1839. The world financial community responded. Alabama's state bank attracted massive quantities of capital from the Rothschilds, perhaps the wealthiest family in the world, proprietors of a powerful merchant bank headquartered in London and Paris. The new issues of bank securities, in turn, allowed banks to loan out more money to southwestern borrowers. Which they did. By 1841, the residents of Mississippi would owe twice as much money—$48 million—to the state's banks as they had at the beginning of 1837.[32]

In December 1837, John Stevens traveled to New Orleans to take soundings at the disaster's epicenter and start buying cotton bales for his employer, Prime, Ward, and King. European factories' stockpiles had finally shrunk. "The Planting States must in a short time recover from the shock of last year," wrote a southern banker. Van Buren wouldn't come to the aid of the cotton-centered entrepreneurial economy, but other players stepped into the breach. First among them was Nicholas Biddle. After the B.U.S. charter expired in 1836, his home state rechartered it as the "Pennsylvania Bank of the United States." Though much reduced in power, the "B.U.S.P." was still the largest private financial entity in the United States, and Biddle had hoarded its cash reserves through the panic.[33]

So now Biddle attempted the greatest creative-destructive play of all time. The B.U.S.P. issued millions of dollars in "post-notes"—promises to pay the holder of the note in a year or eighteen months for the face value of the note plus 6 percent interest. This was a bet placed by both parties on the revival of the cotton trade. The post-notes would remonetize the cotton trade and serve as a currency to be traded for the next year and a half, by which time Biddle's revenues from the sale of the cotton he bought would allow him to redeem the post-notes. Biddle and his intermediaries (other high-level commercial banks, such as Brown Brothers) provided the state-chartered banks with post-notes on credit. Taking the place of the bankrupt southwestern merchants, they bought up local planters' crops. The Commercial Bank of Natchez bought $643,000 of cotton for Liverpool on its own account, for instance, while the Planters' Bank of Mississippi purchased 60,000 bales of cotton from local planters and shipped the bales to Liverpool. There Biddle's allies sat on the cotton.[34]

Cotton climbed from 9 cents a pound at the beginning of 1838 to almost 13 cents as enslavers across slavery's frontier prepared to plant for 1839. And they planted a lot, because they'd soon need cash. As William Rives wrote from Clinton, Mississippi, eventually "immense sums have to be made by the Sheriffs . . . and much of it will be made by the sale of property." So enslavers drove their right and left hands hard in the summer of 1839. "The number of hands I have gathering cotton," wrote A. G. Alsworth in Mississippi, "frequently average over 200 and on the 4th inst they picked as high as 214[,] two of them picked [a combined] 625." James Haywood went into the field and, beside his slaves, "picked cotton from August to the term, because I knew our situation and was anxious to be extricated from debt. . . . No overseer [would have] toiled as I have."[35]

When all was said and done, enslavers shipped 1,650,000 bales of cotton in 1839—225,000 more than in any previous year. But once again, a rise in supply shook the commodity's price, and it started downward. Cotton dropped from a high of 14 cents per pound in the spring of 1839. By September it was at 10 cents. Once the scope of the vast 1839 crop emerged, the price plummeted all the way to 7 cents a pound. As it fell, it crushed Biddle's

B.U.S.P., which had bet everything on being able to redeem post-notes by selling cotton at high prices. The end came fast. On October 9, Biddle's last bank shut its doors. With it fell all the other institutions that had participated in his leveraged bet.[36]

"Our Banks are likely to fall to pieces," wrote Robert Carson, an Alabama enslaver, in August 1839. The Panic of 1839 was an even deeper collapse than the one two years earlier, and from this one, most southwestern banks never reopened. In Tallahassee, when the officers of the Union Bank of Florida ignored a legal judgment ordering them to pay an outstanding bill of $197.23, the court dispatched marshals to auction off its building, the bank's only remaining asset. As the marshals approached the front steps, followed by a crowd of onlookers ready to gloat, the door opened. Officials emerged, carrying sacks of nickels, dimes, and pennies they'd literally scraped off the bottom of the vault. It barely covered the debt. Meanwhile, the money that the Mississippi Union Bank had received for its bonds in late 1838 washed away like a sand castle when the tide of falling cotton prices came in. One observer predicted that "Mississippi will get out of debt about the year of Christ 1897." As it turned out, this was an overoptimistic prediction.[37]

Martin Van Buren's presidency had been ambushed by first one panic and then another. Congress, sensing weakness, abolished the president's independent treasury. To the Whigs, the upcoming national election looked like a perfect opportunity to take the White House and unwind the effects of twelve years of Democratic executive dominance. Using the Democrats' own techniques of popular organization and populist message, the Whigs' 1840 campaign depicted "Martin Van Ruin" as a contradictorily androgynous Casanova who ate from a ballerific gold table service and ordered the construction of a breast-shaped mound (complete with nipple) in the White House garden. They named as their presidential candidate Ohio's William Henry Harrison, who had been born into the Virginia aristocracy but portrayed himself as a frontiersman and claimed credit for victory over Tecumseh at the Battle of Tippecanoe in 1811. Pairing him with John Tyler, a Virginia planter who had stayed home in the Old Dominion, the Whigs' leaders proclaimed a ticket of "Tippecanoe and Tyler Too." The Democratic machine continued to turn out votes. Van Buren took almost 47 percent of the popular vote in the presidential election, which turned out 80 percent of eligible voters—still the highest ever. But the Whigs swept the panic-devastated southwestern core of Old Hickory's support, taking Louisiana, Mississippi, Georgia, and even Tennessee, hauling in 234 electoral votes to Van Buren's 60.[38]

Now in control of both the legislative and executive branches of the federal government, the Whigs immediately forced their first agenda item through

Congress. They passed a national bankruptcy law that would allow federal courts to stop chaotic deleveraging and rationalize the process of debt liquidation and financial recovery. Under it, a debtor could relinquish his property to a court-appointed agent who would sell everything and distribute the proceeds to the creditors. After this, the debtor would be legally free of debt and able to restart business. Samuel Thompson, for example, was the member of a New Orleans cotton-trading partnership that collapsed in 1839. His insolvent firm, according to the documents he filed, owed more than $400,000—not atypically much. It was, also typically, entangled with likewise-flattened creditors, owing $16,000 to the Union Bank of Louisiana, $60,000 to other banks, and even $20,000 for post-notes the firm had borrowed so that it could engage in 1839's last gasp of cotton speculation. The firm, and Thompson, offered a varied portfolio of real-estate assets to offset debts: a lot on the corner of Camp Street in New Orleans; half an interest in 1,500 acres on Bayou Black; 1,111 never-seen Texas acres. If creditors insisted on cash, the properties were auctioned to the highest bidder. This is what happened to Thomas, Henry, Peter, and Evelina and her son James, who were appraised at $3,000. Although these five brought only $1,125 on the block, the firm also held $100,000 in "receivables"—debt others owed to the firm. Smart creditors could pick through these receivables and figure out which ones were most likely to yield value when squeezed, then grab the juiciest ones in return for canceling out the bankrupt's debts.[39]

Fully implemented, the Bankruptcy Act might have limited the financial devastation that southwestern entrepreneurs had brought upon themselves. However, after a month in office, President Harrison, who had contracted a severe cold at his inauguration, died of pneumonia. Now, for the first time, a vice president would succeed a president. Many Whigs assumed that John Tyler, who had, after all, not been elected to lead, would meekly take his direction from Congress. Tyler, however, proved to be mulish in disposition, revealing that he was, after all, essentially a Virginia Democrat. He vetoed the Whig Congress's 1842 bill for a new B.U.S. The next year, the more Democratic Congress elected at the midterm overturned the bankruptcy bill.

Now, all along slavery's frontier, the process of collecting debts from individuals began to roll forward with redoubled speed. All had to fend for themselves against desperate banks, bankrupt merchants, outside creditors, and, above all, each other. On every circuit of every southwestern state's court system, judges and lawyers rode on the appointed day to whichever county courthouse was next in the rotation and heard the debt docket. Often, little else in the way of business had happened since the court's last visit, except the filing of thousands of cases. One Alabamian wrote: "Montgomery is completely run down, there is nothing a-doing here but the courts." Lawyers brought protested notes and unpaid mortgages forward, judges' gavels came down, and clerks issued legal documents empowering sheriffs to seize property for sale. Some debtors were "sold out by the shff.," their slaves and land deeds auctioned from the courthouse steps. Although "a great many negros will be sold on the block in the course of this and the next [session]," most expected prices to fall further and were "waiting till the thing comes to the worst." Certainly no one paid prices that would actually pay debts from the "flush times," especially when measured in gold and silver dollars, the only currency accepted at face value. "I wonder how Old Virginia stands the hard times," wrote one southwesterner about slave sellers who had profited from the rise in asset prices. "I expect Negroes can be bought cheap in the old Dominion. They [Virginians] have reaped the benefits of the folly of the Missns [Mississippians] but I think that harvest is over." Slave trader Tyre Glen came back to collect the $50,000 that Alabamians owed him. In Mississippi, Rice Ballard forced sales and bought the auctioned assets himself. And slave traders were themselves pursued: a letter to Ballard detailed hundreds of thousands of dollars that a dozen slave traders owed to major Virginia banks.[40]

THE FEDERAL BANKRUPTCY COURT that sold Evelina and James to pay Samuel Thompson's debts did not sell James's father. Despite the separations inflicted by forced migration, the slave frontier was actually teeming with fathers. Indeed, it was full of all kinds of relationships—new, rebuilt, flexible, as creative as the left hand. For fathers, brothers, friends, and lovers, the new relationships of flesh, of blood, and of pretend-blood were foundations on which they could stand and feel like men. But relationships were also gateways to more vulnerability. Many enslaved men were more willing to retreat in order to protect their roles as husband and father than they would have been to protect their own bodies alone. One couldn't live out these ties unless one was still alive. Yet achieving survival by sometimes retreating from self-assertion and self-defense required a psychologically difficult sort of thinking about oneself.[41]

These conundrums are explicit in what we know of the life of Joe Kilpatrick, a man whose enslaver sold him to a trader passing through North Carolina in the 1830s. Watching him disappear over the southern horizon were his wife and their two daughters, Lettice and Nelly. Bought near Tallahassee, Joe built a cabin on his enslaver's cotton labor camp. There he took in and raised George Jones, a five-year-old orphaned by the trade. Thirty years passed. George Jones grew up. He got married. He fathered two daughters.

He named them Lettice and Nelly. What stories had Kilpatrick told George in their cabin? When did the boy decide that the girls were his sisters? And what does this story of blood that was not blood say about how Joe Kilpatrick decided to live his life? We cannot guess what played in Kilpatrick's mind as he watched a child turn into a man, or as he watched the little girls who bore his long-lost blood daughters' names play in the dirt before his cabin. Yet Kilpatrick registered choice in his actions. He sought redemption for his own losses not in domination, nor in acceptance of despair, but in long-term, patient hope. This was how he lived out an idea of manhood incompatible with the readiness-for-vengeance that had long defined manhood, not only for whites in the antebellum South, but throughout much of Western history.[42]

Writing about twentieth-century concentration camps, the author Tzvetan Todorov identifies those few who fought to the death, such as the Jews and Communists who rose up against the Nazi occupation of Poland in 1943 and 1944, as exemplars of "heroism." The resistance fighters of the Warsaw ghetto were willing to die for the value of freedom, even if they could not achieve its reality. "To the hero," argued Todorov, "death has more value than life"—certainly more than life under conditions in which one cannot claim freedom. Without the willingness to seek out death to avoid domination, the heroes of the revolts believed, life was not worth living. From the tale of Gilgamesh and *The Iliad* to apocalyptic films, Western epics have been stories about such heroes. They are men who resist, who shed the blood of opponents, who accept no limitations or insults, who will never be slaves. Sometimes they are willing to shed blood and die so that people in general can be free, but always they are willing to do this so that they are free themselves—free most of all from the imputation that anyone could dominate them. Free like Robert Potter, free like the twenty thousand men who came to watch Andrew Jackson become the president. Or free as those men imagined themselves to be.

White men, South and North, viewed the alleged nonresistance of enslaved men as evidence that they were not heroes, proof that they were not really men. They mocked black men as cringing Sambos in jokes, literature, and minstrel shows. The need to disprove the symbolic emasculation that slavery represented has impelled some portion of black cultural creativity for all the years since. And historians have repeatedly confused "manhood" and "resistance" when they have written about slavery.[43]

Joe Kilpatrick was no hero. He could not construct his life as he would have done in freedom. He was not willing to die just to show he had the freedom to die. Yet he did make choices, and the ones he made were important both for the beliefs about manhood they reveal and for what they did for George Jones, for Lettice, and for Nelly. Instead of honor, Kilpatrick chose what Todorov called "ordinary virtues." Heroes deal out vengeance, wiping out insults, and in an existential sense denying their own death. In twentieth-century camps, however, Todorov found, some people instead found transcendence by displaying kindness toward other people. Through small, everyday acts that committed them to the survival of other human beings—even at the cost of lowering their own chances—they demonstrated their own commitment to an abstract yet personal value. Although heroic acts were as suicidal in twentieth-century death camps as they were in nineteenth-century slave labor camps, even in hell there was still room to be a moral human being.[44]

In the slave labor camps of the Southwest, an adult man's commitment to ordinary as opposed to heroic virtues could mean the difference between life and death for children like George Jones. Such choices could have the same result for the men themselves. Rebuilt blood ties could provide a reason not to die fighting in one's chains. Amid the disruptions and dangers of the 1830s, enslaved men frequently became caretakers of others. Caring is not central to most definitions of masculinity. But just as the kindness of enslaved men had breathed life back into Lucy Thurston's soul when her spirit was as dead as a zombie in that Louisiana cotton field, the kindness of men like Joe Kilpatrick led them to create families of all sorts, and to care for them, feed them, and teach them. Because these choices placed them in relationships as husbands or lovers, fathers or brothers, these men often made ordinary virtues central to their own identities, despite all the cultural noise that told them that as men they had failed. And perhaps—perhaps—a man who lived in that way also undermined the white ideal of the man as vengeful hero.

Men's pursuit of ordinary virtue in the context of the devastations of forced migration was already visible by the Panic of 1837, shaping life in ways that even influenced the planters' record books. First is simply the rising rate of marriages on southwestern slave labor camps during the 1830s. At Alexander McNeil's Magnolia, for instance, twenty-one of the thirty-seven women over the age of twenty were married to men who lived there. Such relationships implied a deliberate choice to start again. Many of these frontier husbands had been married to other women back in the old states. In the middle of the 1830s cotton boom, Peter Carter was sold from Maryland to Florida. An older man by the standards of the trade—over forty—he left a whole family behind. But in Florida he remarried, in his fifties, and raised three more children.[45]

Being a husband or father mattered because enslaved men who wanted to live in a way defined by moral choice rather than fear had to turn to the long view, to thinking of the people who would one day be left behind them. Even those who did not marry could establish new ties of blood, or pseudo-blood. Charles Ball had left his family behind in Maryland. In South Carolina he became a contributing member of Nero's household and critiqued Lydia's husband for not being much of a caretaker. Then he adopted a trade-orphaned little boy, "the same age [as] my own little son, whom I had left in Maryland; and there was nothing that I possessed in the world, that I would not have divided with him, even to my last crust." What mattered was to matter—to count, to be essential in the life of another person. No need was greater than that of an orphan child for an adult—except, perhaps, Charles Ball's need for a child.[46]

The full fruition of these efforts appeared decades later in the wake of emancipation. Women did amazing things to keep life going during the Civil War, and they pushed for freedom's fullest measure afterward. But in those days, men also made their own sacrifices—some of them brutally difficult ones—to make and remake hundreds of thousands of free households. Nettie Henry's father tramped back from Texas to Mississippi to rejoin her and her mother. Others chose to stay with the people among whom they had rebuilt a life. Jack Hannibal, a man sold decades prior to the 1870s, wrote from Alabama to his North Carolina onetime owner: "Dear Mistress . . . : Please be so kind to write to Florida to my two sisters to let them know where I am, so that they may know where to post their letters." He believed she knew where they had been sold. Then he told her how many children he had, that he'd buried one wife and married a second, and that he was ready to gather under his wings all those whom she had wounded: "Please write to my two sisters in Florida that if they are not doing well, they must write to me, for I am now doing like Joseph of old, preparing corn now for them if they should come out."[47]

Like Hawkins Wilson, who wrote from Texas to the sister from whom he'd been separated as a little boy to tell her that he'd survived to become a "grown man," and that, "like Joseph," he would be overjoyed to see her again, Hannibal was patriarch and mother hen both. He measured himself by what he had lost, what he had endured, and what he had found again—and not by what he had been unable to resist from enslavers who had called him a "boy." What such men got by surviving and caretaking was not always enough to replace the other hopes that they held in their hearts. They paid a psychological cost no one can measure. Nor were all enslaved men exemplars of ordinary virtue. But Joe Kilpatrick, Jack Hannibal, and uncounted others chose to shelter under their wings far-off futures that might only arrive long after their own deaths. They hoped that in that future, children or children's children—their own blood—would be free. For this future to arrive, however, someone had to survive. In a billion acts of quiet love that kept children and others alive, such men had been challenging southern white and Western definitions of manhood, even as the boom in planter power swelled to 1837's peak.

ONCE A YOUNG ALABAMA man, told to carry a letter, instead took it halfway down the path to town and then stopped. He made sure no one could see him. Then he buried the envelope in the sand next to the road. The information in the letter stayed in the ground for a month. But somehow his enslaver "found it out." The news was coming. Letters and notes from creditors, courts, banks, and sheriffs were all on their way. And there was almost nothing that enslaved men, or the other people in the families they had helped to build, could do to stop the letters from destroying what they had built.[48]

There was also nothing John Devereux could do to stop the letters that were coming for his son, Julien. John, who lived in Alabama, was still an eighteenth-century Virginia gentleman at heart. In good Jeffersonian style, he rose on January 1, wrote the number of the new year in both the Christian and the Muslim reckoning, and added a lyrical description of the day's weather. He fed every white man who called at his door. He spent evenings reading works of natural history. At his advanced age, Devereux preferred for "Scot Negro" to wield the whip.

By 1839, however, a maelstrom of failed schemes was sucking Julien under. There was his botched speculation in land claims swindled from Creek Indians. Political enemies discovered the scam and denounced it in the state legislature. Julien's friends shouted down the whistle-blowers with threats, but the documents revealed that he owed vast sums of money to multiple banks. His business partnership with brother-in-law Henry Holcombe—a slave labor camp and a Mobile cotton brokerage—collapsed. Despite "our long indulgence," growled a merchant firm's letter, Julien's account remained in the red. A few weeks later, a sheriff's employee brought a document certifying that Julien was being sued for $10,000 by another creditor. More demands rolled in by mail: "Will you make some arrangement for payment"; "I take the liberty of reminding you of the promises made to me"; and, "This bill of exchange on *Julien S. Devereux*, in the amount of *$3500.00* is PROTESTED." Even his marriage was collapsing.[49]

Julien sold his land to raise cash and then moved himself and his children—and his remaining slaves—in with John. Julien's divorce from Adaline was a rare event in antebellum Alabama. The legal system believed that only extreme humiliation was sufficient to justify white divorce. John had to claim, in a deposition supporting his son's divorce petition, that Adaline's propensity to argue, beat house servants, and wail on the couch when her will was checked had become the "notorious . . . subject of general remark and gossip," to the "mortification of all her friends." The façade of John's family broke open. Everyone could see the failure inside.[50]

Panic strained and ruptured the bonds that had held schemes together, creating a crisis of planter society—and manhood—that imperiled white social and familial ties in ways that the geographical separations of physical migration had never done. As dawn rose on a ruined financial landscape scattered with useless paper—"Business very dull here, but few speculations going on. Little or no money in circulation"—the light revealed once-dominating men being pursued like fugitives. They could no longer, for instance, use their pet banks to stand between themselves as borrowers on the one hand and world credit markets on the other. Insolvent slave-frontier banks owed massive heaps of debt to northeastern institutions, such as the B.U.S. of Pennsylvania. The B.U.S.P., itself bankrupt, was in the hands of trustees who sent John Roberts down to Mississippi to make collections from the state's banks. But he soon discovered that he had no choice but to try to collect himself the immense quantities of debt that individual Mississippians owed to their Planters' Bank, which in turn it owed to the B.U.S.P.[51]

"The condition of the people in their pecuniary concerns," Roberts soon learned, was impossibly tangled: "Even mortgage[-secured] debts are quite uncertain, the slaves which make mortgaged debts most safe, are frequently removed and disposed of beyond our reach." The mortgage for a piece of land was recorded at the Woodville courthouse, he was told. Or maybe it was recorded in Natchez. Or was it Yazoo City? "'Tis all design!" Roberts exploded, exasperated at run-arounds that circled other run-arounds. Everyone, it seemed, was lying and cheating each other in the scrabble to escape the traps they'd built for themselves: "I would not believe the first man" in Mississippi, he wrote: "Saint or sinner there is no difference, they all lie and cheat." Alabama was no better: "The people are getting all most desperate—More shooting and killing each other here than you have any idea of." Soon Roberts was writing, "I would not ask anyone in Mississippi to become security on a bond." He now regarded Mississippi whites as people without ethics, lacking honor, deserving of their suddenly subordinate status in national credit networks.[52]

Roberts spent the next ten years sifting through bad paper and lies, suing hundreds of enslavers and forcing thousands of slave sales. Under that kind of pressure, white proprieties and interpersonal bonds dissolved. Governor Hiram Runnels owes us money, wrote one of his Mississippi allies, and he won't pay. He's about to fight a duel, and "is likely to be slain." Bad news. But wait: "Would Mrs. Runnels facilitate you in paying it if he is killed?" Maybe a bullet in a friend's chest was good news after all. As entrepreneurs scrabbled to preserve as much of their stake in the game as they could, even family ties snapped. In 1838, William Thompson and his sister, Indiana, had bought slaves from their brother, Darwin, a gambler in both private and entrepreneurial life, to save him from bankruptcy. Now, in 1842, Darwin wanted to regain possession of them, probably by repaying only part of what they would cost on the open market. But William and Indiana suspected that Darwin would turn around and mortgage the slaves again, as if he held full and clear title to them: "He would not keep them two years before he or the sheriff would sell them," his sister predicted. In a moment of candor, he had admitted to William that he planned to sell one boy right away. "Well what will you do with the money?" William reported asking. Darwin admitted he planned to go to Texas, another country, where he would be sheltered from collection of his Mississippi debts. "Of course I retained the boy," William said. That time he managed to protect his own and his sister's financial interests. But when William traveled away for business a few months later, and his wife fell deathly ill, Darwin swooped down to pester her on her deathbed. His sister heard the conversation: "I'll tell what I'll do sister," Darwin told the dying woman. "All I want is my nigers give me them." He promised to use their labor to pay his debts. "Ha ha ha ha," interjected Indiana in her sarcastic account. Everyone knew Brother Darwin was headed far away, leaving creditors to harass his brother and sister. Thus, enslaved people, once the magic seeds of white dreams, became the currency of contention within white families.[53]

White southern women had occasionally raised doubts about slavery. But when pressures caused women to fear not only for family enterprises but for their own individual financial futures, they felt the usefulness of slave property with new intensity. Take northern Louisiana enslaver Nancy Bieller, entangled with husband Jacob Bieller in the tendrils of their own messy divorce case. Long-standing problems between them had intensified back in 1833, she claimed, when he hit her in the head with a stick. He denied that charge, counterclaiming that she had engineered the elopement of their daughter. Nancy then charged that he had "kept a concubine in their common dwelling." Jacob denied all. Nancy vanished and reappeared in her daughter's household, demanding the division of the scores of slaves he owned, regardless of family ties. Jacob could game a public auction, colluding with his friends to keep bids low so he could buy back the undervalued slaves. Instead, she said, appraise the first-rate hands, the women, and the children; balance them all by their book value so that each spouse would get exactly the same; and split them up, for "they are susceptible to a division in kind without injury to us." As the divorce wound on and panics erupted, she stuck to her guns, demanding her share and threatening to get her son-in-law to assault the nearly seventy-year-old Jacob. She offered but one concession: she'd let Jacob buy Mary and Coulson from her if they fell to her in the division by lot. (In an 1835 will, Jacob had given de facto freedom to "my slaves Mary Clarkson and her son Coulson, a boy something more than five years old, both bright mulattoes.")[54]

Planter women's active support for proslavery positions increased dramatically during the 1840s, in both private letters and public writings. Scholars usually attribute this support to a reaction against outsiders' criticism of the South. But perhaps this shift actually grew from the recognition, in the midst of post-panic struggles, of how much right-handed power a Nancy Bieller could get from owning commodified human beings.[55]

In the wake of the collapse of the rag empire of banks and bonds, white people cheated each other left and right with such frequency that southerners came up with the term "G.T.T.," a special acronym to denote the tactic. With bankruptcy only a fleeting option, with everyone grabbing for assets, this tactic made a mockery of the law. But it kept enslaved people in enslavers' right hand so they could try again to create empires. And it swept away castles built by the ordinary virtue of enslaved women and men.

The acronym requires some explanation. In 1841, as the threatening letters mounted up on his desk, John Devereux's son Julien sought advice. One of his business partners was about to go bankrupt. How, he asked a friend, could he save himself from losing all his property to their mutual creditors? First, the friend replied, *do not trust the man*. He was probably hiding the truth from Julien, and would act to preserve himself without any regard for him. Next, find out how bad the man's debts are: "Go ahead and see into the very bottom, *deep* as it may be & *write me* confidentially after you find all out—but don't delay." Finally, get assets from the desperate man: "Take papers; notes; negroes; land, or anything." Things were bad—"I really am afraid it is a scrape—but don't be rash about it"—so threaten to move and leave him holding the bag: "Tell him you act upon your own desires to square up the business for emigration [to Texas]—but you need not emigrate after all." Of course, the advice-giving friend, another of Julien's creditors, didn't realize that Julien wouldn't just bluff. Julien had already bluffed *him*, by sending a group of slaves across the Texas-US border and beyond the reach of Alabama's debt-collection laws. Shortly afterward, leaving both Julien's wife and many debts behind, father and son Devereux headed to Mobile with some of their remaining Alabama slaves. There they boarded a ship for New Orleans and the St. Louis Hotel. After a comfortable and expensive stay in the same building where many New Orleans slave auctions now took place, the white men booked a cabin on a ship headed for Galveston. Any of their slaves that remained unsold went, too, by deck passage. Julien was "G.T.T."—gone to Texas.[56]

Slaves "run off" to escape debt were one reason why the enslaved population of the republic across the Sabine River increased from 4,000 in 1837 to more than 27,000 by 1845. Others took their slaves to a metaphorical Texas. Women sneaked slaves out past vigilant lawmen watching their husbands, delivering them to brothers-in-law, who headed to Texas. Slave owners paid overseers to march enslaved people up into the hills overlooking the Black Warrior River until the courts moved on from one Alabama county to the next and left local debt cases alone for a while. In response, creditors struck back—for instance, kidnapping a borrower's slaves, taking them to New Orleans, and turning them into cash on the auction block under the dome of the St. Louis Hotel before a countersuit could be filed.[57]

Eventually, Mississippi-based lawyers went to the US Supreme Court to argue in the most tortured and causuistic way that every white man in the state had a right to G.T.T. without even leaving their home county. Written in the wake of Nat Turner, the 1832 Mississippi state constitution had barred the domestic slave trade. But the state legislature never passed an act "enabling" the ban, and thousands of Mississippians bought southeastern slaves in the ensuing boom years. Among them was Moses Groves, who went into debt to New Orleans–based trader Robert Slaughter. When the crash came, Groves refused to pay, claiming that the sale had been illegal because it violated the state constitution.[58]

No one knows what happened to the specific individuals whom Slaughter had sold to Groves. The scholarly attention focused on the case has been more concerned with the personalities who argued *Groves v. Slaughter* in front of the Supreme Court. Henry Clay and Daniel Webster represented the slave trader,

Image 8.3. The actual experience of the early 1840s on the cotton frontier was that of living through the clearing-out of the "debt overhang" built up during the boom years of the 1830s. Unceasing slave sales and forced movements were typical, like those depicted in this "Sale of Estates, Pictures and Slaves in the Rotunda, New Orleans," in James Buckingham, *The Slave States of America* (London, 1842), vol. 1, facing title page.

while Groves's defenders—who were really arguing that *all* white Mississippians could G.T.T. their debts without having to leave the state—included Mississippi Senator Robert Walker. After taking George Poindexter's Senate seat from him in 1836, Walker had parlayed political power into privileged access to credit, which now meant that he owed thousands of dollars for his own purchases of slaves. His plea for Groves was for the right of individual debt repudiation. On the other hand, Rice Ballard paid Henry Clay's bill. For the great slave trader, this class-action case would determine whether he could collect on debts still owed him by Mississippi slave buyers. (Several similar cases made it to the Mississippi and Louisiana state supreme courts during the first half of the 1840s.) And the US Supreme Court delivered for Webster, Clay, and Ballard, rejecting slave-buyers' claims that failure to enforce the state constitution gave them the right to cancel their debts by unilateral action.[59]

In the environment of intense popular democracy that had emerged during Jackson's presidency, the next step may have been inevitable. By

1840, streams of slave-produced income had dried up, borrowers could not pay the banks, and sale of their mortgaged property—when it wasn't run off to Texas—brought little cash. The bondholders had fronted the banks millions, and the banks were not making their interest payments. In flusher times, state legislatures had pledged their states' "faith and credit" to redeem the bonds. Bondholders and bank insiders began to demand that the states extract the money from the people via taxes. Contracts had been made, just like the one between Slaughter and Groves. If the states went along, as pro-bank politicians often believed they should in order to maintain the ability to borrow in the future, they would have to commit to taxing their citizens at a very high rate. In Florida, for example, the amount owed to the holders of the state-issued "faith bonds" worked out to approximately $120 per man, woman, and child in the territory, white or black. This meant that the average slaveless farmer would have to pay more in taxes than his farm was worth. In Mississippi, wrote the *Columbus Democrat*, "the beds on which your wives and children sleep, the tables on which you eat your daily bread will be taken by the excise men for the benefit of those who sleep in splendid brick palaces, who sleep in mahogany bedsteads, eat with gold knives and forks, and drink champagne as the ordinary beverage of the day."[60]

Privatizing the gains of investment, socializing the risk. This is a classic strategy for politically powerful entrepreneurs. After generations of struggle to force politicians to respond to them, southwestern yeomen already suffering from the bad economic times that the entrepreneurial class had created were not about to hand over what remained of their livelihoods in order to bail out rich men. Increasingly they and their most radical politicians agitated for states and territories to refuse to pay the bonds. Anti-bank anger also split the northern wing of the Democratic Party. Opponents described the reaction as backward-looking. But many voters saw it as a matter of white equality. They wanted to tell "cormorants and sharks," as a Mississippi newspaper called "bonders," that rich men couldn't force the public to pay their debts. Wherever the anti-bank Democrats got the upper hand, they launched financial investigations that documented the banks' rampant insider lending and completely irresponsible behavior. It emerged, for instance, that the directors of Mississippi's Union Bank had lent themselves $1 million of the first $5 million generated by the sale of the state bonds.[61]

So southwestern anti-bank politicians now launched a crusade for G.T.T. by entire states. Mississippi governor Alexander McNutt, the same governor who in 1838 had supported the Union Bank, by 1841 advocated for repudiating the $5 million in state bonds he had helped to sell in the great 1838–1839 cotton speculation. In that fall's elections, Mississippi elected a repudiationist majority to the state legislature, which immediately decided that it would not pay the bonds. The Mississippi legislators who voted against paying the bondholders collectively owed between $500,000 and $1 million to the Union Bank. Those who voted against repudiation owed about half that amount. Both Florida and Arkansas also repudiated their bonds. Louisiana technically did not repudiate its bonds, but Democratic legislatures refused for years to make interest payments on C.A.P.L., Union, and Citizens' Bank bonds. The state had committed to back $21 million in bonds. Banks sold the securities and lent out the proceeds to their friends, yet as of the Civil War, $6 million remained unredeemed, the interest still unpaid.[62]

Bond repudiation outraged investors. Outrage fermented quickly to contempt. When he traveled to New York in 1839, John Knight discovered that "Mississippi and Mississippi men, bank, &c" already stood "in horrible odour." Wall Street's banks had survived the Panic of 1839, effectively winning the battle with Nicholas Biddle and the southern entrepreneurs for control of America's financial future. But Wall Street men and City of London types alike were shocked that the southwestern frontier, in which they had invested so much money, would so shamelessly steal. European bondholders fired off endless pamphlets criticizing the repudiating governments. The *London Standard* called Mississippi citizens "a set of atrocious scoundrels." The *London Times* claimed in 1847 that it would be fifty years until another European would be fool enough to lend money to the United States.[63]

The bondholders launched endless lawsuits. Despite a withering storm of criticism and lawsuits, however, the bankrupt states continued to refuse to pay. The US Supreme Court dodged involvement. As late as the 1930s, the Principality of Monaco, which had inherited some Mississippi Union Bank bonds, was still trying to sue Mississippi in the Supreme Court. And Congress also declined to act. Neither party wanted to demolish its own electoral chances in the half dozen repudiating states. The states' citizens, meanwhile, solaced themselves against the slings and arrows of an angry financial world in a number of ways. Less wealthy whites took satisfaction in the discomfort of bank cliques. The governor of Mississippi and some of its leading newspapers turned to an ancient Western excuse. A Mississippi newspaper dismissed the *London Times* as "the organ of Jew brokers," while Alexander McNutt sneered that the Rothschilds, who held both Alabama and Mississippi bonds, should be denied payment because they were of "the blood of Shylock and Judas."[64]

So southern popular culture, once as open to Jewish participation as any-place in Christendom, had now been cynically injected with an anti-Semitic virus that would last for many decades. But that was only the start of repudiation's poisoned gift-giving. True, reaction to the bank bonds had produced the most significant political uprising of class-based resentment to elite domination that would ever emerge from the poor and small-farming white men of the plantation frontier. No politician associated with the property banks had a viable political future. Yet G.T.T. on the grand scale was a self-inflicted choking-off of ties to worldwide credit markets. After this, southwestern entrepreneurs would never again participate as equal partners in the worldwide expansion of capitalism. These elites had used popular anger to turn the power of the state into a shield against foreclosures—but at the cost of losing future control over their own credit. Common white southerners, who had not experienced the boom of the 1830s in the same way as their self-appointed "betters," cared little about all that, but credit would shape their futures, too.

REPUDIATION OF ONE FORM or another had called a white man named Paskall to a slave labor camp on the far side of the Brazos. The camp's owner, Richard Blunt, lived twenty miles away in the coastal town of Matagorda. Blunt, in debt in Mississippi, had run his slaves west across the line into Texas, where his creditors' arms were too short to reach. Paskall had come west to find a job. Overseeing paid cash. Now he had to control the people whom Blunt's decisions had separated from anything they'd built, and everyone they'd built it with, back in Mississippi.

Paskall complained to the other white men in the neighborhood that "the Negroes were very unruly." Perhaps the disruption of their lives had shifted the terms of the daily calculus of obeying or fighting back. Go along to get along, get yanked out of one's cabin in the middle of the night, and be herded west all over again. One's husband was back on the next plantation along the Yazoo; or one's wife and child; so were the Bible and the bag of hoarded coins, both hidden under the roots of that old cottonwood.

Or maybe this: there had been that day in Mississippi when Blunt called everyone in from the field and lined them up for the man from the bank, who counted them off and wrote down dollar values and fake ages for his mortgage ledger. A mortgage is technically a sale, so by running to Texas Blunt had stolen each mortgaged slave from his or her legal owner. One day Blunt was the representative of the Law, the hard edge of a giant monolith bearing down. Then, that night, he was slipping away with stolen property. He and his agents now seemed less imposing and united.

So there was Paskall, pushing a man to keep up with the cotton-chopping line. And this spring day, that man had enough. He "knocked [Paskall] in the head with a grubbing hoe and buried him in the field, and ploughed over him." The man took Paskall's gun, and, gritting his teeth, shot himself in the hand. He staggered from the field and walked twenty miles to Matagorda, where he gave Blunt his story. Paskall had shot him in a rage, "thought he killed [the slave], and [Paskall] rode one of his horses off."

Blunt was too busy with drinking and cards to worry about the details. But the story sounded fishy to his neighbor James Hawkins. A few days later the horse came wandering back, saddle still on. Hawkins convinced other local whites to have the slaves interrogated. "It was some time," he reported, "before we could make the Negroes tell anything about [Paskall]." But they did. Hawkins took the men out to the field and made them dig Paskall's body out from under the cotton furrows. "The negroe" with the hand wound, Hawkins reported, "was in jail" and "will surely be hung." Hawkins's overseer, terrified by the neighborhood murder, was barricading himself in his cabin every night.[65]

Perhaps the terrified man couldn't erase the image: blood pooling in dirt; Paskall's shattered head half-covered by the plow's first run; black man frantically whipping balking mule around for one more pass, scanning the horizon. Borrowing and slave purchases in Mississippi, a son leaving Paskall's father's home back East: these ordinary decisions had led to the death of two men on the next and maybe last frontier for cotton slavery. Murder wasn't what these men had imagined as the outcome of their long ride and march west. On slavery's bleeding edge, overly ambitious plans made years earlier led to blowback. But no one bled as much as enslaved people. And no one's life was as disrupted by the principles of G.T.T.

From 1837 to the mid-1840s, desperately indebted enslavers looted the riches stored and nurtured by enslaved people's blood relationships. Alexander McNutt, Mississippi's repudiationist governor, had—back in 1835—purchased $20,000 worth of enslaved people from fellow Virginia native George Rust. McNutt promised to pay Rust principal plus 10 percent annual interest over the next several years. Ten years later, McNutt had entered and left office, and some of the twenty-odd men and women who had survived the adjustment to life in his Mississippi slave labor camp had married and had children. For instance, Lewis and Mary, preteens in 1835, were now married and raising four-year-old Anderson and toddler Louisa. Between the endless hours they spent toiling in McNutt's cotton field, Lewis and Mary had also spent years working to make sure their blood survived. But the governor had not paid Rust back. Fearing that McNutt would slip away to Texas with the slaves, the Virginia creditor demanded that the now ex-governor cash out his debt. So in May 1845, early enough that potential buyers could use them to pick that year's cotton crop, twenty-two survivors of the group that had come out from Virginia a decade before were auctioned. Families, new and old, were broken on the block, like the one whose seven-year-old Nathan was sold off on his own to a bidder named A. J. Paxton for $300. Another couple—Nelson and Prissy—were sold together, but their son, Jefferson, a boy of less than ten, was sold to a different buyer.[66]

Enslaved people in the southwestern states talked about the ways in which whites' decisions and failures inflicted consequences on the enslaved themselves, as if they were commodities. "He drank us up." "He said: 'I'll put you in my pocket.'" If one enslaved person heard a white man and a woman in the house "talking about money," everybody in the quarters understood that "money" meant "slaves," and that "slaves" were about to be turned into "money" ("Massa say: 'they's money to me'"). "They [black folks] knew that mean they [white folks] gonna sell some slaves to the next nigger trader that come round."

The talk showed how well the enslaved understood the forces that structured their lives. But they experienced financial manipulation and devastation as men and women with blood pulsing in every vein. When historians have written about the role of family in the lives of the enslaved, they have talked about the way blood relationships gave structure to life; ensured care for children, even when parents were lost; and provided knowledge about the world that was a true alternative to the system of lies spun by planters. Indeed, kinship could do some of those things, sometimes. Even when the early-1840s disruptions, coming after a quarter-century of a growing slave trade, created a cumulative set of challenges not seen since the heyday of the Middle Passage, many adults could scramble and gamble in response to disrupted situations. And sometimes by doing so, they could protect their families. Already sold once, from Georgia to Alabama, Josiah Trelick heard that his enslaver, Charles Lynch, was in serious financial trouble and planning to sell him again. Lynch thought Trelick's "abroad" wife, "a small dark skind woman," as Lynch described her, "was very homely and ignorant." But she and her child were everything to Josiah. So Trelick dug up some money he'd buried, bought a small wagon and team, and slipped away along back roads to get his family from the other enslaver who owned them.

Then there was the clever light-skinned slave about whom Felix Street's stepmother told stories: this man started an impromptu auction when his owner was in the vicinity but not paying much attention. Before anyone realized it, the "white-looking" slave had sold off the owner. Or there was

Cynthy, a midwife in Tennessee—free, but "apprenticed" to white guardians who skimmed off her earnings. While on a job a day's journey from the cotton labor camp where her enslaved husband lived, she consulted a fortune-teller, whose cards told Cynthy that her husband's indebted owner had "run" him to Mississippi. The cards spoke true, but luckily there was a happy ending: her husband was stubborn and not worth much in the cotton field, and his owner was glad when Cynthy's employers made an offer to buy him.[67]

But enslavers still held the aces. A story told by one formerly enslaved person showed white folks' willingness to manipulate the powers of ownership, breaking any and every relationship, starting with bonds they gave to their creditors. "Old Cleveland," said the former slave, "takes a lot of his slaves what was 'in custom' and brings them to Texas to sell. You know, he wasn't supposed to do that, cause . . . he borrowed money on you, and you's not supposed to leave the place until he paid up. 'Course Old Cleveland just tells the one he owed money to, you had run off, or expired out there." Newspapers and court documents recorded the details of how freshly reestablished blood ties in slave communities could be broken as a result of crises in white families created by the financial collapse or other factors. So-and-so's slaves, valued at $23,845, for example, went for $16,000. And African Americans remembered their own histories of the crash. In the 1930s, a white employee of the Works Progress Administration in Jasper, Texas, typed up a summary of his interview with an elderly woman named Milly Forward. "She has spent her entire life in [this] vicinity," he began. But the text of her interview reveals something different. "I's born in Alabama," she recalled. "Mammy have just got up," from giving birth, "when the white folks brung us out west. Pappy's name Jim Forward and Mammy name May. They left Pappy in Alabama, because he belonged to another master."[68]

That "Mississippi men" were untrustworthy liars may have been news to John Roberts the debt collector, but it was not exactly a revelation to enslaved people, for whom slavery itself was "stealing." But this historical epoch was devastating all the same. If their first movement to the cotton frontier had brought revelation, this second one went down in enslaved people's vernacular history as a storm of chaos that swept away much of the work that survivors of the first round of disruptions had accomplished. Men had created new ways of being men, and the consequence of both women's and men's efforts coursed through children who lived, relationships that bloomed, blood ties linked in presence and remembered absence. But now stepparents and half-siblings were split in the dark of night. And whites' mutual deceptions meant that enslaved children weren't sure about the basic facts of what had occurred. "He stole me," remembered an aged Betty Simmons, of her in-debted Alabama owner who made her hide in the woods. Then "he sell me [in New Orleans] so the creditors couldn't get me." In Mississippi, toddler Henri Necaise wandered every day down to the gate where he last saw his mother leaving. But he never found her. Only his sister was there to comfort him, and he was lucky to have her.[69]

"They was always fearing something terrible was going to happen, from some sign they had saw, or something they had heard," Robert Laird remem-bered of parents and grandparents. As such children looked back from old age, they sometimes felt that these secondary forced migrations during the decade of planter disaster had isolated and atomized them, stealing their opti-mism and teaching them the devastating lesson that their blood ties could be broken into unknowable pieces. One Louisiana ex-slave told the tale he had "heard" of Pierre Aucuin—who was sold by his mother's owner at the age of two. Years later, when freedom came, Aucuin married a woman named Tamerant. The couple had three children. One day, his regular barber was unavailable, so he sat down and Tamerant got out the scissors. As she stood behind him, cutting it close to the scalp, she saw something she had never before noticed. "You know, Pierre, this scar on the back of your head sets me a-thinking way back when I was a gal . . . I had a little brother then. . . . [T]he master sold my little brother from us, and five years later they sold me from my ma and pa. Since then I ain't seen none of my folks." Tamerant continued, not yet realizing what she was saying: "One day my little brother and me was playing, and he hit me and hurt me. I took an oyster shell and cut him on the back of his head right where you got that scar."[70]

In their quest to make something beautiful, two people who had lost their personal and family histories stumbled, terribly, over the shards of the past. And variations of this brother and sister story appear several times in the Works Progress Administration interviews. In each case, the storyteller is saying: Listen, enslaver-generated chaos could ultimately, if it went on long enough, steal one's capacity to recognize even one's closest kin. If you didn't know your family, you didn't know yourself. And if you didn't know your-self, what sort of disasters could you bring down on yourself and others? So history taught orphaned children to hold such fears alongside all their bravery. Adult survivors of whites' financial disaster saw their own new lives, built through the practice of ordinary virtues to each other and through the rebuilding of ties of blood, ripped apart again. They found themselves alone, bearing another set of survivors' scars. This does not agree with the pic-ture of southern African Americans as a traditional people comforted by a deep and resilient web of kinship. Yet it is precisely what happened to people whose family trees had been clear-cut.[71]

DESPITE THEIR STINGING DEFEATS, southwestern entrepreneurs who had been through previous crises knew how to survive a downturn. Slave property was mobile, self-supporting, more liquid than any store of value short of sterling bills, and perhaps the most attractive kind of collateral in the entire Western world. If they could keep possession of their slaves, they could take advantage of those elements of enslaved property, especially if new geographical expansion convinced investors to lend their credit—as they always had before—to entrepreneurially minded planters. And yet, even with all of those reasons to feel confidence in the future, after 1839, as external pressures from abolitionist critics and northern creditors began to increase, a growing number of southern politicians and voters began to show clear symptoms of a deepening siege mentality. A small group of northern congressmen—most notably John Quincy Adams of Massachusetts and Joshua Giddings of Ohio—repeatedly introduced antislavery petitions to test Congress's "gag rule." Although their measures failed, the northern radicals slowly opened cracks in the interregional alliances between southern slavery-expanders and northern expansion-enablers that were the essence of both the Whig and Democratic parties. Meanwhile, the 1840 US Census showed that high population growth in the free states was erasing the slave states' ability to control the House. Reapportionment would give northern Whigs and Democrats less reason to do what southerners demanded. The only obvious hope for increasing the number of southerners in Congress was to add Texas, but after Jackson maneuvered the government into recognition of the Lone Star Republic's independence in 1837, the Whig Party had blocked its annexation.

Texas annexation looked dead, and there were other problems, too. International pressures, generated by Britain, also threatened future expansion, thus imperiling slavery's survival. In 1834, Parliament—persuaded by powerful bureaucrats who insisted that free labor would prove more efficient than slave labor—imposed emancipation in all the empire's far-flung domains. Still, southern enslavers might have taken comfort in the fact that even as Britain freed 700,000 Caribbean slaves, slavery continued to expand, not only in the United States, where statehood was on the docket for Arkansas and Florida, but in two other places—Cuba and Brazil. Between 1810 and 1840, Cuba had taken the lead in world sugar markets, underselling sugar producers on the far-less-efficient British islands. Meanwhile, Brazil's coffee plantations expanded at an astronomical rate, feeding the world market's soaring demand for caffeine.

In contrast to the United States, however, internal trades were insufficient to supply the needs of enslaver-entrepreneurs on Cuba's and Brazil's frontiers of production. Instead, in almost every year of the 1830s, slave traders carried between 80,000 and 100,000 enslaved Africans across the Atlantic to Havana and Rio de Janeiro. Three decades after the much-ballyhooed closing of the Anglo-American Middle Passage, and in violation of existing treaties signed by Spain and Brazil, the open wound in Africa's side was flowing faster than ever. In 1840, British Prime Minister Robert Peel began to push other European nations to accept a treaty called the Convention of London. This agreement would allow the Royal Navy to search and seize ships flying non-British flags if they were suspected of participating in the Atlantic slave trade.[72]

The British had already extended this kind of pressure to Texas, which, in return for diplomatic recognition from Britain, had agreed to allow the Royal Navy to stop ships bringing slaves from Cuba to Texas. And actual enforcement of existing treaties banning the Atlantic slave trade would threaten slavery's viability in Brazil and Cuba. Enforcement would also eviscerate the profits that US citizens were making from the illegal trade. US mercantile firms invested indirectly in slaving voyages to present-day Angola and Nigeria. Slave ships often employed captains from the United States. Many such vessels flew the Stars and Stripes, because British ships were reluctant to strong-arm vessels sailing under that flag. North American shipbuilding firms sold 64 ships in Rio between 1841 and 1845, most of them for the slave trade.[73]

In 1842, Britain sent Lord Ashburton, a.k.a. Alexander Baring, one of the directors of Baring Brothers, as an ambassador to the United States. His mission was to secure US submission to the terms of the Convention of London. Cynics pointed out that the British Empire's sugar producers, comparatively disadvantaged by the parliamentary abolition, would benefit from removing Cuban and Brazilian competition. On first glance, small revenue gains in sugar would hardly seem to balance out the losses that Britain—whose economy depended on an endless supply of cheap, high-quality cotton—might suffer by blocking the further expansion of US slavery. But British politicians wanted to win the votes of reforming evangelicals, who saw worldwide abolition of slavery as a moral goal. Moreover, the recently demonstrated ability of US planters to leverage British dependence on their cotton into credit bubbles and financial crises worried British industrial cities. British chambers of commerce petitioned Parliament to incentivize the growth of Indian cotton. Indian peasants had not been able to stand up to competition from southwestern slaves, but in the early 1840s the British colonial government launched experimental farms across western India. They hired twelve American men who claimed to be southern planters and cotton experts. If Indian cotton failed, an independent Texas might be the solution, freeing British industry from dependence on US planters. Texas land, claimed British agents there, "will yield 3 times as much Cotton as the Carolinas or Georgia to the acre." Even as Lord Ashburton arrived in Washington, British agents were trying to convince Lone Star citizens to remain outside of the United States.[74]

Had Daniel Webster (or John Quincy Adams) been making foreign policy, slavery's expansion in the New World might have been definitively halted in 1842. Instead, many southeastern enslavers were in the process of turning US foreign policy into an engine that would drive the slave South's further growth. One was President John Tyler himself, whom Whig critics, resentful of his activity to undermine their program, had taken to calling "His Accidency." Tyler replaced pro–Convention of London appointees and Cabinet members—such as Webster, who resigned—with fanatically proslavery men, including the new secretary of state, Abel P. Upshur. Like Tyler, Upshur was a planter from one of the oldest counties of eastern Virginia. Although Upshur was the author of arcane constitutional writings that insisted, like early-1830s nullifiers, on the separate sovereignty of the individual states, once inside the executive branch he showed no compunction about using centralized power to advance expansionist enslavers' particular agenda.

Despite the fact that the Senate had the power to approve or reject treaties negotiated by the executive branch, and that the Senate's Whig majority opposed Texas annexation, Upshur and Tyler were determined to see slavery's expansion resume. They began negotiations with the Texas government, and Upshur plotted a strategy that would allow the executive branch to sneak an annexation through Congress. They simply had to figure out how to present annexation as an imperative to two groups: slaveholders who feared an end to expansion; and American nationalists who feared British interference. Southerners of both parties and the northern wing of one party would then cooperate and annex slaveholding Texas.[75]

While Tyler foolishly believed that annexation would convince either the Whigs or the Democratic Party to nominate him for the presidency in 1844, Upshur was actually acting on stage-managing letters from another politician—one who also wanted to use "the Texas question" to make himself the champion and candidate of all who supported national expansion.[76] This secret director was John C. Calhoun. He owned more than one hundred slaves, as well as gold mines in Georgia and the Fort Hill labor camp in South Carolina (now the site of Clemson University), and he had once been the nationalist secretary of war under President James Monroe. Supporting antinationalist nullification, Calhoun had spoken for the fears of declining South Carolina's enslavers rather than to the needs of migrating entrepreneurs. But new realities had made Calhoun rethink his point of view. These included both the flood of petitions that allowed abolitionism to seep into congressional business and his now-intimate experience with the ongoing project of expanding slavery's frontiers. His son Andrew had driven dozens of forced migrants to a new slave labor camp in Alabama, and now he and John together were trying to bring their family fortunes successfully through the broader storm of indebtedness. Calhoun would spend the remainder of his life as the greatest slavery-expansionist in the United States, providing both the theory and the practical political maneuvers that would allow enslavers to launch another wave of creation and destruction.

A student's first encounter with Calhoun often comes in the form of a daguerreotype from Calhoun's last years. Look it up: his eyes glare robotically at the student, his face set like that of an undead despot, skeletal from the tuberculosis that was killing him. The student hears about nullification, and listens to quotations from unpublished disquisitions found in Calhoun's papers after death. The quotations contain impossible abstractions, such as the suggestion that the United States should shift to a two-person executive, one northern president and one southern, who could each veto the other, or veto Congress, if he liked. By the time the professor ties the lecture off with language about the supposedly antimodern, inefficient nature of the slaveholder economy, the student has received the complete image of Calhoun as, at best, "the Hector of a Troy fated to fall" (to quote abolitionist Wendell Phillips)—the champion of an inevitably-to-be-defeated southern ruling class. Calhoun ought to have known, the conventional story suggests, that the South would lose in the struggle for economic, political, and eventually military predominance.[77]

Maybe so. But enslavers were very powerful. The idea that slavery would inevitably end is less incontrovertible once we recognize the dynamism of their economy. Even if they struggled in the early 1840s, enslavers knew how to revive dynamic growth—with more expansion. The theories that Calhoun was developing to justify further expansion were actually modern, tailored to a market economy that saw economic entities as "people," that measured people as factors of production, and whose most innovative actors believed that entrepreneurs should be able to wield private property without restraint. In the meantime, however, he was also an adroit practical politician who was about to maneuver the nation into following his particular entrepreneurial minority's program. For when Upshur died in a freak February 1844 accident aboard a US naval vessel in the Potomac River, Tyler invited Calhoun to become the new secretary of state.[78]

Going through Upshur's correspondence, Calhoun found a letter that Britain's new ambassador, Richard Pakenham, had delivered. Speaking for the British government, the letter informed the Tyler administration that Her Majesty would object to the annexation of Texas, and that Great Britain "desires, and is constantly exerting herself to procure, the general abolition of slavery throughout the world." Sensing opportunity, Calhoun wrote a response, sending a copy of both his and Pakenham's messages to the Senate, whose Whig majority had recently blocked a proposed treaty of annexation suggested by Tyler and Upshur. This "Pakenham Letter" was Calhoun's devious ploy to force both voters and politicians to choose either to support British interference or add more slave territory to the United States. After criticizing British meddling in Texas, Calhoun insisted that slavery was not only expedient, but the best thing for black people. Statistics from the 1840 federal census supposedly proved that a high proportion of free African Americans in the North were insane, so "experience has proved" that slavery must be the proper state for people of African descent. If Britain wanted to end slavery in its own dominions, that was its problem. But Britain had no business keeping Texas out of the United States, for submission to British meddling would inflict "calamity"—freedom—on "the race which it is the avowed object of her exertions to benefit."[79]

Calhoun believed that most northern whites were nationalist and racist. And indeed, many northern Democrats were both, as well as deeply pro-annexation—such as Illinois Congressman Stephen Douglas, an ardent supporter of national expansion whose platforms usually featured extensive race-baiting. Or John L. O'Sullivan, editor of the pro-expansionist *Democratic Review*, who coined the term "Manifest Destiny" to describe what he saw as the white US citizens' God-given right to take the remainder of North America from Indians and mixed-race Mexicans. But Calhoun's letter was a piece of bad behavior that aggravated many other people, as well, even provoking southern Whigs to help kill Tyler's Texas treaty when it finally came up for a Senate vote.

Ultimately, the letter's open insistence that the expansion of slavery was a good thing put each major party's frontrunner to the test—and then

destroyed their candidacies. Democratic frontrunner Martin Van Buren released a public letter that backed away from annexation—killing his chances
of winning southern support for one more presidential run. Henry Clay, the
clear leader among the potential Whig candidates, released a similar document. The Whigs had already made anti-annexation their party line, so Clay
easily collected their nomination, but he had laid up trouble for the fall.[80]

The Democratic convention, however, played out along the fracture lines
Calhoun had struck. Pro-annexation forces—some southern, some expansionist northerners who followed Douglas and read O'Sullivan—seized control of the rules committee and changed the process to require a two-thirds
majority for nominating a presidential candidate. Once the balloting began,
Van Buren could not convince enough southern delegates to get his vote to
the required two-thirds. The convention settled on James K. Polk, Tennessee protégé of Andrew Jackson, former Speaker of the House of Representatives, and indebted owner of dozens of slaves and several Mississippi labor
camps. An alleged moderate who had stood by the party through the panic
years, he seemed to be the second-best choice for all factions. Polk promised
not only to add Texas to the Union, but also to demand most of what is today
British Columbia in his negotiations with the British over the Oregon Territory's border with Canada.[81]

After the Democrats wrote double expansion into their platform, the
South, plus northern expansionists, faced off against northerners who opposed annexation. The Democrats pummeled Clay with his anti-annexation
letter. He faced a relentless series of attacks, like the one launched by Mississippi Senator Robert Walker—he of the *Groves v. Slaughter* advocacy of the
idea that enslavers could repudiate what they owed. Walker, who owned lots
of Texas land, wrote a pamphlet aimed at the northern market claiming that
the expansion of US authority into Texas would actually *reduce* the scope and
life span of slavery—the old diffusion trick again. Walker presented a very
different argument in a South-marketed pamphlet called *The South in Danger*,
which depicted Clay as the tool of antislavery northern Whigs.[82]

When the election was held, Polk lost some of the non-cotton southern
states, plus—by a mere 133 votes—his home state of Tennessee. But he
made a clean sweep of the cotton states, many of the states north of the Ohio
and west of the Appalachians, and the highly populous states of Virginia
and Pennsylvania. The antislavery Liberty Party probably tipped the New
York election to Polk by taking votes from Clay. Although Polk led Clay
by only 1.5 percent in the total national popular vote, his expansionism won

enough key states to give him a substantial electoral-college majority of 170 to Clay's 105.[83]

Calhoun's ingenious strategy of maximizing the confrontation with Britain and asserting the racist case for slavery as a positive good had split the Whig Party in half, producing victory for a southern expansionist. Even before the election, land prices in Texas, anticipating Polk's victory, had begun to rise. National financial markets, meanwhile, anticipated that the federal government would annex Texas and pay off the Lone Star Republic's bonds at full face value once Polk took office. Tyler, however, did not want to leave the credit for Polk, so when the lame-duck Congress gathered in December 1844, he told it that the American people had recorded a mandate for expansion. Annexation-by-treaty had failed, so Tyler suggested a fine-print measure called a "joint resolution" that would require a simple majority in each house. The constitutionality was suspect, but (surprisingly) Tyler and Calhoun did not bring up their usual strict-interpretation principles. In January 1845, the House passed a resolution admitting Texas—and accepting its bonds, its slavery, and its more than 300,000 square miles, which were to be divided into as many as four (slave) states. One of the crucial switch votes that put annexation over the top in the Senate was that of Ohio's Benjamin Tappan. Though his brothers were Lewis and Arthur Tappan, abolitionism's wealthiest supporters, Benjamin had major Texas bondholdings.[84]

The outgoing president, refusing to wait for Polk, immediately signed annexation into law. Thus in the last two years of Tyler's accidental term, enslavers committed the momentum of the federal government and the Democrats' core constituencies (even though Tyler was ostensibly a Whig) to a specific vector of national expansion. This vector, by the realities of geography, would inevitably privilege territorial growth on the southern side of the Missouri Compromise line.

Now the administration was in the hands of James K. Polk. As a product of the Jackson–Van Buren machine, Polk remembered Calhoun as a troublesome character and left him out of the new Cabinet. But the new president still constructed an expansion policy almost identical to what anyone dedicated to the expansion of slavery would have implemented. He quickly compromised with London on the northwestern border, agreeing to split the Oregon country more or less equally along the forty-ninth parallel to the Pacific. Although many southern Democrats celebrated the deal, the 54°40'-or-fight northern Democrats thought they had been promised something else: "Is it treachery? Is it bad faith?" wrote one to another. At the same time,

Polk pushed aggressively on the southwestern border for expansion beyond Texas. Mexico was weak, and Texas was only the first of its distant provinces to be lopped off. The vast region of Alta California, stretching from the north end of the Baja California peninsula to an incompletely determined line somewhere north of the bay of San Francisco, was almost as hard to govern, and already, American settlers were infiltrating. Polk also had designs on disputed territory west of Texas's traditional border on the Nueces River. In the early autumn of 1845, he sent Louisiana politician John Slidell to Mexico City with an offer: give us the disputed territory, and sell us New Mexico and California for a total of $28 million. He also sent General Zachary Taylor and his troops across the Nueces into territory claimed by Mexico on the east bank of the Rio Grande. They spent the winter with their guns pointed across the river at Matamoros.[85]

In May 1846, news reached Washington that Mexico had rejected the Slidell offer three months earlier. Polk and his Cabinet prepared a war message to be sent to Congress. But the message was superseded by the sudden arrival of news from Texas: US and Mexican troops had fought a battle in the disputed territory. "American blood has been shed on American soil," was the way Polk spun it to Congress. He asked for a "war bill" (not, technically, a declaration of war). He got it, despite vocal dissent from Joshua Giddings, John Quincy Adams, and other antislavery Whigs. To them, this war was proof that an expansionist slaveholding cabal was controlling US policymaking. To much of the rest of the country, war promised fulfillment: of the nationalist dream of placing the United States among the great expansive powers of the world; of massive new opportunities for settlement and land ownership; of the strange hunger for collective effort that sometimes reveals itself in the fevered early days of a war. Northern Democrats forgot for the moment Polk's compromises on the Oregon line. Across the nation, men rushed to form volunteer military companies. This was the first chance in more than a generation to achieve military glory in the field against a regular, European-style army. The war, eager patriots believed, would be the making of many kinds of fortune.

BACK ON THE FIRST day of January, American troops had been digging in along the Rio Grande five hundred miles to the west of where old John Devereux, Julien Devereux's Virginia-bred father, had been starting another volume of his diary in Rusk County, Texas. The day opened year 1846 of the Christian era, noted the old gentleman from his desk at the family's new slave labor camp, but also year 1259 "of the Higera or flight of Mahomet" from Mecca to Medina. John on the page still lived in the curious eighteenth-century Enlightenment, but John the old enslaver dwelled on the rough leading edge of the nineteenth-century economy's commodity frontier. Between environment and advancing age, John's language had become less complex, his capitalization sporadic and syntax roughshod. Meanwhile, his son Julien, who like many of their old neighbors had run away from his debts, was preparing to mix up another brew of credit leverage from worldwide financial networks, heated and transformed by the fuel of labor productivity extracted from commodified people.[86]

John had fired the previous year's overseer. Although it was New Year's Day, all "hands commenced grubbing . . . under management of Negro Scot." They were clearing land steadily. On the 2nd he heard them "in good spirits and happy singing & caroling at their work except poor henry who will soon be emancipated from slavery by death." "It's a cool frosty morning, and the niggers go to work," Harriet Jones remembered the men singing on a similar Texas labor camp, "with their hoes on their shoulders and without a bit o' shirt." On they toiled to prep as many acres of bare dirt as they could for cotton seeds. This effort became more high-pitched once John Devereux decided to hire a white overseer. Meanwhile, forced migrants tried once more to shape their lives so that they could survive in this next new place. At the end of January, Devereux captive Eliza Henry Maria married Sam Loftus, a man owned by another local enslaver. On February 23, a runaway from a nearby labor camp, "Bill L.," showed up "Choctaw'd drunk." The "hands" convinced Bill to go back to his owner. Down on the Brazos, where enslavers had already developed a substantial complex of sugar and cotton labor camps, runaways could hope to reach the Mexican border. Bill was too far north and east for that. The people at Devereux's labor camp probably warned him that his fate could be akin to that of another runaway, a woman who had been re-captured in nearby Tyler County. Her owner dragged her back home behind his horse and tied her to the bedstead. The next morning he tried to cut off her breasts. Then he rammed a hot iron poker down her throat. Survivors of these East Texas camps remembered that out there on that frontier, one could always "hear the whip a-poppin'."[87]

On March 12, John also had a guest: "An old man on foot"—a white man—"called this morning and got breakfast," John wrote. The man "had laid out all night in the rain—says he is a millwright and was born in Augusta," in the Shenandoah Valley into which southwest-bound coffles descended after crossing the Rockfish Gap through the Blue Ridge. He knew "the Springers and the Landrums," old Augusta families from John's

Image 8.4. After the wreck of so many entrepreneurial plans in the wake of the bursting of the slave credit bubble, enslavers increasingly portrayed their own operations as being driven by paternalist, familial impulses—rather than pecuniary ones. And, as the title of this illustration suggests, enslavers rejected abolitionists' claims that their society was somehow an un-American tumor that should be excised from the national body. Edward William Clay, "America, 1841." Library of Congress.

childhood. But from there the barriers of fortune and class lowered on the conversation. The sun rose higher. The poor man stood up and said his good-bye. He walked silently down the road, in his own way representing another life ground under by the rolling frontier of the modern slave economy.

John knew that he, too, would die a thousand miles from home. He had more to hope for than an old age of sleeping rough and begging for manual-labor jobs. But the conversation with the wanderer led him to assess his life. John had lost four of his six children, and he was a widower twice over. Yet he admitted that he was much better off than, for instance, Job. Each of his own wives had been "worth a cowpen full such as" the complaining spouse who had burdened the Old Testament figure. And perhaps Julien's second bride would be better than the first. John hadn't heard from Julien in months, but he was on his way. After the worst of the legal storm blew over, the younger Devereux had returned to Alabama to pick up several dozen slaves who had been stashed on an ally's place since 1841. Now, on March 20, "about 12 o'clock," a white employee arrived with "three wagons and the negroes from Montgomery," and John relished both their "excitement at meeting with the Negroes here and Julien's letter giving information that he had sold out and all was coming." Even better, the letter told "of the birth of a son." The news "operated powerfully on my sympathies," John wrote. Tears choked the old man. Julien, remarried, now had an heir of his blood, and thus John did as well. A new generation of enslavers was emerging.

Just a few days more, and Julien arrived. Overseer, three other employees, Julien, and John: six white men were now at the new house, where only a few months ago there had been none but the old man. All day and into the evening, the slaves worked the raw East Texas soil around the new cotton shoots. The United States had stretched its borders to incorporate these acres, these white men, and their property. Slave prices were climbing. With the promise that the US government would fund Texas bonds, surely credit would pump again through the veins that oxygenated the endeavors of southwestern entrepreneurs. Further southwest, cannon boomed and men marched, pushing the border onward. Here, a woman set supper out. All six men sat down to eat, "which," John noted, "filled all our chairs and table." The world had come right side up again.

# 9

# BACKS

## *1839–1850*

THE GIRL GIGGLED IN her pew, looking back at seventeen newly emancipated Louisianans, frozen in the church entrance. Mid-step between the doorway and a sea of staring faces stood Anna and her four children; Sarah and Frankey, both eleven, no parents; Betsy and her son; Maria, Margery, and their daughters; Little Sam; Jose; Rose; nine-year-old Amos. The big red turbans the women wore had been stylish decades ago in New Orleans, when they'd been sold. Now they screamed *country* and *slave* to the Boston streets.[1]

A hand tightened on the knowing girl's arm, jerked down, pulled her around to face the pulpit. She needed to remember. Here at Unitarian King's Chapel, on Beacon Street, she was also a visitor—black Bostonians usually spent their Sundays elsewhere, such as the new A.M.E. church. The day's assigned lesson was solidarity. Like many of the other visitors in the pews, her mother was what we'd today call an activist. She might have been at 1843's huge Faneuil Hall protest meeting, two years earlier. Slave-catchers had come up to Boston in disguise. They had found George Latimer, an escapee from Virginia slavery. He and his wife, Rebecca, were living like free people. The kidnappers had seized the Latimers and thrown them into the Boston jail. But word had gotten out, and soon three hundred free black men were surrounding the Boston courthouse. Their aim was to keep George and Rebecca there until the meeting at Faneuil could raise $600. Eventually, George's Virginia owner decided that taking the money and making out George's manumission papers might be his best option.

Like these seventeen, many of the other African Americans in the church had also been adjusting to Boston. Some were runaways. Others had been forced to leave the South by laws that were designed to make life unbearable for free people of color. They were all in their way forced migrants, driven by slavery's expansion, driven to a place that they had built. If these newest Bostonians looked up in wonder at King's Chapel's austerely magnificent vaults, which soared like white wedding cake from pillars to roof, and if they felt intimidated by the rich variety of clothes on the congregants—clothes unavailable on the backwaters of the Attakapas—the migrants had nevertheless spent their lives constructing exactly this world.

They had certainly built the Palfrey family. John Palfrey the elder had owned them. He was the Massachusetts merchant whose slaves had joined the 1811 rebellion when he lived in St. John the Baptist Parish along the Mississippi River. Palfrey had moved to St. Martin Parish, pursued by debts. The sheriff repossessed some of his slaves. He sold his silver candlesticks and hand-tooled pistols. But after 1815, he could borrow again, so he bought more enslaved people.

The separations that the seventeen, or their parents, had endured as they had traveled from the Chesapeake Bay area to Maspero's place in New Orleans, and then the work they had endured in the crop fields of the Attakapas, had rebuilt John Palfrey's twice-destroyed financial self. His own family was also divided, though not exactly like the families of the people he bought. His oldest son, John Gorham Palfrey, lived in Louisiana briefly with his father, but then returned to Massachusetts. Talents and birth destined John the son to be a Harvard prodigy. At nineteen, he was ordained a Unitarian minister. Then, in 1830, he became a Harvard professor. Later in the decade he took over the *North American Review*. Economic growth was producing a well-educated bourgeois that wanted to participate in a national high culture distinct from that of old Europe. Under Palfrey, the *Review* published the authors of America's emerging literature, from James Fenimore Cooper to William Cullen Bryant.[2]

Young John's four brothers stayed in Louisiana. Henry became a cotton broker; William, a Bayou Teche planter. In 1816, however, Edward died of yellow fever in the New Orleans counting-house where he worked. George caught a pistol ball in an 1824 duel. Death by hot-blooded dueling did not happen in the orderly, morally improving Boston of the *North American Review*. But the brothers stayed in contact. John G. Palfrey visited at the height of the 1830s boom, traveling on the steamboat *Southerner*. The letters he sent to Louisiana afterward asked ironically after enslaved people in the terms of racist parody: How are "my sooty friends?" When William contemplated visiting Boston, John the younger warned him to bring his own slave: "The black servants you can hire here are good for nothing." The Palfreys agreed on national politics. All were sensible Whigs, supporters of the party's project of national social and moral uplift. Henry sold copies of John's *Review* to his planter clients, who perhaps squirmed to read an English author's claim that "the continuance of slavery" in the United States was a disaster. But the author's claim that American problems were caused by too much democracy surely found secret assent.[3]

Of course, the *Review* didn't pay the bills any better than serious magazines ever have. When the Panic of 1837 hit, subscriptions dropped and bills multiplied. Henry helped the *Review* stay afloat, sending young John $1,000 from Louisiana and convincing their father to lend $5,000 to the magazine. Slavery financed John Palfrey's Massachusetts literary project. However, the question of whether slavery should grow or shrink was about to strain the brothers' bonds. As John the elder aged, the Louisiana Palfreys took care to advise their brother that he would, by the terms of their state's Napoleonic civil code, inherit one-third of his father's property. Most of the value of that property was in slaves. The best way to turn this share into money usable in Massachusetts would be to sell the people he inherited. But "you might incur the risk," wrote William, "of some busy abolitionist . . . report[ing] that the Revd. Dr. P. had been selling human flesh etc etc or living on the income of slave labor."[4]

Ties of blood linked John G. Palfrey to the southern slave-owning elite, and so did ties of economic growth. Northern growth in general and the fortunes of its middle and upper classes in particular were built on the forced labor of people like those whom John would inherit from his father. But moderate northern Whigs had grown increasingly disturbed by southern politicians' domineering aggression. By late 1843, Louisiana Whigs were salivating over impending Texas annexation, but the constituents of the Massachusetts Whigs were holding a rash of angry meetings. They were spewing anger at New England "Cotton Whigs" whose close ties to the state's textile manufacturing interests supposedly predisposed them to cave in to enslavers' endless demands.[5]

In the autumn of 1843, one of the season's first cotton ships arriving in Boston also brought news from New Orleans. Old John Palfrey had died. John Gorham Palfrey now owned twenty human beings, a mixed crew ranging in age from Margery's unnamed infant child to Old Sam, sixty-five. At the current price level in New Orleans slave markets, their value approached $7,000—but John the younger had decided that he didn't want any more money from slavery. This new conviction tells us something about his conscience. But it also tells a story about the outcomes of cotton-driven change in the United States over the first half of the nineteenth century, one in which northern and southern brothers began to argue uncontrollably in the 1840s precisely because they had helped each other to thrive for the preceding half-century.

From the 1790s, the continually increasing productivity of enslaved hands had generated the most important raw material in the world economy at a constantly declining real price. This had made southern enslavers incredibly wealthy, and powerful, too. They were able to attract massive quantities of investment capital in the 1830s. Enslavers also exerted disproportionate influence over the national government, ensuring the creation and implementation of policies that benefited them. Yet the same work of hands that built a wealthy South enabled the free states to create the world's second industrial revolution. This one began in the cotton mills of Massachusetts and Rhode Island. From the mills, the development of the northern economy spiraled outward to transform wider sectors. After the South's economy grew into a bubble, and then exploded, the North recovered while the South floundered. And the main reason for the North's quicker recovery was that northerners had reinvested profit generated from the backs of the enslaved in creating a diversified regional economy.

Now, having built a brave new world on the product of the cotton fields, northerners such as John G. Palfrey were convincing themselves that slavery was a premodern, inefficient drain on the national economy. This was an inaccurate generalization from an accurate observation. Northern observers and antislavery activists saw the slower recovery of the southern economy and thought it proved that slavery was an economic incubus and not an engine of growth. But they also had some powerful emotional reasons to look at slavery in this way. By 1843, enslaver-politicians had begun to lunge at Texas and beyond, hoping to implement once again their classic formula: new land, new credit sources, a new boom. This time around, however, northern brothers decided that there was a "Slave Power" bent on tyrannical domination, and not just of enslaved hands.

So Palfrey consulted with several Boston acquaintances. The first was a political and legal mentor, US Supreme Court Justice Joseph Story. Just the previous year, Story's opinion in the case of *Prigg v. Pennsylvania* had strengthened southerners' claims that the US Constitution protected slavery. Edward Prigg, a Maryland enslaver, had tried to recover an enslaved woman who had run to Pennsylvania with her children to escape sale to slave traders. State authorities blocked him. The case went to the Supreme Court. It put Story under pressure from two sources: slavery expansionists, on the one hand, and African Americans who resisted being stolen, on the other. He did not want to write the ruling, but he had no choice. In *Prigg*, the Court ruled that the Constitution required northern states to hand over escapees, undermining northern states' laws that ended slavery within their own borders.

Palfrey also met with the young "Conscience Whig" politician Charles Sumner. If Story warned him of the difficulty of getting the moral responsibility of slavery off one's back, Sumner helped stiffen John's spine for heavy lifting. Without notifying his brothers, John petitioned the Louisiana state legislature to let him free the twenty slaves and allow them to stay in the state. The brothers learned of John's actions from a New Orleans newspaper story reporting the legislature's rejection of his request. Henry wrote angrily to John: the whole story would "be published in the Attakapas paper on Saturday." Local planters would read it. William and Henry would hear questions. Their Attakapas neighbors knew that meddlers were choking Congress with petitions accusing slaveholders of being rapists, torturers, and slave traders. If the Palfreys' brother was an abolitionist, the local Whig Party, in which the brothers were stalwarts, would suffer. Meanwhile, proposing emancipation for twenty people at old John's camp would render the other forty unmanageable. They'd send the news up and down the Attakapas by the grapevine telegraph, talk back to overseers, or run to New Orleans to find a lawyer for a freedom suit. "Better to let them remain quietly at work and time will gradually settle all difficulties," Henry insisted.[6]

Henry knew that enslaved people acted as someone else's hands because they had no other choice. If the grip slackened, African Americans seized opportunities. As the domestic slave trade surged in the 1830s and the flood of new bodies taxed whites' ability to surveil the captives, the number of southwestern fugitives also spiked. Some made it all the way to the North. These new fugitives, who were also migrants—though against the grain of slave-trade and credit-circle flows—invigorated northern antislavery organizations. William Lloyd Garrison, taught by slavery-survivors, had helped to mobilize politically effective petition campaigns that portrayed enslavers as opponents of whites' freedom—particularly whites' freedom to disagree with policies promoting the expansion of slavery. Still, Garrison insisted that abolitionists should reject politics, which required compromises of the sort that in his view rendered the Constitution "a covenant with death and an agreement with hell." But by 1840, a new wave of survivors of slavery's frontier, including activist fugitives such as William Wells Brown and Henry Bibb, was steadily pushing abolitionism into the current of political fight.

Runaways pressured Judge Story, and runaways pushed enslaver-politicians to demand that other whites never disagree with them about slavery or its expansion. Palfrey's brothers didn't think he needed to contribute to the fuss. Especially not when his grandstanding with their father's inheritance would cause them trouble. They had heard that Massachusetts Whigs were squabbling, but they were shocked by the force of the leverage that John was willing to apply to enforce his changing convictions. In 1843, their world was one of hard times and G.T.T., and Henry's firm was bankrupt. They could not fathom how John—who only a few years ago had been asking for *their* help—could leave $7,000 on the table.

John G. Palfrey's personal route to rejecting slave ownership, direct or indirect, was ironic. But it was only somewhat unique. His willingness to act on his own convictions, even at the cost of a substantial sum of money, was unusual, though his changing convictions were not. Yet he still had to make a literal journey of rejection. Louisiana state legislators had denied his request that they allow the people he inherited to stay among the community they had built in the wake of forced migration. So Palfrey decided to bring them back with him to Massachusetts. In 1844, worried that they would not be able to support themselves, he visited Massachusetts author Lydia Maria Child and asked her to help him find them new homes in Boston. Child, a women's rights activist, and also one of the first white women publicly identified as an abolitionist, promised to help. Then he traveled to Lexington, Kentucky, and visited Cassius Clay, a relative of Henry Clay and a rare surviving southern proponent of emancipation. Clay had repeatedly fought off attempts at silencing. One of his speeches degenerated into a knife fight, with attackers rushing the stage. To deter mobs, he loaded a cannon and parked it on his front porch.

Emotionally fortified by Clay's example, Palfrey traveled to the Ohio River and boarded a steamboat headed to Louisiana. After enjoying a pleasant visit in New Orleans, Palfrey traveled out into the hinterland to brother William's home. He found that Attakapas whites were not very tolerant. They threatened him, and William was less cordial than usual as well. Eager to conclude his business, John met privately with each adult slave. All were willing to go North, but they wanted to wait until the end of the year. Cotton prices were low in the early 1840s, and William—like many other southwestern enslavers—was allowing enslaved people more time to cultivate their own patches of cotton, corn, and garden crops. In turn, they'd eat fewer planter-furnished rations, meaning less ink on the debit side of ledgers. Men and women with small amounts of cash in their hands could also buy their own cloth, clothing, tobacco, and liquor. Like potential runaways waiting until the corn was ripe, Palfrey's slaves didn't want to lose their investments of time and labor. And if they were to venture into the unknown in the hands of another John Palfrey, they wanted cash in their pockets.

John left for Boston. His brothers had insisted that it would "demoralize" their own labor forces if John's slaves mixed with theirs once word of impending freedom got out, but William was happy that the short-timers stayed. They helped gather William's cotton harvest—for which John promised to pay them back wages for 1844 once they reached Massachusetts. When 1845 arrived, three of the oldest—Amos (age sixty-one), Clara (fifty-five), and Old Sam (sixty-five)—balked at leaving their children and grandchildren, so John had parish officials bribed to permit these three to stay, despite their manumission. The other seventeen said goodbye to everyone and traveled to New Orleans. From the same levee where they and/or their parents had arrived, they boarded the bark *Bashaw* and set sail for Boston.

After their ceremonial welcome at King's Chapel, John began to send the newly emancipated people to various "placements" arranged by his abolitionist friends. With Child's help, he placed Anna and her four children in Canandaigua, New York, with a nice Quaker lady who needed a maid, and boys to chop her firewood. Amos Marshall was sent to work as a servant in Brooklyn, as was Henry. The others, however, found employment in Boston before Palfrey could disperse them. Local African Americans who remembered their own difficult transitions helped the country migrants to put down roots in Boston's black neighborhoods.[7]

Like most northern whites who adopted antislavery convictions in the 1840s, Palfrey didn't seem to be antislavery because of a belief in black equality, of either capacity or right-to-choose. Freeing his slaves over his brothers' objections, however, allowed Palfrey to demonstrate that southern whites could not silence him, as they had tried to silence his fellow Harvard alum John Quincy Adams with the Gag Rule. Southerners' political bullying had pushed him into a new conviction that replaced his previous implicit belief in an America where slave-owning and slavery-profiting brothers were united across geographic distance. Now, he concluded—as did other northern whites—that slavery was wrong and that its growth must be stopped because it enabled southern brothers to bully northern ones.

BACK IN 1819, RACHEL had climbed the New Orleans levee and then descended into a floodplain forested by pylons of cotton bales, silos of British metalware, and screes of calico bolts from Manchester. By then, Britain was clearly already becoming a new kind of society and economy, escaping the old Malthusian trap with the help of the New World's ghost acres. Its transformations began with the creation of a cotton textile industry. On the capital that sector earned, piggybacking technologies and industries emerged. Soon more people worked in commerce and industry than in agriculture, producing a market of millions of consumers. Raw materials imported from overseas—such as cotton—were essential, but by 1834 the empire concluded it no longer needed its own slaves.[8]

Although the United States and Britain spoke (mostly) the same language, the two nations found themselves in different situations. Britain lacked key natural resources, and therefore cotton made by enslaved US hands was essential to industrialization. Now Britain led the development race by a full quarter-century. Indeed, British-made goods still towered on the levee as the Palfrey people embarked for Boston, for in many manufacturing sectors, such as high-quality textiles, Britain's dominance had starved American competitors of market oxygen. Some northern Whigs, believing the United States should be further on the path that Britain had blazed, blamed enslavers for forcing the young nation to implement policy choices that pushed the republic away from replicating the empire's success. To them, the national investment in territorial expansion was a proof-text. Endless robbery of Indian lands in the Louisiana Purchase, Florida, and Texas also meant that land would remain cheap. Immigrants might move to the cheap-land frontier instead of working in factories, keeping industrialists' labor costs high.[9]

Still, a quarter-century after Rachel's 1819 arrival in New Orleans, some sectors of the US economy were changing dramatically. One way to measure this transformation is to look at historical estimates of how fast the economy was expanding. Between 1774 and 1800, the annual rate of economic growth per capita in the United States was less than 0.4 percent. From 1800 to 1840, the average rate of increase climbed to between 0.66 percent and 1.13 percent per year—spiking in the mid-1830s, of course, but then crashing into the negative range for several years after the Panic of 1837. By the 1850s, it rose to almost 2 percent per year. By comparison, the per capita growth rate of the US economy in the 1990s, its most successful decade since the 1950s, was about 2.5 percent per year.[10] Traditional explanations for this metamorphosis into a post-Malthusian regime assume that the ultimate cause of growth was some characteristic unique to the North's free-labor economy. Writers have credited an individualistic culture, Puritanism, open land and high wages, amorphous "Yankee ingenuity," government intervention in the economy, and government nonintervention in the economy. Yet we now also know that even as the entire economy became more productive, from 1800 to 1860 raw cotton production gained in efficiency still more quickly than other sectors of the economy. The increasing speed of cotton-picking yielded a productivity increase of slightly more than 2 percent per year from 1800 to 1860.

In 1832, the US government compiled a fascinating document that reveals the way that cotton not only dominated US exports and the financial sector but also drove the expansion of northern industry. Jackson's secretary of the treasury, Louis McLane, hoping to find evidence that the 1828 "Tariff of Abominations" was protecting the emergent US manufacturing sector, asked Democratic insiders across the free states to visit manufacturing establishments in their neighborhoods. They interviewed proprietors such as the manager of the Old Sable Iron Works in Delaware County, Pennsylvania, who warned that if the tariff was reduced, "our nail establishments could not be sustained."

McLane's data not only showed that foreign iron was too cheap, but also revealed the crucial role of cotton textiles in driving the expansion of manufacturing. Over the preceding four decades, cotton mills yoked to water power had multiplied along the rivers and creeks of Massachusetts, Rhode Island, and Connecticut. They relied on labor from southern New England's worn-out agricultural sector, machinery designs stolen from Britain, and ever-cheaper southern cotton. Early factories had mechanized the process of spinning cotton, but still "put-out" thread to families who used home hand looms to weave it into cloth. Mill-based powered looms would enable the next transition to take place.[11]

In the 1820s, the "Boston Associates," a group that included men such as Nathan Appleton and Abbot Lawrence, who would become Cotton Whigs and John G. Palfrey's political enemies, planted a factory town on the Merrimack River in eastern Massachusetts. They named it Lowell, after an industrial spy who had stolen loom designs from British factories. By 1832 four massive mills were in operation there. Each integrated spinning and weaving under a single roof. Collectively the mills contained $1 million worth of machinery, and these machines were tended by 3,000 workers, of whom three-quarters were women and girls. Each year, the mills used 5.5 million pounds of cleaned cotton: more than 13,000 bales, close to 15 million pounds as weighed on cotton-stand balance beams. Thus Lowell consumed 100,000 days of enslaved people's labor every year. And as enslaved hands made pounds of cotton more efficiently than free ones, dropping the inflation-adjusted price of cotton delivered to US and British textile mills by 60 percent between 1790 and 1860, the whipping-machine was freeing up millions of dollars for the Boston Associates. They invested it in other machines, higher pay for factory workers, and the finery and architecture that overwhelmed Palfrey's freedpeople in the church on Beacon Street. They also lowered the price of textiles, expanding both Lowell's markets and the access of ordinary people all over the world to factory-made cotton textiles. An entire planet's consumers shared in the welfare of the growing margin between the price of raw cotton and what the price would have been if picked by free labor.[12]

In 1820, only 3.2 percent of the US labor force had worked in manufacturing—maybe 75,000 workers in all. By 1832, the date of McLane's report, factories and workshops across the North employed about 200,000 workers. The biggest share was in cotton mills, which were the most mechanized, capital-heavy, *industrial* kind of industry in the entire United States. Their 20,000 employees represented something new in US history: an unpropertied, nonagricultural, free working class, the growth of which created demand for goods. In fact, both cotton labor camps and cotton mills generated increased demand for such things as iron goods, ready-made clothes, rope, furniture, and shoes. By the time of the 1832 McLane census, American industry was beginning to produce more of these goods. Non-textile production still usually took place in relatively small-scale workshops. These included the small but flexible workshops of New York's "sweated trades," such as clothes-making, furniture, leather goods, and hats. Then as now, the city attracted a stream of hungry immigrants willing to toil long hours in cramped conditions. Small size also reflected limited technology, for most industries had not yet found substitutes for human power and hand production. The tiny workshops scattered through rural areas near Philadelphia and Pittsburgh still dominated the iron industry. A rare exception was the Ousatonic Manufacturing Company of Litchfield County in Connecticut, which in 1831 employed more than one hundred laborers and made 600 tons of iron.[13]

Textiles made from southwestern cotton continued to lead the way: above all, in employing a working class whose wages created a consumer market that encouraged ever more dynamic market production in other areas. In his response to McLane's questionnaire, David Anthony of Fall River, Massachusetts, wrote that the town's mills employed 4,000 textile workers—"all depending directly or indirectly on the manufacturing business . . . requiring as much agricultural produce as any other class of people in the country." Growing markets for food accelerated a commercialization of daily life that reached into the free states' rural districts. Farmers grew crops for the market, rather than for subsistence. In Ohio and Indiana, farmers reached southwestern markets via the Mississippi River, and once New York completed the

Erie Canal in 1824, upstate farmers could ship produce to New York City. Now that efficiency reaped rewards, northern farmers became more efficient: their farms became larger, farmers began to specialize, and they demanded improved seeds and implements.[14]

McLane created his document for the political advantage of northern manufacturers, but it shows that as of 1832, cotton made by enslaved people was driving US economic expansion. Almost all commercial production and consumption fed into or spun out from a mighty stream of white bolls. Politicians and entrepreneurs used the force of cotton's flood like a millrace to turn other wheels. Politicians, for instance, created a tariff system whose core principle was the protection of New England textile manufacturing. After the War of 1812, the British allegedly tried to smother America's infant industries by dumping goods below cost on US markets. In response, Congress added a surcharge of almost 35 cents per yard to low-quality imported cloth. The tariff redistributed the productivity of enslaved hands to northern manufacturers and merchants (in the form of profits) and millworkers (in the form of wages). And it allowed American mills to specialize. While finely woven British products filled wardrobes like the ones displayed in Boston churches, American mill towns produced cheap, rough cloth protected by the tariffs on lower-grade textiles.[15]

In fact, the same cotton that hands picked returned, spun and woven, in the shape of the rough New England cloth that enslavers bought to cover the backs of African Americans. On his "Southdown" and "Waterloo" slave labor camps in Louisiana, for instance, entrepreneur John Minor issued a yearly "ration" of about ten to fifteen yards of cloth. With over a million slaves in the cotton and sugar areas in 1832, entrepreneurs might have bought 15 million yards of cloth, or all of Lowell's annual output. There was enough market space in the Mississippi Valley. Every year, one of the Hazard brothers, the owners of Rhode Island's Peace Dale Manufacturing Firm, traveled down to New Orleans and then out to the countryside to sell their cloth, hats, and other goods. Planters measured women's shoe sizes, decided whether to buy ready-made clothes or bolts of cloth that year, and sent lists of men by rough measures of size, such as "No. 1" and "No. 2." The cotton-picking sacks the Hazards offered, made of sturdy cloth from Peace Dale's steam-powered looms, were "by far the very best" he had "ever seen," said customer John Routh. Even heavier grades of cotton woven with hemp were needed as wrappings for processed cotton, whether in the more backward "round bale districts" or among up-to-date planters whose newer equipment forced ginned cotton into solid cubes.[16]

The specialized workforces of the southwestern slavery frontier didn't just transfer British money paid for raw cotton into infant US textile firms. They also used American-made shovels, plows, ropes, hats, shoes, and hoes. In fact, one estimate suggests that 30 percent of the "transportable" goods made in the Northeast in the 1830s were sold to the West and South. Thousands of northern women braided palm leaves from Cuba into the wide-brimmed disposable hats that enslavers issued, one to each hand, at the start of the picking season. In 1832 in Suffolk County, Massachusetts, alone, 47 different palm-hat-making firms reported a total of 863,000 hats made, costing 28 cents each wholesale, employing 2,500 women year round. Although they were paid 30 cents or less a day, these women in all earned over a quarter of a million dollars—which, measured differently, was in turn paid by 50,000 person-days of cotton-picking.[17]

Another example of the way that southwestern efficiencies provided markets for the infant industries of the Northeast is the story of the Collins Axe Works along the Farmington River in Connecticut. In around 1827, Samuel Collins's brilliant craftsman Charles Morgan mapped the axe-making process into specific tasks: forging, tempering, grinding, polishing, each carried out by an individual worker. Classical economist Adam Smith, who illustrated the division of labor by showing how the production of a pin could be broken into dozens of steps to increase efficiency a hundredfold, would have been proud. So the Collins works ramped up production to 1,000 axes a day, albeit at the cost of an epidemic of silicosis, or "grinders' asthma," a fatal disease caused by constant exposure to the dust generated by grindstones spinning against metal axe-heads. Collins's southwestern traveling agents quickly generated huge sales, such as the order for 30,000 axes placed by one merchant firm. By the middle of the decade, the Collins works was turning out a quarter of a million axes every year.[18]

Collins axes came ready-ground, so they could replace cheap British axes that came at a tariff-inflated price and did not have edges. (Purchasers had to hire or buy blacksmiths to grind edges onto the British blades before use.) Two thousand miles from Connecticut, along the Mississippi River, enslaver Haller Nutt broke open a couple of crates—$20.00 each, containing twelve Collins axes—and put them right into the hands of his male hands. In those hands, Collins axes literally remapped the natural world, felling hundreds of millions of southwestern hickories, oaks, cottonwoods, gums, and pines. An experienced overseer from Tipton County in West Tennessee, who said that there, "the timber [is] I think easier to clear" than in other areas, calculated that a "full hand," a healthy and strong man, working exclusively at clearing, would only open about four acres in a year. By 1860, after thirty years of settlement, Tipton County had 65,570 improved (cleared) acres. Sixteen thousand man-years of swinging Collins axes had made Tipton into a giant organic machine for growing cotton and corn. And Tipton County was one of about 250 similar cotton and sugar counties across slavery's frontier.[19]

At every stage of the march from seed to mill to consumer, entrepreneurs of one kind or another sliced into tranches the margin of profit generated on the backs of enslaved African Americans, plated each slice, and distributed it to an actor in the world economy. Measuring all the elements of this dynamic process, which combined ever-cheaper access to the world's most essential commodity with increasingly efficient manufacturing processes to drive the northern economy in new directions, might be impossible. But here's a back-of-the-envelope accounting of cotton's role in the US economy in the era of slavery expansion. In 1836, the total amount of economic activity—the value of all the goods and services produced—in the United States was about $1.5 billion. Of this, the value of the cotton crop itself, total pounds multiplied by average price per pound—$77 million—was about 5 percent of that entire gross domestic product. This percentage might seem small, but after subsistence agriculture, cotton sales were the single largest source of value in the American economy. Even this number, however, barely begins to measure the goods and services directly generated by cotton production. The freight of cotton to Liverpool by sea, insurance, and interest paid on commercial credit—all would bring the total to more than $100 million (see Table 4.1).

Next come the second-order effects that comprised the goods and services necessary to produce the cotton. There was the purchase of slaves—perhaps $40 million in 1836 alone, a year that made many memories of long marches forced on stolen people. Then there was the purchase of land, the cost of credit for such purchases, the pork and corn bought at the river landings, the axes that slaves used to clear land and the cloth they wore, even the luxury goods and other spending by slaveholding families. All of that probably added up to about $100 million more.

Third-order effects, the hardest to calculate, included the money spent by millworkers and Illinois hog farmers, the wages paid to steamboat workers, and the revenues yielded by investments made with the profits of merchants, manufacturers, and slave traders who derived some or all of their income either directly or indirectly from the southwestern fields. These third-order effects would also include the dollars spent and spent again in communities where cotton and cotton-related trades made a significant impact. Another category of these effects is the value of foreign goods imported on credit sustained by the opposite flow of cotton. All these goods and services might have added up to $200 million. Given the short terms of most commercial credit in 1836, each credit dollar "imported" for cotton would be turned over about twice a year: $400 million. All told, more than $600 million, or almost half of the economic activity in the United States in 1836, derived directly or indirectly from cotton produced by the million-odd slaves—6 percent of the total US population—who in that year toiled in labor camps on slavery's frontier.

THE NORTHERN ECONOMY'S INDUSTRIAL sector was built on the backs of enslaved people. And yet by the 1840s, northerners like John G. Palfrey were increasingly likely to think—from their new vantage point where they stood on those people's backs—that their business endeavors did not need slavery. As early as the 1830s, Americans in the non-slave states were using cotton-generated wealth to develop a more diversified industrial sector that owed less to trade with the South. For instance, in 1832, the Collins Axe Works, one of the first large-scale manufacturing employers in Connecticut, accounted for almost a quarter of all non-textile manufacturing investment and employment in the state. But by 1845, when Robert Walker, Polk's secretary of the treasury, commissioned another survey of manufacturing, Connecticut contained about twenty-five different axe manufacturers. Axes themselves were now only a fraction of the state's industrial production. New brass foundries, firearms manufacturers, and factories for hardware, clocks, hats, and carpet now employed thousands of Connecticut residents. And the vast majority of the brassware, machine tools, and consumer goods that came out of Connecticut foundries and shops were being sold to urban centers, factory cores, and commercial farming zones across the North.[20]

Although Connecticut had become the most densely industrialized state in the United States, it was not alone in shifting toward an industrial economy. By 1840, 500,000 Americans toiled in the manufacturing sector, almost all in the North. By 1850, their total number was 1.2 million, and manufacturing's share of all workers had risen from 9 percent to 15 percent. A significant number of these workers were women, especially in the textile mills. The share that manufacturing contributed directly to value added in the national economy increased from 17 percent in 1839 to 29 percent a decade later, while the corresponding percentage for agriculture fell from 72 percent to 60 percent. Many economic sectors—some of which were completely new, such as railroad construction—depended heavily on the northern consumer markets that manufacturing labor forces were creating with their new cash wages.[21]

True, in the 1840s, cotton was still powerful. No one source of northern revenue was as massive as the rush of British paper that returned west each year in exchange for the cotton bales that had sailed east. No kind of manufacturing was as purely profitable as the hand picking a cotton boll, if prices exceeded about 10 cents per pound: not the segment of northern commercial agriculture that fed the free states' rapidly growing cities, not the mills, not even the shops where mechanics built the latest version of the steam locomotive. Yet the increasing diversification of the northern economy enabled it to grow more consistently and resiliently than its southern counterpart. Even if the annexation of Texas reignited the expansion of slavery, southern economic health depended on the price of cotton.

And northerners depended less on the cotton margin than they had before the late 1830s. Instead, they were creating an industrial margin. The textile industry, for instance, was shifting production into larger, more capital-intensive operations that could turn major investment into rapid revenues at high or low raw material costs. Between 1820 and 1860, New England textile mills increased their average capital investment by 600 percent. This is what historical economists call "capital deepening." The average number of spindles per mill grew from 780 to 6,770, and the number of power looms from 5 to 164—and in both cases, the machinery grew more efficient at processing fiber into thread and cloth. Just like the increasing sleight of left hands in the cotton fields, the accumulation of machinery increased the productivity of millworkers, enabling the typical textile worker of 1860 to make cloth five or six times more quickly than his or her counterpart of 1820.

By the late 1830s, northern textile manufacturing was creating new spin-off industries as well. The machinists who built and repaired textile machinery not only improved power looms and spindles, but also invented and then produced stationary steam engines that could be harnessed to factory machinery. Before the 1830s, steam engines were almost exclusively used to power river craft. By 1845, steam-powered factories were becoming the rule. Increasingly, they burned coal. In 1820, Pennsylvania had sent 365 tons of anthracite coal to market; by 1844 that number had climbed to more than 1.6 million tons. (Eventually, fossil fuels would enable windfall profits parallel to those stolen from enslaved labor.) Meanwhile, machine shops kept nurturing new skills and ideas: improved steam-powered sugar mills that completed the revolution in sugarcane processing and sucrose extraction that had begun twenty years before with the vacuum pan, for instance. By the early 1850s, over half of the 1,500 sugar mills in Louisiana were driven by steam power. The same networks of machinists created increasingly more sophisticated locomotives, and by the early 1840s they were building a coherent railroad industry. This created new efficiencies through a rapid transportation network as well as a demand for steel rails, fuel, and credit.[22]

As northern factories grew, employers could not hire enough workers. In response, European immigration to the North soared. One and a half million came to the United States in the 1840s alone. The Irish were the paradigm. By 1845, 220,000 had already come in a decade not half over, and the second half saw 550,000 Irish refugees arrive in the United States, fleeing British oppression and a famine that killed millions. A few of the Irish went to New Orleans, whose levees and cotton presses offered plenty of opportunity for laborers. But although many came west in American ships that had been loaded with cotton bales on the way east, this was not an unfree migration. Now that Manhattan had achieved financial hegemony over the cotton trade, ships passing between Liverpool and New Orleans usually turned off their old direct course to stop in New York Harbor, and there the immigrants disembarked. Outside of the cotton ports, jobs were scarce for immigrants in the slave states during the 1840s, and they had no desire to compete with workers driven by the whipping-machine. The immigrants' choice to move to the North had a significant demographic impact, raising the northern population from 7.1 million in 1830 to 10 million in 1840, and then to over 14 million by 1850. In the same period, the South grew much more slowly, from 5.7 million in 1830 to almost 9 million.

Immigration, the main source of the free states' population growth, held down labor costs and created massive markets for consumer goods. Most immigrants began at the bottom rungs of northern society and economy, where they were canal-diggers, housemaids, or coal miners. But in the distribution of political representation, they each counted as 5/5 of a person, which meant increased northern power in the House of Representatives. The number of congressional representatives determined the number of electoral votes a state could cast in the presidential election, so reapportionment shaped the influence of states—and regions—in the executive branch as well. In 1820, 42 percent of the House members came from slave states. Along with southern equality in the Senate, enslavers had thus needed only a handful of free-state allies to block any proposal they did not like. But after the 1840 US Census, the number of slave-state representatives dropped below 40 percent. After 1850, free-state representatives would make up two-thirds of the House.

The accelerating growth of the North's economy made northerners less likely to act like southerners' dependents in politics. In the two years after John G. Palfrey's seventeen slaves made their migration to freedom and

Boston, his increasing frustration with Massachusetts Cotton Whigs, and their willingness to compromise with their southern allies (who were backing Polk's policy of slavery expansion), drew him into the political arena on the side of the Conscience Whigs. He wrote and published *Papers on the Slave Power*, an indignant pamphlet with chapter titles such as, "The North Defrauded and Brow-beaten." It described the South as a unitary political bloc that was "enslaving" northern whites' political selves. With both Justice Story's ruling in *Prigg v. Pennsylvania* and the memory of the attempted kidnapping of the Latimers still fresh in his mind, Palfrey claimed that southerners could travel to Boston and alleged that even a white Massachusetts citizen was merely a light-skinned runaway slave. "*There is the law*; it says nothing of color; and by it the Governor of Massachusetts is just as liable to be carried away and sold in the Southern shambles, as the blackest or least considerable citizen in the Commonwealth . . . Harrison Gray Otis [the richest lawyer in Boston] as much as his boot-black." Palfrey singled out Nathan Appleton and Abbot Lawrence, Massachusetts textile magnates and Cotton Whigs, blaming them for persuading northerners to let Texas into the Union.[23]

Palfrey's *Papers* offended proper Bostonians who had once supported him as clergyman, professor, and editor. Some ignored his greetings in the street or barred him from their homes. But Palfrey was not the only one accusing New England cotton lords of collusion with their suppliers in the Mississippi Valley. The newly emerging northern critique of enslavers and their allies was different from that of immediatists, such as William Lloyd Garrison, who demanded that America purge itself of sins. Instead, the new critics argued that southern slavery damaged the national economy. Two decades earlier, in the midst of the Missouri crisis, some expansion opponents had made similar claims, but over the intervening years, the rapidly increasing wealth in every sector touched by cotton rendered the claims that slavery undermined economic progress unpersuasive. Certainly New England's lords of the loom had used slave-made cotton and slavery's market to become the wealthiest people in the free states.

Yet in the early 1840s the increasing sense of northern economic dynamism and southern doldrums emboldened many northerners to assert that they owed slavery nothing—certainly not fealty to the political sway of what Palfrey was calling "The Slave Power," a term he probably learned from clergyman, newspaper editor, and Liberty Party activist Joshua Leavitt. Leavitt's journal, *The Emancipator*, argued that "slavery reigns by fomenting the strife of party at the North." The new alignment of interregional coalitions shaped by Van Buren, Jackson, and their opponents meant that if

Democrats in Vermont, for instance, wanted to win national elections, they had to avoid antagonizing their party brethren from Alabama. The latter made it clear that support for slavery was the price of party alliance. So the Vermont Democrats motivated voters by emphasizing their differences from Whig neighbors at home, rather than from enslavers in the South.

Here, however, was the most distinctive piece of Leavitt's attack: "[I] consider slavery," Leavitt told an Ohio audience in 1840, to be "the chief source of the commercial and financial evils under which the country is groaning." At the time he made the speech, the US economy had not yet recovered from the Panics of 1837 and 1839, and Leavitt insisted that the Slave Power's distortion of public policy was a major cause of the depression. "We find ourselves," Leavitt announced, "subject to the exhausting operations of slavery," a series of policies and patterns that drew the wealth of the free states into the slave ones. Sure, the southwestern slave frontier had *appeared* profitable in the 1830s, as investment and forced migrants flowed into the Mississippi Valley at an unprecedented velocity: "Everyone wanted stock in the Vicksburgh, Grand Gulf, Brandon, and other South-west banks," Leavitt recalled. But "the great drain of northern capital to the South" to meet the "demands of the Domestic Slave Trade"—$100 million to Mississippi alone, Leavitt calculated—was just another one of the "ordinary defalcations of slavery"—layers of theft and fraud, from the theft of labor to the rampant dishonesty of enslavers toward their northern creditors. Although never had trade throughout the national economy appeared "so vast and profitable" as it had in 1836, "the bubble burst, and all that capital is gone, sunk, irrecoverable." Enslavers owed uncountable millions to northern merchants, bondholders, factory owners, and banks, and had no plans to pay much of it, and yet even "the South has nothing to show for it." The South's problem was slavery, Leavitt insisted, for it was in essence opposed to saving, productive investment, and the kinds of technological improvements (specifically, the introduction of labor-saving machinery) that were transforming the North.[24]

Palfrey repeated Leavitt's critiques, for he and other northern whites—and some southern ones, too—were starting to believe that reality was demonstrating the accuracy of his economic analysis. Everyone could see that the North was surging ahead in prosperity and population. Enslaver-politicians had long used their power in Congress to expand unfree territory, steer northern capital south, shut off discussion, destroy monetary systems so that enslavers wouldn't have to repay their creditors, and tear down tariff protections for the northern industrial sector. But now, enterprising northern manufacturers no longer needed the South. So there was no justification for acceding to continued southern dominance over the political process.

And yet, though still stuck in what northerners increasingly considered self-inflicted economic depression at mid-decade, southern politicians were still demanding that the major focus of US foreign policy be the expansion of slave territory. And the Slave Power still exerted disproportionate political influence. Polk, the current occupant of the White House, was a slave owner, like his predecessor. Northern Democrats still obediently tried to silence abolitionists, and the need to get southern votes in order to compete with Democrats trapped northern Whigs in similar binds. Leavitt insisted that northerners needed to raise the electoral cost, to their politicians, of concili-ating the South. This meant drawing voters to anti-slavery-expansion third parties or factions by "develop[ing] the true nature of slavery," as Leavitt put it: showing how the South opposed northern white men's political rights and economic prosperity. "Direct resistance to the political domination of the Slave Power" would then replace party interests with regional ones.[25]

Indeed, by the time Palfrey published his own pamphlets on the Slave Power, a few years after Leavitt, changing economic and political circum-stances were about to make more northern whites than ever suspect that Leavitt and Palfrey might be right about the South. Congress had approved the declaration of war with Mexico on May 13, 1846. A few months later, on August 8, and with war well under way, President Polk asked Congress for $2 million to fund his administration's negotiations with Mexico. Northern Democrats had backed Polk and his war. But plans for expensive negotiations suggested that he was now thinking of extracting still more territory from Mexico. At the same time, he was compromising with Britain, abandoning his promise to assert a claim to present-day British Columbia. Representa-tive Hugh White, a Whig from upstate New York, seized this opportunity to challenge northern Democrats to prevent the appropriations bill from paying for the expansion of slavery. David Wilmot, a freshman Democrat from Pennsylvania, took the bait. He offered an amendment that mandated that all territory acquired in the war with Mexico must become free. If im-plemented, the "Wilmot Proviso" would permanently block slavery's geo-graphic expansion.[26]

African Americans had been saying for years that slavery's power built on the acquisition of new territory. On the frontier, enslavers could destroy old standards of production, disrupt families, securitize the individuals ex-tracted from them as commodities, sell the financial instruments thus created on markets around the world, and ride the resulting boom of excitement.

Some whites had listened, including Gamaliel Bailey, editor of the antislavery *National Era*: "What does the past teach us? That slavery lives by *expansion*," he wrote. Close off new territory, and one closed the veins that pulsed excitement into credit markets. Close off the land that might come from Mexico, and one put a term limit upon the political stranglehold of slave owners over the larger and more rapidly expanding northern population.[27]

Because Wilmot's proviso promised to close off southern expansion in every sense, it placed extreme pressure on the two major parties, which were complex interregional alliances that depended on balancing the interests of politicians on both sides of the Mason-Dixon line. Southern Whigs opposed the proviso, while northern Whigs—who knew they faced potential Conscience Whig revolts back home—supported it. Southern Democrats opposed the proviso, but northern Democrats—supporters of national expansion, yet anxious about the voters at home—froze in the oncoming headlights of the midterm elections: ultimately, most bolted in panic. When the proviso came to a vote in the House, only four free-state Democrats opposed the bill, which passed 85 to 80 in a sectional vote. Then, in an apparent replay of the 1819–1820 Missouri debates, the Senate blocked the proviso.

But 1819 and 1846 were different years. In 1819, many in both North and South saw a future in which exported cotton would drive economic growth. Now, expectations of the economic future had evolved. And just as Joshua Leavitt had hoped, David Wilmot and other northern Democrats—most of whom hated both Whigs and black people—were voting against the Slave Power and with antislavery Whigs. Such developments could destabilize the delicate balances inside US politics. One immediate consequence was that opposition to slavery expansionism became a newly viable political identity for many northern candidates for office. In 1847, John G. Palfrey ran for Congress in a special election to fill a seat in a district once dominated by Cotton Whigs. Supporters proclaimed that he had "shown his faith by his works, having emancipated a large number of slaves in Louisiana who came to him by inheritance." Palfrey won, joining a freshman congressional class that also included a newly elected Illinois Whig named Abraham Lincoln.

Through 1847, however, neither pro– nor anti–Wilmot Proviso forces could gain the upper hand in Washington. And meanwhile, on the far side of the Rio Grande, US troops were winning battles against Mexican forces. General Zachary Taylor, a veteran of counterinsurgency struggles against the Florida Seminoles, defeated one Mexican army in the north of the country. California fell to US troops and US settlers. General Winfield Scott landed an army of 12,000 men on Mexico's Gulf Coast. Among Scott's junior officers were names like Robert E. Lee, Ulysses S. Grant, and Thomas Jackson. Retracing Hernando Cortez's 1519 route, Scott's troops fought their way west toward Mexico City. After winning a crucial battle at Cerro Gordo, they circled west of the city. On September 12, US troops stormed Chapultepec Castle, the capital's last strongpoint, and then occupied a city that had been a capital a millennium before Washington's founding.[28]

As news came back that the halls of Montezuma had been conquered, the Polk administration became entranced by the idea of annexing all of Mexico. But the New York State Democrats, the largest and oldest branch of the party, split in two over whether the new territories should be open to slavery. As southern constituents grew more agitated about the crisis, John C. Calhoun stepped forward to offer a doctrine that had been developing for a few years now—but that was peculiarly suited to the current situation. This idea re-amplified slavery's leverage in the political equations of expansion, using constitutional interpretation to highlight the declining relative demographic and financial force of cotton. It was not a rehash of nullification, which Calhoun had abandoned after his defeat by Jackson in the 1830s. It was far more significant than nullification.

Back in 1819, Calhoun had told the rest of Monroe's Cabinet that he believed that the Constitution allowed Congress to ban slavery from federally controlled spaces, such as new territories. But by 1836, abolitionist petitions were calling for Congress to use its power over federal territory to end the slave trade and even to ban slavery itself in the District of Columbia. In January 1836, Senator Calhoun responded to these demands with a speech that outlined a foundational idea. He told the Senate that he did not find in the Constitution the right of petition to which the anti–Gag Rule forces kept referring. But he did find the Fifth Amendment, and it limited federal power over individuals' property by decreeing that no one could be "deprived of his property without due process of law." Calhoun now proceeded to build a sweeping principle on the back of this sentence. "Due process," he insisted, could mean only "trial by jury" of a specific criminal. Here was the opposite of due process: legislative fiat that erased the property claims of a whole class of people. And, "were not the slaves of this District property," Calhoun asked, and were not their enslavers a whole class of property-owners? Presumably Congress could not prevent people from buying or selling said property, either, since salability is usually one of property's characteristics.[29]

Calhoun was stating an idea that would eventually be known as the doctrine of substantive due process. The "due process" requirement to which the Constitution referred could not be fulfilled simply by passing a law, for a law that invaded the rights of property-owners ran up against something too fundamental for procedure to alter. In Calhoun's vision, the Fifth Amendment was a geological outcropping that confirmed that beneath the Constitution lay an underlying substantive, tectonic plate of natural law that allowed owners to hold and use property. In 1844, a Mississippi congressman named William Hammett even argued that this federal right also protected enslavers from the actions of state legislatures. Thus the state-mandated emancipations completed by northern states were unconstitutional. Shocked northern congressmen foamed in anger at Hammett's claim. But enslavers seemed to accept it instinctively as soon as they heard it.[30]

After the Civil War, pro-big-business legal thinkers from the North would, ironically enough, take up a version of Calhoun's idea. From the 1890s through the New Deal era, the Supreme Court repeatedly used substantive due process to strike down legislative attempts to regulate Gilded Age industry, protect workers' rights, or break up monopolies. Substantive due process shaped (and continues to shape) the political economy of the United States in enduring ways. Like his modern cousins, Calhoun offered in his argument for substantive due process a doctrine of radically unfettered property ownership. It implied that enslavers were forever protected from popular majorities that might try to prevent them from taking full advantage of the boundless resources of a conquered continent and an ever-growing world market. Nor is it clear that southern partisans had the worse argument in the terms of precedents available in their time. Justice Story's 1843 opinion in *Prigg v. Pennsylvania* gave an anchor point to the claim that the Constitution recognized enslavers' fundamental rights to property in human beings and compelled the federal government to protect those claims, even against state legislatures.[31]

The ur-version of substantive due process had been fermenting slowly since 1836, but it had usually stayed in the shadows. How awkward it would have been in the early 1840s if, in the midst of G.T.T. escapes and bond-repudiation, enslaver-entrepreneurs had claimed that governments could not impair the rights of property and contracts. However, war and conquest had by 1847 created new incentives for politicians to find justifications for new slavery territory. Calhoun's argument went even further than that, of course, envisioning an alternative and highly radical version of economic modernity.[32]

The ambient friction of the Wilmot Proviso debate gave Calhoun and his allies the opportunity to use their logic on audiences that were ready to hear about how the North was trying to strangle the constitutional rights of the South, on the back of whose success the free states' own growth built. In February 1847, Calhoun offered the Senate a set-piece exposition of his argument that enslavers had a fundamental right to use and move and exploit enslaved human beings. In this, the most significant speech of his long career, he laid out the constitutional and political argument behind which increasing numbers of enslavers would unite over the next fourteen years.[33]

First, Calhoun insisted that the territories were the equal possession of all the states, free or slave. He also rejected Congress's right to require that new states' constitutions outlaw slavery. And then he swung his sledgehammer: "*Resolved. That the enactment of any law which should directly, or by its effects, deprive the citizens of any of the States of this Union from emigrating, with their property, in to any of the territories of the United States, will make such discrimination* [between citizens from different states of the Union, coding those from free states as worthy and those from slave states as unworthy] *and would therefore be a violation of the Constitution.*" This resolution referenced the "common blood and treasure" argument—that the slave states had shared equally with the free in the costs and dangers of conquest—but it ultimately depended on his claim that the Constitution protected enslavers' ability to hold, move, sell, buy, and exploit people as property. He implied that the federal government should pass laws to enact the institution of slavery on federal territory, for to do otherwise would be to deprive individual slave owners, and indeed all southern whites—who were, after all, potential property-holders—of their rights. Thus, the *only* constitutional fate for the territories was a future in which federal marshals rounded up runaways in California, federal attorneys defeated freedom suits in New Mexico, and federal customs officials regulated and protected the interstate slave trade into Utah.

Thus Calhoun offered a viable alternative to the claim that southern political bullying was protecting an economically backward institution. Southern politicians could now claim that constitutional rights mandated political solutions to their own decline in relative political power. And at the moment when Calhoun made this move, the vision of perpetually expanding slavery as an alternative but still modern economy was once again becoming plausible. The second half of the 1840s brought a small uptick in cotton prices. Enslavers always believed that fresh territory would yield a future of creative-destructive bonanzas. Lest one claim that Calhoun's intervention was irrelevant, because the frontier farther southwest was too arid to slake enslavers' thirst for cotton booms, remember that a century later, Arizona would be the nation's biggest cotton producer. California's Central Valley, using a labor force that was barely free, would then be the most profitable agricultural district in the world. And after these 1847 resolutions, southern newspapers and magazines began to shape a fantasy in which a new generation of right-handed entrepreneurs opened up northern Mexico, yet un-seized lands in the Caribbean, or Pacific islands such as Hawaii, on whose volcanic soil sugarcane had thrived since the first Polynesian settlers planted it.

"I give no advice," concluded iron-faced old Calhoun. "But I speak as an individual member of that section of the Union. There I drew my first breaths. There are my hopes"—hopes not just in South Carolina, as in the days of nullification, but also in Alabama, at his son Andrew's slave labor camp, hopes of an ever-expanding South. "I am," said Calhoun, "a planter—a cotton planter. I am a southern man and a slaveholder; a kind and merciful one, I trust—and none the worse for being a slaveholder. I say, for one, I would rather meet any extremity on earth than give up one inch of our equality—one inch of what belongs to us as members of this great republic." He knew others would agree.[34]

STILL, AS OF 1847, the game Calhoun played was a long con. The bonds of loyalty linking non-planter southern white men to national parties had been forged in the hot fires of the 1830s. And many still hoped that their party's leadership would put forward a viable interregional consensus candidate for the next presidential election. James Polk did not plan to be one of those candidates. The president had grown weary of the gridlock over the territories. He was also preoccupied by negotiations in Mexico City, which had been going on almost as long as those in Congress. One reason for their delay was the Polk administration's increasing desire to persuade domestic public opinion into demanding that the United States swallow the entire conquered nation.

John G. Palfrey's Massachusetts Whigs protested that the annexation of Texas had "stimulated the appetite" of the (rest of) the American people for more territory. "If the Slave Power continues to be strong enough," wrote Palfrey, states carved from Mexico would be "admitted to the Union with constitutions, forced on them through artifice and intimidation, recognizing and perpetuating slavery," and adding to the Slave Power's strength in Congress. About the only thing upon which Calhoun and Palfrey could agree was that all of Mexico was too much. "We have never dreamed of incorporating into our Union any but the Caucasian race," Calhoun proclaimed. "More than half of the Mexicans are Indians, and the other is composed chiefly of mixed tribes. . . . Ours, sir, is the government of the white race." Palfrey also thought that Mexico's "nameless and mongrel breeds" would fit poorly into the United States.[35]

Just as Calhoun tried to convince southern Whigs and Democrats to align with each other along sectional lines, Palfrey and his fellow Massachusetts Conscience Whigs were splitting their party's 1848 state convention by insisting that it should reject any presidential nominee who did not state clear opposition to adding new slave territories. When the resolution failed, Palfrey and his Conscience allies left the party. Meanwhile, the New York Democrats also divided. One faction, led by Martin Van Buren and called "Barnburners" by their opponents (after an apocryphal farmer who burned down his barn to kill off the rats), argued that the expansion of slavery hurt the "free white laborers of the North and South." Proclaiming allegiance to "Free Trade, Free Labor, Free Soil, and Free Men," these dissident Democrats gathered with Whig splinter groups and Liberty Party activists and created the Free Soil Party. They named Van Buren, a man who had spent decades displaying his allegiance to southern planters, as their presidential candidate. His running mate was Charles Francis Adams, son of original Conscience Whig John Quincy Adams, who had been felled by a fatal stroke on the floor of the House earlier in 1848.[36]

Back in Washington, the Senate had finally received the Treaty of Guadalupe Hidalgo, the result of negotiations with the representatives of defeated Mexico. In addition to confirming Texas annexation, the treaty gave the United States 525,000 additional square miles of the conquered nation-state—13 acres for each of the 23 million people in the Union. This was the third-biggest acquisition of territory in US history, after the Louisiana Purchase and Alaska. The Senate eliminated an article that promised recognition of land claims granted by the Spanish or Mexican governments. The treaty opened the new southwest to a massive Anglo real-estate grab. If that wasn't enough incentive for settlers to start dispossessing Mexicans and Indians, gold was discovered at Sutter's Mill, California, in January 1848.

Yet the great giveaways promised by Guadalupe Hidalgo did not turn a controversial war into a success. In the course of two years of debate over the fate of the conquered territory, southerners, anxious to protect their future access to political leverage and entrepreneurial possibilities, had moved toward arguing that a slave West was the price of union. Meanwhile, northerners, convinced that southern enslavers were treating them the way they treated their slaves, had already destabilized electoral calculations. The political system had depended since the bank war on the stability created by two party alliances, each one balancing regional interests. Those coalitions might not survive the election chaos coming in the fall. Even if they did, it was unclear that the parties could persuade enough southerners or enough northerners to accept compromise and resolve the question of organizing the new territories.

In fact, 1848 was putting immense pressure on political arrangements on both sides of the Atlantic. Parisians barricaded the streets and fought the French army. When the smoke cleared, the terrified bourgeoisie was welcoming a second Napoleon, the first one's nephew, as the leader of a new republic that would soon become an empire. Across the Rhine, people rose up against the rulers of various German states, demanding a liberal, unified nation in some cases, and more radical outcomes in others. When the revolutions collapsed, political refugees fled the European mainland, including one named Karl Marx. He landed in London and spent the rest of his life holed up in British libraries, but many "Forty-Eighters" came to the United States. Meanwhile, in July, in the little Erie Canal town of Seneca Falls, several hundred reformers gathered for an impromptu "Woman's Rights Convention." Among the organizers was Elizabeth Cady Stanton. Frederick Douglass, escapee from slavery and one of the most effective conduits of enslaved people's critiques of white power, was in attendance. The convention drafted a "Declaration of Rights and Sentiments," a document that claimed for women the right to vote.

The Seneca Falls gathering helped launch a movement for women's rights in the United States. This development would have long-term effects on politics that would be as radical as anything done in Europe in 1848. At the time, few male politicians took the Seneca Falls gathering seriously. The revolutionary ferment in Europe was more widely discussed, yet it seemed far away. Far more pressing, judging from the obsessive interest of newspapers and the inflammatory rhetoric of politicians both inside and outside the Capitol dome, was the still unresolved question of the Mexican territories and its potential effect on the fall presidential election. National party leaders, seeking to contain destabilizing confrontations, tried to nominate centrists who could appeal to both sections. The Whig convention chose Zachary Taylor, one of the Mexican War's victorious generals. Virginia-born, first cousin to James Madison, Taylor was a southwestern planter who owned more than one hundred people in Louisiana, and he had the useful virtue of possessing no political biography. The Democrats did something similar. Brushing off a convention walkout by southern extremist William Lowndes Yancey, they nominated Lewis Cass of Michigan.[37]

Cass's campaign circulated region-specific campaign biographies—one for the North and another for the South, with predictably targeted emphasis. But the new Free Soil Party still won 10 percent of the national popular vote, showing that pressure initiated by the Wilmot Proviso had opened seams in the party system. Ironically, Free Soil votes helped put a slaveholder in the White House: in New York, Van Buren and the Barnburners pulled enough ballots from the Empire State's Democrats to allow Taylor to collect all thirty-six of the state's electoral votes. The general also swept most of the South. Southern whites assumed that the president-elect would support slavery's expansion into the Mexican Cession.

Yet Calhoun did not trust either Taylor or the party system. In January 1849, he and four other southerners in Congress issued a printed "Address": it warned that if the North's anti-southern attitudes continued to grow, and the South did not respond, slavery's expansion—and slavery itself—would end. A Congress dominated by the likes of John Palfrey the younger would ban the interstate slave trade. Then there would be no injections of new capital, and no stick to hold over enslaved people's heads. An expanding black population would demographically drown whites, and forced emancipation would follow. After that, interfering northern whites would demand for ex-slaves "the right of voting and holding public office," resulting in "the prostration of the white race"—political servility and forced interracial marriage—"a degradation greater than has ever yet fallen to the lot of a free and enlightened people."[38]

The only way to avoid this disastrous future was for southern whites to unite in demanding equal access to the territories. As Calhoun argued in a southern caucus called to discuss the address, "the South could take their slaves into California and New Mexico. . . . Congress was bound . . . to put it [slavery] on the same footing with other property. It required no law of Congress to authorize slavery there." A united southern front behind this substantive-due-process interpretation would force the North to a "calculation of consequences." Inevitably, the North would back down, and the expansion of slavery would be implanted permanently in the nation's constitutional landscape, even as new territories became slave states. Most of all, political victory would compensate enslavers for the economic losses they had suffered since the late 1830s, which had lost them control over the economic rudder of the United States, since new slave-state recruits in the halls of Congress would block all future antislavery measures.[39]

One might be tempted to view pro-slavery-expansion zealots as extremists who were more interested in intellectual abstractions than in actually expanding slavery. But in little more than a decade, these people would launch a war to achieve a redefinition of the United States in which the national government made an explicit and perpetual commitment to defend and spread slavery. They were serious. And they were inking these ideas about slavery as a fundamental property right protected by the Constitution, with all that implied, into the common assumptions of southern politics. In 1849, the propagandizing so far by advocates of substantive due process as a southern right was already working. The "Address" drew widespread support in the southern press. Editors reminded common whites that the struggle to keep slavery's borders open was their fight, too. If the slave frontier closed, the risk of a repeat of the Haitian Revolution would increase. Even without a massive rebellion, poor whites would be taxed to compensate enslavers for mandated emancipation. Afterward, the rich man could use wealth "to maintain his position," but the common white man would lose "that native, free-born, and independent spirit which he now possesses." Constituents responded to this kind of talk, and Mississippi state politicians organized a "Slaveholders' Convention" for October 1849. Senator Henry Foote, Calhoun's Mississippi ally, began to organize an 1850 region-wide convention—an implied threat, a gathering that could be repurposed into a body ready to deliberate on nation-un-making.[40]

In Congress, meanwhile, southern Democrats maneuvered to commit the federal government to new guarantees of expansive definitions of slaveholders' property rights. They started with the recovery of fugitive slaves. Justice Story had conceded in *Prigg* that the South had constitutional leverage on this question. Proslavery Democrats were determined to make the federal government take ownership of enforcing the Constitution's fugitive clause. If they operationalized the federal government's commitment to protecting enslavers' ownership of property when said property ran away into another state, Congress would also find it hard to deny enslavers the right to move property into federal territory. Senator James Mason offered a bill that would eliminate the trial of accused fugitives by northern local juries, a bill that potentially would allow white southerners to accuse anyone of escaping from slavery, with little proof of ownership, and haul them south.[41]

Southern enslavers were coalescing around key principles, raising their demands, and increasing the pressure to find a solution to the territorial issue. Meanwhile, news from California made it clear that gold veins first struck in 1848 would dramatically enhance the US financial system's ability to promote growth. But the fevered migration of more than 80,000 American "49ers" to California in 1849 increased the tension of the territorial debates. The majority of the migrants were northerners, yet southern whites who came often brought slaves to work the mines. Mexico had abolished slavery in California some twenty years prior, but enslavers saw no reason why California had to be a free state. It even could be two states: north and south; free and slave. Yet Congress couldn't create a territorial government until it resolved its ongoing impasse, so for now lawless uncertainty reigned in California.[42]

The Congress elected in November 1848 would not be officially seated until December 1849. But shortly after his March 1849 inauguration, President Taylor secretly encouraged some California and New Mexico settlers, mostly northerners, to hold conventions. The state constitutions they'd write would ban slavery. When southern Whigs, who would soon face their own very southern constituents, found out, they rushed to condemn Taylor's betrayal. Back home, politicians and editors began to plan an all-South convention, scheduled for Nashville in July 1850. As the thirty-first Congress finally convened in December, many wondered if this would be the last gathering of all the states' representatives in Washington. Party alliances showed little sign of cohering again. The House took sixty-four ballots to name a Speaker, finally changing its rules so that a Georgia Democrat won. Relieved, it turned to the business of hiring an official "door-keeper"—an employee position similar to sergeant-at-arms. But then northern and southern representatives turned that, too, into a fight: Should they hire a proslavery or antislavery man? Then, in his official Presidential Message, Taylor boldly asked the gathered representatives and senators to admit California and New Mexico under constitutions that banned slavery. Congress collapsed into a chaos of roiling, seething rhetoric: threats of disunion (the southerners); proclamations of joy at the prospect of slave rebellion (a few Free Soil men); insistent claims that northerners would not be bullied (Democrats and Whigs from the free states); shrieks of "bad faith" and "cheating"; and complaints of insults and dishonorable exclusion from territories won by southern blood (the southerners again).[43]

After two months of shouting that threatened to rend all comity forever, a troop of wrinkled old men rode into the breach. On the night of January 21, 1850, Henry Clay had visited Daniel Webster at his lodgings in Washington to confirm that his fellow old Whig would back his play. On the 29th, the Kentuckian rose in the well of the Senate Chamber, where he had spent much of the last four decades. Clay presented eight resolutions that set off advantages for one section with those granted to the other, and he offered them all together, a pill to swallow, all-or-nothing. Historians often say that the Compromise of 1850, which these resolutions initiated, provided the North with a crucial decade in which to become strong enough to defeat the South when war eventually came. Whether that is true or not, Clay himself came close to scuttling his own union-protecting efforts. He insisted that the unitary nature of his proposals forced the warring sides to commit to all the bargains at once, but opponents accused him of egotistical motives—pointing out that a single large proposal identified the compromise with its author. Moreover, while a real compromise is a win-win solution, in which each side can claim victory, it is also possible for parties in conflict to view a bundle of alternating surrenders as a lose-lose solution. Such an outcome might be not the end of conflict but the fertile source of new ones.[44]

So what did Clay propose, in order to achieve what became called, ominously, a "final resolution" of the territorial conflict? First, he said, admit California as a free state. Second, New Mexico and the rest of the new southwest would be organized as territories "without respect to slavery"—that is, the choice on slavery would be deferred until a territory's actual population could choose. The hope here was that southern partisans would accept this plan as nonexclusion of slavery by Congress. Clay and others denied that slavery could prosper in New Mexico and Utah. Many assumed that this expedient would allow the territories themselves to ask quietly for admission as free states.

Although the loss of California was going to be a hard pill for southerners to swallow, Clay had some goodies for them as well. The United States would fund the outstanding debts of the Republic of Texas. This would make New Orleans investors happy, fourteen unpaid years after they had financed the enslavers' war against Santa Anna. Clay did suggest something that abolitionists had desired for years: a ban on the slave trade inside the District of Columbia. But he paired that with a resolution stating that Congress had no power to obstruct the internal slave trade between states. And one final resolution might also make northern partisans likely to think that they had "lost" the compromise. This was a call for an ironclad, watertight fugitive slave bill like the one recently introduced by James Mason. Enslavers complained that their territorial concessions left them hemmed in by free states that would drain the slave population by a kind of unchecked osmosis. A fugitive slave act would put teeth into *Prigg*, making the federal government the servant of enslavers by helping them to control their property in human beings, as if Calhoun's substantive-due-process interpretation of the Fifth Amendment was the legitimate one.

Clay had thus built his proposed compromise on the backs of African Americans, whom he condemned to an endless future of slavery—the expansion of which would be limited, but which would still continue. And by bundling together the issues, Clay pre-twisted northern votes for compromise into legitimation of extreme southern viewpoints, making a free-state congressional majority normalize ideas that to many northerners seemed antithetical to the Constitution. Debate on his bill was in consequence long and bitter. Taylor demanded California's immediate admission, without slavery. Southerners demanded half of California, all of New Mexico, and more territory for Texas. Jefferson Davis, Henry Foote, James Mason, and a host of southerners, preaching a proslavery Constitution, paraded the full array of substantive-due-process claims through the House and the Senate. The climax of their drama came when Calhoun, dying of tuberculosis, was carried into the Senate chamber on a stretcher. The South Carolinian shivered under blankets as Mason read his final speech for him. This one laid out no arguments about due process, instead warning in emotional terms that the long conflict over slavery and its expansion was snapping the cords of union that bound southern and northern whites. Religious, intellectual, and now political associations were fracturing along the lines of slave and free labor. (He did not add financial associations, which were being repaired.) The gist of the speech was this: the hardest of hard-core southerners were ready to accept a fugitive slave bill, to be sure, but little else of Clay's compromise.

A few days later, William Seward, a New York senator, delivered a speech insisting that constitutional guarantees or not, a "higher law"—the law of God—impelled antislavery northerners to block the expansion of the institution. Still more galling to enslavers was Seward's air of arrogance about the other "higher law" that had supposedly given greater power to the free states: the laws of political economy. The free labor system, he stated, had enabled New York, "by her own enterprise, [to secure] to herself the commerce of the continent, and is steadily advancing to command the commerce of the world." It was as if New Yorkers had never bought or sold a bale of cotton.[45]

Yet southerners in Congress and at home were unsure about how far to go. In the states where expansion mattered most, the debate over whether or not to send delegates to the Nashville Convention—and which delegates to send—ran white hot during early 1850. At the same time, pro-compromise meetings sprang up across the South. Many southern whites weren't ready for secession, which was what the extremists suggested. When the Nashville Convention gathered on June 3, far fewer delegates were present than radicals had anticipated. None came from Louisiana, and only one from Texas. Clay's compromise would pay off Texas debts, many of them held by Louisiana-based creditors.[46]

There was still hope for a Washington compromise. Months of debate had passed with little change in positions, but time moved the pieces on the board all the same. Calhoun, exhausted, died on March 31, depriving the southern radicals of the one figure who could have welded them into a weapon. Clay's increasingly bitter confrontation with Taylor, whose "treachery" to southern enslavers had helped fire up radicalism in Congress and in the southern press, ended on July 5, when the president suddenly died. Vice President Millard Fillmore, an upstate New Yorker with close ties to Clay, succeeded the maverick Taylor. The Whigs still could not unite behind Clay's bill, however, and the Senate defeated it at the end of July. The Nashville Convention delegates, sitting by the telegraph, had nothing to reject.

To judge from his letters to his wife, Clay had spent all spring basking in premonitory adulation. Now he gave up on compromise and fled north to Newport, Rhode Island, his favorite resort town, where the spent old man could play cards, bet the ponies, and flirt. Back in Washington, a new force, Illinois Democratic Senator Stephen Douglas, appointed himself the floor general of compromise. Separating the omnibus into its constituent parts, he deftly assembled a series of coalitions—southerners and a few northerners for the pro-southern aspects, the opposite for elements like the admission of California as a state—and pushed the compromise through the Senate as multiple bills. At the beginning of September, he drove the Senate bills through the House, from whence they were sent back to the Senate for reconciliation. On September 20, almost ten months after the Thirty-First Congress had first been seated, Fillmore signed the compromise bills into law. Cannons boomed in Washington, DC. Crowds outside of boardinghouses and hotels serenaded the congressional leaders, who were inside drinking themselves into stupors of relief.[47]

In communities like Springfield, Illinois, newspapers called for "national jubilation." The New Orleans *Picayune* said the territorial question was "definitely settled." In December, in his message to Congress as it opened a new session, President Fillmore referred to the Compromise of 1850 as "in its character final and irrevocable." Around the country, both northerners and southerners seemed to be cooling down and accepting the results. In the South, organizers quietly canceled state secessionist conventions. The white southern electorate was obviously relieved not to have to consider armed resistance to the Wilmot Proviso, although that, of course, did not stop Democratic congressional candidates in Mississippi, Alabama, Georgia, and South Carolina from doing well that fall by running against the Compromise.[48]

Still, the questions provoked by the Mexican War and northerners' more persistent opposition to the expansion of slavery had not been solved, despite four years of devoting the entire political process to solving them. The newly confident North, angered by Texas and all the other issues that men like John Palfrey had branded with the label "Slave Power," had stumbled upon the Wilmot Proviso as a line to draw, and then united behind it. The proviso promised to corral slavery, leaving it to decay, and end enslavers' attempts to dominate the North and the nation. The slave South, battered by depression and demographic sluggishness, had seen a moment of great danger. It codified the mode by which it would defeat danger and then regain lost relative power: the federal government itself would be made to guard enslavers' property rights, which were protected (southerners argued) by the Constitution, especially in new territories.

What hung on the political question of whether slavery would expand as a legally defined institution into new territories, first and foremost, were the futures of 3 million enslaved people. Neither side had succeeded in imposing its solution on them and on their futures. And both sides were still well-armed and primed, not only with adrenaline, but with literal powder. During one of the 1850 debates, Missouri Senator Thomas Hart Benton, an old Potterite brawler, bull-rushed Henry Foote as the Mississippian gave a speech. Foote pulled out a pistol, but fellow legislators dragged the two men apart. But loaded weapons were planted everywhere in the Compromise. One of its least-discussed but most important elements was the "organization" of the New Mexico and Utah territories. Taylor's attempt to establish New Mexico as a free state had provoked southern outrage, so Clay suggested these territories be organized without protections for or restrictions on slavery. Most textbooks speak of the final outcome as if Clay's proposal prevailed: New Mexico and Utah were to be testbeds for a demographic contest between slave and free-soil settlers. Yet while the committee that hammered out the New Mexico and Utah acts gave territorial legislatures power to legislate on slavery, proslavery and free-soil committee members cooperated to bake something else into the law. Their clause stated that if someone brought a lawsuit challenging the territory's slavery laws—perchance a disgruntled enslaver whose property ownership was not protected by a territory that had enacted laws denying him the "right" to own slaves—the lawsuit would be fast-tracked straight to the Supreme Court. And then the Court would decide whether slave ownership and its expansion were protected by the Fifth Amendment, or the Fifth actually protected people's ownership of themselves.[49]

Both sides in the debate thus gambled that their particular constitutional interpretation would prevail in the courts. Calhoun's ghost would have placed his side's bet with confidence. The Supreme Court had recently stated that the Constitution's framers had insisted on protecting enslavers' property outside of their home states. Now Congress, with the Fugitive Slave Act, had concurred. Due process of law might not, after all, permit the legislative emancipations that northern politicians like Palfrey believed would keep the Slave Power from capturing New Mexico. Moreover, a series of southern and southern-sympathizing Democrats had appointed the members of the Court. What would a reasonable person expect them to decide? And then, how would the increasingly confident North react? The New Mexico and Utah provisions of the Compromise of 1850 were in no way final. Instead, they built a platform for future rounds of conflict. Nor, as it turned out, was much else final about the Compromise.

# 10

# ARMS

*1850–1861*

F OR THE REST OF his life, which was far longer and more successful
than anyone would have predicted when he was a boy, Richard Slaughter insisted that this story was true. It starts with Richard and his cousin Ben
on the James River, thirty miles upstream from the place where American
slavery began. The year was about 1850; Ben was ten and Richard eight.
In a Virginia devoted to raising cotton-pickers, not cotton, enslaved boys
were a little older than their Alabama counterparts when they began their
careers as full-time laborers. So that day they wandered, "catching tad-
poles, minnows." Down by the caved-in clay riverbank, Richard saw "a big
moccasin snake," a poisonous cottonmouth, "hanging in a sumac bush just
a-swinging his head back and forth." Like generations of other southern
boys, Richard and Ben loved to hunt snakes, so they began to beat it with
sticks. It opened its mouth as if to strike, but instead, "a catfish as long as
my arm jumped out, just a-flopping." "The catfish had a big belly too," so
they pounded on the fish. "He opened his mouth and out come one of those
women's snapper pocketbooks," clenched like a slavemaster's heart. They
twisted open the snap. "Guess what in it? Two big copper pennies." "Now
you mayn't believe it," said Slaughter to his interviewer, eighty years later,
"but it's true."

Only Richard and Ben were there. But the most important question about
a miracle isn't whether it happened, but what it meant. For without meaning
a miracle is just a convenient accident. Richard and Ben had surely heard, in
a Virginia Baptist church, the Gospel of Matthew, chapter 17. That fish story
has a meaning. It begins with Jesus's disciples asking if they should pay taxes
to the Romans. The children of God don't have to pay taxes, Jesus responds,
"but so that we may not cause offence, go to the lake and throw out your

line. Take the first fish you catch; open its mouth, and you will find a four-drachma coin. Take it and give it to them for my tax and yours."

One way to interpret Matthew's text is to read it as instruction on how to live as a saint in a world of sinners. There's another interpretation. In this one, the fish is itself the parable, a sign that tells disciples that God will provide what they need, even enough to survive an oppressive regime. Grace will come in prosaic ways, like the ways that working men catch fish, or the way that two boys kill a snake.[1]

But fish swim in dark waters. Down there hide monsters. Eighteen centuries had rolled after Matthew was written by the time Richard and Ben's ancestors crossed the waters. Spit out on the Virginia shore, sticky and gasping from the slave-ship's belly, somehow they survived. To them were born children. To their children were born children. Until at last this day another beast came from the deep for their great-great-grandchildren. And its purse held a fortune as forked as the serpent's tongue.

"I gave my cousin one and I took one," Richard remembered. Richard's penny grew lucky and luckier still as the years ran, as if its grace kept the serpent from swallowing him. As the domestic slave trade reached a new peak in the 1850s, he grew to adulthood unsold. One day, he looked down to the same river's edge to see boats full of blue-clad men. They marched up to Richard Eppes's big house, and on that day Slaughter claimed his freedom. Soon he put on his own blue uniform. For two years he carried a musket in the US Army, fighting battles, bringing freedom to his people. Afterward he made his own, richer life, learning to read and write, traveling the world, eventually returning to Virginia and settling into a routine as a fisherman who plied the same waters beside which he had once played.[2]

Richard reclaimed the parable. But Ben had drawn the other penny. Eppes "never sold but one man, that I can remember," Richard told his interviewer. "That was my cousin Ben. Sold him South." Ben carried his unlucky coin to Richmond. A third generation of dealers in young humans now worked from Bacon Tait's old jail in Shockoe Bottom, where another round of innovations was under way. There, an enslaver could send instructions like these, which were received by slave broker Richard Dickinson: "If you have not sold Charles, try and get him to talk higher," and that meant getting him to say the kinds of things that made him seem earnest and hardworking. "Probably you will have to get him whipped a few times before he will do." Take out an insurance policy in the meantime—an economic innovation that, like the slave broker's business of holding and selling without owning, reduced risk. So Ben played his role, too, talking high and higher as another sellable product of old Virginia. A few days later he was sweating in a boxcar, rolling toward the cotton belt. The South had missed out on railroad-building in the 1840s. The North surged ahead, and the slave states wallowed. But now the South was back on track, laying rails faster than the northeastern states during the 1850s. Iron roads and horses carried bales, planters, and hands, all at a far higher speed than Charles Ball's raw feet walked the coffle-machine's brass locks south to Congaree.[3]

They sold Ben in Alabama. As his years mounted, his reach grew longer, and the pounds he put up on the slate climbed higher. When weighing-up ended, he crept back to his cabin, pulled a soft, furtive cloth from between the logs, unwrapped the hidden penny. Lying down in darkness, he rubbed the copper, praying as it hummed with connection to the far-off state of his birth. Outside, through the starlit woods, in the dark cut where the railroad ran, extruded copper newly strung from pole to pole was talking circles around him. The telegraph hauled instant news of politicians' fights over slavery's expansion, descriptions running faster than the fugitives they named, price quotes for cotton pounds, purchase-orders for twelve-year-old boys.

For seventy years so far of slavery's second life in the United States, the people who raised Ben and Richard had wrestled with the snake. They struggled each in their way with the evil that confronted them. Some ran. Some gave up. Some died. And some died and were yet reborn in new friendships, new marriages; new God, new self. But in the 1850s slavery's expansion revived, too. Another 250,000 were on the slave trail to the southwest.

Over the years since Abraham Lincoln's election in 1860, which prompted the secession of cotton states that led to the Civil War and emancipation, authors have unleashed floods of ink attempting to explain white southerners' actions. The authors already know how the story ends: with the blue-coated soldiers, Abraham Lincoln, and Richard Slaughter winning. Often, borrowing from the economic analysis of 1840s critics such as Joshua Leavitt, they assume that the South was a premodern economic system, and therefore that its defeat was inevitable—both on the field of economic competition, and on that of war. To cite again the words of the white abolitionist and orator Wendell Phillips, the South was a Troy destined to fall. Which then raises the question: What sort of madness would prompt supposedly conservative planters to start a war that would hasten the collapse of their own walls? Perhaps even more puzzling, what led the three-quarters of the white southern population who didn't own slaves to fight, and hundreds of thousands to die, for such doomed madness?

From the 1780s onward, enslavers, along with other white southerners who supported them with votes and participated in the coercion of enslaved people, had consistently pressed to expand slavery's territory. Lifetimes of experience had taught all of these white people to associate slavery's expansion with its prosperity, with the growth of their own wealth and power, and even of their own pleasure. The Compromise of 1850 did not clearly permit future expansion, so enslaver-politicians spent the 1850s trying relentlessly to advance their agenda, even though many Americans had celebrated the Compromise because they were told it offered a "final" end to argument about precisely that issue. Such leaders were trying to implement a strategy that Calhoun and others had initiated in the previous decade: that of using political capital in the Democratic Party, the institutional power of the federal government, the threat of disunion, and constitutional argument to force the rest of the United States to acknowledge a southern "right" to expand slavery as far as enslavers wanted it to go. Their goals were evolving, but over the course of the 1850s, enslavers concluded that they wanted to see slavery expansion written into the laws of the nation and the covenants of its political parties, enforced in the territories by executive policy, and stated as constitutional fact by the Supreme Court. They convinced themselves that anything less meant that their future in the Union would not be secure.

For so long as active antislavery opposition could possibly shape government policies in the future, nothing could reassure anxious entrepreneurs that expansion could continue forever. This was despite a rupture between idealist older white abolitionists, who wanted to keep the antislavery movement untainted by party politics, and increasingly independent and pragmatic African-American abolitionists such as Frederick Douglass, who sought to inject antislavery ideas into northern party politics. Indeed, during the 1850s, Douglass and others who saw an opening in the political party system that had bound national interests to the expansion of slavery were proved correct. A growing number of white northerners heard stories carried by cotton-frontier refugees, or remained angry about post-1837 frauds and repudiations, or reacted to the enforcement of the Fugitive Slave Act of 1850. Whatever the reason, they left the collapsing Whig coalition. As an electoral vehicle, the new political formation they created—the Republican Party— could contain most of the enslavers' free-state opponents, at least for a while. And northern economic and demographic growth had now made it possible that such an anti-southern party could, in theory, lose every southern vote and yet win national elections.

But enslavers did not see their own system as something antique, destined to fall before the onrushing future. Instead, they saw themselves as modern people who were running a highly successful, innovative sector of a world economy that was growing faster than ever before. For all the while, through all of the nagging political conflicts of the decade of the 1850s, slavery's productivity kept expanding. Demand for their products stayed high in the longest sustained cotton-price boom of the pre–Civil War era. Slavery's entrepreneurs kept making more money. The only question was, Which fork in the road would the South choose, the one that kept it in the United States by securing a deeper national commitment to the expansion of slavery, or the one in which the region as a whole seceded in order to gain control of expansion for themselves?

Thus, from the vantage point of a post-1865 world, after the day when Richard Slaughter put on the blue uniform and shouldered a gun, after the day when survivors danced in Danville, it can be hard to see how the world looked before the cotton states seceded. But from the perspective of the 1850s cotton field, the account book, the train full of slaves, and the dark cabin where Ben clutched the unlucky penny, the future looked like one long rising serpent-curve of expansion. For the snake by the river ate parables. And all decade long, it never got full. Never once did Richard see his beloved cousin again. Yes, as they had always done in the selling states, they continued marrying and being given in marriage, being born, giving birth. But mothers disappeared faster than ever. Others raised the babies, and then the babies vanished, too. In those days, Lulu Wilson, along with her mother and siblings, lived in a Kentucky cabin. First the white folks disappeared Lulu's father down the river on a steamboat. As cotton prices stayed high down at the bottom of the map, the older siblings trickled down, too. Clever, clever owner. He showed the merchandise, negotiated the deal, shipped the child off with the trader—all in one workday. Every time, Lulu's mother got home from the field to find it was already over. "Oh Lord," she screamed, falling on the cabin's dirt floor, begging on her knees by the empty bed, "let me see the end of it before I die."[4]

Lulu never forgot the scream, or the fear that the end of the begging and losing would never come. Her mother had little power, as an individual, to achieve freedom. She had less still to save her children. Under the new Fugitive Slave Act passed as an element of the Compromise of 1850, white people and their federal government were now obligated to pursue runaways from one end of the country to another. Collective revolt against slavery also seemed long since foreclosed by patrols, militias, armories full of powder and ball that ensured that any future Nat Turner was like a bug waiting for the hammer. And the rebels would wait alone. Relentless rhetoric had convinced almost all white Americans that African-American rebellion was unacceptable. Sure, white critics of slavery depicted slavery's immorality, and sneered at the allegedly backward economy that slavery produced. They may have felt better. But they had no endgame to offer.

Maybe Frederick Law Olmsted, who during the Civil War would run the American Sanitary Commission—a quasi-governmental agency that tried to ameliorate the squalid living conditions endured by federal soldiers— thought he was the slaves' ally. Yet he was just another Yankee tourist in the South. As he traveled from Virginia to Texas in the 1850s, gathering material for a book, thousands of other northerners roamed the South: railroad mechanics, cotton brokers, women on their way to marry planters' sons whom they had met in New York. Most of them managed to get along fine, especially if their services added to southern whites' balance sheets.[5]

Along the trails of Mississippi's northern delta, poor northern men backpacked factory goods—ribbon, thread, locks—into a wilderness of cotton too new for stores. Rich men weren't interested and shooed the tramping Yankees away from the big houses. The peddlers passed a field where a hundred people (heads down) picked like machines. Dripping, the travelers sat down on their packs, in the treeline at the end of a row. The peddlers "were treated badly by the rich planters," remembered Louis Hughes, and "hated them, and talked to the slaves. . . . 'Ah! You will be free someday.'" But the white-haired ones looked up from their sacks, saying, "We don't b'lieve dat; my grandfather said we was to be free, but we aint free yet." Far across the field, the slumped overseer lurched awake in his saddle. The peddlers shrugged their packs up onto their shoulders and were gone.[6]

Olmsted could hardly have hidden the way his ears pricked up every time a companion at the steamboat rail or the men in the train seat behind him brought up the subject of slavery. He primed himself to find evidence that slavery was inefficient. So when he saw twenty-two enslaved men on a New Orleans street who had just been bought by an enslaver, it made him think, but not simply about the remarkable fact that some southern white men could borrow $20,000 and drop it on one gang of "hands" who would make cotton faster than any forty free men. He believed that a society laid down on a foundation of slavery had a limited capacity for expansion. So, "Louisiana or Texas," he thought, counting the fingers of his mind's right hand, "pays Virginia twenty odd thousand dollars for that lot of bone and muscle," but beyond the levee a steamboat of German immigrants was chugging up the river toward Iowa. These free laborers, who cost nothing to import, built a society diverse in its production and consumption, laced together by "mills and bridges, and schoolhouses, and miles of railroad," because they had incentive to work, to save, and to rise. The only thing left behind those

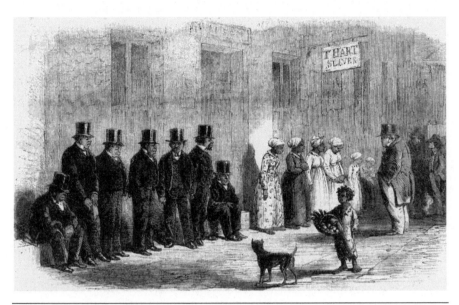

Image 10.1. Slave traders in New Orleans continued to receive and sell enslaved people whom they "packaged" as commodity "hands" in various ways—including by making them wear identical clothes. *Illustrated London News*, January–June 1861, vol. 38, p. 307.

twenty-two enslaved Virginians—when, after twenty years of mining Texas soil for cotton, their enslavers marched them west and south again to some new frontier—would be decaying cabins, divided families, and tangled debit accounts.[7]

Olmsted wrote four volumes about his journeys, relentlessly hammering home the argument that slavery's inefficiency retarded southern growth and national development. During the preceding decade, as slaveholders' collective finances collapsed, educated northerners had concluded that this belief was a fundamental truth. Former Illinois congressman and lawyer Abraham Lincoln insisted that only "free labor gives hope to all, and energy, and progress, and openness of condition." Lincoln himself had escaped unpaid toil in his father's muddy Indiana cornfields by walking to an Illinois frontier town, where he could work for a wage. On the way down to New Orleans, piloting his employer's flatboats, he watched slaves toiling in the fields behind the delta levees. Returning to Illinois, he read law books, stood for elections, and turned himself into someone who hired other people.[8]

Even though slavery supposedly undermined the will to improve, northerners like Olmsted continually found southern whites pushing for efficiency.

"Time's money, time's money!" he heard a white man say on a Gulf steamboat. Pacing anxiously as enslaved and free Irish longshoremen loaded his cotton bales, the man worried about getting back to Texas in time for planting. The rush of the annual cotton cycle predisposed such men to feel tardy, to push themselves to work harder at pushing other people harder. Yet maybe too much time had been lost in the 1840s, or maybe northern critics were right when they claimed that slaveholders had turned away from the path of progress, down some dead-end of history. Olmsted heard those questions lurking in conversations over dinner on steamboats. Southern whites raised such worries in a printed conversation that filled newspapers and monthly journals, such as *DeBow's Review*, published in New Orleans by James DeBow. [9]

Ultimately, however, despite something of a northern consensus that slavery was backward and inefficient, and despite the hard times of the previous decade, plenty of southern readers and talkers answered the question of whether or not the South could continue to use slavery as its recipe for modern economic development with a resounding *yes*. Take Josiah Nott, an Alabama racial theorist and a physician, who argued that mosquitoes, not swampy mists, transmitted malaria and yellow fever. In 1851, he wrote that "7,000,000 people" in the North, Britain, and France, "depend for their existence upon keeping employed the 3,000,000 negroes in the Southern states." Emancipation would be in such circumstances "the most stupendous example of human folly." A "network of cotton" wove enslaved people into the web of "human progress," and without their forced labor, it would unravel. [10]

Over the decade, in fact, the ability of hands to undercut free and serf labor with ruthless efficiency reconfirmed the idea that whether or not Nott was right, Olmsted was wrong. In the hands of cotton entrepreneurs, slavery was a highly efficient way to produce economic growth, both for white southerners and for others outside the region. In the 1850s, southern production of cotton doubled from 2 million to 4 million bales, with no sign of either slowing down or of quenching the industrial West's thirst for raw materials. The world's consumption of cotton grew from 1.5 billion to 2.5 billion pounds, and at the end of the decade the hands of US fields were still picking two-thirds of all of it, and almost all of that which went to Western Europe's factories. By 1860, the eight wealthiest states in the United States, ranked by wealth per white person, were South Carolina, Mississippi, Louisiana, Georgia, Connecticut, Alabama, Florida, and Texas—seven states created by cotton's march west and south, plus one that, as the most industrialized state in the Union, profited disproportionately from the gearing of northern factory equipment to the southwestern whipping-machine. [11]

Although the whipping-machine could be astonishingly good at extracting productivity increases, some southern enslavers worried that dependence on world demand for cotton left the South vulnerable to two dangers: first, to the global economy's vagaries, and second, to a future in which the northern states' immigration-driven population growth steadily sapped southern political power. Regional newspapers and magazines regularly featured articles arguing that the South should create a diversified economy that included a profitable factory sector, which could provide jobs that would attract white labor to the South. In an 1855 issue of *DeBow's Review*, for instance, William Gregg described his Graniteville, South Carolina, manufacturing complex, which he claimed was earning a profit of more than 11 percent. Others insisted that mining, iron-forging, and factory work could employ enslaved black labor. In quantitative terms, slave labor in southern factories produced as high a rate of net profit as slave labor in the fields. It was also as productive as free labor in the Northeast. Slaves staffed most of the expanding iron foundries of Virginia. From the 1830s onward, industrial activity had increased significantly in the South, and enslaved labor was one reason why.[12]

Industrially produced iron railroad tracks were redrawing the cotton frontier's landscape. In the 1840s, southern railroads had expanded from 683 miles in total length to 2,162 miles. But this increase was much lower than that in the free states, which in the same time period created a 7,000-mile network concentrated in the Northeast and Middle Atlantic states. During the 1850s, good times returned, and southern railroad construction projects increased the regional network there to 10,000 miles in length. Corners of Alabama and Georgia, interior Florida, and East Texas had been too many days of wagon-hauling away from steamboat landings to become profitable cotton belts. But the railroads snaking up into hill counties made areas dominated by yeomen and poor whites ripe for transformation. Land speculation companies began to evict squatters. As total southern wealth increased, a new generation of poor whites found themselves turned into unwanted drifters, despised and feared by planters moving into the new railroad-opened regions. When Olmsted visited Columbus, Georgia, men told him that the local textile factory's 20,000 cotton spindles were tended by displaced "cracker girls," whose jobs supposedly saved them from the temptations of prostitution. Southern factories would occupy whites newly forced into landlessness, ameliorating the disruptive impact of the modern market on the Jeffersonian ideal of the independent small farmer as the backbone of the white republic.[13]

Still, southern cotton planters realized that their own increased dependence on financial decisionmakers from outside their region was a thorny problem. Financial collapses and the sovereign defaults that southwestern states had executed during the era of repudiation made it impossible for would-be southern bankers to recapitalize themselves in the 1840s. But cotton demand began to climb again after 1848, leading to the longest period of high prices in the nineteenth century. Although southern state governments were rated as poor credit risks after their legislative repudiations, every year southern entrepreneurs sold the vast majority of the world's most widely traded commodity, so there was profit to be made from investing in the whipping-machine. Moreover, the 3.2 million people enslaved in the United States had a market value of $1.3 billion in 1850—one-fifth of the nation's wealth and almost equal to the entire gross national product. They were more liquid than other forms of American property, even if an acre of land couldn't run away or kill an overseer with an axe.[14]

Yet since the debt-and-repudiation crisis of the early 1840s, enslaved people were no longer being fully tapped as collateral by world financial markets. One untold story of US prosperity and global economic growth in the 1850s would be the creation of a new set of credit flows that used enslaved people's bodies, lives, and hands as the basis for lending in the cotton economy and profit-sharing by investors outside of it. This new financial ecology replaced the chaos of the 1840s, which in turn had succeeded the credit structures of the 1830s. In the 1830s, the securitization of mortgages on enslaved people through the medium of bonds sold on distant financial markets by planter-controlled, state-chartered banks had dominated and organized the flow of credit into the southwestern cotton frontier. The new system of the 1850s would finance massive new expansions in the southwestern United States while also allowing world capital markets to take advantage of the massive collateral held by enslavers. But this new system would not give enslavers what they had lost with the panics of 1837 and 1839, and with repudiation, and this was the control over the flow of credit and repayment that enslavers had once been able to exert.

The new financial ecology was brought into being by start-up firms launched by northerners with small amounts of capital, who moved to southern ports in the wake of 1839 to buy cotton. These were companies such as, for instance, Lehman Brothers of Mobile, Alabama. In the disrupted environment left by the destruction of the old mercantile firms, these new organisms acquired an old name, "factor," which had a long history in the Atlantic slave trade, and their role in the cotton economy evolved quickly. They began to lend money to enslavers on the security of ensuing crops and mortgages on slaves. Factors also arranged for transportation, secured insurance for crops in transit, and bought supplies for clients' labor camps. Any collection of mid-nineteenth-century personal and business documents from the South will be stuffed with the account sheets generated by factors, blue paper, covered in ferrous ink dried to rusty red and black. By the mid-1850s, the hinterland of every cotton port had several large firms—such as Buckner, Stanton, and Co., of New Orleans—standing head and shoulders above the rest.[15]

In the 1850s, the factor mediated between cotton producers and the world market, channeling credit and taking the immediate risk of lending. The factors themselves needed credit, and their financing came from New York banks, such as Brown Brothers. Factors alone could not satisfy all the borrowing needed to generate a cotton crop that increased in total value 450 percent between 1840 and 1859. The lenders depended on personal relationships that allowed them to evaluate the creditworthiness of potential borrowers, so small-scale cotton producers were often kept on a short tether, when they could get tied in at all. Bigger planters and small-town merchants found that they could take their own incoming flow of credit from factors, repackage it, and pass it on at more capillary levels, thus making money from their own investments in other people's enslavement of still other people. Thus, $1 lent by Philadelphia-based factor Washington Jackson became $2 lent by Natchez megaplanter Stephen Duncan to his neighbors. Repackagers usually demanded a mortgage on individual slaves as security, and as locally powerful residents, they were in a position to enforce this requirement. While slave mortgages had been made since the seventeenth century, they now became ubiquitous. During 1859, Louisiana enslavers raised $25.7 million, 75 percent of the value of cotton produced in the state that year, by mortgaging slaves.[16]

The world market's willingness to lend reveals its continued faith in the long-term profitability of slavery. The new system of credit delivery was capillary, as opposed to the arterial system of the 1830s, and so defaults and other breaks in its flow were less catastrophic. It certainly profited lenders up and down the chain, even the little old ladies in Mayfair townhouses who let London men of business put their inheritances into the hands of other men of business. Passing through a chain of intermediaries, that money would be lent on a slave in Mississippi, usually generating 8 percent interest, the highest allowed in many states that had passed usury laws. The collateral of enslaved bodies profited investors around the globe once again in the 1850s. But the new system also connected each borrower to the world economy primarily as an indebted individual property owner, rather than as a member of a unified group controlling a bond-issuing state as sovereign citizens, and a

state bank as stockholders, as had been the case in the 1830s. The disempow-
ering experience of mortgaging without local control over the entrance and
exit of credit into statewide economies might have increased enslavers' recep-
tivity to the Calhounian substantive-due-process doctrine. And so southern
public intellectuals' cries for diversification were not just about where one's
shoes were made (Massachusetts), but about where one's credit came from,
and where one's interest charges went (London, New York).

There was one possibility that, if it had become real, might have shifted
the relationship between the enslavers and the world's credit markets. In the
past, the recipe of collusion between financiers, hard men with guns, and
ambitious politicians had worked to expand both the United States and the
power of southern enslavers. More than once, such groups had teamed up to
break juicy chunks like Florida off the edges decaying of empires. When that
happened, enslavers suddenly controlled the territory and the enslaved labor
necessary to generate speculative gains, and in such situations they had often
been able to get credit under favorable terms from investors who were eager
to get in on the ground floor of the next big thing. There was an exceptionally
attractive possibility of this sort right off the coast of Florida. If the South had
acquired Cuba, the history of the expansion of slavery in the United States,
including the history of investment in the expansion of slavery, would surely
not have ended in 1865.

For by 1850, Cuba was the one real jewel yet to be pried from the crown
of the Spanish Empire. It had become to sugar what Mississippi now was to
cotton. Sugar production in the New World had moved from one island to the
next, with new islands replacing old ones as the ones most desirable to investors, but the physical technology of making sugar had hardly improved over
three centuries. Soon after Saint-Domingue, planters fleeing the Haitian
Revolution brought enslaved laborers and entrepreneurial expertise to Cuba;
however, they began to transform sugar production in ways parallel to the
creative destructions within the whipping-machine. In this case, using new
machine technology, Cuban planters rebuilt processes in ways that shattered
the bottleneck on productivity imposed by the fact that the sucrose in cane
begins to spoil if it isn't extracted within twenty-four hours of harvesting.
After harnessing the power of steam to turn cane-grinding mills fast enough
to keep up with almost any number of enslaved cutters harvesting the raw
cane, Cuban enslavers added vacuum pans to boil extracted cane syrup. This
took the process of crystallizing sugar out of the control of skilled slave artisans. The new *ingenios*, as Cubans called mill complexes, led to a 400 percent
increase in the acres of cane that a mill could turn into sucrose crystals, an

efficiency increase in one generation greater than that of the preceding half-millennium of sugar production.[17]

Cuba was vast, as large as England and Wales together, and in 1791 it had only 86,000 slaves who made but 16,000 metric tons of sugar. Despite an 1835 Anglo-Spanish treaty that was supposed to stop the Atlantic slave trade, between 1800 and the 1860s, Cuban enslavers imported 700,000 enslaved Africans, with 300,000 arriving after the 1835 treaty was signed. Already by 1830, the new *ingenio* system had made Cuba the world's biggest sugar producer, and then, using British credit, the colonial government began to extend railroad lines down the island's spine, opening vast new areas for exploitation. By 1850, the slave population had climbed to more than 435,000, more than in any US slave state but Virginia, and Cuba was shipping 300,000 metric tons of sugar annually—one out of every four pounds of sugar made on the planet. And still the huge island was only partly developed.[18]

In 1848, the Polk administration offered Spain's impoverished government $100 million for the island. Political conflict over the Mexican Cession dissuaded the executive branch from carrying negotiations further at that time. But over the four years after 1848, pressure began to build for Cuban annexation from within the United States. This pressure came from sources in both the North and the South. One was the Cuban exile community in New York, whose Havana Club proclaimed that rule from Madrid denied free Cubans basic natural rights, like that of free speech and political assembly, and denied them the right to trade freely. Spanish imperial officials also periodically held the threat of emancipation over Cuban enslavers' heads; this threat in turn caused a defensive reaction among southern enslavers, who also wanted to acquire the island because an "Africanized" "free negro colony" off the Florida coast would "destroy the efficiency of mainland slaves," as a Tennessee newspaper put it. The newspaper meant that freedom in Cuba would suggest to enslaved people on the mainland that their emancipation was next. Such fears seemed more than imaginary because, in 1839, fifty-three recently enslaved Africans had overthrown the white crew of the Cuban slave-ship *Amistad* as they were being transported from Havana to the island's eastern sugar frontier. Trying to sail to Africa, the rebels made an accidental landfall on the Connecticut coast. State authorities charged them with murder, but abolitionists intervened and pushed the case into the Supreme Court. Concluding that the *Amistad*'s cargo had been illegally transported across the Atlantic, the Court made its only pre-twentieth-century antislavery decision. It ruled that the rebels had been kidnapped, that they had freed themselves, and that they could return to Africa.[19]

After the Wilmot Proviso, however, southern expansionists were determined to regain the offensive. A Virginia-born State Department official, writing to Secretary of War Jefferson Davis in around 1853, said that expansion into Cuba was "essential to the South both in a political and a geographical point of view." Because of Cuba's size and population, it could be carved into multiple states, each one sending proslavery senators and representatives to Washington to rebalance Congress. Bringing Cuba's ultramodern sugar plantations inside American tariff walls would reduce Louisiana sugar's market share, but then, as southern entrepreneurs anticipated, they could simply move operations to "the untouched soil of Cuba," and thus find "the means of underselling the world in sugar." The *New Orleans Delta* believed that "wresting [Cuba] from the mongrelism which now blights and *blackens* it" would make the enslaved population "yield its riches up to the hands of *organized and stable industry and intelligent enterprise.*" This would be "*manifest destiny* accomplished."[20]

Many northern Democrats also supported American acquisition of the "Queen of Islands," as pro-expansion *New York Sun* journalist "Cora Montgomery" (pen name of Jane McManus Cazneau, daughter of a New York congressman) described Cuba. She was one of many aggressively pro-expansion New York journalists whose support for "Manifest Destiny"—a term the expansionists coined—was frankly chauvinist. But annexation also drew support from idealistic refugees from the failed European revolutions of 1848, or so Jane Cazneau claimed. She wrote that "the native Cubans are wild for annexation," because they hoped its incorporation into the United States would make "Young America" a multilingual republican empire to eclipse the Old Europe that had forced out revolutionaries and still sought to shackle Cuba to a European throne. Above all, New York City had a deep economic interest in Cuba. Steam-driven sugar mills were the most significant heavy industrial product made in the city itself. Wall Street powerbrokers such as August Belmont, the so-called "King of Fifth Avenue," who founded (and bankrolled) the national Democratic Party Committee, knew that Cuba was already the mainland's third-biggest trading partner, and he enthusiastically supported acquisition.[21]

White southerners were happy to see northern Democrats demanding a bigger empire for slavery. And in the 1850s, southern enslavers and northern allies didn't just demand new territories. They acted. When the Whig-run executive branch didn't move toward acquiring Cuba between 1849 and 1853, many Cuba expansionists supported extralegal tactics called "filibustering," a term that in the mid-nineteenth century did not mean obstructionist legislative behavior, but still held its seventeenth-century meaning deriving from the activity of Caribbean pirates. Cuban exiles, Wall Street money, New York publicists, and Mississippi power-brokers supported a series of attempted "filibuster" expeditions intended to overthrow the island's Spanish colonial government. The most substantial ones were led by Narciso Lopez, an exiled Cuban planter, in 1850 and 1851. Drawing on financial support from the money-men of New York and the Mississippi Valley (including R. C. Ballard and New Orleans–based millionaire enslaver John Henderson), Lopez recruited his foot soldiers among young men from Louisiana, Ohio, Kentucky, and the northeastern states. But his second invasion ended in disaster. The Spanish government captured his force and brutally executed Lopez and about fifty American prisoners in Havana's public square.[22]

"American blood has been shed! It cries aloud for vengeance," shouted the *New Orleans Courier*. "Cuba must be seized!" Angry mass meetings erupted in US cities, leading in New Orleans to riots that attacked Spanish property. The New York *Democratic Review*, the organ of the "Young America" movement, argued that the party needed a "States-Rights" candidate who would make the 1852 presidential election a referendum on the Whigs' passive expansion policy. When Franklin Pierce of New Hampshire won the Democratic nomination, he adopted Cuba acquisition as a key platform plank. August Belmont threw his money behind Pierce, who demolished Whig Winfield Scott, 253 electoral votes to 44. One victory parade banner proclaimed "The Fruits of the Late Democratic Victory—Pierce and Cuba," and when March 1853 rolled around, the new president's inaugural address proclaimed that his administration would "not be controlled by any timid forebodings of evil from expansion."[23]

Southern and northern Democrats sensed that the time had come. At last they could fulfill the hopes of Manifest Destiny, provide an expansion pie big enough for all of their party's interests, and, of course, frustrate the plans of Whigs, abolitionists, free blacks, and everyone else they collectively despised. Pierce, described in the press as a "Northern Man of Southern Principles," announced that the executive branch would not attempt to stop citizens who chose to "emigrate" to Cuba. Spain could reflect on what happened when US citizens had "emigrated" to Mexican Texas. Pierce sent expansionists as the government's official emissaries to the courts of Europe—such as Louisiana Senator Pierre Soulé, who went to Spain, and Belmont, appointed to the Netherlands. In April 1854, Secretary of State William Marcy instructed the emissaries to "detach that island" from Spain, authorizing them to offer $130 million for Cuba. Belmont already planned to manipulate European financial markets in order to bring Spain's heavily indebted government to its knees.

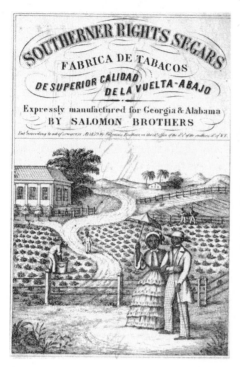

Image 10.2. By the 1850s enslavers had their eyes on expansion into Cuba in order to expand Southern political power. Here we see an idyllic image of a Cuba tobacco plantation, plus the idea of "Southern rights" being used to sell cigars. "Southerner rights segars. Expressly manufactured for Georgia & Alabama by Salomon Brothers. Fabrica de tabacos, de superior calidad de la vuelta-abajo," Broadside, 1859. Library of Congress.

In October, the US ministers gathered at Ostend in Belgium, where they crafted a policy paper called the Ostend Manifesto. This report, which Belmont et al. sent back to Marcy and Pierce, proclaimed that if Spain refused to sell Cuba, "the law of self-preservation"—a euphemism here for protecting mainland slavery from the alleged destabilization that offshore emancipation would inflict—entitled the United States to seize the island. But even as they wrote, on the other side of the Atlantic Pierce was learning that the survival of the Democratic Party itself depended so heavily on alliance behind the cause of expanding slavery that he wasn't going to be allowed to wait for Spain to sell Cuba.[24]

IN 1852, A YEAR after Rice Ballard's business partner Samuel Boyd helped to buy arms for Narciso Lopez's invasion of Spanish territory, other things that Boyd had been doing caught up to him. Boyd, a Natchez lawyer and judge, and former slave trader Ballard had been buying distressed properties through the trough of the 1840s. As the new decade opened, they began to buy dozens of new "hands" through a New Orleans slave-consignment agent named C. M. Rutherford. Pre-1850s financial innovations had worked in tandem with new slave trades, from coffle-chain and Georgia-men to the supertraders and the securitization of hands. Now the factors' capillary credit created demand, to which the domestic slave trade responded with a new business model. Unlike 1830s' supertraders who owned enslaved hands from one end of the pipeline to the other, new players, such as Richmond's Richard Dickinson, behaved more like consignment agents or commodities traders. Using the tools of faster communication—instant telegraph, or mail carried by rail—to gauge demand and supply, they held slaves in their jails for owners who wanted to sell, graded captives, provided clothes and insurance, found remote buyers, and put captives like Ben Slaughter on trains headed southwest. Sellers often waited until final sale to get their money, but they benefited from more predictable prices. Dickinson sent employees around the selling states to gather market data—"No.1 women $1300 to 1350 and girls size of Margaret and Edmony $1025 to 1100. . . . [S]ome think No. 1 men will go as high as $1600 to 1700." He repackaged this data into regular price circulars, which he mailed to potential sellers and brokers across Virginia. The new pattern of trade reduced opportunities for arbitrage but didn't require a single middle party to bear all the risk. Capital requirements for entry declined, and there was demand to fill. The price of an adult man in New Orleans climbed from $697 in 1850 to $1,451 in 1860. The reorganized slave trade moved about 70 percent of the decade's 250,000 forced migrants.[25]

Rising prices, returning credit, and the efficiencies of the newest iteration of the domestic slave trade enabled wealthy cotton enslavers to expand their operations dramatically. US cotton production reached 4 million bales by 1859, an incredible testimony to the seemingly unlimited capacity of both the southern economy to increase its production, and the world economy to absorb it. Boyd and Ballard, who owned almost a dozen labor camps, did their share. On one of them near Natchez, Ballard owned a woman named Virginia. She wasn't a girl, for she had a teenage daughter, and she began to call herself Boyd because Samuel carried on a relationship with her. It doesn't take much imagination to understand why she carried on with "the Old Man," as she later called him. In the early 1850s, Boyd and Ballard were sending enslaved people to carve new labor camps out of the land they now owned on the heavily forested western shore of the Mississippi River: Elcho, Brushy Bayou, Pecan Grove, and Outpost in northeastern Louisiana, and Wagram in Arkansas. In 1852, the partners sold 2,000 bales to their factors. By 1855, a memo showing returns from only six of the partners' ten camps recorded 3,319 bales made—1.34 million pounds of clean ginned cotton.[26]

The partners were not alone. In contrast to the 1810s or 1830s, in the 1850s the borders of slavery's empire were not expanding, even though southern whites hoped for Cuba. In the Mississippi Valley, much of the expansion of cotton production was driven by high capitalization to fill in the vast stretches of untapped rich soil.

On this set of internal frontiers, some of the entrepreneurs who had survived the last crash in good shape achieved a kind of superplanter status. Ballard wasn't the only one who realized old slave-trading profits in the form of massive new projects. For instance, take Tennessee lawyer Joseph Acklen, who married the widow of Ballard's former business partner Isaac Franklin in 1849. Franklin had built up "Angola" and several other labor camps in West Feliciana Parish, Louisiana. By 1860, Acklen had added one hundred newly purchased people to the labor force acquired by marriage, and his Angola complex made over 3,100 bales a year. Across the river, where armies of enslaved people were being deployed to turn Carroll, Concordia, and Tensas Parishes into a new lobe of the world economy's cotton-breathing lung, four camps owned by the Routh family generated 5,000 bales a year by 1859. Back on the Mississippi side, another new frontier opened in the vast stretch from Vicksburg north to Memphis, which had been mostly unexploited before the late 1840s. Issaquena County, for instance, did not exist before 1849. By 1860 its median slaveholding had reached an astonishing 118.[27]

Issaquena County is today one of the poorest counties in the United States, but in those days that whole region was being turned with industrial rapidity into a wealth-generating landscape of endless cotton fields. The Chickasaws had been driven out during the 1830s, leaving a citadel of 7,000 wild square miles, "a chaos of vines and cane and brush" untouched by axe or plow and patrolled by wildlife that included bears, wolves, cougars, and even a few jaguars. But the roots of trees (their trunks up to six feet in diameter) twined through some of the richest dirt for cotton on the surface of the planet—"pure soil endlessly deep, dark, and sweet," as the journalist David Cohn put it a century later. Unlike all preceding North American slavery frontiers, most of the delta's entrepreneurs came from a small group of the most heavily capitalized men in the country. Few settled in the region. Instead they operated massively productive slave labor camps as if by remote control. You can see that in the new delta's demographics. From 1850 to 1860, the enslaved population in its six core counties almost doubled, from 17,000 to 30,000. The white population, which had not yet reached 7,000, stood at roughly 20 percent of the slave population—a fact revelatory of a commitment to large-scale specialized cotton production as complete as the Saint-Domingue enslavers' commitment to sugar.[28]

As the number of enslaved people on this internal frontier grew, so, too, did the demands on them. In 1849, the Issaquena slaveholdings of Robert Turnbull, a Westchester, New York, resident, amounted to 200 slaves who made 300 bales of cotton. By 1859, Turnbull's estate in Issaquena exploited 400 captives who made 2,000 bales of cotton—an increase from 1.5 to 5 bales per enslaved person, which is evidence of how hard they were driven in the new fields. George Young was born on a similar labor camp in that same decade. If he'd had a birth certificate, it would have given a date within a year or two on either side of the Ostend Manifesto. But Young's elders always told him he was born in "The Lawler Year," because enslaved people sometimes remembered years by the names of the annually changing overseers, and Lawler was memorably violent. Indeed, across the South, the 1850s were a Lawler Decade. As slavery's center of gravity lurched south and west, the number of enslaved African Americans who lived in cotton districts grew from 1.6 million to 2.2 million. The re-acceleration of forced migration, the shift of the population into disease-friendly ecologies, and the increasing pace of labor brought hunger, alienation, and death. Life expectancy for African Americans, which had climbed in the less market-frenzied 1840s, now dropped again, as it had in the 1810s and 1830s.[29]

Virginia Boyd was able to avoid the most Lawler-like places as long as Samuel Boyd wanted to keep her handy. They were certainly together in the summer of 1852 outside of Natchez. Just a few months later, she knew she was definitely pregnant. But then someone else—maybe Samuel's wife in Natchez—found out what they had been doing. Ballard also found out. That old and "smooth hand at Cuff" went into action. He wrote a letter ordering Virginia's overseer to send her up to Karnac, a labor camp he and Boyd owned near Port Gibson on the Mississippi River. And, Ballard warned Boyd, Virginia had to be sent farther still. Samuel didn't put up an argument, even replying that he didn't want "to be bothered with her, & if she will not behave, put her in the stocks until you start her off."[30]

Somehow, however, the information in one of Ballard's letters had gone astray, because Virginia, who was literate, had clearly learned many details about his plans. Then, she tried to send a note to Boyd.

In response Ballard's letters began to fly around her, weaving a web that wrapped her tight. His agents moved her, first up the river to Karnac, leaving her daughter near Natchez; then down to New Orleans in February, where Ballard's agent, C. M. Rutherford, was waiting for her. She'd be sent too far away to ever trouble Boyd again—to Mobile, or to the slave market in

Houston. Virginia told Rutherford that the child was due soon, trying to delay the inevitable sending-away, and she snuck out of his store whenever she could to try to find her own buyer in New Orleans. Samuel Boyd, meanwhile, may have had second thoughts, for (as Ballard discovered) he traveled down to New Orleans. But by April, Virginia was consigned on board a Texas-bound ship, guarded by a white man, like a fugitive being escorted by a marshal.

Texas was not a good option for Virginia Boyd, but it was a good one for bootstrapping white men on the make. In the 1850s, they moved 100,000 enslaved people into eastern Texas, a region as big as Mississippi or Alabama. Many of these migrant white entrepreneurs were small slave owners, such as S. G. Ward. In 1850, Ward left Warren County, North Carolina, and, as he explained in a letter, "carried all my negroes, save 3 or 4 and as many children, to Texas," to rent them to his brother, "because they were making nothing clear here." The immediate application of crowd-tested techniques of production gave life on the East Texas frontier to the familiar tang of a society composed of undercapitalized men committed to creative destruction: "Cotton is the leading idea here and men neglect everything else," wrote one migrant. They "lay out all their money on negroes and land. You frequently see men worth $100,000 who seem no better off than our own mountain people."[31]

Virginia was to be sold to one of those men. She had lost everything except her unborn child and her literacy. Somehow she obtained pen and paper, convinced someone to mail a letter, and on May 6, 1853, wrote a remarkable message to Ballard from "the city of Houston at a Negro traders yard." She confronted Ballard with what the relationship between her and her child's father should mean: "Do you think that after all that has transpired between me and the old man (I don't call names) that it is treating me well to send me off among strangers to be sold . . . for the father of my children to sell his own offspring, yes his own flesh and blood." "Is it possible," she asked, testing every rhetorical switch she knew in an attempt to flip Ballard's choice, "that any free born American would hand his character with such stigma as that?" What would slavery's critics say, and couldn't he sympathize with her as a caring father? "You have a family of children & no how to empathize with others in distress." She begged to be reunited with her daughter, for her children to be set free, that she might be permitted to raise the money to buy her own freedom. "If I am a servant"—and slavery's defenders were industriously cranking out articles insisting that the South was built upon a paternalistic relationship between kindly masters and loyal "servants," not slaves—then "there is something due me better than my present situation." And don't worry, she closed, with both promise and threat, she knew how to send letters back to Adams County, but "I shall not seek ever to let anything be exposed, unless I am forced by bad treatment."

In August, C. M. Rutherford wrote to Ballard, who was in Louisville, Kentucky, far from the malarial floodplain where the nearly 1,000 people whom he and Boyd owned toiled at another year's cotton-picking. "I recd a letter" from Houston today, Rutherford told him, "informing me of the sale of Virginia & her child." This was the newborn child. The teenage daughter, purposely not sent to Texas with her mother, was to be sold in Mississippi for at least $1,000. Boyd had created a problem. Ballard had solved it. In fact, he gave all the white men involved some money—Rutherford, for instance, got a $200 commission. And if Virginia Boyd sent any more letters, they did not survive. She does not appear in the 1870 US Census, the first one to record the individual names of most African Americans. Although she may have changed her name, it is also possible that once "the author of my suffering," her child's father, had "thrown [her] upon the charity of strangers," mere charity had been insufficient.

MOST LIKELY, VIRGINIA WILTED and died in a Texas field. Whether in East Texas or among the Mississippi Delta's felled forests, people brought to the newest cotton frontiers were expected to yield massive profits. Sarah Benjamin recalled the games she and all the other children had played in the gin yard during the 1850s: "Some of us were slave owners and some of us were speculators." All the grownups, meanwhile, were in the field, and the pace was quick as the prices were high, under August's brutal sun. At night, the parents of another child, Sarah Wells, reported that the overseer had told them that if they "didn't pick 250 pounds of cotton in a day," he would whip them, and then they fell dead asleep. The children had seen more of how this was accomplished than the grownups ever wanted to believe. Many of those whom we would call children were dragging picksacks in the fields, anyway: Sarah Ashley, born in Mississippi in 1844, was in the Texas fields by the age of twelve and had to make her 300 pounds—and get it to the cotton house, too. All in all, the number of pounds of cotton produced per slave in the cotton region increased by 30 percent between 1850 and 1860.[32]

Typical among the entrepreneurs who helped to shape this new frontier was North Carolina enslaver Paul Cameron, who bought land in Greene County, Alabama, in the 1840s and transferred several score of his hundreds of enslaved African Americans there. But this project disappointed Cameron, though he was already one of the two wealthiest men in his home state. By the early 1850s, the Greene County labor camp was still yielding only 180 bales of cotton per year. Cameron began doodling slave names in the margins of letters: potential lineups for the project he now had in mind. Land speculators got wind of his plans and started to write ingratiating letters. Cameron ultimately bought a huge Tunica County tract in the Mississippi Delta. In late 1856, he selected some of the younger adult slaves from Alabama and North Carolina and moved them to Tunica. They were supposed to build levees, clear trees, and make cotton under the kind of hard driving needed to realize the ten-bales-per-hand yield he had heard about. Cameron hired an overseer named Jeter. Local reputation measured Jeter as "too tight" even for delta enslavers, and Cameron's agent returned from the new site saying, "Youre slaves were very much dissatisfied when I left."[33]

Soon Jeter drove them beyond their ability to endure. One day in the field, Jacob tackled Jeter and held him down. The other men took his whip and tried to flog him. They knew they would suffer for it, but they could not endure his wild, unpredictable violence. But every overseer armed himself with multiple weapons before he left the house in the morning, and Jeter had a hidden knife to pull. He tried to stab Jacob, who fled to the woods. Jeter leapt up, ran to get his dogs, and soon had not only recaptured Jacob but beaten the other rebels as well. "Complete subordination" had been achieved, reported Cameron's business agents in Memphis.[34]

Yet the reality was that no matter how many times Jeter snapped his whip across arms shaking with malaria-induced chills, he never quite beat the Cameron people down. So once all the land was cleared and ditched and ready to yield ten bales to the hand, Cameron dismissed Jeter and got another overseer. The boss now wanted each hand to reach 200 pounds of cotton picked per day. The new man tried to make it happen, but the enslaved pushed back. In the hard picking season of 1859—the best ever for enslavers, the most Lawler-like of all years yet, in which enslaved people gathered in 4.5 million bales of cotton—Lem and Betsy snuck out of the quarter in the middle of the night, reached the river, and stole a canoe. A couple of weeks later, Cameron's overseer, W. T. Lamb, got the message that they'd been caught in Arkansas. "After getting them," Lamb wrote Cameron, "will manage Lem to the best of my ability (but not cruelly)." Two weeks passed before he let Lem out of the iron box and "put hobbles"—heavy iron ankle weights—on him. Lamb also hammered a heavy iron staple into the exterior logs of his own house, and—this was in December—chained Lem to the staple all night. Lamb did suggest that Cameron could use the slave market to liquidate the risk represented by this "troublesome negro that you might probably loose by being drowned or meet his death at some other way." (Perhaps it was far too late; an appraiser had already advised that Lem's health was "so bad and he had been so badly cut with the whip that it was impossible to sell him for anything like his value.")[35]

In a letter he wrote to his friend Paul Cameron, lawyer D. F. Caldwell said, "I often wish my slaves were in Africa." In the early 1850s, men like Caldwell and Cameron were usually still Whigs. So were their sisters and wives. Wealthy southern women had favored the Whigs for years, even though they couldn't vote. From their politics, white men and women of this class came into a heritage of politely poor-mouthing the institution of slavery. But when he finished up his legal work on the day after Christmas in 1854, Caldwell wrote to Cameron that he was heading to Alabama to check on his cotton crop. To his wish that the people he owned were "returned" to Africa, he added just one little caveat: "provided that I could realize two thirds of their value." By the time Caldwell returned four weeks later he had sold one of his two Alabama labor camps and now had "an eye on the Mississippi lowgrounds."[36]

Great investments, of course, demanded greater increases in productivity. Men like Paul Cameron could get them at arm's reach, from the far remove of their home state, tuning the whipping-machine by remote control. And as long as Cameron and his peers could make money by slavery, and would lose their wealth by its ending, they were going to make the kinds of moves that big wealth makes: investing, expanding operations and their margins, finding new sources of credit and new markets. Cameron, Caldwell, Ballard, and other megaplanters, already among the wealthiest Americans, got wealthier still as their reinvigorated investments began to pay off. They invested so much more in captive human beings in the 1850s, in fact, that one can put aside any belief that men like Cameron or Caldwell truly feared (much less hoped for) an end to the enslavement of African Americans. They seemed, instead, increasingly confident in slavery's future.[37]

To at least some extent, the success of the richest also came at the expense of other whites—and not just by pushing subsistence farmers off land made marketable by the railroad, but also by raising barriers to entry in larger-scale cotton production through increased prices for hands, high-quality land, and credit. Over the course of the 1850s, cotton production and slave ownership became increasingly concentrated among those who owned fifteen or more slaves.[38] This skewing of white southerners' benefits from slavery and of their investment in it inspired forebodings in enslavers, practical political economists who depended on white unity. So did the continued southward shift of enslaved human beings. Perhaps the declining percentage of slaves and slave owners in the upper southern states would eventually lead to border-state legislatures filled with non-slaveholders, who might decide to impose emancipation. Such anxieties inspired interest in economic diversification to create slave labor industries in Virginia, Kentucky, and Missouri, raising the in-state price of slaves and slowing out-migration. Other southwestern enslavers suggested that the South force Congress to reopen the international slave trade in order to bring down the price of slaves and allow other whites to buy into the system.[39]

The Compromise of 1850 did not mean either peace or an end to pressure for the expansion of slavery. White southerners assumed that new territory was what they needed to ignite a new, inclusive economic boom. The only problem was that they couldn't agree on where to focus their efforts. Many wanted Cuba. Some talked of splitting California into two states. In the meantime, almost by happenstance, southern politicians lined up behind a different strategy, one based on Calhoun's substantive-due-process insistence that slavery should be legal in all US territories. Their choice determined Ben Slaughter's fate, and Richard's as well.

BY 1853, WHEN FRANKLIN Pierce took office as the fourteenth president, South Carolina native James Gadsden had been promoting the idea of a transcontinental railroad from New Orleans to Los Angeles for five years. This line would spread slaveholding along its path, Gadsden hoped, for he believed that "Negro slavery, under educated and Intelligent masters," has always "been the Pioneers and basis of the civilization of Savage countries," and also that "without an enduring & well regulated labor the agriculture of the Pacific will never be developed." California's state constitution prohibited slavery, but a group of politicians known as the "Chivalry" was pressing the state to reconsider. Indeed, despite existing law, about 1,000 African Americans were already enduring extremely well-regulated labor as slaves in the California goldfields. Nor did the Chivalry plan to stop with converting California into a slave state. They plotted to acquire land on the other side of the Mexican border for a slaveholding settlement that would, Gadsden anticipated, "add Cotton corn and rice to the Gold export." The Pierce administration joined in, sending Gadsden to Mexico City to negotiate for enough Mexican land to ensure that a southern railroad route would run well within US territory, and Secretary of War Jefferson Davis sent military surveying parties to map out this pathway for the iron horse.[40]

Gadsden arrived in the Mexican capital just as a gang of mercenary adventurers, recruited in San Francisco by a megalomaniacal Tennesseean named William Walker, invaded northwestern Mexico. Walker declared the independent republic of Lower California. However, only sixty-two locals renounced their Mexican citizenship and swore allegiance to his flag. Soon Walker and his filibuster band heard that the Mexican army was on its way. They fled across the Sonoran Desert toward the United States. Eventually they staggered into Fort Yuma, "nearly in a naked and starving condition," as one observer put it.[41]

Walker's incursion soured Gadsden's chance to make the southern route the most obvious one. Mexican officials refused to sell more than a fraction of what Gadsden had wanted to acquire for both Baja cotton colonies and railroad. And though it seemed that all politicians believed that the federal government should help to build an iron link between the Mississippi Valley and the Pacific Coast, they all also realized that the route chosen would create path-dependence by tying the West Coast into national markets along a specific geographic axis. The future orientation of the American political economy was in the balance. In spring 1853, congressional opponents blocked federal funding for a southern intercontinental railroad line. Advocates of the southern route now vowed to spoil the northern ones, which were being championed, above all, by Senator Stephen Douglas of Illinois.[42]

Douglas's Chicago landholdings would rise dramatically in value from federal commitment to a northern route, but success on a transcontinental scale would also dwarf the political value of all previous internal improvement projects. Political reporters called Douglas the "Little Giant" because, at five-foot-five, and built like a sweaty tank, he managed with energy and invective to dominate a Congress filled with taller, better-looking, and better-born men. He only had to solve one legislative problem in order to unite a coalition behind one route—although he'd been trying to solve that problem since Polk was president.

Douglas had repeatedly proposed a bill to organize a federal territory west of Missouri and Iowa, because the railroad needed to run through a territory and not an "unorganized" Indian land. But in each of the previous eight years, southerners had blocked him, because the creation of a free territory on Missouri's western flank would leave that state an isolated slaveholding salient. Only 10 percent of Missouri's white households still owned slaves. Working-class St. Louis whites usually voted against those they considered to be representatives of slaveholder power. Yet many wealthy Missourians remained invested in slavery, such as US senator David Atchison, a Democrat whose power base lay in the state's slavery-dense western counties that locals called "Little Dixie." He wanted to keep them from the dilemma reported by a Missourian who moved "to Mississippi on account of the Negroes," because "he was near the Illinois line and his negroes became too troublesome running over to Illinois."[43]

The struggle over the western border was being waged by enslaved people long before 1853. Over the preceding decade, hundreds of African Americans—such as Elsa Hicks—had launched freedom suits in the St. Louis courts. In 1834, Hicks's owner took her from Virginia to Wisconsin. Seven years later, he moved her to St. Louis—back to slave territory as a slave. This was, her petition argued, "contrary to the Ordinance of 1787 passed by the Congress of the United States that had established the Northwest territory as free." In her claim that residing in a free territory had changed her own status, Hicks had precedent on her side. By the 1840s, state and federal courts had repeatedly ruled that when their owners took them to free territory with the intention of "relocating," as opposed to mere "sojourning," enslaved people became free. Both here, and in the possibility of a new free territory on Missouri's western border—one that would more quickly dissolve Missouri slavery—a question arose that Calhoun's idea of substantive due process also highlighted. Did the Constitution protect slave property nowhere, or everywhere?[44]

By 1854, forced migrants Harriet Scott and her husband, Dred, had been waiting for years to hear how their own freedom suit would turn out. Born in Virginia in 1795, Dred was moved to an Alabama cotton camp, and then, in the 1820s, to Missouri. His enslavers sold him to an army doctor named Emerson, who then moved to present-day Minnesota—free territory by virtue of the Missouri Compromise slavery-exclusion line. There Dred met Harriet Robinson. They married, she changed her name to Scott, and Emerson bought her. The doctor then took the couple by steamboat down the Mississippi River to Fort Jesup in Louisiana, where the doctor courted a visiting St. Louis woman named Eliza Irene Sanford. These two also married. The doctor died in 1843, after which Harriet, Dred, and their children lived with the widow in St. Louis.

The Scotts' experience of multiple migrations to slavery's many frontiers was not unusual, and they knew of the dozens of lawsuits launched by enslaved people whose commodification had taken them through free territory. In fact, Harriet and Dred first asked Emerson's widow, Eliza, to let them purchase their freedom, avoiding a freedom suit. Instead, staking out a position as a Calhounian political activist, Eliza asserted her "right" to take property wherever she pleased. When the Scotts responded by suing for their freedom, Eliza fought back with a commitment that surpassed her own specific financial stake in them. When she lost at one level of the judiciary, she pushed for an appeal to the next higher court. She was attempting to impose a constitution that universalized slavery on her own household.[45]

During March 1853, in Congress, Senator Atchison called the Missouri Compromise and the Northwest Ordinance the two greatest "errors committed in the political history of this country." Together these outlawed slavery on three sides of his home state and made the Scotts' freedom suit possible. It was radical enough to call 1819's compromise an error, for the Missouri Compromise was the central congressional bargain between North and South in the history of slavery. But by the end of the year, Atchison and his congressional allies perceived that they could use Douglas's desire to build a railroad as the fulcrum on which to bend a lever that would overturn the Missouri Compromise. Atchison's Washington allies included his three "messmates," senators with whom he shared a rented house on F Street: James Mason and Robert M. T. Hunter of Virginia, and South Carolina's Andrew Butler. The three southeasterners were ideologically committed disciples of Calhoun's substantive-due-process doctrine—Mason, for instance, had written the 1850 Fugitive Slave Act. Together, the F Street messmates decided to fight like Eliza Emerson for the protection of enslavers' power, in Missouri and everywhere, by forcing the Illinois Democrat and his party to commit to the doctrine of slavery as a Fifth Amendment property right that must be imposed in all federal territories.[46]

The railroad was foremost on Douglas's agenda when a new session of Congress opened at the beginning of December 1853, and he quickly drove a new Nebraska Territory bill through committee. But sometime before January 4, 1854, Atchison told the Illinois senator that southern senators would not support the organization of a free territory. Douglas recognized immediately that the southerners had trapped him. He rewrote the bill and, on January 4, offered Congress one that now included, unlike the committee version, language used in 1850 for New Mexico, saying that the Nebraska Territory's slavery status would be that which "their constitution may prescribe at the time of their admission." Again the southerners told Douglas that this was not enough. So then Douglas inserted a little notice in the January 10 edition of the *Washington Union* newspaper, claiming that "clerical error" had omitted another clause from the bill. This clause was an offer of ransom for his kidnapped railroad. It stated that "all questions pertaining to slavery in the Territories . . . are to be left to the people residing in them."

Douglas was still trying to do what he was compelled to do and no more, but the southerners shook their heads again. The bill still did not explicitly repeal the Missouri Compromise.

The next chance to speak on the territorial bill was on January 16, and Archibald Dixon, a Whig Senator from Kentucky, got the floor. He proceeded to propose an amendment. The portions of the Missouri Act of 1820 that denied "the citizens of the several states and Territories" the "liberty to take and hold their slaves within any of the Territories of the United States, or of the States to be formed therefrom" shall now be invalidated "as if the said act . . . had never been passed." This was an explicit repeal of the Compromise. In fact, it implied that slavery should be protected by law in all territories and states formed from the Louisiana Purchase. Douglas consented to incorporate Dixon's amendment, but warned, "It will raise a hell of a storm."[47]

On Saturday, January 21, the Cabinet discussed Douglas's bill. Not even Attorney General Caleb Cushing, a Massachusetts Democrat long known for obsequious devotion to southern interests, could stomach it. He knew it would cost the Democrats dozens of northern constituencies, and perhaps their House majority as well. But the southerners, especially Secretary of War Jefferson Davis, loved the new bill. And they decided they wanted President Pierce, the Democratic Party's official leader, to commit himself to the bill. So the next day Mason, Atchison, Hunter, Douglas, and Davis piled into two carriages and drove to the White House to pay a call on President Pierce. They found him in his parlor, observing the Sabbath, and they laid out the situation.

At his inauguration, Pierce had expressed northern Democrats' hopes when he said, "I fervently hope that the question [of slavery's expansion] is at rest, and that no sectional or fanatical excitement may again threaten the durability of our institutions or obscure the light of our prosperity." Most white Americans, shaken by the capital's constant struggle from 1846 to 1850, had agreed. Yet it only took an hour to persuade Pierce to saw into the republic's most important load-bearing pillars. Pierce even took out his pen and personally crafted the language that would doom him, his party, and the delicate political balances of the antebellum United States. The Missouri Compromise, he wrote, "had been superceded by the principles of the legislation of 1850"—in other words, the rest of the West would be something like New Mexico after the Compromise of 1850: open to slavery until either local elections or court decisions decided otherwise. The president was all in. What remained was to convince enough northern Democratic congressmen to vote for the bill.[48]

The next day, Monday, January 23, Douglas formally introduced the bill under a new name, for he now proposed two territories. One, Kansas, stretched west from the Missouri border; the other, Nebraska, from the latitude of Iowa north to Canada. Listeners took Douglas as implying that Kansas would be slave territory, and more northerly Nebraska free. Observers might also have mused that only a month before, they had assumed that Kansas was too far north to be a slave territory. Douglas and Pierce tried to make the bill seem palatable in the North by proclaiming to the press that the "great principle of the Nebraska bill" was not slavery extension, but self-determination. But the same observers might also consider that everywhere that slavery was permitted to go since 1787, it had gone.[49]

Yet opponents of slavery also saw opportunity in the Kansas-Nebraska bill. A group of congressmen seized it by publishing a document they called the "Appeal of the Independent Democrats"—although its primary authors were not actually Democrats, but Free Soil Ohioans Joshua Giddings and Salmon Chase. The "Appeal" deployed Free Soil arguments from the 1840s, backed now with proof in the form of Douglas's craven treason. Legalized slavery in the Nebraska Territory—for the "Appeal" didn't believe Kansas could contain it—would extend the slave lords' domain all the way north to the Canadian border and box freedom in. Overturning once "sacred" compromises, Douglas's "enormous crime" would enable slavery to block wage laborers and independent farmers from new territories, for "labor cannot be respected when any class of laborers is held in bondage." The "Independent Democrats" promised to fight Kansas-Nebraska to the end in Congress. And "if overcome in the impending struggle," they wrote, "we shall not submit. We shall go home to our constituents, erect anew the standard of freedom, and call on the people to come to the rescue of the country from the domination of slavery. We shall not despair, for the cause of human freedom is the cause of God."[50]

The battle that followed the introduction and simultaneous denunciation of the Kansas-Nebraska Act was the most thunderous in the history of congressional debate over the expansion of slavery. All the great Senate lions roared: Charles Sumner of Massachusetts, William Seward of New York, and Chase against the bill; and in its favor Douglas, Douglas, and again Douglas. The southern supporters sat back and let Douglas do his work. His squat, furious figure was on the floor almost every day, denouncing ministers who preached sermons against him, cursing the anti-slave-expansion *New York Tribune*, and recalling minute details of the Missouri Compromise debate in order to make his points. Eventually, on March 3, he forced a Senate vote and won it, 37 to 14. Most of the no votes were northern Whigs, while 14 northern Democrats joined 23 southerners in voting yes.[51]

The battle moved into the House. By now, "anti-Nebraska" mass meetings were being held across the North. "We went to bed one night, old-fashioned, conservative, compromise Union Whigs," textile-mill heir and former Cotton Whig Amos Lawrence recalled, "and waked up stark mad Abolitionists." In New York, merchants who had fought for the Compromise of 1850 now organized public meetings against the 1854 bill. There were ominous rumors of a new political party.[52] Northern Democrats strained against party-line pressure, but Douglas and the administration herded them relentlessly. Finally, Douglas's floor managers broke a filibuster. On May 22, the Kansas-Nebraska Act passed the House, 113 to 100, with 44 northern Democrats voting for and 42 against. After three bruising months, Douglas—his arms bound by his F Street captors—had repealed the Missouri Compromise.

The act destroyed the two-party system that had existed for the previous two decades. The Whig Party split along North-South lines and collapsed in the fall midterm elections. The new "Know-Nothing" Party, also known as the American Party, which captured 62 congressional districts, picked up many former Whigs with a "nativist," or anti-immigrant, message. But 37 of the 44 northern Democratic congressmen who had supported Kansas-Nebraska fell, most of them before the scythe of another new party. This was the Republicans, who suddenly emerged in 1854, coalescing around the ideals of the "Appeal of the Independent Democrats" and winning 46 House seats. Compared to their Free Soil or Liberty predecessors, Republicans appealed to a wider audience. They opposed the expansion of slavery both on moral grounds and because they believed the white man's frontier should be unsullied by black slaves. They also espoused a pro-industry policy, and eventually they would incorporate many of the nativists.[53]

It soon became obvious that the Republican coalition had the potential to win a commanding majority of northern voters. The Kansas-Nebraska Act destroyed not only the Missouri Compromise but also many of the other structures that had encouraged compromise on the question of the expansion of slavery. But the rise of the Republicans did not yet portend a new equilibrium between two national parties. Southern voters and politicians now believed more than ever that they would be able to make the expansion of slavery normative. In the debates, Douglas had tried to highlight the allegedly democratic essence of "popular sovereignty," insisting that Kansas citizens were free to choose against slavery. This was a smokescreen for what the act meant as both policy and politics. Salmon Chase insisted that

"Southern gentlemen" in Congress were now claiming that "they could take their slaves into" Kansas and "hold them there by virtue of the Constitution," no matter what the voters decided. Southern House members, in particular, agreed. They insisted that repeal of the Missouri Compromise meant the federal government's acknowledgment of their substantive-due-process doctrine. They planned to get final confirmation of the right of enslavers to take their "property" into federal territory by either victory in the demographic competition for control of the Kansas plains or success in getting the Supreme Court to overturn a territorial act forbidding slavery.[54]

Salmon Chase also insisted that those "southern gentlemen" did not speak for "the great majority" of white southerners. Yet the southern press, at least, agreed with the F Street vision. It wanted the expansion of slavery. The *Nashville Union and American* said the Kansas-Nebraska Act "saved [the South] from unconstitutional proscription and insult by Congress," while a Florida editor described it as a "mere act of justice," an acknowledgment of all citizens' "right to carry property" into the territories. For many southern whites, Kansas-Nebraska confirmed the substantive-due-process doctrine as law, even if they knew not all northerners would agree. From 1854 forward, the right to expand slavery into the territories would be an article of faith in southern popular politics. And no wonder—many of them had already lived its essence, the use of enslaved African Americans as the tools of their entrepreneurial pursuits. Even to those who did not own slaves, the unlimited use of enslaved African Americans as chattel property was associated with freedom, modernity, and liberal economic life.[55]

The southern white voting public was, however, uncertain about the best way to proceed: Was immediate enforcement of the ideas that John Calhoun had championed more important than remaining in the Union, or was more patience necessary for the ultimate extraction of one's natural right to transport slaves? One door had already closed. Kansas would not grow cotton, much less sugar, but Kansas-Nebraska's passage destroyed any chance to get Cuba. The island, momentarily in Young America's grasping reach, would have delivered enslavers tangible benefits. Southern enslavers would have exploited the island together with northern white allies, and Cuba would have become two or three Democratic states. The remainder of the nineteenth century would then have proceeded very differently.

But while the Young America and Mississippi Valley supporters of Cuba acquisition had waited for the island to fall into US hands, by means diplomatic or not-so-diplomatic, the F Street mess and their allies had moved. Even before the hammer of the 1854 fall elections fell on the Democrats, the

conflict over the Kansas-Nebraska bill had raised doubts about the possibility of acquiring Cuba during Pierce's presidency. "No More Slave States,"
proclaimed a New Jersey newspaper article. "There was a time when the
North would have consented to annex Cuba, but the Nebraska wrong has
rendered annexation forever impossible." The Ostend Manifesto, written by
Pierce's ambassadors to the Old World to push both Madrid and Washington to carry out the sale of Cuba, arrived on US shores right at the time of
the northern Democrats' stunning fall 1854 electoral defeat. The *New York
Tribune* quickly leaked its contents. Northern reaction was scornful. The administration—though it had run on Cuba in 1852—quickly disowned the
manifesto and seized the Cuban junta's New York–based ship. Over the next
few years, other filibustering schemes would entice young male adventurers—such as William Walker, whose 1856 invasion of Nicaragua ended in
his execution. But Cuba had been the real prize, and slave-owning expansionists had knocked it out of their own reach by forcing northern allies to
risk all their political capital on the Kansas-Nebraska bill.[56]

Now, concluded southern hard-liners like James Mason, Kansas controlled the "destiny" of the South. Yet free-soil settlers already outnumbered
pro-slave ones on the plains. Supposedly, "nine-tenths of the whole number of [land] claimants" who had squatted on the Kansas public domain by
the summer of 1854 planned to vote to exclude slavery. That fall, President
Pierce established a territorial government staffed by southerners and compliant northerners, such as Governor Andrew Reeder, who told southern
congressmen that he hoped to bring slaves to Kansas himself. He scheduled
an 1855 election for the territorial legislature. Senator Atchison urged white
Missourians to "do their duty" and secure "peace and quiet" at the Kansas
ballot box. The 5,000 Missourians who crossed the border to vote illegally
accounted for 75 percent of the ballots. All but one of the legislators elected
were proslavery. Reeder, feeling betrayed by the way southern radicals had
overturned even the façade of popular sovereignty, resigned.[57]

Meanwhile, the northern press and Republicans in Congress charged that
Democrats had adopted the idea that "the subjugation of white freemen may
be necessary that African slavery may succeed" in Kansas. In response to
electoral cheating, Amos Lawrence used his textile-mill fortune to fund the
"New England Emigrant Aid Company," an operation that paid free-state
settlers to move to Kansas—and armed them. In contrast, although an Alabama editor claimed that "every mail brings tidings of the gallant young
men buckling on their armor for the struggle that is to give Kansas to the
South," few southern slaveholders were willing to take that risk. Instead,

slavery expansionists relied on the Missourians—whom northerners called "border ruffians" and "pukes"—to win the battle through intimidation and illegal voting.[58]

Above all, slavery expansionists counted on their control over the levers of power in Washington to make the results of border-ruffian elections permanent. Stephen Douglas was already obediently pushing Kansas statehood through Congress. It looked like another fraudulent election would soon make Kansas the sixteenth slave state. On May 21, 1856, proslavery forces sacked and burned the free-soil town of Lawrence. In response, Massachusetts Senator Charles Sumner gave an outraged speech in which he denounced the administration, Douglas, and the South for what he called "the crime against Kansas." He threw in what sounded like personal attacks on Senator Andrew Butler, of the F Street mess. A couple of days later, Butler's South Carolina cousin, US representative Preston Brooks, assaulted Sumner at his Senate desk with a cane, beating the Massachusetts man into bloodied unconsciousness. "We much regret that the insolence of such men as Sumner renders such scenes occasionally necessary" to defend one's honor, wrote a Georgia editor. Northern newspapers, even racist ones like the *New York Herald*, took a different view—that southern "slave lords" respected free-state whites so little that they would inflict "nigger-driving" whippings on them, even in the Senate.[59]

During 1855, slave-state settlers had murdered several Kansas free-soil men as part of a campaign of intimidation. "Thick-headed bullies in the West [think] that the Northern and Eastern men will not fight. Never was a greater mistake," wrote one free-soil editor, for "the Free State men in Kansas will fight before they are disfranchised. . . . Mark the word." When a Kansas free-soil leader counseled patience, recently arrived Connecticut native John Brown called him "a perfect old woman." Brown brought his many sons, the financial backing of wealthy New York land magnate Gerrit Smith, and also weapons. On the night of May 24, 1856, Brown and his sons went on a killing spree. They stormed into proslavery cabins along Kansas's Pottawatomie Creek, pulled men out, and murdered them execution-style. Brown, who believed he was the agent of a vengeful God who hated slavery, intended the murders as exemplary political terrorism. The inevitable eruption of violence would force free-state men to fight for their convictions. Indeed, settlers spent the summer hunting each other across the territory. While another governor fled, nearby US Army units blocked armed northerners from entering Kansas. By the summer of 1856, in-migration had virtually stopped.[60]

THE "BLEEDING KANSAS" DRAMA took place against the backdrop of the 1856 presidential election. This was the first one contested by the brand new Republican Party, which nominated John Frémont. Although he was the grandson of a Virginia planter, Frémont ran on a platform focused on the single issue of blocking slavery's further expansion. The Americans, or Know-Nothings, who nominated ex-president Millard Fillmore of New York, were split between their northern and southern wings. General economic prosperity also had lessened the perceived relevance of their anti-immigrant message. The Democratic convention rejected both the disgraced Franklin Pierce and the compromised Stephen Douglas in favor of Pennsylvanian James Buchanan, who had spent the past four years overseas as an ambassador. But southern delegates knew him well. They expected him to cave to their dictation.[61]

During the summer of 1856, local Democratic activists began to report that party members were returning to the fold. The states in which slavery was legal contained 120 of the 149 electoral votes needed for victory. The southern Whigs were gone, so the Democrats could expect to win all 120 slave-state votes. This left them needing only a few northern states for victory. On election day, they managed to win Pennsylvania (Buchanan's home state), New Jersey, Indiana, and Illinois—and thus, the presidency. But southern expansionists could see that the old balance was gone. Population shifts meant that a Republican president could be elected without a single southern electoral vote. And Buchanan had won a minority of the popular vote, even though Frémont had received only 600 votes from southerners brave or inattentive enough to cast their ballots for a sectional party aimed at their section.[62]

Some northern Democrats, meanwhile, convinced themselves that Buchanan would be less subservient to the slave power than Pierce. They misread the willingness of the southerners to implement strategies aimed at forcing the entire nation to accept slave property as a truly national institution while they still had the leverage to extract such an outcome. Harriet and Dred Scott, however, had a much clearer sense of what they were dealing with. In 1852, the Missouri's supreme court's proslavery activist justices—reversing their own precedents in dozens of successful freedom suits—ruled that territories' antislavery laws did not overrule the property claims of Eliza Emerson, a Missouri citizen. The Scotts appealed to federal court, and Emerson handed off her property claim to her brother, changing the case's name to *Dred Scott v. Sanford*. It reached the US Supreme Court in 1856. Some of the questions were technical, but the biggest issues were as timely as it was possible for a case to be. Did Congress have the power to pass the slavery restrictions of the Missouri Compromise? Could the federal government extinguish or limit enslavers' property claims?[63]

Over the past thirty years, a series of presidents, starting with Andrew Jackson, had loaded the Court with a southern majority. Although Chief Justice Roger B. Taney had voluntarily manumitted all his human property decades earlier, the Court under his leadership, in cases ranging back to *Prigg v. Pennsylvania* and beyond, had steadily moved toward establishing enslavers' property claims as a fundamental, natural right. This Court increasingly ranked the property claims of entrepreneurial, mobile enslavers higher than the rights of legislative majorities—even congressional ones. The Court was coming to accept the claims, enunciated by Calhoun and others, that slaveholders' property rights meant that neither the federal nor the state governments could limit enslavers' mobility, and that neither could refuse to help enforce enslavers' power over forced migrants or fugitives.[64]

On March 4, 1857, James Buchanan took the oath of office—the fifteenth consecutive president for whom the issue of forced migration had been an irritant. In his inaugural address, Buchanan announced that there was no need for Americans to feel agitated about Kansas, or about whether it had been just for Congress to revoke the Missouri Compromise. For soon the Supreme Court would settle all key questions about slavery and expansion. Two days later, Taney's Court issued a decision. Six of the nine justices agreed that the Scotts had no standing to sue for their freedom. Taney himself delivered an opinion that laid out the case against the Scotts' freedom in its most extreme form, including a claim that the Court's majority agreed with him that the Missouri Compromise was unconstitutional. While Justice Peter Daniel (a Virginian) restated the "common-property" doctrine to explain why Congress could not exclude slavery from territories, Taney's argument was a sophisticated and lengthy rendering of Calhounian substantive due process. "The Federal Government can exercise no power over person or property" belonging to a migrant into the territories, including the forced migrants they brought with them, "beyond what [the Constitution] confers, nor lawfully deny any right which it has reserved"—including the right to have one's property protected from unreasonable search and seizure, such as by legislative emancipation.[65]

The decision immediately came in for massive criticism. Many Republicans rejected as illegitimate the Court's attempt to overrule majority opposition to the expansion of slavery. They insisted that the Constitution gave Congress the power to make basic law for the territories. Some rejected the

Court itself as illegitimate. Horace Greeley's *New York Tribune*, the most famous paper in the United States at the time, described the Court's decision as "false statements and shallow sophistries" no better than what one could gather in any "Washington Bar-room." The concept of due process had been around since the Magna Carta, one critic pointed out, but only in the 1830s had anyone discovered that it prevented legislatures from abolishing the use of human beings as property.[66]

Historians have generally sustained the dissenters' insistence that Taney was incorrect to claim that the Scotts could not sue because no people of African descent had ever been accounted as US citizens. Indeed, at least five states clearly counted free African Americans as citizens in 1789 when they ratified the Constitution. On other grounds, historians and contemporary critics alike are less persuasive. For instance, some insist that the due-process clause in the Fifth Amendment, which mentions "property," does not include slave property, and hence does not protect slavery from seizure by congressional lawmaking. But as Justice Peter Daniel pointed out, with its fugitive slave clause the Constitution does more to specify enslaved people as a specific type of "property" than it does for any other kind. In such a case it seems less reasonable to think that the enslavers who wrote the due-process clause would not have intended it to encompass enslaved human beings.

Some critics insisted that in his most sweeping claims Taney did not speak for the whole Court. However, the fact is that he could assemble a majority of the justices behind almost every conclusion. Other critics insisted that Taney wrote as a mere partisan. *Dred Scott* was emphatically a political decision, of course, but then, so are most Court decisions. The justices could easily have ruled against the Scotts on procedural grounds and left the deeper issues alone. Instead, like the widow Eliza Emerson, and like the congressmen who demanded Kansas-Nebraska, Taney and his Court allies sought out a constitutional Armageddon: a final battle to settle all questions and usher in an age in which the enslaved had no allies. They wanted to stand in the place of God, hear a Kentucky woman's prayer—Will I live to see the end?—and reply: No, you will not.[67]

Moreover, Taney and his allies made the *Dred Scott* decision partisan in favor of everybody but African Americans and Republicans. Taney's attack on black citizenship recycled Stephen Douglas's rhetorical strategy of focusing northern white anger on black people. When the New Orleans *Picayune* said *Scott v. Sandford* (the court misspelled the enslaver's last name) rendered unconstitutional "the whole basis of the Black Republican organization," northern Democratic newspapers concurred: the Court had shattered "the anti-slavery platform of the late great Northern Republican party into atoms," said the *New York Herald*. While some furious Republicans advocated extralegal action to overrule the use of the judicial branch to advance a minority's political agenda, they should not have been surprised by the court's decision. The decision reaffirmed one of the most significant traditions in the history of the United States: the construction of white people's futures on the backs and from the hands of enslaved African Americans, a process piloted by southerners, who always found many northern allies. The Constitution's most important compromises had been created by enslavers and their closest northern allies to sustain slavery's expansion. The constitutional system had sustained that process for seventy years. And Taney's Court was insisting more clearly than ever that the price of union was still the right of enslavers to treat enslaved people as fully chattel property.[68]

*"All the powers on earth seem rapidly combining against him. Mammon is after him . . . philosophy follows, and the Theology of the day is fast joining the cry,"*— and Law had brought Dred and Harriet Scott and their daughters down as prey. So said ex-congressman Abraham Lincoln in an Illinois speech in the summer of 1857. He pushed his listeners to see how enslavers were engineering an ever-tighter perimeter around 4 million human beings; collectively a Gulliver tied down, stretched out on a continent that was now to be one giant whipping-machine. *"One after another they have closed the heavy iron doors upon him,"* said Lincoln, continuing the metaphor. Partisan politics, the constitution, half the churches in the country, and a vast array of business interests had all been twisted and leveraged to bind the enslaved as if in a prison cell *"bolted with a lock of a hundred keys, which can never be unlocked without the concurrence of every key; the keys in the hands of a hundred different men, and they scattered to a hundred different and distant places; and they stand musing as to what invention, in all the dominions of mind and matter, can be produced to make the impossibility of his escape more complete than it is"* (italics added).[69]

After returning to Illinois in 1849 from his single term in Congress, Lincoln had stepped back from the political whirl. But in 1854 news of Douglas's Kansas-Nebraska Act had rendered him "thunderstruck." He helped organize the Illinois Republican Party, and, freed from the need of cooperating with southern Whigs, he found his distinctive voice. He began to insist, in every speech he gave, that the expansion of slavery would always escape the categories and compromises in which white America tried to contain and store it. The entrepreneurial destruction and re-creation of everything that forced migration touched went beyond white abolitionists' moral critique of slavery as a sin. It went beyond the regional arrogance that insisted slavery was archaic, for, efficient or not, slavery had locked southerners to the continued expansion of the institution. "We would be as they were," he warned northerners, were all our wealth invested directly in the cotton machine. What was now happening, Lincoln insisted, was that in order to protect slavery's future growth, the principles and institutions which had offered people like Lincoln opportunities for freedom unprecedented in the history of ordinary tillers of soil and hewers of trees were being twisted. Shut every door and arm every bolt, and you would replace possibilities still undreamed with slavery everlasting. Immeasurable misery was the future for those locked in the prison house. And for the millions of people around the globe who hoped the modern world would bring liberation from ancient tyrannies, the death of the promise of freedom for all in the United States meant the death of the world's hopes for liberation.

Lincoln's fears might have come true. Many factors already rendered the situation of southern expansionists more promising than at any point since 1837. Support for national expansion remained high, and an unparalleled stretch of economic prosperity sustained enslavers' revenues at previously unimagined heights. Enslavers had in their pocket an opinion from the Supreme Court and an act of Congress (Kansas-Nebraska) that opened new possibilities. Democrats, North and South, could have been satisfied to lay the Dred Scott decision as the last brick on a constitutional and political-economic edifice that ended the debate about the expansion of slavery. That could have left "the Democracy," the Democratic Party, as the dominant national political organization.

Once the mechanisms of 4 million locks were armed, the entire array of defenses against freedom might never have been unlocked. Yet once again, as in 1837, the overuse of leverage—this time political, rather than financial—created a disastrous outcome for southern enslavers. In the summer of 1857, Kansas had held an election for delegates to a constitutional convention. The free-state majority boycotted the election, while Missourians again poured over the border to vote illegally. Of 19,000 actual male residents, 85 percent did not cast ballots. So when 60 delegates assembled in October 1857 at the town of Lecompton, all 60 were proslavery. They proceeded to write the most proslavery state constitution in US history. Its Article VII parroted the Calhounian doctrine: "The right of property is before and higher than any constitutional sanctions, and the right of the owner of a slave to such slave and its increase is the same and as inviolable as the right of the owner to any property whatsoever." (Number 23 in the constitution's "Bill of Rights" read "Free negroes shall not be permitted to live in this State under any circumstance.") The convention decreed that the 200-odd slaves already in Kansas could never be freed, even by constitutional amendment.[70]

Free-staters boycotted the ratification ballot as well, and the proslavery voters who participated approved the Lecompton constitution by a tally of 6,000 to 600. As northerners watched this travesty unfold each day on the pages of their telegraph-updated newspapers, southern Democrats pressed for instant congressional acceptance of the undemocratic document, which would be the last step in confirming Kansas as a slave state. The Buchanan administration fell humbly into line. But northern Democrats, led by Stephen Douglas, realized that "the Lecompton fraud" rendered absurd their previous claim that the "popular sovereignty" idea they'd used to sell the Kansas-Nebraska bill was about giving the choice to the voter. If these Democrats wanted to win elections in Illinois, New York, or New Hampshire, they had to repudiate Lecompton. Douglas knew he was fighting for his political life. He turned his thunderous energy against the Democrats who were loyal to Buchanan and his pro-southern administration.

At the same time that the Democratic Party began to scratch and claw itself to pieces in Congress, the fighting in Kansas began to generate economic fallout. The number of emigrants riding the rails west through Chicago toward Kansas plummeted from 100,000 in 1856 to 10,000 in 1858. The market for Kansas land warrants vanished, imploding speculative schemes, while railroad stocks plunged in price. Major northern banks collapsed under the weight of failed investments in both. The collapses became the Panic of 1857, which put hundreds of thousands out of work in the North. Yet factors continued to buy southern cotton, because international demand remained high. Remembering how northern debt collectors had wagged their fingers during the 1840s, proslavery writers chortled that this time, "the *slave labor staples of the South* will furnish the means for extrication from commercial indebtedness." Still, while southern nationalists savored schadenfreude, Republicans, true to their own dogma, insisted that somehow "slavelords" must have caused the panic. And Lecompton kept political wind in their sails. Northern Democrats up for reelection in 1858, including Stephen Douglas, were vulnerable.[71]

Abraham Lincoln decided to challenge Douglas for his Senate seat. Lincoln used the election to test his arguments, in particular his claim that any policy that enabled further forced migration to occur—like Douglas's "popular sovereignty"—inevitably led to the subordination of all political and economic freedom to the needs of enslavers. In the seven Lincoln-Douglas debates of August to October 1858, the challenger grounded the antislavery argument on a foundation that held true whether the listener was an open racist like David Wilmot, an abolitionist, or something in between. Lincoln insisted that slavery contradicted what he understood to be the fundamental truths of American identity, particularly the natural-rights claims of the Declaration: "If slavery is not wrong, nothing is wrong." Lincoln acknowledged the difficulty of ending slavery in a day, a week, or a year. Slavery, he said, was like a gruesome metastatic cancer growing on a man's neck. "He dares not cut it out. He bleeds to death if he does, directly." Slavery, he said, was also like a rattlesnake that crawled into "a bed where the children are sleeping. Would I do right to strike him there? I might hurt the children." Or the awakened serpent "might bite the children." But leave it coiled in the bed, let the cancer grow, and the result was also death. Permit expansion, and, as the past seventy years had shown, you deepen American slavery's severity, entrench more securely its "immense pecuniary interest."[72]

For the Union, Lincoln insisted, cannot "endure permanently half slave and half free. . . . It will become all one thing or the other." His ultimate opponents, the slavery-expansionist politicians of the South, agreed with his analysis of slavery as a system that needed geographic growth in order to function. And, Lincoln warned, they would try to ensure that growth would happen by trying to turn the entire United States into slave territory. This would limit all Americans' rights, making people in the free states as subservient to the thought-policing of proslavery orthodoxy as those in the South. Historians have dismissed the idea that slavery could have returned to the free states. But perhaps his claim was not implausible. At the Ottawa, Illinois, debate, Lincoln asked: "What is necessary for the nationalization of slavery? It is simply the next Dred Scott decision. It is merely for the Supreme Court to decide that no *State* under the Constitution can exclude it, just as they have already decided that under the Constitution neither Congress nor the Territorial Legislature can do it." Even as Lincoln and Douglas squabbled, the case of *Lemmon v. People of New York* was moving toward the Supreme Court. In it, a Virginia slaveholder who was taking his slaves to Texas via New York protested that the latter state had violated his rights when it declared his slaves to be free because he had kept them in Manhattan during an extended visit. A Taney-led Supreme Court might well rule, on the broadest substantive-due-process grounds, that no state could deny slaveholding citizens of the United States the right to hold their human property.[73]

Lincoln acknowledged that most northern whites were reluctant to imagine a society in which African Americans could claim the rights of the free, much less the rights of the equal. In recent years, Lincoln critics have cherry-picked quotations from these acknowledgments to "prove" that Lincoln was a "racist." He did use cagey qualifications here, especially during the debates in "Little Egypt" in southern Illinois, where Douglas was particularly successful at using race-baiting to fire up virulently anti-black crowds. But he stuck to his central points. Slavery undermined freedom's future for whites as well as blacks. It could not be allowed to expand, or it would go everywhere and change everything. Though its excision must not be rushed destructively, it must begin, and excision should begin with the defeat of the Douglas Democrats who had long enabled southern expansionists to get their way.[74]

Douglas fought both at home and in Washington to prove that the northern wing of the Democratic Party had not been turned into a front by which enslavers defrauded northerners of votes. Through late 1857 and the first part of 1858, southerners in Congress and the supine Buchanan administration demanded a vote on Kansas's admission as a slave state under the Lecompton constitution. Douglas and his loyalists among the northern Democrats in Congress now made a stand. In April 1858, after a furious debate that featured a brawl between thirty congressmen, which, among other things, dislodged Mississippi Congressman William Barksdale's previously unsuspected toupee, the House rejected the Lecompton bill. The Senate insisted (over Buchanan's protests) on returning the proposed constitution to the territory's actual residents for another opportunity to reject or ratify. In August, free-state Kansas voters, finally turning out to vote—now that they had a fair chance—turned down the Lecompton constitution.[75]

Douglas's stand against Lecompton held Illinois Democrats' votes to the party line in November 1858. The party eked out a narrow victory that translated into his reelection as US senator. But southern Democratic strategists, seeing that powerful elements of the northern wing were trying to muster enough defiance to preserve themselves, planned a test that would require either commitment to slavery's expansion or full-scale breakup of the national party.[76]

IN MAY 1858, PROSLAVERY Kansans murdered five settlers outside their cabins at a free-state settlement. John Brown responded with a raid into Missouri, killing one enslaver and carrying off eleven enslaved people to Canada. Early the next year, Brown went to Boston and met with a group of wealthy abolitionists who admired his Kansas work. They included his backer Gerrit Smith, abolitionist Unitarian minister Theodore Parker, and Thomas Wentworth Higginson, the epitome of a Boston aristocrat. The "Secret Six," as they called themselves, seduced by Brown's Old Testament–prophet manner of carrying himself, agreed to support the plan he unfolded. Brown proposed that he and a group of raiders seize the federal armory at Harpers Ferry, Virginia, where the Blue Ridge Mountains meet the Potomac River. If he controlled the armory, Brown believed, slaves from fifty miles around would flock to his vanguard.

The backers tingled vicariously, righteously. Here was a northerner truly willing to meet southern bullying with unblinking violence. They agreed to send Brown money and weapons, and he established a hideout near Chambersburg, Pennsylvania. From there he began recruiting commandos: his sons, a dozen or so other white men, and five African Americans. The Secret Six also set up a secret meeting between the scourge of Kansas and Frederick Douglass, the most prominent African °American of the era. In a quarry outside of Chambersburg, Brown tried to °persuade Douglass to join him. Douglass, whose two decades in slavery had given him a far more realistic understanding of enslavers' massive power, warned him that Kansas bushwhacking against soft targets, plus abolitionist propaganda, had led Brown and his backers to the unrealistic belief that slaveholding society would crumble easily. An abolitionist attack on the federal government not only was futile but might turn public opinion against a movement that many northern whites already saw as irresponsibly radical.

On the evening of October 16, 1859, without Douglass, Brown and eighteen warriors slipped into Harpers Ferry, a small town in Virginia (now West Virginia) perched on high cliffs over the main routes into the rich Shenandoah Valley—including the slave-driver route to Kentucky. Brown and his men quickly seized the town's federal armory, which held a massive cache of arms. He sent detachments to nearby plantations to try to recruit rebels willing to rise up against slavery, and also cut telegraph lines and stopped the eastbound evening train.

The attack went wrong from the start. Brown's men killed a train conductor—ironically, a free African American—and then inexplicably let the train continue down the tracks to Washington, bringing news of the raid. Brown's recruiting parties brought only four people back from nearby slave quarters. The next morning, local militia forced their way into town, shooting one of Brown's men—an ex-slave named Dangerfield Newby. As he fell, Newby clutched at the despairing letters in his pocket. They came from his wife, Harriet, who was enslaved with their children in northern Virginia. Her last one had been written on August 16: "It is said Master is in want of monney if so I know not what time he may sell me an then all my bright hopes of the futer are blasted." The price of slaves at the Richmond consignment market had risen above $1,000 for women like Harriet, and her owner had changed his mind about letting Newby buy her freedom. Now some militiamen paused to mutilate Newby's corpse, cutting off his testicles and his ears as souvenirs. The rest forced Brown and his remaining men to make their stand in the armory.[77]

The next morning, US Marines from Washington under an army colonel named Robert E. Lee stormed the stronghold. The federals killed many raiders, including two of Brown's sons, and captured the badly wounded Brown. Though Brown's crimes were clearly federal, Buchanan allowed the state of Virginia to try him. The trial was a procedural travesty, but there was no lack of evidence for his conviction for inciting insurrection. Before his sentencing, Brown was allowed to speak. The New Testament on which he had sworn to tell the whole truth, he noted, commanded him to "remember them that are in bonds, as bound with them." As if he were bound himself, he had taken up arms to defend slaves' right to freedom. If his sacrifice brought justice closer, then he would gladly now "mingle my blood further with the blood of my children and with the blood of millions in this slave country whose rights are disregarded by wicked, cruel, and unjust enactments." On December 2, 1859, with hundreds of militia guarding the execution site at Charles Town against a rescue attempt that never came, the state of Virginia hanged John Brown. Brown's wife recovered his corpse and sent it to their farm in New York for burial. The bodies of the two African Americans executed with him—South Carolina fugitive Shields Green and freeman John Copeland—were taken by medical students and used as dissection cadavers.[78]

For seventy years, southern and northern economic and political elites—and many average white citizens—had cooperated to extract profit and power from the forced movement and exploitation of enslaved people's bodies and minds. Always, the proslavery forces had made the rest of the United States choose between profitable expansion of the slave country or economic slowdown. Between slavery and disunion. Between supporting a party turned into a colonized host for viral proslavery dogma, or defeat in national elections. Between bills for expanding slavery into Kansas, or passing up the opportunity to build a transcontinental railroad.

John Brown and his band of futile revolutionaries signaled that the game was changing. The clarity of Lincoln's arguments had also raised the warning, but he at least had lost in 1858, and perhaps northerners would once more flinch from containing the expansion of slavery in 1860. But somehow, in losing, Dangerfield Newby, Shields Green, John Copeland, and John Brown had won. For now southerners believed they had to choose: run the risks created by making good on the threat to leave the Union, or remain in the Union and risk another Harpers Ferry. Someone discovered a map at Brown's Maryland hideout. Newspapers breathlessly detailed the additional targets marked on it. Whites began to look at any neighbor of uncertain origin, eyeing them as potential John Browns, seeing every newspaper report of a local murder as part of a wider plot. William Keitt, Florida slave owner and brother of secessionist politician Lawrence Keitt, had his throat slit in the middle of the night by his own slaves. A traveler from South Carolina was seized in deepest Alabama by a local mob—although eventually, when he proved that he owned slaves back home, they let him go. A Massachusetts map-dealer, peddling his wares in Georgia, was picked up by "vigilance committees." An Irishman in Columbia, South Carolina, dared to express the opinion that slavery drove down wage rates for white laborers. A mob stripped him naked. State legislators ordered a slave to beat him, and then they poured boiling tar on his bleeding skin and doused him with feathers. The northern newspaper that interviewed the Irishman when he made it back to New York reported that "he had always voted with the Democratic Party."[79]

Rumors of slave conspiracies and news of lynchings competed with each other throughout the anxious winter and spring of 1859–1860, and alongside them were stories about northern whites who heaped hagiographic praise on John Brown as he dangled. National Republican politicians disavowed the raid, but even moderate opponents of slavery expansion adopted Brown as a symbol of uncompromising resistance against much-resented slavelords. The city of Albany, New York, fired one hundred salutes to John Brown on December 2, starting at the scheduled time of his execution. Northern middle-class public culture depicted him as Christlike. Ralph Waldo Emerson wrote that John Brown would "make the gallows as glorious as the cross." And Henry David Thoreau, last heard from as a pacifist proponent of nonviolence, and a non-taxpaying protestor against the Mexican War, said that "for manly directness and force, and for simple truth," all the talk of politicians could not equal "the few casual remarks of crazy John Brown." Brown was, Thoreau believed, "the first northern man whom the slaveholder has learned to respect."[80]

Certainly Brown had forced slaveholders to make new calculations. And now the long tide of slavery's expansion across the continent and hegemony over national politics seemed to poise at a crest: Crash, or roll on forward? The crop of cotton in 1859 was astonishing—almost 2 billion pounds of clean fiber in 4 million bales. Slavery's productivity was higher than ever—some

700 pounds per enslaved man, woman, and child in the cotton country, twenty-two times the rate in 1790. The old rules of political gravity—the way 4 million slaves multiplied by three-fifths of a vote for each, plus 4 million (and climbing) bales of cotton, plus the needs of northern politicians to maintain interregional coalitions—had all worked to keep a national minority at the controls of national policy.

But as southern Democrats looked toward the upcoming 1860 national party convention, they feared that the failure of Lecompton, the rise of the Republicans, and the possibility of an emerging consensus in the North had seemingly arrested their project of writing entrepreneurial slavery expansion permanently into the rules of the American political system. They had told themselves that their ultimate recourse was the right to secede from the Union. Secession had become a truism of southern public discourse, and disunion now seemed far more attractive than it had in the 1850 crisis. The boom decade had erased southerners' fears that their economic system was either weak or decaying. Because "Cotton Is King," as South Carolina's James H. Hammond brayed in 1858 on the floor of the Senate, "no power on earth dare make war on cotton." The North would not dare to resist their going, and cotton would allow the South to continue its decade of prosperity indefinitely.

Although Mississippi Senators Jefferson Davis and Albert Gallatin Brown introduced Senate resolutions operationalizing *Dred Scott* by requiring the federal government to impose a slave code on all territories, many politically active southern citizens had by early 1860 abandoned the idea of seeking solutions from normal politics. State legislatures across the South were stocking their militia armories. Some southern representatives in Washington were plotting a coup: they themselves would seize the Capitol, and then would call their home states to send in their militias to defend a provisional government. The South Carolina legislature sent an emissary to Virginia counterparts shaken by Harpers Ferry to discuss a cooperative secession from the Union. The Mississippi legislature called for a southern convention to be held at Atlanta to consider mass exit from the Union. Florida and Alabama counterparts voted for cooperative secession.[81]

In the end, the coup that southwestern Democrats led was against their own party. Luck—or doom—had scheduled Charleston, South Carolina, as the site of the Democratic Party's April 1860 national convention. There, the heirs of three score and ten years of entrepreneurship on the cotton and sugar frontiers planned to force the party to bow before them and commit to making slavery's endless expansion a matter of national policy. Or else, as the Alabama state party had instructed its delegates, secede from the convention—what South Carolina's Robert Barnwell Rhett called "demolition of the party."[82]

The southerners opened the convention by insisting that the national party's platform had to incorporate the federal slave code that Brown and Davis had proposed in the US Senate. The northern delegates—a majority in the convention hall—refused. Take a slave-code platform before the free-state electorate, they warned, and when the dust settled there would be left "of the Democratic party of the North scarcely one [candidate] to tell that there were Democrats living there." You are "telling us," said a delegate from Ohio, "that we are an inferior class of beings, that we shall not assume to have or express any opinions," but only serve the southerners' interests. "Gentlemen," he said, "you mistake us. We will not do it." The delegations of Alabama, Mississippi, Louisiana, South Carolina, Florida, Arkansas, and Texas stomped out. The Georgians complained that their cotton-growing counterparts should have left over a different issue—the reopening of the international slave trade—and then they, too, left. Caleb Cushing, chairing the convention, ruled that a presidential nominee needed two-thirds of the *original* delegates. It was mathematically impossible for Stephen Douglas, who after successfully defying Buchanan on Lecompton had the virtually united support of northern Democrats, to get the required number of delegates.[83]

The remaining delegates decided to reconvene in Baltimore on June 18. There the northern Democrats refused to reseat the Charleston seceders, who decided to meet across the street. Northern delegates in the main convention voiced their anger: Slave owners wanted to "rule or ruin"; "ruling niggers all their lives, [they] thought they could rule white men just the same." They nominated Douglas. In the other convention, the secessionist Democrats wrote a pro-slavery-everywhere-and-forever platform. They nominated John Breckinridge—Buchanan's Kentucky vice president. Meanwhile, a group of old Whigs—most of them well over sixty—added a third presidential candidate to the mix by naming Tennessee's John Bell to the ticket of their so-called Constitutional Union Party. Many in the border states would vote for Bell as a possible way out of the madness.[84]

But the Black Republicans, as the race-baiting Democrats called them, had already nominated their candidate. Meeting in Chicago, the party's chieftains rejected their most prominent national figures, William Seward and Salmon Chase. Although these men were popular among loyalists in party strongholds, in Pennsylvania and the Northwest they were viewed as radical abolitionists. The Republicans needed an electoral-vote majority. So the party turned to Abraham Lincoln. He could appear to lower North voters as a moderate who didn't exude the moral triumphalism that clung to Chase and Seward. Yet he could also maintain the Republican case against further compromise. In 1858 against Douglas and in a widely reprinted speech at New York's Cooper Institute in early 1860, Lincoln had argued that ending expansion would kill off slavery over the course of the next century. This solution and timeframe meant that white voters did not have to wrap their minds around an immediate transformation of racial hierarchies.[85]

Lincoln's nomination may have decided the outcome of the election of 1860. The South was going to split its votes between Breckinridge and Bell. The Republicans counted on New England, Ohio, Illinois, and the far Northwest. If they also won New York and Pennsylvania, they'd have the presidency. The party organized clubs of "Wide-Awakes"—young male Lincoln supporters—who made it their business to rumpus and campaign "wherever the fight is hottest," as the Hartford, Connecticut, club put it. State party bosses, such as Simon Cameron of Pennsylvania and Thurlow Weed of New York, also unleashed their grimy turnout mechanisms. On November 6, Lincoln carried every free state except New Jersey. In a four-way contest, he won 40 percent of the popular vote, collecting 180 of the 303 electoral votes.[86]

Despite Democrats' claims that Republican victory would mean both the end of slavery and the handing-over of white women to black men, Breckinridge had not won the upper South. Some Union sentiment survived there. Without those states and their large white populations, an independent South would be smaller, its army far weaker. Now that the national electorate had chosen a "Black Republican" president, would the cotton states now back down from their politicians' threats to secede from the Union? If they did secede, would their white citizens really resort to arms if the federal government moved—like Jackson in the nullification winter of 1832–1833—to coerce the states?

In late October, South Carolina governor William Gist had written his fellow slave-state executives to ask if they were prepared to call secession conventions if Lincoln won. The Republicans frankly stated that they intended to block the expansion of slavery, with the goal of bringing about the ultimate extinction of slavery. Alabama, Mississippi, Georgia, and Florida all replied affirmatively but hoped South Carolina would take the lead. Now, on November 10, the South Carolina state legislature set an early December date for a state convention of delegates to consider secession. The other cotton states did the same. The South Carolina election was held, the convention met, and on December 20, delegates voted unanimously for secession. Within three weeks, conventions in Mississippi and Florida also voted for secession. Alabama, Georgia, and Louisiana followed, and then, on February 1, 1861, Texas also seceded.[87]

Perhaps the majority of whites in the cotton states really felt the same imperatives as the entrepreneurs who were threatened by the closing-off of expansion, and perhaps they did not. But political leaders manipulated convention elections to make sure they would yield the desired result. The options offered to voters were limited to one pathway to secession or another—either "immediate," or "cooperative," the latter meaning they preferred to wait for other states to secede first. Even those choosing "cooperationist" secession were derided as "submissionists" willing to truckle under to Yankee tyranny. Convention delegates were also significantly wealthier than the overall white population. The median Mississippi delegate owned fifteen slaves, the Alabama delegate thirteen, the Georgians fourteen, and the South Carolinians thirty-seven. Slaveholder cooperationists elected from non-planter districts often went to state capitals under instruction from their constituents: slow down secession. Yet once they were surrounded by their economic peers, they changed their positions and gave their conventions near-unanimous outcomes.[88]

Still, even if the enslavers who dominated the conventions rigged the process of secession in order to defend the proslavery state they were creating, they ultimately had to appeal to the yeomen and poor whites whose doubts (and, in some cases, commitment to the Union) they had procedurally suppressed. Ever since the end of the Civil War, Confederate apologists have put out the lie that the southern states seceded and southerners fought to defend an abstract constitutional principle of "states' rights." That falsehood attempts to sanitize the past. Every convention's participants made it explicit: they were seceding because they thought secession would protect the future of slavery. Lincoln's victory led Deep South slaveholders to claim that only secession could save the South from being "stripped," as one Alabama editor, a former Douglas supporter, said, "of 25 hundred millions of slave property & to have loose among us 4,000,000 of freed blacks."[89]

From Missouri to Texas, from Wilmot through Kansas-Nebraska and Lecompton, political debates had been about whether or not slavery could expand, not whether or not the federal government would interfere with it in the states where it existed. But secessionists feared that they could not convince the non-slaveholding white southern majority to abandon the Union just to protect entrepreneurs' access to future cotton frontiers. Instead, they proclaimed that by electing Republicans, the North had declared its commitment to "equality between the white and negro races," as an emissary sent from the Mississippi convention told his Georgia counterparts. Not only had the Republican Party declared its goal to be abolition, but it "now de-mand[s] . . . equality in the right of suffrage, equality in the honors and emoluments of office, equality in the social circle, equality in the right of matrimony." Not only would emancipation mean that non-planters would lose the chance to move up in the world—a chance that ownership of even one slave could represent. Worse, the everyday distinctions that gave status to all whites, especially men, would vanish. Lincoln's victory left only one choice. Secede, or your neighbor's field "hand" will marry your daughter. Secede, or offer up your "wives and daughters to pollution and violation to gratify the lust of half-civilized Africans." Republican domination, the emissary concluded, meant a "saturnalia of blood," "a war of extermination" that would lead to the destruction of the white people by "assassinations" and "amalgamation," or rape.[90]

If racial fears led non-slaveholders to accept the proslavery argument, en-slavers could continue to plan for slavery to resume its modernist, capitalist, entrepreneurial, creative, destructive, right-hand-empowering course of ex-pansion. They could continue to deploy the apparatus of forced migration and slave trading that commodified black bodies, rhetorically breaking them into pieces for more profitable use by white people, and creating isolated and rapeable black women. Yet the rhetoric of fear makes one wonder if the speakers knew that common white men feared the South's volatile, highly unequal, extractive, exploitative economy, and knew that without the safety net of racial privilege—and slavery was that net's strongest cord—they would fall into complete poverty and degradation. Perhaps, too, the speakers' horrors projected their own scrambled-together desires and anxieties about life in a migratory, expanding modern economy where fortunes were made and lost at a drop; the conflation of sexual force and political power; and the mixing of sexual pleasure with the use of enslaved bodies for making wealth.

While these arguments worked well enough in the seven cotton-focused states, non-slaveholder majorities in upper-South states stomped on the brakes. The February 4 election for a Virginia state convention produced only 32 immediate secessionists out of 153 total delegates. Despite the com-mitment of James Mason and others to Calhounite ideology, less wealthy, less ideologically committed citizens of the Old Dominion were not ready. In the same month, the voters of Arkansas, Tennessee, Kentucky, Missouri, and North Carolina also rejected secession—at least for the time being.[91]

Meanwhile, in Washington, senators and representatives scrambled to resurrect interregional compromise at the federal level. Kentucky's John

Crittenden put together a committee of thirteen senators whose task was finding a way out of the crisis. In the tradition of Henry Clay, Crittenden offered an "omnibus" of six constitutional amendments and four resolutions. Most significant was the amendment that would restore the Missouri Compromise line and commit the federal government to enforcing slavery south of 36°30' North forever. Another would have forbidden any future change to these amendments, the three-fifths clause, or the fugitive-slave clause of the Constitution.[92] If adopted by Congress—and three-fourths of the state legislatures would also have had to approve them to add them to the Constitution—Crittenden's proposals would have made slavery perpetual in the United States. They would have added new enticements to filibustering. Here was the pattern of compromise, reasserted: a placating response to southern brinksmanship.

The passage of these amendments might not have persuaded the cotton states to reverse their charge toward political independence. The white population of those seven states was now swept up in a level of violent political fervor that made it hard for anyone to suggest a change in course. A commitment to the idea that southerners constituted a separate political community was already becoming its own justification. In the meantime, southern political leaders still in Washington over December 1860 and January 1861—such as Mississippi's Jefferson Davis—remained cool toward the various plans for compromise.

While many Republican Party leaders anxiously participated in the compromise negotiations, the president-elect took a different position. To Thurlow Weed, master of the New York Republican machine, Lincoln wrote, "Let there be no compromise on the question of *extending* slavery. If there be, all our labor is lost, and ere long, must be done again." The people had spoken. They voted for a platform that opposed all expansion of slavery. Lincoln refused to abandon the results of the election. His insistence that "the tug has to come, and better now," stiffened the resolve of congressional Republicans, who decided to reject the 36°30' extension—though they did offer to admit New Mexico as a slave state.

Some historians have criticized Lincoln for these moves. He and other northerners allegedly misread the South, believing that secessionists were only bullies playing a game of chicken to force the North to back down again. The result of the failure to compromise, this line of thinking argues, was mass death. Such critics of Lincoln's "interference" with compromise bolster their claims with cost/benefit analyses that assume that slavery would have ended in a few decades even without war. Thus the primary positive gain of the war is accounted as thirty years of freedom for several million people, versus, in the loss column, the deaths of about 700,000 Americans, plus the massive financial cost of the war.[93]

Yet the assumption that slavery would have ended is based on the idea that it was an inefficient form of labor that would soon be weeded out by economic realities. By 1860, this system had been growing for seventy years at a rate unprecedented in human history. It had broken its supposed limits again and again. Moreover, in very practical terms, the Crittenden plan itself would have rendered the end of slavery far more difficult to accomplish. And, as Lincoln wrote in January, adopt Crittenden, and the past tells us that "a year will not pass, till we shall have to take Cuba as a condition upon which they will stay in the Union." In any case, the seceding states sent no emissaries to Washington or Springfield that winter, offered no bargains that included renunciation of disunion.[94]

On March 4, Lincoln stood before a crowd in Washington to take the same oath that Andrew Jackson had taken. Thirty-two years later, the democracy that Jackson's crowd drank in had dissolved. Since late January, armed men had seized most of the federal institutions in the lower South. Representatives of the seven cotton states had met in Montgomery, Alabama, and declared themselves the "Confederate States of America." They named Mississippi senator Jefferson Davis as their president. Striking a most un-Jacksonian pose, outgoing president James Buchanan had done nothing about any of this. And by Inauguration Day, a crisis was sharpening to a swordpoint. Federal troops evacuated their fort near Charleston Harbor's old slave-trade wharf and moved to Fort Sumter—a new installation that was much farther offshore. Confederate officials demanded Sumter's surrender. So far, its commandant, Colonel Robert Anderson, had refused, but his troops were running out of food.

The rawboned, Kentucky-born lawyer took the oath of office from emaciated old Roger Taney. Lincoln then turned to face the crowd. His six-foot-four frame towered over the podium. This president, a lifelong opponent of Jackson and his followers, was taking office as the most "common" man to hold the office, before or since. No president had been poorer in his youth. Yet here was Lincoln. And here, too, was another irony. The president-elect had made Jackson's great enemy Henry Clay his "beau ideal of a statesman." But Lincoln had been studying Andrew Jackson's words from the 1832–1833 nullification crisis in preparation for facing down the rebellious enslavers.

Just as he had pointed out to his wavering Republican colleagues, when he refused surrender disguised as compromise, Lincoln now told the nation and the world that consent to secession meant agreement to the principle that the loser can overrule the outcome of an election. The secessionists' demand, Lincoln argued, ripped the fabric of democratic government, replacing it with the principle that a slaveholder's threat is the ultimate right-handed veto. The claim that states that were controlled by slavery entrepreneurs could break up the United States by unilaterally revoking the contract of the Constitution was analogous to scrawling a "G.T.T." on every key document of the Union.

At the same time, Lincoln warned, "The certain ills you fly to, are greater than all the real ones you fly from." If enslavers wanted to protect their property and power, their own decisions were counterproductive. In the War of 1812, thousands of slaves had fled to the British. An army raised in the free states, on the ground in the slave ones, would by its mere presence disrupt enslavers' power. It is certainly strange that few enslaver-politicians considered this possibility. Among the few exceptions to this self-induced blindness were ex-Whig megaplanters such as Stephen Duncan and Paul Cameron, who remained Unionists deep into the crisis. But in general, the more enslaved people secession delegates owned, the more radical were their demands.

In the face of a clear decision by slaveholders and the non-slaveholding whites who appeared to support them, Lincoln counseled patience. He insisted that the Union remained unbroken, but that he would not use his executive power as president to retake seized federal property, send troops into the states, or appoint officeholders "obnoxious" to local communities. Here he accepted the limits of the then possible. In March 1861, the US Army numbered in the few tens of thousands. Moreover, the upper South states remained on the fence. Let Lincoln seem to coerce, and he would shift leverage into the hands of secessionists in those wavering states. So the new president deftly played the ball back into the enslavers' court. "In *your* hands, my dissatisfied fellow countrymen, and not in *mine*, is the momentous issue of civil war." Perhaps nationalist loyalty and reason would persuade states like Virginia, North Carolina, Missouri, and Kentucky not to join the ranks of secession. So he closed with his famous invocation of the emotional ties of a common history: "Though passion may have strained, it must not break our bonds of affection. The mystic chords of memory, stretching from every battle-field, and patriot grave . . . will yet swell the chorus of Union, when again touched, as surely they will be, by the better angels of our nature."

The paths of the future were at that moment unlighted. It seemed unlikely that enslavers would accept the new normal that Lincoln offered and remain part of a nation that had decided to insist that they accept that their desires and dreams would shrink rather than expand. Their inevitable rejection meant that suddenly the future of millions of enslaved African Americans and of their enslavers—these twinned bodies who spread across a subcontinent in a vast embrace of suffering and power—was more uncertain than it had been since the moment when Andrew Jackson looked out across the sugarcane stubble and January mire at Pakenham's scarlet lines. Or then again, as open as at any one of the millions of moments when enslaved men and women pushed their minds and nerves and hands to pick one or two more pounds before twilight fell, to save their backs from the cowhide verdicts of slate and chalk. In those moments, entrepreneurs had revolutionized the world. They had always done so. This time, instead of trying to sweep away old market patterns, traditional ways of making things, or African Americans' families, it was the Union that they would try to sweep aside. And then, as with all of those other creations and destructions, they would try to replace it with a new arrangement that was far more conducive to their own profit and power.

Back when John Brown's attack began to make the possibility of a resort to arms seem less like a distant fantasy, Henry David Thoreau had written these prophetic words about the imminent execution of the martyr: "When you plant . . . a hero in his field, a crop of heroes is sure to spring up." Still, the white South did not believe the North would fight. Lincoln's caution seemed unheroic. Perhaps it fed the Confederate leaders' confidence about war as a solution. But in the month after the inauguration, the new president demonstrated that he was canny enough to outmaneuver enslavers on the field of peace. Instead of forcing his way into Charleston's harbor with blazing guns, he sent a resupply fleet sailing from New York with instructions to resupply the Fort Sumter garrison—but not to reinforce it with troops and weapons. The South's decisionmakers decided to move the game onto a different board. They would assert their independence by eliminating the Union presence off the coast of the state where the cotton frontier had started. On April 10, the local Confederate commander heard from Montgomery: tell the Union troops to evacuate Fort Sumter immediately. If they refuse, begin the bombardment before supplies can arrive. At 4:30 a.m. on April 12, the first cannon boomed. Fort Sumter surrendered at first light on the 14th, after thirty-three hours of shelling that produced not a single fatality.[95]

Afterword

# THE CORPSE

*1861–1937*

L IZA MCCALLUM WALKED SLOWLY back from the lawyer's office.
Just a few days had passed since her second husband, Cade, had died.
Now he lay in a whitewashed, above-ground New Orleans tomb. The February wind, cold for Louisiana, bit her seventy-three-year-old bones. It
blew a freak flurry across the city of the dead, sweeping stray flakes like tiny
sheets of paper over the whitewashed wall and toward Liza's slow walk along
nearby Oak Street.

She was probably thinking about the cold mechanics of how to keep living. Since 1890, Cade had been receiving a pension from the federal government as a former soldier of the Union Army. To get it transferred to her, she
had to prove they had been legally married. So now the lawyer would mail
her deposition to Washington, where bureaucrats would judge it. A clerk
would eventually file the document with all the other paper that made up the
McCallum case. Then he would put Bundle 11, Can 53367, back in its place
between 53366 and 53368 on the shelf, in a warehouse full of shelves.

On those shelves still sleep the biographies of a million men who had defended the nation against those who had fought for the slaveholders' right
to expand slavery. The bundles and cans also contain the stories of soldiers'
families, friends, fellow-soldiers, and communities. And yet they hold clouds
of silence, too, fogs that seep from their pages and weigh on the dark air between and under the shelves. For instance, Liza's own life story, which she
told in the depositions she gave to support her claim to Cade's pension, also
revealed that she simply couldn't know all of Cade's biography. Cade McCallum, Liza told the lawyer, had been born somewhere near the Atlantic. An
army friend, who also submitted to an interview for the pension claim, had
once said Cade was born in North Carolina, but all Liza remembered was

stories about catching fish from a boat. Maybe he had told her Maryland. Like each of the millions of individuals whose biographies together composed the great epic of the expansion of slavery's body, he could have explained to Liza how forced migration had destroyed the life into which he'd been born. He could have told her that story every night for decades. But when they both closed their eyes to sleep, no one but Cade—to borrow the words of another survivor of enslavement—could truly "guess the awfulness of it" for him in his own life. Perhaps half of every story is forever unheard.[1]

Yet Liza knew some essential facts. She knew that in 1850, when Cade was already a grown man, his enslaver sent him to Richmond. Turned into money, shipped on to New Orleans, and sold as a hand, by 1861 Cade was toiling on the Iberville Parish slave labor camp of a woman whom he remembered as "Madame Palang." Liza, for her own part, was in 1861 the property and chief capital investment of a Boonville, Missouri, storekeeper. When news of Fort Sumter came, the Missouri state government immediately split in two halves, pro-Union and pro-Confederate. When the Union Army gained control over the area around St. Louis, antislavery writers in the northern press pushed President Lincoln to use war powers for emancipation. Lincoln refused, announcing, "I hope to have God on my side, but I must have Kentucky," and countermanding Union general John Frémont's preemptive assertion of emancipation in Missouri—like Kentucky, a border state. But Liza's enslaver already saw how (just as at Fortress Monroe in Virginia) the presence of Union troops at St. Louis could tempt enslaved African Americans to escape. Hearing that a man named Daniel Berger was buying up slaves to take them south, he cashed Liza out for US dollars. By the late summer of 1861, she was "in the traders' yard" in the town of Plaquemine, coincidentally in Iberville Parish.

By that time, Cade McCallum was still on Palang's farm, though he was probably no longer picking cotton. In 1861 and 1862, southern cotton producers, believing that their collective monopoly on the international cotton market gave them leverage that would sway European powers to their side if they induced a "cotton famine," quit planting and selling their great staple. Most grew food crops for Confederate Armies instead. By early 1862, the number of bales received at Liverpool fell to 3 percent of the 1860 level. The sudden dearth of cotton on the world market raised prices, ironically rendering cotton from other production zones price-competitive with the yield of enslaved hands for the first time in the nineteenth century. In West Africa and in Brazil, cotton production expanded dramatically. And in Egypt, farmers turned the rich soil of the Nile delta into a huge cotton plantation. They took their earnings from 1861 to Cairo and purchased slaves brought down the Nile from Sudan or across the desert in caravans from Darfur. One historian estimates that the slave trade to Egypt expanded from less than 5,000 per year in the 1850s to more than 20,000 by 1865.[2]

Even before the end of 1861, the Confederacy lost control of its oldest cotton region, South Carolina's Sea Islands. When Union ships bearing an invasion force arrived off the coast south of Charleston in the summer of 1861, enslavers fled. Union forces occupied the coast around Hilton Head. African Americans, who made up over 90 percent of the local population, began talking about dividing the plantations where they had toiled for generations into individual farms. But federal and other northern policymakers feared that the South would follow the Jamaican precedent. There, after Britain's 1834 empire-wide emancipation, formerly enslaved people refused to participate in sugar-plantation labor, wrecking Jamaica's commodity-export economy. To prevent a repetition of that process, as the 1862 crop season loomed, the Treasury Department claimed authority over the abandoned lands and rented them to northern entrepreneurs who proposed to reorganize and revive cotton production on the Sea Islands.

Often the lessees' agenda went beyond profit alone. For example, there was the group of Vermont entrepreneurs who assured the Treasury that their "New England skill and energy" could "direct these persons [to] grow cotton 25% cheaper when employed by fair wages than when compelled to do it as slaves." Thus they could prove that enslavers not only were politically imperialistic, destroying the rights of other white people, but also had operated an inefficient, backward system. Indeed, they believed, "so faforable [*sic*] an opportunity to prove this will probably not occur again for ages." Should $6 per month prove insufficient motivation to convince newly liberated African Americans to enter the cotton wage-labor market, instead of growing corn and yams to eat, the New Englanders also asked permission to use "the ball and chain" to enforce "authority."[3]

The experiment didn't work, at least not on the terms of northern plantation lessees. They signed contracts to pay workers by the month, only to find that at the end of 1862, half of the cotton was rotting in the fields—cotton that could have been picked only at whip-driven speed. Unwilling to admit that wage labor might not be as efficient in all cases as slave, some experimented with paying pickers by the pound, withholding monthly wages until the end of the harvest, or haranguing the workers—telling them that if they failed to work well, "I shall report them to Massa Lincoln as too lazy to be free." Yet neither Sea Island experiments nor distant continents came close to spinning Lancashire's mills back up to speed. Cotton remained scarce on the world market, and cotton prices sky-high.[4]

Across this particular continent, the Union and the Confederacy fought bigger and bloodier battles with almost every passing month. By late 1862, the two warring republics, one slave and the other still part-slave, had between them almost a million men under arms. The Union barely blunted a southern invasion in a battle when 3,600 soldiers died and 17,000 were wounded on a single September day at Antietam Creek in western Maryland.

Most of the press focused on the eastern theater of war. Much of the nation's historical memory continues to focus on the drama and the generals of that front of battle. Yet the war was also decided on the cotton frontier of the Mississippi Valley, the theater where many of the fundamental dramas of American economic development had been played out. And the key event here occurred at the end of April 1862, when a Union fleet—succeeding where the British had failed—broke through the Mississippi River's collar of forts and reached New Orleans. Confederate officials fled the South's biggest city, and Union troops disembarked on the same levee where Rachel and so many others had landed.

Soon after the Union captured New Orleans, "contrabands" began to leave nearby slave labor camps and stream into the army's Camp Parapet just west of the city. Parapet's Union commandant resisted enslavers' entreaties for him to sort out the bondpeople of "loyal" masters and send them back. So many thousands of runaways thronged the facility that the army soon built a second camp in St. Charles Parish at Bonnet Carré, not far from the 1811 slave revolt's epicenter.

Since the beginning of the war, Lincoln had been working to convince politicians in the loyal border states to agree to gradual or compensated emancipation plans. His efforts already represented a more active support for freedom than those of all previous presidents combined. In April 1862, Congress passed a law freeing—in return for payments to enslavers totaling $1 million—all 3,000 people enslaved in the District of Columbia. Maryland, Delaware, and Kentucky politicians refused to bend, holding out for permanent slavery. Yet after the Union won its narrow victory at Antietam, Lincoln felt that he could act more decisively against slavery. He released a document he'd written months before.[5]

The Preliminary Emancipation Proclamation would prove to be the most important executive order ever issued by an American president. It announced that as of January 1, 1863, any slaves in rebel-held areas would be free. The Proclamation wasn't complete. It excluded the enslaved in Union-held territory, which meant not only the border states, but also the western Virginia counties that were forming themselves into a separate pro-Union state. Also exempted was southern Louisiana, where Union leaders were trying to create a "reconstructed" state government and didn't want to antagonize local whites.

Yet the Emancipation Proclamation offered the possibility of freedom to enslaved people held in the giant prison that was the Confederacy. So its tide ran ahead of the blue-coated army. Liza's Iberville Parish enslaver tried to move Liza farther from the flood, to Texas. African Americans called this maneuver "refugeeing." At any moment after early 1862, thousands of people were being refugeed all over the South to make it more difficult for them to trek to Union lines. But as the column of slaves was passing through Opelousas, Union raiders swooped down, scattering the Confederate guards. Marching the newly liberated people back to the river, the soldiers put Liza and hundreds of liberated African Americans onto boats bound for New Orleans.

Because Liza had been in the Confederate zone, the Proclamation officially freed her. But after being disembarked on the New Orleans levee, she and the others were herded into the city's cotton warehouses. "From there," Liza remembered, decades later, "we were all scattered about" to different Union-controlled plantations to do forced labor: "I went on the McCall place near Donaldsonville." There she met a man named Thomas Faro. They started a relationship. They went out into the field every day, demonstrating to Union officials "a disposition to work" that entitled them to receive government rations. Others resisted, and went hungry. This was not quite freedom. Still, enslaved people had been knocking on the portal of freedom for decades, in any way possible. Now, in a single moment, the Emancipation Proclamation had unbarred the door. Next, African Americans would force it all the way open.

That opportunity was even more tangible because, as Lincoln made emancipation the policy for a long-term war that could only end with the fall of slavery's empire, another policy shifted, too. Since the beginning of the war, free northern blacks had been pushing for enlistment. The federal government, afraid of the reaction of the border states, resisted. Policymakers knew that as much as many northern whites hated the idea of disunion, many feared even more that Frederick Douglass had been right when he'd insisted that "let the black man get upon his person the brass letters US . . . a musket on his shoulder, and bullets in his pocket, and there is no power on earth or under the earth which can deny that he has earned the right of citizenship in the United States."[6]

Image A.1. Interior of former slave trader's pen in Alexandria, Virginia, partially disman-
tled. This was probably the same structure used by John Armfield in the 1830s, though
other traders had used it in the ensuing years before Union soldiers captured the city
in 1861. Today the structure is the site of the Freedom House Museum, operated by the
Northern Virginia Urban League. Photo c. 1861–1865. Library of Congress.

On January 1, 1863, Lincoln reaffirmed the Emancipation Proclamation.
He also confirmed that the executive branch would fulfill Congress's summer 1862 mandate, allowing the Union Army to enlist African Americans.
Many had already been drilling under individual states' authority—such as
the soldiers of the famous 52nd Massachusetts Regiment. The new U.S.C.T.
(United States Colored Troops) also included numerous new enlistees from
places such as Fortress Monroe and Camp Parapet. Soon some enslaved men,
drawn by word of mouth passed from one side of the battle lines to the other,
were leaving slavery and enlisting immediately in the Union Army. One
night in 1863, for instance, Cade McCallum and his friend James Douglass
crept out of Madame Palang's slave quarters and set off east through the
deep woods. To the north, the Union was trying to encircle Vicksburg. They
reached the Mississippi and found a tiny skiff lodged against the west side.

Douglass, who couldn't swim, climbed into the skiff. McCallum, in the water, held the boat's edge as he kicked it out into the stream. They drifted downriver. In the morning light, someone from the Confederate-controlled west bank took a shot. Douglass lay in the bottom of the skiff. McCallum ducked like a turtle. A couple of other bullets whistled past. Then the shooting stopped.

Around a bend loomed a Union gunboat. Seeing the Stars and Stripes, Douglass and McCallum hailed the crew, and kicked and paddled that way. The sailors hauled the two men up the sloping iron-plated side of the *Essex* and told the river-soaked runaways they had a choice. They could go to Bonnet Carré and do plantation labor. Or they could serve in the US Army. Douglass and McCallum immediately enlisted in the 80th Regiment of the U.S.C.T.

Over the next two years, almost 200,000 other African-American soldiers—many of them former slaves—did mighty things that defined the rest of their lives. McCallum and Douglass's 80th Regiment took part in the siege of Port Hudson, one of the first Civil War battles in which black troops played a major role. Union victory there helped ensure the fall of Vicksburg in July 1863, which cut the Confederacy in half along the Mississippi. At the same time, at Gettysburg, the Union defeated the South's second invasion of the North.

Now slavery began to crumble more quickly. Blue-coated troops ranged ever more widely through the cotton belt. A column raided through the bayous of central Louisiana, where they rounded up Eliza and Andre Dupree, Felo Battee, and hundreds of other African Americans from the parishes where Solomon Northup had toiled after he had been kidnapped from freedom. The soldiers "drove us like cattle," Battee later remembered. He and the liberated men were herded onto the tops of the boxcars, while the women were crowded inside them. The train unloaded Eliza Dupree and the other women onto steamers bound to leased-out "Government farms," while the soldiers marched Andre Dupree, Battee, and the remaining men overland to the Mississippi, offering them the same choice that had been presented to James Douglass and Cade McCallum.

Andre Dupree and Felo Battee joined the 81st U.S.C.T. regiment. Meanwhile, Eliza Dupree appreciated the plentiful rations available on the "Old Hickory" labor camp—food was getting scarce in the Confederate-held areas—but she had little interest in toiling under armed supervision any longer. She slipped away, walked fifty miles to Baton Rouge, and got a job in an army hospital. A few months later, as she stirred a giant iron pot of boiling laundry outside the tents, Andre walked up to her through the billowing steam. His regiment was at Camp Parapet, completing its training. Someone had told him where she was, and he came to find her on a one-day pass.[7]

By 1864, the crippled Confederate Army was too weak to launch major offensives. But it could still make the Union spend oceans of blood for every advance in Virginia, Tennessee, and Georgia. The pro-war resolve of the white northern press began to sag. Volunteering declined. Resistance to the draft increased. The weaker-willed began to talk of a negotiated peace, which was exactly what Jefferson Davis and the Confederacy were now playing for. Instead, Andre Dupree, James Douglass, Cade McCallum, and 200,000 other African-American men kept the faith, becoming the increment that helped the war-weary Union to persist in its effort through 1864 and 1865. They paid a high collective price: 40,000 black soldiers died, and a similar number of African Americans may have died in the camps and in the chaos of the war-devastated South. One day, Andre's brother-in-arms Sylvester Caffery came to Eliza and told her that Andre had died of cholera.

Yet there was birth as well as death in the refugee and army camps. Here the once-enslaved found each other for the first time, or again. Here they laid the groundwork for African Americans' claim to civic and political identity in a postslavery society. For instance, take Lucinda Howard, who had been shipped from Virginia to New Orleans for sale right before the war—along with her sisters Emily and Margaret. An agent bought all three for a Mrs. Welham, who owned the "Oneida" labor camp in St. James Parish. Lucinda was only fifteen when the Yankees came in 1862. She ran first. When her sisters and other girls whom they knew followed her, they found Lucinda at the Bonnet Carré camp, doing the heavy labor of levee repair and making a wage. They also met her man, a black soldier named Abram Blue. And they stood with her as the provost marshal, the military commandant who governed civilians living in the camp, married Lucinda to Abram "under the flag," as the saying went.

The certificate that the commandant gave them proved that Abram and Lucinda had been married in a legal ceremony, one sanctioned by the national state itself. Unlike prewar marriages, which enslavers erased at whim, these weddings had the force of law. They established the claim of a man and a woman to choose to stay together, to not be separated by the desires of a white person, to make decisions for their own lives and their own blood. Abram and Lucinda brought the certificate with them when they joined a new church in Mississippi after the war. It showed that they were serious—not merely cohabiting. It made Abram the legitimate father of the fifteen children Lucinda bore. And it gave Lucinda recognition as someone who

Image A.2. An enslaved man's journey to escape, freedom, and death as a Union soldier martyred for the twin causes of the United States and freedom. Depicted by artist James Queen, who may have made the panel for *Harper's Weekly*. Library of Congress.

had already earned citizenship by supporting Abram, a soldier-citizen. That would entitle her to a claim to his pension, for she, too, had put her shoulder to the wheel of the nation.[8]

By 1864, once-enslaved people were marching through almost every southern state, not in tatters and chains, but bearing arms and wearing blue uniforms with the confidence of people who believed that the federal government would back their claims to rights. Their presence encouraged still-enslaved people to refuse to work for their owners, or to run to the woods. The growing number of U.S.C.T. enlistees also provided a crucial increment for a North that was running out of soldiers. Congress passed the Thirteenth Amendment in March 1865, just before Lincoln's second inauguration. The amendment ended slavery throughout the United States forever, freeing people even in areas not covered by the Emancipation Proclamation, such as the 425,000 African Americans who had still been enslaved in the border states. Soon afterward, Richmond fell, and Robert E. Lee's Army of Northern Virginia surrendered at Appomattox in Southside Virginia on April 9, 1865. Confederate President Jefferson Davis had already fled Danville. Like the sold and stolen whom Lorenzo Ivy had seen flow by, and of whom he had spoken in his interview with Works Progress Administration worker Claude Anderson, Davis now carried his all in a little bag.

After four years, the war was over. Although 700,000 Americans had died, mixed with the sorrow was joy. As Union troops spread throughout the remaining areas of the slave states in May and June of 1865, they found properties where people were still being held in slavery. Again and again, the scene of celebration was repeated, on days still remembered in African-American communities across the country as the holiday "Juneteenth," for June 19. People broke into spontaneous song and dance. Some told enslavers what they really thought. Some set off on the road with everything they had, looking for lost ones, heading back to Tennessee or Virginia, or simply looking to get away. Some literally picked up their cabins and moved them out of sight of the big house. When landowners could get the attention of those whom they had once ruled, they sometimes offered to share the proceeds of the crop fifty-fifty. And more than one former enslaver, their world turned upside down, committed suicide on the day of jubilee.

There was one final casualty, of course. In the surviving photo from March 4, 1865, the triumphant and solemn day of Lincoln's second inauguration, you can see among the massive crowd of people covering the Capitol portico a mustached figure leaning against a pillar. For John Wilkes Booth was present for Lincoln's astonishing second inaugural address. This was, perhaps, the greatest speech ever given in the English language. It was itself a history of the half untold. It named slavery and the incessant pressure for its expansion as the reason why oceans of blood had drowned the battlefields of the Civil War. When he turned over the last page of his so-brief text, Lincoln had only forty days to live.

After Richmond fell, the president went to visit. He walked through Shockoe Bottom in wonder, among throngs of people celebrating freedom on the very docks from which thousands of their kin had been shipped to the cotton country. Four million African Americans—most of whom had been enslaved when the first cannonballs plunged into Fort Sumter—had raised over four years of war a claim to freedom, to citizenship, and to relationships no one could sell. When he returned to Washington, Lincoln gave another speech, in which he acknowledged this indisputable claim. Then the president announced his support for extending the vote to African-American men. Their service in battle had saved the nation. Booth was in the crowd at that speech, too. He turned to a friend. Lincoln's announcement, Booth snarled, "means nigger citizenship. Now, by God, I'll put him through." And on Good Friday 1865, April 14, he murdered the president.

ABRAHAM LINCOLN WAS EITHER the last casualty of the Civil War or one of the first of a long civil rights movement that is not yet over. He was succeeded by his vice president, Andrew Johnson, who was unfortunately an alcoholic racist bent on undermining emancipation. Johnson spent the summer signaling to southern whites that they could build a new white supremacy that looked much like the one African Americans had fought to end. In the fall of 1865, southern white voters made it clear that they did not plan to come to terms with freedom. In elections intended to reseat southern states in Congress, they sent a host of sullen Confederates back to Washington. At the same time, whites in southern legislatures were trying to keep the status of African Americans as close to slavery as possible, passing vagrancy laws to limit mobility, proposing apprenticeship laws binding black youths as unfree laborers in white families, and making troubling threats about bringing back the whip as cotton-picking rates declined.

Angered by southern whites' unwillingness to admit that they had lost the verdict of war, northern Republicans in Congress, led by a faction called the "Radicals," took control of Reconstruction. Overriding Johnson's objections, they refused to seat the newly elected southern representatives and senators. They passed a series of bills that took the vote away from most ex-Confederate officers, and they extended the power of the army and the "Freedman's Bureau" to impose new labor systems on the cotton South. The Freedman's Bureau sent agents into southern counties to mediate between land-owning, cash-poor planters and the formerly enslaved. African Americans wanted, above all, to avoid anything like the pushing-system or the whipping-machine: no more driver's lash, no weighing-up and recording, nothing that resembled that. They wanted mothers to have a chance to care for their babies and tend their gardens. They wanted men to be able to plow without other men riding behind them with guns on their hips. They wanted children to go to school instead of doing field work all year. And African Americans throughout the South usually wanted their own land, on which they could grow subsistence crops and live as what, in another country, we would call independent peasant farmers.

The freedpeople's dream of land went largely unfulfilled. The US economy still needed the overseas earnings generated by the South's power in the world cotton market. Therefore, just as had been presaged in South Carolina and Louisiana during the early years of the war, neither postwar federal policymakers nor white landowners were interested in seeing the freedpeople become landowning small farmers. Instead, Freedman's Bureau agents—including many with "Radical" political views—forced formerly enslaved people and former enslavers to sign and keep wage-labor contracts for 1866. Over the next few years, a compromise system emerged across the South: various permutations of "sharecropping," which meant that African-American households worked individual plots of land as tenants, in exchange for paying the landlord a share of the cotton crop they grew. Landowners and local store owners advanced goods on credit to the sharecroppers, but at high interest rates, often trapping freedpeople in permanent debt. For sharecroppers, however, there was no scale, no chalk, and no whip at the end of the day. And that was no small thing.[9]

Yet the Radicals also convinced Congress to pass the Fourteenth Amendment, which by making former slaves equal citizens of a multiracial republic did what no other postslavery settlement had ever done. It wrote into the Constitution a nationwide standard of birthright citizenship that would eventually enable future generations—descendants of slaves and immigrants alike—to undermine racial and cultural supremacy. Although the Fourteenth Amendment didn't extend the vote to women, Congress, state constitutional conventions, and the press all debated the possibility. In that heady postwar time of rewriting the basic bargains of American political economy, anything seemed possible.[10]

In the short term, African-American voting permitted male former slaves to make policy in state legislative halls where once deals had been brokered to securitize their own blood and seed. African Americans represented southern states in the same Congress where compromises had formerly kept the door open for more slave trades, more first days in the cotton field, more stained dirt by the gin stand. Between 1866 and the early 1870s, Reconstruction in the South seemed like it might produce a radically transformed society. White resistance was brutal and widespread, but the national commitment to emancipation kept federal troops stationed in the South. But after 1873, when the industrial economy fell into a deep depression, white America's conscience wavered. Consumed by labor disputes in the North, Republican leaders were increasingly unlikely to see the free laborers of the South as people with whom they shared interests.

African Americans were watching the promise of emancipation, the heady days of eagles on brass buttons and unions under the flag, slowly begin to sag and fade—like Thomas Faro and Liza, who moved to New Orleans after the war. She built up a business selling food to travelers on steamboats, and she bore Thomas two children. They struggled on to make free lives, but the world turned, compounding the universal tragedies of human life, amplifying failures and speeding hope's decay.

Thomas died in the 1870s during a smallpox epidemic that swept through black Louisiana. Liza then moved to St. John the Baptist Parish and got a steady job working on the plantation of John Webb. She met Cade McCallum, who was a supervisor there. The war had battered his body, and he could only do hard labor sporadically, but he drew the workers' respect. One day in the late 1870s, Cade's old army brother Amos Gale came to see him, at "rice-cutting time." He met Liza, who had moved herself and her two children in with Cade. Although there was nothing to eat in the house but "a dried alligator hanging up there," Cade and Liza cut it down, cleaned it, and shared it with Amos.

Outside the cabin, the dark was coming down. Across the South, night riders went out—hooded in white, burning, raping, beating, and killing. They stole one state's elections after another. They torched the houses of black folks bold enough to buy land, or even bold enough to paint their own house, for that matter. They rode to Washington and made deals. To resolve the disputed presidential election of 1876, northern Republicans made a corrupt bargain with the South's Democratic rulers to let the latter have "home rule." The "Redeemers," as the white southern Democrats called themselves, changed the laws to roll back as much of Reconstruction as they could. By 1900, they had taken away the vote from most black men, and many of the less reliable white men as well. They also lowered the boom of segregation—"Jim Crow," as people would come to call it—an array of petty and brutal rules. This forbade African Americans from, for instance, drinking from the same water fountains as whites, eating at the same restaurants, and attending the same schools—that is, from enjoying the civil right to move in public spaces as equals or have access to the same educational and economic opportunities as whites.

Southern whites built monuments to the defeated generals of their war for slavery, memorialized the old days of the plantation, and wrote histories that insisted that the purpose of the war had been to defend their political rights against an oppressive state. They were so successful at the last goal that they eventually convinced a majority of white Americans, including most historians, that slavery had been benign and that "states' rights" had been the cause of the Civil War. Yet the kingdom that the South's white lords had regained was a starved one. They themselves were much poorer than they had once been. Their violence was more self-destructive, and less profitable.

Even the new story about the old past was a kind of fool's gold. The valorization of causes lost, the delusional praising of fathers' treason—these things did not make one better adapted to the modern world. White entrepreneurs vigorously promoted a "New South." But the region's economic decisionmakers struggled to adapt to two postslavery realities. First, neither African Americans nor anyone else would do hand labor at the breakneck, soul-scarring pace of the whipping-machine. Many white yeoman farmers, impoverished by war and unable to pay debts or taxes, lost their land and became tenants and sharecroppers themselves. The total number of bales produced in the United States didn't surpass 1859's peak until 1875, despite a significant increase in the number of people making cotton in the South after emancipation. Cotton productivity dropped significantly. Many enslaved cotton pickers in the late 1850s had peaked at well over 200 pounds per day. In the 1930s, after a half-century of massive scientific experimentation, all to make the cotton boll more pickable, the great-grandchildren of the enslaved often picked only 100 to 120 pounds per day.[11]

Second, both because productivity was now declining instead of rising, and because of the political-economic isolation that the South's white rulers inflicted upon their region in order to protect white power, the South sank into subordinate, colonial status within the national economy. Although many southerners wanted to develop a more diverse modern economy that went beyond cotton, for nearly a century after emancipation they failed to do so. Despite constant attempts to industrialize, the South could only offer natural resources and poverty-stricken laborers. It did not have enough local capital, whether of the financial or the well-educated human kind, and it could not develop it. Although a textile industry sprang up in the piedmont of the Carolinas and Virginia, and an iron and coal industry in Alabama, they offered mostly low-wage jobs. Non-textile industries suffered in the competition with more heavily capitalized northern industries, which literally rigged the rules—such as the price structures that corporations used to ensure that Pittsburgh's steel would cost less than Birmingham's. Extractive industries, including coal mining and timber, devastated the landscape and depended on workforces oppressed with shocking violence. The continued small size and poverty of the nonagricultural working class also limited urban and middle-class development. Thus, in the 1930s, a lifetime after the Civil War, the majority of both black and white southerners were poor and worked on farms—often farms that they did not own.[12]

LIZA WAS IN HER forties when she and Cade got together. Sarah to his Abraham, she still bore two children by him. In 1882, the couple finally got officially married. A few years later they moved to New Orleans. In 1890, sixty-eight years old, he first applied for an invalid pension from the federal government, which had committed itself to support old soldiers and their widows after the soldiers died. On his application he listed many ailments. Some were typical of old age. Some were especially likely among those who had suffered through forced migration, hard labor, and soldier's service in mud and rain: intestinal disorders, old injuries, a fluttering heart that left him exhausted. After sixteen years in the Carrolton neighborhood, he died. It was February 1906. The family laid him out in his blue uniform. The old veterans from the neighborhood came by to pay their respects, and they slowly walked him to his tomb.

On that cold day as Liza walked back from the cemetery to the house where she would now have to live with her son and his family, not only was Cade McCallum lying dead in his tomb; what was worse was that he seemed to have been defeated, and Liza, too. Slavery was gone, but Jim Crow was alive. Almost all southern African Americans were shut out of the ballot box and the political power it could yield. Segregated public accommodations and schools promised that they and their descendants would be second-class citizens for the foreseeable future. The young people who took the train north to Chicago and New York found that even outside of the South, they faced segregated workplaces and neighborhoods, a door of opportunity only intermittently and partially open.

But the body of African America, stretched, and chained, and stretched again, the body whose tongue and spirit and blood had developed alongside slavery's expansion, was still alive. For the history in which Cade and Liza and millions of others had been caught up, the history that had been stolen from them and which people were always trying to steal from them, was not over, and in many ways, still is not. Slavery and its expansion had built enduring patterns of poverty and exploitation. This legacy was certainly crystal clear in Liza's early twentieth-century South. African-American households had virtually no wealth, for instance, while a substantial portion of the wealth held by white households, even after emancipation, could be traced to revenue generated by enslaved labor and financing leveraged out of their bodies before 1861.

More broadly, the history of feet and heads, hands, tongues, breath, seed, blood, and backs and arms had made all of African America, the United States, and the modern world. The shaping began in the 1780s. The

Image A.3. Convention of former slaves, left to right: unidentified, Anna Angales, Eliza-beth Berkeley, and Sadie Thompson, 1916. Library of Congress.

possibility of profit from forced migration kept the United States together through the lean years after the American Revolution. The Constitution's compromises built a union on slavery and embedded its expansion—some thought temporarily, some thought permanently—in the fabric of the American political economy. For the three score and ten years that followed, a full biblical lifespan, enslaved people were marched and shipped south and west. African Americans' hands and creativity, turned against themselves and even against each other at times, made commodities and built an archipelago of slave labor camps, a literal organism of economic production.

From markets built on the labor and the bodies of enslaved people, and from the infrastructure laid down to ship the product in and out, came economic growth. But from this economic growth came not only wealth, but also political power in the councils of the nation. Poor white men insisted that they, too, should enjoy the psychic rewards of right-handed power on slavery's frontier, and from that came temporary defeat for arrogant planters. Yet clever political entrepreneurs, most notably Andrew Jackson, turned assertively populist energies into the channels of political power, too. They created a new interregional political alliance that yielded decades more of compromise and that enabled the South to maintain its disproportionate power within the federal government. Still, both South and North depended on slavery's expansion. The products generated from the possibilities of co-exploitation explain much of the nation's astonishing rise to power in the nineteenth century. Through the booms and the crashes emerged a financial system that continuously catalyzed the development of US capitalism. By the 1840s, the United States had grown into both an empire and a world economic power—the second greatest industrial economy, in fact, in the world—all built on the back of cotton.

Dependence on cotton stretched far beyond North American shores. A world greedy for a slice of the whipping-machine's super-profits had financed the occupation of the continent, and the forced migration of enslaved African Americans to the southwestern cotton fields helped to make the modern world economy possible. The steadily increasing productivity of hands on the cotton frontier kept cheap raw materials flowing to the world's newest and most important industry, the cotton textile factories of Britain, Western Europe, and the North. Theft of days, years, labor, of the left hand's creative secrets helped provide the escape velocity for the fledgling modern world to do what no other historical society had done before and pull away from the gravitational field of the Malthusian cul-de-sac. Slavery's expansion was the driving force in US history between the framing of the Constitution and the beginning of the Civil War. It made the nation large and unified, and it made the South's whites disproportionately powerful in that nation. Enslavers had turned right hand against left to achieve not only productivity but also power that few other dominant classes in human history had possessed.

Yet from the epic of theft and survival, of desire and innovation, came the Civil War, too. Expansion's profits and power made southerners willing to push for more expansion. This made some northern whites into allies who recognized their dependence on cotton profit and were willing to do what was necessary to keep it flowing. These were southern whites' allies. But southern power frightened other northern whites. Some feared that slavery, acceptable enough when it remained a southern institution, would invade the places they lived or wanted to live. Others believed that slavery corrupted everything, and that its expansion fed the rot in American society, American freedom, the American soul—whatever category was their touchstone for everything good. Still others believed that the financial disasters of the late 1830s and early 1840s showed that slavery was economically derelict, doomed, a drag on the capitalist economy's future.

All those groups united in the Republican Party of the late 1850s behind the one policy position on which they could all agree: that slavery's expansion must be stopped. For white southerners, who had always been able to find new frontiers, the victory of that party in a national election was too much.

Buoyed by their other successes in the 1850s, by the nearly complete consensus of white southerners behind the slaveholder political bloc, and their overwhelming power within the national Democratic Party, enslaver-politicians made decisions for secession and then for war.

It has been said that the Civil War was "unnecessary" because slavery was already destined to end, probably within a few decades after the 1860 election. Yet this is mere dogma. The evidence points in the opposite direction. Slavery yielded ever more efficient production, in contrast to the free labor that tried (and failed) to compete with it, and the free labor that succeeded it. If slave labor in cotton had ever hit a wall of ultimate possibility, enslavers could have found new commodities. Southern enslavers had adapted slavery before, with incredibly profitable results. Forced labor that is slavery in everything but name remained tremendously important to the world economy well into the twenty-first century. And the lessons that enslavers learned about turning the left hand to the service of the right, forcing ordinary people to reveal their secrets so that those secrets could be commodified, played out in unsteady echoes that we have called by many names (scientific management, the stretch-out, management studies) and heard in many places. Though these were not slavery, they are one more way in which the human world still suffers without knowing it from the crimes done to Rachel and William and Charles Ball and Lucy Thurston; mourns for them unknowing, even as we also live on the gains that were stolen from them.[13]

Nor is it obvious that slavery's expanders would have been politically defeated, outnumbered, or boxed in. In the 1850s, slavery-expansion's promoters were making continued expansion defensible in constitutional terms that the North found quite acceptable long after the war. In addition, the vast enslaved body was the biggest store of wealth in the American economy. So long as law and normal politics reign, wealth-holders typically find ways to preserve their wealth. Successful revolt from within was impossible, so war was the only way slavery would end in the United States. War is what the enslavers, in their right-handed arrogance, launched, and it was—for them—a tremendous mistake.

YET CADE MCCALLUM WAS dead in his tomb. So were many of the men and women who with him had seized the finally-here chance that enslavers' overreach had opened up to enslaved men and women—a generation that had made sure that they would finally see the end of it. But dead, too, it seemed, were the dreams of equality, independence, of redeeming the thefts of slavery's deepest, longest journeys. Liza, toiling up the street in the cold, might have seen little chance of reversing that process of decay. In 1937, when Claude Anderson came to talk to Lorenzo Ivy, she might have still said the same thing.

Indeed, though former enslavers and their descendants had lost much of their power through defeat in the Civil War, they had regained some of it by the early twentieth century. Southern white elites continued to wield disproportionate power through the next one hundred years. The willingness of many white southerners to unite around the idea of hanging on to racial power made the South a swing region, and white southerners a defined interest group, willing to join whichever national party was willing to cater to its demands. That was only one of the ways in which the bitter fruit of the southern elites—and their defense of slavery and of their own power—continued to gall democracy everywhere in the country. In another case, the federal judiciary took the Calhounian argument for the independence of slave property from majority control and made it, in the form of the so-called Lochner Doctrine, a defense of rampant industrial power in the face of attempts to regulate workers' safety, consumer health, and environmental impact. In yet another case, scientific racism had a long history after the fall of the Confederacy. It was used to justify anti-Semitism, the extermination of native peoples around the world, brutal forms of colonialism, and the exclusion of immigrants. And it continued to be used to justify discrimination against the descendants of the enslaved.

Meanwhile, the unbending anger of former Confederates against Reconstruction morphed into their grandchildren's suspicion of the New Deal, and the insistence on the part of white southern Democrats that measures against the Depression could do nothing to alleviate black poverty or lessen white supremacy. Compared to their dominance of US politics through much of the antebellum period, and their ability to consume disproportionate quantities of the fruits of antebellum national economic growth, the postwar southern white upper class achieved only a truncated triumph. Yet white folks still kept the black folks who toiled for them in poverty, forcing African Americans to take the implicit and explicit insults of life in the Jim Crow South in silence, lest they die brutally at the hands of mobs with or without badges. No wonder so many African Americans saw no chance for freedom but to leave.[14]

Still, there were things that for all their power, even the pre–Civil War enslavers themselves had not been able to control. They could create a system that seemed to reduce African Americans to body parts: feet walking like a chained machine, hands on the block and hands picking, minds and nervous systems yielding revenue, providing entertainment and pleasure. Yet there were two ways to look at the body of African America, sutured together in the trauma of slavery's expansion. The body had two forms, two instances. One profited enslavers, and in fact, white America, North and South, had again and again agreed to co-exploit this body, which was the new slavery of the cotton fields. This African America, created by expansion, was marked by vast suffering. In it, hundreds of thousands of people died early and alone, separated from their loved ones. Millions of people were lost by millions of people. By the water's edge, they parted.

But tongues also spoke words that enslavers did not hear. Lungs breathed a spirit that would not yield. Enslaved men and women watched and guarded and stilled their blood, and trained their seed to wait. Even when enslavers realized, in particular moments, that enslaved people had created something else, an identity, a political unity, a common culture, a story, and a sense of how it shaped them and made them one, enslavers had forgotten, or willed themselves to forget. So people survived, and helped each other to survive, and not only to survive but to build. Thus, another body grew as the invisible twin of the one stretched out and used by white people. Eventually, the waiting had its reward. The body rose. African Americans took up arms and defeated the enslavers.

Survival, and this kind of survival, made victory possible. Unlike its predecessors on the North American mainland, and unlike counterparts in most of the New World, the African-American culture that emerged from the crucible of nineteenth-century forced migration within the United States had no alternative but to think of itself as a political unity. Assimilation, sought by enslaved Africans and their descendants in both Brazil and in many Spanish-speaking societies, was impossible. Escape through individual manumission, an option pursued by enslaved strivers throughout the rest of the New World, was usually impossible. Escape through revolt, relying on old African identities and concepts—the Haitian option—was likewise impossible. All of these options closed, enslaved African Americans had to develop a sense of unity or crumble. And they did develop that unity, bending a narrative of history that bound them together around a clear-eyed assessment of their situation as victims of a vast crime. They had to recognize that without solidarity they would live only at the whim of a set of structures and practices designed to exploit them in every possible way.

The political agenda that enslaved people developed, and that they exported in the words of survivors and runaways, was not assimilation, not manumission, but destruction for the whipping-machine and everything that made it work, and the transformation of America into a place that would redeem its thefts. This agenda, smuggled north in the minds and on the tongues of an intrepid and lucky few escapees, resurrected a dead antislavery movement in the United States. This agenda set a group of progressive whites on a political collision course with the slavelords and their many northern allies. Even as that political trajectory unfolded, in spaces sacred and secular, during the day and during the night, in pain and in joy, enslaved people were still finding new ways to protect and defend the human soul in the midst of the still-unfolding chaos of creative destruction. They made survival and form out of terror, theft, and death. They learned to be fast but not hurried, to lose themselves without losing their souls. All this was also the legacy of slavery's expansion. This was the collective body that survived forced migration even as many bodies did not survive it, or died in the war that ended it, or suffered through impoverishment and disfranchisement in the wake of Reconstruction.

In the war, survivors ended slavery. When the survivors began to die off, they could pass on to their descendants very little in the way of material wealth. So much had been stolen from them. But African Americans had a story that made them a people. They had a unity that was ultimately political. This had led them to choose solidarity over individual deals. They had lodged their claim to citizenship in the Constitution, a precedent that would grow in leverage as the century went on and the United States found itself up against enemies eager to point to the hypocrisy of first-class language and second-class practice of civil and political equality. They had, with white allies, created in the form of abolitionism the ideological template of American dissent, of progressivism, of the faith that social change, pursued with a religious zeal, could make America truer to its ideal self.

At the same time, from lands devastated by forced migration, creativity continued to boil forth in the years after Reconstruction's collapse. African-American cultural forms permeated and reworked American popular culture, which then exported these cultural forms to the entire globe. Over the century that followed Cade McCallum's burial, using all these tools, working in all sorts of métiers, African-American people transformed the world. They remade the social, cultural, and political geography of the United States through their own volition in the course of the Great Migration. They changed the South and the United States and the world forever through the civil rights movement. And they built a tradition of community organization that eventually led the American electorate, in an astonishing development, to elect a black president who was the son of an African immigrant. As a political force, the solidarity that African Americans first built while still

Image A.4. Alfred Parrott, formerly enslaved man, photographed in 1941, when he was ninety-one. Jack Delano, Farm Security Administration. Library of Congress.

Image A.5. Formerly enslaved woman, living on a farm near Greensboro, Alabama. Jack Delano, Farm Security Administration, 1941, Library of Congress.

enslaved remains impressively coherent, generations later, despite two centuries of temptations to give up, turn aside, or dissolve into nihilism.

The descendants of enslaved African Americans could do these mighty deeds for many reasons, but one root of every reason was this: those who survived slavery had passed down what they had learned. The gifts, the creations, the breath of spirit, songs that saved lives, lessons learned for dimes, the ordinary virtues, and the determination to survive the wolf. The lessons came down in the strong arms that held babies in sharecroppers' cabins, in the notes of songs, in the rocking of churches, in jokes told around the water bucket on hot days of cotton-picking, and in lessons taught in both one-room schoolhouses and at places like Hampton. Day after day, year after year, the half untold was told. And in the tomb, the body stirred.

The wind washed the sun clear of clouds. Claude Anderson scribbled the last few words with his pencil, and then noticed that the old man had come to a stop. The sunlight had marched far across the pine board floor. It must be well past noon. Glancing up, Anderson saw Lorenzo Ivy looking at him with a calm smile, one that belied the catalog of horrors he had detailed. Outside, children were calling to each other in wild play. Anderson heard two pairs of bare feet shooting down the street in chase. He could feel the dirt kicking out behind his own heels, only a few years since.

Somewhere, across the sea, people peered up through the barbed wire at guard towers. The story being told to justify the machine guns was one of the prisoners' subhuman race. It was a story told with phrases that the defenders of slavery had coined to claim their righteous hold on Ivy when he had been a child. Somewhere, across the sea, a man in a gulag huddled under a blanket woven from cotton picked by Anderson's and Ivy's lost cousins. Somewhere, across the ocean, a child in a tavern entrance heard a record playing, heard a shocking combination of correctness and violation, a trumpet singing a new song. Somewhere, in fact at the far end of the same old slave trail that led through Danville and over the mountain, a mother huddled by Mississippi's Highway 61 with her children. Put out with the coming of the tractor, she clutched a Chicago address in her hand. And somewhere—not far from Danville—law students three generations from slavery huddled, planning the next move against Jim Crow and lynching.

Another shift of wind shook the curtains, another minute had marched the sun further, to an angle that suddenly cast the deep wrinkles on Ivy's face into relief. He rose, creaking audibly. Sometimes these old men wanted chewing tobacco; Anderson often gave the women snuff. Ivy's hand only asked for a grip. "I know a lot more I can tell you some other time; I'll write

Image A.6. Great-grandchildren of enslaved men and women, preparing to leave the cotton South, 1930s. Marion Wolcott, Works Progress Administration, 1939. Library of Congress.

it out. Just send me an envelope like you said and I'll write it all down and send it to you."[15] Anderson thanked him, and he stepped through the door the old man held open. He walked down the steps, opened the door of his black Ford, dropped his notepads on the passenger side, and slid into the driver's seat. He started the engine and leaned his head out through the rolled-down window. The old man was still on the porch. "Be good now," Lorenzo Ivy said, and turned back through the open door.

# ACKNOWLEDGMENTS

Any book that takes this long to write inevitably leads one to incur multiple debts. The power of compound interest eventually renders those debts completely unpayable. I'll just consider this a statement of bankruptcy. In this list of debts, I must begin with the fact that this book would never have seen the light of day without the unflagging support of Lara Heimert, editor and director of Basic Books. I can't thank her enough for her support, patience, careful readings, and pointed questions. Other sources of support and expertise at the press and in the production process include Sandra Beris and Leah Stecher of Basic, line editor Roger Labrie, and copyeditor Kathy Streckfus. Linda Beltz Glaser and Syl Kacapyr of Cornell helped with promotion ideas, David Ethridge did the maps, and Lillian Baptist helped create the cover concept.

Research funding came above all from Cornell University, the National Endowment for the Humanities, and the University of Miami, but also from the University of São Paulo, Tulane University, the Gilder Lehrman Institute of American History, the University of North Carolina, and Duke University.

No work of history is possible without the support of the librarians, archivists, and institutions that make original research possible. Support and assistance came from: Cornell University Library and its entire staff; Duke University Library and its staff, especially Elizabeth Dunn, Nelda Webb, and Janie Morris; the University of North Carolina's Southern Historical Collection, especially Laura Clark Brown, Tim West, Tim Pyatt, Shayera Tangri, and John White; Tulane University's Howard-Tilton Library and its Special Collections Department; the New Orleans Notarial Archives; the New Orleans Public Library, especially Greg Osborne; the New York Public Library; the New York Historical Society; Louisiana State University's Hill Memorial Library; the National Archives (Washington, DC, and Fort Worth); the Chicago Historical Society; the Newberry Library; the Virginia Historical Society; and the University of Miami Library. The Natchez Historical Collection deserves special mention for the intellectual and moral support given to scholars by Mimi Miller, as does the University of West Alabama's Center for Study of the Black Belt. I thank Zachary Kaplan, Gregg Lightfoot, and Sam Robinson for research assistance. Thanks go as well to Jonathan Pritchett, James Wilson, Richard H. Kilbourne, Dale Tomich, and Mimi Miller for sharing data, to CISER (Cornell Institute for Social and Economic Research) for help in storing and analyzing data, especially Bill Block,

Lynn Martin, and Jeremy Williams; and also to Jordan Suter, Nancy Brooks, Peter Hirtle, Bob Kibbee, and Michelle Paolillo for help in analyzing data.

I was able to get useful feedback from audiences and co-panelists at numerous presentations of portions of the materials contained here, so I thank those who participated in and organized such events, including the Southern Historical Association, Social Science History Association, Humboldt Foundation, American Philosophical Society, Fernand Braudel Center at Binghamton University, Federal University of São Paulo, University of Rio de Janeiro, University of São Paulo, British-American Nineteenth-Century History Conference, Cambridge University, Cornell University Society for the Humanities, Harvard University, Brown University, University of North Carolina, Tulane University, University of Pennsylvania, University of Southern Mississippi (Gulfport), University of the West Indies (St. Augustine), Georgetown University, the Huntington Library, and Columbia University.

Then there is the group of people who read and commented on all or on significant parts of the book as it was being written and revised. These include Sarah Franklin, and Rafael Marquese and his students and colleagues at the University of São Paulo, including Waldimiro Lourenço, Leo Marques, and Tamis Parron. The group also includes Richard Dunn, Chuck Mathewes, Joshua Rothman, Tom Balcerski, Eric Tagliacozzo, Adam Rothman, Julia Ott, Dale Tomich, and Tony Kaye. I thank others who not only engaged with the arguments in the book, but from whom I have learned on a journey that has been going on so long that some of you have probably forgotten. But I remember: Lauren Acker, Rosanne Adderley, Ligia Aldana, Tony Badger, Whitney Battle-Baptiste, Sven Beckert, Catherine Biba, Ser Seshs Ab Heter-Clifford M. Boxley, Jeff Brosco, Vince Brown, the late Clark Cahow, Corey Capers, Mickey Casad, Catherine Clinton, Mari Crabtree, Fred D'Aguiar, Edwidge Danticat, Christine Desan, Doug Egerton, the late Robert F. Engs, Freddi Evans, Susan Ferber, Laura Free, Johan Grimm, Gwendolyn Midlo Hall, Will Harris, Maurice Jackson, Walter Johnson, James Lake, Triwa Lee-Chin, Jonathan Levy, David Libby, Gregg Lightfoot, Mary Maples Dunn, Stephanie McCurry, John H. McNeill, Delores McQuinn, Alice Michtom, Stephen Mihm, Daegan Miller, Duncan Morgan, Brent Morris, Chris Morris, Viranjini Munansinghe, Michael O'Brien, Sarah Pearsall, Dylan Penningroth, David Perry, Larry Powell, Marcus Rediker, Elizabeth Pryor Stordeur, Olivia Robba de Rocha, Pharissa Robinson, Seth Rockman, Dan Rood, Ricardo Salles, Manisha Sinha, Adriane Lentz-Smith, Jason Scott Smith, Nicole Spruill, Daisybelle Thomas-Quinney, Darla Thompson, Phil Troutman, Rob Vanderlan, Harry Watson, Jonathan Wells, Mark Wilson, Betty Wood, Kirsten Wood, and Michael Zakim.

Here at Cornell University, I've benefited from a wonderful and supportive group of colleagues. I especially appreciate the friendship and intellectual exchange I have enjoyed with Holly Case, Derek Chang, Duane Corpis, Jeff Cowie, Ray Craib, Maria Cristina Garcia, Robert Harris, Louis Hyman, the late Michael Kammen, Walter LaFeber, Fred Logevall, Tamam Loos, Vladimir Micic, Larry Moore, Mary Beth Norton, Jon Parmenter, Gabriele Piccoli, Mary Roldan, Aaron Sachs, Nick Salvatore, Suman Seth, Joel Silbey, and Eric Tagliacozzo.

I appreciate the confidence of Cornell's History Department, especially a series of supportive chairs: Sandra Greene, Victor Koschmann, Barry Strauss, and Isabel Hull. The History staff, above all Katie Kristof and Maggie Edwards, not only did a great job, but also taught me a lot about friendship. In my other life on campus, on West Campus and especially at Carl Becker House, I have to thank Cindy Hazan and Laura Schaefer Brown in particular, but also Renee Alexander, Garrick Blalock, Rick Canfield, Isaac Kramnick, and Elmira Mangum. Above all, when it comes to Becker House I am deeply grateful to our incredible assistant dean, Amanda Carreiro. Along with her, I thank our assistants Jesse Hilliker and Victoria Gonzalez, as well as Tony Kveragas and Eileen Hughes, and the wonderful graduate and undergraduate student staff members with whom I have worked. Among the latter, I want to name in particular Neal Allar, Tinenenji Banda, Fritz Bartel, Joyce Chery, Ryan Edwards, Kelsey Fugere, Jeremy Fuller, Aziza Glass, Darvin Griffin, Louis Hopkins, Janice Chi-lok Lau, Javier Perez Burgos, Jon Senchyne, and Kavita Singh.

I have benefited for many years from the teaching, guidance, and mentoring of Drew Gilpin Faust, Richard Dunn, the late John Hope Franklin, David Johnson, Robert F. Moore, and my parents Ed and Lynda Baptist. I would forget my own self without my friends Luther Adams, Stephen Bumgardner, and Justin Warf to remind me of who I am.

As this book was going to press, my friend Stephanie M. H. Camp passed away. She was a great historian of slavery, and in this book, she would see much that she had shaped. But to me, she was my older, wiser sister, always there for me when things were at their lowest ebb. I will miss her grace and her laughter as long as I live. I still hear her voice in the words that she wrote, and I see her in the inspiration she gave to so many others. To feel those things is its own kind of grace, sweet and painful, a left hand that holds me up in its palm.

This book would have remained forever entombed in my computer without Donnette's unflagging support, enthusiasm, and love. Now it lives, because she helped breathe the spirit back into me.

Above all, the book is for my children Lillian and Ezra, who have known this story from before-times. In many ways it has made us. But stories change with each passing day. Now we are writing our own chapters.

# ABBREVIATIONS

| | |
|---|---|
| *AHR* | *American Historical Review* |
| AS | George P. Rawick, ed., *The American Slave: A Composite Autobiography*, 18 vols. (Westport, CT, 1971–1979) |
| ASAI | Theodore Weld, *American Slavery As It Is* (New York, 1839) |
| BD | Baptist Database, collected from Notarial Archives of New Orleans |
| BIELLER | Alonzo Snyder Papers, LLMVC |
| CAJ | *Correspondence of Andrew Jackson*, ed. John Spencer Bassett, 7 vols. (Washington, DC, 1926–1935) |
| CATTERALL | Helen T. Catterall, ed., *Judicial Cases Concerning American Slavery and the Negro*, 5 vols. (Washington, DC, 1926–1937) |
| *CG* | Washington *Congressional Globe* |
| CHSUS | Susan B. Carter, Scott Sigmund Gartner, Michael R. Haines, Alan L. Olmstead, Richard Sutch, and Gavin Wright, eds., *Cambridge Historical Statistics of the U.S.* (Cambridge, MA, 2006) |
| Duke | David M. Rubenstein Rare Books and Manuscripts Library, Duke University, Durham, North Carolina |
| *GHQ* | *Georgia Historical Quarterly* |
| GSMD | *God Struck Me Dead* [vol. 19 of AS] |
| HALL | Gwendolyn Midlo Hall, ed., *Afro-Louisiana History and Genealogy, 1719–1820*, www.ibiblio.org/laslave/, accessed January 6, 2014 |
| HAY | Haywood Family Papers, SHC |
| HSUS | *Historical Statistics of the United States: 1789–1945* (Washington, DC, 1949) |
| *JAH* | *Journal of American History* |
| JCC | John C. Calhoun, *The Papers of John C. Calhoun*, ed. Clyde Wilson, 28 vols. (Columbia, SC, 1959–2003) |
| *JER* | *Journal of the Early Republic* |
| JKP | James K. Polk Papers, Library of Congress |
| JQA | John Quincy Adams, *Memoirs of John Quincy Adams*, ed. Charles Francis Adams (Philadelphia, 1875–1877) |

| | |
|---|---|
| JRC | Jackson, Riddle, & Co. Papers, SHC |
| JSD | J. S. Devereux Papers |
| *JSH* | *Journal of Southern History* |
| LC | New Orleans *Louisiana Courier / Courier de Louisiane* |
| LG | New Orleans *Louisiana Gazette* |
| LINCOLN | Abraham Lincoln, *Collected Works of Abraham Lincoln*, ed. Roy E. Basler, 9 vols. (New Brunswick, NJ, 1953) |
| LLMVC | Lower Louisiana and Mississippi Valley Collections, Louisiana State University, Baton Rouge |
| MCLANE | *Documents Relative to the Manufactures in the United States*, transmitted to the House of Representatives by Secretary of the Treasury Louis McLane (Washington, DC, 1833) |
| MW | R. W. Clayton, ed., *Mother Wit: The Ex-Slave Narratives of the Louisiana Writers' Project* (New York, 1990) |
| NA | National Archives |
| *NOP* | *New Orleans Picayune* |
| NOPL | New Orleans Public Library |
| *NR* | *Niles Register* |
| NSV | Benjamin Drew, ed., *The Refugee: A North-Side View of Slavery* (Reading, MA, 1855) |
| NYHS | New York Historical Society |
| NYPL | New York Public Library |
| PALF | Palfrey Family Papers, LLMVC |
| PCC | Cameron Family Papers, SHC |
| RASP | Records of Antebellum Southern Plantations, microfilm series collected from multiple archives. See: www.lexisnexis.com/academic/upa, accessed January 6, 2014 |
| RCB | Rice C. Ballard Papers, SHC |
| SCPOA | St. Charles Parish Original Acts |
| SHC | Southern Historical Collection, University of North Carolina, Chapel Hill |
| ST | John Blassingame, ed., *Slave Testimony: Two Centuries of Letters, Speeches, Interviews, and Autobiographies* (Baton Rouge, LA, 1977) |
| TASTD | Trans-Atlantic Slave Trade Database, www.slavevoyages.org/tast/assessment/estimates.faces, accessed June 16, 2012 |
| TP | Clarence E. Carter, ed., *Territorial Papers of the United States*, 26 vols. (Washington, DC, 1934–1975) |
| Tulane | Special Collections, Howard-Tilton Library, Tulane University |
| VHS | Virginia Historical Society |
| WCCC | William C. C. Claiborne, *Official Letterbooks of W. C. C. Claiborne*, ed. Dunbar Rowland, 6 vols. (Jackson, MS, 1917) |

# NOTES

INTRODUCTION. THE HEART: 1937

1. Robert F. Engs, *Educating the Disfranchised and Disinherited: Samuel Chapman Armstrong and Hampton Institute, 1839–1893* (Knoxville, TN, 1999); Lorenzo Ivy: Charles L. Perdue Jr., Thomas E. Barden, and Robert K. Phillips, eds., *Weevils in the Wheat: Interviews with Virginia Ex-Slaves* (Charlottesville, VA, 1976), 151–154; personal communications with Rev. Doyle Thomas, January 2012.

2. Stephen Small and Jennifer Eichstedt, *Representations of Slavery: Race and Ideology in Southern Plantation Museums* (Washington, DC, 2002); cf. Stephanie E. Yuhl, "Hidden in Plain Sight: Centering the Domestic Slave Trade in American Public History," *JSH* 79, no. 3 (2013): 593–625.

3. Ralph Ellison, "Twentieth-Century Fiction and the Black Mask of Humanity," *Shadow and Act* (New York, 1964).

4. Many recent historians of slavery, preferring the published autobiographies, have discounted the WPA narratives. Systematic critiques of the use of such interviews include the following: John Blassingame, "Introduction," in ST, xliii–lxii; Donna J. Spindel, "Assessing Memory: Twentieth-Century Slave Narratives Reconsidered," *Journal of Interdisciplinary History* 27 (1996): 247–261; Damian Alan Pargas, "The Gathering Storm: Slave Responses to the Threat of Interregional Migration in the Early Nineteenth Century," *Journal of Early American History* 2, no. 3 (2012): 286–315. I find these critics less persuasive than those who argue that the twentieth-century narratives are extremely useful. The WPA narratives contain rich personal observation remembered by the interviewees themselves, which can be read carefully and successfully with an understanding of the interview dynamic. Just as importantly, the narratives also transmit collectively held stories that in some cases are even older than the interviewees. The latter reflect the culture, beliefs, and vernacular history of the enslaved—including concepts and beliefs that clearly predate and make their way into the nineteenth-century narratives. See Mia Bay, *The White Image in the Black Mind: African-American Ideas About White People, 1830–1925* (New York, 2000), esp. 113–116; George Rawick, "General Introduction" to AS, S1, 11, xxxix; Edward E. Baptist, "'Stol' and Fetched Here': Enslaved Migration, Ex-Slave Narratives, and

Vernacular History," in Edward E. Baptist and Stephanie M. H. Camp, eds., *New Studies in the History of American Slavery* (Athens, GA, 2006), 243–274. For links between vernacular storytelling by slaves and former slaves, on the one hand, and literary production by African Americans, on the other, see William L. Andrews, *To Tell a Free Story: The First Century of Afro-American Autobiography, 1760–1865* (Urbana, IL, 1985), 274; Marion W. Starling, *The Slave Narrative: Its Place in American History* (Boston, 1981, repr. of 1946 diss.); Charles T. Davis and Henry Louis Gates, eds., *The Slave's Narrative* (New York, 1985); Henry Louis Gates, *The Signifying Monkey: A Theory of Afro-American Literary Criticism* (New York, 1988).

## CHAPTER I. FEET: 1783–1810

1. In this book, some of the vignettes told from the perspective of enslaved people incorporate not only the specific content of the historical documents cited, but also details from other sources, as is the custom with evocative history. By drawing upon a wide variety of sources, I attempt to provide a richer depiction of the landscape, work practices, and cultural practices of the time and a more intimate portrait of the enslaved African Americans whose experience is the center of this history. These sources include the testimony of other formerly enslaved people who went through virtually identical experiences. This particular story, for instance, is drawn from Charles Ball, *Slavery in the United States: A Narrative of the Life and Adventures of Charles Ball* . . . (New York, 1837), but it was written in the light of dozens of other accounts, including descriptions of people's reactions to coffles, descriptions of slavery in early nineteenth-century Piedmont North Carolina, reports of the family demography of enslaved people during the era of the early domestic slave trade, and enslaved people's stories of their experience during the era of the domestic slave trade. All of these are cited copiously in the coming pages, but for firsthand accounts of enslaved people's reactions to the slave trade, see Charity Austin, AS, 14.1 (NC), 59; Ben Johnson, AS, 14.1 (NC); Dave Lawson, AS, 15.2 (NC), 49; Lila Nichols, AS, 14.1 (NC), 147–150; Mary Hicks, AS, 14.1 (NC), 184; Josephine Smith, AS (NC); Alex Woods, AS, 15.2, (NC), 416–417; Jeremiah Loguen, *The Rev. J. W. Loguen, As Slave and Free* Man (Syracuse, 1859), 65–67; "Recollections of a Runaway Slave," *Emancipator*, September 20, 1838; Isaac Williams, *Aunt Sally: The Cross, the Way of Freedom* (Cincinnati, 1858), 10–15; ASAI, 76; and, for rich documentation of enslavement and the domestic slave trade in the area of North Carolina through which Ball was driven in chains, see Tyre Glen Papers, Duke; Jarratt-Puryear Papers, Duke, and Isaac Jarratt Papers, SHC. Unless otherwise noted, italics, underlining, and boldface type within quotations are reproduced from the original.

2. Edmund Morgan, *American Slavery, American Freedom: The Ordeal of Colonial Virginia* (New York, 1975); Kathy Brown, *Good Wives, Nasty Wenches, and Anxious Patriarchs: Gender, Race, and Power in Colonial Virginia* (Chapel Hill, NC, 1996); Lorena Walsh, *Motives of Honor, Pleasure, and Profit: Plantation Management in the Colonial Chesapeake, 1607–1763* (Chapel Hill, NC, 2010).

3. Again, a few starting points: Philip Curtin, *The Rise and Fall of the Plantation Complex: Essays in Atlantic History* (Cambridge, UK,1990); Richard Dunn, *Sugar and Slaves: The Rise of the Planter Class in the English West Indies, 1624–1713* (Chapel

Hill, NC, 1972); Peter Wood, *Black Majority: Negroes in Colonial South Carolina from 1670 Through the Stono Rebellion* (New York, 1973); Leonardo Marques, "The United States and the Transatlantic Slave Trade to the Americas, 1776–1867" (PhD diss., Emory University, 2013).

4. Robert Olwell, *Masters, Slaves, and Subjects: The Culture of Power in the South Carolina Low Country, 1740–1790* (Ithaca, NY, 1998), 270.

5. David Brion Davis, *The Problem of Slavery in the Age of Revolution, 1775–1820* (Ithaca, NY, 1975); Donald Robinson, *Slavery in the Structure of American Politics, 1765–1820* (New York, 1970); Christine Heyrman, *Southern Cross: The Beginning of the Bible Belt* (New York, 1997); Thomas Jefferson, *Notes on the State of Virginia* (New York, 1984 [Library of America]), 289.

6. Rachel Klein, *Unification of a Slave State: The Rise of the Planter Class in the South Carolina Backcountry* (Chapel Hill, NC, 1990); Richard Beeman, *The Evolution of the Southern Backcountry* (Philadelphia, 1984); Allan Gallay, *The Indian Slave Trade: The Rise of English Empire in the Colonial South* (New Haven, CT, 2002); James Merrell, *The Indians' New World: Catawbas and Their Neighbors from European Contact Through the Era of Removal* (Chapel Hill, NC, 1989).

7. John Filson, *Adventures of Colonel Daniel Boone* (Norwich, CT, 1786), and his *Discovery, Settlement, and Present State of Kentucky* (New York, 1793), 74; Daniel Blake Smith, "'This Idea in Heaven': Image and Reality on the Kentucky Frontier," in Craig Thompson Friend, ed., *The Buzzel About Kentuck: Settling the Promised Land* (Lexington, KY, 1998), 78; *Massachusetts Spy*, January 27, 1785; *Philadelphia Gazetteer*, November 27, 1784; Ellen Eslinger, "The Shape of Slavery on the Kentucky Frontier," *Kentucky Historical Society Register* 92 (1994): 1–23, esp. 4; Steven Aron, *How the West Was Lost: The Transformation of Kentucky from Borderland to Daniel Boone* (Baltimore, 1996).

8. Thomas Hart to [N. Hart], August 3, 1780, "Shane Collection, No. 22"; *Philadelphia Gazetteer*, November 27, 1784, May 16, 1788; *Massachusetts Spy*, May 29, 1782; *Connecticut Journal*, November 4, 1789; *New York Packet*, October 22, 1789; *New York Weekly*, June 20, 1792; *Philadelphia Advertiser*, October 4, 1792; *Norwich Western Register*, May 20, 1794.

9. Abraham Lincoln to Jesse Lincoln, April 1, 1854, in LINCOLN, 2:217; cf. Richard L. Miller, *Lincoln and His World: The Early Years* (Mechanicsburg, PA, 2006), 5n17.

10. Joanne Pope Melish, *Disowning Slavery: Gradual Emancipation and "Race" in New England, 1780–1860* (Ithaca, NY, 1998); Arthur Zilversmit, *The First Emancipation: The Abolition of Slavery in the North* (Chicago, 1967); Eva Sheppard Wolf, *Race and Liberty in the New Nation: Emancipation in Virginia from Jefferson to Nat Turner* (Baton Rouge, LA, 2006); Jefferson, *Notes on the State of Virginia*, 288; cf. Annette Gordon-Reed, *Thomas Jefferson and Sally Hemings: An American Controversy* (Charlottesville, VA, 1997).

11. Patricia Watlington, *The Partisan Spirit: Kentucky Politics, 1779–1792* (New York, 1972), 17–18; Janet A. Riesman, "Money, Credit, and Federalist Political Economy," in Richard Beeman, Stephen Botein, and Edward C. Carter II, eds., *Beyond Confederation: Origins of the Constitution and American National Identity* (Chapel Hill, NC, 1987), 128–161.

12. Peter Onuf, *Statehood and Union: A History of the Northwest Ordinance* (Bloomington, IN, 1987); Robinson, *Slavery in American Politics*, 379–380; Malcolm C. Rohrbough, *Land-Office Business: The Settlement and Administration of American Public Lands* (New York, 1968), 8–14.

13. David Libby, *Slavery and Frontier Mississippi, 1720–1835* (Jackson, MS, 2004); Walter LaFeber, *The American Age: United States Foreign Policy at Home and Abroad Since 1750* (New York, 1989), 30–31; Andrew R. L. Cayton, "'Separate Interests' and the Nation-State: The Washington Administration and the Origins of Regionalism in the Trans-Mississippi West," *JAH* 79, no. 1 (1992): 39–67; Jefferson to Madison, April 25, 1784, *Jefferson Papers: Digital Edition*, ed. Barbara Oberg and J. Jefferson Looney, http://rotunda.upress.virginia.edu/founders/TSJN-01-07-02-0129 (accessed February 24, 2014).

14. Paul S. Finkelman, "Slavery and the Northwest Ordinance: A Study in Ambiguity," *JER* 6, no. 4 (1986): 343–370.

15. Woody Holton, *Unruly Americans and the Origins of the Constitution* (New York, 2007); Pauline Maier, *Ratification: The People Debate Their Constitution, 1787–1789* (New York, 2010).

16. *The Founders' Constitution*, ed. Philip Kurland and Ralph Lerner (Chicago, 1987), 3:280.

17. *Founders' Constitution*, 3:279–281. Cf. George Van Cleve, *A Slaveholders' Union: Slavery, Politics, and the Constitution in the Early American Republic* (Chicago, 2010).

18. Hazel Dicken-Garcia, *To Western Woods: The Breckinridge Family Moves to Kentucky in 1793* (Rutherford, NJ, 1991); 177–178; CHSUS, 1:Aa3644–3744.

19. Aron, *How the West Was Lost*, 82–95; Frederika Teute, "Land, Liberty, and Labor in the Post-Revolutionary Era: Kentucky as the Promised Land" (PhD diss., Johns Hopkins University, 1988), 102–130, 185, 227–275; Watlington, *Partisan Spirit*, 220–222; David Rice, *Slavery Inconsistent with Justice and Good Policy; Proved by a Speech Delivered in the Convention, Held at Danville, Kentucky* (Philadelphia, 1792); John Craig Hammond, *Slavery, Freedom, and Expansion in the Early American West* (Charlottesville, VA, 2007); John Craig Hammond, "Slavery, Settlement, and Empire: The Expansion and Growth of Slavery in the Interior of the North American Continent, 1770–1820," *JER* 32, no. 2 (2012): 175–206.

20. Dicken-Garcia, *To Western Woods*, 177–178; Marion Nelson Winship, "Kentucky *in* the New Republic: A Study of Distance and Connection," in Craig Thompson Friend, ed., *Buzzel About Kentuck: Settling the Promised Land* (Lexington, KY, 1998), 100–123; Gail S. Terry, "Sustaining the Bonds of Kinship in a Trans-Appalachian Migration: The Cabell-Breckinridge Slaves Move West," *Virginia Magazine of History and Biography* 102 (1994): 455–476.

21. Francis Fedric, *Slave Life in Virginia and Kentucky, Or, Fifty Years of Slavery* . . . (London, 1853), 15.

22. Terry, "Sustaining the Bonds of Kinship," 465–466.

23. Fedric, *Slave Life*, 15–17; Dicken-Garcia, *To Western Woods*, 116–118, 173; Daniel Drake, *Pioneer Life in Kentucky: A Series of Reminiscential Letters* (Cincinnati, 1870), 176–177.

24. Fedric, *Slave Life*, 16; Washington (PA) *Herald of Liberty*, September 2, 1799.

25. Stanley Harrold, *Border War: Fighting over Slavery Before the Civil War* (Chapel Hill, NC, 2010); *Philadelphia Advertiser*, February 17, 1792.

26. William Hayden, *Narrative of William Hayden, Containing a Faithful Account of His Travels for Many Years Whilst a Slave* (Cincinnati, 1846), 20–26; Teute, "Land, Liberty, and Labor," 209–210.

27. Teute, "Land, Liberty, and Labor," 212; Monica Najar, "'Meddling with Emancipation': Baptists, Authority, and the Rift over Slavery in the Upper South," *JER* 25, no. 2 (2005): 157–186.

28. Barbara Fields, *Slavery and Freedom on the Middle Ground: Maryland During the Nineteenth Century* (New Haven, CT, 1985); Seth Rockman, *Scraping By: Wage Labor, Slavery, and Survival in Early Baltimore* (Baltimore, 2009); Max Grivno, *Gleanings of Freedom: Free and Slave Labor Along the Mason-Dixon Line, 1790–1860* (Urbana, IL, 2011); Jennifer Hull Dorsey, *Hirelings: African American Workers and Free Labor in Early Maryland* (Ithaca, NY, 2011); US Bureau of the Census, *Negro Population, 1790–1815* (Washington, DC, 1918), 57.

29. Ball, *Slavery in the United States*, 36.

30. Leonard Black, *The Life and Sufferings of Leonard Black, a Fugitive from Slavery* (New Bedford, CT, 1847), 24–26; Ball, *Slavery in the United States*, 15–18; Thomas Culbreth to Gov. Maryland, February 21, 1824, 818–819, in "Estimates of the Value of Slaves, 1815," *AHR* 19 (1914): 813–838.

31. David Smith, *Biography of the Rev. David E. Smith of the A.M.E. Church* (Xenia, OH, 1881), 11–14; William Grimes, *Life of William Grimes, Written by Himself* (New York, 1825), 22; cf. Abraham Johnstone, *The Address of Abraham Johnstone, a Black Man Who Was Hanged at Woodbury, N.J.* (Philadelphia, 1797); Michael Tadman, "The Hidden History of Slave-Trading in Antebellum South Carolina: John Springs III and Other 'Gentlemen Dealing in Slaves,'" *South Carolina Historical Magazine* 97 (1996): 6–29, esp. 22. For the complex origins of the cotton gin, see Joyce Chaplin, *An Anxious Pursuit: Agricultural Innovation and Modernity in the Lower South, 1730–1815* (Chapel Hill, NC, 2013); Angela Lakwete, *Inventing the Cotton Gin: Machine and Myth in Antebellum America* (Baltimore, 2003).

32. Cf. *New York Advertiser*, September 24, 1790.

33. "Charleston" from *Pennsylvania Packet*, February 25, 1790; C. Peter Magrath, *Yazoo: Law and Politics in the New Republic: The Case of Fletcher v. Peck* (Providence, RI, 1966), 2–5.

34. Jane Kamensky, *The Exchange Artist: A Tale of High-Flying Speculation and America's First Banking Collapse* (New York, 2008); "Charleston" from *Pennsylvania Packet*, February 25, 1790.

35. Shaw Livermore, "Early American Land Companies: Their Influence on Corporate Development" (PhD diss., Columbia University, 1939).

36. Magrath, *Yazoo*, 6–19; Kamensky, *Exchange Artist*, 35–36.

37. John Losson to John Smith, 1786, Pocket Plantation Papers, RASP. Series E.

38. G. Melvin Herndon, "Samuel Edward Butler of Virginia Goes to Georgia, 1784," *GHQ* 52 (1968): 115–131, esp. 123; "The Diary of Samuel E. Butler, 1784–1786, and the Inventory and Appraisement of his Estate," ed. G. Melvin Herndon, *GHQ* 52 (1968): 208–209, 214–215; *Heads of Families at the First Census of the United States Taken in the Year 1790* (Washington, DC, 1908), 32; Grimes, *Life*, 25; cf.

Thomas Johnson, *Africa for Christ: Twenty-Eight Years a Slave* (London, 1892), 10–11; Moses Grandy, *Life of Moses Grandy, Late a Slave in the United States of America* (Boston, 1844), 55–56; Hayden, *Narrative*, 57–59; Julius Melbourn, *Life and Opinions of Julius Melbourn* (Syracuse, NY, 1847), 9–10; James Pennington, *The Fugitive Blacksmith* (London, 1849), vi, 24, 82; James Watkins, *Narrative of the Life of James Watkins, Formerly a "Chattel" in Maryland* (Bolton, UK, 1852), 26; Lewis Charlton, *Sketches of the Life of Mr. Lewis Charlton* (Portland, ME, n.d.), 1; James Williams, *Life and Adventures of James Williams, a Fugitive Slave* (San Francisco, 1873), 11.

39. For definition of "coffle," see Oxford English Dictionary Online, www.oed.com.

40. James Kirke Paulding, *Letters from the South, Written During an Excursion in the Summer of 1816* (New York, 1817), 126–127.

41. Grimes, *Life*, 22; *Alexandria Gazette*, June 22, 1827; Damian Alan Pargas, "The Gathering Storm: Slave Responses to the Threat of Interregional Migration in the Early Nineteenth Century," *Journal of Early American History* 2, no. 3 (2012): 286–315; Frederic Bancroft, *Slave-Trading in the Old South* (Baltimore, 1931), 23–24. Some of the chains were literally repurposed from Atlantic slave-trading vessels. See Gardner, Dean, to Phillips, Gardner, April 10, 1807, Slavery Collection, NYHS.

42. *New Hampshire Gazette*, October 13, 1801; *Alexandria Times*, January 10, 1800.

43. ASAI, 69–70; John Brown, *Slave Life in Georgia* (London, 1855), 17–18.

44. Parker Autobiography, Rankin-Parker Papers, Duke; "Aaron," *The Light and Truth of Slavery* (Springfield, MA, 1845).

45. Matthew Mason, *Slavery and Politics in the Early American Republic* (Chapel Hill, NC, 2006); John C. Hammond and Matthew Mason, eds., *Contesting Slavery: The Politics of Bondage and Freedom in the New American Nation* (Charlottesville, VA, 2011).

46. Jesse Torrey, *A Portraiture of Domestic Slavery in the United States* (Philadelphia, 1817), 39–40, 33–34.

47. Jesse Torrey, *American Slave-Trade* (London, 1822), 66–71.

48. Robert Goodloe Harper, *The Case of the Georgia Sales Reconsidered* (Philadelphia, 1797); Abraham Bishop, *The Georgia Speculation Unveiled* (Hartford, CT, 1797).

49. "Charleston" from *Pennsylvania Packet*, February 25, 1790.

50. Thomas Hart Benton, *Abridgement of the Debates of Congress, from 1798 to 1856*, 223 (March 1798).

51. Magrath, *Yazoo*, 34–35.

52. Klein, *Unification*, 252–254; John Cummings and Joseph A Hill, *Negro Population 1790–1915* (Washington, 1918), 45, available at http://www2.census.gov/prod2/decennial/documents/00480330_TOC.pdf; Watson Jennison, *Cultivating Race: The Expansion of Slavery in Georgia, 1750–1860* (Lexington, KY, 2012).

53. *NR*, September 29, 1821; Gerald T. Dunne, "Bushrod Washington and the Mount Vernon Slaves," *Supreme Court Historical Society Yearbook* (1980); Robert Gudmestad, *A Troublesome Commerce: The Transformation of the Interstate Slave Trade* (Baton Rouge, LA, 2003), 6–8.

54. Thomas Jefferson to John Holmes, April 22, 1820; *Founders' Constitution*, 1:156; Jefferson, *Notes on the State of Virginia*, 264.

55. *NR*, September 1, 1821.

56. Ball, *Slavery in the United States*, 86–91.

### CHAPTER 2. HEADS: 1791–1815

1. Benjamin Latrobe, *Impressions Respecting New Orleans: Diary and Sketches, 1818–1820*, ed. Samuel Wilson Jr. (New York, 1951), 13–14; Frances Trollope, *Domestic Manners of the Americans*, ed. Pamela Neville-Sington (repr. London, 1997), 9–11; John Pintard to Sec. Treasury, September 14, 1803, TP, 9:52–53. Cf. Amos Stoddard, *Historical Sketches of Louisiana* (Philadelphia, 1812), 159–160; James Pearse, *Narrative of the Life of James Pearse* (Rutland, VT, c. 1826), 16; H. Bellenden Ker, *Travels Through the Western Interior of the United States* (Elizabethtown, NJ, 1816), 36; Pierre-Louis Berquin-Duvallon, trans. John Davis, *Travels in Louisiana and Florida in the Year 1802* (New York, 1806), 8.

2. TASTD; James McMillin, *The Final Victims: Foreign Slave Trade to North America, 1783–1810* (Columbia, SC, 2004), 23; Stephen Behrendt, David Eltis, and David Richardson, "The Costs of Coercion: African Agency in the Pre-Modern Atlantic World," *Economic History Review* (n.s.) 54, no. 3 (2001): 454–476.

3. Approval Alex. Clark, Bill of Lading, March 9, 1807, Reel 1, Inward Manifests, New Orleans, RG 36, NA; John Lambert, *Travels Through Canada and the United States of America, In the Years 1806, 1807, and 1808* (London, 1816), 2:166.

4. David Eltis, *The Rise of African Slavery in the Americas* (New York, 2000); Joseph C. Miller, *Way of Death: Merchant Capitalism and the Angolan Slave Trade* (Madison, WI, 1988); Robin C. Blackburn, *Origins of New World Slavery: From the Baroque to the Modern, 1492–1800* (London, 1997).

5. Sidney Mintz, *Sweetness and Power: The Place of Sugar in Modern History* (New York, 1985); Stuart Schwartz, *Sugar Plantations in the Formation of Brazilian Society: Bahia, 1550–1835* (New York, 1985).

6. M.L.E. Moreau de St. Méry, *Description topographique, physique, civile, politique et historique de la partie francaise de l'isle Saint-Domingue . . .* , 2 vols. (Paris, 1797); Antonio Benitez-Rojo, *The Repeating Island: The Caribbean and the Postmodern Perspective*, trans. James Maraniss (Durham, NC, 1992).

7. Mintz, *Sweetness and Power*; Kenneth Pomeranz and Steven Topik, *The World That Trade Created: Society, Culture, and the World Economy, 1400 to the Present*, 2nd ed. (Armonk, NY, 2000); Kenneth C. Pomeranz, *The Great Divergence: China, Europe, and the Making of the Modern World Economy* (Berkeley, CA, 2000), 31–68; David Eltis, "Nutritional Trends in Africa and the Americas: Heights of Africans, 1819–1839," *Journal of Interdisciplinary History* 12 (1982): 453–475.

8. Berquin-Duvallon, *Travels in Louisiana*, 35–37.

9. Alexander DeConde, *This Affair of Louisiana* (New York, 1976), 61–62, 107–126; William Plumer, *William Plumer's Memorandum of Proceedings in the U.S. Senate, 1803–1807*, ed. Edward Sommerville Brown (Ann Arbor, MI, 1923).

10. Carolyn Fick, *The Making of Haiti: The St. Domingue Revolution from Below* (Knoxville, TN, 1990).

11. Michel-Rolph Trouillot, *Silencing the Past: Power and the Production of History* (Boston, 1995); Susan Buck-Morss, "Hegel and Haiti," *Critical Inquiry* 26 (2000):

821–865; Alfred N. Hunt, *Haiti's Influence on Antebellum America: Slumbering Volcano in the Caribbean* (Baton Rouge, LA, 1988).

12. C. L. R. James, *The Black Jacobins: Toussaint Louverture and the San Domingo Revolution* (New York, 1963).

13. Stephen Englund, *Napoleon: A Political Life* (New York, 2004); Laurent Du-Bois, *Avengers of the New World* (New York, 2004); Robin Blackburn, *The Overthrow of Colonial Slavery* (London, 1988).

14. Roger Kennedy, *Mr. Jefferson's Lost Cause: Land, Farmers, Slavery, and the Louisiana Purchase* (New York, 2003).

15. Jefferson to Robert Livingston, April 18, 1802; Jon Kukla, *A Wilderness So Immense: The Louisiana Purchase and the Destiny of America* (New York, 2003), 235–259.

16. DeConde, *Affair of Louisiana*, 161–166.

17. P. L. Roederer, *Oeuvres du Comte P. L. Roederer* (Paris, 1854), 3:461; Comté Barbé-Marbois, *The History of Louisiana: Particularly of the Cession of That Colony to the United States of America*, trans. "By an American Citizen (William B. Lawrence)" (Philadelphia, 1830), 174–175, 263–264.

18. Dubois, *Avengers of the New World*, 297–301.

19. Christopher Brown, *Moral Capital: Foundations of British Abolitionism* (Chapel Hill, NC, 2006).

20. *Annals of Congress*, 1806, 238; Donald Robinson, *Slavery in the Structure of American Politics, 1765–1820* (New York, 1970), 331; David Brion Davis, *Slavery and Human Progress* (New York, 1984), 162–163.

21. DeConde, *Affair of Louisiana*, 205–206; Jared Bradley, ed., *Interim Appointment: William C. C. Claiborne Letter Book, 1804–1805* (Baton Rouge, LA, 2003), 13; Alexander Hamilton, in *New-York Evening Post*, July 5, 1803, *Papers of Alexander Hamilton*, 26:129–136. An exception to historians' cover-up: Henry Adams, *History of the Administrations of Jefferson and Madison* (New York, 1986 [Library of America]), 1:2, 20–22. Cf. Edward E. Baptist, "Hidden in Plain View: Haiti and the Louisiana Purchase," in Elizabeth Hackshaw and Martin Munro, eds., *Echoes of the Haitian Revolution in the Modern World* (Kingston, Jamaica, 2008).

22. Peter J. Kastor, *Nation's Crucible: The Louisiana Purchase and the Creation of America* (New Haven, CT, 2004); Lawrence Powell, *The Accidental City: Improvising New Orleans* (Cambridge, MA, 2012); Plumer, *Proceedings*, 223–224, notes three Louisiana French planters' visits to Congress complaining about Claiborne.

23. Berquin-Duvallon, *Travels in Louisiana*, 28–29, 80; Vincent Nolte, *Memoirs of Vincent Nolte* (New York, 1934); Sarah P. Russell, "Cultural Conflicts and Common Interests: The Making of the Sugar Planter Class in Louisiana, 1795–1853" (PhD diss., University of Maryland, 2000); Kenneth Aslakson, "The 'Quadroon-Placage' Myth of Antebellum New Orleans: Anglo-American (Mis)interpretations of a French-Caribbean Phenomenon," *Journal of Social History* 45 (2012): 709–734; Jennifer Spear, *Race, Sex, and Social Order in Early New Orleans* (Baltimore, 2009).

24. Peter C. Hoffer, *The Treason Trials of Aaron Burr* (Lawrence, KS, 2008); James Madison to Gov. Claiborne, January 12, 1807, TP, 9:702.

25. J. P. to J. Johnston, February 1, 1810, Folder 1, PALF; Adam Rothman, *Slave Country: American Expansion and the Origins of the Deep South* (Cambridge, MA, 2005).

26. J. Carlyle Sitterston, *Sugar Country: The Cane Sugar Industry in the South, 1763–1950* (Lexington, KY, 1953), 3–11; Ira Berlin, *Many Thousands Gone: The First Two Centuries of Slavery in North America* (Cambridge, MA, 1998), 325–357; Stoddard, *Sketches*, 332–333; C. C. Robin, *Voyages dans L'Intérieur de la Louisiane,* (Paris, 1807), 109–110; Russell, "Cultural Conflicts," 55.

27. James Pitot, *Observations of the Colony of Louisiana, from 1796 to 1802* (repr. Baton Rouge, LA, 1979), 9; Claiborne to President Jefferson, November 25, 1804, TP, 9:340; Gilbert Leonard to Claiborne, January 25, 1804, TP, 9:172. On Louisiana importing only a few thousand slaves before 1801 to 1804: TASTD; Rothman, *Slave Country*, 89–91.

28. John Watkins to Claiborne, February 2, 1804, WCCC, 2:10–11; Claiborne to Madison, July 5, 1804, March 10, 1804, ibid.; cf. Claiborne to Albert Gallatin, May 8, 1804, ibid., 2:235–237, 25–26, 134; *Annals of Congress*, vol. 14, 1595–1608; W. E. B. DuBois, *Suppression of the African Slave-Trade to the United States* (New York, 1896), 89–90; James E. Scanlon, "A Sudden Conceit: Jefferson and the Louisiana Government Bill," *Louisiana History* 9 (1968): 139–162; Sarah P. Russell, "Ethnicity, Commerce, and Community on Lower Louisiana's Plantation Frontier," *Louisiana History* 40 (1999): 396–399; Robinson, *Slavery in American Politics*, 398; Claiborne to President Jefferson, November 25, 1804, TP, 9:340; "Act for Organization of Orleans Territory," March 26, 1804, TP, 9:202–213. Southerners and their congressional allies, including John Quincy Adams, defeated an effort to free all slaves imported into the territory.

29. McMillin, *Final Victims*, Appendix B; Claiborne to Madison, May 8, 1804, WCCC, 2:134, 358–361; Claiborne to President Jefferson, November 25, 1804, TP, 9:340; Rothman, *Slave Country*, 92–95; Brown to Gallatin, December 11, 1805, TP, 9:545–547.

30. Frederic Bancroft, *Slave-Trading in the Old South* (Baltimore, 1931), 300n19; Claiborne to A. Jackson, December 23, 1801; John Hutchings to Jackson, December 25, 1801, CAJ, 1:265, 266.

31. Claiborne to R. Smith, May 15, 1809, WCCC, 4:354–355; Paul Lachance, "The 1809 Immigration of the St. Domingue Refugees," in Carl Brasseaux and Glenn Conrad, eds., *The Road to Louisiana: The Saint-Domingue Refugees, 1792–1809* (Lafayette, LA, 1992), 246–252; Paul Lachance, "The Foreign French," in Arnold Hirsch and Joseph Logsdon, eds., *Creole New Orleans: Race and Americanization* (Baton Rouge, LA, 1992), 101–130; Extrait des documents, 1804; Dautouville to Miltenberger, July 1806, both Miltenberger Papers, SHC. Some of the French nationals came to Cuba from Saint-Domingue shortly after 1791, and some as late as 1803. Some of those denominated as "slaves" in the migration to Louisiana had been transported to Cuba from Saint-Domingue, while others had been bought there as slaves in the up to eighteen years that French nationals had spent in Cuba. See Rebecca J. Scott, "Paper Thin: Freedom and Re-Enslavement in the Diaspora of the Haitian Revolution," *Law and History Review* 29, no. 4 (2011): 1061–1087.

32. Claiborne to R. Smith, July 29, 1809, WCCC, 4:391–393.

33. James Mather to Claiborne, July 18, 1809, WCCC, 4:387–409; Claiborne to Julien Poydras, May 29, 1809, ibid., 4:371–372; Claiborne to R. Smith, May 20, 1809, ibid., 4:363–367; Claiborne to William Savage, November 10, 1809, ibid., 5:4–6;

*Annals of Congress*, 11th Cong., Pt. 1, 462–465, "House Debate on Emigrants from Cuba."

34. "Aux Arrivans de Cuba: On prendrait à loyer . . . une trentaine de nègres de hache & quelques négresses de travail," *Moniteur de la Louisiane*, August 5, 1809; "Vente a L'Encan," ibid., October 7, 1809; HALL, 60131, 54165; F. Carrere à Miltenberger, April 18, 1809, and Miltenberger to N. Fournier, September 27, 1809, Miltenberger Papers, SHC. Italics added.

35. Don Dodd and Wynelle Dodd, *Historical Statistics of the United States* (Tuscaloosa, AL, 1973–1976); R. Claiborne to Madison, December 31, 1806, TP, 9:692–702.

36. *LC*, November 19, 1810; *LG*, December 6, 1810, July 24, 1810.

37. Quartier Générale, January 13, 1811, "Interrogation du Cupidon," January 13, 1811, SCPOA; HALL; Thomas Marshall Thompson, "National Newspaper and Legislative Reactions to Louisiana's Deslondes Slave Revolt of 1811," *Louisiana History* 33 (1992): 5–29; James H. Dormon, "The Persistent Specter: Slave Rebellion in Territorial Louisiana," *Louisiana History* 18 (1977): 389–404; *Richmond Enquirer*, February 22, 1811, reported as leader "Charles, a yellow fellow, the property of Mr. Andre"; *LG*, January 11, 1811; Albert Thrasher, *On to New Orleans! Louisiana's Heroic 1811 Slave Revolt* (New Orleans, 1996), 297; Rothman, *Slave Country*.

38. Trial Augustin, February 25, 1811, SCPOA, 1811, no. 20; Glenn Conrad, *The German Coast: Abstracts of the Civil Records of St. Charles and St. John the Baptist Parishes, 1804–1812* (Lafayette, LA, 1981), 108.

39. Claiborne to Wade Hampton, January 7 (1 & 2), 1811, WCCC, 5:91–92.

40. Interrogation "Koock," January 14, 1811, SCPOA; Mary Ann Sternberg, *Along the River Road: Past and Present on Louisiana's Historic Byway* (Baton Rouge, LA, 1996), 130; *Moniteur*, January 15, 1811; Thrasher, *On to New Orleans*, 268.

41. Jupiter interrogation from "Jugement du Nègre de M. Andry," February 20, 1811, no. 17, SCPOA.

42. Numbers from HALL; Deposition of Hermogène Trepagnier, SCPOA, no. 20.

43. Thrasher, *On to New Orleans*, 119n42, n46, n49, 52–53.

44. *Moniteur*, January 17, 1811.

45. Destrehan's compensation claim, SCPOA, 160.

46. *Moniteur*, January 17, 1811; Manuel Andry to Claiborne, *LC*, January 15, 1811; Hampton to Sec. of War, January 16, 1811, TP, 9:918–919; Hampton to Claiborne, January 12, 1811, TP, 9:916–917.

47. Conrad, *German Coast*.

48. *Moniteur*, January 17, 1811; Barthelemy compensation list from SCPOA; Samuel Hambleton to David Porter, January 15, 1811, in Stanley Engerman, Seymour Drescher, and Robert L. Paquette, eds., *Slavery* (New York, 2001), 326.

49. January 14, 1811, SCPOA: *"Amar, chef de brigandes, dénoncé comme tel par tous les autres brigandes, n'a pas peu répondre aux questions quand lui a adressées, parce qu'il l'était bless'e à la gorge, de manière à être pincé de l'usàge de la parole"* (Amar, chief of rebels, denounced as such by all the other rebels, was not able to respond to questions when asked, because he had been wounded in the throat, in such a way as to prevent him from speaking.")

50. SCPOA, "State of the Work Forces"; Thrasher, *On to New Orleans*, 64–65.

51. SCPOA Act 2, 3–4.

52. TP, 9:923, 702; and a key point of Rothman, *Slave Country*.

53. Claiborne to Andry, December 24, 1811, WCCC, 6:15; Junius P. Rodriguez, "Always 'En Garde': The Effect of Rebellion upon the Louisiana Mentality, 1811–1815," *Louisiana History* 33, no. 4 (1992): 399–416. Just to be certain that free people of color could not assist rebellion, Louisiana passed new laws that increased taxes on free men of color and forbade them to carry weapons—even walking sticks, which could hide saber blades.

54. Matthew Mason, *Slavery and Politics in the Early American Republic* (Chapel Hill, NC, 2006); Speech of Josiah Quincy, *Annals*, 11th Cong., 3rd sess., 525, 540.

55. Robert Remini, *Andrew Jackson and the Course of American Empire, 1767–1821* (New York, 1977), 247–250; Alexander Walker, *Jackson and New Orleans: An Authentic Narrative of the Memorable Achievements of the American Army* (Cincinnati, 1856).

56. Remini, *Jackson and American Empire*, 133–216; James Parton, *Life of Jackson* (New York, 1860), 1:88–94.

57. Remini, *Jackson and American Empire*, 246–254.

58. For Indian slave owners, see, among many other excellent works, Christina Snyder, *Slavery in Indian Country: The Changing Face of Captivity in Early America* (Cambridge, MA, 2010); Tiya Miles, *Ties That Bind: The Story of an Afro-Cherokee Family in Slavery and Freedom* (Berkeley, CA, 2005).

59. Remini, *Jackson and American Empire*, 187–233.

60. Arsène Latour, *Historical Memoir of the War in West Florida and Louisiana in 1814–1815*, ed. Gene Smith (Gainesville, FL, 1999), 294–297; Caryn Cossé Bell, *Revolution, Romanticism, and the Afro-Creole Protest Tradition in Louisiana, 1718–1868* (Baton Rouge, LA, 1997), 51–59.

61. Parton, *Life of Jackson*, 2:63; CAJ, 2:118–119.

62. Latour, *Historical Memoir*, 137–152; Remini, *Jackson and American Empire*, 276–289.

## CHAPTER 3. RIGHT HAND: 1815–1819

1. Manifests of the *Temperance* from Reel 1, Inward Manifests of New Orleans, RG 36, NA; *LC*, January 25, 1819; for McDonogh being rowed across the river, cf. "McDonogh's Last Trip," Lithograph by Dominique Canova, c. 1850, Historic New Orleans Collection, New Orleans, Louisiana; Ari Kelman, *A River and Its City: The Nature of Landscape in New Orleans* (Berkeley, CA, 2003).

2. Maspero's advertisements and announcements were ubiquitous in New Orleans between 1806 and 1833. See John Adems Paxton, *The New-Orleans Directory and Register* (New Orleans, 1822), frontispiece, and multiple newspapers, e.g., *LG*, February 10, 1816.

3. *LG*, April 2, 1818; Henry C. (Henry Cogswell) Knight, *Letters from the South and West* (Boston, 1824), 115–124; James Pearse, *Narrative of the Life of James Pearse* (Rutland, VT, c. 1826), 17; Timothy Flint, *Recollections of the Last Ten Years . . . in the Valley of the Mississippi* (Boston, 1826), 218; Darla Jean Thompson, "Circuits of Containment: Iron Collars, Incarceration, and the Infrastructure of Slavery" (PhD diss., Cornell University, 2014).

4. Henry C. Castellanos, *New Orleans as It Was* (New Orleans, 1978), 146–148; Christian Schultz, *Travels on an Inland Voyage* (repr. Ridgewood, NJ, 1968), 190–191; Knight, *Letters from the South and West*, 115–123; Flint, *Recollections*, 222–223; HALL; *New-York Columbia*, August 6, 1818; *Westchester Herald*, August 11, 1818.

5. Kenneth C. Pomeranz, *The Great Divergence: China, Europe, and the Making of the Modern World Economy* (Berkeley, CA, 2000); Joel Mokyr, *The Enlightened Economy: An Economic History of Britain, 1700–1850* (New Haven, CT, 2009); Frederick Engels, *The Condition of the Working Class in England* (New York, 1987); Immanuel Wallerstein, *The Modern World-System*, 3 vols. (Berkeley, CA, 1974–1989); Charles Tilly, *Coercion, Capital, and European States, 990–1992* (Cambridge, MA, 1992); C. A. Bayly, *The Birth of the Modern World, 1789–1915: Global Connections and Comparisons* (Malden, MA, 2004).

6. Thomas R. Malthus, *An Essay on the Principle of Population* (London, 1798); Drew McCoy, *The Elusive Republic: Political Economy in Jeffersonian America* (Chapel Hill, NC, 1980), 108.

7. D. A. Farnie, *The English Cotton Industry and the World Market, 1815–1896* (Oxford, 1979), 3–44.

8. *LC*, January 1, 13, 22, 29, 1819, February 10, 15, 18, 22, 1819.

9. Edwin A. Davis and John C. L. Andreassen, eds., "From Louisville to New Orleans in 1816: Diary of William Newton Mercer," *JSH* 2 (1936): 390–402, qu. 396.

10. W. N. Mercer to J. Ker [1816], Fol. 4, Ker Family Papers, SHC; Robert G. Albion, *The Rise of New York Port, 1815–1860* (New York, 1939), 390–391; Pierre-Louis Berquin-Duvallon, trans. John Davis, *Travels in Louisiana and Florida in the Year 1802* (New York, 1806), 127–129.

11. W. Kenner to S. Minor, May 19 and 29, 1815, Wm. Kenner Papers, LLMVC; Barclay, Southeld, to S. Minor, September 14, 1815, Minor Papers, SHC; Albion, *Rise of New York Port*, 390–391; *LG*, September 2, 1815, January 1, 1818.

12. Flint, *Recollections*, 222; *LC*, January 29, 1819, February 22, 1819.

13. Knight, *Letters*, 117; *LC* and *LG* for 1815–1820, passim; Thomas H. Whitney, *Whitney's New-Orleans Directory and Louisiana and Mississippi Almanac for the Year 1811* (New Orleans, 1810), 38; Carol Wilson, *The Two Lives of Sally Muller: A Case of Mistaken Racial Identity in Antebellum New Orleans* (New Brunswick, NJ, 2007).

14. William Hayden, *Narrative of William Hayden, Containing a Faithful Account of His Travels for Many Years Whilst a Slave* (Cincinnati, 1846), 54–58.

15. Josiah Henson, *The Life of Josiah Henson, Formerly a Slave . . .* (Boston, 1849), 37–41; William Grimes, *Life of William Grimes, Written by Himself* (New York, 1825), 22; Hayden, *Narrative*, 124. The idea that slave traders were anomalous is demolished by Michael Tadman, *Speculators and Slaves: Masters, Traders, and Slaves in the Old South* (Madison, WI, 1989); Frederic Bancroft, *Slave Trading in the Old South* (Baltimore, 1931), 314–320; and Walter Johnson, *Soul by Soul: Life Inside the Antebellum Slave Market* (Cambridge, MA, 1999).

16. Vincent Nolte, *Memoirs of Vincent Nolte* (New York, 1934), 86–87; Henry B. Fearon, *Sketches of America: A Narrative of a Journey of Five Thousand Miles Through the Eastern and Western States of America* (London, 1819), 279; Lewis E. Atherton, "John McDonogh—New Orleans Capitalist," *JSH* 7 (1941): 451–481; McDonogh Papers, Tulane.

17. George Dangerfield, *The Era of Good Feelings* (New York, 1952), 80–81; Nolte, *Memoirs*, 268–280; Ralph Hidy, *The House of Baring in American Trade and Finance: English Merchant Bankers at Work, 1763–1861* (Cambridge, MA, 1949), 35.

18. Nolte, *Memoirs*; Robert Roeder, "New Orleans Merchants, 1790–1837" (PhD diss., Harvard University, 1959).

19. The classic statement of the capitalist-as-Puritan is Max Weber, *The Protestant Ethic and the Spirit of Capitalism* trans. Talcott Parsons (New York, 1930).

20. John Cassidy, *How Markets Fail: The Logic of Economic Calamities* (New York, 2009); Joseph Schumpeter, *Capitalism, Socialism, and Democracy* (New York, 1947).

21. Nolte, *Memoirs*, 69, 274–275, 311–313; Stephen Palmié, "A Taste for Human Commodities," in Palmié, ed., *Slave Cultures and the Culture of Slavery* (Knoxville, TN, 1995), 40–54; Roeder, "New Orleans Merchants."

22. George Green to J. Minor, January 15, 1820, Minor Papers, SHC. Instead of offices, many merchants carried commercial paper in wallets. Cf. *LC*, January 17, 20, 1817, February 28, 1817, March 14, 1817, March 15, 29, 1819.

23. J. Wetherstrandt to S. Minor, November 23, 1814, and J. Minor to Kitty, May 24, 1816, Minor Papers, SHC; R. Claque to Dear Major, February 26, 1821, William Kenner Papers, LLMVC; *LG*, October 23, 1816; Benjamin Latrobe, *Impressions Respecting New Orleans: Diary and Sketches, 1818–1820*, ed. Samuel Wilson Jr. (New York, 1951), 9–10; *LG*, September 30, 1815, December 13, 1817, April 28, 1818; W. Flower to J. Vinot, 1818, Flower to Dugue Bros. & Harang, 1820, and Flower to C. Bouchon, 1820, HALL, 85325, 96018–96022, 97346–97348.

24. *LC*, October 4, 18, 1819, November 24, 1819; HALL, 93012.

25. Henson, *Life*, 41–45; *LG*, April 28, 1818, May 13, 1818; *LC*, January 29, 1818. Local slaves were typically sold privately. Cf. *LC*, January 31, 1817, November 3, 1819.

26. Slaves "on hand": J. Garner to A. Cuningham, February 1, 1830, and Brown and Armistead to E. B. Hicks, August 1, 1821, Alexander Cuningham Papers, Duke. Slave-sale money "in hand": Brown and Armistead to E. B. Hicks, August 1, 1821, Alexander Cuningham Papers, Duke; Kenner & Co. to J. Minor, January 26, 1826, Minor Papers, SHC. "Cotton": David Ker to Mary Ker, May 7, 1812, Ker Family Papers, SHC. Letter "come to hand": E. Fraser to M. White, August 28, 1806, Maunsel White Papers, SHC; Fol. 1834–1835, Jarratt-Puryear Papers, Duke. Slaves also "came to hand": e.g., Tyre Glen to Isaac Jarratt, December 23, 1833, Jarratt-Puryear Papers, Duke; J. Richards to Cashier of Bank of United States, March 14, 1815, Box 2E949, Bank of State of Mississippi Records, Natchez Trace Collection, RASP; Abijah Hunt to R. Sparks, June 14, 1809, Ker Family Papers, SHC.

27. Robert Farrar Capon, *The Parables of Grace* (Grand Rapids, MI, 1988).

28. M. Tournillon to Nicholas Trist, February 28, 1821, Nicholas Trist Papers, SHC.

29. *LC*, January 25, 1819, February 10, 15, 1819; Thomas Henderson to Stephen Minor, June 4, 1819, Minor Family Papers, SHC; John Minor in Acct. with Kenner and Henderson, 1816–1818, William Kenner Papers, LLMVC.

30. Sean Wilentz, *The Rise of American Democracy: Jefferson to Lincoln* (New York, 2005), 205–209; W. Meriwether to Brother, September 28, 1814, Meriwether Family Papers, SHC; Daniel Walker Howe, *What God Hath Wrought: The Transformation of America, 1815–1848* (New York, 2007).

31. Martha Brazy, *An American Planter: Stephen Duncan of Antebellum Natchez and New York* (Baton Rouge, LA, 2006), 15–16, 21; Collector, Port of New Orleans, 1806–1823, v. 2, Mf #75–109, NOPL; Dangerfield, *Era of Good Feelings*, 180; Bray Hammond, *Banks and Politics in America: From the Revolution to the Civil War* (Princeton, NJ, 1957), 282; *New York Courier*, September 24, 1816.

32. Jesse Hunt to Jeremiah Hunt, April 1, 1815, Folder 4, Ker Papers, SHC; F. E. Rives Ledger, Rives Papers, Duke.

33. John Read to Josiah Meigs, April 17, 1817; TP, 18:83–84; J. Brahan to J. Meigs, February 18, 1818; TP, 18:260–261; Israel Pickens to W. Lenoir, December 18, 1816, C. S. Howe Papers, SHC; J. W. Walker to L. Newby, February 28, 1817, Larkin Newby Papers, Duke; M. E. Williams to Mary K. Williams, September 10, 1823, Hawkins Family Papers, SHC; *New-York Columbian*, April 21, 1818; J. Mills Thornton, *Politics and Power in a Slave Society: Alabama, 1800–1860* (Baton Rouge, LA, 1978); NSV, 249; Anne Royall, *Letters from Alabama* (Washington, DC, 1830), 114; J. Campbell to D. Campbell, December 16, 1817, Campbell Papers, Duke; Daniel Dupre, *Transforming the Cotton Frontier: Madison County, Alabama, 1800–1840* (Baton Rouge, LA, 1997), 41–86; *Carolina Republican*, March 8, 1817; cf. Thomas Chase Hagood, "'I Looked Upon the Long Journey, Through the Wilderness, with Much Pleasure': Experiencing the Early Republic's Southern Frontier," *Journal of Backcountry Studies* 6, no. 1 (2011), www.partnershipsjournal.org/index.php/jbc/issue/view/25 (accessed December 26, 2013).

34. See Table 1.1.

35. *Baltimore Patriot*, July 16, 1819; *LC*, April 15, 1817, March 12, 1819; *LG*, June 14, 1817, June 9, 1818.

36. *Baltimore Patriot*, July 16, 1819.

37. Lawrence J. Kotlikoff, "The Structure of Slave Prices in New Orleans, 1804 to 1862," *Economic Inquiry* 17 (1979): 496–518; Jonathan Pritchett, "Quantitative Estimates of the U.S. Interregional Slave Trade, 1820–1860," *Journal of Economic History* 61, no. 2 (2001): 467–475; and my analysis (with assistance from Jordan Suter) of slave sales reported in HALL.

38. Henry Watson, *Narrative of Henry Watson: A Fugitive Slave* (Boston, 1848), 12; J. Sain to Obadiah Fields, May 25, 1821, O. Fields to Jane Fields, November 29, 1822, Acct. O. Fields, 1822, Obadiah Fields Papers, Duke; Certificate issued to William Haxall, Petersburg Insurance Company, 1823, Mss 1H3203d, Haxall Papers, VHS; Grandmother Trist to Nicholas Trist, April 25, 1822, N. P. Trist Papers, SHC; Adam Hodgson, *Remarks During a Journey Through North America in the Years 1819, 1820, 1821* (New York, 1823), 55–56. James Kirke Paulding, in *Letters from the South, Written During an Excursion in the Summer of 1816* (New York, 1817), 124–125, reports a trader paying $500 for a mulatto Virginia woman. According to Robert W. Fogel and Stanley L. Engerman (in *Slave Sales and Appraisals, 1775–1865*, ICPSR07421-v3 [Rochester, NY: University of Rochester (producer), 1976; Ann Arbor, MI: Inter-University Consortium for Political and Social Research (producer and distributor)], 2006-10-11, doi:10.3886/ICPSR07421.v3), twenty-three men were sold in Maryland (1815–1819) at a mean price of $220 and a mean age of twenty-one. HALL shows average male price in New Orleans in 1815 to 1819 as $810 (mean age twenty-five). Jonathan Pritchett and Herman Freudenberger, "The Domestic United States Slave

Trade: New Evidence," *Journal of Interdisciplinary History* 21 (1991): 447–477, notes $17 shipping per slave, 1830s, p. 473.

39. *A Narrative of the Life and Labors of the Reverend G. W. Offley* (Hartford, CT, 1859), 5–6; W. C. Whitaker to J. Whitaker, January 16, 1835, Coffield-Bellamy Papers, SHC. On competitive bidding, see Ariela J. Gross, *Double Character: Slavery and Mastery in the Antebellum Courtroom* (Princeton, NJ, 2000); Johnson, *Soul by Soul*.

40. Louis Hughes, *Thirty Years a Slave: The Institution of Slavery as Seen on the Plantation and in the Home of a Planter* (Milwaukee, WI, 1897), 7–8.

41. Watson, *Narrative*, 12–13; L. M. Mills, ST, 502–503.

42. ST, 503, 507, 727, 744. Johnson, *Soul by Soul*, emphasizes give-and-take between slave and buyer.

43. Delicia Patterson, AS, 11.2 (MO), 270–271; Dickson, ST, 507.

44. MW, 103; Hodgson, *Remarks*, 55–56; Maria Clemons, AS, 8.2 (AR), 17; Charlotte Willis, AS, 11.1 (AR), 198; Sella Martin, ST, 727.

45. Charles L. Perdue Jr., Thomas E. Barden, and Robert K. Phillips, eds., *Weevils in the Wheat: Interviews with Virginia Ex-Slaves* (Charlottesville, VA, 1976), 14–15; Knight, *Letters*, 78.

46. Tabb Gross, Lewis Smith, ST, 347; Paulding, *Letters*, 1:124–130; Perdue et al., eds., *Weevils in the Wheat*, 325–326; Henson, *Life*, 44; Allen Sidney, ST, 522; John Lambert, *Travels Through Canada and the United States of America, In the Years 1806, 1807, and 1808* (London, 1816), 1:167–169; William N. Blane, *An Excursion Through the United States and Canada During the Years 1822–1823, by an English Gentleman* (London, 1824), 226–227; ASAI, 153–155; Bancroft, *Slave Trading*, 108–112; Thomas Hamilton, *Men and Manners in America* (Philadelphia, 1843), 347. Knight, in *Letters*, 101–102, 127, refers to sellers as "slave-jockies."

47. Bancroft, *Slave Trading*, 106; Edward E. Baptist, "'Cuffy,' 'Fancy Maids,' and 'One-Eyed Men': Rape, Commodification, and the Domestic Slave Trade in the United States," *AHR* 106 (2001): 1619–1650; ST, 503–507, 727, 744; Perdue et al., eds., *Weevils in the Wheat*, 48–49, 166; Cornelia Andrews, AS, 14.1 (NC), 29.

48. *LG*, April 2, 1816, November 20, 1817, June 3, 1818; *NR*, April 26, 1817, 144; J. Perkins to J. Minor, August 20, 1814, Minor Papers, SHC.

49. Aristotle, *Nicomachean Ethics*, trans. David Ross (London, 1980), 212; David Brion Davis, *Slavery and Human Progress* (New York, 1984), 25.

50. Wm. Kenner to J. Minor, March 1, 1816, Wm. Kenner Papers, LLMVC.

51. J. Knight to Wm. Beall, January 27, 1844, Box 2, John Knight Papers, Duke; E. B. Hicks to John Paup, August 6, 1837, 1830–1846 Folder, E. B. Hicks Papers, Duke; Philip Troutman, "Slave Trade and Sentiment in Antebellum Virginia" (PhD diss., University of Virginia, 2000).

52. J. Knight to Wm. Beall, January 27, 1844, Box 2, John Knight Papers, Duke. French-language advertisements for slave sales in the 1810s did not use *main*, the translation of the word "hand," but *négres de pioche*—"Negroes of the pickaxe," or, colloquially, "Blacks who sweat": Vente de l'Encan, *LC*, June 25, 1817.

53. HALL; Philip D. Morgan, *Slave Counterpoint: Black Culture in the Eighteenth-Century Chesapeake and Low Country* (Chapel Hill, NC, 1999); Dylan Penningroth, *Claims of Kinfolk: African-American Property and Community in the Nineteenth-Century South* (Chapel Hill, NC, 2003); Roderick A. McDonald, *The Economy and Material*

*Culture of Slaves: Goods and Chattels on the Sugar Plantations of Jamaica and Louisiana* (Baton Rouge, LA, 1993).

54. *LC*, January 1, 1819; bills of sale, Compagnie Assurance de la Nouvelle-Orleans, to multiple purchasers, HALL, 89554–89607, 90226, 90405, 91505, 90046, 927161, 90279, 92761. The *Louisiana Courier* ad for William and Rachel's sale listed sixteen of twenty-eight as skilled, but none of the bills of sale identified skills: *LC*, January 25, 1819.

55. ST, 695–697; Perdue et al., eds., *Weevils in the Wheat*, 71; J. Stille to Mrs. Gayoso, August 29, 1805, Fol. 10, R. R. Barrow Papers, Tulane.

56. *LC*, January 25, 1819; HALL; Richard H. Steckel, "A Peculiar Population: The Nutrition, Health, and Mortality of U.S. Slaves from Childhood to Maturity," *Journal of Economic History* 46, no. 3 (1986): 721–741.

57. Herbert Gutman and Richard Sutch, in "The Slave Family: Protected Agent of Capitalist Expansion or Victim of the Slave Trade?" in Paul A. David, *Reckoning with Slavery: A Critical Study in the Quantitative History of American Negro Slavery* (New York, 1976), 94–133, esp. 112–120, rely on Fogel and Engerman's samples of New Orleans notarial records; I rely on HALL's complete sales through 1820.

58. *LC*, January 1, 1819; HALL, 89554–89607; Pearse, *Narrative*, 85.

59. Melinda, MW, 167. Cf. Helen Odom, AS, 10.5 (AR), 227; Cora Poche, AS, 9.4 (MS), 1726; Clarissa Scales, AS, 5.4 (TX), 3; Robert Laird, AS, 8.3 (MS), 1292; Milton Ritchie, AS, 10.6 (AR), 271.

60. Milton Ritchie, AS, 10.6 (AR), 271; Carry Allen Patton, AS, 10.6 (AR), 298; Eyre Crowe, quoted in Bancroft, *Slave Trading*, 116.

61. HALL, 91162–91163, 91173–91178, 91249, 91250, 91279–91289, 91300–91304.

62. Thomas Buchanan, *Black Life on the Mississippi: Slaves, Free Blacks, and the Western Steamboat World* (Chapel Hill, NC, 2004); "Dick Eggleston Diary," vol. 72, Roach-Eggleston Papers, SHC.

### CHAPTER 4. LEFT HAND: 1805–1861

1. Charles Ball, *Slavery in the United States: A Narrative of the Life and Adventures of Charles Ball* . . . (New York, 1837), 125–136.

2. Peter H. Wood, "Slave Labor Camps in Early America: Overcoming Denial and Discovering the Gulag," in Carla Gardina Pestana and Sharon V. Salinger, eds., *Inequality in Early America* (Hanover, NH, 1999), 222–238.

3. William Grimes, *Life of William Grimes, Written by Himself* (New York, 1825), 26.

4. James Scott, *Domination and the Arts of Resistance: Hidden Transcripts* (New Haven, CT, 1990).

5. Ball, *Slavery in the United States*, 106–119.

6. Ibid., 47–48, 128–131; ASAI, 101.

7. Ball, *Slavery in the United States*, 117–119; Grimes, *Life*, 25.

8. Israel Campbell, *An Autobiography, Bound and Free* (Philadelphia, 1861), 33; Philip D. Morgan, *Slave Counterpoint: Black Culture in the Eighteenth-Century Chesapeake and Low Country* (Chapel Hill, NC, 1999), 179–186; Peter Coclanis, "How the Low Country Was Taken to Task: Slave-Labor Organization in Coastal South

Carolina and Georgia," in Robert L. Paquette and Louis Ferleger, eds., *Slavery, Secession, and Southern History* (Charlottesville, VA, 2000), 59–78; Philip D. Morgan, "Task and Gang Systems: The Organization of Labor on New World Plantations," in Stephen Innes, ed., *Work and Labor in Early America* (Chapel Hill, NC, 1988), 189–220.

9. Latrobe Sketchbook, III, 33, Maryland Historical Society; "The Atlantic Slave Trade and Slave Life in the Americas: A Visual Record," Jerome S. Handler and Michael L. Tuite Jr., Digital Media Lab, University of Virginia, image at http://hitchcock.itc.virginia.edu/SlaveTrade/collection/large/NW0048.JPG (accessed October 18, 2013); Richard S. Dunn, "A Tale of Two Plantations: Slave Life at Mesopotamia in Jamaica and Mount Airy in Virginia, 1799 to 1828," *William and Mary Quarterly*, 3rd ser., vol. 34, no. 1 (1977): 32–65, esp. 36–37; James Curry, ST, 134.

10. William Anderson, *Life and Narrative of William Anderson . . .* (Chicago, 1857), 19; Thomas Spalding, *Farmers' Register*, November 1834, 353–363; *The Narrative of Amos Dresser . . . and Two Letters from Tallahassee, Relating to the Treatment of Slaves* (New York, 1836); Steven F. Miller, "Plantation Labor Organization and Slave Life on the Cotton Frontier: The Alabama-Mississippi Black Belt, 1815–1840," in Ira Berlin and Philip D. Morgan, eds., *Cultivation and Culture: Labor and the Shaping of Slave Life in the Americas* (Charlottesville, VA, 1993), 155–169. On connections with military systems, see Michel Foucault, *Discipline and Punish: The Birth of the Prison* (New York, 1977), 135–169. Two works that appeared as this book went to press and have much to say about enslaved migrants and labor in the cotton fields include: Walter Johnson, *River of Dark Dreams* (Cambridge, MA, 2013); Damian Alan Pargas, "In the Fields of a 'Strange Land': Enslaved Newcomers and the Adjustment to Cotton Cultivation in the Antebellum South," *Slavery and Abolition* 34, no. 4 (2013): 562–578.

11. "Almost," *American Farmer*, December 14, 1821, 298–299; *Farmers' Register* 2, no. 6 (1834): 353–363; Jn. Stewart to D. McLaurin, June 30, 1831, Duncan McLaurin Papers, Duke.

12. *Farmers' Register* 3, no. 3 (1835): 16; N. P. Hairston to J. Hairston, December 4, 1822, P. Hairston Papers, SHC; J. Knight to Wm. Beall, January 27, 1844, John Knight Papers, Duke.

13. Sidney, ST, 524; cf. Laura Clark, AS, 6.1 (AL), 72–73; [John] Neal to Mother, August 6, 1829, Neal Papers, SHC.

14. Mark Smith, *Mastered by the Clock: Time, Slavery, and Freedom in the U.S. South* (Chapel Hill, NC, 1997).

15. Ball, *Slavery in the United States*, 148–151; Campbell, *Autobiography*; Henry Bibb, *Narrative of the Life and Adventures of Henry Bibb, an American Slave* (New York, 1849), 115; Jacob Metzer, "Rational Management, Modern Business Practices, and Economies of Scale in Antebellum Southern Plantations," in Robert William Fogel and Stanley L. Engerman, eds., *Without Consent or Contract: Technical Papers* (New York, 1992), 1:191–215. Cf. Smith, *Mastered by the Clock*, which argues for a post-1830 timepiece revolution. While Fogel argues, in *Without Consent or Contract*, that southern slaves' work breaks were longer than northern ones (p. 79), ex-slaves' accounts disagree: Sarah Wells, AS, 11.1 (AR), 89; Charlie Aarons, AS, 6.1 (AL), 1; Angie Garrett, AS, 6.1 (AL), 133.

16. H. Lee to R. Brown, July 17, 1827, Henry Lee, VHS. But many enslavers only let men plow.

17. Ball, *Slavery in the United States*, 150. HALL reveals the flattening of job descriptions: of slaves sold to Louisiana in 1804 to 1821, 95 percent of those described by a job title were listed as "hand" or "laborer," not identified by Chesapeake-acknowledged skills.

18. Ball, *Slavery in the United States*, 67, 160–162; Okah Tubbee, *A Sketch of the Life of Okah Tubbee* (Toronto, 1852); John Warren, NSV, 184; Philemon Bliss, ASAI, 104; William N. Blane, *An Excursion Through the United States and Canada During the Years 1822–1823, by an English Gentleman* (London, 1824), 150–151. For Chesapeake cat-o'-nine tails, see Charles Crawley, AS, 16.5 (VA), 8–9.

19. Song notes, undated, Fol. 9, James Bailey Papers, SHC; Ball, *Slavery in the United States*, 160–162. Cf. Charlie Aarons, AS, 6.1 (AL), 1; NSV, 301–304, "I lived," William Hall, NSV, 134. Cf. James Curry, ST, 128–144, qu. 134; Lunsford Lane, *The Narrative of Lunsford Lane* (Boston, 1842), 19.

20. "Before," Aaron Siddles, NSV, 272; Tubbee, *Sketch*, 23; Anderson, *Life and Narrative*, 17.

21. Ball, *Slavery in the United States*, 67, 150, 161; Bibb, *Narrative*, 116–117, 132; Louis Hughes, *Thirty Years a Slave: The Institution of Slavery as Seen on the Plantation and in the Home of a Planter* (Milwaukee, WI, 1897), 15–24, 46; Blane, *Excursion*, 67, 161; Anderson, *Life and Narrative*, 17; John Brown, *Slave Life in Georgia* (London, 1855), 39, 43; Willie Vester to B. H. Vester, March 19, 1837, Benjamin Vester Papers, Duke; Campbell, *Autobiography*, 33; A. K. Bartow to J. J. Phillips, April 23, 1849, Ivan Battle Papers, SHC. Contrast with Richard Follet, *The Sugar Masters: Planters and Slaves in Louisiana's Cane World* (Baton Rouge, LA, 2005), which emphasizes positive incentives; Robert Fogel and Stanley Engerman, *Time on the Cross: The Economics of American Negro Slavery* (Boston, 1974), 193–210; and Paul A. David and Peter Temin, "Slavery: The Progressive Institution?" in Paul A. David, Herbert G. Gutman, Richard Sutch, Peter Temin, and Gavin Wright, *Reckoning with Slavery: A Critical Study in the Quantitative History of American Negro Slavery* (Oxford, 1976), 206–207n46, which claims that the "rhythm" of enslaved work generated efficiencies supposedly found in Haitian *coumbite* and West African collective labor.

22. Ball, *Slavery in the United States*, 160.

23. Jack Ericson Eblen, "New Estimates of the Vital Rates of the United States Black Population During the Nineteenth Century," *Demography* 11 (1974): 301–319; Richard H. Steckel, "A Peculiar Population: The Nutrition, Health, and Mortality of U.S. Slaves from Childhood to Maturity," *Journal of Economic History* 46, no. 3 (1986): 721–741; Richard H. Steckel, "Fluctuations in a Dreadful Childhood: Synthetic Longitudinal Height Data, Relative Prices, and Weather in the Short-Term Health of American Slaves," NBER Working Paper no. 10993, December 2004, National Bureau of Economic Research, www.nber.org/papers/w10993. My own research shows that enslaved men born in the southwestern states that grew the least corn per capita in 1839 were, on average, shorter by half an inch than those born farther up the Mississippi Valley and in Georgia. That difference is significant.

24. Ball, *Slavery in the United States*, 139–183.

25. Abigail Slack to Eliphalet Slack, January 6, 1829, Slack Papers, SHC.

26. W. C. Wirt to Dabney Wirt, December 10, 1835, Wirt Papers, SHC.

27. Ball, *Slavery in the United States*, 184–187; Solomon Northup, *Twelve Years a Slave* (Auburn, NY, 1853), 134–143; Anderson, *Life and Narrative*, 19.

28. Ball, *Slavery in the United States*, 217; cf. J. Ker to I. Baker, November 19, 1820, Ker Papers, SHC; J. S. Haywood to Dear Sister, May 3, 1839, Fol. 156, HAY; A. K. Barlow to J. J. Phillips, April 23, 1849, Ivan Battle Papers, SHC; James Harriss to Th. Harriss, September 14, 1845, 1843–1847 Fol., Thomas Harriss Papers, Duke; Jn. Knight to Wm. Beall, February 7, 1844, April 14, 1844, Box 2, John Knight Papers, Duke; R. B. Beverley to Robert Beverley, September 3, 1833, Beverley Papers, Mss. 1B4678a, VHS; Mary Ker to Isaac Baker, November 19, 1820, Ker Papers, SHC.

29. P. A. Bolling to Edmund Hubard, February 24, 1837, Hubard Papers, SHC; C. Jameson to H. Clark, January 15, 1833, Henry Toole Clark Papers, Duke; Delilah H. H. to Sarah, January 31, 1834, Young Allen Papers, SHC; cf. R. Dalton to J. Dalton, July 2, 1835, Placebo Houston Papers, Duke; P. Barringer to D. Barringer, January 10, 1848, Daniel M. Barringer Papers, SHC. The disproportion between the amount of cotton a hand could grow and the amount a hand could harvest was a regular theme: J. S. Haywood to G. Haywood, May 22, 1836, Fol. 146, HAY; N. P. Hairston to J. Hairston, December 4, 1822, P. Hairston Papers, SHC; Jno. W. Paup to E. B. Hicks, October 17, 1841, E. B. Hicks Papers, Duke; L. R. Starks to R. C. Ballard, February 5, 1833, Fol. 8, RCB.

30. John Ker to Isaac Baker, November 19, 1820, Ker Papers, SHC; James Magruder Account Book, 1796–1818, Magruder Papers, series N, RASP; R. & M. Timberlake to Mother, December 26, 1829, Neal Papers, SHC; W. R. Arick to J. S. Copes, October 22, 1846, Fol. 82, J. S. Copes Papers, Tulane; Elley Plantation Book, 1855–1856, Mississippi Department of Archives and History; Alan L. Olmstead and Paul W. Rhode, "Biological Innovation and Productivity Growth in the Antebellum Cotton Economy," June 2008, NBER Working Paper no. 14142, National Bureau of Economic Research, www.nber.org/papers/w14142, 1–2, 22; Alan L. Olmstead and Paul W. Rhode, "'Wait a Cotton Pickin' Minute': A New View of Slave Productivity," August 2005, www.unc.edu/~prhode/Cotton_Pickin.pdf (accessed December 19, 2013).

31. Olmstead and Rhode, in "Biological Innovation," postulate that the answer lies in the introduction and improvement of new breeds of cotton, especially the Mexican "Petit Gulf" seeds, from the 1820s onward. "Petit Gulf" plants supposedly offered a cotton boll optimized for "pickability." The pickability/bioengineering story substitutes seeds for machines and builds on the commitment of agricultural historians to credit science for increased yields. See, e.g., John Hebron Moore, *Agriculture in Ante-Bellum Mississippi* (New York, 1958), 27–36, 145–160; J. A. Turner, *The Cotton Planter's Manual: Being a Compilation of Facts from the Best Authorities on the Culture of Cotton; Its Natural History, Chemical Analysis, Trade, and Consumption; And Embracing a History of Cotton and the Cotton Gin* (New York, 1857), 36; L. C. Gray and Esther K. Thompson, *History of Agriculture in the Southern United States to 1860* (Washington, DC, 1933), 2:703; J. L. Watkins, *King Cotton: A Historical and Statistical Review* (New York, 1969 [1908]), 172; *American Farmer*, passim; *Farmer's Register*, passim. Increased yield led to increased expectations for labor: "Nothing would astonish you more than the difference in the work of a hand in cotton yielding 2000 lbs to the acre

[than] where not more than 700 lbs can be had," wrote a North Carolina native visiting his Alabama slave labor camp. Paul Cameron to D. Cameron, December 13, 1845, Fol. 974, PCC; Charles Lewellyn to PC, August 16, 1845, Fol. 962, PCC. A handful of economists and one or two historians have noted the increase in cotton productivity over time, but most of those who have focused on picking have credited the adoption of Petit Gulf seeds. See Franklee Gilbert Whartenby, "Land and Labor Productivity in United States Cotton Production, 1800–1840" (New York, 1977); Stanley Lebergott, *The Americans: An Economic Record* (New York, 1984); John Douglas Campbell, "The Gender Division of Labor, Slave Reproduction, and the Slave Family Economy on Southern Cotton Plantations, 1800–1864" (PhD diss., University of Minnesota, 1988). Fogel and Engerman noted output increases, as noted above, but did not succeed in explaining them. Johnson, in *River of Dark Dreams*, gives more credit to Petit Gulf seeds than does this account.

32. Gray and Thompson, *History of Agriculture*, 2:692–693; Kenneth C. Pomeranz, *The Great Divergence: China, Europe, and the Making of the Modern World Economy* (Berkeley, CA, 2000). Early adopter George Matthews of Louisiana reported that his "hands" were picking 160 pounds of cotton each by 1826, but other Mississippi Valley enslavers would report significantly greater amounts just ten years later with the same kind of cotton. The Prudhomme plantation in Terrebonne Parish, Louisiana, however, reported daily picking numbers around 100 pounds per person in the 1830s, even with new seed. But by the 1850s, new methods drove the numbers into the 200s, with some individuals averaging more than 300 pounds daily. Turner, *Cotton Planter's Manual*, 99–102; George Matthews to Harriet Matthews, October 7, 1827, Folder 2/1, Matthews-Ventress-Lawrason Papers, LLMVC; Folders 267, 271, Prudhomme Papers, SHC.

33. Pomeranz, *Great Divergence*, 274–278; D. A. Farnie, *The English Cotton Industry and the World Market, 1815–1896* (Oxford, 1979), 199. Cf. Seymour Shapiro, *Capital and the Cotton Industry in the Industrial Revolution* (Ithaca, NY, 1967).

34. E.g., Levi Woodbury, "Cotton: Cultivation, Manufacture, and Foreign Trade of," *House Executive Documents*, 24th Cong., 1st sess., vol. 4, no. 146 (Washington, DC, 1836). Sugar mills were the first enterprises to use the conveyor belt, the classic device of twentieth-century factories. Follett, *Sugar Masters*; Daniel Rood, "Plantation Technocrats: A Social History of Knowledge in the Slaveholding Atlantic World, 1830–1865" (PhD diss., University of California at Irvine, 2010).

35. E. F. Barnes Cotton Book, RASP, Series G, 5/17. Occasionally enslavers held "races" to see who could pick the most cotton in a day: Cull Taylor, AS, 6.1 (AL), 364. Ball, in *Slavery in the United States*, 212, 271–272, mentions pay for overpicking or Sunday picking in two cases.

36. Mary Younger, NSV, 258; Allan Sidney, ST, 524.

37. Ball, *Slavery in the United States*, 215–216; Jn. Knight to Wm. Beall, August 12, 1844, Box 2, John Knight Papers, Duke.

38. Campbell, *Autobiography*, 33–35.

39. Brown, *Slave Life in Georgia*, 128–132; Anderson, *Life and Narrative*, 19–20; Henry Watson, *Narrative of Henry Watson: A Fugitive Slave* (Boston, 1848), 19–20; ST; Works Progress Administration interviews from the 1930s, e.g., GSMD, 199;

Gus Askew, AS, 6.1 (AL), 15; Rufus Dirt, AS, 6.1 (AL), 117; Sarah Wells, AS, 11.1 (AR), 89; Sarah Ashley, S2 2.1 (TX), 87; Jesse Barnes, S2, 2.1 (TX), 175. Also J. Monett, Appendix C, J. W. Ingraham, *The South-West, by a Yankee* (New York, 1836), 2:285–286.

40. Rules from Box 3, May–-December 1820 Fol., A. P. Walsh Papers, LLMVC; Miller, in "Plantation Labor Organization," 163–165, points out that some historians have confused cotton minimums with low-country "tasks," e.g., Moore, *The Emergence of the Cotton Kingdom in the Old Southwest* (Baton Rouge, LA, 1988), 95–96. For ledgers, five good examples: Ballard Papers, SHC; Prudhomme Papers, SHC; U. B. Phillips and James Glunt, *Florida Plantation Records from the Papers of George Noble Jones* (St. Louis, 1927); F. T. Leak Papers, SHC; Edwin Davis, ed., *Plantation Life in the Florida Parishes of Louisiana, 1836–1846, as Reflected in the Diary of Bennett H. Barrow* (New York, 1943). "So many pounds," ASAI, 96, 98; Ball, *Slavery in the United States*, 216–218; Campbell, *Autobiography*, 33–39; Sarah Wells, AS, 11.1 (AR), 89; Jn. Knight to Wm. Beall, February 10, 1844, April 14, 1844, John Knight Papers, Duke; R. B. Beverley to Robert Beverley, September 3, 1833, August 28, 1842, Sec. 17, MssıB4678a, Beverley Papers, VHS. Cf. Kelly Houston Jones, "'A Rough, Saucy Set of Hands to Manage': Slave Resistance in Arkansas," *Arkansas Historical Quarterly* 71 (2012): 1–21.

41. Anderson, *Life and Narrative*, 18–19; ASAI, 47; NSV, 140–141; Jn. Haywood to G. W. Haywood, February 5, 1842, March 17, 1839, May 22, 1836, HAY; P. Cameron to D. Cameron, December 2, 1845, Fol. 973, PCC; Betsy Clingman to I. Jarratt, January 8, 1835, Jarratt-Puryear Papers, Duke. Cf. GSMD, 215.

42. These lists of pounds picked would not help scholars to identify best seed types. They were offshoots of a slate or memory system designed to carry numbers for individual slaves: Charles Thompson, *Biography of a Slave* (Dayton, OH, 1875), 41–42; Brown, *Slave Life in Georgia*, 128–129; Campbell, *Autobiography*, 33–35.

43. Ball, *Slavery in the United States*, 186–187, 212. Early daily totals are from *American Farmer*, December 14, 1821, 298; August 31, 1838, Magnolia Pltn. Jnl., Fol. 429, RCB. "Bresh heap" from B. Fox to Eliza Neal, September 25, 1835. For 100–130 lbs./day, see R. and M. Timberlake to Mother, December 26, 1829, Neal Papers, SHC; cf. Phanor Prudhomme Cotton Books, 1836 and 1852, Prudhomme Papers, SHC; "Dunk," D. W. McKenzie to D. McLaurin, September 26, 1840, Fol. 1838–1840, Duncan McLaurin Papers, Duke; J. F. Thompson Diary, July 6, 1841, [51], Benson-Thompson Papers, Duke; R. B. Beverley to R. Beverley, September 3, 1833, Sec. 13, and August 28, 1842, Sec. 41, Beverley Papers, VHS; Northup, *Twelve Years a Slave*, 125, 135. By 1860, Paul Cameron expected two hundred pounds per hand per day in the Mississippi delta: W. T. Lamb to P. Cameron, September 16, 1860, Fol. 1210, PCC. For increased southwestern extraction of labor, L. A. Finley to Caroline Gordon, February 17, 1853, Gordon-Hackett Papers, SHC; T. J. Brownrigg to R. Brownrigg, January 29, 1836, Brownrigg Papers, SHC; A. K. Barlow to J. J. Philips, April 23, 1849, Ivan Battle Papers, SHC; J. S. Haywood to G. W. Haywood, April 4, 1835, Fol. 144, and J. S. Haywood to Sister, May 3, 1839, Fol. 156, HAY; A. P. Cameron to D. Cameron, December 13, 1845, Fol. 974; W. T. Lamb to P. Cameron, December 1, 1860, PCC.

44. *Farmers' Register*, June 1836, 114–116, and November 1934, 353–363; cf. James Pearse, *Narrative of the Life of James Pearse* (Rutland, VT, c. 1826), 24–37; Philip Younger, NSV, 249.

45. Northup, *Twelve Years a Slave*, 159; John Haywood to G. W. Haywood, February 5, 1842, HAY; Ingraham, *The South-West*, 2:286.

46. Campbell, *Autobiography*, 36–39.

47. Martha Bradley, AS, 6.1 (AL), 47; Northup, *Twelve Years a Slave*, 134, 142–143.

48. I. C. McManus, *Right Hand, Left Hand: The Origins of Asymmetry in Brains, Bodies, Atoms, and Cultures* (Cambridge, MA, 2002).

49. ASAI, 69; Ball, *Slavery in the United States*, 215; Northup, *Twelve Years a Slave*, 188–189.

50. ASAI, 69; Ball, *Slavery in the United States*, 218; Anderson, *Life and Narrative*, 29; William Wells Brown, *Narrative of William Wells Brown, a Fugitive Slave* (Boston, 1849), 20; GSMD, 199.

51. Adeline, AS, 6.1 (AL), 181; Frank Hawkins to Wm. Hawkins, August 29, 1849, Fol. 84, Hawkins Papers, SHC; Araby Journal, Haller Nutt Papers, Duke; Magnolia Journal, 1848–1851, Fol. 442, RCB; Gray and Thompson, *History of Agriculture*, 2:702–703.

52. AS, v. 18, GSMD, 199; cf. B. L. C. Wailes, *Report on the Agriculture and Geology of Mississippi* (Philadelphia, 1854), 154. Historians argue that the acceptability and practice of torture declined in the Western world after the mid-eighteenth century: Foucault, *Discipline and Punish*; Elizabeth Clark, "'The Sacred Rights of the Weak': Pain, Sympathy and the Culture of Individual Rights in Antebellum America," *JAH* 82 (1995), 463–493. But if the whippings common on southwestern plantations were torture, then in the United States, white people inflicted torture far more often than in almost any human society that ever existed. Meanwhile, though, a late-antebellum "paternalistic" move made it a crime to kill a slave: Peter Kolchin, *American Slavery, 1619–1877* (New York, 1993), 130–131. Ariela J. Gross, in *Double Character: Slavery and Mastery in the Antebellum Courtroom* (Princeton, NJ, 2000), 105–120, finds that defendants presented themselves as using torture for the "rational" purpose of compelling labor. Thomas R.R. Cobb, in *An Inquiry into the Law of Negro Slavery* (Philadelphia, 1858), argues that non-"wanton" violence can enforce "subordination" (90–99).

53. Many historians of torture hold this definition: Page DuBois, *Torture and Truth* (New York, 1991); John Langbein, *Torture and the Law of Proof: Europe and England in the Ancien Regime* (Chicago, 1977); Edward Peters, *Torture*, 2nd ed. (Philadelphia, 1996); Foucault, *Discipline and Punish*. But by the United Nations Convention Against Torture, deliberate violence against an imprisoned and/or bound individual becomes torture when it is designed to extract information or a confession, to serve as a punishment, or to inflict intimidation, or is based on discrimination. Cf. William F. Schulz, ed., *The Phenomenon of Torture: Readings and Commentary* (Philadelphia, 2007).

54. Herbert Gutman, *Slavery and the Numbers Game: A Critique of Time on the Cross* (Urbana, IL, 1975), 17–35; Davis, ed., *Plantation Life*. Barrow's journal also reveals that he whipped 75 percent of the sixty-six working "hands" at one point or another, and Patsey's skills did not save her from being beaten: Northup, *Twelve Years a Slave*,

142–143, 196–199; Ball, *Slavery in the United States*, 217–218; Brown, *Slave Life in Georgia*, 150.

55. R. B. Beverley to R. Beverley, September 3, 1833, Sec. 13, August 28, 1842, Sec. 41, Beverley Papers, VHS; Frederick Law Olmsted, *A Journey in the Back Country* (New York, 1860), 1:44, 83–84; Ball, *Slavery in the United States*, 59; Bibb, *Narrative*, 115.

56. Thomas Jefferson, *Notes on the State of Virginia* (New York, 1984 [Library of America]), 288–289; Nancy Howard, NSV, 50; cf. NSV, 54, 132, 158, 225–227, 243; James Fisher, ST, 236; Brown, *Slave Life in Georgia*, 230–240.

57. Lavinia Bell, ST, 342–345; cf. ST, 180, 433; NSV, 382; Anderson, *Life and Narrative*, 16; S. Haywood to G. W. Haywood, December 1, 1837, Fol. 151, HAY; Themy to T. Harriss, May [1846], Undated Fol., Thomas Harriss Papers, Duke; W. H. Fox to J. Fox, September 9, 1856, John Fox Papers, Duke; Johnson, NSV, 383–384; Gowens, NSV, 140–141; Brown, *Slave Life in Georgia*, 28–30. For a failed-overseer counter-example, see Pearse, *Narrative*, 35–37.

58. Henry Clay, AS, S1, 12 (OK), 111–112.

59. D. Jordan to Malvina, August 3, 1833, D. Jordan Papers, Duke; ST, 435; NSV, 78; Robert W. Fogel and Stanley Engerman, "Explaining the Relative Efficiency of Slave Agriculture in the Antebellum South," 241–265, and Fogel and Engerman, "Explaining the Relative Efficiency of Slave Agriculture in the Antebellum South: Reply," in *Without Consent or Contract: Technical Papers*, vol. 1; Stuart W. Bruchey, *Cotton and the Growth of the American Economy, 1790–1860: Sources and Readings* (New York, 1967), 7–21; S. Duncan to J. Ker, n.d., Fol. 12, Ker Papers, SHC; *Farmers' Register*, November 1834, 353–363; James L. Huston, *Calculating the Value of Union: Slavery, Property Rights, and the Economic Origins of the Civil War* (Chapel Hill, NC, 2003).

60. Ball, *Slavery in the United States*, 216–217.

61. Wm. Kenner to J. Minor, August 23, 1819, William Kenner Papers, LLMVC.

## CHAPTER 5. TONGUES: 1819–1824

1. Lucy Thurston, AS, S1, 10.5 (MS), 2113.

2. Sophia Word, AS, 16.2 (KY), 67; Silas Jackson, AS, 16.3 (MD); Ank Bishop, 6.1 (AL), 37; Lucinda Washington, 6.1 (AL), 410; cf. Vincent Brown, *The Reaper's Garden: Death and Power in the World of Atlantic Slavery* (Cambridge, MA, 2008).

3. Ann Ulrich Evans, AS, 11.2 (MO), 118.

4. Lucy Thurston, AS, S1, 10.5 (MS), 2113.

5. Jos. Sheppard to Jas. & Jn. Sheppard, October 17, 1843, James Sheppard Papers, Duke; Sophia Nobody to Sally Amis, June 7, 1858, Fol. 45, Eliz. Blanchard Papers, SHC; Margaret Nickens, AS, 11.2 (MO), 264; GSMD, 45–46, 202.

6. L. A. Finley to Hackett, May 18, 1854, Gordon-Hackett Papers, SHC; Jordan Connelly[?] to H. Brown, October 17, 1833, Fol. 55, Hamilton Brown Papers, SHC; S. Amis to Grandmother, December 22, 1836, Fol. 40, Eliz. Blanchard Papers, SHC; "Hermitage" Account 1820–1822, Miltenberger Papers, SHC; Sim Neal to Mother Sisters Brothers, [1827], Neal Papers, SHC; William Anderson, *Life and Narrative of William Anderson . . .* (Chicago, 1857), 18.

7. Brian W. Thomas, "Power and Community: The Archaeology of Slavery at the Hermitage Plantation," *American Antiquity* 63 (1998): 531–551; Henry C. Bruce, *The New Man: Twenty-Nine Years a Slave* (York, PA, 1895), 52–56; Henry Bibb, *Narrative of the Life and Adventures of Henry Bibb, an American Slave* (New York, 1849), 25–28; William Grimes, *Life of William Grimes, Written by Himself* (New York, 1825), 29.

8. Charles Ball, *Slavery in the United States: A Narrative of the Life and Adventures of Charles Ball* . . . (New York, 1837), 157, 165; Octavia Albert, *The House of Bondage: Or, Charlotte Brooks and Other Slaves* (New York, 1890), 6.

9. Albert, *House of Bondage*, 4–5; Prudhomme Family Papers, SHC; Brashear Family Papers, SHC; Slack Family Papers, SHC; Michael D. Picone, "Anglophone Slaves in Francophone Louisiana," *American Speech* 78 (2003): 404–443; Elisha Garey, AS, 12.2 (GA), 2.

10. Sarah P. Russell, "Cultural Conflicts and Common Interests: The Making of the Sugar Planter Class in Louisiana, 1795–1853" (PhD diss., University of Maryland, 2000), 327–328; Herbert Gutman, *The Black Family in Slavery and Freedom, 1750–1925* (New York, 1976), 165; Edgar Schneider, *American Earlier Black English: Morphological and Syntactic Varieties* (Tuscaloosa, AL, 1988), 231–235, 255, 275–278; Salikoko Mufwene, "Some Inferences About the Development of African-American English," in Shana Poplack, ed., *The English History of African-American English* (Malden, MA, 2000), 246–248; John McWhorter, "Recovering the Origin," 337–366, in his *Defining Creole* (New York, 2006).

11. Ball, *Slavery in the United States*, 189, 264–266.

12. John Brown, *Slave Life in Georgia* (London, 1855), 23–24, 28–30.

13. Ball, *Slavery in the United States*, 192–193.

14. T. Bryarly to S. Bryarly, February 26, 1847, Bryarly Papers, Duke; Margaret Brashear to Frances, July 10, 1832, Brashear Papers, SHC; G. Henry to [wife], December 2, 1837, Gustavus Henry Papers, SHC; Isham Harrison to T. Harrison, January 20, 1837, James Harrison Papers, SHC; Roderick C.McDonald, "Independent Economic Production," in Ira Berlin and Philip D. Morgan, eds., *Cultivation and Culture: Labor and the Shaping of Slave Life in the Americas* (Charlottesville, VA, 1993), 200–204; Dylan Penningroth, *The Claims of Kinfolk: African American Property and Kinship in the Nineteenth-Century South* (Chapel Hill, NC, 2003).

15. Anthony Abercrombie, AS, 6.1 (AL), 7; Dylan Penningroth, "My People, My People," in Edward E. Baptist and Stephanie M.H. Camp, eds., *New Studies in the History of American Slavery* (Athens, GA, 2006).

16. Willentz, *Rise of American Democracy*, 72–140; William Lee Miller, *Arguing About Slavery: The Great Battle in the United States Congress* (New York, 1996), 168–169.

17. Matthew Carey, *A Calm Address to the People of the Eastern States, on the Subject of the Representation of Slaves* (Boston, 1814); Worthington C. Ford, ed., *Writings of John Quincy Adams* (New York, 1913–1917), 3:71; Sidney E. Morse, *The New States: Or, A Comparison of the Wealth, Strength, and Population of the Northern and Southern States* (Boston, 1813); James Pearse, *Narrative of the Life of James Pearse* (Rutland, VT, c. 1826); H. Bellenden Ker, *Travels Through the Western Interior of the United States* (Elizabethtown, NJ, 1816), 43–50; Glover Moore, *The Missouri Controversy, 1819–1821* (Lexington, KY, 1953), 11.

18. Boynton Merrill, *Jefferson's Nephews: A Frontier Tragedy* (Princeton, NJ, 1976); James Simeone, *Democracy and Slavery in Frontier Illinois: The Bottomland Republic* (DeKalb, IL, 2000); Suzanne Cooper Guasco, "'The Deadly Influence of Negro Capitalists': Southern Yeomen and Resistance to the Expansion of Slavery in Frontier Illinois," *Civil War History* 41, no. 1 (2001): 7–29.

19. R. Douglas Hurt, *Agriculture and Slavery in Missouri's Little Dixie* (Columbia, MO, 1992).

20. William R. Johnson, "Prelude to the Missouri Compromise," *Arkansas Historical Quarterly* 24, no. 1 (1965): 47–66.

21. Moore, *Missouri Controversy*; "Mr. King's Speeches," *NR*, December 4, 1819; JQA, February 20, 1820, 4:528–529; Stuart Leiberger, "Thomas Jefferson and the Missouri Crisis: An Alternative Interpretation," *JER* 17, no. 1 (1997): 121–130.

22. Daniel Webster et al., *A Memorial to the Congress of the United States, on the Subject of Restraining the Increase of Slavery in States to Be Admitted to the Union* (Boston, 1819); Joseph D. Learned, *A View of the Policy of Permitting Slaves in the States West of the Mississippi* (Baltimore, 1820); William Plumer, quoted in Sean Wilentz, *The Rise of American Democracy: Jefferson to Lincoln* (New York, 2005), 231.

23. JQA, February 11, 1820, 4:524, July 5, 1819, 4:398.

24. JQA, February 24, 1820, 4:530–531.

25. Wilentz, *Rise of American Democracy*, 232–234; Matthew Mason, "The Maine and Missouri Crisis: Competing Priorities and Northern Slavery Politics in the Early Republic," *JER* 33, no. 4 (2013): 675–700.

26. Matthew Crocker, "The Missouri Compromise, the Monroe Doctrine, and the Southern Strategy," *Journal of the West* 43 (2004): 45–52. The crisis was not over. Missouri passed a state constitution banning free people of African descent—violating, said free-state congressmen, the US Constitution's "rights and privileges" clause.

27. Francis Fedric, *Slave Life in Virginia and Kentucky, Or, Fifty Years of Slavery . . .* (London, 1853), 47–51; Harry Smith, *Fifty Years of Slavery in the United States of America* (Grand Rapids, MI, 1891), 37–38; cf. L. A. Horton to R. Horton, October 3, 1830, Wyche-Otey papers, SHC, reporting Alabama corn-shucking; Roger D. Abrahams, *Singing the Master: The Emergence of African-American Culture in the Plantation South* (New York, 1992).

28. Shane White and Graham White, *The Sounds of Slavery: Discovering African American History Through Songs, Sermons, and Speech* (Boston, 2006), 66–68; "Dark," Frank Monefee, AS, 6.1 (AL), 280; "Speculator," Eliza Washington, AS, 11.1 (AR), 52; "Polk," Joseph Holmes, AS, 6.1 (AL), 193; "Boss man," Lucindy Jurdon, AS, 6.1 (AL), 243.

29. Henry Walker, AS, 11.1 (AR), 34; Eliza Washington, AS, 11.1 (AR), 52.

30. Fedric, *Slave Life*, 50–51.

31. Josiah Henson, *Truth Stranger Than Fiction: Father Henson's Story of His Own Life* (Boston, 1858), 6–7; Benjamin Latrobe, *Impressions Respecting New Orleans: Diary and Sketches, 1818–1820*, ed. Samuel Wilson Jr. (New York, 1951), 49–51; William Wells Brown, *My Southern Home, Or the South and Its People* (Boston, 1880), 121–124; Dena Epstein, *Sinful Tunes and Spirituals: Black Folk Music to the Civil War* (Urbana, IL, 1977), 95–99; cf. Henry B. Fearon, *Sketches of America: A Narrative of a Journey of Five Thousand Miles Through the Eastern and Western States of America*

(London, 1819), 276–278; Henry C. Knight, *Letters from the South and West* (Boston, 1824), 127; Freddi W. Evans, *Congo Square: African Roots in New Orleans* (Lafayette, LA, 2011).

32. James K. Kinnaird, "Who Are Our National Poets?" *Knickerbocker Magazine* 26 (1845): 331–341.

33. Ibid.; Portia Maultsby, "Africanisms in African-American Music," from Joseph Holloway, ed., *Africanisms in American Culture* (Bloomington, IN, 1990).

34. Eli Sagan, *Citizens and Cannibals: The French Revolution, The Struggle for Modernity, and the Origins of Ideological Terror* (Lanham, MD, 2001), 187–190; Marshall Berman, *All That Is Solid Melts into Air: The Experience of Modernity* (New York, 1982). A classic claim that African Americans were merely imitators, not creators, appears in Thomas Jefferson, *Notes on the State of Virginia* (New York, 1984 [Library of America]), 266–267; cf. Ronald Radano, "Hot Fantasies: American Modernism and the Idea of Black Rhythm," in Ronald Radano and Philip V. Bohlman, eds., *Music and the Racial Imagination* (Chicago, 2000), 459–480. This lack, the story implied, had consequences in the economic realm. Primitive economies were allegedly stuck on starvation-mode because incompletely realized individuals were unwilling to try new ideas, accepting stale orthodoxies rather than seeking growth through entrepreneurial innovation.

35. Hattie Nettles, AS, 6.1 (AL), 297–298; Eliza White, AS, 6.1 (AL), 412; Solomon Northup, *Twelve Years a Slave* (Auburn, NY, 1853), 166–168.

36. Sara Colquitt, AS, 6.1 (AL), 88; White and White, *Sounds of Slavery*, 67; William Piersen, *Black Legacy: America's Hidden Heritage* (Amherst, MA, 1993); George Tucker, *Valley of Shenandoah, Or, Memoirs of the Graysons* (New York, 1824), 2:116–118; T. C. Thornton, *An Inquiry into the History of Slavery; Its Introduction into the United States; Causes of Its Continuance; and Remarks upon the Abolition Tracts of William E. Channing, D.D.* (Washington, DC, 1841), 120–122; John Bernard, *Retrospections of America, 1797–1811* (New York, 1887), 207, 214; Epstein, *Sinful Tunes*, 139.

37. George Strickland, AS, 6.1 (AL), 359; Jacob D. Green, *Narrative of the Life of J. D. Green* (Huddersfield, UK, 1864), 12–13.

38. J. W. Loguen, *The Rev. J. W. Loguen as a Slave and a Freeman* (Syracuse, NY, 1859), 115; Northup, *Twelve Years a Slave*, 216–222; Albert Murray, "Improvisation and the Creative Process," in Robert O'Meally, ed., *The Jazz Cadence of American Life* (New York, 1998), 111–113.

39. William D. Piersen, personal communication; Northup, *Twelve Years a Slave*, 180–182; cf. Tommie Shelby, *We Who Are Dark: The Philosophical Foundations of Black Solidarity* (Cambridge, MA, 2005).

40. Eric Lott, *Love and Theft: Blackface Minstrelsy and the American Working Class* (New York, 1993); David Roediger, *Wages of Whiteness: Race and the Making of the American Working Class* (New York, 1991).

41. Robert Cantwell, *Bluegrass Breakdown: The Making of the Old Southern Sound* (Urbana, IL, 1984).

42. Ball, *Slavery in the United States*, 122–124, 382.

43. John Hope Franklin and Loren F. Schweniger, *Runaway Slaves: Rebels on the Plantation* (New York, 1999), 279.

CHAPTER 6. BREATH: 1824–1835

1. Hettie Mitchell, AS, 10.5 (AR), 111; Nicey [West?], AS, 6.1 (AL), 324; Foster Weathersby, AS, S1, 10.5 (MS), 2228; Toby James, AS, 4.2 (TX), 250; Smith Wilson, AS, S2, 10.9 (TX), 4239.

2. Robert Falls, AS, 16.6 (TN), 13; Rezin Williams, AS, 16.3 (MD), 76–77; Marilda Pethy, AS, 11.2 (MO), 277; Nancy East, 16.4 (OH), 35. Here is a crucial point to understand: formerly enslaved people interviewed in the 1930s, most of them illiterate, used the same terminology one finds in pre-emancipation published narratives. Since the former were unlikely to have learned the terminology from narratives to which they did not have access, their words, though chronologically newer, actually transmit an older set of terms and ideas about slavery, one originating prior to the narratives published between the 1830s and 1860s. In fact, the vernacular history of slavery shaped around the fires of the southwestern plantations, and passed on to children who would use such terms in the 1930s interviews, shaped the ideas and expressions used by the fugitive narrators who wrote nineteenth-century autobiographies.

3. Lawrence J. Kotlikoff, "The Structure of Slave Prices in New Orleans, 1804 to 1862," *Economic Inquiry* 17 (1979): 496–518. By comparison, if we look at the cost of the labor it would have taken to buy a slave, in 2014 dollars the 1820 slave would cost between $230,000 and $500,000, depending on the assumptions and algorithms used. This makes one "hand" the cost-equivalent of an ordinary 2014 American single-family house in the less pricey real-estate markets. See MeasuringWorth.com, www .measuringworth.com/index.php, accessed December 27, 2013.

4. BD, #423; Jonathan Pritchett and Herman Freudenberger, "The Domestic United States Slave Trade: New Evidence," *Journal of Interdisciplinary History* 21 (1991): 448; *Richmond Enquirer*, March 26, 1829; US Department of Commerce, US Census Bureau, 1830 US Census of Population, R174/p 217.

5. Cf. Pritchett and Freudenberger, "Domestic United States Slave Trade." My database records all 5,500-odd interstate slave sales in New Orleans between the summer of 1829 and the end of 1831, whether or not they are associated with certificates.

6. HALL; Louis Hughes, *Thirty Years a Slave: The Institution of Slavery as Seen on the Plantation and in the Home of a Planter* (Milwaukee, WI, 1897), 11.

7. David Hackett Fischer and James Kelly, *Bound Away: Virginia and the Westward Movement* (Richmond, 1993), 137.

8. Henry C. Knight, *Letters from the South and West* (Boston, 1824), 101–102; Robert Falls, AS, 16.6 (TN), 13.

9. Jacob D. Green, *Narrative of the Life of J. D. Green* (Huddersfield, UK, 1864), 5; Frederick Douglass, *My Bondage and My Freedom* (New York, 1855), 448; *Easton Star*, November 27, 1827, May 26, 1829.

10. *Easton Star*, September 27, 1831; cf. *Easton Star*, April 12, 1825, May 8, 1827, November 27, 1827, April 7, 1829, May 28, 1829, September 7, 1830; Stanley Harrold, *The Rise of Aggressive Abolitionism: Addresses to the Slaves* (Lexington, KY, 2004); BD. Not all slaves sold in Kent County were from Kent County: many were like the fourteen-year-old girl named Anne, whom Caleb Dorsey brought across the Chesapeake from Anne Arundel County to sell to John Maydwell in the fall of 1830.

11. Richard Watson, John Wesley, and John Dixon Long, *Pictures of Slavery in Church and State* (Philadelphia, 1857).

12. William G. Shade, *Democratizing the Old Dominion: The Second Party System in Virginia, 1824–1861* (Charlottesville, VA, 1996), 22.

13. Herbert G. Gutman, Richard Sutch, Peter Temin, and Gavin Wright, *Reckoning with Slavery: A Critical Study in the Quantitative History of American Negro Slavery* (Oxford, 1976), 109–112; Michael Tadman, *Speculators and Slaves: Masters, Traders, and Slaves in the Old South* (Madison, WI, 1989), 301; Moses Grandy, *Life of Moses Grandy, Late a Slave in the United States of America* (Boston, 1844), 46.

14. S. C. Archer to R. T. Archer, July 28, 1833, Box 2E652, Fol. 6, Richard T. Archer Papers, Center for American History, University of Texas at Austin.

15. Harriet Jacobs, *Incidents in the Life of a Slave Girl, Written by Herself* (Boston, 1861); Calvin Schermerhorn, *Money over Mastery, Family over Freedom: Slavery in the Antebellum Upper South* (Baltimore, 2011).

16. Sarah Byrd, AS, 12.1 (GA), 168; John Majewski, *A House Dividing: Economic Development in Pennsylvania and Virginia Before the Civil War* (Cambridge, UK, 2000); John Bezis Selfa, *Forging America: Ironworkers, Adventurers, and the Industrious Revolution* (Ithaca, NY, 2004); Ledger, 1829–1855, Alfred Rives Papers, Duke.

17. US Census Bureau, 1830, R54/p429; Robert Falls, AS, 16.6 (TN), 13; Viney Baker, AS, 14.1 (NC), 71; Charley Barbour, AS, 14.1 (NC), 76.

18. Grandy, *Life*, 44; Steven Deyle, *Carry Me Back: The Domestic Slave Trade in American Life* (New York, 2005), 98–99; Robert Gudmestad, *A Troublesome Commerce: The Transformation of the Interstate Slave Trade* (Baton Rouge, LA, 2003), 25–30; Frederick Douglass, "The Meaning of the Fourth of July for the Negro," *Selected Addresses of Frederick Douglass* (Lanham, MD, 2013); Rezin Williams, AS, 16.3 (MD), 76–77; Ethan A. Andrews, *Slavery and the Domestic Slave-Trade in the United States* (Boston, 1836), 80–81.

19. Allen Parker, *Recollections of Slavery Times* (Worcester, MA, 1895), 9; BD.

20. Robert Falls, AS, 16.6 (TN), 13; B. S. King to Joel King, February 23, 1824, Joel King Papers, Duke.

21. Christopher Brown, *Moral Capital: Foundations of British Abolitionism* (Chapel Hill, NC, 2006), 165–206.

22. David Brion Davis, *The Problem of Slavery in the Age of Revolution, 1775–1820* (Ithaca, NY, 1975); John C. Hammond and Matthew Mason, eds., *Contesting Slavery: The Politics of Bondage and Freedom in the New American Nation* (Charlottesville, VA, 2011).

23. JQA, 9:35; Robert Pierce Forbes, *The Missouri Compromise and Its Aftermath: Slavery and the Meaning of America* (Chapel Hill, NC, 2007); Lacy K. Ford, *Deliver Us from Evil: The Slavery Question in the Old South* (New York, 2009), 149; cf. Kari J. Winter, *The American Dreams of John B. Prentis, Slave Trader* (Athens, GA, 2011).

24. Margaret Nickerson, AS, 17 (FL), 251; Jane Sutton, AS, 7.2 (MS), 152; Cora Gillam, AS, S2, 1.3 (AR), 68; Adaline Montgomery, AS, S1, 9.4 (MS), 1514; Lewis Brown, AS, 8.1 (AR), 292; Grandy, *Life*, 10–11.

25. Jane Sutton, AS, 7.2 (MS), 152; George Ward, AS, S1, 10.5 (MS), 100; Harry Johnson, AS, 4.2 (TX), 212–213; George Fleming, AS, S1, 11 (SC), 127–133; William Wells Brown, *Narrative of William Wells Brown, a Fugitive Slave* (Boston, 1849), 13; Edward E. Baptist, "'Stol' and Fetched Here': Enslaved Migration, Ex-Slave Narratives, and Vernacular History," in Edward E. Baptist and Stephanie M. H. Camp,

eds., *New Studies in the History of American Slavery* (Athens, GA, 2006), 243–274; Charles L. Perdue Jr., Thomas E. Barden, and Robert K. Phillips, eds., *Weevils in the Wheat: Interviews with Virginia Ex-Slaves* (Charlottesville, VA, 1976), 115; Greta Elena Couper, *An American Sculptor on the Grand Tour: The Life and Works of William Couper (1853–1942)* (Los Angeles, 1988). *Weevils in the Wheat* refers to a 1907 statue of a Confederate soldier near the Norfolk docks.

26. Helen Odom, AS, 10.5 (AR), 227; Lettie Nelson, AS, 10.5 (AR), 209; William Grose, NSV, 83. On slaves' vernacular storytelling as the root of literary production, see William L. Andrews, *To Tell a Free Story: The First Century of Afro-American Autobiography, 1760–1865* (Urbana, IL, 1985); Marion W. Starling, *The Slave Narrative: Its Place in American History* (Boston, 1981, repr. of 1946 diss.); Henry Louis Gates, *Signifying Monkey: A Theory of Afro-American Literary Criticism* (New York, 1988).

27. John Brown, *Slave Life in Georgia* (London, 1855), 18–19. For claims that ancestors were kidnapped free people, see Spence Johnson, AS, 4.2 (TX), 228–229; Clayton Holbrooke, AS, S2, 1 (KS), 286; Carey Davenport, AS, 4.1 (TX), 284; Ann Clark, AS, 4.1 (TX), 223; Ambrose Douglass, AS, 17 (FL), 101; Samuel Smalls, AS, 17 (FL), 300–301; Douglas Dorsey, AS, 17 (FL), 93; Florida Clayton, AS, S1, 6.1 (MS), 143; Mary Reynolds, S2, 8.7 (TX), 3284, and 5.3 (TX), 236; Julia Blanks, 4.1 (TX), 93. Philadelphia cases: Joseph Watson Papers, Louisiana State University; cf. *Freedom's Journal*, June 22, 1827, September 14, 1827, January 18, 1828; Jonathan Evans et al. May 30, 1825, and Th. Kennedy to Geo. Swain, September 11, 1826, Manumission Society Papers, Duke; *John (a negro) vs. George Williams*, 1821, Box 6/101, Adams Co. [MS] Court Files, one of eighteen cases from the 1820s in the Natchez Historical Collection. Cf. Carol Wilson, *Freedom at Risk: The Kidnapping of Free Blacks in America, 1780–1865* (Lexington, KY, 1995); James Gigantino II, "Trading in New Jersey Souls: New Jersey and the Interstate Slave Trade," *Pennsylvania History* 77, no. 3 (2010): 281–302.

28. Evie Herrin, AS, 8.3 (MS), 988; Sim Greeley, AS, 2.2 (SC), 190; J. Green, AS, 4.2 (TX), 87, and S2, 5.4 (TX), 1577–1583.

29. Shang Harris, AS, 12.2 (GA), 119; Josephine Hubbard, AS, 4.2 (TX), 163; Henry Benjamin Whipple, *Bishop Whipple's Southern Diary, 1843–1844*, ed. Lester B. Shippee (Minneapolis, 1937), 17. Uses of "stole" to describe the Middle Passage: John Jea, *The Life and Unparalleled Sufferings of John Jea, the African Preacher* (Portsea, UK, 1811), 3; Martin Diagney, MW, 62; Carlyle Stewart, MW, 206; Victor Duhon, AS, 4.1 (TX), 307, and 18 (TN), 152, 198; Charley Barbour, AS, 2.1 (SC), 30–31; Susan Snow, AS, 7.2 (MS), 136; Brown, *Narrative of William Wells Brown*, 1, 64; John Andrew Jackson, *The Experience of a Slave in South Carolina* (London, 1862), 7; Frederick Douglass, *Narrative of Frederick Douglass, an American Slave, Written by Himself* (Boston, 1845), 40; Henry C. Bruce, *The New Man: Twenty-Nine Years the Slave, Twenty-Nine Years the Free Man* (York, PA, 1895), 129–131; Francis Fedric, *Slave Life in Virginia and Kentucky, Or, Fifty Years of Slavery* . . . (London, 1853), 4.

30. Charley Barbour, AS, 2.1 (SC), 30–31; Venus in Emma Hurley, AS, 12.2 (GA), 274; Mariah Snyder, AS, 5.4 (TX), 53. A few of the endless references to stealing and sale in Works Progress Administration interviews include: Jake Terriel, AS, 5.4 (TX), 79; Mary Thompson, AS, 5.4 (TX), 101; William Rooks, AS, 10.6 (AR), 76–77; J. T. Travis, AS, 10.6 (AR), 336; Mollie Barber, AS, S1, 12 (OK), 29–30;

Amy Chapman, AS, 6.1 (AL), 58; Nelson Cameron, AS, 2.1 (SC), 173; "Mrs. Sutton," AS, 18 (TN), 31, 81, 105, 204–205, 216, 298–299; Jim Allen, AS, 7.2 (MS), 1; Maria Clemmons, AS, 8.2 (AR), 15; Wash Allen, AS, 12.1 (GA), 10; Lucretia Hayward, AS, 2.2 (SC), 280; Amanda Jackson, AS, 12.2 (GA), 292. See also Perdue et al., *Weevils in the Wheat*, 161 (Katie Johnson), 185 (Louise Jones), 211, 250 (Sis Shackelford), 318 (Nancy Williams). Cf. Mia Bay, *The White Image in the Black Mind: African-American Ideas About White People, 1830–1925* (New York, 2000), 117–149.

31. *Natchez Gazette*, March 11, 1826; John Hope Franklin and Loren F. Schweniger, *Runaway Slaves: Rebels on the Plantation* (New York, 1999).

32. Elisha Winfield Green, *Life of Elisha Winfield Green . . .* (Maysville, KY, 1888), 3.

33. *Emancipator*, 1820; Hiram Hilty, *North Carolina Quakers and Slavery* (Richmond, IL, 1984), 93; Stephen Weeks, *Southern Quakers and Slavery: A Study in Institutional History* (New York, 1968); Ryan P. Jordan, *Slavery and the Meetinghouse: The Quakers and the Abolitionist Dilemma* (Bloomington, IN, 2007), 7.

34. Benjamin Lundy, *Life, Travels, and Opinions of Benjamin Lundy* (Philadelphia, 1847), 15–24.

35. Phineas Norton, Haiti trip notebook, 1826, Th. Kennedy to Meeting for Sufferings, 1826, and "Account of Negroes," Manumission Society Papers, SHC.

36. *Emancipator*, September 1820, 86; Merton Dillon, *Benjamin Lundy and the Struggle for Negro Freedom* (Urbana, IL, 1966), 117–120; *Genius of Universal Emancipation*, September 12, 1825.

37. *Genius of Universal Emancipation*, January 20, 1827, February 24, 1827, March 31, 1827; Gudmestad, *Troublesome Commerce*, 155–156.

38. Henry Mayer, *All On Fire: William Lloyd Garrison and the Abolition of Slavery* (New York, 1998); C. Peter Ripley, *The Black Abolitionist Papers: The United States, 1830–1846* (Chapel Hill, NC, 1991), 7–10; Lundy, *Life*; John L. Thomas, *The Liberator: William Lloyd Garrison* (Boston, 1963), 106–113.

39. *Freedom's Journal*, March 16, 1827. The asterisk indicates that this was an abbreviation, but it was understood that the name was "Woolfolk."

40. Stephen Kantrowitz, *More Than Freedom: Fighting for Black Citizenship in a White Republic, 1829–1889* (New York, 2013), 13–40; Peter Hinks, *To Awaken My Afflicted Brethren: David Walker and the Problem of Antebellum Slave Resistance* (University Park, PA, 1997).

41. David Walker, *Appeal to the Coloured Citizens of the World* (Boston, 1829), 12–26, 43, 62–75.

42. David E. Swift, *Black Prophets of Justice* (Baton Rouge, LA, 1989), 23–41; Walker, *Appeal*, 65, 71–72.

43. Ford, *Deliver Us from Evil*, 332–338.

44. Hinks, *Awaken My Afflicted Brethren*, 269–270; *Liberator*, January 22, 1831.

45. The literature on the abolitionist movement is vast. Within it, a few good starting points that do not silence the voices of the formerly enslaved include: Benjamin Quarles, *Black Abolitionists* (New York, 1969); R. J. M. Blackett, *Building an Antislavery Wall: Black Abolitionists in the Atlantic Abolitionist Movement, 1830–1860* (Baton Rouge, LA, 1983); Paul Goodman, *Of One Blood: Abolitionism and the Origins of Racial Equality* (Berkeley, CA, 1998); James Oliver Horton and Lois E. Horton, *In Hope of Liberty: Culture, Community, and Protest Among Northern Free Blacks, 1700–1860*

(New York, 1997); Julie Roy Jeffrey, *The Great Silent Army of Abolitionism: Ordinary Women in the Abolitionist Movement* (Chapel Hill, NC, 1998); Richard S. Newman, *The Transformation of American Abolitionism: Fighting Slavery in the Early Republic* (Chapel Hill, NC, 2002); James Brewer Stewart, *Abolitionist Politics and the Coming of the Civil War* (Amherst, MA, 2008); J. Brent Morris, "'All The Wise and Truly Pious Have One and the Same End in View': Oberlin, the West, and Abolitionist Schism," *Civil War History* 57 (2011): 234–267; Margaret Washington, *Sojourner Truth's America* (Urbana, IL, 2009); Stanley Harrold, *Border War: Fighting Over Slavery Before the Civil War* (Chapel Hill, NC, 2010); Kantrowitz, *More Than Freedom*.

46. Brown, *Narrative of William Wells Brown*, 13, 51; cf. Thomas Smallwood, *A Narrative of Thomas Smallwood* (Toronto, 1851), 19; Isaac Williams, *Aunt Sally, Or, the Cross the Way of Freedom* (Cincinnati, 1858), 89; Charles Ball, *Slavery in the United States: A Narrative of the Life and Adventures of Charles Ball . . .* (New York, 1837), 36; Moses Roper, *A Narrative of the Adventures and Escape of Moses Roper* (Philadelphia, 1838), 62; J. W. Loguen, *The Rev. J. W. Loguen as a Slave and a Freeman* (Syracuse, NY, 1859), 14–15; Charles Wheeler, *Chains and Freedom, Or, the Life and Adventures of Peter Wheeler, a Colored Man* (New York, 1839), 36–45; *Running a Thousand Miles for Freedom, Or, The Escape of William and Ellen Craft from Slavery* (London, 1860), 3–7; Henry Brown, *Narrative of Henry Box Brown* (Boston, 1849), 15; Kate E. R. Pickard, *The Kidnapped and the Ransomed: Being the Personal Recollections of Peter Still and His Wife "Vina"* (Syracuse, NY, 1856), passim; Lunsford Lane, *The Narrative of Lunsford Lane* (Boston, 1842), 20. Cf. Elizabeth Clark, "'The Sacred Rights of the Weak': Pain, Sympathy and the Culture of Individual Rights in Antebellum America," *JAH* 82 (1995): 463–493; Karen Halttunen, "Humanitarianism and the Pornography of Pain in Anglo-American Culture," *AHR* 100, no. 2 (1995): 303–334.

47. *Freedom's Journal*, March 16, 1827.

48. GSMD, 99–100.

49. Nathan O. Hatch, *The Democratization of American Christianity* (New Haven, CT, 1989).

50. Albert Raboteau, *Slave Religion: The "Invisible Institution" in the Antebellum South* (New York, 1978), 129–132, 223–225; Christine Heyrman, *Southern Cross: The Beginning of the Bible Belt* (New York, 1997), 217–225.

51. NSV, 137; Charles F. Irons, *The Origins of Proslavery Christianity: White and Black Evangelicals in Colonial and Antebellum Virginia* (Chapel Hill, NC, 2008); Jeffrey Young, *Domesticating Slavery: The Master Class in Georgia and South Carolina, 1670–1837* (Chapel Hill, NC, 1999); David Barrow, *Involuntary Slavery Examined* (Lexington, KY, 1808), 22; Betsey Madison, ST, 185–186; Betty Crissman, ST, 468–469; Ball, *Slavery in the United States*, 164–165.

52. On Cane Creek: John B. Boles, *The Great Revival, 1787–1805: The Origins of the Southern Evangelical Mind* (Lexington, KY, 1972); Ellen Eslinger, *Citizens of Zion: The Social Origins of Camp Meeting Revivalism* (Knoxville, TN, 1999); Paul Conkin, *Cane Ridge, America's Pentecost* (Madison, WI, 1990).

53. John F. Watson, *Methodist Error, Or Friendly Christian Advice to Those Methodists Who Indulge in Extravagant Religious Emotions and Bodily Exercises* (Trenton, NJ, 1819); Jane Alexander to Mary Springs, July 24, 1801, Springs Papers, SHC; R. C. Puryear to Isaac Jarratt, November 16, 1832, Jarratt-Puryear Papers, Duke.

54. Jon Butler, *Awash in a Sea of Faith: Christianizing the American People* (Cambridge, MA, 1990).

55. Adam Hodgson, *Remarks During a Journey Through North America in the Years 1819, 1820, 1821* (New York, 1823), 200; Randy J. Sparks, *On Jordan's Stormy Banks: Evangelicalism in Mississippi, 1773–1876* (Athens, GA,1994), 61–66; Ellen Eslinger, "The Beginnings of Afro-American Christianity," in Craig Thompson Friend, ed., *The Buzzel About Kentuck: Settling the Promised Land* (Lexington, KY, 1998), 206–207; Daniel Walker Howe, *What God Hath Wrought: The Transformation of America, 1815–1848* (New York, 2007).

56. Sparks, *On Jordan's Stormy Banks*, 66–71, 116–117, 125–139; David T. Bailey, "A Divided Prism: Two Sources of Black Testimony on Slavery," *JSH* 46 (1980): 392; Randolph Scully, "'I Come Here Before You Did and I Shall Not Go Away': Race, Gender, and Evangelical Community on the Eve of the Nat Turner Rebellion," *JER* 27, no. 4 (2007): 661–684; Janet Duitsman Cornelius, *Slave Missions and the Black Church in the Antebellum South* (Columbia, SC, 1999); Isaac Johnson, *Slavery Days in Old Kentucky* (Ogdensburg, NY, 1901), 25–26; Solomon Northup, *Twelve Years a Slave* (Auburn, NY, 1853), 94.

57. June 26, 1821, Neill Brown Papers, Duke.

58. GSMD, 36, 71, 98; cf. GSMD, pp. 41, 53–55, 81–83, 146.

59. GSMD, 215. The screaming mothers and abandoned babies are frequent elements in Works Progress Administration accounts of the domestic slave trade as-told-to-the-interviewee: e.g., Dave Harper, AS, 11.2 (MO), 163; Alice Douglass, AS, 7.1 (OK), 73–74.

60. GSMD, 99–100.

61. William Webb, *History of William Webb* (Detroit, 1873), 5.

62. Lula Chambers, AS, 11.2, (MO), 79–81; Robert Falls, AS, 16.6 (TN), 16; Henry Bibb to Albert G. Sibley, September 23, 1852, ST, 50–51; Hannah Davidson, AS, 16.4 (OH), 32.

63. Ball, *Slavery in the United States*, 221.

64. Brown, *Slave Life in Georgia*, 3.

65. Scully, "'I Come Here,'" 675; Ira Berlin, *Generations of Captivity: A History of African-American Slaves* (Cambridge, MA, 2003), 209.

66. Nat Turner, *Confessions of Nat Turner* (Baltimore, 1831), 10–11.

67. Scot P. French, *The Rebellious Slave: Nat Turner in American Memory* (Boston, 2004), 83; Patrick Breen, "Contested Communion: The Limits of White Solidarity in Nat Turner's Virginia," *JER* 27, no. 4 (2007): 685–703; Anthony E. Kaye, "Neighborhoods and Nat Turner: The Making of a Slave Rebel and the Unmaking of a Slave Rebellion," *JER* 27, no. 4 (2007): 705–720; estimate from Patrick Breen, "Nat Turner's Revolt: Rebellion and Response in Southampton County, Virginia" (PhD diss., University of Georgia, 2005).

68. *New Orleans Bee*, September 15, 1831; Rachel O'Connor to Brother, October 13, 1831: Allie B. W. Webb, ed., *Mistress of Evergreen Plantation: Rachel O'Connor's Legacy of Letters, 1823–1845* (Albany, NY, 1983), 62–63.

69. *New Orleans Bee*, November 19, 1831; Office of the Mayor, List of Slaves Arrived, 1831, NOPL; W. M. Drake, "The Mississippi Constitutional Convention of

1832," *JSH* 23 (1957); Stephen Duncan to Thomas Butler, September 4, 1831, Butler Papers, LLMVC.

70. "Individuals Importing Slaves, 1831–1833," Orleans Parish Court Records, NOPL; Alison Goodyear Freehling, *Drift Toward Dissolution: The Virginia Slavery Debate of 1831–1832* (Baton Rouge, LA, 1982); Ford, *Deliver Us from Evil*, 373–374.

71. Marshall's speech: Ford, *Deliver Us from Evil*, 369.

72. Ford, *Deliver Us from Evil*, 459.

73. John Floyd, quoted in Ford, *Deliver Us from Evil*, 351; Freehling, *Drift Toward Dissolution*, 83; *Mobile Register*, November 7, 1831.

74. *Mobile Register*, November 7, 1831; J. F. H. Claiborne, *Mississippi as Territory and State* (Jackson, MS, 1880), 1:385; ST, 267, 185–186.

75. Annie Stanton, AS, 6.1 (AL), 354; Janet Duitsman Cornelius, *When I Can Read My Title Clear: Literacy, Slavery, and Religion in the Antebellum South* (Columbia, SC,1991).

76. Ephesians 6:5, Colossians 3:22; James Smylie, *Review of a Letter, from the Presbytery of Chillicothe, to the Presbytery of Mississippi, on the Subject of Slavery* (Woodville, MS, 1836), 3.

77. For the 1835 rebellion scare, see Joshua Rothman, *Flush Times and Fever Dreams: A Story of Capitalism and Slavery in the Age of Jackson* (Athens, GA, 2011); Christopher C. Morris, "An Event in Community Organization: The Mississippi Slave Insurrection Scare of 1835," *Journal of Social History* 22, no. 1 (1988): 93–111; David Libby, *Slavery and Frontier Mississippi, 1720–1835* (Jackson, MS, 2004); James Lal Penick, *The Great Western Land Pirate: John A. Murrell in Legend and History* (Columbia, MO, 1981); Laurence Shore, "Making Mississippi Safe for Slavery: The Insurrectionary Panic of 1835," in Orville Vernon Burton and Robert McMath, eds., *Class, Conflict, and Consensus: Antebellum Southern Community Studies* (Westport, CT, 1982), 96–120.

78. Israel Campbell, *An Autobiography, Bound and Free* (Philadelphia, 1861), 71–74; Rothman, *Flush Times*.

## CHAPTER 7. SEED: 1829–1837

1. Jonathan F. Wendel, Curt L. Brubaker, and A. Edward Percival, "Genetic Diversity in *Gossypium hirsutum* and the Origin of Upland Cotton," *American Journal of Botany* 79, no. 11 (1992): 1291–1310.

2. Cf. *Arkansas Gazette*, June 30, 1821.

3. Tyre Glen to Isaac Jarratt, February 11, 1832, Box 2, Jarratt-Puryear Papers, Duke.

4. Oakley Neils Durfee Barber, "Honor, Gender, Violence and the Life of Robert Potter" (Master's thesis, Southwest Texas State University, 2000); Ernest Fischer, *Robert Potter: Founder of the Texas Navy* (Gretna, LA, 1976); Harry L. Watson, *Jacksonian Politics and Community Conflict: The Emergence of the Second American Party System in Cumberland County, North Carolina* (Baton Rouge, LA, 1981); Lacy K. Ford, *Origins of Southern Radicalism: The South Carolina Upcountry, 1800–1860* (New York, 1988); Alexander Keyssar, *The Right to Vote: The Contested History of Democracy in America* (New York, 2000), 332.

5. Edwin Miles, *Jacksonian Democracy in Mississippi* (Chapel Hill, NC, 1960); Craig T. Friend, *Along the Maysville Road: The Early American Republic in the Trans-Appalachian West* (Knoxville, TN, 2006); Joseph Tregle, *Louisiana in the Age of Jackson: A Clash of Cultures and Personalities* (Baton Rouge, LA, 1999).

6. Ernest Shearer, *Robert Potter: Remarkable North Carolinian and Texan* (Houston, 1951), 9–12.

7. Manuel Eisner, "Long-Term Historical Trends in Violent Crime," *Crime and Justice* 30 (2003): 83–142, esp. 99; Randolph Roth, *American Homicide* (Cambridge, MA, 2009), 162–225.

8. Shearer, *Robert Potter*, 12–28; Joseph Cheshire, *Nonnulla: Memories, Stories, Traditions, More or Less Authentic* (Chapel Hill, NC, 1930).

9. *Richmond Enquirer*, September 30, 1831; *Indiana Democrat*, September 18, 1831; *Baltimore Patriot*, October 18, 1831; R. S. to John D. Hawkins, August 30, 1831, Fol. 48, Hawkins Family Papers, SHC.

10. Robert Potter, *Mr. Potter's Appeal to the Citizens of Nash, Warren, Franklin, and Granville* (Hillsborough, NC, 1831); *Richmond Enquirer*, March 27, 1832.

11. *Richmond Enquirer*, December 28, 1831; *Baltimore Patriot*, July 28, 30, 1834; August 8, 1834; *Barre* (MA) *Farmers' Gazette*, February 13, 1835; *Norfolk* (VA) *Advertiser*, March 14, 1835; *New Hampshire Patriot*, March 16, 1835; Shearer, *Robert Potter*, 34–36.

12. Roth, *American Homicide*, 162–225.

13. P. W. Alston to J. D. B. Hooper, December 22, 1833, John D. Hooper Papers, SHC; Wm. Hardies to Sarah Hardies, April 11, 1833, Fol. 1/5, BIELLER; D. McKenzie to Jn. McLaurin, March 29, 1838, August 23, 1845, Duncan McLaurin Papers, Duke; Wm. Southgate to Wm. P. Smith, May 17, 1837, Wm. P. Smith Papers, Duke; B. F. Duvall to Martha Wattairs, May 2, 1843, Box 2, James Tutt Papers, Duke; D. Ker to J. Ker, August 1, 1817, Ker Papers, SHC; *NOP*, March 19, 1837, July 5, 1846; cf. Jos. Hazard to I. Hazard, November 30, 1841, Hazard Company, LLMVC; Sam Sutton to Fred. Harris, August 14, 1820, Frederick Harris Papers, Duke; L. Taylor to W. H. Hatchett, September 26, 1836, William Hatchett Papers, Duke; Letter of August 24, 1823, David Leech Papers, Duke.

14. Henry Benjamin Whipple, *Bishop Whipple's Southern Diary, 1843–1844*, ed. Lester B. Shippee (Minneapolis, 1937), 24–25; C. A. Hentz Diary, vol. 1, February 24, 1849, Hentz Papers, SHC; Lewis Clarke, ST, 157; cf. Wm. Slack to Ch. Slack, December 1838, Slack Papers, SHC.

15. John Pelham to E. Dromgoole, February 20, 1833, Dromgoole Papers, SHC.

16. H. Watson to Mother, December 2, 1836, Henry Watson Papers, Duke; Edward E. Baptist, *Creating an Old South: Middle Florida's Plantation Frontier Before the Civil War* (Chapel Hill, NC, 2002), 103–105; J. F. H. Claiborne, *Mississippi as Territory and State* (Jackson, MS, 1880), 361–414.

17. *Natchez Gazette*, May 11, 1832; Miles, *Jacksonian Democracy*, 45.

18. Claiborne, *Mississippi*, 423–427.

19. *NR*, March 12, 1825.

20. Webster to Mrs. Webster, February 19, 1829, in Daniel Webster, *Private Correspondence* (Boston, 1857), 1:470; Robert V. Remini, *Andrew Jackson and the Course of*

*American Freedom, 1822–1832* (New York, 1981); Edwin Miles, "The First People's Inaugural—1829," *Tennessee Historical Quarterly* 37 (1978).

21. James Parton, *Life of Jackson* (New York, 1860), 3:169–170.

22. Remini, *Andrew Jackson and American Freedom*, 2:132; Robert V. Remini, *Andrew Jackson and the Course of American Democracy* (New York, 1984), 227–230; James Wyly to J. K. Polk, January 11, 1833, JKP, 2:15–17.

23. Remini, *Andrew Jackson and American Freedom*, 200.

24. A. Jackson to J. Overton, June 8, 1829, *The Papers of Andrew Jackson*, ed. Sam B. Smith and Harriet Fason Chappell Owsley (Knoxville, TN, 1980), 7:270–271.

25. *NR*, March 8, 1828, 19–22. Historians still argue about whether or not the plot existed, and if so, what it entailed: Michael P. Johnson, "Denmark Vesey and His Co-Conspirators," *William and Mary Quarterly*, 3rd ser., vol. 58, no. 4 (2001): 915–976; James O'Neil Spady, "Power and Confession: On the Credibility of the Earliest Reports of the Denmark Vesey Conspiracy," *William and Mary Quarterly*, 3rd ser., vol. 68 (2011): 287–304.

26. Nicholas Biddle to J. Harper, January 9, 1829, 67–68; Wm. Lewis to Biddle, October 16, 1829, 79–80, *The Correspondence of Nicholas Biddle Dealing with National Affairs, 1807–1844*, ed. Reginald McGrane (Boston, 1919).

27. Margaret Bayard Smith to Maria Kirkpatrick, March 12, 1829, in Gaillard Hunt, ed., *The First Forty Years of Washington Society in the Family Letters of Margaret Bayard Smith* (New York, 1906), 424.

28. Historians often misidentify southwestern anti-Jackson politicians as "nullifiers." Most, like Poindexter, were simply Jackson-haters: Elizabeth Varon, *Disunion: The Coming of the American Civil War, 1789–1859* (Chapel Hill, NC, 2008), 55–57. For nullification, among many other excellent works, see Brian Schoen, *The Fragile Fabric of Union: Cotton, Federal Politics, and the Global Origins of the Civil War* (Baltimore, 2009).

29. Kirsten Wood, "One Woman So Dangerous to the Public Morals: Gender and Power in the Eaton Affair," *JER* 17 (1997): 237–275; Anthony F. C. Wallace, *The Long, Bitter Trail: Andrew Jackson and the Indians* (New York, 1993).

30. CHSUS, Ca 9–19.

31. *Correspondence of Nicholas Biddle*, 93.

32. J. Springs to Wife, September 23, 1806, Springs Papers, SHC.

33. H. B. Trist to N. Trist, May 18, 1825, Nicholas Trist Papers, SHC; Undated note, Fol. 1824, A. P. Walsh Papers, Louisiana State University.

34. Fritz Redlich, *The Molding of American Banking: Men and Ideas* (New York, 1968), 1:270fn8–9; Sean Wilentz, *The Rise of American Democracy: Jefferson to Lincoln* (New York, 2005), 365.

35. I. Franklin (IF) to R. C. Ballard (RB), January 9, 1832, February 10, 1832, Fol. 4 & 5, RCB.

36. *Baltimore Patriot*, January 1, 1829; Richard H. Kilbourne, *Slave Agriculture and Financial Markets in Antebellum America: The Bank of the United States in Mississippi, 1831–1852* (London, 2006).

37. Wilentz, *Rise of American Democracy*, 366; Redlich, *Molding of American Banking*, 1:21; Biddle to Thomas Swann, March 17, 1824, Exhibit No. 1-L, p. 297, in

report of the Senate Committee on Finance, 23rd Cong., 2nd sess., Congressional Serial Set.

38. March 19, 1832, Discounts A-L #1, vol. 19, Bank of the United States (Natchez Branch) Records, LLMVC; Bank of Mississippi, RASP; US Department of Commerce, US Census Bureau, 1830 Census, Adams County, MS; Miles, *Jacksonian Democracy*, 23; Martha Brazy, *An American Planter: Stephen Duncan of Antebellum Natchez and New York* (Baton Rouge, LA, 2006), 20–21; Robert Roeder, "New Orleans Merchants, 1790–1837" (PhD diss., Harvard University, 1959); Ralph Catterall, *The Second Bank of the United States* (Chicago, 1902), 137–143.

39. McKay W. Campbell to James K. Polk, November 23, 1833, JKP, 2:136–138; A. O. Harris to James K. Polk, November 16, 1833, JKP, 2:131–132.

40. Jesse Cage to William Cotton, August 27, 1839, Fol. 28, RCB.

41. IF to RB, September 27, 1834, Fol. 15, RCB; cf. Walter Johnson, *Soul by Soul: Life Inside the Antebellum Slave Market* (Cambridge, MA, 1999).

42. Daniel Kahneman, *Thinking, Fast and Slow* (New York, 2011); Dan Ariely, *Predictably Irrational: The Hidden Forces That Shape Our Decisions* (New York, 2008); Geoffrey Miller, *Spent: Sex, Evolution, and Consumer Behavior* (New York, 2009), 106–111.

43. Annette Gordon-Reed, *Thomas Jefferson and Sally Hemings: An American Controversy* (Charlottesville, VA, 1997); Jan Lewis and Peter Onuf, eds., *Sally Hemings and Thomas Jefferson: History, Memory, and Civic Culture* (Charlottesville, VA, 1999); "Bawdy Poem," n.d. [1820s–1830s], Fol. 10, Young Allen Papers, SHC.

44. Bryan Edwards, "The Sable Venus: An Ode," from his *Poems, Written Chiefly in the West-Indies* (Kingston, 1792); cf. Regulus Allen, "The Sable Venus and Desire for the Undesirable," *Studies in English Literature, 1500–1900* 51, no. 3 (2011).

45. Trevor Burnard, "The Sexual Life of an Eighteenth-Century Jamaican Slave Overseer," in Merril D. Smith, ed. *Sex and Sexuality in Early America* (New York, 1998), 163–189, esp. 173.

46. Cf. Patricia Cline Cohen, *The Murder of Helen Jewett: The Life and Death of a Prostitute in Nineteenth-Century New York* (New York, 1998); Karen Halttunen, *Confidence Men and Painted Women: A Study of Middle-Class Culture in America, 1830–1870* (New Haven, CT, 1982).

47. Harriet Jacobs, *Incidents in the Life of a Slave Girl, Written by Herself* (Boston, 1861); Calvin Schermerhorn, *Money over Mastery, Family over Freedom: Slavery in the Antebellum Upper South* (Baltimore, 2011).

48. Drew Gilpin Faust, *James Henry Hammond and the Old South: A Design for Mastery* (Baton Rouge, LA, 1982).

49. Henry C. Knight, *Letters from the South and West* (Boston, 1824), 127; *NR*, 29 (November 5, 1825), 160; Tregle, *Louisiana in the Age of Jackson*, 37.

50. IF to RB, November 14, 1831, December 10, 14, 1831, Fol. 3; IF to RB, January 9, 1832, Fol. 4; IF to RB, February 10, 1832, Fol. 5; IF and James Franklin to RB, April 24, 1832, Fol. 6; IF and James Franklin to RB, June 9, 1832, Fol. 7; IF to RB, October 26, 1831, Fol. 2; Samuel Franklin to RB, June 1, 1831, Fol. 1; IF to RB, May 31, 1831, Fol. 1; John Armfield to RB, July 23, 1831, August 15, 1831, Fol. 2, RCB. Biddle: H.R. 460, 22nd Cong., 1st sess., 316–317; Catterall, *Second Bank*,

143n2, cf. 502–508; Richard H. Kilbourne, *Slave Agriculture and Financial Markets in Antebellum America: The Bank of the United States in Mississippi, 1831–1852* (London, 2006), 28–32.

51. IF to RB, December 8, 1832, Fol. 8; IF to RB, January 29, 1833, Fol. 10; C. M. Rutherford to RB, December 23, 1832, Fol. 9; IF to RB, June 8, 1832, Fol. 7; IF to RB, June 9, 1832, Fol. 7; IF to RB, June 11, 1833, Fol. 11, RCB.

52. Ethan A. Andrews, *Slavery and the Domestic Slave-Trade in the United States* (Boston, 1836), 136; E. S. Abdy, *Journal of a Residence and Tour in the United States* (London, 1835), 2:179–180; Wendell Stephenson, *Isaac Franklin: Slave Trader and Planter of the Old South; With Plantation Records* (University, LA, 1938), 29–30; J. W. Ingraham, *The South-West, by a Yankee* (New York, 1836), 2:245; RB to Franklin & Co., September 7, 1832, Fol. 7, RCB; Ariela J. Gross, *Double Character: Slavery and Mastery in the Antebellum Courtroom* (Princeton, NJ, 2000), 57.

53. IF to RB, January 11, 1834, Fol. 13, RCB.

54. *Norfolk Democrat*, December 1, 1848; William Bowditch, *Slavery and the Constitution* (Boston, 1849), 89; Henry Clarke Wright, *American Slavery Proved to Be Robbery and Theft* (Edinburgh, 1845), 21; *Farmers' Gazette*, March 6, 1835.

55. Andrews, *Domestic Slave-Trade*, 166; ASAI, 16; Ronald Walters, "The Erotic South: Civilization and Sexuality in American Abolitionism," *American Quarterly* 25, no. 2 (1973): 177–201; Elizabeth Clark, "'The Sacred Rights of the Weak': Pain, Sympathy and the Culture of Individual Rights in Antebellum America," *JAH* 82 (1995): 463–493; Carol Lasser, "Voyeuristic Abolitionism: Sex, Gender, and the Transformation of Antislavery Rhetoric," *JER* 28, no. 1 (2008): 83–114; Gregory Smithers, "American Abolitionism and Slave-Breeding Discourse: A Re-Evaluation," *Slavery and Abolition* 33, no. 4 (2012): 551–570; IF to RB, November 1, 1833, Fol. 12; IF to RB, January 11, 1834, Fol. 13; J. Franklin to RB, March 7, 1834, Fol. 13, RCB.

56. Wood, "One Woman So Dangerous"; Johnson, *Soul by Soul*, 114; IF to RB, January 11, 1834, Fol. 13; Sam Wakefield to RB, August 16, 1836, Fol. 17; Bacon Tait to RB, August 13, 1839, Fol. 28, RCB.

57. R. B. Beverley to W. B. Beverley, July 2, 1842, Sec. 46, Beverley Papers, VHS; Nancy Bieller to Jacob Bieller, August 16, 1836; Jacob Bieller Will, December 8, 1834; *Bieller v. Bieller* notes, BIELLER; Robt. Hairston to G. Hairston, April 13, 1852; P. Hairston to G. Hairston, June 8, 1852, Fol. 2, George Hairston Papers, SHC; Jas. Hairston to P. W. Hairston, May 13, 1852, vol. 9, P. W. Hairston Papers, SHC; Henry Wiencek, *The Hairstons: An American Family in Black and White* (New York, 1999).

58. Louisa Picquet and Hiram Mattison, *Louisa Picquet, The Octoroon: Or, Inside Views of Southern Domestic Life* (New York, 1861), 10–19; N. E. Benson to E. Benson, May 3, 1837, Benson-Thompson Papers, Duke.

59. IF to RB, January 9, 1832, Fol. 4; C. M. Rutherford to RB, February 19, 1853, Fol. 187, RCB; Philip Thomas to Finney, July 24, 1859; P. Thomas to Jack, November 26, 1859, William Finney Papers, Duke.

60. Jas. Franklin to RB, March 27, 1832, Fol. 5, RCB.

61. Moses Alexander to Wm. Graham, July 8, 1836, *Papers of William Graham* (Raleigh, NC, 1957–1992), 1:432–435. Discussions of "animal spirits" in the economy

have usually left out sex, from Charles Mackay, *Memoirs of Extraordinary Popular Delusions and the Madness of Crowds* (London, 1852), all the way to John K. Galbraith, *A Short History of Financial Euphoria* (New York, 1993), and beyond.

62. Undated note, Fol. 1824, A. P. Walsh Papers, LLMVC.

63. Irene Neu, "J. B. Moussier and the Property Banks of Louisiana," *Business History Review* 35, no. 4 (1961): 550–557; Redlich, *Molding of American Banking*, 1:206–207; Earl S. Sparks, *History and Theory of Agricultural Credit in the United States* (New York, 1932), 6.

64. *New Orleans Argus*, February 26, 1828.

65. George Green, *Finance and Economic Development in the Old South: Louisiana Banking, 1804–1861* (Palo Alto, CA, 1972), 113–117; Lavergne à Manuel Andry, September 14, 1828, Fol. 1A/1; Interr. Oliver Morgan with John R. Dewitt, March 19, 1829; J. DeWitt application, March 24, 1829, Fol. 1A/4; Mortgage Book, vol. 68, CAPL Papers, LLMVC.

66. "Slaves' Deaths on Ste. Sophie, October 1824–March 1829," Ste. Sophie / Live Oak Records, Tulane.

67. Robert Carson to Henderson Forsyth, December 3, 1836, John Forsyth Papers, Duke; *Natchez Gazette*, October 20, 1830; Miles, *Jacksonian Democracy*, 24; James Silver, "Land Speculation Profits in the Chickasaw Cession," *JSH* 10 (1944): 84–92.

68. Wilentz, *Rise of American Democracy*, 364, 874–875n13; Catterall, *Second Bank*, 243–286; *Baltimore Patriot*, July 12, 1831; *New York American*, July 10, 1819; Frank Otto Gathell and John McFaul, "The Outcast Insider: Reuben Whitney and the Bank War," *Pennsylvania Magazine of History and Biography* 91 (1967): 115–144; Frank Otto Gathell, "Sober Second Thoughts on Van Buren, the Albany Regency, and Wall Street," *JAH* 53 (1966): 19–40.

69. Biddle to Thomas Cadwalader, July 3, 1832, *Correspondence of Nicholas Biddle*, 192–193; Samuel Smith to Jackson, June 17, 1832, CAJ, 4:449.

70. Donald B. Cole, *A Jackson Man: Amos Kendall and the Rise of American Democracy* (Baton Rouge, LA, 2004).

71. John Anderson to Polk, January 25, 1833, JKP, 2:47–49; Jackson's Veto Message, http://avalon.law.yale.edu/19th_century/ajveto01.asp, accessed May 3, 2012.

72. Biddle to William G. Bucknor, July 13, 1832, *Correspondence of Nicholas Biddle*, 195; Martin Van Buren, *The Autobiography of Martin Van Buren*, ed. John Fitzpatrick (Washington, DC, 1920), 625; Remini, *Andrew Jackson and American Freedom*, 2:366; Daniel Walker Howe, *What Hath God Wrought: The Transformation of America, 1815–1848* (New York, 2007); William Lee Miller, *Lincoln's Virtues: An Ethical Biography* (New York, 2002).

73. Biddle to Henry Clay, August 1, 1832, *Correspondence of Nicholas Biddle*, 196–197.

74. Baptist, *Creating an Old South*; J. Mills Thornton, *Politics and Power in a Slave Society: Alabama, 1800–1860* (Baton Rouge, LA, 1978); Harry L. Watson, *Liberty and Power: The Politics of Jacksonian America* (New York, 1990).

75. Jackson to Polk, August 31, 1833, JKP, 2:106–107.

76. Pet banks increased from seven to thirty-five between 1833 and 1836: Frank Otto Gathell, "Spoils of the Bank War: Political Bias in the Selection of the Pet Banks," *AHR* 70 (1964): 35–58; Harry N. Scheiber, "Pet Banks in Jacksonian

Economy and Finance, 1833–1841," *Journal of Economic History* 23 (1963): 196–214; Miles, *Jacksonian Democracy*, 74–75; Peter Temin, *The Jacksonian Economy* (New York, 1969), 73–76; US Congress, House of Representatives, "Condition of Banks, 1840," 26th Cong., 2nd sess., H. Doc. 111 (Serial 385), 1441; D. W. Jordan to Emily Jordan, August 3, 1833, and D. W. Jordan to Richard Evans, October 15, 1833, D. W. Jordan Papers, Duke; IF and J. Franklin to RB, October 29, 1833, Fol. 11; IF to RB, November 5, 1833, Fol. 12, RCB; Knight to William Beall, February 8, 1834, John Knight Papers, Duke; Green, *Finance and Economic Development*, 90–94.

77. Thomas Govan, *Nicholas Biddle: Nationalist and Public Banker, 1786–1844* (Chicago, 1959), 253; Howe, *What Hath God Wrought*, 391n61; IF to RB, February 7, 1834; James Franklin to RB, Fol. 13, RCB; S. S. Prentiss to Mother, March 23, 1834, in George L. Prentiss, *A Memoir of S. S. Prentiss* (New York, 1856), 1:139.

78. Miles, *Jacksonian Democracy*, 76; Tregle, *Louisiana in the Age of Jackson*, 281–284; cf. J. Franklin to RB, December 19, 1833, Fol. 12, RCB; Claiborne, *Mississippi*, 409–416; John Wurts to Polk, December 19, 1833, JKP, 2:186; John Welsh to Polk, December 28, 1833, JKP, 2:200–202; Parton, *Life of Jackson*, 2:549–550; Biddle to Poindexter, February 22, 1834; IF to RB, February 7, 1834; James Franklin to RB, Fol. 13, RCB; Terry Cahal to Polk, January 2, 1834, and William Jenkins to Polk, January 3, 1834, JKP, 2:209–211, 217.

79. US Congress, "Condition of Banks," 249, 299, 535; R. T. Hoskins to R. T. Brownrigg, December 19, 1835, Brownrigg Papers, SHC; Thomas Abernethy, "The Early Development of Commerce and Banking in Tennessee," *Mississippi Valley Historical Review* 14 (1927): 321–322; R. W. Hidy, "The Union Bank Loan of 1832: A Case Study in Marketing," *Journal of Political Economy* 47 (1939): 232–352; Miles, *Jacksonian Democracy*, 140–141; Roeder, "New Orleans Merchants," 334.

80. Jane Knodell, "Rethinking the Jacksonian Economy: The Impact of the 1832 Bank Veto on Commercial Banking," *Journal of Economic History* 66 (2006): 541–574; Edward E. Baptist, "Borrowed by the Lash: Enslaved People as Collateral in the Great Divergence," Paper presented at Capitalizing on Finance Conference, Huntington Library, Pasadena, CA, April 13, 2013.

81. *American State Papers: Land*, 2:495–497; Claiborne, *Mississippi*, 411–417; US Congress, "Condition of Banks," 290, 325–344; Henry Clay to Wm. Mercer, August 13, 1834, William Mercer Papers, Tulane.

82. Anna Whitteker to Emily Dupuy, May 10, 1835, Emily Dupuy Papers, Mss1D9295b, Sect. 1, VHS.

83. Miles, *Jacksonian Democracy*, 118–119; [?] to Thomas Wyche, February 9, 1835, Wyche-Otey Papers, SHC; IF to RB, March 30, 1834, Fol. 13; James Blakey to RB, August 6, 1834, Fol. 15; IF to RB, September 17, 1834, Fol. 15, RCB.

84. Thomas Dorsey to J. Bieller, April 15, 1835, Fol. 1/7, BIELLER; Isham Harrison to Thomas Harrison, October 14, 1834, Fol. 3, James Harrison Papers, SHC.

## CHAPTER 8. BLOOD: 1836–1844

1. William Colbert, AS, 6.1 (AL), 81–82.

2. Lewis Clarke, "Leaves from a Slave's Journal of Life," ed. Lydia Maria Child, *National Anti-Slavery Standard*, October 20, 27, 1842, 78–79, 83; Orlando Patterson, *Rituals of Blood: Consequences of Slavery in Two American Centuries* (New York, 1999);

S. Ford to Bieller, n.d., Fol. 2/15, BIELLER; Archibald Hyman to L. Thompson, June 30, 1860, Lewis Thompson Papers, SHC.

3. Ford to Bieller, n.d. Fol. 2/15, BIELLER; Jos. Labrenty to J. Waddill, September 22, 1838, Elijah Fuller Papers, SHC.

4. Wiley Childress, AS, 16.6 (TN), 9; Martha Bradley, AS, 6.1 (AL), 47; Anthony Abercrombie, AS, 6.1 (AL), 7.

5. Peter Corn, AS, 11.2 (MO), 87; Henry Waldon, AS, 11.1 (AR), 15–16; Columbus Williams, AS, 11.1 (AR), 155; William Read to Downey, August 18, 1848, S. S. Downey Papers, Duke; cf. Thomas Foster, "The Sexual Abuse of Black Men Under American Slavery," *Journal of the History of Sexuality* 20, no. 3 (2011): 445–464.

6. David Walker, *Appeal to the Coloured Citizens of the World* (Boston, 1829), 14–15, 23, 28, 32; 1842 Speech of Lewis Clarke, ST, 152, 157–158; Robert Falls, AS, 16.6 (TN), 16; "Violence, Protest, and Identity: Black Masculinity in Antebellum America," in James O. Horton, *Free People of Color: Inside the African-American Community* (Washington, DC, 1993); Orlando Patterson, *Slavery and Social Death: A Comparative Study* (Cambridge, MA, 1982); Claude Meillassoux, *The Anthropology of Slavery: The Womb of Iron and Gold* (Chicago, 1991); Ann Clark, AS, 4.1 (TX), 223–224; George Cato, AS, S2, 11 (SC), 98; AS, 18 (TN), 95; Francis Burdett to R. C. Ballard (RB), July 3, 1848, Fol. 130, RCB.

7. "Mrs. Webb," MW, 209; Charity Bowers, ST, 266; Scott Bond, AS, S2, 1 (AR), 33.

8. CHSUS, 3:24, 599.

9. Andrew V. Remini, *Andrew Jackson and the Course of American Democracy* (New York, 1984), 3:418–419, 367–368.

10. Sean P. Kelley, "'Mexico in His Head': Slavery and the Texas-Mexico Border, 1810–1860," *Journal of Social History* 37 (2004): 709–723; Sean P. Kelley, "Blackbirders and Bozales: African-Born Slaves on the Lower Brazos River of Texas in the Nineteenth Century," *Civil War History* 54, no. 4 (2008): 406–424; Randolph Campbell, *An Empire for Slavery* (Baton Rouge, LA, 1989), 54; Dudley G. Wooten, *A Comprehensive History of Texas, 1685 to 1897* (Austin, TX, 1986), 1:759; J. F. Perry to Lastraps & Desmare, January 15, 1834, *Stephen Austin Papers*, 3:39–40; Paul D. Lack, "Slavery and the Texas Revolution," *Southwestern Historical Quarterly* 89 (1985): 181–202.

11. *Richmond Enquirer*, October 27, 1835, January 4, 1836; Ernest Shearer, *Robert Potter: Remarkable North Carolinian and Texan* (Houston, 1951), 49; *Essex Gazette*, May 14, 1836; Thomas Hardeman to Polk, March 31, 1836, 3:567–668, JKP. Harrison's son was released unharmed and died in Ohio, genitalia intact, in 1840. Twenty-five Alamo dead were New Orleans volunteers: Edward L. Miller, *New Orleans and the Texas Revolution* (College Station, TX, 2004), 154.

12. Jn. Lockhead to W. H. Hatchett, August 26, 1836, William Hatchett Papers, Duke. White southerners saw Texas as a new empire for slavery; cf. Eugene Barker, *Mexico and Texas, 1821–1835* (Dallas, 1928); *Alexandria Gazette*, May 19, 1836; Wm. Christy to Jos. Ellis, March 22, 1836, Miller, *New Orleans and the Texas Revolution*; *New York Express*, April 4, 1837; *Washington Intelligencer*, April 30, 1836.

13. Farish Carter and R. S. Patton, April 4, 1835, Fol. 20, Eliz. Talley Papers, SHC; J. G. Johnson to G. W. Haywood, May 18, 1836, Fol. 146, HAY; James Huie,

Case File 258, Bankruptcy Act of 1841, RG 21, NA; E. B. Hicks to Alex. Cuningham, March 29, 1838, Texas Land Scrip, Cuningham Papers, Duke; Geo. Johnson to Wm. Johnson, August 22, 1838, Wm. Johnson Papers, SHC; Missi. River Diary, Duke; James D. Cocke, *A Glance at the Currency and Resources Generally of the Republic of Texas* (Houston, 1838), 7–15.

14. Campbell, *Empire for Slavery*, 35; *New Hampshire Sentinel*, April 21, 1836; *Alexandria Gazette*, May 10, 1836.

15. William Lee Miller, *Arguing About Slavery: The Great Battle in the United States Congress* (New York, 1996); Joel H. Silbey, *Storm over Texas: The Annexation Controversy and the Road to the Civil War* (Oxford, UK, 2005), 10–14.

16. Changes to the Treasury's gold-silver exchange rate, plus overseas sales of slave-backed bonds, attracted specie, while the British trading practices that provoked the 1839–1843 Opium War unlocked Chinese "hoards" of silver. Peter Temin, *The Jacksonian Economy* (New York, 1969); Silbey, *Storm over Texas*; Burrell Fox to Elizabeth Neal, September 25, 1835, Neal Papers, SHC; R. T. Hoskins to Richard Brownrigg, December 19, 1835, Brownrigg Papers, SHC; H. P. Watson to A. B. Springs, January 24, 1836, Springs Papers, SHC.

17. Isham Harrison to Thos. Harrison, June 16, 1834, Thos. Harrison to Jas. Harrison, January 4, 1836, October 20, 1836, August 28, 1836, James Harrison Papers, SHC; R. Hinton to Laurens Hinton, October 16, 1836, Laurens Hinton Papers, SHC; P. A. Bolling to Edm. Hubard, February 24, 1837, Fol. 72, Hubard Papers, SHC; William Ashley to Chester Ashley, April 10, 1836, Chester Ashley Papers, SHC.

18. Ballard and Franklin to Jacob Bieller, Fol. 2/15, BIELLER; R. H. M. Davidson to Dear Brevard, November 8, 1836, Davidson Papers, SHC.

19. Charles P. Kindleberger, *Manias, Panics, and Crashes: A History of Financial Crises* (New York, 1978); John K. Galbraith, *A Short History of Financial Euphoria* (New York, 1993). Free states also borrowed money to pump into local economies, e.g., Reginald C. McGrane, *Foreign Bondholders and American State Debts* (New York, 1935), 129.

20. Byrne Hammond and Co. to Jackson, Riddle, March 26, 1836, JRC; John Cassidy, *Why Markets Fail: The Logic of Economic Calamities* (New York, 2009), 239; Henry Draft to Wm. Miller, June 4, 1835, John Fox Papers, Duke; Samuel Faulkner to Dear Fitz, September 2, 1835, Wm. Powell Papers, Duke.

21. Henry Watson to Father, December 15, 1836, Henry Watson Papers, Duke; *New Orleans Price-Current*, August 20, 1836, Fol. 3, JRC; Thomas Harrison to James Harrison, August 28, 1836, Fol. 3, James Harrison Papers, SHC; Robert Carson to Henderson Forsyth, December 3, 1836, N. E. Matthews to H. Forsyth, March 31, 1836, John Forsyth Papers, Duke; Peter Martin to Susan Capehart, December 5, 1836, Capehart Papers, SHC.

22. With 200,000 slaves at, on average, $1,000 each (sold or moved, they represented investment), $40 million in government land, $75 million in bank investments, plus removals and wars costing $50 million. Production totals from CHSUS, 4:110; T. Bennett to Jackson, Riddle, October 7, 1836, Fol. 7, JRC.

23. "We had better take the market prices," instead of holding out for a rise, ruminated a savvy Alabama planter: N. B. Nolwinther to J. S. Devereux, October 24, 1836, JSD; T. Bennett & Co. to Jackson, Riddle, October 7, 1836, Fol. 7, JRC; L. C.

Gray and Esther K. Thompson, *History of Agriculture in the Southern United States to 1860* (Washington, DC, 1933), 2:1027.

24. CHSUS, 3:354 (land sales); Temin, *Jacksonian Economy*, 123; Richard Timberlake, "The Specie Circular and Distribution of the Surplus," *Journal of Political Economy* 68 (1960): 109–117. The belief that the Circular was solely responsible for economic troubles was created by Jackson's Whig opponents. Daniel Walker Howe, *What Hath God Wrought: The Transformation of America, 1815–1848* (New York, 2007), 503, presents a fairly undigested Whig version. Bank of England: Ralph Hidy, *The House of Baring in American Trade and Finance: English Merchant Bankers at Work, 1763–1861* (Cambridge, MA, 1949), 206–207.

25. *NOP*, February 4, 1837, February 9, 1837; S. E. Phillips to J. A. Stevens, February 5, 1837, John A. Stevens Papers, NYHS; John Forsyth to Brother, February 19, 1837, John Forsyth Papers, Duke.

26. Hidy, *House of Baring*, 214–219; Vol. 50, Brown Brothers, NYPL. For a recent cultural and political history of the Panic of 1837, see Jessica Lepler, *The Many Panics of 1837: People, Politics, and the Creation of a Transatlantic Financial Crisis* (New York, 2013).

27. *NOP*, March 16, 1837, April 20, 1837; John Elliott to Lucy, April 8, 1837, Samuel Bryarly Papers, Duke; D. W. McLaurin to John McLaurin, April 10, 1837, Duncan McLaurin Papers, Duke; Vol. 50, Brown Brothers, NYPL.

28. Albert Gallatin to J. A. Stevens, May 10, 1837, Fol. April–July 1837, John Stevens Papers, NYHS; "Comparative Statement . . . Banks of New Orleans, 1835 and 1836," Fol. 5, Citizens' Bank of Louisiana Records, Tulane; Champ Terry to Nathaniel Jeffries, October 15, 1836, Fol. 345, RCB.

29. D. W. McKenzie to D. McLaurin, June 18, 1837, November 1, 1837, Duncan McLaurin Papers, Duke; Wm. Southgate to W. P. Smith, May 17, 1837, Wm. Smith Papers, Duke; J. Rowe to J. Cole, February 8, 1837, Cole-Taylor Papers, SHC.

30. In April, New Orleans banks allowed some commercial debtors to renew debts every sixty days until November, with a 10 percent fee, but required most individual borrowers to make regular payments on mortgage loans: City Bank Resolution, April 1, 1837; A. Beauvais to Pres. C.A.P.L., April 6, 1837, Fol. 7/47B, C.A.P.L. Papers, Louisiana State University; J. R. Miller to William Miller, July 19, 1837, John Fox Papers, Duke; James Harrison to [?], July 12, 1837, James Harrison Papers, SHC; Joseph Amis to [?], May 6, 1837, S. S. Downey Papers, Duke; K. M. King to Uncle, November 1, 1837, Duncan McLaurin Papers, Duke; Stephen Duncan to W. Mercer, August 7, 1837, William Mercer Papers, Tulane.

31. Leland Jenks, *Migration of British Capital to 1875* (New York, 1927), 90–92; John Niven, *Martin Van Buren: The Romantic Age of American Politics* (New York, 1983).

32. S. Duncan to W. Mercer, August 7, 1837, William Mercer Papers, Tulane; US Congress, House of Representatives, "Condition of Banks, 1840," 26th Cong., 2nd sess., H. Doc. 111 (Serial 385), 1441; W. Bailey to Washington Jackson, June 4, 1838, Fol. 10, JRC; John J. Wallis, "What Caused the Crisis of 1839," NBER Historical Paper no. 133, April 2001, National Bureau of Economic Research, www.nber.org/papers/h0133.pdf; C. L. Hinton to Laurens Hinton, April 17, 1839, Laurens Hinton Papers, SHC; Bacon Tait to RB, Fol. 24, RCB.

33. J. A. Stevens to T. W. Ward, August 5, 1837, September 15, 1837; T. W. Ward to H. Lavergne, December 1837, T. W. Ward to J. A. Stevens, December 8, 1837, December 16, 1837, John Stevens Papers, NYHS; W. W. Rives to Thomas Smith, June 15, 1837, Wm. Smith Papers, Duke; R. Hinton to Laurens Hinton, July 23, 1837, Laurens Hinton Papers, SHC; E. B. Hicks to A. Cuningham, January 10, 1838, Cuningham Papers, Duke.

34. John Killick, "The Cotton Operations of Alexander Brown and Sons in the Deep South, 1820–1860," *JSH* 43 (1977): 185; H. H. G. to J. A. Stevens, February 16, 1838, Baring Brothers to J. A. Stevens, March 14, 1838 (I), March 14, 1838 (II), T. W. Ward to G. B. Milligan, March 11, 1838, John Stevens Papers, NYHS; Bray Hammond, *Banks and Politics in America: From the Revolution to the Civil War* (Princeton, NJ, 1957), 467–477; W. Bailey to Washington Jackson, June 4, 1838, JRC; Bennett Ferriday & Co. to Jackson, Riddle, January 24, 1838, JRC; Joseph Eaton to Thomas Jeffrey, May 20, 1838, Bank of State of Georgia Papers, Duke.

35. J. Knight to Wm. Beall, October 21, 1838, February 10, 1839, John Knight Papers, Duke; J. S. Haywood to G. W. Haywood, November 25, 1838, Fol. 155, HAY; W. R. Rives to J. Harris, March 18, 1838, Fol. 22, RCB; A. Cuningham to E. B. Hicks, May 14, 1838, Cuningham Papers, Duke; J. S. Haywood to G. W. Haywood, March 17, 1839, Fol. 155, HAY.

36. A. G. Alsworth to J. S. Copes, September 10, 1839, Box 1, Fol. 64, Copes Papers, Tulane; R. C. O. Matthews, *A Study in Trade-Cycle History: Economic Fluctuations in Great Britain, 1833 to 1842* (Cambridge, UK, 2011), 65–68; Wallis, "What Caused the Crisis of 1839," 40.

37. Edward E. Baptist, *Creating an Old South: Middle Florida's Plantation Frontier Before the Civil War* (Chapel Hill, NC, 2002), 154–155; *Tallahassee Floridian*, March 20, 1841; Robert Carson to Dear Sir, August 30, 1839, John Forsyth Papers, Duke; Rich. Faulkner to Wm. Powell, May 8, 1839, William Powell Papers, Duke.

38. Sean Wilentz, *The Rise of American Democracy: Jefferson to Lincoln* (New York, 2005), 502–510.

39. Rowland Bryarly to S. Bryarly, May 5, 1838, Bryarly Papers, Duke; Edward Balleisen, "Vulture Capitalism in Antebellum America: The 1841 Federal Bankruptcy Act and the Exploitation of Financial Distress," *Business History Review* 70 (1996): 473–516; S. Thompson, Case 12, 1841 Bankruptcy Case Files, ELA37; 1841 Bankruptcy Sales Book 1, p. 93, E39, RG 21, NA.

40. Michael F. Holt, *The Rise and Fall of the American Whig Party: Jacksonian Politics and the Onset of the Civil War* (New York, 1999), 122–161; James Donnelly to J. S. Devereux, 1839, JSD; Rich. Faulkner to Wm. Powell, May 8, 1839, Wm. Powell Papers, Duke; Robert Carson to Dear Sir, August 30, 1839, John Forsyth Papers, Duke. For prices, cf. *Carson v. Dwight* [LA, 1843]; *Erwin v. Lowry* [LA, 1849]; *Stacy v. Barber* [MS, 1843]; all CATTERALL, 3:554, 595, 297–298; IF to RB, May 23, 1838, Fol. 22, RCB; Jos. Alsop to RB, January 18, 1839, Fol. 24, Bacon Tait to RB, May 1, 1838, RCB; IF to RB, May 23, 1838, both Fol. 22, RCB; "Memo. of . . . Debts Due in Ala," Tyre Glen Papers, Duke.

41. Herbert Gutman, *The Black Family in Slavery and Freedom, 1750–1925* (New York, 1976); Anthony G. Kaye, *Joining Places: Slave Neighborhoods in the Old South* (Chapel Hill, NC, 2007), 74; Ann P. Malone, *Swing Low, Sweet Chariot: Slave Family*

*and Household Structure in Nineteenth-Century Louisiana* (Chapel Hill, NC, 1992); Dep. Victoria Burrell, 455.869, Union Veterans' Pension Files, NA; George Jones, #1184, *Register of Signatures of Depositors*, Tallahassee Branch of Freedmen's Savings and Trust Company, National Archives Microfilm M816, Roll 5.

42. Wm. C. Bryarly to S. Bryarly, February 17, 1848, Bryarly Papers, Duke; Richard Trexler, *Sex and Conquest: Gendered Violence, Political Order, and the European Conquest of the Americas* (Ithaca, NY, 1995); Amy Greenberg, *Manifest Manhood and the Antebellum American Empire* (Cambridge, UK, 2005), 1–16.

43. ST, 152; Jim Cullen, "'I's a Man Now': Gender and African-American Men," in Darlene Clark Hine and Earnestine Jenkins, eds., *A Question of Manhood* (Bloomington, IN, 1999), 489–501; Walter Johnson, "On Agency," *Journal of Social History* 37, no. 1 (2003): 113–124; James Scott, *Domination and the Arts of Resistance: Hidden Transcripts* (New Haven, CT, 1990); François Furstenberg, "Beyond Freedom and Slavery: Autonomy, Virtue, and Resistance in Early American Political Discourse," *JAH* 89, no. 4 (2003): 1295–1330; Edward E. Baptist, "The Absent Subject: African-American Masculinity and Forced Migration to the Antebellum Plantation Frontier," in Craig T. Friend and Lorri Glover, eds., *Southern Manhood: Perspectives on Manhood in the Old South* (Athens, GA, 2004).

44. Tzvetan Todorov, *Facing the Extreme: Moral Life in the Concentration Camps*, (New York, 1996). Pioneering works on the history of women in American slavery include the following: Deborah Gray White, *Ar'n't I a Woman? Female Slaves in the Plantation South*, 2nd ed. (New York, 1999); Angela Davis, *Women, Race and Class* (New York, 1981), 3–29; Brenda Stevenson, *Life in Black and White: Family and Community in the Slave South* (New York, 1996); Hortense Spillers, "Mama's Baby, Papa's Maybe: An American Grammar Book," *Diacritics* 17 (1987): 65–81; Catherine Clinton, "Caught in the Web of the Big House: Women and Slavery," in Walter J. Fraser Jr., R. Frank Saunders Jr., and Jon L. Wakelyn, eds., *The Web of Southern Social Relations: Women, Family, and Education* (Athens, GA, 1985), 19–34; Jacqueline Jones, *Labor of Love, Labor of Sorrow: Black Women, Work, and the Family from Slavery to the Present* (New York, 1985); Thelma Jennings, "'Us Colored Women Had to Go Through a Plenty,'" *Journal of Women's History* 1 (1990); Nell Irvin Painter, "Soul Murder and Slavery: Toward a Fully Loaded Cost Accounting," in Linda K. Kerber, Alica Kessler-Harris, and Kathryn Kish Sklar, eds., *U.S. History as Women's History: New Feminist Essays* (Chapel Hill, NC, 1995), 125–146; David Barry Gaspar and Darlene Clark Hine, *More Than Chattel: Black Women in the Americas* (Bloomington, IN, 1996); Stephanie M. H. Camp, *Closer to Freedom: Enslaved Women and Everyday Resistance in the Plantation South* (Chapel Hill, NC, 2004); Jennifer L. Morgan, *Laboring Women: Reproduction and Gender in New World Slavery* (Philadelphia, 2004); Thavolia Glymph, *Out of the House of Bondage: The Transformation of the Plantation Household* (Cambridge, UK, 2008); Daina Ramey Berry, *Swing the Sickle for the Harvest Is Ripe: Gender and Slavery in Antebellum Georgia* (Urbana, IL, 2007).

45. Magnolia, 1838–1840, Fol. 429, RCB; Richard S. Dunn, *A Tale of Two Plantations: Slave Life at Mesopotamia in Jamaica & Mount Airy in Virginia, 1762–1865* (New York, 2014); Gutman, *Black Family*; Peter Carter, *Register of Signatures*, #359; for conundrums of remarriage, see Jeff Forret, "Slaves, Sex, and Sin: Adultery, Forced Separation and Baptist Church Discipline in Middle Georgia," *Slavery and Abolition*

33, no. 3 (2012): 337–358, also cf. Damian Alan Pargas, *The Quarters and the Fields: Slave Families in the Non-Cotton South* (Gainesville, FL, 2010).

46. Charles Ball, *Slavery in the United States: A Narrative of the Life and Adventures of Charles Ball . . .* (New York, 1837), 263–265, 275; cf. Dickson D. Bruce, *The Origins of African-American Literature* (Charlottesville, VA, 2001).

47. Nettie Henry, AS, S.1, 8.3 (MS), 975–976; Jack Hannibal to Dear Mistress, August 9, 1878, Jack Hannibal Letter, Duke.

48. Eliz. Koonce to Eliz. Franck, December 18, 1849, Cox and Koonce Papers, SHC.

49. E.g., Notice to Sampson Lanier, JD, and Wildredge Thompson, January 11, 1838, JSD; Memo of Debts, JSD; John Devereux to JD, January 26, 1839, JSD; Bank of Milledgeville to JD, February 14, 1840, JSD; Notice of Protest, April 24, 1840, JSD; S. Grantland to JD, September 14, 1840, JSD; *Executions v. JD*, Macon County, Alabama, October 24, 1840, JSD.

50. Petition of JD, February 10, 1843, and Deposition JD, JSD.

51. J. S. Short to T. P. Westray, August 1, 1838, Battle Papers, SHC; John Roberts to John Bacon et al., December 13, 1841, and John Roberts to H. D. Mandeville, January 3, 1842, both in Bank U.S. of Penna. Papers, LLMVC. I thank Richard Kilbourne for generously sharing his transcription of this difficult collection.

52. Fol.: Papers: 1839, JSD (passim); Rich. Faulkner to Wm. Powell, May 8, 1839, William Powell Papers, Duke; John Roberts to Bacon et al., April 12, 1842, and John Roberts to Geo. Connelly, February 26, 1843, both in Bank of U.S. of Penna. Papers, LLMVC; Joseph Baldwin, *The Flush Times of Alabama and Mississippi* (New York, 1854).

53. R. W. Cook to J. S. Copes, July 5, 1840, Joseph Copes Papers, Tulane; Wm. Thompson to John Bassett, July 19, 1839, Fol. 3, Indiana Thompson, 1842, Fol. 4, John Bassett Papers, SHC.

54. Jacob Bieller Will, December 1835, Fol. 1/15, BIELLER.

55. Louisiana Supreme Court, *Bieller v. Bieller*, 1845; Jacob Bieller Will, December 1835, Fol. 1/15, BIELLER. However, Nancy Bieller, at least, did not get to divide and monetize people whom she had claimed. When the divorce case finally made it to the state supreme court, Jacob was dead, as was his son, whose heirs successfully argued that Jacob's *earlier* divorce from his son's South Carolina mother in 1808 was never legally completed. Hence Nancy was never really married and her daughter was illegitimate, so Jacob's white son's heirs were his legitimate legatees.

56. "N.B.N." [?] to JD, July 14, 1841, JSD; Andrew Scott to JD, June 22, 1841, JSD; Wm. Bond to JD, October 22, 1841, JSD; "Memo" [210], Diary 1833–1846, JSD.

57. *Irish v. Wright*, 8. Rob. La. 428, July 1844 [431], 3:561; *Pleasants v. Glasscock*, Ch. 17, December 1843 [21], 3:297; *Cawthorn v. McDonald*, 1 Rob. La. 55, October 1841 [56], 3:541; *Tuggle v. Barclay*, 6 Ala. 407, January 1844 [408], 3:561, 297, 541, 153, all CATTERALL; Campbell, *Empire for Slavery*, 55.

58. *Groves v. Slaughter*, 40 U.S. Pet. 449 (1841), CATTERALL, 3:533–535, January 1841; *Green v. Robinson*, ibid., 3:289, December 1840; David Lightner, *Slavery and the Commerce Power: How the Struggle Against the Interstate Slave Trade Led to the Civil War* (New Haven, CT, 2006), 72–84.

59. *Brien v. Williamson* (MS), 3:294; *Green v. Robinson* (MS), 3:289; cf. *Carson v. Dwight* (LA), 3:554, all CATTERALL; Bacon Tait to RB, January 1, 3, 1840, Fol. 31, RCB; H. Donaldson Jordan, "A Politician of Expansion: Robert J. Walker," *Mississippi Valley Historical Review* 19, no. 3 (1932): 362–381; Robert Gudmestad, *A Troublesome Commerce: The Transformation of the Interstate Slave Trade* (Baton Rouge, LA, 2003), 193–200.

60. Edwin Miles, *Jacksonian Democracy in Mississippi* (Chapel Hill, NC, 1960), 150–151; Rich. Faulkner to Wm. Powell, June 16, 1839, Wm. Powell Papers, Duke; John J. Wallis, Richard Sylla, and Arthur Grinath, "Sovereign Debt and Repudiation: The Emerging-Market Debt Crisis in the U.S. States, 1839–1843," NBER Working Paper no. 10753, 2004, National Bureau of Economic Research, www.nber .org/papers/w10753; Baptist, *Creating an Old South*, 154–190; *Columbus Democrat*, February 20, 1841; McGrane, *Foreign Bondholders*, 201.

61. US Congress, "Condition of Banks"; *Mississippi Free-Trader*, October 28, 1843, November 1, 1843.

62. *Albany Argus*, November 26, 1841. In 1852, Mississippi's legislature also defaulted on the $2 million principal of the Planters' Bank bonds of 1831. Florida and Arkansas repudiated in 1843. Only Alabama levied taxes and continued payments in the antebellum era, though after the Civil War both Alabama and Tennessee repudiated their prewar debts. McGrane, *Foreign Bondholders*, 178–192, 241–257, 282–291, 357–364.

63. John Knight to Wife, July 14, 1839, John Knight Papers, Duke; *Circular to Bankers*, December 10, 1841, McGrane, *Foreign Bondholders*, 203, 265–281, 382–391.

64. McGrane, *Foreign Bondholders*, 201–205.

65. J. B. Hawkins to W. J. Hawkins, June 5, 1847, Fol. 76, Hawkins Papers, SHC.

66. Miles, *Jacksonian Democracy*, 139; G. Rust and A. McNutt, [1835], E. Mason to Wm. Rust, June 2, 1845, E. Mason to G. Rust, April 5, 1844, June 2, 1845, McNutt Papers, MDAH; Malone, *Sweet Chariot*.

67. Jim Allen, AS, 7.2 (MS), 1; Tempie Lummins, AS, 4.1 (TX), 264; Charles L. Perdue Jr., Thomas E. Barden, and Robert K. Phillips, eds., *Weevils in the Wheat: Interviews with Virginia Ex-Slaves* (Charlottesville, VA, 1976), 211, 318; Anonymous, AS, 18 (TN), 298–299; Mollie Barber, AS, S1, 12 (OK), 29–30; C. G. Lynch to JD, August 16, 1840, JSD; Felix Street, AS, 10.5, (AR), 250; Carrie Pollard, AS, 6.1 (AL), 318–319; Clayton Holbert, AS, 16.1 (KS), 1. Gutman, *Black Family*, represents the classic "strong patriarchal family" position, while Wilma A. Dunaway, *The African-American Family in Slavery and Emancipation* (Cambridge, UK, 2003), argues that kinship ties were tenuous. Brenda Stevenson, *Life in Black and White: Family and Community in the Slave South* (New York, 1996), and White, *Ar'n't I a Woman*, describe women-centered networks.

68. *Erwin v. Lowry*, Louisiana cases 1849; *Comstock v. Rayford*, 1 S. and M. 423, 1843, [424]; *Hardeman v. Sims*, 3 Ala. [747], 1840; *Blanchard v. Castille*, 19 La. 362, September 1841 [363], 595, 297, 147, 539, all CATTERALL 3; Milly Forward, AS, 4.2 (TX), 45; Mary Anderson, AS, 4.1 (TX), 26–27; Tom Harris, AS, 9.4 (MS), 1579; Annie Penland, AS, S1, 12 (OK), 257; William Holland, AS, 4.2 (TX), 145; AS, 18 (TN), 98–99.

69. Betty Simmons, AS, 5.4 (TX), 20; Henri Necaise, AS (MS); Ellaine Wright, AS, 11.2 (MO), 378; cf. AS, 10.5 (AR), 203; Iran Nelson, AS, 7.2 (MS), 199.

70. Robert Laird, AS, 8.3 (MS), 1292; Wash Hayes, AS, 8.3 (MS), 963–964; John McCoy, AS, 5.3 (TX), 32; Pierre Aucuin, MW, 21–23.

71. Gutman, *Black Family*, 88–93, mentions incest tales but does not discuss their symbolic aspects. See also Perdue et al., *Weevils in the Wheat*, 89, 105; Henry Brown, AS, 2.1 (SC), 124–125; Cora Horton, AS, 9.3 (AR), 321–324; Lizzie Johnson, AS, 9.3 (AR), 102–103; Liza Suggs, *Shadow and Sunshine* (Omaha, 1906), 75, retells the same story, though born in 1875.

72. Dale W. Tomich, *Through the Prism of Slavery: Labor, Capital, and World Economy* (Lanham, MD, 2004); Rafael de Bivar Marquese, *Feitores do Corpo, Missionários da Mente: Senhores, Letrados e o Controle dos Escravos nas Américas, 1660–1860* (São Paulo, 2004).

73. Steven Heath Mitton, "The Free World Confronted: Slavery and Progress in American Foreign Relations, 1833–1844" (PhD diss., Louisiana State University, 2005); Maxwell, Wright, & Co., *Commercial Formalities of Rio De Janeiro* (Baltimore, 1841).

74. David Brion Davis, *Slavery and Human Progress* (New York, 1984), 236–237; Walter R. Cassels, *Cotton: An Account of Its Culture in the Bombay Presidency* (Bombay, 1862); K. L. Tuteja, "American Planters and the Cotton Improvement Programme in Bombay Presidency During the Nineteenth Century," *Indian Journal of American Studies* (1998); Lelia M. Roeckell, "Bonds over Bondage: British Opposition to the Annexation of Texas," *Journal of the Early Republic* 19 (1999): 269n29; Madeline Stern, *The Pantarch: A Biography of Stephen Pearl Andrews* (Austin, TX, 1968); Benjamin Lundy, *Life, Travels, and Opinions of Benjamin Lundy* (Philadelphia, 1847).

75. Mitton, "Free World Confronted"; William W. Freehling, *The Road to Disunion* (New York, 1990), 1:390–391.

76. Virgil Maxcy to Calhoun, December 3, 10, 1844, in JCC, 17:586, 599–603; Wilentz, *Rise of American Democracy*, 565.

77. Harriet Martineau, *Retrospect of Western Travel* (London, 1838), 1:147–148; Irving H. Bartlett, *John C. Calhoun: A Biography* (New York, 1994), 379; William W. Freehling, "Spoilsmen and Interests in the Thought and Career of John C. Calhoun," *Journal of American History* 52 (1965): 25–42; Richard R. John, "Like Father, Like Son: The Not-So-Strange Career of John C. Calhoun," *Reviews in American History* 23, no. 3 (1995): 438–443.

78. Edward Crapol, "John Tyler and the Pursuit of National Destiny," *Journal of the Early Republic* 17 (1997): 467–491.

79. Calhoun to Richard Pakenham, April 18, 1844; Documents relative to Texas, Serial Set vol. 435, session vol. 5, 28th Cong., 1st sess., S.Doc. 341; Charles Wiltse, *John C. Calhoun: Sectionalist* (Indianapolis, 1951), 168.

80. Silbey, *Storm over Texas*, 62–68. Van Buren's letter responded to William Hammet, former University of Virginia chaplain, now Mississippi congressman and unpledged Democratic convention delegate.

81. Joel Silbey, "'There Are Other Questions Besides That of Slavery Merely': The Democratic Party and Anti-Slavery Politics," in Alan Kraut, ed., *Crusaders and*

*Compromisers: Essays of the Relationship of the Antislavery Struggle to the Antebellum Party System* (Westport, CT, 1983), 143–175.

82. Robert J. Walker, *Letter of Mr. Walker, of Mississippi: Relative to the Reannexation of Texas. In Reply to the Call of the People of Carroll County, Kentucky, to Communicate His Views on that Subject* (Washington, DC, 1844); Robert J. Walker, *The South in Danger: Being a Document Published by the Democratic Association of Washington, D.C., for Circulation at the South, and Showing the Design of the Annexation of Texas to Be the Security and Perpetuation of Slavery* (Washington, DC, 1844); Frederick Merk, *Fruits of Propaganda in the Tyler Administration* (Cambridge, MA, 1971).

83. Silbey, *Storm over Texas*, 77; Holt, *Whig Party*, 196–206.

84. Nell Mick Pugh, "Contemporary Comments on Texas, 1844–1847," *Southwestern Historical Quarterly* 62 (1959): 267–270; Frederick Merk, *Slavery and the Annexation of Texas* (New York, 1972), 152–166; Holman Hamilton, "Texas Bonds and Northern Profits: A Study in Compromise, Investment, and Lobby Influence," *Mississippi Valley Historical Review* 43 (1957): 579–594. When the bonds were paid off (1856–1857, at 0.75 on the dollar), 60 percent went to northern holders.

85. Silbey, *Storm over Texas*, 111–112.

86. Following paragraphs: John Devereux Diary, 1833–1846, January 1 to March 23, 1846, JSD. The 1845 Texas state constitution enabled homestead exemptions that protected slaves from debt seizure. Mark Nackman, "Anglo-American Migrants to the West: Men of Broken Fortunes? The Case of Texas, 1821–1846," *Western Historical Quarterly* 5 (1974): 441–455. Attempts to pursue debtors into Texas postannexation apparently failed. *Endicott v. Penney*, 1850, 325; *McIntyre v. Whitfield*, 1849, 322, all CATTERALL, vol. 3.

87. Harriet Jones, AS, S2, 6.5 (TX), 2095; Frank Adams, AS, S2, 2.1 (TX), 2–10; Sean Kelley, *Los Brazos de Dios: A Plantation Society on the Texas Borderlands* (Baton Rouge, LA, 2010), 99–102.

## CHAPTER 9. BACKS: 1839–1850

1. Hannah Palfrey Ayer, *A Legacy of New England: Letters of the Palfrey Family* (Milton, MA, 1950), 1:145.

2. Frank Otto Gatell, *John Gorham Palfrey and the New England Conscience* (Cambridge, MA, 1963), 76–87; Frank Otto Gatell, "Doctor Palfrey Frees His Slaves," *New England Quarterly* 34 (1961): 74–86.

3. *Baltimore Patriot*, November 8, 1824; Rev. Wm. Trotter, "Observations on State Debts," *North American Review* 51 (1840): 316–337; J. G. Palfrey (JGP) to Wm. Palfrey, March 11, 1836, PALF.

4. Henry Palfrey to JGP, January 8, 1838, September 3, 1838, January 9, 1839, December 4, 1838, all in PALF; Gatell, "Doctor Palfrey," 75–76.

5. Kinley J. Brauer, *Cotton Versus Conscience: Massachusetts Whig Politics and Southwestern Expansion, 1843–1848* (Lexington, KY, 1967); Thomas O'Connor, *Lords of the Loom: The Cotton Whigs and the Coming of the Civil War* (New York, 1968).

6. Gatell, "Doctor Palfrey," 80; *Washington Daily Intelligencer*, March 3, 1842; Melvin Urofsky and Paul Finkelman, *March of Liberty: A Constitutional History of the*

*United States* (New York, 2002), 1:352–353; Brauer, *Cotton Versus Conscience*; Gatell, *John Gorham Palfrey*, 111–114; H. W. Palfrey to JGP, March 12, 1844, PALF.

7. Preceding paragraphs: Ayer, *Legacy*, 1:145–146; Gathell, "Doctor Palfrey"; Stephen Kantrowitz, *More Than Freedom: Fighting for Black Citizenship in a White Republic, 1829–1889* (New York, 2013); Cf. J. Brent Morris, "'We Are Verily Guilty Concerning Our Brother': The Abolitionist Transformation of Planter William Henry Brisbane," *South Carolina Historical Magazine* 111 (2010): 118–150; Sydney J. Nathans, *To Free a Family: The Journey of Mary Walker* (Cambridge, MA, 2012).

8. Boyd Hilton, *A Mad, Bad, and Dangerous People? England, 1783–1846* (Oxford, 2006); Joel Mokyr, *The Enlightened Economy: An Economic History of Britain, 1700–1850* (New Haven, CT, 2009).

9. John G. Palfrey, *Papers on the Slave Power: First Published in the Boston Whig in July, August, and September, 1846* (Boston, 1846), 31–35.

10. Thomas Weiss, "U.S. Labor Force Estimates and Economic Growth, 1800–1860," in Robert Gallman and John J. Wallis, eds., *American Economic Growth and Standards of Living Before the Civil War* (Chicago, 1992).

11. MCLANE, 2:225.

12. Robert Dalzell, *Enterprising Elite: The Boston Associates and the World They Made* (Cambridge, MA, 1987); MCLANE 2:342–343; Robert Fogel and Stanley Engerman, *The Reinterpretation of American Economic History* (New York, 1971); C. Knick Harley, "Cotton Textile Prices and the Industrial Revolution," *Economic History Review* 51 (1998): 49–83. In "The Relative Productivity Hypothesis of Industrialization: The American Case, 1820–1860," NBER Working Paper no. 722, July 1981, National Bureau of Economic Research, www.nber.org/papers/w0722, Claudia Goldin and Kenneth Sokoloff find that in industries dependent on southwestern cotton fields, female labor was highly profitable.

13. Mark Bils, "Tariff Protection and Production in the Early U.S. Cotton Textile Industry," *JER* 44 (1984): 1033–1045; MCLANE, 1:1015; David R. Meyer, *Roots of American Industrialization* (Baltimore, 2003), 240.

14. Meyer, *Roots of Industrialization*, 3; MCLANE, 1:70; cf. Charles Sellers, *The Market Revolution: Jacksonian America, 1815–1846* (New York, 1991); John L. Larson, *The Market Revolution in America: Liberty, Ambition, and the Eclipse of the Common Good* (Cambridge, UK, 2010); Harry L. Watson, "'The Common Rights of Mankind': Subsistence, Shad, and Commerce in the Early Republican South," *JAH* 83 (1996): 13–43.

15. Douglas A. Irwin and Peter Temin, "The Antebellum Tariff on Textiles Revisited," *JER* 61 (2001): 777–798; Israel Andrews, *Communication from the Secretary of the Treasury . . . Notices of the Internal Improvements in Each State, of the Gulf of Mexico and Straits of Florida, and a Paper on the Cotton Crop of the United States*, US Congress, Senate, 32nd Cong., 1st sess., Doc. 112 (Serial 622–623), 818–821. By 1845, Massachusetts mills consumed 7 percent of the US crop.

16. 1847 Diary, vol. 2, William Minor Papers, LLMVC; Thos. Byrne to R. G. Hazard, July 8, 1839; Joel Small to J. P. Hazard, May 17, 1841; J. P. Hazard to Isaac Hazard, November 30, 1841, December 13, 1841, Hazard and Co., all LLMVC.

17. MCLANE, 1:950, 2:470–577.

18. Janet Siskind, *Rum and Axes: The Rise of a Connecticut Merchant Family, 1795–1850* (Ithaca, NY, 2002), 92–117.

19. Araby Jnl., 88, Haller Nutt Papers, Duke; Henry Kauffman, *American Axes: A Survey of Their Development and Makers* (Brattleboro, VT, 1972), 33–34; Anderson Ralph to J. D. Hawkins, July 18, 1847, Hawkins Papers, SHC; Magnolia Jnl., 1851–1852, Fol. 444, RCB; Laurel Jnl., 1850–1851, Fol. 445, RCB; Plantation Jnl., 1849–1866, McCollam Papers, SHC.

20. Meyer, *Roots of Industrialization*, 268–270; MCLANE; *Report of the Secretary of the Treasury, Dec. 3, 1845*, 29th Cong., 1st sess.

21. Meyer, *Roots of Industrialization*, 3; Robert Gallman, "Commodity Output, 1839–1899," in *Trends in the American Economy in the Nineteenth Century* (New York, 1960), 24:43, Table A-1/A.

22. J. D. B. DeBow, *Industrial Resources, etc., of the Southern and Western States . . .* (New Orleans, 1852), 3:277, 287; David R. Meyer, *Networked Machinists: High-Technology Industries in Antebellum America* (Baltimore, 2006).

23. Palfrey, *Papers on the Slave Power*, 8–9; Nathan Appleton et al., *Correspondence Between Nathan Appleton and John G. Palfrey* (Boston, 1846); Leonard Richards, *The Slave Power: The Free North and Southern Domination* (Baton Rouge, LA, 2000).

24. Joshua Leavitt, *The Financial Power of Slavery* (New York, 1841).

25. Reinhard O. Johnson, *The Liberty Party, 1840–1848: Antislavery Third-Party Politics in the United States* (Baton Rouge, LA, 2009); Eric Foner, *Free Soil, Free Labor, Free Men: The Ideology of the Republican Party Before the Civil War* (New York, 1970); Jonathan H. Earle, *Jacksonian Antislavery and the Politics of Free Soil, 1824–1854* (Chapel Hill, NC, 2004); Betty Fladeland, *James Gillespie Birney: Slaveholder to Abolitionist* (Ithaca, NY, 1955).

26. Sean Wilentz, *The Rise of American Democracy: Jefferson to Lincoln* (New York, 2005), 596.

27. *National Era*, February 4, 1847, June 24, 1847.

28. Robert Merry, *A Country of Vast Designs: James K. Polk, the Mexican War, and the Conquest of the American Continent* (New York, 2009); Paul Foos, *A Short, Offhand, Killing Affair: Soldiers and Social Conflict During the Mexican-American War* (Chapel Hill, NC, 2002).

29. William Lee Miller, *Arguing About Slavery: The Great Battle in the United States Congress* (New York, 1996), 27–42 and passim; *Richmond Enquirer*, January 23, 1836. The first recorded use of this doctrine with slavery is by James Gholson, who argued to the 1832 Virginia constitutional convention that state legislative emancipation would violate the Fifth Amendment's restriction of confiscation of private property without just compensation. See *Register of Debates*, 24th Cong., 4025–4026; Arthur Bestor, "State Sovereignty and Slavery: A Reinterpretation of Proslavery Constitutional Doctrine, 1846–1860," *Journal of the Illinois State Historical Society* 54 (1961): 117–180, esp. 172n113.

30. *Washington National Intelligencer*, February 7, 1844; cf. numerous instances of such reasoning recorded in James L. Huston, *Calculating the Value of Union: Slavery, Property Rights, and the Economic Origins of the Civil War* (Chapel Hill, NC, 2003), 49–57.

31. *Washington National Intelligencer*, February 17, 1844; Donald Fehrenbacher, *The Slaveholding Republic: An Account of the U.S. Government's Relations with Slavery* (New York, 2001), 220–221. Story tried to limit the scope of his decision to fugitive slave cases, but he concurred that constitutional protection of the property rights of enslavers was a bargain without which "the Union could never have been formed." For a pro-*Lochner* take on the later use of substantive due process, see David E. Bernstein, *Rehabilitating Lochner: Defending Individual Rights Against Progressive Reform* (Chicago, 2011); for a critical view, see Cass Sunstein, "Lochner's Legacy," *Columbia Law Review* 87 (1987): 873–919.

32. Wilentz, *Rise of American Democracy*, 533–539.

33. Thomas Hart Benton, *Thirty Years' View, Or, A History of the Working of the American Government for Thirty Years, from 1820 to 1850* (New York, 1854–1856), 2:695–696.

34. *CG*, February 19, 1847, 453–455.

35. *New Bedford Mercury*, October 1, 1847; *Gloucester Telegraph*, October 28, 1846; *CG*, January 4, 1848; Reginald Horsman, "Scientific Racism and the American Indian in the Mid-Nineteenth Century," *American Quarterly* 27 (1975): 152–168.

36. Joseph G. Rayback, *Free Soil: The Election of 1848* (Lexington, KY, 1971); Wilentz, *Rise of American Democracy*, 608–610.

37. Joel Silbey, *Party over Section: The Rough and Ready Election of 1848* (Lawrence, KS, 2009).

38. David Potter, *The Impending Crisis, 1848–1861* (New York, 1976), 83–85; "Address . . . ," JCC, 26:239–241.

39. "Remarks . . . Southern Caucus," January 15, 1849, JCC, 26:216–217.

40. J. Mills Thornton, *Politics and Power in a Slave Society: Alabama, 1800–1860* (Baton Rouge, LA, 1978), 206–207: *Montgomery Advertiser*, November 21, 1849, February 12, 1851; Collin S. Tarpley to John C. Calhoun, May 9, 1849, JCC, 26:395–396; Calhoun to Tarpley, July 9, 1849, JCC, 26:497–498; William W. Freehling, *The Road to Disunion* (New York, 1990), 1:479–486; Thelma Jennings, *The Nashville Convention: Southern Movement for Unity, 1848–1851* (Memphis, TN, 1980), 3–40.

41. *CG*, January 8, 1849, 188; Ralph Keller, "Extraterritoriality and the Fugitive Slave Debate," *Illinois Historical Journal* 78 (1985): 113–128; Bestor, "State Sovereignty"; Fehrenbacher, *Slaveholding Republic*, 226–227.

42. *Jackson Mississippian*, November 30, 1849, October 5, 1849, in Freehling, *Road to Disunion*, 1:480–481.

43. *New Hampshire Patriot*, January 18, 1850; Jennings, *Nashville Convention*, 13–42; Holman Hamilton, "The 'Cave of the Winds' and the Compromise of 1850," *JSH* 23 (1957): 331–353.

44. Wilentz, *Rise of American Democracy*, 637–645; Potter, *Impending Crisis*.

45. *CG*, Senate, 31st Cong., 1st sess., March 11, 1850, 269.

46. Holman Hamilton, "Texas Bonds and Northern Profits: A Study in Compromise, Investment, and Lobby Influence," *Mississippi Valley Historical Review* 43 (1957): 579–594.

47. Potter, *Impending Crisis*, 114.

48. Holman Hamilton, *Prologue to Conflict: The Crisis and Compromise of 1850* (Lexington, KY, 1964), 166; *CG*, December 2, 1850, 5; Potter, *Impending Crisis*,

125–128; Christopher J. Olsen, *Political Culture and Secession in Mississippi: Masculinity, Honor, and the Antiparty Tradition, 1830–1860* (New York, 2000).

49. Robert R. Russel, "What Was the Compromise of 1850?" *JSH* 22 (1956): 292–309.


CHAPTER 10. ARMS: 1850–1861

1. Robert Farrar Capon, *The Parables of Grace* (Grand Rapids, MI, 1988), 19–30.

2. Charles L. Perdue Jr., Thomas E. Barden, and Robert K. Phillips, eds., *Weevils in the Wheat: Interviews with Virginia Ex-Slaves* (Charlottesville, VA, 1976), 270–273.

3. S. Wilkes to D. & H., July 11, 1855, R. H. Dickinson Papers, Chicago Historical Society; Sharon Ann Murphy, *Investing in Life: Insurance in Antebellum America* (Baltimore, 2010); Jonathan Levy, *Freaks of Fortune: The Emerging World of Capitalism and Risk in America* (Cambridge, MA, 2012); W. A. Britton Record Book, LLMVC; *NOP*, January 26, 1854; Calvin Schermerhorn, *Money over Mastery: Family over Freedom: Slavery in the Antebellum Upper South* (Baltimore, 2011).

4. Lulu Wilson, AS, 5.4 (TX), 192.

5. Frederick Law Olmsted, *The Cotton Kingdom: A Traveler's Observations on Cotton and Slavery in the American Slave States* (New York, 1861); Jonathan D. Wells, *The Origins of the Southern Middle Class, 1800–1861* (Chapel Hill, NC, 2004). Later, Olmsted became America's most famous landscape architect; he was the creator of Manhattan's Central Park, among other famous places.

6. Louis Hughes, *Thirty Years a Slave: The Institution of Slavery as Seen on the Plantation and in the Home of a Planter* (Milwaukee, WI, 1897), 78.

7. Olmsted, *Cotton Kingdom*, 216–217, 229–230.

8. "Address Before the Wisconsin State Agricultural Society," September 30, 1859, LINCOLN, 3:471–482.

9. Olmsted, *Cotton Kingdom*, 278; Robert McCardell, *The Idea of a Southern Nation: Southern Nationalists and Southern Nationalism, 1830–1860* (New York, 1979), 122–123; L. Diane Barnes, Brian Schoen, and Frank Towers, eds., *The Old South's Modern Worlds: Slavery, Region, and Nation in the Age of Progress* (New York, 2011).

10. "J.C.N.," "Future of South," *DeBow's Review* 2, no. 2 (1851): 132–146, 142; US Department of Commerce, US Census Bureau, 1860 Census, vol. 4, 295; J. D. B. DeBow, *Statistical View of the United States, Being a Compendium of the Seventh Census* (Washington, DC, 1854), 190–191.

11. James L. Huston, *Calculating the Value of Union: Slavery, Property Rights, and the Economic Origins of the Civil War* (Chapel Hill, NC, 2003), 26, 30, 32n10; Robert William Fogel, *Without Consent or Contract: The Rise and Fall of American Slavery* (New York, 1989), 85–86; Richard Easterlin, "Interregional Differences in Per Capita Income, Population, and Total Income, 1840–1950," *Trends in the American Economy in the Nineteenth Century* (Princeton, NJ, 1960).

12. "Southern Manufactures," *DeBow's Review*, June 1855, 777–791; "Autaugaville Factory, Alabama," *DeBow's Review*, May 1851, 560; Fogel, *Without Consent*, 106–108; Fred Bateman and Thomas Weiss, *A Deplorable Scarcity: The Failure of Industrialization in the Slave Economy* (Chapel Hill, NC, 1981).

13. Aaron Marrs, *Railroads in the Old South: Pursuing Progress in a Slave Society* (Baltimore, 2009), 5; William G. Thomas, *The Iron Way: Railroads, the Civil War, and the Making of Modern America* (New Haven, CT, 2011); Charles C. Bolton, *Poor*

*Whites of the Antebellum South: Tenants and Laborers in Central North Carolina and Northeast Mississippi* (Durham, NC, 1994); J. Mills Thornton, *Politics and Power in a Slave Society: Alabama, 1800–1860* (Baton Rouge, LA, 1978); Lacy K. Ford, *Origins of Southern Radicalism: The South Carolina Upcountry, 1800–1860* (New York, 1988); "A Vagabond's Tale: Poor Whites, Herrenvolk Democracy, and the Value of Whiteness in the Late Antebellum South," *JSH* 79 (2013): 799–840.

14. Robert E. Gallman, "The United States Capital Stock in the Nineteenth Century," in Stanley L. Engerman and Robert E. Gallman, eds., *Long-Term Factors in American Economic Growth* (Chicago, 1986), 165–214; Richard H. Kilbourne, *Debt, Investment, and Slaves: Credit Relations in East Feliciana Parish, 1825–1885* (Tuscaloosa, AL, 1995), 26–68. Kilbourne shows how factors became middlemen for credit relationships collateralized by enslaved bodies.

15. Ralph Hidy, *The House of Baring in American Trade and Finance: English Merchant Bankers at Work, 1763–1861* (Cambridge, MA, 1949), 355–450; John Killick, "The Cotton Operations of Alexander Brown and Sons in the Deep South, 1820–1860," *JSH* 43 (1977); Harold D. Woodman, *King Cotton and His Retainers: Financing and Marketing the Cotton Crop of the United States, 1800–1925* (Lexington, KY, 1968), 39; Ballard Account with Nalle, Cox, 1852, Fol. 387, RCB; Pope & Devlin to W. M. Otey, July 4, 1852, Wyche-Otey Papers, SHC.

16. Bonnie Martin, "Slavery's Invisible Engine: Mortgaging Human Property," *JSH* 76 (2010): 817–856.

17. Oscar Zanetti and Alejandro García, et al., *Sugar and Railroads: A Cuban History, 1837–1959* (Chapel Hill, NC, 1998); Dale W. Tomich, *Through the Prism of Slavery: Labor, Capital, and World Economy* (Lanham, MD, 2004), 75–95; Michael Zeuske and Orlando García Martínez, "La Amistad de Cuba, Ramón Ferrer, Contrabando do Esclavos, Captividad y Modernidad Atlántica," *Caribbean Studies* 37, no. 1 (2009): 119–187.

18. Jose Piqueras, ed., *2009 Trabajo Libre e Coactivo en Sociedades de Plantación* (Madrid, 2009); Tomich, *Prism of Slavery*, 81–83.

19. Amy Greenberg, *Manifest Manhood and the Antebellum American Empire* (Cambridge, UK, 2005), 225–230; Robert E. May, "Lobbyists for Commercial Empire: Jane Cazneau, William Cazneau, and U.S. Caribbean History," *Pacific Historical Review* 48, no. 3 (1979): 383–412; Gregg Lightfoot, "Manifesting Destiny" (PhD diss., Cornell University, 2014); Robert E. May, "Young American Males and Filibustering in the Age of Manifest Destiny: The United States Army as a Cultural Mirror," *JAH* 78 (1991): 857–886; A. D. Mann to L. Keitt, August 24, 1855, Keitt Papers, Duke; Robert E. May, *The Southern Dream of a Caribbean Empire, 1854–1861* (Baton Rouge, LA, 1973), 31–38; *Clarksville* (TN) *Jeffersonian*, January 29, 1853, September 28, 1853; Howard Jones, *Mutiny on the Amistad: The Saga of a Slave Revolt and Its Impact on American Abolition, Law, and Diplomacy* (New York, 1987).

20. *Democratic Review*, September 1, 1849, 203; Louis A. Perez Jr., *Cuba and the United States: Ties of Singular Intimacy* (Athens, GA, 1990); Olmsted, *Cotton Kingdom*, 331–333; *New Orleans Delta*, May 31, 1856; Charles Henry Brown, *Agents of Manifest Destiny: The Lives and Times of the Filibusters* (Chapel Hill, NC, 1980), 41.

21. Yonathan Eyal, *The Young America Movement and the Transformation of the Democratic Party, 1828–1861* (New York, 2007), 159–162; Daniel Rood, "Plantation Technocrats: A Social History of Knowledge in the Slaveholding Atlantic

World, 1830–1865" (PhD diss., University of California at Irvine, 2010); Robert E. May, "Reconsidering Antebellum U.S. Women's History: Gender, Filibustering, and America's Quest for Empire," *American Quarterly* 57 (2005): 1155–1188; Philip S. Foner, *Business and Slavery: The New York Merchants and the Irrepressible Conflict* (Chapel Hill, NC, 1941); Irving Katz, *August Belmont: A Political Biography* (New York, 1968); Barbara Weiss, *The Hell of the English: Bankruptcy and the 19th-Century Novel* (Lewisburg, PA, 1986), 160.

22. *Democratic Review*, January 1850, September 1849, 203; Robert E. May, *John Quitman: Old South Crusader* (Baton Rouge, LA, 1985); Christopher J. Olsen, *Political Culture and Secession in Mississippi: Masculinity, Honor, and the Antiparty Tradition, 1830–1860* (New York, 2000); S. Boyd to RB, April 10, 1850, April 14, 1850, Fol. 150, and April 24, 1850, Fol. 151, RCB.

23. Brown, *Agents of Manifest Destiny*, 53–54; J. S. Thrasher to D. M. Barringer, July 26, 1852, D. M. Barringer Papers, SHC; *Washington National Intelligencer*, March 5, 1853.

24. *Arkansas Gazette*, December 16, 1853; *Cleveland Plain Dealer*, October 26, 1853; *Alexandria Gazette*, November 4, 1853; J. F. H. Claiborne, ed., *Life and Correspondence of John A. Quitman* (New York, 1860), 2:206–208.

25. C. M. Rutherford to RB, February 19, 1853, Fol. 187, RCB; May 18, 1860, Hector Davis Acct. Book, Chicago Historical Society; Bolton Dickens Acct. Book, NYHS; Philip Thomas to Wm. Finney, December 24, 1858, January 12, 1859, November 8, 1859, William Finney Papers, Duke; D. M. Pulliam to L. Scruggs, July 27, 1857, D. M. Pulliam Letters, Duke; Schermerhorn, *Money over Mastery*, 178–180; Michael Tadman, *Speculators and Slaves: Masters, Traders, and Slaves in the Old South* (Madison, WI, 1989), 77–79, appx. 2; Laurence J. Kotlikoff, "Quantitative Description of the New Orleans Slave Market," in William Fogel and Stanley L. Engerman, eds., *Without Consent or Contract: Technical Papers* (New York, 1992); Maurie McInnis, *Slaves Waiting for Sale: Abolitionist Art and the American Slave Trade* (Chicago, 2011).

26. Rects. Sales, 1852, Fol. 384; Memo of Sales, 1855, Fol. 397, RCB.

27. Joseph K. Menn, *The Large Slaveholders of Louisiana, 1860* (New Orleans, 1964); Wendell Stephenson, *Isaac Franklin: Slave Trader and Planter of the Old South; With Plantation Records* (University, LA, 1938); William K. Scarborough, *Masters of the Big House: Elite Slaveholders of the Mid-Nineteenth-Century South* (Baton Rouge, LA, 2003), 124–135.

28. James Cobb, *The Most Southern Place of Earth: The Mississippi Delta and the Roots of Regional Identity* (New York, 1992), 3–5, 30.

29. George Young, AS, 6.1 (AL), 432; Scarborough, *Masters of the Big House*, 124–135; Jack Ericson Eblen, "New Estimates of the Vital Rates of the United States Black Population During the Nineteenth Century," *Demography* 11 (1974): 301–319.

30. Folders 183–196, December 1852–August 1853, RCB.

31. S. G. Ward to E. Malone, May 24, 1850, Ellis Malone Papers, Duke; Wm. Williams to G. W. Allen, September 12, 1850, G. W. Allen Papers, SHC; J. Ewell to Alice Ewell, February 5, 1861, John Ewell Papers, Duke.

32. Statement of G. S. Bumpass, Bolton, Dickens, & Co., Acct. Book, NYHS; Sarah Benjamin, AS, S2, 2.1 (TX), 256–257; Sarah Wells, AS, 11.1 (AR), 89; Sarah Ashley, AS, 16.1 (TX), 34–35.

33. "List of Slaves Oct. 1845," vol. 124; Fols. 932–937, passim; Benjamin Barber to Paul C. Cameron (PC), August 1, 1853, Fol. 1103; John Beard to PC, February 14, 1853; J. W. Bryant to PC, February 2, 1853, Fol. 1126; John Webster to PC, November 24, 1856, Fol. 1163, and December 24, 1856, Fol. 1164, all in PCC.

34. S. Tate to PC, December 26, 1856; Jas. Williamson to PC, December 26, 1856, Fol. 1164, and January 2, 1856; S. Tate to PC, January 16, 1857, Fol. 1165, all in PCC.

35. W. T. Lamb to PC, September 16, 1860, Fol. 1210, and December 4, 18, 24, 1859, Fol. 1201; A. Wright to PC, November 6, 1858, Fol. 1188, all in PCC.

36. D. F. Caldwell to PC, Fol. 1136, PCC.

37. Fol. 33, A. H. Arrington Papers, SHC; L. C. Gray and Esther K. Thompson, *History of Agriculture in the Southern United States to 1860* (Washington, DC, 1933), 1:530.

38. Lee Soltow, *Men and Wealth in the United States, 1850–1870* (New Haven, CT, 1975), 57, 142; Gavin Wright, *The Political Economy of the Cotton South: Households, Markets, and Wealth in the Nineteenth Century* (New York, 1978), 30–36; James Oakes, *The Ruling Race: A History of American Slaveowners* (New York, 1982).

39. Manisha Sinha, *The Counterrevolution of Slavery: Politics and Ideology in Antebellum South Carolina* (Chapel Hill, NC, 2000); Ronald Takaki, *A Proslavery Crusade: The Agitation to Reopen the African Slave Trade* (New York, 1971).

40. "Isthmus," *DeBow's Review*, July 1852, 43–52; Jere Robinson, "The South and the Pacific Railroad, 1845–1855," *Western Historical Quarterly* 5 (1974): 163–186; Stacey L. Smith, "Remaking Slavery in a Free State: Masters and Slaves in Gold Rush California," *Pacific Historical Review* 80 (2011): 28–63; Susan Lee Johnson, *Roaring Camp: The Social World of the California Gold Rush* (New York, 2000); John C. Parish, "A Project for a California Slave Colony in 1851," *Huntington Library Bulletin*, no. 8 (1935): 171–175; Leonard L. Richards, *The California Gold Rush and the Coming of the Civil War* (New York, 2007).

41. Brown, *Agents of Manifest Destiny*, 174–218.

42. David Potter, *The Impending Crisis, 1848–1861* (New York, 1976), 146–156; William Cronon, *Nature's Metropolis: Chicago and the Great West* (New York, 1991).

43. J. A. Reinhart to Jn. Dalton, January 20, 1851, Placebo Houston Papers, Duke; William W. Freehling, *The Road to Disunion* (New York, 1990), 1:540.

44. Case 55, April 1845 term, Office of Circuit Court Clerk–St. Louis, Missouri State Archives–St. Louis, http://stlcourtrecords.wustl.edu, an excellent resource, initiated by Lea VanderVelde, accessed June 24, 2011.

45. Don E. Fehrenbacher, *The Dred Scott Case: Its Significance in American Law and Politics* (New York, 1978); Lea VanderVelde, *Mrs. Dred Scott: A Life on Slavery's Frontier* (New York, 2009).

46. Freehling, *Road to Disunion*, 1:547–549; Thomas G. Balcerski, "The F Street Mess Reconsidered: A Homosocial History of the Kansas-Nebraska Act," Unpublished paper presented at the Fall 2010 Americanist Colloquium, Cornell University.

47. Robert W. Johannsen, *Stephen A. Douglas* (New York, 1973); *CG*, 28:1, 33rd Cong. 1st sess., 115, January 4, 1854; Susan Bullit Dixon, *The True History of the Missouri Compromise and Its Repeal* (Cincinnati, 1899), 442–445; Potter, *Impending Crisis*, 160.

48. Michael F. Holt, *Franklin Pierce* (New York, 2010), 77–80, 53; Dixon, *True History*, 457–460.

49. Douglas to N. Edwards, April 13, 1854, in Robert W. Johannsen, ed., *The Letters of Stephen A. Douglas* (Urbana, IL, 1961), 322–323; Johannsen, *Stephen A. Douglas*, 420.

50. "Appeal of the Independent Democrats, to the People of the United States. Shall Slavery Be Permitted in Nebraska?" (Washington, DC, 1854); Sean Wilentz, *The Rise of American Democracy: Jefferson to Lincoln* (New York, 2005), 673–674.

51. *CG*, March 3, 1854, 532; Roy F. Nichols, "The Kansas-Nebraska Act: A Century of Historiography," *Mississippi Valley Historical Review* 43, no. 2 (1956): 187–212; Alan Nevins, *Ordeal of the Union* (New York, 1947), 2:129–130.

52. Thomas O'Connor, *Lords of the Loom: The Cotton Whigs and the Coming of the Civil War* (New York, 1968), 98; Foner, *Business and Slavery*, 91–100.

53. Potter, *Impending Crisis*, 175.

54. *CG* [appendix], March 30, 1854 (L. Keitt), 464–467; February 23, 1854 (Robert Toombs), 347–349; April 24, 1854 (Peter Phillips), 532–534; May 10, 1854 (James Dowdell), 705–706; April 27, 1854 (Wm. Smith), 553.

55. *Washington National Intelligencer*, June 7, 1854; *Nashville Union*, June 7, 1854, September 20, 1854; Jonathan Atkins, *Party, Politics, and Sectional Conflict in Tennessee, 1832–1861* (Knoxville, TN, 1997), 193; *Tallahassee Floridian*, January 28, 1854; *Alexandria Gazette*, April 15, 1854.

56. *Trenton Gazette*, October 5, 1854; *New York Weekly Herald*, December 16, 1854; *Tallahassee Floridian and Sentinel*, November 18, 1854; Brown, *Agents of Manifest Destiny*, 267–457; Freehling, *Road to Disunion*, 2:166; *NOP*, December 13, 1854.

57. *New York Tribune*, September 25, 1854; Nicole Etcheson, *Bleeding Kansas: Contested Liberty in the Civil War Era* (Lawrence, KS, 2004), 67.

58. Etcheson, *Bleeding Kansas*, 97; *New Hampshire Sentinel*, December 28, 1855; *Eufaula* (AL) *Spirit of the South*, in *Charleston Mercury*, January 25, 1856.

59. *Augusta Constitutionalist* repr., *Charleston Mercury*, May 28, 1855; *New York Weekly Herald*, May 24, 1856.

60. Repr. *St. Albans* [VT] *Herald*, September 20, 1855; Etcheson, *Bleeding Kansas*, 109, 113–138.

61. Potter, *Impending Crisis*, 248–265.

62. Joel Silbey, *The Partisan Imperative: The Dynamics of American Political Life Before the Civil War* (New York, 1985); *Richmond Enquirer*, October 20, 1856; Freehling, *Road to Disunion*, 2:104.

63. Austin Allen, *Origins of the Dred Scott Case: Jacksonian Jurisprudence and the Supreme Court, 1837–1857* (Athens, GA, 2006), 146–147; VanderVelde, *Mrs. Dred Scott*, 288–289; Kenneth Stampp, *1857: A Nation on the Brink* (New York, 1990), 149–170.

64. Fehrenbacher, *Dred Scott*, 50–61.

65. Allen, *Origins of the Dred Scott Case*, 179.

66. *New York Tribune*, March 7, 9–12, 16–17, 19–21, 25, 1857, April 11, 1857; Fehrenbacher, *Dred Scott*, 403–414.

67. Fehrenbacher, *Dred Scott*, is the most obvious critique and collates the opinions of various historians.

68. *Washington Union*, March 6, 11, 12, 1857; *New York Journal of Commerce*, March 11, 1857; *New York Herald*, March 8, 1857; *NOP*, March 20, 1857; Fehrenbacher, *Dred Scott*, 418–419.

69. Speech at Springfield, Illinois, June 26, 1857, LINCOLN 2:404.

70. "Lecompton Constitution," Daniel Wilder, *Annals of Kansas* (Topeka, 1875), 183; Stampp, *1857*, 171, 271.

71. Charles Calomiris and Larry Schweikart, "The Panic of 1857: Origins, Transmission, and Containment," *Journal of Economic History* 54, no. 4 (1991): 807–834; *Mississippi Free Trader*, November 6, 1857; James L. Huston, *The Panic of 1857 and the Coming of the Civil War* (Baton Rouge, LA, 1987), 63 (cf. 60); Foner, *Business and Slavery*, 139–147.

72. "Speech at Hartford, Conn., Mar. 5, 1860," LINCOLN, 4:5–6.

73. "House Divided Speech," June 18, 1858, LINCOLN, 2:461; August 21, 1858, LINCOLN, 3:27.

74. For examples of selective reading of Lincoln to "prove" his racism, see George Frederickson, *Big Enough to Be Inconsistent: Abraham Lincoln Confronts Slavery and Race* (Cambridge, MA, 2008); Lerone Bennett, *Forced into Glory: Abraham Lincoln's White Dream* (Chicago, 2000).

75. LINCOLN, 2:461; Freehling, *Road to Disunion*, 2:130–135; Robert Remini, *The House: The History of the House of Representatives* (New York, 2006), 155; *Alexandria Gazette*, April 4, 1858.

76. Douglas to J. McClernand, February 21, 1858, in Johannsen, *Douglas Letters*, 417.

77. Harriet Newby to Dangerfield Newby, August 16, 1859, in *Governor's Message and Reports*, 116–117, Library of Virginia, Richmond, www.lva.virginia.gov/public /trailblazers/res/Harriet_Newby_Letters.pdf, accessed March 7, 2014.

78. Four escaped, and three others fled the Maryland farm hideout where they had stayed as a rear guard. Two of these seven were captured and hanged. Four of the surviving five fought for the Union, of whom two were killed.

79. *Charleston Mercury*, January 4, 1860: Freehling, *Road to Disunion*, 2:214; *Barre Gazette*, December 23, 1859; *Farmers' Cabinet*, January 11, 1860; Ollinger Crenshaw, "The Psychological Background of the Election of 1860," *North Carolina Historical Review* 19 (1942): c. 260; Peter Wallenstein, "Incendiaries All . . . etc.," in Paul Finkelman, ed., *His Soul Goes Marching On: Responses to John Brown and the Harpers Ferry Raid* (Charlottesville, VA, 1995).

80. Henry David Thoreau, "A Plea for Captain John Brown," 1859, www .gutenberg.org/files/2567/2567-h/2567-h.htm, accessed October 26, 2013.

81. Potter, *Impending Crisis*, PIC, 403; Nevins, *Ordeal of the Union*, 2:179; *Baltimore Sun*, April 17, 1860; Ph. Thomas to Finney, January 24, 1859, W. Finney Papers, Duke; Freehling, *Road to Disunion*, 2:220–221, 246–287.

82. *Montgomery Confederation*, April 26, 1860; Robert B. Rhett to William P. Miles, January 29, 1860, Miles Papers, SHC; Thornton, *Politics and Power*, 381–391.

83. *Wisconsin Daily Patriot*, May 9, 1860; *Cleveland Plain Dealer*, May 9, 1860.

84. William Hesseltine, *Three Against Lincoln: Murat Halstead Reports the Caucuses of 1860* (Baton Rouge, LA, 1960), 230; Freehling, *Road to Disunion*, 2:318; *Annapolis Gazette*, June 21, 1860.

85. David Donald, *Lincoln* (New York, 1995); Douglas Wilson, *Honor's Voice: The Transformation of Abraham Lincoln* (New York, 1998); Harry V. Jaffa, *Crisis of the House Divided: An Interpretation of the Issues in the Lincoln-Douglas Debates* (Garden City, NJ, 1959); Harry V. Jaffa, *A New Birth of Freedom: Abraham Lincoln and the*

*Coming of the Civil War* (Lanham, MD, 2000); and especially William Lee Miller, *Lincoln's Virtues: An Ethical Biography* (New York, 2002).

86. Jon Grinspan, "'Young Men for War': The Wide Awakes and Lincoln's 1860 Presidential Campaign," *JAH* 96 (2009): 357–378; Potter, *Impending Crisis*, 432–447.

87. Sinha, *Counterrevolution*, 219–220.

88. Ralph Wooster, "An Analysis of the Membership of Secession Conventions in the Lower South," *JSH* 24, no. 3 (1958): 360–368; Stephanie McCurry, *Confederate Reckoning: Power and Politics in the Civil War South* (Cambridge, MA, 2010); Wilentz, *Rise of American Democracy*, 768–773, 944n3; Stephen Channing, *Crisis of Fear: Secession in South Carolina* (New York, 1970); William L. Barney, *The Secessionist Impulse: Alabama and Mississippi in 1860* (Princeton, NJ, 1974); Michael P. Johnson, *Toward a Patriarchal Republic: The Secession of Georgia* (Baton Rouge, LA, 1977); Edward E. Baptist, *Creating an Old South: Middle Florida's Plantation Frontier Before the Civil War* (Chapel Hill, NC, 2002); Douglas R. Egerton, *Year of Meteors: Stephen Douglas, Abraham Lincoln, and the Election That Brought the Civil War* (New York, 2010); Shearer Davis Bowman, *At the Precipice: Americans North and South During the Secession Crisis* (Chapel Hill, NC, 2010).

89. John Forsyth to Stephen Douglas, December 28, 1860, in Johannsen, *Stephen A. Douglas*, 246. Charles B. Dew, in *Apostles of Disunion: Southern Secession Commissioners and the Causes of the Civil War* (Charlottesville, VA, 2001), explains the "states' rights" revisionists' argument and then demolishes it by demonstrating that the conventions' message was that by electing Lincoln, "revolutionary" Republicans had signaled that they planned to destroy slavery and white supremacy. See also David Blight, *Race and Reunion: The Civil War in American Memory* (Cambridge, MA, 2003), for the roots of reinterpretation of secession's causes.

90. Dew, *Apostles of Disunion*, 56–58, 85. "Equality," etc., is from address of William Harris, Commissioner from Mississippi, to Georgia General Assembly, December 17, 1860.

91. Daniel W. Crofts, *Reluctant Confederates: Upper South Unionists in the Secession Crisis* (Chapel Hill, NC, 1989); Potter, *Impending Crisis*, 508–510.

92. Potter, *Impending Crisis*, 528–533.

93. Potter, *Lincoln and His Party in the Secession Crisis* (New Haven, CT, 1942).

94. Lincoln to James T. Hale, January 11, 1861, LINCOLN 4:172.

95. Thoreau, "Plea for Captain Brown." One Confederate soldier would be killed after the fort surrendered, while setting off celebratory cannon salutes.

## AFTERWORD. THE CORPSE: 1861–1937

1. Delia Garlic, AS, 6.1, (AL), 129.

2. Sven Beckert, "'Emancipation and Empire': Reconstructing the Worldwide Web of Cotton Production in the Age of the American Civil War," *AHR* 109 (2004): 1405–1438; Gabriel Baer, "Slavery in Nineteenth-Century Egypt," *Journal of African History* 8, no. 3 (1967): 426.

3. Vermont Investors to Sec'y of the Treasury, February 3, 1862, *Freedom: A Documentary History of Emancipation, 1861–1867* (Freedom and Southern History Project, University of Maryland, 1985–2013), ser. 1, vol. 3, 124–151; E. S. Philbrick to a Massachusetts Businessman, April 12, 1862, FSSP, ser. 1, vol. 3, 182–187; HQ 2 Brigade

SC Expeditionary Corps to Supt. Contrabands at Beaufort, SC, April 4, 1862, FSSP, 1/3, 180–181.

4. E. S. Philbrick to MA businessman, April 12, 1862, FSSP, ser. 1, vol. 3, 182–187; R. Saxton, Military Govr., Gnl. Order #12, December 20, 1862, FSSP, 1/3, 222–224; E. S. Philbrick to Direct-tax Commissioner for SC, January 14, 1864, FSSP, 1/3, 278–279.

5. James Oakes, *Freedom National: The Destruction of Slavery in the United States, 1861–1865* (New York, 2013), emphasizes the Republican Party's commitment to a national ideal of emancipation.

6. Frederick Douglass, "Should the Negro Enlist in the U.S. Army," speech delivered July 6, 1863.

7. Dep. of Felo Battee, May 29, 1865, in Thomas Hamilton, #255536, and Andre Dupree, #492774, both Record Group 15, Records of the Department of Veterans Affairs, National Archives, Washington, DC.

8. Abram Blue, #131.901, #946.653, Record Group 15, Records of the Department of Veterans Affairs, National Archives, Washington, DC; cf. Nancy Bercaw, *Gendered Freedoms: Race, Rights, and the Politics of Household in the Delta, 1861–1875* (Gainesville, FL, 2003).

9. This, plus a long slow decline in agricultural commodity prices after 1870, helped to ensure that for many people, sharecropping became a kind of debt peonage that eventually trapped three consecutive generations of African Americans in the cotton country in extraordinary poverty. See Gavin Wright, *Old South, New South: Revolutions in the Southern Economy After the Civil War* (New York, 1986).

10. Laura Free, *Gendering the Constitution: Manhood, Race, Woman Suffrage, and the Fourteenth Amendment* (Philadelphia, 2014).

11. Harry Bates, *Cotton: History, Species, Varieties, Morphology, Breeding, Culture, Diseases, Marketing, and Uses* (New York, 1927), 151–152, 323; Warren C. Whatley, "Southern Agrarian Labor Contracts as Impediments to Cotton Mechanization," *Journal of Economic History* 47, no. 1 (1987): 45–70; William L. Shea and Edwin Pelz, "A German Prisoner of War in the South: The Memoir of Edwin Pelz," *Arkansas Historical Quarterly* 44, no. 1 (1985): 42–55, esp. 52–53; Steven Hahn, *A Nation Under Our Feet: Black Political Struggles in the Rural South from Slavery to the Great Migration* (Cambridge, MA, 2003), 424–425; David Blight, *Race and Reunion: The Civil War and American Memory* (Cambridge, MA, 2003).

12. It would be impossible to list all of the great works on the post–Civil War history of the South, but these two paragraphs build above all on traditions of scholarship that include the following: W. E. B. DuBois, *The Souls of Black Folk* (Chicago, 1903); W. E. B. DuBois, *Black Reconstruction in America: An Essay Toward the Part Which Black Folks Played in the Attempt to Reconstruct Democracy in America, 1860–1880* (New York, 1935); C. Vann Woodward, *Origins of the New South, 1877–1913* (Baton Rouge, LA, 1951); Eric Foner, *Reconstruction: America's Unfinished Revolution, 1863–1877* (New York, 1988); Edward L. Ayers, *The Promise of the New South: Life After Reconstruction* (New York, 1992); Glenda Gilmore, *Gender and Jim Crow: Women and the Politics of White Supremacy in North Carolina, 1896–1920* (Chapel Hill, NC, 1996); David Cecelski and Timothy Tyson, eds., *Democracy Betrayed: The Wilmington Race Riot of 1898 and Its Legacy* (Chapel Hill, NC, 1998); Laura F. Edwards,

*Gendered Strife and Confusion: The Political Culture of Reconstruction* (Urbana, IL, 1998); Gregory Downs, *Declarations of Dependence: The Long Reconstruction of Popular Politics in the South, 1861–1908* (Chapel Hill, NC, 2011).

13. Bill Cooke, "The Denial of Slavery in Management Studies," Paper No. 68, Institute for Development Policy and Management, University of Manchester, http://ageconsearch.umn.edu/bitstream/30566/1/dp020068.pdf, accessed December 18, 2013.

14. Ira Katznelson, *Fear Itself: The New Deal and the Origins of Our Time* (New York, 2013). Among many excellent works on lynching, see Crystal Feimster, *Southern Horrors: Women and the Politics of Rape and Lynching* (Cambridge, MA, 2009); Mari Nagasue Crabtree, "The Devil Is Watching You: Lynching and Southern Memory, 1940–1970" (PhD diss., Cornell University, 2014).

15. Susie King, AS, 2.4 (AR), 213; Charles L. Perdue Jr., Thomas E. Barden, and Robert K. Phillips, eds., *Weevils in the Wheat: Interviews with Virginia Ex-Slaves* (Charlottesville, VA, 1976), esp. 151–154.

# INDEX